LET'S GO:
PARIS

is the best book for anyone traveling on a budget. Here's why:

No other guidebook has as many budget listings.

In Paris, we found over 75 hotels or hostels for under $20 a night. Our food listings let you experience the culinary marvels of Paris without going broke. We tell you how to get there the cheapest way, whether by bus, plane, or thumb, and how to get around the city once you've arrived. There are hundreds of money-saving tips for everyone plus lots of information on student discounts.

LET'S GO researchers have to make it on their own.

Our Harvard-Radcliffe researchers travel on budgets as tight as your own—no expense accounts, no free hotel rooms.

LET'S GO is completely revised every year.

We don't just update the prices, we go back to the places. If a charming café has become an overpriced tourist trap, we'll replace the listing with a new and better one.

No other budget guidebook includes all this:

Coverage of both the city and daytrips into the countryside; directions, addresses, phone numbers, and hours to get you there and back; in-depth information on culture, history, and the people; listings on transportation between and within regions and cities; tips on work, study, sights, nightlife, and special splurges, detailed neighborhood maps; and much, much more.

LET'S GO is for anyone who wants to see Paris on a budget.

Books by Let's Go, Inc.

Let's Go: Europe
Let's Go: Britain & Ireland
Let's Go: France
Let's Go: Germany, Austria & Switzerland
Let's Go: Greece & Turkey
Let's Go: Israel & Egypt
Let's Go: Italy
Let's Go: London
Let's Go: Paris
Let's Go: Rome
Let's Go: Spain & Portugal

Let's Go: USA
Let's Go: California & Hawaii
Let's Go: Mexico
Let's Go: New York City
Let's Go: The Pacific Northwest, Western Canada & Alaska
Let's Go: Washington, D.C.

LET'S GO:

The Budget Guide to

PARIS

1993

Zachary M. Schrag
Editor

Cecily Anne Morgan
Assistant Editor

Written by
Let's Go, Inc.
a wholly owned subsidiary of
Harvard Student Agencies, Inc.

ST. MARTIN'S PRESS
NEW YORK

Helping Let's Go

If you have suggestions or corrections, or just want to share your discoveries, drop us a line. We read every piece of correspondence, whether a 10-page letter, a tacky Elvis postcard, or, as in one case, a collage. All suggestions are passed along to our researcher/writers. Please note that mail received after May 5, 1993 will probably be too late for the 1994 book, but will be retained for the following edition. Address mail to:

Let's Go: Paris
Let's Go, Inc.
1 Story Street
Cambridge, MA 02138

In addition to the invaluable travel advice our readers share with us, many are kind enough to offer their services as researchers or editors. Unfortunately, the charter of Let's Go, Inc. and Harvard Student Agencies, Inc. enables us to employ only currently enrolled Harvard students.

Quotations from Marcel Proust, *Remembrance of Things Past,* trans. C. K. Scott Moncrieff and Terence Kilmartin, © 1981, are used with the kind permission of Random House, Inc.

Maps by David Lindroth, copyright © 1993 by St. Martin's Press, Inc.

Distributed outside the U.S. and Canada by Pan Books Ltd.

ISBN: 0-312-08246-0

First edition
10 9 8 7 6 5 4 3 2 1

Let's Go: Paris is written by the Publishing Division of
Let's Go, Inc., 1 Story Street, Cambridge, Mass. 02138.

Let's Go® is a registered trademark of Let's Go, Inc.
Printed in the U.S.A. on recycled paper with biodegradable soy ink.

Editor	Zachary M. Schrag
Assistant Editor	Cecily Anne Morgan
Managing Editor	Christopher Capozzola
Publishing Director	Paul C. Deemer
Production Manager	Mark N. Templeton
Office Coordinator	Bart St. Clair
Office Manager	Anne E. Chisholm

Researcher-Writers

Paris, Versailles, Chartres, Fontainebleau	
Vaux-le-Vicomte, Château-Thierry, Beauvais	Heather Lynn Bell
Paris, EuroDisneyland, St-Ouen	Carla Deykin
Paris, Giverny, Malmaison, Chantilly	Marina Harss
Paris, La Défense, St-Denis	Jadran Lee

Sales Group Manager	Tiffany A. Breau
Sales Group Representatives	Frances Marguerite Maximé
	Breean T. Stickgold
	Harry James Wilson
Sales Group Coordinator	Aida Bekele
President	Brian A. Goler
C.E.O.	Michele Ponti

About Let's Go

A generation ago, Harvard Student Agencies, a three-year-old non-profit corporation dedicated to providing employment to students, was doing a booming business booking charter flights to Europe. One of the extras offered to passengers on these flights was a 20-page mimeographed pamphlet entitled *1960 European Guide,* a collection of tips on continental travel compiled by the HSA staff. The following year, students traveling to Europe researched the first full-fledged edition of *Let's Go: Europe,* a pocket-sized book with tips on budget accommodations, irreverent write-ups of sights, and a decidedly youthful slant.

Throughout the 60s, the series reflected the times: a section of the 1968 *Let's Go: Europe* was entitled "Street Singing in Europe on No Dollars a Day." During the 70s *Let's Go* evolved into a large-scale operation, adding regional European guides and expanding coverage into North Africa and Asia. In the 80s, we launched coverage of the United States, developed our research to include concerns of travelers of all ages, and finetuned the editorial process that continues to this day. The early 90s saw the introduction of *Let's Go* city guides.

1992 has been a big year for us. We are now Let's Go, Incorporated, a wholly owned subsidiary of Harvard Student Agencies. To celebrate this change, we moved from our dungeonesque Harvard Yard basement to an equally dungeonesque third-floor office in Harvard Square, and we purchased a high-tech computer system that allows us to typeset all of the guides in-house. Now in our 33rd year, *Let's Go* publishes 17 titles, covering more than 40 countries. This year *Let's Go* proudly introduces two new entries in the series: *Let's Go: Paris* and *Let's Go: Rome.*

But these changes haven't altered our tried and true approach to researching and writing travel guides. Each spring 90 Harvard University students are hired as researcher-writers and trained intensively during April and May for their summer tour of duty. Each researcher-writer then hits the road for seven weeks of travel on a shoestring budget, researching six days per week and overcoming countless obstacles in the quest for better bargains.

Back in Cambridge, Massachusetts, an editorial staff of 32, a management team of six, and countless typists and proofreaders—all students—spend more than six months pushing nearly 8000 pages of copy through a rigorous editing process. By the time classes start in September, the typeset guides are off to the printers, and they hit bookstores world-wide in late November. Then, by February, next year's guides are well underway.

A NOTE TO OUR READERS

The information for this book is gathered by Let's Go's researchers during the late spring and summer months. Each listing is derived from the assigned researcher's opinion based upon his or her visit at a particular time. The opinions are expressed in a candid and forthright manner. Other travelers might disagree. Those traveling at a different time may have different experiences since prices, dates, hours, and conditions are always subject to change. You are urged to check beforehand to avoid inconvenience and surprises. Travel always involves a certain degree of risk, especially in low-cost areas. When traveling, especially on a budget, you should always take particular care to ensure your safety.

Acknowledgments

In the Navy they call them "plank-owners," the first crew to take out a new vessel, to appreciate her strengths, fix her flaws, and love her quirks. The plank-owners of Let's Go: Paris worked themselves past exhaustion to perform their duty with precision, grace, and humor. Future editions of this book may improve their work, but will never exceed their efforts.

Judging from the quality of her research and writing, **Heather Bell,** C.O.T., carried with her a library of several thousand volumes, rewrote mulitple drafts of each batch, and through some supernatural means, went without sleep for seven weeks. Whether in a hallway bathroom or the Hall of Mirrors, she combined a Holmesian regard to detail with a mischievous wit, and left me cursing because there was nothing left to add. **Carla Deykin** never missed a chance to insert that tiny nugget of essential information that is the difference between a smooth trip and hours of frustration. Grimy hotels fell by the score, victim to her uncompromising standards. **Marina Harss,** beating off her suitors, surveyed the club scene and scaled Montmartre before setting out to the Nord. Even before he crossed the Atlantic, **Jadran Lee** did crucial work, helping plan the book's overall design and setting up Let's Go's Paris HQ. Once there, he talked to cops, he talked to bouncers, he talked to waiters, then he sent back more facts than I knew could fit on a floppy disk. *Soldats! Je suis content de vous!*

The real power behind the throne was Parisienne-in-spirit **Cecily Morgan**—indispensible, Daedalian, heaven-sent Cecily—who made it all possible. Functioning as a fifth researcher and a second editor, she brought fluent French, a profound knowledge of Paris, and never-flagging laughter to the office and the book. My own personal nightmare will always be having to do this job without Cecily's help. Never complaining, she combined the vision of Jeanne d'Arc, the courage of Ney, and the creativity of Baudelaire, meanwhile enduring more absurdity and longer hours than anyone on a Let's Go salary should have to. Her contribution is evident in every paragraph.

Along with Cecily, **Becca Knowles** and **Patrick La Rivière,** the gallant provincials, made this summer one to savor. They invited me into their homes, saved my tuchus as the book came due, and in general made me eager to go into work every day. Well, most days. If you guys are ever pursued by the Tooth Ferry or the Border Patrol, you can hide in my basement. **Chris Capozzola** managed with a firm hand, a keen eye, and sometimes an air of martyred resignation, but never a sharp voice. Without the electronic necromancy and tortoise-like patience of **Mark Templeton,** *Let's Go: Paris* would be nothing but a pile of papers and Macintosh disks. **Pete Deemer** presided over what has to have been the happiest, smoothest year in Let's Go history. I won't try to name everyone in the office who made this summer a terrific Hundred Days in power; their names wouldn't fit. Speaking of close fits, *Vive* St. Martin's Press! for color maps and extra signatures.

Outside the office, wisdom, advice, and support came from Will Bachman, Steve Burt, Boris Dolgonos, Claudia Gonson, Tony Lee, Cynthia Rapacke, John Stilgoe, Rebecca Tushnet, Liz Temin, Ian Watson, Judy Vichniac, and various Schrags, Fenichels, Lermans, and Davidsons. My vision of Paris, such as it is, owes a great deal to such scholars, writers, and artists as Ferdinand Braudel, Alfred Cobban, Jacques-Louis David, H. Sutherland Edwards, Norma Evenson, Alistair Horne, Alan Jay Lerner, A. J. Liebling, Cole Porter, Waverly Root, Irwin Shaw, Simon Schama, and François Truffaut. I salute the defenders of Paris, notably Generals Trochu and Gallieni; the martyrs of the barricades; and all scientists who are working to prove that roast goose, Camembert cheese, and Bordeaux wine are health foods after all. I thank all readers who sent mail about Paris—we read and mull over all of it. Most of all, I applaud Ms. Audrey Hepburn, whose performances in *Charade, Sabrina,* and *Love in the Afternoon* define the true magic of Paris.

—ZMS

To Zach, the Brutal Lexicon of Death, who has called me, among other things, a "queer potato" and a "fanatic" and has implied that it takes no more than a flimsy puff of air to make me laugh, I offer my eternal, grateful, obsequious, properly subservient-thanks. May the Commune live forever and in all the future editions of this book. Ah, Zach, who glorified Ramen by calling it "K-rations;" who hid under his desk after trying to decipher the hours at Vaux-le-Vicomte; who rode around the office squealing on Patrick's seatless bike, at 3am the night before the deadline. You have made me, Yes!, enjoy military history, and brought Napoleon, Général Trochu, Général Gallieni, and their many fellow soldiers to life. Nor will I forget your striking pose of the Maréchal Ney and dramatic rendering of *"Tirez sur moi, et visez juste!"*

Some memorable quotes: "I don't think you can be really enthusiastic about Paris without some taste for Blood;" "No uprising will get past me! From 1293 to 1968 is but an uninterrupted story of struggle in the streets;" "The history of Paris is one of elaborate city planning, punctuated by moments of extreme violence;" "To say that a paper is on my desk is like saying I'm looking for a person in the People's Republic of China." And finally, the piéce de résistance: "It'd be kind of fun to replace all the Rococos with rocky-the-flying squirrel" (10:20pm, deadline eve, with a manic gleam in his eye)

To Carla, of the 8½ century-long sentences, Heather of the firm mattresses, perma-dirt, and tile, Marina of the nightclubs, and Jad of the "Is this really marble? Knock against it and see." You're all wonderful! This book belongs to you.

To Chris, who dealt so stoically with our utter lack of Organization, who gave up on our Task Sheets and 10-day planner, who suffered with the Bubonic Plague while reading our copy, but who nevertheless did not lose hope. May this prove you justified.

Ah yes, the France book—crazybec and official Reference Librarian of the France Room and soon-to-be-insane youngster Patrick. I would mention red-haired Irishmen and incomprehensible Québecois French, but a natural tact and delicacy holds me back.

Mom, Dad, Doug, Steve, and my second family at 50 Holyoke street: the Bosserts, Kim, Bonnie, Anju, Greg, Rusty, Tash, and Megan. Thanks for making this summer wonderful and for understanding that food is the most important of all resources for an up-and-coming Publishing Magnate!

And of course, to Bohemia and Baudelaire, and René's coffee, where would I be without you? Additional keeping-Cecily-sane recognition goes to Colin, Linda, Amee, John, Gabrielle, la famille Beaugiraud et la famille Raby, Christine, Alice, Judy and Stéphan, Jessica, and Michelle Lambert.

I dedicate this book to those in France who showed me Paris for the first time and whose memories fill its pages.

So after all, whose desk was messier, Zach's or mine?

—CAM

CONTENTS

x   **Contents**

LIST OF MAPS

LET'S GO: PARIS

General Introduction

It has been at least two centuries since a human being saw Paris through unveiled eyes. The myth of Paris is not merely strong, it is inescapable. The *communards* of '71 imitated the revolutionaries of '48 imitating the Jacobins of '89. The Grand Arche de La Défense gazes humbly down on the Arc de Triomphe, which is itself an imitation of a Roman form. Young artists still crowd into cafés where Picasso and Matisse met and relived the careers of the Bohemians a century before, and lovers, having seen photographs of other couples along the Seine and in the Jardin du Luxembourg, stroll and kiss in the same places. Baudelaire called Paris a "teeming city, city full of dreams, where the specter in full daylight, accosts the passerby." The specters may be more solid than even he guessed. So strong are the associations that many observers are driven to absurd superlatives, describing Paris as the most, the only, the best, the perfect, the heavenly. In one sense, none of this is true—while Paris is a very nice city, a handsome city, and a justifiably popular destination, a perfect city would not have so much canine excrement on its sidewalks, nor would its drivers cut in front of ambulances. It is in fact quite possible to go to Paris and not fall in love; you may not even finish your novel. But these are trivial matters. Paris's ability to deprive the observer of reason and scale is one of its charms, and the web of myth is part of the reality.

History

> Human nature shrinks in horror from the deeds that
> have been done in Paris.
> —The Times of London, June 1, 1871

Paris slakes the human thirst for blood. Its history is a saga of grand schemes of urban design, punctuated by bursts of artistic genius and outbreaks of unrestrained violence. Over the centuries, the warp of creation and the woof of death have combined to form a fabric of beauty, heroism, cruelty, and greatness. Oh yes, and treachery. It is an epic that disgusts as it inspires, and thrills as it drives to despair.

The importance and centrality of Paris to France cannot, and has not, been overstated. It has shaped the destiny of its country more than any other capital. In England, dynasties were chosen on the battlefields of Hastings and Bosworth Field. In France, they were decided in Paris. America built its industrial might around Pittsburgh and Detroit. France's grew around Paris. Japan has a modern capital in Tokyo, but its ancient, spiritual center is Kyoto. France knows only Paris. The very flag of France is derived from the city's colors—blue and red—and recently Jacques Chirac served simultaneously as mayor of the capital and prime minister of the nation.

Yet it is a mistake to assume that the history of France and the history of Paris are identical. Certainly such decisive events as the Revolution and the birth of Impressionism are inexplicable without reference to Paris. And the history of France, from Vercingétorix to De Gaulle is recorded in the street names and monuments of the capital. But Paris also has a quieter history, a local history. Its appearance and its essence reflect both these histories. On one hand, there is great Paris, the cauldron of France, the capital of Europe, a bastion of civilization. But there is also local Paris, home to families, traffic jams, and cats.

Paris

1 Accueil Central de France:
  127 Champs Elysée
2 Transalpino: 16, rue La Fayette
3 American Express: 11, rue Scribe
4 Post Office: 52, rue du Louvre

 5 Musée Marmottan
 6 l'Arc de Triomphe
 7 Sacré-Coeur
 8 Musée d'Art Moderne
   de la Ville de Paris
 9 Grand Palais
10 Petit Palais
11 Opéra Garnier
12 Place Vendôme
13 Comedie Française
14 Palais Royal
15 Orangerie
16 St-Eustache
17 Centre National d'Art et
   Culture George Pompidou
18 Hôtel de Ville
19 Musée Picasso
20 Musée Carnavalet

21 Place des Vosges
22 Opéra Bastille
23 Sainte Chapelle and Palais de Justice
24 Notre Dame
25 St-Germain-des-Prés
26 Musée de Cluny
27 Sorbonne
28 Panthéon
29 Palais du Luxembourg
30 Musée d'Orsay
31 Musée Rodin
32 Les Invalides

33 Tour Eiffel
34 Cité Internationale
   de l'Université de Paris
35 Louvre

bd. Ney
bd. Ney
bd. Macdonald

Canal de l'Ourcq

rue Championnet
rue Ordener
Marcadet
Caulaincourt
rue Dunesme
rue Custine
rue de Clignancourt
bd. d'Ornano
Poissonnières
rue de la Chapelle
r. l'Evangile
rue d'Aubervilliers
rue Riquet
rue Archereau
rue de l'Ourcq
av. Corentin Cariou
av. Jean Lolive

7

bd. de Clichy
PL. Rochechouart
PIGALLE
av. Trudaine
rue de Châteaudun
Barbès
bd. de la
Chapelle
rue Max Dormoy
Gare
du Nord
RER
Gare de
l'Est
RER
rue La Fayette
rue Poissonnière
r. Paradis
rue du Fg. St-Denis
rue de Flandre
rue de Crimée
Bassin de la Villette
PL. DE
STALINGRAD
PL. DU
COLONEL
FABIEN
av. Secrétan
Canal St-Martin
Chapelle
r. Armand Carel
av. Jean
Jaurès
rue Martin
r. David d'Angiers
Parc de
la Villette
bd. Sérurier
bd. Indochine
bd. d'Algérie

N

2
bd. Montmartre
bd. des
Italiens
4 Sept.
rue Montmartre
Etienne Marcel
3 14
16
CHÂTELET
LES HALLES
17
RER
35
rue de Rivoli
pont Neuf
d. Louvre
18
rue de Rivoli
5
rue St-Michel
ST-
MICHEL RER
t-Germain
26
29
27
28
LUXEMBOURG
RER
PL. DE LA
CONTRE-
SCARPE
Poissonnière St-Denis
Réaumur
rue du Fg. d'Hauteville
rue de Fg. St-Denis
rue de Strasbourg
bd. de Magenta
blvd. St-Martin
PL. DE LA
RÉPUBLIQUE
rue St-Denis
bd. de Sébastopol
rue St-Martin
rue du Turbigo
rue Beaubourg
rue des Archives
rue Vieille du Temple
rue St-Honoré
rue de Rivoli
Beaumarchais
quai de
la Cité
lle de
la Cité
quai de la Tournelle
ST-Louis
PL.
MAUBERT
des Ecoles
quai St-Bernard
PL. DE LA
Jardin
des Plantes
bd. de la Villette
rue du Temple
av. du Temple
rue du Faubourg
rue St-Maur
rue Parmentier
av. de la République
rue Oberkampf
bd. du
bd. de Belleville
rue du Chemin Vert
R. Lenoir
rue de la Roquette
Voltaire
rue de Charonne
rue St-Antoine
Henri
IV
Ledru Rollin
rue du Faubourg
St-Antoine
rue de Montreuil
av. de Lyon
Pont
de Sully
Gare
de Lyon
RER
PL. DE LA
NATION
av. Daumesnil
bd. Diderot
NATION
Cours de Vincennes
av. Philippe Auguste
bd. de Charonne
bd. Davout
Ménilmontant
av. Gambetta
rue des Pyrénées
PL.
GAMBETTA
bd. Mortier
av. Gambetta
Cimetière
du
Pere Lachaise
Parc des
Buttes Chaumont

19
20
21
22
23
24

PORT
ROYAL
RER
ENFERT
ROCHEREAU
Montsouris
Parc
Jourdan
RER CITÉ
UNIVERSITAIRE
34
bd. Kellerman
rue d'Alésia
bd. A. Blanqui
PL
D'ALÉSIA
rue de Tolbiac
Av. de Choisy
Av. d'Ivry
Av. d'Italie
bd. de Massena
bd. Arago
bd. de Port Royal
bd. St-Jacques
bd. de Port Royal
rue Mouffetard
rue Monge
rue St-Jacques
rue d'Ulm
rue G. St-Hilaire
rue Censier
rue Buffon
rue St-Marcel
bd. St-Marcel
Av. des Gobelins
rue de l'Hôpital
rue de la Gare
rue Jeanne d'Arc
rue du
rue de Tolbiac
Chevallet
rue Regnault
rue National
BD. RER
MASSÉNA
Gare
d'Austerlitz
RER
Pont
de Bercy
Pont de
Tolbiac
Pont
National
quai
bd.
de Bercy
rue de Bercy
rue de Charenton
av. Daumesnil
PL. FÉLIX
ÉBOUÉ
av. du Gén
bd. Poniatowski
Dr. Arnold Netter
bd. Soult
Mi. Bizot
av. du
rue de Picpus
bd. de Picpus
Parc
Zoologique
Bois de
Vincennes
rue de Paris

0   1 mile
0   1 km

Mere words can suggest the history of a place, but they are better accompanied by the music of old stone and bronze. With this in mind, we have emphasized those elements of the city's history that can still be traced on its time-worn visage. For each chapter in the glorious tale, we point out a few sights that bear witness to that era. At the end, we suggest works of history and literature relevant to Paris. Any one of them will give you a better feel for the city than a broad survey of French history. The story of Paris is too big to be confined to one book or to be understood in any one tour. Ernest Hemingway called Paris a "moveable feast." It is a rich treat, to be sampled in small bites.

Lutetia (the primordial past to 476 AD)

Politics

In the beginning, there was a crossroads and an island. Thousands of years ago, the rue St-Jacques/rue St-Martin was one segment of a road that ran all the way from the Mediterranean to Northern Europe. It crossed another ancient road, now the rue St-Honoré, at a point just north of the Seine. And in the Seine itself, named after Sequana—a Gallic river goddess—lay the Ile de la Cité, where a tribe called the **Parisii** caught fish and grew crops. The city's site had much to recommend it: an island fortress, many nearby navigable rivers, and the chance to extract tolls from boats traveling the Seine. Moreover, the hinterland, the Ile-de-France, was composed of loess: a light soil, well-drained and easily plowed. As Ferdinand Braudel points out, other cities—Rouen, perhaps even Lyon—could have served France as well or better as a capital. But as luck would have it, Paris was the nucleus.

The Parisii called their home *Loutonheze,* "a dwelling in the midst of the waters." When the Romans conquered Gaul in 52 BC, they Latinized the name to *Lutetia,* later Frenchified into *Lutèce*. Though far from the Mediterranean heart of the Roman Empire, Lutetia was an important administrative center for northern Gaul, a springboard for invasions of Germany, and the residence of several emperors in their tours of the region. In the mid-3rd century, Christianity arrived in the person of **St-Denis,** who tried to convert the Gauls, and was beheaded for his efforts. **St-Martin,** preaching a century later, was more successful. In 451, a provincial girl named **Geneviève** deflected Atilla's approaching hordes to Orleans. In gratitude, Parisians adopted her as the city's patron saint.

Architecture and Urban Design

Paris began as a series of fishing huts. Then came the Romans, who rebuilt the city in their own image, with vineyards, an arena, and a perpendicular street plan. Suddenly, Paris became a place of civilization—a destiny it has prided itself on (to excess) ever since. Even more importantly, the Romans brought their new colony clean water, with a complex system of aqueducts, and connected it to Rome with an equally complex system of roads. The Arènes de Lutèce, modeled after Rome's Coliseum, were flooded and used for naval battles, as well as the more prosaic (dry) gladiator fights and throwing of Christians to the lions. The Thermes, now part of the Musée de Cluny, provided the requisite public baths for the city's new patrician population, centered around the Left Bank's Montaigne Ste-Geneviève. Renovations in the 1960s in the square outside Notre-Dame revealed a network of elaborate Roman houses. Yet all of this was, essentially, only a side-show for the Romans, whose main center in France was farther south in Vienne, and for whom the 28,000 Parisians remained only a slightly civilized barbaric race.

The Arts

Little art remains from this period, yet France's entire proud classical tradition is based upon it. The Romans brought to the barbarians their own Greek-inspired worship of pristine forms and simple geometry, a style France has perpetuated in such diverse buildings as the 17th-century Cour Carrée of the Louvre, or the triumphal arches of Napoleon. Since the time of Roman domination, the classical columns and pediments of Greek architecture have been synonymous wth power and authority. Witness the imposingly classical façade of Versailles, or the Greek-temple form of the 19th-century Bourse de Valeurs (the stock market). Radicals, from the Gothic architects, to more modern "heretics" like Eugène Delacroix or Marcel Duchamp, have tried to escape from this imposing heritage. Dictators, from Louis XIV to Napoleon, have embraced it.

See: Arènes de Lutèce, Hôtel de Cluny, Archeological Museum at Notre-Dame.

Middle Ages (476-1328)

Politics

Even after the collapse of Roman Gaul in the 4th century and the fall of the Western Roman Empire in 476, Paris remained under Roman administration. Finally the Roman leader Syagrius was defeated by **Clovis,** the great Frankish king, in 487. The Franks shortened "Lutetia Parisiorum" to a simple "Paris" and, in 508, made it their capital. Clovis's descendants, the **Merovingians,** followed suit. The Merovingians left the real administration of the country to the "mayors of the palace," including **Charles Martel.** Martel's son Pepin overthrew the Merovingians and founded the **Carolingian** dynasty. His son **Charlemagne** was one of the greatest military leaders in history, and in 800 had himself crowned Holy Roman Emperor. But the illiterate Emperor abandoned Paris to the scholars and held court at Aix-la-Chapelle. With the loss of its status as capital, the city went into decline. Throughout the 9th century, Norman raiders repeatedly pillaged the city. The city's greatest break came in 987 with the election of **Hugh Capet,** duke of Ile-de-France (the area around Paris) to the throne of France. Building outward from his power base in the Ile-de-France, Capet expanded his authority across a much larger territory. His descendants, the **Capetians,** were to continue this process, gradually winning more and more feudal lords to their allegiance.

In 1129, a fever swept through the city, killing 14,000 inhabitants. In 1176, the Seine flooded, carrying away bridges, houses, and people. But overall, the 12th century was one of great prosperity. The nearby Champagne fairs, where the goods of the Mediterranean were swapped for those of Northern Europe, gave power and wealth to the kings of France and their capital. **Philippe II (Philippe-Auguste),** who reigned from 1180-1223, was the greatest unifier of France. During his long reign he married into the Artois, Valois, and Vermandois families, and conquered Normandy and Anjou back from the English. Historian André Maurois writes, "in the course of two centuries the Duke of Ile-de-France had become the King of France." Though it would take centuries more, the government and language of the Ile-de-France would eventually spread over such diverse, separate nations as Brittany, Burgundy, and Provence.

Louis IX spent much of his long reign (1226-1270) crusading in the Middle East, but he spent enough time in Paris doing works of charity that he was later canonized as **St-Louis.** In 1261, he gave the powers of local administration over to the city's merchants. As France became militarily more secure, Paris became a central, rather than a frontier city. The first attempt to dethrone a king came in 1293, when Philippe le Bel was besieged in the headquarters of the Knights Templar. He survived and executed his enemies, but a precedent had been set. More serious for the Capetians was their inability to live very long. After a series of short-lived monarchs, the line came to and end in 1328.

Architecture and Urban Design

With monumental buildings like his palace at Aix-la-Chapelle (c. 800), Charlemagne inspired a style of architecture modeled after early Roman basilicas. Early Carolingian structures, spreading through Western Europe, blossomed suddenly into the huge, massive **Romanesque** cathedrals of the 11th century. The oldest parts of St-Germain-des-Prés, notably the main tower and sections of the choir, show the massive walls and semicircular arches characteristic of this style.

The prosperity of the 12th century allowed the invention of a new, far more ornate architectural style—the **Gothic** (for a discussion of Gothic architecture, see St-Denis in the Daytrips section). Europe's first Gothic cathedral, St-Denis, was built just outside of Paris and inaugurated in 1144. Rebuilding of Notre-Dame in this style began a mere 19 years later; Chartres, rebuilt after the 1194 fire, became one of the most eloquent expressions of high Gothic; Sainte-Chapelle, begun in 1243 and finished in a record five years, became "the pearl among them all." The Gothic spread quickly from northern France to influence and meld with the native styles of England, Germany, and Italy—all that was then seen as the "civilized" world—culminating spiritually when the cathedral at Beauvais, planned as the largest and tallest cathedral in the world, was abandoned after three dramatic collapses; only the tower remains as a monument to human hubris in an age that preached humility.

Philippe-Auguste did as well by Paris as he did by France, embellishing the city's streets, fortifications, and public works, including Notre-Dame and two aqueducts. Most importantly he built the city's first set of walls, not counting the fortification of the Ile-de-la-Cité itself, to protect it from the English forces, who had a garrison nearby. The western end of this wall was anchored by a fortress called the Louvre. During his time in Paris, Louis IX ordered the construction of Ste-Chapelle, improved the royal road of the rue St-Jacques/rue St-Martin, and granted permission for residents to build outside of Philippe-Auguste's walls.

The Arts

During this period, the **Sorbonne** (recognized by the pope in 1209) and other academies attracted such intellectual giants as **Thomas Abelard** (of the celebrated romance with **Héloïse), St-Thomas d'Aquin,** and **Roger Bacon** to a city that had become Europe's most prestigious center for theological study. Aquinas claimed that material objects were merely "corporeal metaphors for things spiritual." Following this precept, lavish attention was paid to the objects of ecclesiastical worship, from the priest's ornate robes to the gold chalice that held the Eucharistic wine. Stunning stained glass illustrated and analyzed the stories of the Bible at Chartres, Sainte-Chapelle, and Notre-Dame. The façades of Chartres and Notre-Dame expressed the depths of human emotion within the rigid confines of stone. Over a century later, **International Gothic,** typified by Notre-Dame's 14th-century statue of Madonna and Child, dominated all of Europe with its emphasis on sinuous lines and delicate, weightless grace.

See: St-Germain-des-Près, Notre-Dame, Chartres, Musée Cluny, Sainte-Chapelle, Hôtel Sens, St-Denis, Beauvais.

Hundred Years War and Renaissance (1328-1559)

Politics

Charles IV, the last of the Capetians, died in 1328. He was succeeded by Philippe VI, founder of the **Valois** dynasty. But Philippe's claim to the throne was disputed by Edward III of England, himself a descendant of the dukes of Normandy. Edward, along with his son, invaded France to claim the throne, initiating the Hundred Years War and an Anglo-French rivalry that would last until the 1830s. In 1358, after the capture of John II (the Good) at Poitiers, Paris rose against the *dauphin* (the heir to the throne). Parisians used stones, chains, and rubbish to improvise strong points in their narrow streets, initiating a tradition of revolutionary barricades that have sporadically blocked Parisian streets ever since. In this case, the *dauphin,* later **Charles V,** triumphed, and built the Bastille to imprison other troublemakers.

Civil war between the Armagnac and Burgunidian factions let to a slaughter of Armagnacs in Paris in May 1418; one witness described corpses "piled up like pigs in the mud." **Henry V** of England took advantage of this internal division by rolling through Normandy on the most successful English invasion yet and defeating the flower of the French chivalry at Agincourt. In 1420, Henry entered Paris, since 1415 the official capital of France, as son-in-law to the king and heir to the throne of France. For the next 16 years, the English ruled Paris, until they were deserted by their Burgundian allies and expelled by the French King **Charles VII** and his ally **Jeanne d'Arc.** After freeing Paris in 1437, Charles forsook the devastated city, he chose to reside on the Loire. To add injury to insult, that same year a pack of wolves swam out of the Seine and devoured many of the inhabitants. As the French economy collapsed under the strain of war, Parisians learned to subsist on the grain, fish, water, and wine produced in the immediate vicinity. Paris almost lost its fortune when, in the 1470s, **Louis XI** toyed with the idea of permanently moving the capital to Tours. But in 1528, **François I** declared

Paris to be his home, and the city's destiny was secure. He let the city keep whatever taxes it raised, bringing power and prosperity to the city government. François's reign also marked the beginnings of religious strife in France, as the Reformation trickled in from central Europe. Protestantism was rejected by the Sorbonne and by the king, who organized a parade of the city's major relics. Dozens of Protestants had their tongues cut out, after which they were slowly burned to death.

Architecture and Urban Design

By the 14th century, Paris's 80,000 inhabitants (including 10,000 students) made it one of the three great cities of Europe, along with Venice and Milan. The **Black Death** of 1351 may well have carried away half the city's population, but the numbers were more than made up by immigration. To cope with this growth, Charles V created a new, larger wall on the Right Bank. (It was destroyed in 1646 by Louis XIV, but its outline remains as the northern and eastern borders of the third *arrondissement.*) The English occupation brought his fine plans to an end, and construction stagnated.

Although François I himself spent most of his time at Fontainebleau, his reign marked a period of resumed growth in the city. The walls of the Right Bank were extended, and aristocratic mansions, influenced by the Renaissance taste for classical motifs and harmonious proportions, began filling the Marais, protected from the marshy dampness by Charles's wall. To live up to its new role, the city began construction of the Hôtel de Ville in 1529. Fire regulations decreed that wooden exteriors had to be plastered over, creating the flat, gray aesthetic that is still characteristic of the city's appearance. But there are plenty of half-timbered houses left in the provinces! (See *Let's Go: France.*) The Renaissance rejected the intricate human-dwarfing vaults of the Middle Ages, which they labeled "Gothic"—after the Goths, synonymous with barbarians—in favor of an architecture based on classical forms and a human scale.

The Arts

Influenced by the Italian Renaissance, a new age of **Humanism** crept into Parisian arts and letters. Dante came to study at the Sorbonne; Pierre de **Ronsard** wrote in the vernacular. **Rabelais** expanded the limits of French prose, with his pungent social satire. **Montaigne** invented the essay form. **Calvin** translated from Latin to French his determination that humanity was utterly corrupt. The *Tres Riches Heures du Duc de Berry,* an illuminated prayer book now in the collection of the Chantilly museum, ushered in the **Northern Renaissance** with its naturalistic portrayal of the labors of the months. A new attention to secular objects and the comforts of life yielded sumptuous tapestries. François I imported Italian artists like Cellini, Rosso, and Primaticcio to Fontainebleau, where they decorated his palace in the best of the **Mannerist** (a late Renaissance style, featuring a consciously "artificial" and mannered form of expression) tradition. **Jean Clouet's** portraits of the French royalty, including his *François I,* provided a fitting background for the ever-strengthening monarchy.

See: The Marais, Fontainebleau, Hôtel de Ville, Musée de Cluny.

Wars of Religion (1560-1642)

Politics

François's son **Henri II** continued his father's treatment of Protestants; he revelled in watching them burn. Henri died a messy death in a jousting accident in 1559, and his widow, **Cathérine des Médicis,** took power as regent for their son, **François II.** He died the next year, and was succeeded in turn by two brothers, though Cathérine remained the real sovereign. Threatened by a rising French Protestant (Huguenot) power, she married off her daughter to the Protestant Henri of Navarre, a member of the **Bourbon** line of Louis IX's descendants, in 1572. When all of the leading Protestants in France had assembled in Paris for the wedding, she signaled the start of the **St. Bartholomew's Day Massacre.** The next day, 2000 Huguenot corpses were fished out of the Seine. In 1588, Catherine's son **Henri III** was chased from Paris by a fiercely anti-Protestant mob opposed to the expected accession of his brother-in-law, Henri of Navarre. Henri III returned the next year and—like an angry parent—revoked all of the city's privileges, including its ability to raise its own revenue. But in 1590 he was assassinated, and for several years the city governed itself in defiance of any king. Henri of Navarre twice besieged the capital (the second siege lasting three months), but was unsuccessful. Finally, in 1593, he converted to Catholicism, winning the acceptance of many Parisians and waving off his transfomation with a nonchalant, "Paris is well worth a mass." Despite his conversion, the new **Henri IV** had to wait a year before sneaking into the city at night, presenting Paris with a fait accompli the next morning.

Upon Henri's death in 1610, **Marie des Médicis,** Henri's second wife and now his widow, became the regent for her son, **Louis XIII.** Marie's councilor, Concini, attempted to subdue the population by hanging gibbets throughout the city. But he was murdered by a courtier, and bits of his body were hung in his own gibbets, while his wife was beheaded for sorcery. In an attempt to keep power, Marie made a cardinal out of Concini's disciple, **Richelieu,** only to have him turn against her (but she, of course, had the Three Musketeers on her side).

Architecture and Urban Design

Years of warfare had left Paris well worth a mass, and well, quite a mess. The fortifications had been blasted by siege, and buildings were collapsing everywhere. But immigrants were still streaming in (the city's population was now about 350,000) and the new Henri IV wanted a gleaming Paris as the symbol of his power. With the help of his minister **Sully,** Henri set about a massive project of reconstruction. First he enlarged the Louvre. Then came the Pont-Neuf, the place des Vosges and the place Dauphine, plus many smaller projects. Henri widened the streets of Paris, making the city accessible to carriages for the first time (Henri himself loathed the new contraptions), and improved the city's water supply with the Pompe de la Samaritaine. To improve the city's ragged appearance (along with war and women, Henri claimed that architecture was his chief hobby), he decreed that buildings must be aligned with the street and encouraged Parisians to build in brick, rather than the more expensive stone, though wood was forbidden. Although the bulk of the program lasted only five years (1605-1610), Henri reestablished Paris's position as the place to be for aristocrats and merchants.

Henri's successors turned to more selfish projects. Marie and Richelieu built themselves palaces—the Luxembourg and the Palais Royal. Meanwhile the city's population skyrocketed, reaching perhaps 400,000 by the end of Louis XIII's reign.

The Arts

French art continued in the style of the Renaissance, unfazed by the violent wars of religion. The early 17th century witnessed the publication of several carefully surveyed maps of the city, prized today not only for the historical information they provide but also their aesthetic beauty. The lion-skin draped image of Henri IV—the "Gallic Hercules"—was painted and printed in large quantities, spreading the belief idea that he had brought peace and unity to the country.

See: Place des Vosges, Pont Neuf, Hôpital St-Louis, Luxembourg Palace, Palais Royal.

The End of the Old Regime (1643-1789)

Politics

Louis XIV ascended to the throne in 1643 at the mature age of five. He gained a harsh exposure to reality in 1648, when an attempt by his councilor, **Mazarin,** to levy fines on Parisian homeowners drove the city to the barricades, in a revolt known as the **Fronde.** The young king never got over the shock of being caught in the midst of a disloyal Paris. As soon as he had escaped the clutches of Mazarin, Louis ordered a new palace to be built outside the city, in the town of Versailles. Despite the absence of the king, Paris continued to thrive as a financial and industrial capital. Immigrants poured in from different provinces and settled into distinctive neighborhoods. Under Louis XIV, the doctrine of **absolute monarchy** reached its apogee. Calling himself the *Roi Soleil* (the Sun King), he eliminated the last powers of the nobility, turning them into a caste of idle hunters and fawning courtiers, and declared that there was no higher law than the will of the sovereign. Taxing France for all its worth, he attacked Holland and the German states to the east in an endeavor to extend his power to the left bank of the Rhine. The War of Spanish Succession, which pitted France against the English and the Prussians, was particularly draining, and by the time the Sun King set after a 72-year reign, the monarchy was getting into trouble.

Louis XV, the Sun King's great-grandson, was one of the most dissolute monarchs in European history, and that's saying a lot. Like his ancestor, he enjoyed expensive wars and lavish entertainment. Unlike Louis XIV, he demonstrated little capacity as a leader and relied on his mistresses, including **Madame de Pompadour** and **Madame du Barry,** for political advice. When he died of smallpox in 1774, he left his grandson with a crippling national debt. , **Louis XVI's** fondness for naval power, his costly support of the Thirteen Colonies in their war of independence from Great Britain, and the expensive habits of his queen, **Marie Antoinette,** all aggravated the situation.

Architecture and Urban Design

The 17th century—reign of the Sun King, Versailles, and the Absolute Monarchy— ushered in the age of the **Baroque. Le Nôtre, Le Brun,** and **Le Vau** reigned as the triumvirate of French art, designing respectively the gardens, architecture, and all-important interior paintings of Vaux-le-Vicomte and Versailles. More prosaic buildings inside the city copied the Mansart roofs invented for Versailles. Gothic architecture was banned by order of Louis XIV, and Italianate domes popped up like toadstools across the city. The dense urban center grew to a height of five or six stories, with the richest Parisians living on the lowest floors and the poor occupying the garrets. This growth concerned the king, but he was powerless to stop it; Paris had become the largest city in Europe, its stench detectable from 15km away. Louis relieved some of the pressure by pulling down Chales V's walls and replacing them with wide streets, as well as by taking his court—and all of its attendant mistresses, servants, nobility, horses, and fleas—out to the suburbs.

Louis XVI ordered the construction of a new wall around Paris. The *fermiers généraux* (farmers-general) wall was not intended to keep out enemy troops; it served as a physical customs barrier to ensure that the proper taxes were paid on goods, such as salt, tobacco, and wine, moving in and out of the city. Of course, the Parisians were just ecstatic about this. Destroyed in the 19th century, this wall was replaced by the "exterior boulevards" that form the outer borders of the eighth, ninth, tenth, and eleventh *arrondissements* as well as the bd. St-Jacques, bd. Grenelle, and other streets on the Left Bank. This project tripled the area of the city, though most building remained within the lines of the older walls for a long time.

Outside the city walls, working-class districts called *faubourgs* housed a growing population of artisans, as workers immigrating from the provinces made Paris the manufacturing center of France. The royal administration met this development with ambivalence, sometimes bestowing privileges on the workers, often trying to limit the growth of the city and the number of factories. Farther suburbs, including many towns that were later to be incorporated into Paris proper, grew rich by provisioning the capital, while wheat and livestock were drawn in from all over northern France.

The Arts

The 17th century established the foundation of the Classical French tradition, and the portrait of Louis XIV, in stone, paint, and relief, loomed as ever-present as Big Brother. Within the walls of the aristocracy's elaborate palaces, a system of patronage tied the age's most respected literati to the merest whim of their ruler. The rigidly rhythmed tragedies of **Corneille** and **Racine** explored the issues of love, honor, and duty. **Molière's** brilliant satires were performed in the gardens of Vaux-le-Vicomte and Versailles and, sponsored by the king's cousin, at the prestigious Comédie Française. **La Fontaine** read his highly moralistic fables in the salons of the immoral aristocracy, who were in turn serenaded by the operas of Jean-Baptiste **Lully. Pascal,** in his pessimistic *Pensées,* anticipated Romanticism when he wrote "the heart has its reasons of which reason knows nothing." His colleague **Descartes** ushered in the Enlightenment with a more intellectual "I think, therefore I am." **Mme. de Sévigné,** collecting a *salon* of leading intellectuals around her, recorded her reflections on her contemporaries in hundreds of letters to her daughter. And all this was regulated by the newly formed **Académie Française** (1635), which ever since has righteously preserved the tradition of classical French letters, with Racine's *Phèdre* as its Bible and the crystal clear poetry of Malherbe as its *Book of Songs*.

The Académie Royale, founded in 1648, performed the same function in the realm of painting and sculpture. **Nicolas Poussin's** classical, "serious-minded" views of historical and Biblical scenes became its highest ideal; **Claude Lorraine's** idyllic landscapes, with ruins, shepherds, and mountains, formed a landscape tradition based on highly structured lyricism. In 1725, the Academy inaugurated annual *Salons,* held in the vacant halls of the Louvre.

In 1666, Colbert founded the **Académie des Sciences** to argue over such important issues as whether a dead fish weighs more than a live fish (actually weighing two such fish was *not* considered conclusive evidence). But the publication of Newton's *Principia* ushered in an era of faith in the power of reason known as the **Enlightenment. Voltaire** declared that "if God did not exist, we would have to invent Him." A generation later, **Diderot** gathered around him a group of young intellectuals, intent on creating an Encyclopedia that would encapsulate all human knowledge, including several articles by their mentor, Voltaire. **Mozart** played his first concert in Paris in 1763, bringing the classical purity and restrained elegance of his music to France, where it found a counterpart in the rationalistic philosophy of the *philosophes*. **Rousseau's** *Social Contract* and autobiographical *Confessions* rejected this rationality entirely, claiming that a return to nature alone could save human nature, long corrupted by modern society.

Beaumarchais's *Marriage of Figaro,* produced in 1784, was hugely popular with nobility and working class alike, yet its sharp wit and eloquent dialogues held an open condemnation of the aristocracy. Louis XVI, when he first heard the play, exclaimed prophetically "the Bastille would have to be destroyed if the performance of the play is not to have dangerous consequences;" the playwright was imprisoned, not in the Bastille as protocol dictated, but in the St-Lazare prison for delinquent boys.

A sober bourgeoisie admired the scenes of everyday life by **Chardin** and **Greuze** before turning its attention to the stirring moral history paintings of **David.** Meanwhile the French aristocracy, continuing on its ruinous course of debauchery and dissolution, employed **Rococo** artists like **Boucher** and **Fragonard** to decorate its gold-embossed salons and bedrooms with flying cherubs and mischevious escapades. **Watteau** painted the *fêtes* and secret *rendez-vous* of the aristocracy as a magnificently theatrical display. **Choderlos de Laclos** illuminated the same world, part sparkling wit, part licentiousness, part tragic emptiness, in his controversial *Dangerous Liaisons*. **Elisabeth Vigée-Lebrun,** a rare female artist, painted the French nobility with a charm that many years later earned her a great success with the court of Russia.

See: Versailles, Vaux-le-Vicomte, Ile-St-Louis, Panthéon.

Revolution and Napoleon (1789-1815)

Politics

The crisis of the French monarchy began with the disastrous harvests of 1787 and 1788, combined with an enormous royal debt that was crippling the economy. Forced to find a new source of income, Louis XVI summoned the old **Estates General,** a representative body that had not met since 1614, but which held the power to tax the nobility and clergy. Once gathered together in Paris, this body declared itself a National Assembly, and the age of absolute monarchy was over. Meanwhile, the high numbers of artisans in the capital felt the sting of recession as their wages bought less and less bread each week. On July 14, 1789, an impatient mob stormed the **Bastille** to seize its gunpowder. For a time, it appeared that a compromise could be reached in the form of a constitutional monarchy. But in October, with no cheap bread forthcoming, a Parisian mob marched out to Versailles and brought the royal family back under the power of the city; power devolved to the National **Convention.** Major reforms, such as the abolition of guilds and the disestablishment of the Church, transformed the nation. In 1791, Louis and his despised queen tried to flee to the border, but were captured and dragged back to Paris again, their legitimacy spent. On September 21, 1792, the French republic was declared. In 1793, the radical **Jacobin** faction, led by brutal merchant of death Maximilien **Robespierre,** took over the Convention and began a period of suppression and mass execution known as the **Terror.** While passing radical legislation to create a new calendar, a new civic religion, and the metric system, the Jacobins guillotined the king and queen, their enemies, and, as things got rough, each other. Such a system could not last, and the leading Jacobins were arrested in the revolutionary month of **Thermidor** (August 1793). A moderate **Directory** took power in late 1795.

The Directory held on as best it could, but it was faced with a disastrous national debt and the invading forces sent by worried monarchs who had been trying to kill the republican disease before its spread. One of the most promising generals of these wars, **Napoleon Bonaparte,** took power in a coup in 1799 and declared a faux-Roman **consulate** with himself as consul. By 1804 he had declared himself **emperor** and, in a series of astonishing victories over various monarchies, proved himself the greatest military commander since Alexander the Great. But the combined power of the Royal Navy, the Russian winter, and various opposing armies proved too much, and on March 30, 1814, the Prussians occupied an undefended Paris. Five days later, Napoleon abdicated and was packed off to the island of Elba while Louis XVI's brother entered the capital as **Louis XVIII.** A bored Napoleon returned to France in early 1815, winning the army's loyalty away from Louis, who was forced to flee. But it was a desperate move, and Napoleon met ultimate defeat at Waterloo. A few weeks later, enemy troops were encamped on the Champs-Elysées and the Bois de Boulogne.

Architecture and Urban Design

Many of the Revolution's most impressive architectural achievements were temporary. An artificial mountain on the Champ de Mars, a cardboard Neoclassical interior for Notre-Dame, and various plaster statues of Liberty. All very Roman. More lasting were the various defacements; kings' statues were torn down and churches ransacked all over the city. Of course, the Revolution had better things to spend its *assignats* on, such as defending French borders and providing bread to the poor. In 1793, the Jacobins opened up to development the one-eighth of the city center previously owned by the Church and nobility. As if to show that tyrants do indeed leave better monuments, Napoleon took time from his pan-European schemes to improve his imperial capital—what he hoped would become the capital of Europe, the home of both emperor and pope. He planned cemeteries, dug sewers, numbered houses, widened the streets, and brought back the plunder of a continent to the Louvre. To the Right Bank's only east-west thoroughfare, the rue St-Honoré, he added the rue de Rivoli, naming it after one of his victories. Water and transport arrived in the form of the Ourcq canal. At the same time, Napoleon replaced the Commune's authority with imperial rule, establishing the office of the prefect to supervise the city.

The Arts

Art during the revolution was characterized by an emphasis on public displays, such as the **Fête de la Fédération,** held on the Champ de Mars on the first anniversary of the storming of the Bastille; subsequent ceremonies, with elaborate Neoclassical props and costumes planned by **David,** fêted such important state occasions as the transfer of Voltaire's body to the Panthéon. David himself joined the Jacobin party, painting such striking works as *The Oath in the Tennis Coart* and *The Dead Marat.* In 1793—the year of the Terror—the Louvre opened the Royal collection to the public, providing the beginnings of what would become the world's most famous art museum. Imprisoned by the Directory in 1794 and subsequently released, David changed allegiance, moving to the camp of the Corsican Emperor-to-be and painting for him the monumental *Le Sacre de Napoléon* (The Coronation of Napoleon).

Napoleon's regime sponsored a Neoclassicism in all realms of visual art, with Egyptian and Greek motifs (the **Empire** style) expressing his role as the spiritual son of the Roman emperors. At the same time, a spirit of **Romanticism** creeping in from Germany, from England, and from Jean-Jacques Rousseau came to a focus in the essays of **Mme. de Staël** and the novels of **Chateaubriand.** Chateaubriand's description of an isolated, melancholy young hero in *René* provided perhaps the first example of the *mal du siècle*—a feeling of disillusionment and alienation among 19th-century literati, rooted in the conviction that their century was a dying age.

See: Bastille, Versailles, Conciergerie, Palais Royal, Fontainebleau, Malmaison.

Restoration and July Monarchy (1815-1848)

Politics

After Napoleon's defeat at Waterloo, he surrendered and was imprisoned on the British island of St. Helena, in the middle of the Atlantic Ocean. The victorious monarchies of Europe reimposed the House of Bourbon upon a prostrate France. This **Restoration,** however, lasted only two monarchs (Louis XVIII and Charles X) and 15 years. In July of 1830, the people of Paris rose up against the monarchy. A terrified Louis-Philippe, Duc d'Orléans and cousin of the king, fled across the fields surrounding Paris, only to be tracked down and offered the throne. His **July Monarchy,** also known as the **Orleanist dynasty,** was seen as a compromise between the Bourbons' autocracy and the Republic's excess. Louis-Philippe was to be a "citizen-king," king not of France, but of the French, and his flag remained the revolutionary tricolor. In 1832, republicans dissatisfied with this arrangement erected barricades on the bd. Bourdon, but were shot down—an event dazzlingly recreated in the smash musical *Les Misérables.* The insurgents suffered thousands of casualties, most of them workers, and for sixteen years Louis-Philippe ruled without another major threat to his authority.

Architecture and Urban Design

Despite two bloody revolutions, the early 19th century was a prosperous time for the city. In 1828, the introduction of cheap horse-drawn omnibuses allowed workers to move to the outer distrcits and the suburbs. Four years later, a deadly cholera epidemic inspired the creation of a new network of sewers. Then in 1842, the French government made a momentous decision that would keep Paris at the center of the French economy in the new industrial age. The major railroads of France would all terminate in the capital. As the center of transportation, Paris thrived as the center of manufacture, where high wages drew thousands of migrants from the provinces. Gas illuminated the streets, and the Bièvre, a dribbling stream that had been stinking up the Left Bank since the Middle Ages, was finally filled in. Louis-Philippe's minister **Adolphe Thiers** created a new line of fortifications around the city, both to keep the enemy out and the troublemakers in (the line of this wall is now marked by the boulevard *périphérique* and the city limits). Meanwhile the city finally began to spread and fill in the area enclosed by the *fermiers généraux* wall.

Under the Restoration, the apartment building, introduced under Louis XVI, first became widespread. Previously, shared dwellings had been haphazard arrangements of owners and tenants living communally in a big building. Only now were buildings subdivided into wholly separate apartments, each with its own kitchen and windows overlooking the street—a form that would be adapted and imitated throughout the world. Many of the four-story buildings of Louis XV's reign had two more stories added on top. As industrialization made glass cheaper, windows proliferated. But unchecked growth continued to swamp improvements, and many of Paris's one million people lived in miserable, congested slums.

The Arts

The period of the Restoration and July Monarchy marked the division that would define the rest of the century: the **Classical** school led by **Jean-Auguste Dominique Ingres,** a student of David, and the **Romantic** school led by **Eugène Delacroix.** Ingres did not merely mimic David; he abandoned the classical proportions and monumental subjects of his master, focusing instead on sinuous lines and sensual surfaces—with subjects ranging from portraits to exotically erotic visions of near-eastern harems. Nevertheless, his use of linear forms, flat planes of color, and invisible brushstrokes was vastly different from Delacroix's emphasis on brilliant colors, dramatic movement, and emotional excess. The duel between the two artists focused into a battle between "line" and "color," the same which had separated Poussin's calculated Classicism from Rubens's emotional Baroque.

The *petite cénacle,* a group of poets led by **Victor Hugo** and including **Gérard de Nerval** and **Théophile Gautier,** espoused an emotional, lyrical style radically opposed to the cooly detached Academic tradition. Hugo's drama *Hernani* sparked an intense debate between Classicists and Romantics in the theater where it was first performed; the play's huge success indicated the triumph of the latter. Now, the idea of a *mal du siècle* came to dominate the field of letters. **Alfred de Vigny's** *Chatterton* blamed society for the tragic suicide of a young, idealistic poet. **Alfred de Musset** eloquently expressed the gloomy outlook of his contemporaries when he declared that "I came too late in a century that is too old." **Chopin,** a Polish-born composer, brought Romanticism to music with his sensitive, highly personal piano serenades. **George Sand,** Chopin's on-again-off-again significant other, was the first important female novelist in France, celebrated for her *romans champâtres* (pastoral novels) and for her scandalous habit of wearing trousers and smoking cigars. A second affair, between Sand and Musset, ended unhappily; in the best of romantic traditions, both used the failed romance as a subject for their next books.

The prolific **Honoré de Balzac** provided an opposite literary movement focusing on the harsh realities of bourgeois society under the "citizen-king." His *Comédie Humaine*—a series of novels that attempted to capture all of Parisian society with its biting wit and powerful sense of observation—covered everyone from the melancholy poet to the bejeweled courtesan and the *nouveau riche* noble. Meanwhile the invention of **photography** by Parisians **Nièpce** and **Daguerre** provided a new artistic medium, sparking an intense debate over the relative merits of painting and photography.

See: Musée des Egouts, Musée Balzac, Rue Rambuteau.

Second Republic and Second Empire (1848-1870)

Politics

A prohibition on political assembly and acute unemployment in the capital proved sufficient to catalyze latent discontent into active rebellion. On February 22, 1848, veterans of 1830 joined students in a march on the Chamber of Deputies, demanding a republic. Louis-Philippe could have quashed the revolt with force, but was unwilling to order his troops to fire on his subjects. Instead, he abdicated peacefully, and the **Second Republic** was declared. Even more than in 1792, the change in regime had been determined solely by events in the capital. The new provisional government did little for the starving workers of Paris, who, feeling betrayed, erected more barricades in the **June Days.** After what Marx called "the most colossal event in the history of European civil wars," the workers of Paris were defeated—thousands were killed or transported to the colonies. An anti-Parisian, conservative peasantry elected to the presidency an ambitious man named **Louis-Napoleon Bonaparte,** the nephew of the late emperor. On December 2, 1851, the anniversary of Napoleon's coronation and of Austerlitz, his greatest victory, Louis-Napoleon betrayed his true ambitions. With the help of generals imported from Algeria, he dissolved the National Assembly and ordered troops to arrest its leaders and suppress the city's newspapers. Two days later, his troops massacred the insurgents who had thrown up the now-traditional barricades against him.

Louis-Napoleon's regime was in many ways a prototype for the dictatorships of the 20th century. The press was more thoroughly censored than at any time since the spread of cheap newspapers. The illusion of democracy was maintained through periodic plebiscites and an elected assembly, but in fact only one party—the Bonapartists—had a chance. In 1852, after a victory in a national referendum, the dictator proclaimed himself Emperor **Napoleon III**—skipping a number in respect to Napoleon I's son, who had died in 1832—and moved from the presidential palace of the Elysée to the imperial palace of the Tuileries. A small amount of dissent was tolerated, and radical Paris kept sending republican representatives to the overwhelmingly Bonapartist legislature. Blights in the wine and silk industries, financial scandals, and a failed attempt to establish a puppet regime in Mexico tarnished the Empire, and the 1869 election revealed diminished support of the regime, especially in Paris.

Architecture and Urban Design

To France, the 1850s and 60s were the decades of Napoleon III. To Paris, they marked the tenure of **Baron Georges-Eugène Haussmann** as Prefect of the Seine. Armed with an 1841 law allowing the expropriation of private property in the public interest, the engineer was commissioned to modernize the city, to give it light, circulation, and safety. Haussmann's solution was to tear long, straight boulevards through the tangled clutter and stenchy, narrow alleys of old Paris, creating a unified network out of the few *grands boulevards* that followed the lines of the old city walls. (An embryonic version of this process had begun under Louis-Philippe and his prefect, Rambuteau.) These avenues were to serve several purposes. First, they were designed to increase circulation of goods and people, making life more pleasant in a crowded city whose widest street was only 12m from building to building. Second, they were to make Paris a work of art, a splendid capital worthy of France, with a street plan reminiscent of Versailles and beautiful boulevards lined with elegant, harmonious buildings. The demolition of old neighborhoods provided the perfect opportunity for the installation of modern water, sewer, and gas lines, and did much to eliminate odor and disease. And finally, the wide avenues and oblique intersections would once and for all make street barricades obsolete, and thus prevent insurrection. All of these "improvements" were funded in part by the imperial purse, mostly by highly unorthodox real estate speculation on the new avenues. Anticipating the Dadaists, Haussmann called himself an *"artiste demolisseur"* (artist-demolisher) and took a hatchet to the helpless city.

From 1852 to 1870, Haussmann transformed Paris from an intimate medieval city to a bustling modern metropolis. The old *fermiers généraux* wall was torn down, and the city expanded to fill the wall of 1840, annexing 400,000 people, doubling its area, and reaching its present total of 20 *arrondissements*. Five of Paris's seven hills were leveled; only Montmartre and the Montagne Ste-Geneviève remain. Twelve thousand structures were destroyed; 136km of straight avenues created. Each new boulevard, unveiled at its opening like a work of art, became more fashionable than the last. Government regulations on even design of façades ensured stylistic harmony of buildings facing the boulevards. Wide sidewalks (demolished in the next century to make room for automobiles) encouraged strollers, not to mention sidewalk cafés, kiosks, peddlers, and general crowds. The street culture of Paris gained fame throughout Europe, and Paris's street plan became an object of admiration, particularly when Napoleon III invited all of Europe to come see it at the Exhibition of 1867. Cast-iron was used for new purposes, such as bridges and pavilions, in anticipation of the modern skyscraper. But the transformation was not without its costs. Intimate neightborhoods were destroyed by the lacerations of the avenue de l'Opéra and the boulevard St-Michel. Their homes demolished to make room for the boulevards and replaced with inaffordable luxury apartments, the workers of Paris were forced eastward to Belleville and beyond. Here, suburban single-family houses were subdivided into tiny, squalid dwellings for the poor, creating a reservoir of misery that would erupt in the Commune.

The Arts

The birth of the Second Republic brought sudden hope to the melancholy circle of Romantics headed by Hugo. **Alphonse de Lamartine,** a poet known for his lyrical, soul-searching verses, turned to radical politics, becoming a member of the provisional government, and then the short-lived Legislature. Hugo himself served in the Assembly, eloquently defending the cause of "Liberty." The coup d'état of December 2 ended their short-lived political careers. Lamartine fled to the country; Hugo was exiled and spent the next 19 years on the isle of Guernsey, where he penned *Les Châtiments,* a book of vehemently anti-Bonaparte poems.

Hugo's exile became the clarion-call for a new generation of artists, utterly disillusioned with a government that no longer represented their ideals. Like the itinerant gypsies after which they were named (mistakenly labeled Bohemians), the **Bohemians** proclaimed for themselves a life free from normal conventions. Following in the footsteps of the *petit cénacle,* this "race of obstinate dreamers for whom art has remained a faith and not a career" gathered in the cafés of the Latin Quarter and starved proudly in the garrets of Paris. **Charles Baudelaire, Champfleury, Nadar** (photographer and aeronaut), and **Rodolphe Bresdin** were but a few of the famous characters whose way of life was made famous in **Henry Murger's** bestselling *Scènes de la Vie de Bohème* (later turned into Puccini's opera, *La Bohème*). Murger described a society of itinerant artists, gay and lighthearted on the outside, faced with poverty, heartbreak, and disillusionment inside. "Bohemia is the apprenticeship for artistic life; it is the preface to the Academy, the Hospital, or the Morgue," he wrote in the preface. His gloomy forecast was substantiated by such famous examples as the suicide of Gérard de Nerval, who hanged himself from an iron grill of the rue de la Vieille Lanterne. Images like these, however, only perpetuated the myth of Bohemia as the last, despairing frontier for the artist in an age where "American" values had overtaken society.

Their world, together with that of the bourgeois society they rejected, was described by **Emile Zola** in his *Rougon-Macquart* series. Inspired by Balzac's *Comédie Humaine*, Zola added a newly "scientific" element of detail and called his movement **Naturalism. Flaubert's** *Madame Bovary*, published in 1857 and charged with "offense to public and religious morality and to good morals," caused a sensational trial. His novel tells the story of a provincial wife who, attempting to escape from her narrow life, takes on a lover and subsequently commits suicide, but the outrage appears to have been more due to the style of his work, its "free indirect form," than the actual story-line.

Following both this new urge for naturalistic detail and the Romantics' urge to escape to nature, artists like **Millet** and **Rousseau** retreated to Barbizon to paint the forêt de Fontainebleau and the French peasantry. Influenced by the social-Utopian theories of Charles Fourier, **Gustave Courbet** rejected Academic historical painting in favor of a "living art" that would portray what he saw around him; he received the same label as Flaubert **(Realist)** and also the same general outrage. As Europe spread its tentacles across the globe, the East became an inspiration for fashion, painting, and the decorative arts. Academic artsits like **Jean-Léon Gérôme** created lush scenes of Turkish baths and snake-charmers. At the opposite end of the spectrum, Japanese *ukiyoe* prints, which inundated the market from 1853 on, brought their asymmetrical compositions, soft colors, and flattened planes to the welcoming eyes of the nascent Impressionists.

Claude Monet, Pierre-Auguste Renoir, and **Frédéric Bazille** (who died before making his name) met during the 1860s in Paris and began to develop their now-famous technique. Used to the smooth surfaces and clear-cut lines of Academic painting, critics objected to the "mess" the soon-to-be Impressionists produced; the sketchy quality of their paintings, together with the rough brushwork, invalidated the hallowed Renaissance concept of the canvas as a smooth, illusionistic window. **Edouard Manet's** *Déjeuner sur l'Herbe* was refused by the Salon of 1863; together with his fellow radicals, he defiantly exhibited his painting just outside in a separate *"Salon des Refusés"* (Salon of the Rejected), with a 50 centimes entrance fee.

Six years earlier, in 1857, **Charles Baudelaire** led the way to modernism with his perverse, disturbingly beautiful *Fleurs du Mal* (Flowers of Evil), a collection of poems describing Paris as a sordid and decaying world, seen through the eyes of the elderly, the poor, the prostitutes, and, amid all these, the poet. With this alternative guidebook to Paris, the *flâneur* (wanderer) came into being—the Bohemian ideal of someone who wanders endlessly without direction, doomed to roam among the crowd, and yet stand apart from it. In August 1857, half a year after the *Madame Bovary* trial, *Les Fleurs du Mal* was put on trial for the same charge; the same prosecutor, Ernest Pinard, this time succeeded. Baudelaire was fined and six poems were censored from his book, not to be reinstated until a second trial in 1949.

See: Opéra Garnier, Compiègne, Bd. Haussmann, Avenue Foch, Bois de Boulogne, Bois de Vincennes.

Siege and Commune (1870-1871)

Politics

As his popularity faded in the spring of 1870, Napoleon III again resorted to that eternal trick of cynical statesmen: start a war. On a flimsy diplomatic excuse, Napoleon launched the **Franco-Prussian War** in July 1870. Lacking allies and steel artillery, the French army was within weeks divided in two, trapped in Metz and defeated at Sedan.

Napoleon, who in farcical imitation of his uncle had decided to participate in the battle himself, personally surrendered to King Wilhelm of Prussia on September 3. When the news of the emperor's capture reached Paris, a mob of National Guardsmen stormed the Palais Bourbon, then carried the Paris representatives to the Hôtel de Ville, where the Third Republic was proclaimed. But the Prussians were fighting France, not the Empire, and they continued on their march. By September 20, Paris was invested.

Général **Louis Trochu,** serving as both military commander and president of the republic, made a few attempts at breaking out, but was repeatedly thrown back. Cut off from the rest of France and the world, resourceful Parisians turned to that Parisian invention, the balloon. They floated out thousands of letters, and even Minister of the Interior **Léon Gambetta** raised an army in the provinces in an unsuccessful attempt to relieve the capital. But there was no way to get food in. Desperate city-dwellers turned their culinary powers on cats, rats, horses, and zoo animals, while the poorest of the poor slowly starved on various forms of adulterated bread. Finally, the hunger was too much. On January 27, 1871, after 129 days of encirclement, the city capitulated.

In a national election held under the terms of the armistice with Prussia, the aristocrats and peasants of France voted in an extremely conservative regime, led by **Adolphe Thiers,** the old Orléanist. Thiers's government negotiated a treaty with Bismarck, under which France agreed to disband most of its army, pay an enormous indemnity, cede the provinces of Alsace and Lorraine, and allow the Germans (until recently Prussians) a triumphal march through Paris. Paris could not endure this government by the provinces. When, on March 18, Thiers tried to disarm the National Guard, the Paris workers who composed the Guard responded with gunfire. Thiers's government fled to Versailles, and ten days later, a committee of leftist politicians installed itself in power and called itself the **Paris Commune,** a name revived from the glory days of 1789. Part workers' state, part reenactment of the great Revolution, part schoolboys' attempt at government, the Commune was feared by the bourgeoisie and orphaned by international socialism. The only thing certain about the Commune is that it set the workers of Paris against the peasant government at Versailles. In response, Thiers received permission from the Germans to assemble a new army of provincials to begin a new siege of the city. The *Versaillais* regulars proved much more efficient than the city's defenders, and on May 21 they pierced the city walls into the friendly, bourgeois, 16th *arrondissement.* The Prussian siege had been a nightmare, but the street fighting of the "bloody week" is by far the low point in the city's violent history. Resorting to old forms, the dying Commune threw up barricades. But Haussmann's boulevards functioned with deadly efficiency, and the regulars easily outflanked the defenders. By the 25th, the *Versaillais* had taken the city. As they swept through and in the following days, they massacred hundreds of *communards* and suspected *communards* without any effort at trial. Over 20,000 Parisians perished, and one leftist newspaper claimed that the Seine was literally streaked with blood. Half the plumbers in the city were dead, imprisoned, or on the lam, and similar numbers in other trades hint at the devestation inflicted upon the working class. The crushing of the Commune broke both the power of Paris over the provinces and of the Paris proletariat over the city.

Architecture and Urban Design

By the time the Prussians arrived, Thiers's 30-year old walls were already obselete, but the ring of forts he had constructed kept the invaders several kilometers away. In spite of their glorified goals, Haussmann's boulevards didn't help much with the defense effort; it still took days for large numbers of troops to get from one side of the city to the other. Although the siege was unpleasant, it left few permanent scars. The Prussian bombardment, raining 12,000 shells on the city in the space of three weeks, was terrifying, but not very destructive: only 97 lives were lost. The real destruction came during the suppression of the Commune. Fires—the result of stray shells, military necessity, and *communard* spite—did a great deal of damage. The *communards* deliberately destroyed the Tuileries palace and the Hôtel de Ville. The city's firefighters were helpless amid the whizzing bullets and broken water mains. But Parisian rain, as dependable as death and taxes, eventually put out the blaze.

The Arts

Among the Parisians trapped by the Prussians were two of history's greatest diarists, the **Goncourt** brothers. Their *Journal* provides a fascinating account of daily life in wartime. Other artists, like Rodolphe Bresdin, participated avidly in the battles of 1870-71. Gustave Courbet was elected to the Commune and put in charge of reopening the Salon. His own special project was the toppling of the Vendôme column, a long-time symbol of Royal and Napoleonic absolute authority. After the fall of the Commune, Courbet's execution was falsely reported by *Le Figaro;* in actuality, he got off far more lightly than many who were far less guilty—six-months imprisonment and a 250,000F fine for the restoration of the Vendôme column. Unable to pay the fine, he subsequently fled to Switzerland.

See: Sacré Coeur, Père Lachaise, Versailles, Hôtel de Ville.

La Belle Epoque (1871-1914)

Politics

Given the decisive defeat of the ultra-republican Commune and the election of a very conservative National Assembly, France expected a return to monarchy. But the monarchists were divided between the legitimists (who supported a return of the Bourbons) and the Orléanists (who wanted Louis-Philippe's heir), so France ambled along under the republican tricolor. The assembly improvised a regime composed of a mostly powerless president as head of state, plus a prime minister as head of government. In the elections of 1877, the republicans triumphed, and the regime solidified. The next year, the government returned to Paris from Versailles. In 1880, the last imprisoned *communards* were given amnesty.

The **Boulanger** crisis of 1888, in which a former minister of war almost seized power, revealed the public's weak enthusiasm for the republic; however, with no real strongman or heir to the throne as a rival, the regime survived. In 1898 the city divided over the **Dreyfus Affair,** which set the Rightists and anti-Semites, who believed Jewish army captain Alfred Dreyfus a traitor (or at least not worth exposing the beloved Army's corruption), against Leftists of various types, who saw through the government's charges and demanded that the cover-up be exposed. In August 1899, the president's attempt to attend the races at Auteuil sparked a riot between Right and Left that left a hundred people wounded. Few observers expected the republic to last, but the Left wasn't ready for another Commune and the Right had no one to offer as dictator. A presidential pardon of Dreyfus gave a limited victory to the Left (Dreyfus's name was not cleared until 1906), but the conservatives had shown their power. In the elections of 1900 and 1902, the Right gained control of Paris's municipal council, an astounding reversal for the traditionally liberal capital. More ominious were the riots of 1908 and 1909, when extremely conservative Catholic students organized into the first political street gangs, protesting the right of a somewhat anti-clerical professor to lecture. While a powerful, industrialized Germany saw itself surrounded by enemies, the French were obsessed with finding enemies among themselves.

Architecture and Urban Design

Although it broke with the politics of the Second Empire, the Third Republic continued the transformation of Paris along its predecessor's lines. What Haussmann was to the Second Empire, **Eugène Hénard** was to the early Third Republic. As an official in the public works department, he conceived and initiated an intensificiation of Haussmann's plan, widening several streets in and radiating from the center of the city. Although he lacked the dicatorial power of his predecessor, Hénard was able to make his vision of traffic circles, muti-level interchanges, and varied façades an important element in the city's appearance. Electricity slowly began to replace gas lighting. Hydraulic elevators, introduced to the world at the 1867 Exhibition, became widespread; suddenly the top floors of buildings became the most desirable. The Exhibitions of 1889 and 1900 brought glory to the city and left several quintessentially Parisian landmarks in their wake: the *Métropolitain,* the Grand and Petit Palais, and of course, the Eiffel Tower. A new building code in 1902 gave architects considerably more freedom than they had enjoyed before. Under the influence of **Art Nouveau,** façades became increasingly fanciful, reaching their stylistic zenith at Hector Guimard's Castel Béranger.

The Arts

The Third Republic is seen by many as the age of **Impressionism.** Monet, increasingly the head of this group of young radicals, and **Camille Pissarro** established their own exhibition in 1874, sick to death of juries, official competition, and establishment taste. Housed in the former photographic studio of Nadar, the exhibit consisted of 165 canvases of which one was Monet's *Impression: Sunrise.* A snide critic made fun of this canvas, labeling its creator an "Impressionist." Monet and his colleagues gleefully extolled their name, and the show became an annual event. The newly dubbed Impressionists set about playing with light and color to capture perceived reality. On the one hand, Impressionism was an aesthetic movement, breaking with the Academy's program of flawless surface, monumental themes, and invisible brush strokes—insisting that art could be made just as easily with swift brushstrokes, broken surfaces, and ordinary themes, and that paintings ought to capture the spirit and sensations of a moment. On the other hand, Impressionism was a movement to capture the new rhythm of bourgeois life—no longer expressible through the tired channels of traditional French painting. Haussmann had created an entirely new city, and an entirely new field of subject matter for the modern-thinking artist. For the first time, the crowd—already so aptly described by Hugo and Baudelaire *Les Fleurs du Mal*—became a subject worthy of painting. Impressionist paintings focused on cafés, balls, cabarets, ballets; works like **Manet's** *A Bar at the Folies-Bergères* (1882) and **Degas's** *The Glass of Absinthe* (1876) illuminated a disquieting emptiness behind the theatricality of the Belle Epoque. At the same time, a new interest in the countryside created an ideal arena for the Impressionists' credo of *plein air* (open-air) painting.

In the last decades of the 19th century, a highly individualistic group of artists, labelled the **Post-Impressionists,** explored more and more abstract issues of color, light, and planar geometry, anticipating the 20th century's movement to Cubism and abstract art. Both **Paul Cézanne** and **Vincent Van Gogh** went past Impressionism to explore their own unique visions—from Van Gogh's brilliant colors and deeply spiritual views of nature to Cézanne's geometric reconstruction of landscape and form. **Paul Gauguin,** to whom Van Gogh mailed his severed ear, left a family and highly successful career as a stockbroker to paint the peasants of Brittany and the "natives" of Tahiti. Declaring that "art is an abstraction," he created a highly symbolic form of painting, attempting to leave behind the "corruption" of the Western tradition. His reliance on non-Western art forms, especially the wooden idols of Tahiti, anticipated Picasso's discovery of African art. Meanwhile, **Pointillists** like **Seurat** explored a highly scientific type of painting, with works made up of tiny dots in primary colors. Their flat, static surfaces took the landscapes and cabaret scenes of Impressionism and imbued them with a simultaneous sense of permanence and lack of depth. In sculpture, official commissions (exemplified by the extravagant, allegorical creations of **Carpeaux)** abounded, while **Rodin,** focusing on a highly energetic, muscular shaping of bronze and stone, provided a counterpart to Michelangelo's *Slaves.*

During this period, Bohemia had moved outside Haussmann's city to the cabarets and cafés of **Montmartre**—an oasis for artists and bourgeois alike from the crowds and sterility of the modern city below. Offenbach composed his celebrated cancan; **Toulouse-Lautrec** captured the spirit and flashy theatricality of the Belle Epoque in the vibrant silkscreen posters that covered Paris, as well as his starkly linear paintings of brothels, circuses, and cabarets. Meanwhile, a circle of **Symbolist** poets—**Verlaine, Rimbaud,** and, later, **Mallarmé**—followed Baudelaire to create a "musical" poetry, founded in sounds and images *(vers libérés)* rather than meaning, reaching its epitome in Mallarmé's *l'Aprés-midi d'un faune.* "Impressionist" composers like **Debussy** and **Ravel** in turn brought the freedom of Symbolist poetry to their music, evoking the sounds of the ocean, the winds, and the rising sun.

In 1884, **J.K. Huysmans,** erstwhile protogée of Emile Zola, published *Against the Grain* heralding the beginning of the **Decadence.** Huysmans described a wealthy hyper-aesthete nobleman who, disgusted with the banality of Parisian society, retires to a suburb and tries to create a perfect aesthetic environment. Huysmans "anti-hero" revels in the artificial and the perverse; instead of fake flowers that imitate the real, he chooses "real flowers that imitate the false." Naturally, the more conservative critics were outraged. "After such a book," recorded one critic, "there is nothing left for the author but to choose between the pistol's mouth or the foot of the cross." (Huysmans chose the cross, turning to a deeply mystical Catholic literature in his later books.)

Nietzsche's philosohpy, rooted in a belief in artifice, in surface, in "cheerfulness," and "dancing," and in the rejection of decayed traditions, formed the basis of a new, extraordinarily style—**Art Nouveau.** Art Nouveau quickly became as universal as the Gothic movement seven hundred years before, embracing architecture, furniture, lamps, jewelry, fashion, and book illustration in its search for an all-conclusive aesthetic where *style* was more important than function. Paris erupted into the violent storm of the Dreyfus Affair in 1898 when Zola published *J'accuse*—a letter that accused the goverment of a huge cover-up that had made Dreyfus into a national scapegoat. Manet, Pissaro, Signac, and Mary Cassat joined Zola in the *dreyfusard* camp; Cézanne, Renoir, Rodin, and the anti-Semitic Degas joined the *anti-dreyfusards.*

The 20th century brought a deeply self-conscious, chaotic art world, following the generation just before in its search for a new and *modern* art. **Erik Satie,** a wandering Bohemian of Montmartre, wrote his pensive, ponderous *Gymnopèdes,* where each piano note has the weight of a spoken word. A young group of artists led by Henri **Matisse** and inspired by Gauguin painted with increasingly brilliant colors, flat planes, and decorative surfaces. Critics labeled them the *fauves* (wild beasts), yet their "wildness" barely hinted at the extreme to which **Pablo Picasso** and **George Braque** would carry art with their **Cubist** experiments of 1907 to 1914. Together with Braque and a poet friend—**Guillaume Apollinaire**—Picasso soon formulated rigid precepts for the movement: Cubist painting sought to overcome traditional attachment to "retinal reality," representing the idea of an object, rather than the object itself. In order to represent a three-dimensional "idea" on a flat canvas, Picasso presented his subjects from several angles at once, deconstructing and reassembling them into their simplest geometric components. **Marcel Duchamp** added an element of dynamic movement and machinism to Cubism with paintings like *Nude Descending a Staircase.* **Utrillo,** painter of Montmartre, and **Man Ray** formed part of the same set, while **Eugene Atget,** a brilliant photographer who documented the streets, buildings, and shop fronts of Paris, provided Picasso and his friends with photographic "sketches" to use as a basis for their art. **Marc Chagall** and **Giorgio de Chirico** immigrated to Paris from Russia and Italy and brought with them their own uniquely child-like visions; Chagall created his Cubist-fairy-tale pictures of Russian villages and Jewish legends, while Chirico painted his strange, often sinister images that anticipated Breton's *Surrealist Manifesto.*

On the eve of World War I, Paris argued and sometimes came to blows over such *Ballets russes* as Debussy's *L'Aprés-midi d'un faune* (1912), danced and choreographed by the famous **Nijinsky.** Debussy's symphonic setting of Mallarmé's poem, with the flute taking the role of Pan, provided perhaps the era's most perfect expression of the union between musical sound and words, while Nijinsky's highly erotic choreography (fitting the tone of the poem) caused a truly magnificent scandal. Yet no one was prepared for the 1913 opening of **Stravinsky's** *Rites of Spring,* blowing apart traditional precepts of music and ballet with its iconoclastic use of atonalities, a non-plot, and violently ungraceful choreography. The opening show, on May 29, 1913, erupted almost immediately into an uproar; to Stravinsky's amazement, the conductor kept going and was able (amid catcalls, fights, whistles, and applause) to finish the show.

See: Eiffel Tower, Moulin Rouge, *Métropolitain* signs, Grand and Petit Palais.

World War and Après la Guerre (1914-1939)

Politics

On August 3, 1914, Kaiser Wilhelm II's belligerent Germany declared war on France. Hoping for a quick victory in the west to be followed by an attack on Russia, an enormous German army swept through neutral Belgium and northern France with startling speed, hellbent on capturing Paris. As their armies fought a desperate retreat,

French generals debated whether to treat Paris as any other city and abandon it if necessary, to declare it an open city to prevent its destruction, or to defend the capital at all costs while preparing for another siege. On August 30, German planes dropped bombs and disheartening leaflets on the city in a new milestone of warfare aimed at civilians. Three days later, the government fled for Bordeaux. But Paris's military governor, Général **Gallieni**, vowed to stay and fight, drafting civilians to dig trenches in the suburbs and entrusting the city's museums to the neutral Americans. Ironically, just as the French decided that Paris was too important to abandon, the Germans decided that it could be ignored and wheeled east in pursuit of the bulk of the French army. Gallieni and Commander-in-Chief **Joffre** took the opportunity to attack the German flank. As the **Battle of the Marne** raged a mere 60km from Paris, 600 of the city's taxis were commandeered to rush reinforcements to the front. This improvised counteroffensive was successful, and the Germans were thrown back to a safe distance from the capital. By the spring of 1916, despite occasional Zeppelin raids, the theaters, cinemas, and galleries of Paris were joyously humming again, much to the disgust of the *poilus* dying in the trenches of Verdun. Then the front returned; from March to August 1918 a hundred-foot-long German cannon, knicknamed "Big Bertha" shelled the city from 130km away, causing over 1000 casualties. By the signing of the Armistice at Compiègne in November 1918, 1,300,000 Frenchmen were dead.

In the immediate aftermath of World War I, Paris shone in the spotlight of victory. On July 14, 1919, troops from the Allied nations marched down the Champs-Elysées, in tribute to France. Delegates from around the world arrived to redraw the map of Europe at the Paris **Peace Conference,** eventually producing the flawed Treaty of Versailles. The rift between Left and Right, so evident during the Commune and the Dreyfus affair, gaped anew during the 1930s. War debts, the bane of French regimes since Louis XIV, were a continuing problem. Uniformed fascist leagues and extreme-right newspapers demanded an overthrow of the government and its Socialist leader **Daladier.** On February 6, 1934, right-wing newspapers called for a march on the Assembly, i.e., an overthrow of the government by force. 40,000 demonstrators—many of them veterans, others with paramilitary training, and some of them Communists who considered the left-wing government reactionary—assembled in the place de la Concorde. Armed with sticks, lead pipes, and razors, they attempted to smash through the police barricade on the pont de la Concorde, but were forced to retreat when the police opened fire, killing 16. The coup was unsuccessful, but Daladier did resign. In response to such challenges and the rise of Nazism in Germany, the Socialists and Communists (who had split in 1920 over the issue of obedience to Moscow) buried the hatchet and founded the **Popular Front,** a coalition of the Left similar to the one fighting Franco in Spain. Led by Socialist **Léon Blum,** the Front won power in April 1936. Blum instituted such social reforms as paid holidays and the 40-hour week, but in the middle of a world depression and a German military buildup, his timing was disastrous; his government fell in 1937. The burden of France's massive national debt, divided citizenry, ravaged population, and obselescent industry became increasingly apparent as Hitler flexed his muscles in Munich.

Architecture and Urban Design

With France's available labor force occupied in either the army or the arms industry, the years 1914-1918 marked a near-complete cessation of building; many half-finished projects were abandoned as they stood. Despite a few air raids, Paris suffered none of the war damage endured by French, Belgian, and Russian cities on the front. After the war, architects finished up many incomplete buildings without any major stylistic changes. A few radical architects began to focus on new building materials, discovering reinforced concrete. Among the pioneers of this new material was a Swiss citizen named **Le Corbusier.** Rather than cursing the concrete's inability to bear intricate ornament, he gloried in its flat, plain surfaces. Le Corbusier's work was so controversial that at a 1925 exposition, the organizers surrounded his pavilion with a 6m-high fence, then prevented him from receiving first prize on the grounds that his work "contained no architecture." Perhaps they were justified; inside the pavilion were plans for demolishing much of the Right Bank and replacing it with a grid of uniform skyscrapers.

Distressed by the poverty, squalor, and disease of the Paris slums, the government took action in the interwar period to surround Paris with a ring of *cités jardins* (garden cities). Other public housing was started on the edge of the city, in the open space that was left by the demolition in 1919 of Thiers's old walls. In the 1930s, the Great Depression slowed building to a crawl, and few new projects (with the notable exception of the Palais de Chaillot) were built.

The Arts

In 1917, in the midst of World War I, came the *Ballet russes*'s final great triumph— *Parade*, written by dreamy young poet **Jean Cocteau,** who had been inspired by the audience "participation" at the opening of *the Rites of Spring,* with music by Erik Satie, Cubist costumes and set by Picasso, and choreography by Nijinsky. As the war continued, however, the Cubists and their circle dispersed, and Apollinaire died at the front. Horrified by the machine-like slaughter of the war, Duchamp switched from his futurist machine-worshiping painting to lead the **Dadaists,** a group of artists who focused on utter nonsense and non-art—drawing a mustache on a picture of the Mona Lisa and exhibiting a urinal, signed by the man who had finished it on the assembly line.

André Gide, whose own novels and journals reflected a pure, classical detachment, founded the *Nouvelle Revue Française,* a journal which would become *the* grounding board for up-and-coming writers in the inter-war period. In the years between 1913 and 1927, **Marcel Proust** wrote his monumental *Remembrance of Things Past,* a semi-autobiographical summation of the Belle Epoque and its complex social undercurrents. Proust sent his first chapter to the *Nouvelle Revue;* in one of history's great miscalculations, Gide refused the piece without even unwrapping the package, claiming that the aristocratic Proust—"a snob, a dilettante, and a man-about-town"—was incapable of producing good literature. **Colette** provided a multi-layered description of the sensual world of Paris in the 20s, focusing on issues of love and sexuality, especially between women. In 1924, **André Breton** published his *Surrealist Manifesto* and launched the **Surrealist** movement among a group of former Dadaists, who now claimed to create an art of the subconscious, seeking out the dream world that was more real than the rational world around them. **René Magritte, Salvador Dalí, Yves Tanguy,** and **Max Ernst** painted and etched their playful images of top hats, castles, angels, misplaced nude bodies, and melting clocks. Cocteau, now a full-fledged surrealist, wrote *Les Enfants Terribles* and produced such dreamily evocative films as *La Belle et la Bête.*

The 1920s and 30s were the decades of the expatriates. Even before the war, the cutting edge had belonged to foreigners, such as Stravinsky and Picasso. After the Armistice, a "lost generation" of literati streamed in from America and western Europe— **James Joyce, Ernest Hemingway, Ford Madox Ford, Ezra Pound, Gertrude Stein,** and **F. Scott Fitzgerald** among them. The Americans, above all, sought a freedom in Paris they could not find at home, including the freedom to drink; the American dollar served them well against the highly devalued French franc. Gertrude Stein expressed the feelings of her fellow expatriates: "America is my country, but Paris is my home town." Soon they were joined by a different kind of migrant: refugees from the tyrannical states that were sprouting up around Europe. **Walter Benjamin,** for example, fled to Paris from Nazi Germany, only to flee again (unsuccessfully) after the fall of France. **Robert Capa,** a Hungarian Jew who grew up in Germany, escaped to Paris before beginning his twenty years as a war photographer.

During the 30s, photographers like **Brassaï** and **Kertész,** both emigrants from Hungary, recorded the streets and *quartiers* of Paris, especially Montmartre, in black and white. **Jean Renoir** (son of the painter) made his poetic, witty films which investigated the state of culture in the 20th century; *Boudu is Saved from Drowning* (the original version of *Down and Out in Beverly Hills)* tells the story of a beggar saved from the Seine and taken in by a book-seller, pitting the staid bourgeois world against the happy anarchy the beggar represents. *La Grande Illusion,* on a more serious level, presents the interactions of three French prisoners of war, each from radically different social backgrounds, with the aristocratic German head of their World War I camp.

The years before World War II were marked by the beginnings of **Existentialism,** led by **Jean-Paul Sartre,** who began with the essentially absurd, incomprehensible world described by earlier novelists like Dostoevsky and André Gide. In 1937, Picasso exhibited his *Guernica* at the Paris International Exposition, in the pavilion of the Spanish Republic. Based on the bombing of the Basque town of Guernica during the Spanish Civil War, the huge, violent mural provided the century's most conclusive condemnation of the horrors of the war—three years before the Germans invaded Paris, bringing on the brutality of World War II.

See: Compiègne, Château-Thierry, Ritz, various cafés in Montparnasse.

World War II And Occupation (1940-1944)

Politics

In 1939, when France declared war upon Germany in response to the invasion of Poland, its army was reckoned one of the greatest in Europe. But in fact, 1940 was to mark the third time in 70 years that France went to war against a German army with more modern equipment, better organization, and a far stronger grasp of strategy. Due to internal division, a mistaken reliance on the fortified Maginot Line, and a fundamental misunderstanding of the use of tanks, France collapsed under the weight of the *Blitzkrieg* in only six weeks. Unwilling to endure another German siege, the government declared Paris an open city before fleeing to Bordeaux. Millions of Parisians evacuated as well, and on June 14, 1940, the *Wehrmacht* rolled in. The Germans wore gray. You wore blue. Eight days later, France surrendered. Because the north of France was to be under direct German administration, the capital of Unoccupied France was moved to the small town of Vichy, while General **Charles de Gaulle,** having escaped to London, organized a Free French Army.

As the effective capital of occupied France, Paris swarmed with officials, diplomats, and spies sent from Berlin, Vichy, and the rest of the world. German troops goose-stepped daily down the Champs-Elysées, the swastika flew from the top of the Eiffel Tower, and rationing prevented cafés from serving wine on certain days. More serious were the imprisonment and murder of thousands of French Communists, Resistance members, and Jews. Well-attended exhibits purported to show the evils of Freemasonry, Bolshevism, and international Jewry, and a concentration camp was set up in the suburb of Drancy. On July 16 and 17, 1942, 13,000 Jews were rounded up in a stadium on the Left Bank and deported to the death camps, the first of many such deportations. The Nazis could never have administered the occupied zone and effected their policies without help from inside; they relied on a network of French informers and collaborators. Whether out of anti-Semitism, frustration with the chaos of democracy, or utter resignation, thousands of Parisians participated in the Nazi regime.

The horror of the Nazi occupation made the liberation of Paris, in contrast, one of the most glorious moments in the city's history. Allied armies, sweeping east from the Normandy beachheads, neared Paris in August 1944. Originally Eisenhower hoped to bypass the city to save precious gasoline for his fast tank marches across France. But the threat that Hitler might destroy the city out of spite, combined with an uprising by the Communist Resistance, forced the Americans' hand. On August 25, 1944, the American-built tanks of the Free French Second Armored Division rolled through the Porte d'Orléans, soon to be joined by the American Fourth Infantry. Amid centuries-old monuments and exultant throngs of Parisians, the opposing forces tried to have their battle. The unenthusiastic German commander, von Choltitz, eventually ordered a surrender, and the city came alive once more.

Architecture and Urban Design

The streets and buildings of Paris were virtually unaffected by Fascist occupation, but they were observed with keen interest by Hitler and his team of architects. Like Napoleon, Hitler wanted to glorify the new capital of Europe. But his capital was to be Berlin, not Paris. Though Hitler himself only spent a few hours in Paris in 1940, "grateful to fate to have seen this town whose aura has always preoccupied me," he sent his architect, Albert Speer, to learn what he could from Napoleon's capital. Paris became the standard that Berlin would have to exceed. Berlin was to have its own noble axes, with triumphal arches and domes to make Paris look like a model-railroad setup.

When, in the summer of 1944, it became clear that Hitler would never see his triumphal Berlin and that he was about to be driven from Paris, he ordered the destruction of the French capital. But his garrison commander evaded the order, and Paris was preserved. Despite the tank shells whizzing down the boulevards, the street fighting of the liberation left few lasting scars.

The Arts

As the Germans advanced on Paris, the masterpieces of the Louvre, except for the *Nike,* which was too heavy, were evacuated to the provinces. Within days of the German entry into Paris, the invaders filled the Opéra and the theaters, which staged uncontroversial farces to avoid offense. Many artists found it easiest to either lie low or continue their careers. Braque and Picasso kept painting, and musicians pulled out their Wagner and Beethoven scores. Edith Piaf and Maurice Chevalier sang in the music halls. Under its collaborationist editor Pierre Drieu la Rochelle, the *Nouvelle Revue* promoted fascism as an alternative to communism. Books by Jewish authors were banned, and on May 27, 1943, hundreds of "degenerate" paintings by Miró, Picasso, Ernest, Klee, and Léger were destroyed in a bonfire in the garden of the Jeu de Paume. Tens of thousands more "respectable" masterpieces belonging to Jewish collectors and dealers were appropriated and shipped to Germany at the direction of Luftwaffe commander Hermann Goering, but were returned after the war.

Albert Camus published *The Stranger* in 1942, telling the story of the young Meursault who is fundamentally incapable of relating to his fellow human beings. Sartre's *Being and Nothingness,* written at Café Le Flore in the midst of the Occupation, became the veritable encyclopedia of Existentialism. **Jacques Prévert** and **Marcel Carné** teamed up to create two great films, *The Devil's Envoy* and *Children of Paradise.* The first, filmed in 1942, contained a subtle condemnation of the regime under which it was shown; the second, made in 1945 just after the Liberation of Paris, focused on the complex relationship between love, art, and theater, with a harlequin as its main hero—reminiscent of the paintings of Watteau.

See: numerous memorial plaques for resistance all over Paris, monuments to the deportations.

Fourth Republic and early Fifth Republic (1945-1981)

Politics

A referendum in October 1945 abolished the already dead Third Republic, but the constitution of the **Fourth Republic** continued the parliamentary system of the Third. The twelve-year reign of the Fourth Republic saw the reconstruction of French transport and industry, the formation of the **European Economic Community** (**EEC**) in 1957, and the collapse of the French Empire in Indochina, Tunisia, and Morocco. By 1958, France had 350,000 troops fighting a nasty war in Algeria against a small number of Algerian rebels. On May 13, 1958, a mob of French-Algerians, assisted by some army officers, stormed government headquarters in Algiers and called for new governments in both Algiers and in Paris. The commanders of the armed forces drew up a detailed plan for paratroopers to seize the nerve centers of Paris and put De Gaulle in power. Although the operation was called off at the last minute, the threat of another coup d'état convinced the leaders of the republic to hand all power over to De Gaulle.

After a period of personal rule by the General, the constitution of the **Fifth Republic** was approved in September of 1958. A blend of traditional European parliamentary systems and the American system of an independent executive, it provides for the president of the republic to be elected by the people, rather than the assembly. In 1959, De Gaulle became the first popularly elected president since Louis-Napoleon in 1851. In May 1968, university students, frustrated by sexual segregation, an outdated curriculum, and the threat of a reduction in the number of students allowed to matriculate, seized the Sorbonne, launching a **student revolt.** Although Paris's streets were by now asphalt, courtyards held enough cobblestones for the students to erect the classic barricades throughout the Latin Quarter. Throughout the month of May, the situation escalated; police used tear gas and clubs to storm the barricades, while students fought back by throwing Molotov cocktails and lighting cars on fire. Hundreds of students and police officers were wounded in the fighting, though none were killed. Workers in state industries went on strike in support of the students, incapacitating the entire country. Government officials, planning for the worst, arranged for tanks and commando units to be brought into the city in the event of a Communist insurrection. But a march of hundreds of thousands of De Gaulle's supporters down the Champs-Elysées confirmed public support of the government, extinguishing the revolt.

George Pompidou, the prime minister during the crisis, succeeded De Gaulle as president in 1969, and was in turn followed by **Valéry Giscard d'Estaing.** The city gained a measure of autonomy in 1977, when it was allowed to elect its own mayor, rather than having the chief executive appointed by the national government. (When the Third Republic quashed the Commune, it had decided to administer the capital itself, just to be sure.) The winner of the election, Jacques Chirac, is still in office today; he remained mayor while serving as Prime Minister of the Republic in the 1980s. Fortunately for the city, the end of direct control by the republic did not mean the end of heavy financial aid: the state still contributes about half of the city's annual budget.

Architecture and Urban Design

In 1947, geographer J.-F. Gravier warned that government policies, if continued, would concentrate all growth in the capital and leave the provinces "a French Desert." The government heeded the warning, and began looking for ways to spread growth more evenly throughout France. Still, Paris continued to grow, creating a serious housing shortage, as well as congestion problems within the city. An influx of immigrants, many of them from North Africa, could find no affordable housing and resorted to building *bidonvilles* (shanty-towns) around the edge of the city. Interest in monumental architecture dwindled, and building continued according to the needs and whims of the moment, rather than based on any grand scheme. But private construction proceeded at a furious pace, making Paris an ever denser center. Meanwhile, despairing of making it easy to drive *through* the city, the Municipal Council built the *boulevard périphérique* in the last available space—along the old lines of Thiers's walls—from 1956 to 1973.

During the postwar years, architects rejected the classical Parisian building-type, which had progressed gradually from the time of Louis XIV and Mansart. Cornice-heights became varied, proportions were ignored, tradition repudiated. Architects began to make buildings that would stand out, rather than blend in: tall buildings in a flat city, severe buildings on streets rich in ornament. In the words of François Loyer, "the urban landscape was shattered." Fortunately, the damage was contained in the outer *arrondissements,* like the 13th and the 17th, leaving the historic core relatively intact (though the Tour Montparnasse ruins views all over town). But Napoleon III's beloved Les Halles was torn down , and the *quais* of the Left Bank, like those of the Right, were almost converted into expressways—acts that inspired calls for conservation.

The real action was in the suburbs. In the 1950s, the government sponsored vast housing projects called *grands ensembles* for the region's workers. Millions of people now live in these enormous, impersonal developments. In 1965, planners seeking more humane suburban growth initiated the development of a ring of "new towns" surrounding Paris, with the intention of reducing crowding in the city and accommodating future growth. These new towns were intended to be employment, as well as residential centers, a hope that has not been fully realized. Five of these towns have been built, including Marne-la-Vallée, now the home of Euro Disneyland. Unlike American suburbs, which are populated by wealthy families fleeing the city, Parisian suburbs house mainly the working class and immigrants. Plagued by long commutes, impersonal architecture, crime, and vandalism, the suburbs are often the only source of affordable housing. As high rents pushed the working class out to the suburbs, Paris's middle class gentrified the old workers' quarters, making them tidy but, some would say, dull.

The Arts

Postwar Paris was still the city of the Existentialists, who met at the cafés of Montparnasse to discuss the absurdity and meaninglessness of the world around them. **Jean-Paul Sartre** published *Huis Clos* in 1945, with its telling assertion that *"L'Enfer, c'est* *les autres."* (Hell is other people.) **Simone de Beauvoir,** his lifetime companion (whom he met at the café Les Deux Magots) wrote *The Second Sex,* one of the century's most important feminist works, as well as existentialist novels like *All Men are Mortal.* Camus's *The Plague* (1947) provided the spiritual summation of the movement, with its description of a town quarantined by a renewed epidemic of the Bubonic Plague; unlike Sartre's pure pessimism, Camus's novel ends with a note of optimism: in the face of absolute despair and sure death, human nature retains an element of goodness that provides for acts of great charity and courage.

The bleak philosophy of the Existentialists was lightened by nights filled with the sounds of Jazz, imported from America to Paris, where musicians like **Louis Armstrong** found a far more receptive audience than they could have hoped for in the States. Paris moved into the 1950s with the plays of **Eugène Ionesco** and **Samuel Beckett,** whose absurdist non-plots illustrated the hilarious inanity of modern life. **New Wave** movies, inspired by American gangster films and Alfred Hitchcock, burst into the cinematic scene in the 50s, using black and white to capture the fragmented, hurried quality of life on the edge. **François Truffaut's** *The 400 Blows,* **Alain Resnais's** *Hiroshima mon Amour,* and **Jean-Luc Godard's** *A bout de souffle,* all made in 1959, marked the hallmark of this style. The script for *Hiroshima Mon Amour* was written by **Marguerite Duras,** who simultaneously initiated the *nouveau roman* (new novel); her novels claim to present the abstract painting of literature, breaking each moment into extracts of conversations, phrases, and momentary visions. **Georges Simenon** described the streets of Paris relentlessly perused by his detective hero, Inspector Maigret. French philosophy in the last few decades has been characterized by a tradition of near incomprehensibilty and ultra-intellectualism, symbolized by a few great names: **Lacan, Foucault, Saussure, Barthes, Baudrillard, Derrida.** These heroes of their time sponsored movements of **Cultural Criticism, Semiology, Structuralism,** and **Deconstructionism,** not necessarily in that order. If you really want to know what these terms mean, look for a good dictionary of literary criticism, such as Terry Eagleton's *Literary Theory,* and hope for the best.

See: Various cafés, Sorbonne, Centre Pomidou, Les Halles.

Mitterrand (1981- present)

Politics

In 1981, the Socialists, one of five major political parties in France, swept to power, capturing both the National Assembly and the Presidency. Within weeks they had raised the mininum wage and added a fifth week to the French worker's annual vacation—thus carrying out some of the long-deferred dreams of Léon Blum. President **François Mitterrand** won re-election to a second seven-year term in 1988, but great support for reducing the presidential term to five years may force him to step down in 1993. Currently, France is debating two big issues: immigration and Europe. Workers from France's African and Asian colonies migrated to the metropolis after World War II. In the early 1970s, amid the oil shock, the government decided to halt the flow, and since then very few have come, except for the families of male workers already in France. Neither the immigrants nor their French-born children are citizens, though the second generation born in France is. Today, 40% of the immigrants in France live in or around Paris—particularly in the 13th, 19th, and 20th *arrondissements,* as well as in the suburbs, making up 13% of the city's population. They have encountered a great deal of hostility, especially by the National Front party of Jean-Marie Le Pen, which has called for citizens to be given preference in housing, jobs, and schooling, and for immigrants to be denied welfare payments. In September 1992, France followed Denmark and Ireland by going to the polls in a national referendum on the Maastricht treaty, which would establish a common currency for the European Economic Community and transfer certain powers from individual countries to the EEC administration in Brussels. French farmers, currently heavily subsidized, oppose the treaty because it would force them to reduce their output. The National Front is against it because, after all, they're nationalists. The Socialists are for it. Whatever happens, it will not be France alone but all of Europe that decides the future.

Architecture and Urban Design

Although new buildings in the city have been limited to seven stories since 1974, the last two decades may go down in history as one of the greatest periods of building in Paris. Presidents Giscard d'Estaing and Mitterrand (also known as Mitterramses) showed themselves as enthusiasts of dramatic architectural endeavors. Mitterrand initiated the famous (some say infamous) 15 billion franc **Grands Projets** program to provide a series of modern monuments in the City of Light—symbolic of France's role at the center of art, politics, and the world economy. To find designs that would be on the cutting edge of architecture, Mitterrand sponsored contests drawing hundreds of entries from around the world; among the winners have been French, Danish, Canadian, and American architects, making the Grands Projets a truly international endeavor. From La Défense to La Villette, these government offices, museums, and public buildings constitute some of the boldest and most successful additions to the city since the Eiffel Tower. Of course, a city is more than monuments, and Paris is more than just a ctiy. Mitterrand has continued the policy of using national funds to pay for the city's local needs, like street-cleaning, schools, and homeless shelters. An enormous budget lets the city keep its streets clean with a legion of sweepers and all sorts of nifty green buggies. As a result, Paris is a very popular, and outrageously expensive, place to live.

The Arts

Look around you, in the contemporary arts galleries all over Paris, to get an idea of the eclecticism that has characterized the visual arts in the last decade, as artists search for a new medium to express the **postmodern** culture of the 1980s and 90s. Minimalist artist **Christo,** originally from Bulgaria, received permission to wrap the Pont Neuf in pink plastic, demonstrating a notion of modern art as ephemeral and essentially performance-related. Recent, hugely popular exhibits on Andy Warhol, Seurat, and Toulouse-Lautrec, illustrate the range of styles Parisians and tourists alike have come to appreciate. The new-age synthesizer music of **Jean-Michel Jarre** is the equivalent of buildings like the Arche de la Défense in its expression of the sleek, commodities-oriented quality of modern French culture. The same idea was expressed in film with **Jean-Jacques Beineix**'s *Diva,* with its complex plot, black humor, refined symbolism, and thrilling scenes of Paris, above-ground and below.
   See: Louvre, La Defense, Parc de la Villette, Opéra de la Bastille.

Recommended Reading

Non-Fiction

Abelard and Héloïse, *Letters*
Walter Benjamin, *Illuminations* and *Charles Baudelaire*
T. J. Clarke, *The Painting of Modern Life*
Larry Collins and Dominique Lapierre, *Is Paris Burning?*
Alistair Horne, *The Fall of Paris: The Siege and the Commune, 1870-71*
John Huizinga, *The Waning of the Middle Ages*
Linda Nochlin, *Realism* and *The Politics of Vision: Essays on 19th-century Art and Society*
David Pinkney, *Napoleon III and the Reshaping of Paris*
Simon Schama, *Citizens: A Chronicle of the French Revolution*
Jerrold Seigel, *Bohemian Paris: Culture, Politics, and the Boundaries of Bourgeois Life*
Eugen Weber, *France: Fin de Siècle*

Fiction

Charles Dickens, *Tale of Two Cities*
Ernest Hemingway, *The Sun Also Rises*
Victor Hugo, *Les Misérables* and *The Hunchback of Notre-Dame*
Choderlos Laclos, *Dangerous Liaisons*
Georges Simenon, the Inspector Maigret novels
Patrick Süskind, *Perfume: the Story of a Murderer*

Planning Your Trip

Note: In Paris addresses "Mo." indicates the nearest metro stop. The postal code of Paris addresses is formed by affixing the two-digit *arrondissement* number to 750. Thus, the postal code of an address in the 8*ème* (eighth) is 75008. An international telephone call to Paris requires 33 (France code) plus 1 (Paris code) before dialing the 8-digit number (see Communications for more information).

US$1 = 4.96F	1F = US$0.20
CDN$1 = 4.17F	1F = CDN$0.23
UK£1 = 9.56F	1F = UK£0.10
IR£1 = 8.97F	1F = IR£.11
AUS$1 = 3.57F	1F = AUS$0.28
NZ$1 = 2.66F	1F = NZ$0.38

A Note on Prices and Currency

The information in this book was researched in the summer of 1992. Since then, inflation will have raised most prices at least 10%. The exchange rates listed were compiled on August 18, 1992. Since rates fluctuate considerably, confirm them before you go by checking a national newspaper.

Useful Organizations and Publications

Research your trip early. The government and private agencies listed below will provide useful information.

French Government Services

The French government is well aware of the benefits of tourism for the country's economy, and will gladly provide prospective visitors a panoply of pamphlets and an inundation of information.

French Government Tourist Office: Write for information on any region of France, festival dates, and tips for travelers with disabilities. **U.S.,** 610 Fifth Ave., New York, NY 10020; 645 N. Michigan Ave., #630, Chicago, IL 60611; 9454 Wilshire Blvd. #303, Beverly Hills, CA 90212 (tel. nationwide (900) 990-0040, costs 50¢ per minute). **Canada,** 1981, av. McGill College, #490, Montréal, Qué. H3A 2W9 (tel. (514) 593-4723); 30 St-Patrick St., #700, Toronto, Ont. M5T 3A3 (tel. (416) 593-6427). **Australia,** B&P Building, 12th Fl., 12 Castlereagh St., Sydney, NSW 2000 (tel. (02) 231 52 44). **New Zealanders** should contact this branch. **U.K.,** 178 Piccadilly, London W1V OAL (tel. (071) 629 1272). **Irish** residents should consult this branch.

Cultural Services of the French Embassy, 972 Fifth Ave., New York, NY 10021 (tel. (212) 439-1400). General information about France including culture, student employment, and educational possibilities.

French Consulates

While not laden with colorful brochures, the French consulate in your home country can supply you with important legal information concerning your trip, arrange for necessary visas, and direct you toward a wealth of other information about tourism, education, and employment in France. Write or call for more information.

U.S., Consulate General: 3 Commonwealth Ave., Boston, MA 02116 (tel. (617) 266-1680); **Visa Section,** 20 Park Plaza, Statler Bldg., 11th Fl., Boston, MA 02116 (tel. (617) 482-3650 for a recording of general information, (617) 482-2864 for specific inquiries). There are 12 branch offices across the U.S.; contact the Consulate General to locate the branch nearest you. **Canada,** 1, pl. Ville Marie, #2601, Montréal, Qué. H3B 4S3 (tel. (514) 878-4381). **U.K.,** 21 Cromwell Rd., London SW7 2DQ (tel. (071) 581 5292); **Visa Section,** 6A Cromwell Pl., London SW7 2EW (tel. (071) 823 9555). **Irish** citizens should address inquiries to this consulate. **Australia,** 31 Market St., 20th Fl., Sydney, NSW 2000 (tel. (02) 261 5931 or (02) 261 5779). **New Zealanders** should address inquiries to this consulate.

Budget Travel Services

Council on International Educational Exchange (CIEE)/Council Travel, 205 E. 42nd St., New York, NY 10017 (tel. (212) 661-1414). Administers programs and distributes information on study, work, voluntary service, and professional opportunities abroad. Administers ISIC, FIYTO, and ITIC cards. Publishes the biannual *Student Travels* (free, postage US$1), a new travel magazine for college students. Among CIEE's books are *Work, Study, Travel Abroad: The Whole World Handbook* (US$12.95, postage US$1.50), *Going Places: The High School Students's Guide to Study, Travel, and Adventure Abroad* (US$13.95, postage US$1.50), and *Volunteer! The Comprehensive Guide to Voluntary Service in the U.S. and Abroad* (US$8.95, postage US$1.50). Budget travel subsidiaries of CIEE include **Council Travel** and **Council Charter.** Council Travel sells Eurail and individual country passes, guidebooks, travel gear, discounted flights, ISIC, FIYTO, ITIC cards, and HI memberships. 205 E. 42 St., New York, NY 10017 (tel. (212) 661-1450); 729 Boylston St., Boston, MA 02116 (tel. (617) 266-1926); 1093 Broxton Ave., Los Angeles, CA 90024 (tel. (310) 208-3551); 1153 Dearborn St., Chicago, IL 60610 (tel. (312) 951-0585); 28A Poland St., London W1V 3DB, UK; 31, rue St-Augustin, 75002 Paris, France. Council Charter, 205 E. 42 St., New York, NY 10017 (tel. (800) 800-8222) operates charter and scheduled flights to major European cities, which can be purchased through any Council Travel office in the U.S.

Let's Go Travel Services, Harvard Student Agencies, Inc., Thayer Hall-B, Harvard University, Cambridge, MA 02138 (tel. (617) 495-9649). Sells railpasses, American Youth Hostel memberships (valid at all HI youth hostels), International Student and Teacher ID cards, YIEE cards for nonstudents, travel guides and maps (including the *Let's Go* series), discount airfares, and a complete line of budget travel gear. All items are available by mail; call or write for a catalog.

Rail Europe Inc., 226 Westchester Ave., White Plains, NY 10604 (tel. (800) 438-7245; in NY, NJ, CT call (914) 682-5172). Sells all Eurail products in addition to 26 national and regional European Rail and Rail 'n' Drive passes. Also available are point-to-point tickets and reservations.

Travel CUTS (Canadian Universities Travel Service), 187 College St., Toronto, Ont. M5T 1P7 (tel. (416) 979-2406). Offices throughout Canada; in London, 295A Regent St. W1R 7YA (tel. (071) 255 1944). Sells discounted transatlantic flights, the ISIC, International Youth Card, and also runs the Canadian Work Abroad Programme. Sells the Eurailpass/Youthpass. Arranges adventure tours and work abroad. Their newspaper, *The Canadian Student Traveler,* is free at all offices and on campuses across Canada.

Educational Travel Centre (ETC), 438 N. Frances St., Madison, WI 53703 (tel. (608) 256-5551). Flight information, HI membership cards, railpasses. Write or call for a free copy of their travel newspaper *Taking Off.*

International Student Exchange Flights (ISE Flights), 5010 E. Shea Blvd., #A104, Scottsdale, AZ 85254 (tel. (602) 951-1177). Budget student flights on major regularly scheduled airlines. International Student Exchange (ISE) cards, *Let's Go* series, traveler's checks, Hostelling International guide books, and railpasses.

International Student Travel Conference (ISTC): In the U.S., they are represented by CIEE. In Canada: Travel CUTS (see address above). In the U.K.: London Student Travel, 52 Grosvenor Gardens, London WC1 England (tel. (071) 730 3402). In Australia: STA/SSA, 222 Faraday St., Melbourne, Victoria 3053, Australia (tel. (03) 347 69 11). In New Zealand: Student Travel, 2nd Fl., Courtenay Chambers, 15 Courtenay, Wellington (tel. (04) 85 05 61). Issues ISICs.

STA Travel, a worldwide youth travel organization. Offers bargain flights, railpasses, accommodations, tours, insurance, and ISICs. Ten offices in the U.S., including 17 E. 45th St., New York, NY 10017 (tel. (212) 986-9643 or (800) 777-0112) and 7202 Melrose Ave., Los Angeles, CA 90046 (tel. (213) 934-8722). In the UK, STA's main office is at 74 and 86 Old Brompton Rd., London SW7 3LQ England (tel. (071) 937 9921 for European travel; (071) 937 9971 for North American). In New Zealand they're at 10 High St., Auckland (tel. (09) 309 9995).

Publications

Forsyth Travel Library, 9154 W. 57th St., P.O. Box 2975, Shawnee Mission, KS 66201 (tel. (913) 384-3440 or (800) 367-7984). A mail-order service that stocks a wide range of city, area, and country maps, as well as guides for rail and ferry travel in Europe. Sole North American distributor of the Thomas Cook *European Timetable* for trains, covering all of Europe and Britain (US$24.95, postage $4). Write for free catalog and newsletter.

John Muir Publications, P.O. Box 613, Sante Fe, NM 87504 (tel. (505) 982-4078 or (800) 888-7504). Publishes more than 12 books by veteran traveler Rick Steves. These include *Europe through the Back Door,* revised winter 1992 (US$16.95), which offers good advice, especially on traveling light and avoiding tourist traps. *Mona Winks* (US$14.95) provides a good-humored, self-guided tour of Europe's top museums.

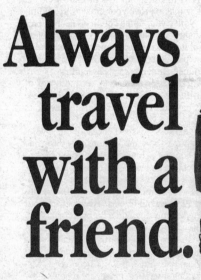

Always travel with a friend.

Get the International
Student Identity Card,
recognized worldwide.

For information call toll-free **1-800-GET-AN-ID**.
or contact any Council Travel office. (See inside front cover.)

Press and Information Division of the French Embassy, 4101 Reservoir Rd. NW, Washington, DC 20007 (tel. (202) 944-6048). Write for information about political, social, and economic aspects of France. Publishes a bi-weekly newsletter, *News from France* and *France Magazine.*

Superintendent of Documents, U.S. Government Printing Office, Washington, DC 20402 (tel. (202) 783-3238). Publishes helpful booklets including *Your Trip Abroad* (US$1), *Safe Trip Abroad* (US$1), and *Health Information for International Travel* (US$5).

Wide World Books & Maps, 1911 N. 45th St., Seattle, WA 98105 (tel. (206) 634-3453). Useful, free catalog listing the most recent guidebooks to every part of the world.

Documents

Remember to file all applications several weeks or even months before your planned departure date. A backlog at any agency could spoil even the best-laid plans.

Passports

You need a valid passport to enter France and to re-enter your own country. Apply well in advance. Most offices suggest that you apply in the winter off-season for speedy service. Be sure to record your passport number in a separate, safe place, and photocopy the pages with your photograph and visas in case of loss or theft. Leave a copy with someone at home. These precautions will help prove your citizenship and facilitate the issuing of a new passport if needed. Notify your home country's nearest embassy or consulate and the local police immediately if your passport is lost or stolen. Registering with the nearest embassy or consulate is wise if you intend an extended stay in France. Some consulates can issue new passports, given proof of citizenship, within two days. In an emergency, ask for an immediate temporary passport.

Bring two extra pieces of identification when traveling abroad. A second proof of citizenship can be anything from your birth certificate to a driver's license. Keep these items separate from your passport. A few extra passport-type photos can also come in handy if you lose your passport or decide to apply for a visa.

U.S. citizens over age 18 may apply for a 10-year U.S. passport at one of the several thousand Federal courts or post offices that accept passport applications, or at any one of the 13 Passport Agencies, located in Boston, Chicago, Honolulu, Houston, Los Angeles, Miami, New Orleans, New York, Philadelphia, San Francisco, Seattle, Stamford, and Washington, DC. Those under 18 can obtain a five-year passport. Parents must apply in person for children under age 13. If this is your first U.S. passport, if you are under 18, or if your current passport is more than 12 years old or was issued before your 18th birthday, you must apply in person. Otherwise, you can renew by mail for US$55.

For a U.S. passport, you must submit the following documents: (1) a completed application; (2) proof of U.S. citizenship, which can be a certified birth certificate, naturalization papers, or a previous passport; (3) identification bearing your signature and either your photo or personal description, e.g., an unexpired driver's license or passport; and (4) two identical, recent, passport-sized photographs. If you are renewing by mail, your old passport will serve as both (2) and (3); do not forget to enclose it with your application. To obtain or renew a passport when ineligible for application by mail, bring items (1-4) and US$65 (under 18 US$40) in the form of a check (cashier's, traveler's, certified, or personal) or money order. Passport agencies will accept cash in the exact amount, but post offices and courts may not. Passport Services also requests that you write your birth date on your check.

Processing usually takes three to four weeks (longer through a court or post office), but it's best to apply several months early. If you are leaving within five working days, the passport office can provide urgent service, but you must have valid proof of your departure date (e.g., an airline ticket) and arrive early at the office. Abroad, a U.S. consulate can usually issue new passports, given proof of citizenship. For more details, call the U.S. Passport Information's 24-hour recording (tel. (202) 647-0518) or write the passport agency nearest you.

Canadian citizens may present their passport application in person at one of the 26 regional offices (addresses are in the telephone directory) or mail it to the Passport Office, Department of External Affairs, Ottawa, Ont. K1A 0G3. Passport applications are available from passport offices, post offices, and most travel agencies. Passport requirements include (1) a completed application; (2) original documentary evidence of Canadian citizenship; and (3) two identical photographs, both signed by the holder and one certified by a "guarantor" from an approved list who has known you for at least two years. Children may be included on a parent's passport; they also need proof of Canadian citizenship. The fee is CDN$35 and may be paid in cash, money order, certified check, or bank draft. Expect a five-day wait if applying in person and three weeks if applying by mail. A Canadian passport is valid for five years. For more information, consult the booklet *Bon Voyage, But...*, available free from the Passport Office. Canadian citizens residing in the U.S. should apply at the nearest Canadian diplomatic mission.

There are two types of **British** passports. The **Visitor's Passport** is available over-the-counter at main post offices; you must bring two photos and identification. It is valid for travel to Western Europe for one year and costs £7.50. For a **Full British Passport,** apply by mail or at any one of the passport offices in London, Liverpool, Newport, Peterborough, Glasgow, and Belfast. You need a completed application, your birth certificate and marriage certificate (if applicable), and two identical copies of recent photos signed by a guarantor. The fee is £15 for a 10-year adult passport (5 years if under 16). A spouse who does not have a separate passport, and those under 16, may be included on one person's passport. Processing averages four to six weeks.

Irish citizens should pick up an application at a local guard station or request one from one of the two passport offices. If you have never had a passport, you must send your birth certificate, the long application, and two identical pictures to Passport Office, Setanta Centre, Molesworth St., Dublin 2 (tel. (01) 711 633) or Passport Office, 1A South Mall, Cork, County Cork (tel. (021) 272 525). To renew, send your old passport, the short form, and the photos. Passports cost IR£45 and are valid for 10 years.

Australian citizens must apply for a passport in person at a local post office, where an appointment may be necessary, through a passport office, or through an Australian diplomatic mission overseas. A parent may file for an applicant who is under 18 and unmarried. With your application you must turn in proof of citizenship, proof of your present name, two photographs, and other forms of identification. Proof of citizenship can be an Australian passport valid for more than two years and issued after November 22, 1984, a birth certificate, or a citizen certificate from the Department of Immigration. The photographs (45mm x 35mm) must be identical, not more than six months old, and signed as instructed in the application. Other forms of ID include driver's license, credit card, rate notices, etc. Application fees are adjusted every three months; call the toll-free information service for current details (tel. (008) 02 60 22). There is also a departure tax when a citizen over 11 years old leaves the country.

New Zealanders must contact their local Link Centre, travel agent, or New Zealand Representative for an application, which must be completed and mailed to the New Zealand Passport Office. Evidence of identity and New Zealand citizenship and two certified passport-sized photos must accompany your application. The fee for a passport is NZ$56.25, NZ$110 if overseas. For children under 16 the fee is NZ$25.30, NZ$49.50 overseas. The application process normally requires three weeks, but the office will speed up processing in an emergency. For more information, write the New Zealand Passport Office, Documents of National Identity Division, P.O. Box 10-526, Wellington (tel. (04) 474 8100).

Visas

A visa is an endorsement or stamp placed in your passport by a foreign government allowing you to visit their country for a specified purpose and period of time. Visas are currently required of **all** visitors to France, except those from EC member countries, the U.S., Canada, New Zealand, Andorra, Austria, Czechoslovakia, Cyprus, Finland, Hungary, Iceland, Japan, Republic of Korea, Liechtenstein, Malta, Monaco, Norway, Poland, San Marino, Sweden, and Switzerland. Note that Australia is distinctly absent from this list. A visa is required for *anyone* planning to stay more than three months (see below). It must be obtained from the French consulate *in your home country*. For more details write to R. Woods, Consumer Information Center, P.O. Box 100, Pueblo, CO 81002, for *Foreign Entry Requirements* (US50¢). Claimants to the throne of France are no longer barred from entering the country, but they will generally want to establish a loyal following in the provinces before marching on Paris.

Requirements for a long-stay visa vary with the nature of the stay: work, study, or *au pair.* Apply to the nearest French Consulate at least three months in advance. For a **student visa,** you must present a passport valid until at least 60 days after the date you plan to leave France, an application with references, a passport photo, a letter of admission from a French university or a study abroad program, a notarized guarantee of financial support for $600 per month, and a fee, which fluctuates according to the exchange rate (currently US$57). To obtain a **work visa,** you must first obtain a work permit. After you secure a job and a work contract from your French employer, your employer will obtain this permit for you and will forward it with a copy of your work contract to the consulate nearest you. After a medical checkup and completion of the application, the visa will be issued on your valid passport. Note that it is illegal for foreign students to work during the school year, although they can receive permission from their local *Direction départementale du travail et de la main-d'oeuvre étrangère* to work in summer (see below). For an *au pair* stay of more than three months, an **au pair's visa** is required and can be obtained by submission of a valid passport, two completed application forms, two passport photos, a fee (varying between US$15-25), a medical certificate of good health completed by a Consulate-approved doctor, two copies of the *au pair's* work contract signed by the *au pair,* and proof of admission to a language school or university program. (See Au Pair Positions, below, for more info.)

In addition to securing a visa, if you are staying longer than 90 days in France—for one of the above three reasons or any other—you must obtain a **carte de séjour** (residency permit) once in France. Report to the **Préfecture de Paris,** 17, bd. Morland, 4ème (tel. 42 76 40 40). Here you must present a valid passport stamped with a long-stay visa, a medical certificate, six (yes, six) application forms completed in French, six passport photos, a letter of financial guarantee, and, if you're under 18, proof of parental authorization. Be prepared to jump through hoops, bark like a dog, and stand in line, perhaps repeatedly. Bring your Proust.

Student, Teacher, and Youth Identification

The **International Student Identity Card (ISIC)** (US$15) is an internationally recognized proof of student status. If you have a student ID from a school in France or from your home country, it will usually qualify you for the same discounts on train and theater tickets and on admission to museums, historical sites, and festivals. The ISIC offers other benefits including lower fares on many forms of local and international transportation—it's essential if you plan to use student charter flights or clubs. The card incorporates the International Union of Students card. If you purchase the card in the U.S., it also provides you with US$3000 medical/accident insurance and US$100 per day for up to 60 days in case of in-hospital illness. The **International Teacher Identity Card (ITIC)** (US$16) offers identical discounts in theory, but many establishments are unfamiliar with the recently introduced card and are reluctant to honor it.

To apply for either, submit the following to one of the student travel services listed above: (1) current, dated proof of student or teacher status (a photocopy of your school ID showing this year's date, a letter on school stationery signed and sealed by the registrar, or a photocopied grade report); (2) a 1½ x 2-inch photo with your name printed in pencil on the back; (3) proof of your birthdate and nationality. The card is valid from September 1 through December of the following year. If you are about to graduate, you can still get a card by proving student status during the same calendar year. You cannot purchase a new card in January unless you were in school during the fall semester.

If you're not a student but are under age 26, inquire about other youth discounts. The **Federation of International Youth Travel Organizations (FIYTO)** issues the **International Youth Card** to anyone under age 26; it is also available from a number of the travel services listed above. The card is internationally recognized and gives you access to over 8000 discounts on international and intra-European transport, accommodations, restaurants, cultural activities, and tours. Applications must include proof of age, a passport-sized photo and a certified check or money order for US$15. For further information and an application, write to FIYTO, Islands Brygge 81, DK-2300 Copenhagen S, Denmark (tel. (45) 31 54 60 80).

International Driver's License

An International Driving Permit (essentially a translation of your driver's license into 9 languages) is not usually required to drive in France, but is recommended if you don't speak French. Most rental agencies will not ask to see the permit but will want to see a valid driver's license. The permit is available at any branch of the **American Automobile Association** or at the main office, AAA Travel Agency Services, 1000 AAA Drive (mail stop 100), Heathrow, FL 32746 (tel. (800) 222-4357). For more information, contact your local AAA. It is also available from the **Canadian Automobile Association (CAA),** 60 Commerce Valley Dr. E., Markham, Ont. L3T 7P9 (tel. (416) 771-3170). You will need a completed application, two recent passport-sized photos, a valid U.S. (or Canadian) driver's license (which must always accompany the International Driving Permit), and US$10. You must be over 18 to apply. If you are going to drive, buy, or borrow a car that is not insured, you will need an **International Insurance Certificate,** or **green card,** to prove you have liability insurance. Inquire at the AAA. If you are renting or leasing, you must get the green card (and the coverage too, if your insurance does not apply abroad) from the rental agency or dealer.

Customs

Unless you plan on hauling back a BMW or a barnyard animal, don't be alarmed by customs procedures. First off, visitors have an allowance of what they can bring into France. Anything exceeding the allowance is charged a duty. Among other things, if you are bringing into France more than 200 cigarettes, 2 liters of wine, 1 liter of alcohol over 38.8 proof, or 50g of perfume, you must declare such items. All travelers must declare articles acquired abroad; only the truly profligate budget traveler must pay duties; time may be spent in better ways than collecting receipts from duty-free shops.

Before leaving, **U.S. citizens** should record the serial numbers of expensive (especially foreign-made) items that will accompany you abroad. Have this list stamped by the Customs Office before you leave. U.S. citizens may bring in US$400 worth of goods duty-free every 30 days; the next US$1000 is subject to a 10% tax. Duty-free goods must be for personal or household use and cannot include more than 100 cigars, 200 cigarettes (1 carton), and 1 liter of alcohol. You must be 21 or older to bring liquor into the U.S. These items may not be shipped. Non-prescription drugs and narcotics, many foods, plant and animal products, pornography, lottery tickets, and harmful items may not be imported into the U.S. Similar restrictions apply in many other countries. You can bring in some plants, non-meat foods, and seeds; they'll just have to be inspected by Agriculture Department employees at the airport when you return. Write for the brochure, *Know Before You Go* (50¢), item 477Y, R. Woods, Consumer Information Center, Pueblo, CO 81009. *Travelers' Tips on Bringing Food, Plant, and Animal Products into the United States* is available from the Animal and Plant Health Inspection Service, U.S. Department of Agriculture, 6505 Belcrest Rd., Attn: Public Information, Washington, DC 20250. They also provide information on restrictions in the wildlife trade. To avoid problems when carrying prescription drugs, make sure the bottles are clearly marked, and have the prescription ready to show the customs officer.

While in Europe, you can mail unsolicited gifts back to the U.S. duty-free if they're worth less than US$50. Mark the package "unsolicited gift" and indicate the nature of the gift and its retail value. Again, you may not mail liquor, tobacco, or perfume into the U.S. If you send back a parcel worth over US$50, the Postal Service will collect the duty plus a handling charge when it is delivered. To mail home personal goods of U.S. origin, mark the package "American goods returned."

Before departure, **Canadian citizens** should identify or list the serial numbers of all valuables on a Y-38 form at the Customs Office or point of departure; these goods can then be reimported duty-free. Once every year after a seven-day absence, you can bring in goods up to a value of CDN$300. After any two-day absence, you can bring in goods up to a value of CDN$100. These two allowances may not be claimed on the same trip. Duty-free goods may not include more than 50 cigars, 200 cigarettes, 1kg of tobacco, or 1.1 liters of alcohol. The minimum age to import tobacco is 16; the age for liquor varies by province. Anything above the duty-free allowance is charged a 20% tax. Shipped items will be taxed at a higher rate and may not include alcohol or tobacco products. You can send gifts up to a value of CDN$40 duty-free, but again, you cannot mail alcohol or tobacco. Canadians traveling to or from Europe via the U.S. should also note that pain-killers containing codeine—available over the counter in Canada—are illegal in the U.S. For more information, get the pamphlet *I Declare,* available from the Revenue Canada Customs and Excise Department, Communications Branch, Mackenzie Ave., Ottawa, Ont. K1A 0L5 (tel. (613) 957-0275) or *Bon Voyage, But...* from External Affairs, Ottawa, Ont., K1A OG2 (tel. (613) 993-6435).

Returning **British citizens** are allowed an exemption of up to £32 of goods. This includes not more than 200 cigarettes; 100 cigarillos; 50 cigars; 250g tobacco; or 2 liters of still table wine plus 1 liter of alcohol over 22% by volume, or 2 liters of alcohol not over 22% by volume. Allowances are about 50% higher for goods obtained tax- and duty-paid in the EC. You must be 17 or over to import liquor or tobacco.

Irish citizens may import a maximum of IR£34 per adult traveler duty-free (IR£17 per traveler under the age of 15). Travelers above the age of 17 may bring in 200 cigarettes or 100 cigarillos or 50 cigars or 250g of tobacco, and 1 liter of alcohol over 44 proof or 2 liters of alcohol under 44 proof. You may import as much currency into Ireland as you wish. For more information, write Division 1, Office of the Revenue Commissioners, Dublin Castle, Dublin 1 (tel. (01) 679 27 27).

Australian citizens over 18 years of age can bring 250g of tobacco (equivalent to 250 cigarettes) and 1 liter of alcohol back into the country duty-free. The duty-free allowance is AUS$400 (under 18 AUS$200). Goods above the limit will be taxed and must be carried into the country with you. You may not import or export more than AUS$5000 (or the foreign equivalent) without filing a special form with customs. You may mail back personal property; mark it "Australian goods returned" to avoid duty.

For additional information, consult the brochure *Customs Information for All Travellers,* available at an Australian Consulate or offices of the Collector of Customs.

Citizens of **New Zealand** may bring in NZ$700 worth of duty-free goods as long as the goods are intended for personal use or as unsolicited gifts. Travelers 17 or older are allowed 200 cigarettes (1 carton) or 50 cigars or 250g of tobacco or a mixture of all three not to exceed 250g. You may also bring in 4.5 liters of beer or wine and 1.125 liters of liquor. The *New Zealand Customs Guide for Travelers* and *If You're Not Sure About It, DECLARE IT* are both available from any customs office. For more information, contact **New Zealand Customs,** P.O. Box 29, Auckland (tel. (9) 773 520).

When to Go

Traveling during the off-season is a great way to minimize the damage to your bank account. Airfares drop and domestic travel becomes less congested. What's more, the off-season includes the world-famous "Paris in the Springtime." In spite of the rain, spring is *the* time to see Paris; go then if you can. In the summer, the tourists move in and the Parisians move out—on vacation. On the other hand, if you stay away from the Champs-Elysées, Versailles, and the Eiffel Tower, August can be pleasingly calm. The noisy schoolkids who crowd the metro during the rest of the year are away with their parents at the beach; traffic on the roads is noticeably less hectic; the sidewalks are less crowded. On August 15, a national holiday, all of Paris (except the tourist areas) is eerily deserted. For the most authentic Paris, try the city in autumn and winter—it's just as beautiful, and free (almost) of the freshets of tourists that flood in during the warmer months. If you want to see the city in celebration come on July 14 or New Year's Eve. Expect crowds, firecrackers going off under your feet, and lots of champagne.

Climate

> It rains softly on the city.
>
> —Arthur Rimbaud

Nobody goes to Paris for the climate. No matter when you go, expect it to be cold and rainy. Don't despair. This is the way Paris is meant to be. Its gray stone buildings are meant to be seen against gray skies. That is why Paris is romantic. It rains in the fall, winter, and spring. Early and late summer are often quite cool. Evenings can be windy and cold throughout the summer, and hot days (in the 80s, 30°C) don't hit Paris until mid-July. Then, you'll discover Paris in the summer, with its high humidity and persistent pollution. Air-conditioning is not as widespread as in America, so the entire city clears out to Deauville and Trouville in the north when the days begin to swelter. You'll be wishing it were cold and rainy. Winters are mild, averaging about 40°F (5°C) during the day, but the ever-present dampness makes them feel much colder.

Time

In general, Paris is 6 hours ahead of North America (Eastern Standard Time) and one hour ahead of the United Kingdom. France springs forward one hour on the last Sunday in March and falls back an hour on the last Saturday in September. Beware: these time changes occur on different weekends than in North America. One stalwart *Let's Go* editor was not aware of this last year and missed his plane home!

Health and Insurance

A little prevention and a lot of precaution should prevent you from falling ill—or into debt—while you tour.

Health

The simplest prescription for staying healthy while traveling is to eat well, drink lots of fluids, keep clean, and avoid excessive exertion. All food, including seafood, dairy products, and fresh produce, is normally safe in Paris. The water is chlorinated and also quite safe; to avoid the infamous traveler's diarrhea, you may want to drink mineral water for the first day or two while your body adjusts to new bacteria. To minimize the effects of **jet lag,** you must "reset" your body clock. Don't consume tea, coffee, alcohol, or large meals the day of your flight, and try to get lots of natural light your first afternoon there. This way, you clear your natural body clock and can reset it once in Europe. Set your watch to the time of your destination and come "morning," eat breakfast. You should be acclimatized to the new time zone by the end of the first day or two.

Although no special immunizations are necessary for travel to France, be sure that your **inoculations** are up-to-date. Typhoid shots remain good for three years, tetanus for 10. *Health Information for International Travel* (US$5) provides U.S. Public Health recommendations and other hints; write the Superintendent of Documents (address under Useful Publications above).

Travelers with **contact lenses** should bring an extra pair, or at least a copy of their prescription. Since the pressurized atmosphere of an airplane can dehydrate soft lenses, clean them just before leaving, and don't drink coffee or alcohol or read for long periods of time while on the plane. Bring along adequate supplies of your cleaning solutions, and don't let them get overheated in luggage. Foreign brands with familiar names may have different formulations than your brand. For heat disinfection you'll need outlet and low-watt voltage adapters. In general, use chemical if you can while you're traveling; even with a converter, heat-disinfecting units don't always work the same way in Europe. Many, for example, will not shut off automatically.

Travelers with a chronic medical condition requiring regular treatment should consult their doctors before leaving. All travelers should carry an ample supply of appropriate **medicines,** since matching a prescription with a foreign equivalent may be difficult. Always carry up-to-date prescriptions (in legible, preferably typewritten form, including the medication's trade name, manufacturer, chemical name, and dosage) and/or a statement (with a translated version) from your doctor, especially if you use insulin, syringes, or any narcotic drug. Keep all medicines and syringes in your carry-on luggage.

If you have a medical condition that cannot be easily recognized (e.g., diabetes, allergies to antibiotics, epilepsy, heart conditions), you should obtain a **Medic Alert identification tag.** This internationally recognized tag indicates the nature of the condition, and provides the number of Medic Alert's 24-hour hotline, through which medical personnel can obtain information about the member's medical history. Lifetime membership, which includes the price of a steel tag, costs US$35; contact Medic Alert Foundation International, P.O. Box 1009, Turlock, CA 95381 (tel. (800) 432-5378, emergency (209) 634-4917).

Paris is a lover's city, and stocks all the necessary equipment. Condoms and other birth control devices are readily available in most pharmacies. The danger of AIDS and other sexually transmitted diseases looms large in Paris, as in any city of its size; take necessary precautions and don't hesitate to consult one of the STD clinics listed under Emergency, Health, and Help below.

If illness does strike, Paris has a number of late-night pharmacies and a handful of English-speaking hospitals. Consult the emergency numbers listed under Safety in the Practical Information section.

Insurance

Beware of unnecessary insurance coverage—your current policies might well extend to many travel-related concerns. For instance, your **medical insurance** policy may cover costs incurred abroad. University term-time medical plans often include insurance for summer travel. Medicare's foreign travel coverage is limited and is valid only in Canada and Mexico. Canadians are protected by their home province's health insurance plan; check with the provincial Ministry of Health or Health Plan Headquarters. Your **homeowners' insurance** (or your family's coverage) often covers theft during travel. Homeowners are generally covered against loss of travel documents (passport, plane ticket, railpass, etc.) up to about US$500.

Claims can only be filed against your home medical or homeowner's insurance upon return to your home country and must be accompanied by the proper documents (i.e., police reports and/or doctor's statements), written in English if possible, and all relevant receipts. Note that some of the plans listed below offer cash advances or guaranteed transferrals, so it is not always necessary to use your own vacation cash to pay doctor bills. Full payment in cash before check-out (and sometimes even before treatment) is virtually the rule at most French hospitals. If your coverage doesn't include on-the-spot payments or cash transferrals, then budget for emergencies.

When purchased in the U.S., the **ISIC** (see above) will provide you with US$3000 worth of accident insurance plus US$100 per day for up to 60 days of in-hospital sickness coverage as long as the card is valid. **CIEE** offers an inexpensive Trip-Safe package that extends coverage of medical treatment and hospitalization, accidents, and even charter flights missed due to illness. ISIC also provides a 24-hour traveler's assistance line for legal and financial aid. American Express cardholders receive automatic car-rental and flight insurance on purchases made with the card.

A number of agencies offer insurance against theft, loss of luggage, trip cancellation/interruption, and medical emergencies; rates average around US$6 per $100 of coverage. Consult your local yellow pages or a travel agency to find an agency that suits you.

Travelers with Specific Needs

Senior Travelers

The freedom of retirement affords many seniors the opportunity to travel, while an assortment of discounts on transportation and tours helps make it affordable. Most museums and concerts in Paris offer reduced prices for visitors over 60. Write the Superintendent of Documents (see Useful Publications, above) for a copy of *Travel Tips for Older Americans* (US$1). The following organizations offer information, assistance, and discounts to seniors.

American Association of Retired Persons (AARP), Special Services Department, 601 E St. NW, Washington, DC 20049 (tel. (800) 227-7737; for travel information, (202) 434-2277). For an annual membership fee of US$8, anyone 50 or over and their spouses can receive benefits from AARP Travel Services and get discounts on hotels, motels, car rental, and sightseeing companies.

Elderhostel, 75 Federal St., 3rd Fl., Boston, MA 02110 (tel. (617) 426-7788). Week-long educational workshops in over 40 countries in the Americas and Europe cover a variety of subjects. US$1500-5000 fee includes room, board, tuition, and extracurricular activities. You must be 60 or over to enroll; companions must be 50 or over.

Gateway Books, 13 Bedford Cove, San Rafael, CA 94901 (tel. (415) 454-5215). Publishes Gene and Adele Malott's *Get Up and Go: A Guide for the Mature Traveler* (US$10.95). Offers recommendations of places to visit and general hints for the budget-conscious senior.

National Council of Senior Citizens, 1331 F St. NW, Washington, DC 20004 (tel. (202) 347-8800). Information on discounts and travel abroad.

Pilot Industries, Inc., 103 Cooper St., Babylon, NY 11702 (tel. (516) 422-2225). Publishes *The International Health Guide for Senior Citizen Travelers* (US$4.95) and the newly revised *Senior Citizen's Guide to Budget Travel in Europe* (US$5.95).

Travelers with Disabilities

The French Tourist Board and the Mairie de Paris provide free handbooks and access guides to travelers with disabilities, but these directories can be misleading since they are not compiled by other travelers with disabilities. Accurate information about ramps, the width of doors, the dimensions of elevators, and so on, remains difficult to secure. The best method is to write or telephone, and directly ask restaurants, hotels, railways, and airlines about their facilities: *"Etes-vous accessibles aux chaises roulantes?"* Most places that are wheelchair accessible will understand the question if you ask in English. In general, modern buildings in Paris are wheelchair acessible, as are the more expensive hotels. The majority of the budget hotels in this book do not have an elevator; exceptions are noted in the listings. It is still better to call ahead, however, because many of the elevators are too narrow to hold a wheelchair.

Travel by metro is facilitated by wider seats reserved for the disabled, although many stations have stairs rather than escalators or elevators. The RER network operates a number of stations with lift access and others with flat/ramped access. If you're going out of Paris, all TGV high-speed trains can accommodate wheelchairs, and guide dogs are transported free. Other trains have a special compartment and an escalator for boarding. It is worth calling or writing to the train station at your destination to alert the conductor of your needs.

If you bring a seeing-eye dog into France, you must carry a vaccination certificate for rabies issued in your home country or a certificate showing there have been no cases of rabies in your country for over three years. Check with the following organizations for more information on accessibilty and traveling with disabilities.

The American Foundation for the Blind, 15 W. 16th St., New York, NY 10011 (tel. (800) 232-5463 or (212) 620-2147). Call from anywhere in the continental U.S. Mon.-Fri. 8:30am-4:30pm EST. Information, travel books, and ID cards (US$10) for the blind. Write for an application.

L'Association des Paralysés de France, Délégation de Paris, 22, rue du Père Guérion, 75013 Paris (tel. 44 16 83 87). Publishes *Où ferons-nous étape?* (180F), which lists French hotels and motels accessible to persons with disabilities.

Disability Press, Ltd., Applemarket House, 17 Union St., Kingston-upon-Thames, Surrey KT1 1RP, U.K. Publishes the *Disabled Traveler's International Phrasebook* (£1.75), listing useful phrases in 8 languages, including French.

Federation of the Handicapped, 211 W. 14th St., New York, NY 10011 (tel. (212) 206-4200). Leads tours as well as an annual summer trip for its members. Annual membership US$4.

The Guided Tour, 613 West Chelterham Ave., #200, Melrose Park, PA, 19126 (tel. (215) 782-1370). Year-round full-time travel program for developmentally and learning-disabled adults as well as separate trips for those with physical disabilities.

Mobility International, USA (MIUSA), P.O. Box 3551, Eugene, OR 97403 (tel. (503) 343-1284, voice and TDD). MIUSA has information on travel and exchange programs, accommodations, organized tours, and study abroad. They recently updated and expanded *A World of Options for the 1990s: A Guide to International Educational Exchange, Community Service and Travel for Persons with Disabilities.* Travel information and referral network for members. In the U.K., contact Mobility International, 228 Burough High St., London SE1 1JX.

Pauline Hephaistos Survey Projects, 39 Bradley Gardens, West Ealing, London W13 8HE. *Access Guides* to Paris, Jersey, and the Channel Ports, detailing ease of access relating to traveling, accommodations, hotels, and points of interest (£4 each). The guides are researched by people with disabilities.

Wings on Wheels, c/o Evergreen Travel Service, 19505L 44th Ave. W., Lynnwood, WA 98036 (tel. (800) 435-2288 or (206) 776-1184, in WA (800) 562-9298). Provides services for travelers with disabilities. Charters buses with on-board wheelchair-accessible facilities and runs White Cane Tours for the blind as well as tours for hearing-impaired travelers and slow walkers.

Gay and Lesbian Travelers

While Paris is not a haven for gays, in general Parisians are unperturbed by homosexuals living openly. Indispensable to the gay or lesbian traveler in Paris is the encyclopedic *Guide Gai 1993,* which lists support groups, hotels, clubs, and restaurants across France that cater to an either uniquely gay, or mixed gay and straight, clientele (45F, available at newstands). From the same publishers comes Paris's weekly journal, *Gai Pied Hebdo,* which is distributed nationally. The best of the lesbian and gay monthly magazines are *Gay International, Gay Men,* and *Lesbia. Illico* is available free in bars and other gay meeting places. **Les Mots à la Bouche,** 6, rue Ste-Croix de la Bretonnerie, 4*ème* (tel. 42 78 88 30; Mo. St-Paul or Hôtel-de-Ville) carries the city's most extensive collection of gay and lesbian literature including novels, essays, books on art, and magazines in French, English, German, and Italian. **Ecoute Gaie,** a gay hot-line, takes calls on Monday through Friday from 6pm until 10pm (tel. 48 06 19 11).

For more general travel information, consult **Ferrari Publications,** P.O. Box 37887, Phoenix, AZ 85069 (tel. (602) 863-2408), which publishes a number of travel books for gay people, including *Places of Interest* (US$12.95), *Places for Men* (US$12.95), *Places of Interest to Women* (US$10) and *Inn Places: USA and Worldwide Gay Accommodations* (US$14.95). The *Spartacus International Gay Guide* (US$27.95) provides information about gay bars, restuarants, hotels, bookstores, and hotlines throughout the world; it is very specifically for men. Order the guide from 100 East Biddle St., Baltimore, MD 21202 (tel. (301) 727-5677) or c/o Bruno Lutzowstrasse, P.O. Box 30 13 45, D-1000 Berlin 30, Germany (tel. +49 (30) 25 49 82 00).

Traveling with Children

Paris is a wonderful place to travel with children, as long as you don't drag them to every possible museum, historic monument, church, and nearby château. Try following them for a change; you'll see the city in a new and very different light. Parks, most of which have playgrounds, fountains, and lots of interesting people-watching, provide an excellent spot for a relaxed, fun, and very Parisian afternoon. **The Jardins du Luxembourg** have a *guignol* (puppet show), pony rides, go-carts, a carousel, boats to rent and sail on the ornamental ponds, and swings with attendants who, for a tip, will push the swings while you vanish into a café. The Luxembourg gardens also maintain some of the few lawns in Paris that children may play on. In the summer, the carnival at the **Tuileries** has a collection of rides suitable for all ages. Parents will enjoy the ferris wheel—with its outstanding view of central Paris—as much as their kids. **La Villette,** a huge science-museum, aquarium, and Omnimax theater complex, offers an entire day (or even several days) worth of innovative, inspirational entertainment. A climb up the tower of **Notre-Dame,** with its steep, winding stairs, its view of Paris at the top, and—most of all—its leering gargoyles, will liven up any child's tour of the cathedral. The **Jardin des Plantes** and the Paris **Zoo** are also fun, and even the most clichéd sights, such as the Eiffel Tower and the *bateaux mouches* (tour boats on the Seine), rejuvenate jaded travelers when seen with children. Remember that not all museums in Paris are devoted to traditional art; flip through our Museum section for some more unusual selections. Finally, for a surrender to international capitalist homogeneity and childrens' occasionally unrefined taste, take the RER out to **Euro Disneyland.**

In the culinary domain, don't fight the siren song of *le hot dog, le croque monsieur* (a grilled ham-and-cheese sandwich), *les frîtes* (french fries), or even the dreaded "McDonalds!" if your kids don't take to the subtleties of *haute cuisine*—they aren't any different from French kids, who dismay their parents by insisting on fast food. France also offers great ice cream, and older children may enjoy a *demi-panaché* (shandy) made half-and-half with beer and an otherwise uninspiring carbonated lemonade *(limonade;* for true mix-it-yourself lemonade, ask for *citron pressé).* In general, it's not very common to see kids in restaurants. Head for the less formal cafeterias, *café-restaurants* and *brasseries.* Not all restaurants have high chairs; you may want to ask first *("Est-ce que vous avez une chaise haute?").*

For bedtime stories before or during your trip, follow the 12 little girls around the sights of Paris in Hugo Bemelmans's *Madeleine* picture books. *Crin blanc* and *Le ballon rouge,* both by Albert La Morisse, are two powerful stories that exemplify a peculiarly French sentimentality regarding early childhood. Kids will enjoy seeing scenes from them come to life on the streets of Paris, especially around Montmartre and the Ile-de-la-Cité. The well-known *Tintin* and *Astérix* comics appeal to a wide range of ages, and the hardbound copies are both travel- and child-proof (well, almost).

For more hints on traveling with children (and parent-survival) write to **Lonely Planet Publications,** 115 Filbert St., Oakland, CA 94607 (tel. (510) 893-8555) for Maureen Wheeler's *Travel with Children* (US$10.95, U.S. postage US$1.50).

Packing

Pack light; the rest is commentary. Lay out everything you think you'll need, pack only half of it, and take more money. Remember that you can buy almost anything you'll need in Paris, and the more luggage you carry, the more alien you'll feel.

Plan on taking **one suitcase** and **one carry-on**—any more will make it very difficult for you to get to your hotel or place of lodging, unless you're planning to shell out for a taxi. If possible, bring a portable luggage carrier; it can be a lifesaver in the mile-long metro stations. Don't forget a small **daypack** to carry your *Let's Go,* lunch, map, umbrella, and camera. If you want to look more Parisian, make it a funky black book-bag instead. For those planning to buy a lot in Paris (not recommended for the low in funds), an extra fold-up duffle bag will allow you to carry back everything you buy.

Pack solid, dark-colored clothes that won't show the wear they'll surely receive. Loose clothes that can be worn in layers are the most versatile. Dress neatly and conservatively and avoid looking American—you'll fare better when dealing with locals. Sturdy cotton-blend pants or a skirt are cooler for summer. For the most chic in Parisian looks, bring jeans, a funky shirt, and a black, leather belt. Light wool clothing is good for autumn and (with a warm coat) will carry you through winter as well. Bring at least one warm sweater; even in the middle of summer, evenings can be quite cool. Also remember that you should dress neatly when visiting any house of worship, whether or not services are being held. Many churches in France will not allow visitors with bare shoulders to enter (i.e., no tank tops). Take clothes that you can wash in a sink and that dry quickly and wrinkle-free; this will save you time and money spent in laundromat visits. No matter what the season, don't forget your **raincoat** and **umbrella.** Comfortable **walking shoes** are a necessity.

Avoid taking electrical appliances, but if you must, remember that electricity in most European countries is 220 volts AC, twice as much as in North America and enough to fry any of your appliances. In France, as in most of Europe, sockets accommodate two-pin round plugs; get an adapter. If the appliance is not dual voltage, you'll also need a **converter** (US$15-18). You can buy adapters and converters when you get to Europe, or order them in advance from the **Franzus Company,** Murtha Industrial Park, P.O. Box 142, Beacon Falls, CT 06403 (tel. (203)723-6664). The company also distributes a pamphlet called *Foreign Electricity Is No Deep Dark Secret.*

The following is a **checklist of items** you should definitely squeeze in the corners of your pack: needle and thread, tissues, a pocket knife, safety pins, rubber bands, soap, a bath towel, bags which seal shut (for damp clothing, soap, or messy foods), a notebook and pens or pencils, a pocket French-English dictionary or phrasebook, and a (non-ticking!) travel alarm clock. If you don't speak French, bring an English-language map, although you should be able to find one in Paris also. Once you're in Paris, buy a small bottle of mineral water and save the bottle—its always a good idea to carry water around with you, especially in the summer. Bring a sleep-sack if you plan to stay in hostels and toilet paper if you don't want to deal with the waxed brown paper some of the budget hotels may give you.

If you take expensive **cameras** or equipment abroad, it's best to register everything with customs at the airport before departure. Buy a supply of film before you leave; it's more expensive in France. Unless you're shooting with 1000 ASA or more, airport security x-rays should not harm your pictures. It never hurts, however, to buy a lead pouch, available at any camera store. Either way, pack film in your carry-on, since the x-rays employed on checked baggage are much stronger. To avoid x-rays altogether, you can have your film and camera hand-inspected at most American airports; French airports may be less accommodating. If you're bringing a laptop or notebook **computer,** be sure to have both computer and floppy discs hand-inspected, lest stray x-rays wipe out your as-yet-unpublished *chef-d'oeuvre.* Officials may ask you to turn it on, so be sure the batteries are fully loaded. A final warning: lost baggage is common, and not always retrieved. Keep all valuables and a change of clothing in your carry-on.

Alternatives to Tourism

If the often madcap, train-changing, site-switching pace of tourism loses its appeal, consider a longer stay in Paris, where through study, work or volunteering you can gain a deeper appreciation for the France that extends beyond cathedrals and cafés.

Useful Publications

Council on International Educational Exchange, 205 E. 42nd St., New York, NY 10017 (tel. (212) 661-1414), publishes a wide variety of books on work, study and volunteering abroad. See listing above under Travel Services for a list of publications.

Institute of International Education (IIE), 809 UN Plaza, New York, NY 10017 (tel. (212) 883-8200). Publishes a number of useful books, including *Basic Facts on Foreign Study* (free), and the very thorough, annual *Academic Year Abroad* (US$39.95, postage US$3), and *Vacation Study Abroad* (US$31.95, postage US$3). You can call or write IIE for information, or visit their reference library (open by appointment). They also publish *Financial Resources for International Study,* available from Peterson's Guides, P.O. Box 2123, Princeton, NJ, 08543-2123 (tel. (800) 338-3282), which lists over 600 foundations providing money to undergrad, grad and post-grad students. Finally, they distribute several books published by the **Central Bureau for Educational Visits and Exchanges** in the U.K., including *Study Holidays* (£8.95 including U.K. postage, £10.40 including postage to mainland Europe, and £13.95 including airmail postage worldwide), **Working Holidays** (£8.95, £10.45, and £13.95), and *Home from Home* (£7.99, £9.49, and £11.99), an annual guide to homestays, termstays and exchanges. Write to the Central Bureau directly at Seymour Mews House, Seymour Mews, London W1H 9PE, England (tel. (071) 486 5101).

Vacation Work Publications, 9 Park End St., Oxford OX1 1HJ, England (tel. (0865) 24 19 78). Distributes books on work and volunteer opportunities, including *Directory of Summer Jobs Abroad* (£7.95), *Work Your Way Around the World* (£9.95), *The Au Pair and Nanny's Guide to Working Abroad* (£7.95), *International Directory of Voluntary Work* (£8.95), and *Emplois d'Eté en France* (£6.95).

Study

If you choose your program well, study in Paris could be one of the most exciting and cosmopolitan experiences you'll ever have. If you're looking for the true France, however, try elsewhere in the country. In Paris, you'll have to be stubborn about speaking French; it's far too easy to hang out exclusively with other English-speakers. Research your options well, as programs vary considerably in academic quality, living conditions and expense. If possible, avoid programs that will place you with a group of other students from your home country. Consider enrolling directly in the French universities—by far the cheapest and most authentic (if least well organized) way to go (see below). A good place to begin investigating study abroad programs is CIEE's *Work, Study, Travel Abroad: The Whole World Handbook. Basic Facts on Study Abroad,* put out by the IIE, CIEE, and **NAFSA: The Association of International Educators,** a free brochure that covers the nitty-gritty of foreign study, from visas to tax

returns. **UNESCO** publishes *Study Abroad* (US$24, postage US$2.50), available from Unipub Co., 4611-F Assembly Dr., Lanham, MD 20706 (tel. (800) 274-4888). French educational terminology and equivalencies are radically different from almost anyone elses. For guidance and information, including free pamphlets on various fields of study in France, contact the **Cultural Services of the French Embassy.** The **American Center for Students and Artists** is a student advisory service that provides information on housing, education, and *au pair* and small jobs. Contact the center at 51, rue de Bercy, 12*ème,* 75592, Paris Cedex 12 (tel. 44 73 77 77).

Language Schools

Language instruction is a booming business in France; semester and year abroad programs are run by American universities, independent international or local organizations, and divisions of French universities. The **tourist office** in Paris maintains a list of member language schools.

> **Cours de Civilisation Française de la Sorbonne,** 47, rue des Ecoles, 75005 Paris (tel. 40 46 22 11). The **Sorbonne** has been giving its French civilization course since 1919. Academic year course can be taken by the semester; 4-, 6-, and 8-week summer programs with civilization lectures and language classes at various levels. The Sorbonne also offers a special course in commercial French during the academic year, and a 4-week session for high-level students during the summer. You can also take the *Cours de Civilisation* through the **American Institute for Foreign Study (AIFS),** 102 Greenwich Ave., Greenwich, CT 06830 (tel. (800) 727-2437), which also arranges accommodations and meals in Paris for its students. In addition the AIFS administers programs in Cannes and Grenoble.

> **Alliance Française,** Ecole Internationale de Langue et de Civilisation Française, 101, bd. Raspail, 6*ème,* 75270 Paris Cedex 06 (tel. 45 44 38 28; fax 45 44 89 42). Mo. Notre-Dame-des-Champs, St-Placide, or Rennes. Offers language courses at various levels, a business course, teacher training, and refresher courses.

> **Institut Catholique de Paris,** 21, rue d'Assas, 6*ème,* 75270 Paris Cedex 06 (tel. 42 22 41 80). Mo. St-Placide. Semester-long and summer classes at all levels, including business French and courses for teachers of French.

> **Eurocentres,** another of the many hats worn by Council Travel. Long and short intensive courses, holiday courses, and teacher refresher courses at centers in Paris at 13, passage Dauphine, 75006 Paris (tel. 43 25 81 40); in La Rochelle at 10ter, rue Amelot, 17000 La Rochelle (tel. 46 50 57 33); and in Amboise at 9, Mail Saint-Thomas, BP 214, 37402 Amboise Cedex (tel. 47 23 10 60). Call or write the nearest Council Travel office for information on centers worldwide.

French Universities

While it is tempting (and comforting) to meet and talk to other Americans, you may regret it later. If your French is already extremely competent, direct enrollment in a French university may be more rewarding than a language or civilization class filled with English-speakers. Enrolling yourself directly can sometimes cost three or four times less than going through an American university's program, but it might be more difficult to receive academic credit at your home university. The French educational system is structured to prepare students for a series of standard examinations that must be passed to earn degrees. After 1969, the **Université de Paris** split into ten isolated universities, each occupying different sites and offering a different range of fields. The famous and century-old Sorbonne is now the Université de Paris IV, focusing on a range of traditional fields in the humanites. For a more experimental approach, try one of the more modern universities. Each of them requires at least a *baccalauréat* degree or its putative equivalents (British A-levels or two years of college in the United States) for admission. For details on application procedures and lists of the fields offered by each Université de Paris, contact the cultural services office at the nearest French consulate or embassy. Start this way ahead of time and expect to be confused—the bureaucracy of the French educational system is notorious.

As a student registered in a French university, you will be given a student card *(carte d'étudiant)* by your school upon presentation of your residency permit and a receipt for your university fees. In addition to the card's standard student benefits (generally in the form of discounts at museums and the like), many additional benefits available to students in Paris are administered by the **Centre Régional des Oeuvres Universitaires et**

Scolaires (CROUS) de Paris. Founded in 1955 to improve the living and working conditions of its members, this division of the Oeuvres Universitaires welcomes foreign students. A student card entitles you to subsidized rates at restaurants, accommodations, and various social and cultural services in Paris. The regional center is at 39, av. Georges-Bernanos, 5ème, 75231 Paris Cedex 05 (tel. 40 51 36 00). CROUS also publishes brochures, *Guide Infos Etudiants*, listing addresses and information on every aspect of student life in Paris. Pick up the helpful guidebook *Je vais en France* (free), available in French or English, from any French embassy or consulate.

Work

Today's strict regulations can make George Orwell's search for work as an unskilled *plongeur* (dishwasher) look like a cakewalk. Because of high unemployment, the French government has become wary of hiring foreigners. Before you can obtain a work permit through normal channels, your employer must convince the Ministry of Labor that there is no French citizen capable of filling your position. Even when a foreigner is considered, EC country members have priority. Long-term employment is difficult to secure unless you have skills in high-demand areas such as medicine, computer programming, or teaching. If you have the appropriate skills or educational background, you might investigate positions with US firms, government agencies, or non-profit organizations that hire Americans for work abroad.

Permits

With the exception of *au pair* jobs, it is illegal for foreign students to hold full-time jobs during the school year. Students registered at French universities may get work permits for the summer with a valid visa, a student card from a French university, and proof of a job. After spending one academic year in France, Americans with a valid student *carte de séjour* can find part-time work if they will be enrolled at a French university again in the fall. Check the fact sheet *Employment in France for Students,* put out by **Cultural Services of the French Embassy,** which provides basic information about work in France and also lists the government-approved organizations through which foreign students must secure their jobs. **CIEE** operates a reciprocal work program with France and is the only U.S. organization so approved. If you are a degree-seeking college or university student, a resident U.S. citizen, and have an intermediate level knowledge of French (at least 2 years of college French), CIEE will issue you a three-month work permit for US$125. Under this system, you do not need a job prior to obtaining a work permit. CIEE will provide information on accommodations and job-hunting, but will not place you in a job. Jobs available are mostly short-term, unskilled work in hotels, shops, restaurants, farms, and factories. Wages should cover food, lodging, and basic living expenses. Complete information and an application are enclosed in their *Work Abroad* brochure.

Useful Publications

A number of firms publish guides that can lead you through the complicated process of finding work abroad.

CIEE: Their *Work, Study, Travel Abroad: The Whole World Handbook* (US$12.95, postage US$1.50), available in bookstores, from any Council Travel office, or from CIEE's New York headquarters, is a comprehensive guide to overseas opportunities that includes a work-abroad section with listings by country. The handbook also includes a section on long-term employment. For more detail specific to France, consult *CIEE's Emplois d'Eté en France* (US$13.95, postage US$1.50). Also available from CIEE is *Working in France: The Ultimate Guide to Job Hunting and Career Success à la Française* (US$12.95, postage US$1.50).

Peterson's, P.O. Box 2123, Princeton, NJ 08543 (tel. (800) 338-3282), publishes the *1992 Directory of Overseas Summer Jobs* (US$14.95, postage US$4.75), which lists 50,000 openings worldwide, volunteer and paid.

World Trade Academy Press, 50 E. 42nd St., #509, New York, NY 10017 (tel. (212) 697-4999), publishes a *Directory of American Firms Operating in Foreign Countries* (look it up in the library—it costs an awe-inspiring US$195), and the more manageable *Looking for Employment in*

Foreign Countries (US$16.50). It also publishes excerpts of listings of American firms in specific countries for about $10-15.

Addison Wesley, 1 Jacob Way, Reading, MA 01867 (tel. (800) 447-2226) makes available another general guide, *International Jobs: Where They Are, How To Get Them* (US$12.95).

Finding a Job

Once in Paris, a good place to start your job search is the **American Chamber of Commerce,** 21, av. George V, 8*ème* (tel. 47 23 80 26; Mo. George or Alma Marceau). The *Membership Directory of the French-American Chamber of Commerce* is available from its office at 509 Madison Ave., #1900, New York, NY 10022 (tel. (212) 371-4466). It is quite expensive, so go through the directory at the office. The **Agence Nationale Pour l'Emploi,** 4, rue Galilés, 93198 Noisy-le-Grand Cedex (tel. 49 31 74 00), has specific information on employment. You could also visit the **Centre d'Information et de Documentation Jeunesse (CIDJ),** 101, quai Branly, 15*ème* (tel. 45 66 40 20; Mo. Champ de Mars/Tour Eiffel), a government-run information clearinghouse on French law, camping, touring, sports, employment, careers, and long-term accommodations. Part-time jobs and housing listings are posted at 9am on the bulletin boards outside. Pamphlets available include *Cours d'été pour étrangers en France, Placement au pair en France,* and *Tourisme en France.* (Open Mon.-Fri. 9am-7pm, Sat. 10am-6pm.) **The American Church in Paris,** 65, quai d'Orsay, 7*ème,* posts a full bulletin board of potential job and housing opportunities. Also check help-wanted columns in newspapers, especially *Le Monde, Le Figaro,* and the English-language *International Herald Tribune*, as well as *France-USA Contacts.* Many of these jobs are unofficial, and won't require a work permit. For more under-the-table work, try giving English lessons (advertise in *France-USA Contacts* or put up notices at *boulangeries, librairies,* etc.). Because there are so many foreigners in Paris already offering lessons, don't expect to support yourself on this alone.

The **International Association for the Exchange of Students for Technical Experience (IAESTE)** program, a division of the Association for International Practical Training (AIPT), is an internship exchange program for science, architecture, engineering, agriculture, and math students who have completed at least two years at an accredited four-year institution. There is a non-refundable US$75 fee. Apply to the IAESTE Trainee Program, c/o AIPT, 10 Corporate Ctr., Ste. 250, 10400 Little Patuxent Parkway, Columbia, MD 21044 (tel. (410) 997-2200). Applications are due December 10 for summer placement.

Teaching English

There are a variety of resources available to those interested in **teaching English** in a foreign school. This may be your best chance at a steady salary and a well-paying job. The U.S. State Department **Office of Overseas Schools,** Rm. 245 SA-29, Department of State, Washington, DC 20522 (tel. (703) 875-7800) maintains a list of elementary and secondary schools abroad and agencies that arrange placement for Americans to teach abroad. Also, check with your local univeristy's career office.

International Schools Services, 15 Roszel Rd., P.O. Box 5910, Princeton, NJ 08543 (tel. (609) 452-0990) publishes a free newsletter, *NewsLinks;* call or write to get on the mailing list. Their Educational Staffing Department, which coordinates placement of teachers in international and American schools, publishes the free brochure *Your Passport to Teaching and Administrative Opportunities Abroad.* The *ISS Directory of Overseas Schools* (US$34.95) is distributed by **Peterson's,** 202 Carnegie Center, Princeton, NJ 08543 (tel. (800) 338-3282).

Leading Tours

Summer positions as tour group leaders are available with **Hostelling International,** P.O. Box 37613, Washington, DC 20013 (tel. (202) 783-6161). You must be over age 20 and are required to take a nine-day training course (US$295, room and board included; in Washington, DC US$395). You must lead a group in the U.S. before taking one to Europe. The **Experiment in International Living (EIL),** P.O. Box 676, Kipling Rd., Brattleboro, VT 05302 (tel. (800) 451-4465 or (802) 257-7751), requires leadership ability and extensive overseas experience (min. age 24). Applications are due in late November for summer positions. CIEE also has group leader positions available; contact its International Voluntary Projects division.

Au Pair Positions

And then there is the old standby—*au pair* work. Positions are reserved primarily for single women aged 18 to 30 with some knowledge of French; a few men are also employed. The *au pair* cares for the children of a French family and does light housework five or six hours each day (1 day off per week) while taking courses at a school for foreign students or at a French university. Talking with children can be a great way to improve your French, but looking after them (and ironing their jeans, underwear, handkerchiefs, etc.) may be extremely strenuous. Make sure you know in advance what the family expects of you. *Au pair* positions usually last six to 18 months; during the summer the contract can be as short as one to three months, but you may not be able to take courses. You'll receive room, board, and a small monthly stipend (around 1300F). Be sure to acquire a visa *long séjour* before arriving in France.

The Cultural Services of the French Embassy offers a detailed information sheet on *au pair* jobs. Organizations offering placement include **L'Accueil Familial des Jeunes Etrangers,** 23, rue du Cherche-Midi, 75006 Paris (tel. 42 22 50 34 or 42 22 13 34) and **Centre d'Echanges Culturels Internationaux (CECI),** B.P. 30171, 69406 Lyon Cedex 3 (tel. (16) 77 27 00 91). *Au pair* jobs can also be arranged through individual connections, but make sure you have a contract detailing hours per week, salary, and living accommodations.

Volunteering

If you have the financial freedom to forgo a salary, volunteering can provide a wonderful opportunity to meet people and might even secure you room and board in exchange for your work. *Volunteer! The Comprehensive Guide to Voluntary Service in the U.S. and Abroad* is co-published by CIEE and the Commission of Religious Volunteer Agencies. It offers advice on choosing a voluntary service program and lists over 200 organizations in fields ranging from social work to construction. Write to CIEE (US$8.95, postage US$1.50). Also try international firms, museums, art galleries, and non-profit organizations like UNESCO; they may have unpaid internships available.

Transportation

Getting There

From North America

Budget air travel began inauspiciously with Icarus, whose no-frills flight to the center of the solar system was fatally turbulent. Survival rates have risen dramatically since then, but air travel has become immensely more complicated. Use the following suggestions as a base for research, but above all, plan ahead and shop around.

Making reservations far in advance gives you access to cheaper fares and a wider choice of dates. Also, try to be flexible. Direct, regularly scheduled flights are notoriously expensive. It may pay to fly to a city other than Paris. Flying to London is usually the cheapest way across the Atlantic, though special fares to other cities—such as Amsterdam, Luxembourg, or Brussels—can cost even less. Off-season travelers will enjoy lower fares and face much less competition for inexpensive seats, but you don't have to travel in the dead of winter to save; peak season rates begin on either May 15 or June 1 and run until about September 15. Midweek (Mon.-Thurs.) flights run about US$30 cheaper each way. It is generally advisable to fix a return date when purchasing your ticket. Traveling with an "open return" ticket can be pricier than fixing a return date and paying to change it. Purchasing a one-way ticket invites the same danger.

Begin by calling **student travel organizations** such as Council Travel, Travel CUTS, or Let's Go Travel (see Useful Organizations). They cut special deals for students not available to regular travel agents, and are often significantly cheaper. If you are not eligible for their fares, look for a knowledgable, sympathetic travel agent. Consulting several is a good idea; some travel agents won't be eager to help you find the cheapest option, since budget flights earn them only a small commission. Another option is the Sunday travel sections of *The New York Times* and other newspapers, where fare brokers advertise incredibly cheap, but erratic fares. Seniors can also get excellent deals; many airlines offer senior-traveler club deals or airline passes, and discounts for seniors' companions as well.

Commercial Airlines

Flying with a commercial airline is usually the most expensive option, but will reward you with a commensurate level of flexibility, reliability, and comfort. The industry is extremely variable: in 1992 prices on commercial flights from the East Coast to Paris ranged from $200-$1000 round-trip. Plan for a ball-park figure of $700-900 high season, $500-700 off-season. Look into smaller carriers such as Icelandair, Virgin Atlantic, and Martinair Holland, which may undercut the fares of large airlines. Most airlines offer price cuts for advance purchase; a small number have **standby** and **three-day advance purchase** youth fares. Check with individual carriers for information on restrictions and availability.

Charter Flights

Charter flights make the most economic sense, especially in the high season. You can book charters up until the last minute, but most flights during the summer fill up months in advance. Later in the season, companies have trouble filling their planes and either cancel flights or charge special fares. Charter flights allow you to stay abroad for as long as you like and often allow you to mix and match arrivals and departures from different cities. Once you have made your reservations with a charter company, however, flexibility flies away. You must choose your departure and return dates when you book the flight, and if you cancel your ticket within 14 to 20 days of departure, you will lose some money. Be aware, however, that charter flights are often inconvenient and require long layovers. Ask a travel agent about your charter company's reliability, since such companies reserve the right to cancel flights until 48 hours before departure.

Council Charter is among the oldest and most reliable charter-flight companies and offers flights to most major European cities with a variety of gateways in the U.S. Tickets can be purchased at any Council Travel office, or through Council Charter in New York (tel. (800) 800-8222). Also try **DER Tours** (tel. (800) 782-2424); and **Travel Avenue** (tel. (800) 333-3335 or (312) 876-1116). In Canada, try **Travel CUTS** (see Useful Organizations above).

Discount Clubs and Ticket Consolidators

Last-minute discount clubs and fare brokers offer savings on European travel, including charter flights and tour packages. Organizations that act as clearing houses for unsold airline, charter, and cruise tickets include **Access International** (tel. (800) 825-3633 or (212) 465-0707); **Discount Travel International** (tel. (215) 668-7184; US$45 membership); **Last Minute Travel Club** (tel. (800) 527-8646 or (617) 267-9800); **Last-Minute Travel Connection** (tel. (708) 498-9216 or (900) 446-8292) for last-minute travel opportunities; **Moment's Notice** (tel. (212) 486-0503, hotline (212) 750-9111); **Unitravel Corporation** (tel. (800) 325-2222); and **Worldwide Discount Travel Club** (tel. (305) 534-2082; US$50 membership). Clubs generally charge a yearly subscription fee of $30-50; fare brokers like Access International do not. Both sell empty seats on commercial carriers and charters from three weeks to a few days before departure. Study their often Byzantine contract—you may prefer not to stop over in Luxembourg for 11 hours.

For the truly flexible budget traveler, **Airhitch** (tel. (212) 864-2000) lets you choose a date range in which you want to travel and a number of possible desitinations; you are then placed with 90% certainty in a vacant spot on a flight in your date range to one of

EUROPE BY YOURSELF

WITH THE YOUTH & STUDENT TRAVEL SPECIALISTS

FROM PARIS TO

	return ✈	return 🚂
Amsterdam	FFR 910	488
Berlin	FFR 1480	1121
Rome	FFR 1100	1008
Madrid	FFR 1580	1042
Moscow	FFR 2900	-
New York	FFR 2450	-
Sydney	FFR 8425	-
Bangkok	FFR 5385	-

FROM ROME TO

	return ✈	return 🚂
Athens	$ 310	200
Cairo	$ 540	-
Istanbul	$ 370	220

FROM LONDON TO

	return ✈	return 🚂
Athens	£ 133	265
Rome	£ 120	170
Venice	£ 150	157

ACCOMMODATION WORLDWIDE

Paris	$ 30
London	$ 30
Amsterdam	$ 28
Athens	$ 18
Madrid	$ 32
Florence	$ 21
Rome	$ 21
Venice	$ 23

Prices are valid for summer '92

 YOUTH & STUDENT TRAVEL CENTRE

PARIS V°	**20, rue des Carmes - Tel. (00331) 43250076** **Metro Maubert Mutualitè**
LONDON	44 Goodge Street, W1P 2AD - Tel. (004471) 5804554/6375601 Metro Goodge Street
LONDON	220 Kensington High Street, W8 7RA - Tel. (004471) 9373265 Metro High Street Kensington
ROME	via Genova, 16 - Tel. (06) 46791
ROME	corso Vittorio Emanuele II, 297 - Tel. (06) 6872672/3/4
ROME	Air Terminal Ostiense - Tel. (06) 5747950
FLORENCE	via dei Ginori, 25/R - Tel. (055) 289721/289570
MILAN	via S. Antonio, 2 - Tel. (02) 58304121
NAPELS	via Mezzocannone, 25 - Tel. (081) 5527975/5527960
VENICE	Dorso Duro Ca' Foscari, 3252 - Tel. (041) 5205660/5205655

your destinations. The trip back also requires such flexibility. While Airhitch's prices are ostensibly low (one-way flights to Europe from New York cost US$169), this is by no means a convenient or reliable means of travel. Be sure to read all the fine print.

Courier Flights

Go-getters who don't mind traveling light might consider flying to Paris as a **courier.** A company hiring you as a courier will use your checked luggage space for freight, leaving you with only the carry-on allowance. Fares vary wildly, depending on proximity to departure date, but are usually standby level or lower—often dramatically lower. Most courier companies offer single round-trip tickets only, leaving from New York with fixed-length stays (usually short). **Now Voyager** (tel. (212) 431-1616) couriers fly to Paris from New York. **Courier Travel Service** (tel. (800) 922-2359 or (516) 374-2299), and **Halbart Express** (tel. (718) 656-8189) advertise similar opportunities. Check the travel section of a major newspaper for other courier companies. For more information, write or call Thunderbird Press, W. Greenway Bd., Suite 112H, Glendale AZ 85306 (tel. (800) 345-0096), for the *Courier Air Travel Handbook* (US$10.70).

From Europe

By Plane

If charters to Paris are booked and commercial flights are too expensive, you can always fly to London and connect with an intra-European flight. **Council Travel** offers rates of around US$75-95 between London or Amsterdam and Paris. In London, check newspapers, travel agencies, and student travel organizations for bargain charter flights. The **Air Travel Advisory Bureau,** Strauss House 41-45, Goswell Road, London EC1V 7DN (tel. (071) 636 2908) puts travelers in touch with the cheapest carriers for free. Also contact **STA Travel** or a **CIEE** office for information about inexpensive flights throughout Europe.

You may want to consider special student fares offered within Europe, which can be competitive with train and ferry ticket prices. See a student travel organization such as CIEE about this option. Finally, check on special deals offered by national airlines if you fly with them across the Atlantic. For continental travel, some of the lowest fares can be found on Eastern European airlines. Note that baggage limitations for intra-European flights (20kg or 32 lbs.) are lower than those for flights to and from North America (44kg or 70 lbs.).

By Train

You can get to Paris from nearly anywhere on the continent by train. Most European trains are fast, punctual, and convenient. Gas is astronomically expensive in Europe, and the train system is a far more popular (and more energy-efficient) mode of transportation than automobiles.

Overnight trains will save you money on accommodations, but spend a few extra dollars for a berth in a *couchette* (bunkbed) car. Bring your own food and drink—it's expensive in the diner cars, and the water from the bathroom faucets is not suitable for drinking. Be mindful of safety as trains are hardly theft-proof: lock the door of your compartment if you can and keep valuables on your person.

Point-to-point tickets can be purchased in Europe or from a travel agent in North America. They are "open" tickets, specifying only points of departure and arrival, not specific dates or seat assignments. Reservations, for which you will be charged a moderate fee, are recommended for longer trips on all international trains, though you can usually find a seat on shorter journeys. It is always advisable to make reservations when traveling during peak periods (weekends and in the summer), unless you enjoy standing for endless hours.

Thomas Cook publishes the incredibly useful *European Timetable,* with schedules for routes all over Europe, available from Forsyth Travel Library (see Useful Organizations—Publications).

By French Train

France has a vast rail network to accommodate its over 15,000 daily departures, and its national rail company, the **Société Nationale de Chemins de Fer (SNCF),** is wondrously efficient. Off the main lines between cities and large towns, however, service is both less frequent and less convenient. Consequently, be prepared for long waits and obscure timetables. Buses fill in shorter gaps in the system, and recently a few unprofitable SNCF train routes have been replaced with SNCF buses, which also honor railpasses. The TGV *(train à grande vitesse)* serves major cities and is faster and more comfortable than normal express trains *("express"* or *"rapide");* it always requires a reservation even if you have a railpass. The reservation fee (about US$8) is waived for Eurailpass holders. Reservations, like the tickets, are available from travel agents (for a slight commission) or from train stations (after a long line) in France.

For domestic travel in France, be sure to validate your ticket in one of the orange ticket punches (with signs marked *"compostez votre billet"*) at the entrance to the platforms. This stamps the date on the ticket making it valid for that day of travel. If you break your journey, you must validate your ticket again after the stopover. Always keep your ticket with you, as you may have to present it during your trip and when you finally leave the train.

French timetables are complicated but organized. They consist of three periods, designated by colors, which depend on the expected volume of passenger traffic. Red (peak) periods generally fall on important long weekends and tickets are more costly. Individual days are generally divided into white (peak) and blue (off-peak) hours; again, prices vary accordingly. Every major railroad station in France carries schedules and provides train information at computer tellers, via representatives at the station, or most commonly, on poster timetables. You can purchase the complete SNCF timetable at newsstands in the stations. SNCF representatives in the U.S. provide material on France Railpasses and Eurailpasses, as well as a booklet of French and European fares.

Train Discounts and Railpasses

Billet International de Jeunesse (BIJ) tickets remain one of the cheapest options for travelers under 26. They cut up to 50% off regular second-class rail fares on international routes and are valid on the vast majority of trains. When you buy a BIJ ticket, you specify both your destination and route and have the option of stopping anywhere along that route for up to two months. BIJ tickets are available in Europe only, from **Eurotrain** outlets and **Wasteels** offices, as well as other student travel agencies. In England, Eurotrain is located at 52 Grosvenor Gardens, London SW1W OAG (tel. (071) 730 8518). In Paris, **Eurotrain** is located at 3, bd. des Capucines, *2ème* (tel. 44 71 30 00; Mo. Opéra); several student travel agencies in Paris also sell BIJ tickets (see Practical Information—Budget Travel Services).

In addition, a number of special discounts can be applied to point-to-point tickets purchased in France. The **Carrissimo,** available for 12- to 25-year-olds traveling alone or with up to 3 friends all under the age of 26, offers discounts of 50% on blue period trips for the traveler and 3 friends or less, or 20% discounts during the white period. (Valid for one year; 190F for 4 trips, 350F for 8 trips max.) This sounds expensive, but just one trip with the Carrissimo will usually save you enough to more than pay for it. The **Carte Vermeille** (165F) entitles travelers 65 and over to 50% off first- or second-class tickets for trips in blue (off-peak) periods. It can be obtained at larger rail stations (valid for 1 year). The Carte Vermeille and Carrissimo are sold only in Europe. For an additional supplement, both of these passes can be used to get discount rates on several other national train systems.

If you are planning to rack up many kilometers on French or European trains, you might consider investing in a **railpass.** Ideally, a railpass allows you to hop on any train in France or Europe (depending on the pass), go wherever you and whenever you want, and change your plans at will. You can ride the TGV or regular trains during peak periods and hours at no extra charge. The handbook that comes with your railpass is designed to tell you everything you need to know, including a timetable for major routes, a map, and details on ferry discounts. In practice, of course, it's not so simple. You must still stand in line to pay for seat reservations, for supplements, and for couchette reservations, and to have your pass validated when you first use it. More importantly, railpasses don't always pay off; unless you're covering a lot of ground in a short amount of time, point-to-point BIJ tickets may be cheaper. Find a travel agent with a copy of the *Eurailtariff* manual (or call Rail Europe at (800) 438-7245), add up the second-class fares for the major routes you plan to cover, deduct 5% (the listed price includes a commission), deduct 30% if you are under 26 and eligible for the BIJ, and compare. The ostensible convenience of a railpass might prove expensive.

For travel across the continent, five flavors of **Eurailpass** exist. The basic **Eurailpass** is valid for unlimited rail travel in Western European countries, including the Republic of Ireland, but not Great Britain or Northern Ireland. You can travel first class for periods ranging from 15 days (US$460) to three months (US$1260). Those under 26 also qualify for the **Eurail Youthpass,** good for one month (US$508) or two months (US$698) of second-class travel. The **Eurail Flexipass** allows you to travel on specific days within a two-month period: five days for US$298, 10 days for US$496, or 15 days for US$676. The **Eurail Youth Flexipass** offers those under 26 the same options for US$220, US$348, and US$474, respectively. Finally, the **Eurail Saverpass** allows two or more people traveling together at all times (3 or more from April-Sept.) to travel first class for 15 days for US$390 per person. You must get your Eurailpass or Eurail Youthpass in North America. Purchase them from a travel agent, CIEE, the Educational Travel Center, or from Let's Go Travel Services. Rail Europe (tel. (800) 438-7245) sells all passes, point-to-point tickets, and reservations for European rail travel.

With a **France Railpass,** travelers can ride for any four days within a one-month period (US$175 first-class, US$125 secondclass). The days of use need not be consecutive. Up to five additional days can be purchased (each US$38 first-class, US$27 second-class). Included is a pass for the Paris metro, covering the city's buses, subways, and RER trains for one day. You also get free transfer from Orly or Roissy Airports to Paris and back. You can buy the railpasses in North America at offices of Rail Europe or from travel agents. France passes cannot be purchased or used by residents of France. If your itinerary includes Britain as well, you might consider purchasing a **BritFrance Railpass.** The pass is good for rail travel in France and Great Britain for 5 days within a 15-day period for US$335, first class, or US$249, second class. A second option allows for 10 days of travel within a one-month period for US$505, first class, or US$385, second class. If you are under 26, a Youthpass, providing second-class travel through the BritFrance Railpass will cost you US$199 for the first option and US$299 for the second. All BritFrance Railpasses include one round-trip hovercraft crossing of the English Channel. For those bit by the travel bug early in life, consider the **Kiwi** pass, which yields a 50% discount off tickets for children under 16. The trips must begin during the white or blue period. Up to 4 adults traveling with the child also receive 50% discounts. The Kiwi pass is sold at French rail stations only.

By Ferry

Many ferries link France with England and Ireland. **Sealink Stena Lines** and **P&O European Ferries** offer extensive service across the English Channel. Sealink ferries leave from Dover to Calais, take about 90 minutes, and are the most frequent (at peak times every 75min.). Alternate routes between England and France include Southampton to Cherbourg (4½hr., night service 6hr.) and Newhaven to Dieppe (3 per day, 4hr.). **P&O European Ferries** operates the fastest crossing by ship—just 75 minutes from Dover to Calais. Other convenient Channel crossings include Portsmouth to Le Havre and Cherbourg. Le Havre has the fastest road connections to Paris, and Cherbourg is ideal for a scenic route through Normandy to Brittany. **Brittany Ferries** run from Plymouth or Cork to Roscoff, from Portsmouth to St-Malo/Caen, and from Poole to Cherbourg. Standard foot passenger fare from all Dover routes is approximately £17.50, with substantial savings available on fixed-period returns. From any of these destinations in France, you should be able to catch a train to Paris. **Irish Ferries** offers service between Cherbourg or Le Havre to Rosslare in Ireland, and to Le Havre from Cork. Irish Continental is rather expensive (price varies between £50-100, depending on season), but Eurailpass holders travel free.

Traveling by **catamaran** is quicker (50min.), but you should book in advance. **Hoverspeed** departs for Calais or Boulogne from Dover. Service is suspended in rough weather, so you may find yourself waiting for a ferry instead. Hoverspeed also offers combination rail/bus and hovercraft service to and from London, Paris, Brussels, Amsterdam, and points in southwestern France. This is often the easiest and cheapest way to get to Paris. Students under 26 travel at youth rates. For information, write Travelloyd, 8 Berkeley Sq., London SW1, or the British Rail Travel Centre, 4-12 Lower Regent St., London SW1Y 4PQ.

Getting In and Out of Paris

From the Airport

Roissy-Charles de Gaulle

Most transatlantic flights land at **Aéroport Roissy-Charles de Gaulle,** 23km northeast of Paris. As a general rule, Terminal 2 serves Air France (info tel. 43 20 14 55; arrivals tel. 43 20 12 55; departures tel. 43 20 13 55), and most other carriers operate from Terminal 1 (info tel. 48 62 22 80).

The cheapest and fastest way to get into the city from Roissy-Charles de Gaulle and vice versa is by the **Roissy Rail** (tel. 43 46 14 14) bus-train combination. Take the free shuttle bus from Aérogare 1 arrival level gate 28, Aérogare 2A gate 5, Aérogare 2B gate 6, or Aérogare 2D gate 6, to the Roissy train station. From there, the **RER B3** (one of the Parisian commuter rail lines) will transport you to central Paris. If you are going to transfer to the metro, be sure to buy an RER ticket that includes metro transfer, and get off at **Gare du Nord** or **Châtelet-Les Halles,** which double as RER and metro stops. To go to Roissy-Charles de Gaulle from Paris, take the RER B3 to "Roissy," and change to the shuttle bus (RER 25-35min., bus 10min., 31F with metro transfer).

Alternatively, **Air France Buses** run to the Arc de Triomphe (Mo. Charles de Gaulle-Etoile) at av. Carnot (every 15min. from 5:40am to 11pm, 40min., 48F, group of 3 passengers 112F, group of 4 140F), and the pl. de la Porte de Maillot/Palais des Congrès (Mo. Porte de Maillot), near the agence Air France (every 20min. from 5:40am-11pm, 40min., same prices). For recorded information about either of these buses, call 42 99 20 18. Air France buses also run to and from a spot near the Gare Montparnasse, 113, bd. du Vaugirard (Mo. Montparnasse-Bienvenue). (To the airport hourly 7am-9pm; from the airport hourly 6:30am-7:30pm, 45min., 64F, group of 3 passengers 144F, group of 4 170F.) Call 43 23 82 20 for recorded info.

The **RATP** (tel. 43 46 14 14) runs city buses from Roissy-Charles de Gaulle into Paris. **Bus #350** plies between the airport and Gare du Nord and Gare de l'Est (every 15min. from 5:30am-11pm, 50min., 30F). **Bus #351** goes to pl. de la Nation (every 30min. from 6am-8:30pm, 40min., 30F). Unless your hotel is near one of these terminals, you'll wind up having to take the metro anyway. **Taxis** take at least 50 minutes to the center of Paris and cost about 210F during the day, 290F at night.

Orly

Aéroport d'Orly (tel. 49 75 15 15), 12km south of the city, is used by charters and many continental flights. From Orly Sud gate H or Orly Ouest arrival level gate F, take the shuttle bus (every 15min. from 5:40am-11:15pm) to the **Pont de Rungis/Aéroport d'Orly** train stop where you can board the **RER C2** for a number of destinations in Paris. (35min., 25F; call RATP at 43 46 14 14 for info).

Air France Buses run to and from Montparnasse, 36, rue de Mienne, 6ème (Mo. Montparnasse-Bienvenue) and the downtown Invalides Air France agency (tel. 43 23 82 20 or 43 23 97 10, every 12min., 32F, group of 3 passengers 83F, group of 4 103F). In addition the RATP runs **Orlybus** to and from metro and RER stop Denfert Rochereau. Board at Orly Sud gate H platform 4 or Orly Ouest level O door D (every 10-15min. from 6am-11pm, 25min., 21F). **Taxis** from Orly to the center cost at least 170F during the day, considerably more at night. Allow at least 45 minutes for the trip.

Le Bourget

Paris's third airport, **Le Bourget** (tel. 48 62 12 12) is notable only because Charles Lindbergh landed there after his historic transatlantic flight. Nowadays, Le Bourget is used for charter flights, generally within France. Should you land at Le Bourget, take **Bus #350** (every 15min. from 6:10am-11:50pm, 2 metro tickets) to Gare du Nord or Gare de l'Est. **Bus #152** also makes these stops, and, for the same price, will take you to Porte de la Villette, where you can catch the metro or another bus.

From the Train Stations

Each of Paris's six train stations is a veritable community of its own, with resident street people and police, cafés, restaurants, *tabacs,* and banks. Locate the ticket counters *(guichets),* the platforms *(quais),* and the tracks *(voies),* and you will be ready to roll. Each terminal has two divisions: the *banlieue* and the *grandes lignes.* **Grandes lignes** depart for and arrive from distant cities in France and other countries—each of the six stations serves destinations in a particular region of France or Europe (see below). Trains to the **banlieue** serve the suburbs of Paris and make frequent stops. Within a given station, each of these divisions has its own ticket counters, information booths, and timetables; distinguishing between the two before you get in line will save you hours of frustration. All train stations are reached by at least two metro lines, with the metro station cleverly bearing the same name as the train station. For train information, call the SNCF at 45 82 50 50; for reservations, call 45 65 60 60 or use the minitel 3615 SNCF (see Communications, below; reservations and minitel both open daily 8am-8pm). The SNCF line may seem perpetually busy—visiting a local travel agency will let you buy your tickets or make your reservations with more personal attention and little to no fee. There is a free telephone with direct access to the stations on the right-hand side of the Champs-Elysées tourist office.

A word on safety: though full of atmosphere, each terminal also shelters its share of thieves and other undesirables. Gare du Nord, for example, becomes rough at night, when drugs and prostitution take over; Gare d'Austerlitz can be similarly unfriendly by moonlight. As in all big cities, be cautious in and around stations; the unsuspecting may be invited out for a drink only to be doped up and ripped off. In each train station metro stop, you will encounter friendly-looking people who will try to sell you a metro ticket at exorbitant prices. Do not purchase anything in the stations except from uniformed personnel. Above all, do not change cash or buy anything from these con artists. Any money you hand over will never be seen again.

Gare du Nord: Trains to northern France, Britain, Belgium, the Netherlands, Scandinavia, the Commonwealth of Independent States, and northern Germany (Cologne, Hamburg). To: Brussels (10 per day, 3hr., 211F); Amsterdam (6 per day., 6hr., 339F); Cologne (6 direct, 6 indirect per day, 5-6hr., 406F); Boulogne (11 per day, 2½hr., 153F); Copenhagen (1 direct, 3 indirect per day, 16hr., 1183F); London (by train and boat, 7hr., return within 5 days 602F, within 2 months 502F).

Gare de l'Est: To eastern France (Champagne, Alsace, Lorraine), Luxembourg, parts of Switzerland (Basel, Zürich, Lucerne), southern Germany (Frankfurt, Munich), Austria, and Hungary. To: Zürich (7 per day, 6hr., 357F); Munich (4 direct, 4 indirect per day, 9hr. direct, 584F); and Vienna (3 per day, 15hr., 898F).

Gare de Lyon: To southern and southeastern France (Lyon, Provence, Riviera), parts of Switzerland (Geneva, Lausanne, Berne), Italy, and Greece. To: Geneva (5 per day, 3½hr., 287F plus 16-80F TGV reservation); Florence (4 per day, 11-12hr., 612F); Rome (3 per day, 14-16hr., 575F); Lyon (12 per day, 2hr., 250F plus 16-80F TGV reservation); Nice (8 per day, 7hr., 443F plus 16-48F TGV reservation); Marseille (10 per day, 5hr., 368F plus 16-48F TGV reservation).

Gare d'Austerlitz: Trains to the Loire Valley, southwestern France (Bordeaux, Pyrénées), Spain, and Portugal. TGV service to southwestern France leaves from Gare Montparnasse. To Barcelona (3 per day, 11-14hr., 485F) and Madrid (5 per day, 12-16hr., 578F).

Gare St-Lazare: To Normandy. To: Caen (10 per day, 2½hr., 150F).

Gare Montparnasse: To Brittany, and the TGV to southwestern France. To: Rennes (15 per day, 2-2½hr., 199F plus 32-80F TGV reservation).

From the Bus Stations

Most buses to Paris arrive at **Gare Routière Internationale,** 3, av. Porte de la Villette, 19*ème* (tel. 40 38 93 93; Mo. Porte de la Villette). Some buses, however, have more bizarre ports of call. The **City Sprint** bus (tel. 42 85 44 55), operating in conjunction with Hoverspeed from England, drops its passengers in front of the Hoverspeed offices, three blocks from Gare du Nord at 135, rue Lafayette (Mo. Gare du Nord). For information about buses to other European countries, call **International Express Eurolines Coach Station** at 40 38 93 93.

By Thumb

Women, even in a group, should never hitchhike. And anyone who values safety and sanity over penny-pinching will take a train or bus out of Paris. Hitchhikers don't wait at a *porte* (city exit); traffic is too heavy for cars to stop safely. The following information is for the desparate few only.

> **Toward the east:** Metz, Strasbourg, Munich. The Autoroute de l'est A4 is accessible from the metro to Porte de Charenton after a walk along bd. Massena. This is reportedly the worst highway on which to hitch.

> **Toward the north:** Lille, Brussels, Cologne, Hamburg, Berlin, Scandinavia. Mo. Porte de la Chapelle, next to the Autoroute du nord A1.

> **Toward the west:** Rouen, Caen, Cherbourg, Mont St-Michel, St-Malo. Hitchhikers take the metro to Porte de St-Cloud and walk up bd. Murat toward pl. de la Porte d'Auteuil, where Autoroute de Normandie A13 begins.

> **Toward the south:** A number of *autoroutes* are accessible from Mo. Porte d'Orléans. **Southeast** A6: Lyon, Marseille, Cannes, Nice, Monaco, Switzerland, Italy, Barcelona. **Southwest** A10: Orléans, Bordeaux, Madrid, Galicia, Portugal. A11 branches off A10 toward Brittany: Chartres, Le Mans, Rennes.

A sign clearly stating the destination, ornamented by the letters "S.V.P." *(s'il vous plaît)* helps ingratiate hitchhikers. Hitchers also sometimes ask customers at gas stations or truck stops if they are going their way.

Ride Sharing

For a more formal "hitch," try **Allostop-Provoya,** 84, passage Brady, 10*ème* (tel. 42 46 00 66; Mo. Strasbourg-St-Denis). They will try to match you with a driver going your way. The cost is 67F per ride and, for rides longer than 500km, 18 *centimes* per km given to the driver. (Round-trip 134F. 8 trips over 2 years 220F.) Also available from Allostop is **Eurostop International** membership, valid in 76 cities in Switzerland, Germany, Spain, France, Hungary, Italy, Netherlands, Belgium, and Canada, which entitles you to a 25% reduction on ride-sharing services. If your home country is one of the nine listed above, you must purchase your card there. At Allostop-Provoya, you can also buy train and bus tickets to points throughout Europe. They sell BIJ/Eurotrain tickets and, via a bus company, arrange special weekend tours in Europe. (Open Mon.-Fri. 9am-7:30pm, Sat. 9am-1pm and 2-6pm.)

Getting Around

> *With a loud rattle and clatter, and an inhuman*
> *abandonment of consideration... the carriage*
> *dashed through streets and swept round corners.*
> —Charles Dickens, *A Tale of Two Cities*

Orientation

Coursing languidly from east to west, the Seine River forms the heart of modern Paris. Perhaps singlehandedly the basis of the city's legendary romance, the river played midwife to Paris's birth on an island, some 2300 years ago. Today, the Ile de la Cité and neighboring Ile St-Louis remain the geographical and sentimental center of the city,

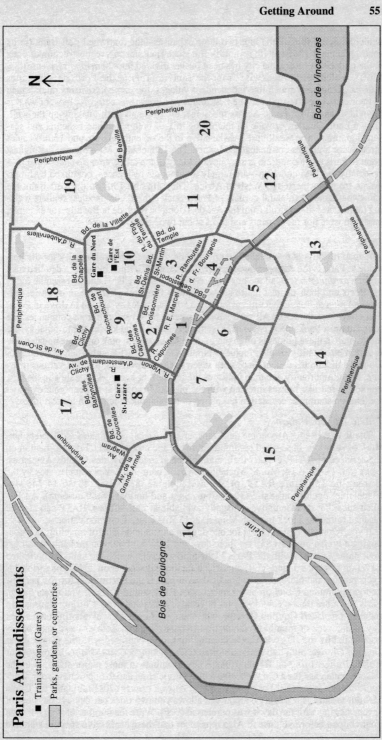

Paris Arrondissements

- ■ Train stations (Gares)
- Parks, gardens, or cemeteries

N ←

Peripherique

Bois de Vincennes

20

19

Peripherique

R. de Belville

11

12

Bd. de la Villette

R. d'Aubervilliers

Gare de
l'Est

Bd. du
Temple

13

Bd. de la Chapelle

Gare du Nord

10

R. du Fbg.
du Temple

3

R. Rambuteau

Bd. Sebastopol

Bd.
St-Martin

d. Fr. Bourgeois

4

Peripherique

18

Bd. de
Rochechouart

9

Bd.
St-Denis

Bd.
Poissonnière

2

R. E. Marcel

1

5

Peripherique

Bd. de
Clichy

Bd. des
Capucines

R.
Capucines

R. Vignon

6

Av. de St-Ouen

Av. de
Clichy

R.
d'Amsterdam

7

14

Bd. des
Batignolles

Gare
St-Lazare

8

17

Bd. de
Courcelles

Peripherique

Av.
Wagram

15

Peripherique

Av. de la
Grande Armée

16

Seine

Bois de Boulogne

Peripherique

while the Seine splits Paris into two large expanses—the renowned Left Bank (to its south) and the Right Bank (to its north). But since Haussmann's reconstruction of Paris in the mid-19th century, the city has been further divided into 20 *arrondissements* (districts), which spiral clockwise from the Louvre (1*er*) to the Porte de Vincennes (20*ème*). Originally much like independent villages, the *arrondissements* retain much of their erstwhile atmosphere. The first four *arrondissements* comprise most of what is thought of as central Paris. Across the Seine, the fifth and sixth, making up the well-known Latin Quarter, provide an interesting mix of both collegiate bohemia and seasoned glamour. The wealthiest Parisians live in the seventh, eighth, and 16th. Wander through for a glimpse of unabashed luxury. The 18th cradles Montmartre, the highest point in Paris and a one-time artists' haven. Many of the other outer *arrondissements*—especially the 19th and 20th—are largely low-income residences, populated by immigrants from Northern and Western Africa. The 14th and 15th on the Left Bank are somewhat tamer residential corners of Paris. Such citified compactness renders walking tours a breeze—a stroll from the Arc de Triomphe to pl. de la Bastille, for example, passes most major monuments and takes about two hours.

Maps

A map of Paris is essential if you plan to do any serious strolling. By far the best guide to Paris is the *Plan de Paris par Arrondissements,* which includes a detailed map of each *arrondissement,* all the bus lines, a wealth of miscellany, and an essential index of streets and their nearest metro stops. Editions Coutarel offers the most basic, red-covered *plan* at 30F. Others run as high as 150F, but unless you plan to drive in Paris, don't pay more than 50F. All such *plans,* marketed by several different companies, are found at most bookstores, *papeteries* (stationery stores), and kiosks. Unfortunately, the metro map in these guides is often out of date. Make sure to pick up a free updated one in any metro station: it also includes bus lines and the RER suburban system. McDonald's distributes decent maps with seven suggested walking tours of various quarters. Most importantly, the map indicates the location of every McDonald's in the city, marked in red like houses infected with the plague. If you're lost, keep your eyes out for a metro station; every station has a map of the neighborhood, with a street index.

Public Transportation

The **RATP** (Régie Autonome des Transports Parisiens) coordinates an efficient network of subways, buses, and commuter trains in and around Paris. For information on the services of RATP, contact their main office at 53ter, quai des Grands-Augustins, 6*ème* (tel. 43 46 14 14; Mo. St-Michel; open daily 6am-9pm). You can also stop by the **Bureau de Tourisme RATP,** pl. de la Madeleine, 8*ème* (tel. 43 46 14 14; Mo. Madeleine; open Mon.-Sat. 7:30am-7pm, Sun. and holidays 6:30am-6pm). An English-speaking representative is usually available at both offices. RATP can also be reached round the clock through Minitel: 3615 RATP (see Communications).

If you're only staying in Paris for one day but expect to do a lot of traveling, consider buying a **metro pass.** At 85F for three days and 135F for five, you probably won't get your money's worth with the **Paris Visite** tourist tickets, which are valid for unlimited travel on bus, metro, and RER, and which facilitate discounts on sightseeing trips, bicycle rentals, and more. A more practical saver-pass is the **Formule 1;** for 25F per day, you get unlimited travel on buses, metro, and RER within Paris. If you're staying in Paris for more than a few days, get a weekly *(hebdomadaire)* **Coupon Jaune** or a monthly *(mensuel)* **Coupon Orange,** which allow unlimited travel (starting on the first day of the week or month) on the metro and buses in Paris. Both of these must be accompanied by the ID-style **Carte Orange** (not to be confused with the flimsy paper *Coupon Orange,* although Parisians often refer to both as *Carte Orange*). To get your *Carte Orange,* bring an ID photo (taken by machines in most major stations) to the ticket counter, ask for a *Carte Orange* with a plastic case, and then purchase your handsome *coupon jaune* (57F) or equally swanky *coupon orange* (201F). Finally, the **Carte Hebdomadaire** is a weekly coupon that allows you two rides per day, six days out of seven, starting with the day it was purchased (37F). Write the number of your *carte* on your coupon before you use it. Also remember that these cards have specific start and end dates and may not be worthwhile if bought in the middle or at the end of the month or the week. *All prices quoted here are for passes in zones 1 and 2* (the metro and RER in Paris and the immediate suburbs). If you intend to travel to the distant 'burbs, you'll need to buy RER passes for more zones (up to 5). Ask at the ticket windows for details.

Metro

Inaugurated in 1898, the Paris Métropolitain (metro) is one of the world's oldest and most efficient subway systems, able to whisk you within walking distance of nearly any spot in the city. Stations are marked with an "M" or the "Métropolitain" in lettering designed by Art Nouveau pioneer Hector Guimard. All trains run frequently, and connections are easy. A disabled metro train is a rare sight. The first trains start running at 5am; the last leave the end-of-the-line stations (the *"portes de Paris,"* i.e., Porte d'Orléans, Porte Maillot) for the center of the city near 12:15am. One exception is the last train leaving from Porte de Balard, which does not travel the length of the line to Porte de Charenton but goes only as far as République. In the other direction, however, the train runs the whole route from Porte de Charenton to Porte de Balard. For the exact departure times of the last trains from the *portes,* check the poster in the center of each station called *"Principes de Tarification"* (Rate Guidelines).

Free metro maps are available in most stations, display maps are posted in all stations, and all have a *plan du quartier.* Connections to other lines are indicated by orange *"correspondance"* signs, and the exits by blue *"sortie"* signs. Metro lines are numbered (1 is the oldest), but referred to by their final destination. Transfers to other lines are free if made in the same station, but it is not always possible to reverse direction on the same line without exiting the station and using another ticket.

Each trip on the metro requires one ticket. Tickets can be bought individually (6F), but a *carnet* of 10 (36F50) is more practical. *Don't buy tickets from anyone except the people in the ticket booths.* **Hold onto your ticket** until you pass the point marked *Limite de Validité des Billets;* a uniformed RATP *contrôleur* (transit inspector) may request to see it on any train. If caught without one, you will be forced to pay a hefty fine. In addition, any *correspondances* to the RER require you to put your validated (and uncrumpled) ticket into a turnstile. Otherwise you may need to buy a new ticket in order to exit. Keep in mind that a standard metro ticket is valid only within Paris. There is no longer first-class metro service; any cars still marked "1" are waiting to be repainted.

Most train lines are well-traveled at night, and Parisian women often travel alone, though their familiarity lends them a confidence you may lack. Violent crime in the metro is on the increase; use common sense. Avoid empty cars. At night, many people choose to ride in the first car, where the conductor is only a door away. Stay away from the most dangerous stations (Barbès-Rochechouart, Pigalle, Châtelet, Trocadéro, and Anvers). Despite the excellent neighborhoods in which some of these stops are located, they are often frequented by thieves and other troublemakers looking to prey on the tourist or the wealthy. Be careful in the long, empty corridors of larger stations. When in doubt, take a taxi.

All metro lines are inaccessible to those in **wheelchairs.** "Gare de Lyon" and "Chatelet-Les Halles" stations have access points to the RER for people in wheelchairs. People who are blind or deaf can get a metro staff person to accompany them while in the metro by calling **Voyages Accompagnés** at 49 59 96 00 three days before they would like to ride the metro.

RER

The **RER** (Réseau Express Régional), is the RATP's local suburban train system, which passes through central Paris. Introduced in 1969, the RER runs through deeper tunnels at higher speeds. Within the city, the RER travels much faster than the metro, and for all intents can be regarded as a set of faster metro lines. The main difference is that you need your ticket to exit the station. Within the city, tickets cost the same as the metro; to go to the suburbs you'll need to buy a special ticket valid for the entire journey (10-40F depending on destination). If you plan to make repeated trips to the suburbs, a *carnet* of 10 will again prove cheaper.

Bus

Because the metro is so efficient and convenient, the Paris bus system is ignored by many visitors and locals alike. Buses, however, offer the distinct advantage of traveling above ground, thereby providing prime sightseeing and a greater familiarity with the city for the cost of one ride. The free bus map *Autobus Paris-Plan du Réseau* is available at the tourist office and some metro information booths. The routes of each line are also posted at each stop. The buses no longer take the same tickets as the metro; you must buy special tickets that cost exactly the same as metro tickets and are available in metro stations, *tabacs,* and from the bus drivers themselves. Most trips within the city and nearest suburbs cost 1 ticket; if your journey takes you out of the city you might need more than 1 ticket—ask the driver. Enter the bus through the front door and punch your ticket by pushing it into the cancelling machine by the driver's seat. If you have a *coupon orange,* flash it at the driver, but **do not** insert the ticket into the machine. As on the metro, *contrôleurs* may ask to see your ticket; hold onto it until the end of the ride. For more information, call the RATP office (tel. 43 46 14 14).

Most buses run from about 7am to 8:30pm, although some (marked *Autobus du Soir)* continue until 12:30am, and others *(Noctambus)* run all night. Night buses (3 tickets, 4 if you use 2 buses) start their runs to the *portes* of the city from the Châtelet stop and leave every hour on the half hour from 1:30 to 5:30am. Buses with three-digit numbers come from or are bound for the suburbs, while buses with two-digit numbers travel exclusively within Paris. Buses with numbers in the 20s come from or are bound for Gare St-Lazare, in the 30s Gare de l'Est, in the 40s Gare du Nord, in the 70s Châtelet/Hôtel de Ville (with exceptions), in the 80s Luxembourg (with exceptions), and in the 90s Gare Montparnasse.

For more detailed diagrams of all bus routes, consult the *Plan de Paris par Arrondissements* (see Maps, above). The pamphlet printed by the RATP, *Paris Bus Métro RER,* lists several bus routes that pass through interesting neighborhoods and by the main sights of Paris (available at metro stops). It also lists directions to major museums, churches, and monuments. Some routes pass by enough sights to make them mini-tours in themselves. Buses worth riding from start to finish include:

Bus #20: From Gare St-Lazare to the Opéra, Montmartre-Poissonière, République, Bastille (50min.). A trip down the *grands boulevards.* Open platform in back.

Bus #21: From Gare St-Lazare to the Opéra, Palais Royal, the Louvre, the Pont Neuf, St-Michel, Gare du Luxembourg, Porte de Gentilly (40min.).

Bus #52: From Opéra to Concorde, Charles-de-Gaulle-Etoile, Auteuil, Pont de St-Cloud (50min.).

Bus #67: From Pigalle to Carrefour de Châteaudun, Louvre, Châtelet, Hôtel-de-Ville, Jussieu, pl. d'Italie, Porte de Gentilly (45min.).

Bus #82: From Gare du Luxembourg to Gare Montparnasse, Ecole-Militaire, Champs-de-Mars, Tour Eiffel, Porte Maillot, Neuilly (45min.).

Bus #83: From pl. d'Italie, along bd. Raspail, Gare des Invalides, pl. des Ternes (50min.). A glimpse of some of Paris's finest real estate and great views of the *quais.* Open platform in back.

Bus #95: From Tour Montparnasse past St-Germain-des-Prés, the Louvre, Palais Royal, the Opéra, and to Montmartre, near Sacré-Coeur (50min.).

Bus #96: From Montparnasse past St-Michel, the Palais de Justice on the Ile de la Cité, Châtelet, Hôtel-de-Ville, Oberkampf, Ménilmontant, Porte des Lilas (50min.).

Taxi

Taxi trips within Paris represent the height of decadence for the budget travel. Rates vary according to time of day and geographical area, but they're never cheap. Tarif A, the basic rate, is in effect in Paris proper from 7am to 7pm (2F62 per km). Tarif B is in effect Mon.-Sat. 7pm to 7am, all day Sunday, and during the day from the airports (4F08 per km). Tarif C, the highest, is in effect from the airports from 7pm to 7am (5F48 per km). In addition, there is a base fee *(prix en charge)* of 11F, and stationary time (such as at traffic lights and traffic jams) costs 108F per hour. All taxis have lights on top indicating the rate being charged, so you can check to see that the driver is playing it straight. Make sure the meter is on when you start the ride. A 15% tip is customary (round up to the nearest 5F). If you must take a taxi, try picking one up at a train station or waiting at a stand *(arrêt taxis, tête de station),* usually found near bus stops. Calling a radio-cab (**ARTAXI,** tel. 42 41 50 50, **Taxis Radio Etoile** tel. 42 70 41 41, or **Taxis G7** tel. 47 39 47 39) is far more expensive, since you must pay for the distance the cab drives to pick you up. Technically, taxis cannot refuse to take a fare if their roof light is on, but can refuse to take more than three people. Illegal overcrowding of cabs can bring heavy fines upon the driver. If you have a **complaint,** write to Service des Taxis de la Préfecture de Police, 36, rue des Morillons, 75015 (tel. 45 31 14 80). If you expect to file a complaint, ask the driver for a receipt.

Bicycle

Although Nazi gas rationing turned Paris into a town of cyclists for four years, with ill-tempered drivers overrunning narrow, congested streets, the center of Paris is no longer the place for a leisurely afternoon pedal. A few intrepid souls, tourists and locals, still venture out into the city *en vélo.* The parks, especially the Bois de Boulogne and the Bois de Vincennes, are well-suited to two-wheeled exploration (see Sports). The metro cannot accommodate bikes, but local trains list specific times when they allow bicycles on board for free.

> **Mountain Bike Tours,** 6, pl. Etienne Pernet, 15*ème* (tel. 48 42 57 87). Mo. Félix Faure. Runs popular English-language bike tours through Paris. Die-hard mountain bike fans have discovered the only way to really *do* Paris in a day—six-hour guided bicycle tours in English to the Eiffel Tower, the Louvre, the Latin Quarter and Montparnasse. You may want to carefully observe Parisian drivers before signing up. Groups limited to 12 people. Helmet and insurance included. March-Oct. daily 11am-5pm. 118F. They also rent mountain bikes for 90F per day.

> **Bicyclub-Roue Libre,** 8, pl. de la Porte-Champerret, 17*ème* (tel. 47 66 55 92; fax 43 80 35 68). Mo. Porte de Champerret. 6 locations, including the Bois de Boulogne (Pré Catalan), the Bois de Vincennes, the Canal de l'Ourcq, and the Forêt de Rambouillet. 3-speed bikes from 25F per hr., 100F per day. 1000F deposit includes insurance that covers you but not the bike. Locks, maps, and baby seats available; bring your own baby. Open daily 9am-7pm; Oct.-June Mon.-Fri. 9am-7pm, Sat. 9am-1pm and 2-7pm.

> **Paris-Vélo,** 2, rue de Fer-à-Moulin, 5*ème* (tel. 43 37 59 22). Mo. Censier Daubenton. Bikes 90-140F per day (depending on the model) or 1000-2000F per week, with a 1000F deposit (including accident insurance). Try to book in advance and ask for any accessories you'll need. Open Mon.-Sat. 10am-12:30pm and 2-7pm.

Mopeds and motorcycles are no longer leased in the city, but you can rent a scooter from **Mondial Scooter,** 20bis, av. Charles de Gaulle (tel. 46 24 63 64; Mo. Porte Maillot) in Neuilly-sur-Seine from 145F per day or 800F per week, with a 2500F deposit.

Car

"Somewhere you have heard a dark apocryphal statistic—that one driver out of every twelve in Paris has killed his man. On foot, the Parisian is as courteous as the citizen of any other city. But mounted, he is merciless." So wrote Irwin Shaw, and he actually liked Parisians. Parisian drivers are notorious for their *"système D"*—D for *débrouiller* (doing whatever works), which includes driving on the sidewalk in traffic jams, ignoring any lane markings that might exist, and passing in small streets at high speeds. The infamous rotary at the Arc de Triomphe has trapped many an unwary tourist with its relentless centripetal force; at rush hour, cars move in any direction they want here, much like a pack of blind sheep. Drivers will even cut in front of ambulances, proving once and for all that Paris is still a barbaric city. *Priorité à droite* gives the right of way to the car approaching from the right, regardless of the size of the streets, and Parisian drivers make it an affair of honor to take this right even in the face of grave danger. Drivers are not allowed to honk their horns within city limits unless they are about to hit a pedestrian, but you will see how often this rule is broken. The legal way to show discontent is to flash the headlights, for which you should be on the lookout in case a law-abiding driver refrains from honking until just before impact. If you do not have a map of Paris marked with one-way streets, the city will be almost impossible to navigate. Street parking is hard to locate (although Parisians do park on side-walks, corners, etc.) and garages are expensive.

Possibly the best excuse for renting a car in Paris is to escape from the city into the provinces. Renting a car for a group of three or four may be even cheaper than buying train tickets. Foreigners need a passport, a license of at least two years, and a credit card to rent in Paris; an international license is not required. None of the agencies in Paris will rent to drivers under 21. The best deal in town is at **ACAR,** 77, rue de Lagny, 20*ème* (tel. 43 79 54 54; Mo. Porte de Vincennes). A two-door SEAT Mirabella costs 218F per day, first 100km free plus 1F15 per additional km; insurance costs 35F. A weekend with 1000km and insurance included is 710F. A week with unlimited mileage and insurance included is 1820F. (Open Mon.-Fri. 8am-12:30pm and 2-7pm, Sat. 8am-12:30pm and 2-6pm.) **Inter Touring Service,** 117, bd. Auguste Blanqui, 13*ème* (tel. 45 88 52 37; Mo. Glacière), rents Renault 4s for 145F per day plus 1F50 per km, insurance included, or 1820F per week, distance and insurance included. (Open Mon.-Sat. 8:30am-6:30pm.) **Autorent,** 98, rue de la Convention, 15*ème* (tel. 45 54 22 45; Mo. Boucicaut), and 3-5, av. Jean Moulin, 14*ème* (tel. 49 92 55 06; Mo. Alésia), rents Fiat Pandas for 199F per day plus 2F40 per km.

Practical Information

Tourist Offices

Though packed in the summer, the following offices are usually able to keep the wait down to an hour at most. Lines are worse in the afternoon. They all stock the requisite reams of brochures, maps, and pamphlets, as well as information on special seasonal events. Tourist offices will help you find a room in a one-star hotel for 15F, two-star for 20F, three-star for 35F, and hostels for 5F. They will also help you reserve rooms in other parts of the country, though no more than seven days in advance, for a 23F minimum charge. All the offices exchange money at decent rates with no commission; they are a sensible option when banks are closed.

Bureau d'Accueil Central: 127, av. des Champs-Elysées, 8*ème* (tel. 47 23 61 72). Mo. Charles-de-Gaulle-Etoile. Helpful English-speaking staff. Mobbed in summer but remarkably efficient. Open daily 9am-8pm. There are 5 smaller *Bureaux d'Accueil,* also operated by the *office de tourisme,* located in the following train stations and at the Eiffel Tower: **Bureau Gare du Nord,** 10*ème* (tel. 45 26 94 82). Mo. Gare du Nord. Open Mon.-Sat. 8am-10pm, Sun. 1-8pm; Nov.-Easter daily 8am-8pm. **Bureau Gare de L'Est,** 10*ème* (tel. 46 07 17 73). Mo. Gare de l'Est. Open Mon.-Sat. 8am-10pm; Nov.-April Mon.-Sat. 8am-1pm and 5-8pm. **Bureau Gare de Lyon,** 12*ème* (tel. 43 43 33 24). Mo. Gare de Lyon. Open Mon.-Sat. 8am-10pm; Nov.-April Mon.-Sat. 8am-1pm and 5-8pm. **Bureau Gare d'Austerlitz,** 13*ème* (tel. 45 84 91 70). Mo. Gare d'Austerlitz. Open Mon.-Sat. 8am-10pm; Nov.-April Mon.-Sat. 8am-3pm. **Bureau Tour Eiffel,** Champs de Mars, 7*ème* (tel. 45 51 22 15). Mo. Champs de Mars. Open May-Sept. daily 11am-6pm.

In addition, both international airports run tourist offices where you can make same-day hotel reservations (with deposit equal to 12% of room rate) and receive information about Paris.

Orly, Sud: Near gate H. **Orly, Ouest:** Near gate F (tel. 48 84 32 63). Both open daily 6am-11:45pm.

Roissy-Charles de Gaulle: Near gate 36 arrival level (tel. 48 62 22 81). Open daily 7am-11:30pm.

Also try the following:

Maison de la France: 8, av. de l'Opéra, 1*er* (tel. 42 96 10 23). Mo. Palais-Royal. A friendly and well-staffed agency that provides tourist information on all of France. If you're planning to tour the rest of the country, come here to get maps and sightseeing brochures; this information will save you countless trips to tourist offices in other cities. Prices for hotels and campgrounds but no reservations. Also free tourist literature and information by mail. Open Mon.-Fri. 9am-7pm.

Tourist Information: tel. 47 20 88 98. A recorded message in English gives the major events in Paris. Updated weekly. Call 47 20 94 94 for French and 47 20 57 88 for German.

Budget Travel

Accueil des Jeunes en France (AJF): 119, rue St-Martin, *4ème,* across from the pedestrian mall in front of the Pompidou Center (tel. 42 77 87 80). Mo. Rambuteau. Open Mon.-Sat. 9am-6pm. Also 16, rue du Pont Louis-Philippe, *4ème,* near the Hôtel de Ville (tel. 42 78 04 82). Mo. Hôtel-de-Ville or Pont-Marie. Open Mon.-Fri. 9:30am-6:30pm. Also 139, bd. St-Michel, *5ème,* in the Latin Quarter (tel. 43 54 95 86). Mo. Port-Royal. Open March-Oct. Mon.-Fri. 9am-6pm. Another in Gare du Nord arrival hall next to Agence de Voyages SNCF (tel. 42 85 86 19). Open June-Sept. daily 8am-10pm; Oct. and March-May Mon.-Fri. 9:30am-6:30pm. The Gare du Nord office only books accommodations. The other offices will give you free maps, sell ISIC cards (45F), and make room reservations in *foyers* in Paris, London, or Spain (72-85F per night). Reduced-price student train and bus tickets, budget weekend holidays in Europe, and meal vouchers for Paris youth hostels. The office across from the Pompidou Center can be used as a mailing address but is so ridiculously crowded that it pays to try one of the other branches—all friendly, centrally located, English-speaking, and, well, crowded.

Office de Tourisme Universitaire (OTU): 39, av. G. Bernanos, *5ème* (tel. 43 36 80 27). Mo. Port-Royal. A French student travel agency. Crowded and English-speaking. The same reduced train and plane tickets for students under 26 that are sold at any travel agent in Paris, but more crowded. Bring an official form of ID. Also sells ISIC (45F), HI card (70F), Carte Jeune (70F), and BIJ tickets. Open Mon. 11am-6:45pm, Tues.-Fri. 10am-6:45pm. **CROUS** next door (tel. 40 51 36 00) has information on student housing, employment, university restaurants, transubstantiation, and health care.

Council Travel: 51, rue Dauphine, *6ème* (tel. 43 26 79 65). Mo. Odéon. Also at 16, rue de Vaugirard (tel. 46 34 02 90; Mo. Odéon) and at 31, rue St-Augustin, *2ème* (tel. 42 66 20 87; Mo. Opéra). English-speaking travel service for young people. Books international flights. Sells student train tickets, guidebooks, and ISIC cards (45F). BIJ/Eurotrain tickets. If you have lost your CIEE charter flight ticket, go to the Opéra office and they will telex the U.S. to authorize a substitute, for which you will pay a penalty depending on your flight. All open Mon.-Fri. 11am-1pm and 2-6:45pm, Sat. 11am-1pm and 2:30-5pm.

Council on International Educational Exchange (CIEE) and Centre Franco-Américain Odéon: 1, pl. de l'Odéon, *6ème* (tel. 46 34 16 10). Mo. Odéon. CIEE's Paris office. See Travel Services under Useful Organizations in the General Introduction for information on CIEE'S services. Open Mon. and Thurs.- Fri. 2-6pm, Tues. 9:30am-12:30pm.

Embassies and Consulates

If anything serious goes wrong—arrest, theft, death of a companion, etc.—make your first inquiry to your country's consulate in Paris. The distinction between an embassy and a consulate is significant: an embassy houses the offices of the ambassador and his or her staff; you won't gain access unless you know someone inside. All facilities for dealing with nationals are in the consulate, and when you call the numbers listed below for information, you should ask to be connected with the consulate. If your passport gets lost or stolen, your status in France is immediately rendered illegal—go to the consulate *as soon as possible* to get a replacement. A consulate is also able to lend (not give) up to 100F per day (interest free), but you will be forced to prove you are truly desperate with no other source of money. The consulate can give you lists of local lawyers and doctors, notify family members of accidents, and give information on how to proceed with legal problems, but its functions end there. Don't ask the consulate to pay for your hotel or medical bills, investigate crimes, obtain work permits, post bail, recite poetry, or interfere with standard French legal proceedings.

U.S.: 2, av. Gabriel, *8ème,* off pl. de la Concorde (tel. 42 96 12 02 or 42 61 80 75). Mo. Concorde, off pl. de la Concorde. **Consulate** at 2, rue St-Florentin (tel. 42 96 12 02, ext. 2613), 3 blocks away. Passports replaced for US$42 (under 18 US$27), or the equivalent in francs. Open Mon.-Fri. 9am-4pm. Closed for both American and French holidays.

Canada: 35, av. Montaigne, *8ème* (tel. 47 23 01 01). Mo. Franklin-Roosevelt or Alma-Marceau. **Consulate** at 16, rue d'Anjou (same phone), around the corner from the embassy. New passport CDN$25, or the equivalent in francs. Open Mon.-Fri. 9-11:30am and 2-4pm.

U.K.: 35, rue du Faubourg-St-Honoré, *8ème* (tel. 42 66 91 42). Mo. Concorde or Madeleine. New passport 158F (must be paid in francs). **Consulate** at 16, rue d'Anjou, around the corner. Visa bureau open Mon.-Fri. 9am-noon.

Australia: Embassy at 4, rue Jean-Rey, 15*ème* (tel. 40 59 33 00). Mo. Bir-Hakeim. New passport 400F. Open Mon.-Thurs. (Fri. in an emergency) 9:15am-noon and 2-5pm.

New Zealand: Embassy at 7ter, rue Léonard-de-Vinci, 16*ème* (tel. 45 00 24 11). Mo. Victor-Hugo. New passport 400F (must be paid in francs). Open Mon.-Fri. 9am-1pm and 2:30-6pm.

Ireland: 12, av. Foch, 16*ème* (tel. 45 00 20 87). Mo. Dauphine. Not a consulate, but in an emergency call this number for instructions.

Money

Currency and Exchange

The basic unit of currency in France is the franc, divided into 100 centimes, and issued in both coins and paper notes. The smallest unit of French currency is the five-centime piece. The new franc, equal to 100 old francs, was issued in 1960.

When looking to change money in Paris, try to approach the event with the spirit of competition. Not every change bureau offers the same rates and most do not charge commission. Don't be fooled by what seem like fantastic rates. Make sure that no strings (like having to sell your soul or exchange at least 15,000F worth of currency) apply. The best rates in town are found around the Opéra on rue de Scribe (close to American Express), rue Auber, and rue de la Paix. The American Express office and currency exchanges on the Champs-Elysées are almost always crowded, especially on summer afternoons. Many post offices will change cash and American Express traveler's checks at competitive rates and without commission; bureaus at train stations and airports tend to offer less favorable rates. Most banks are open 9am-noon and 2-4:30pm, but not all exchange currency. Check before you get in line. Before leaving home, convert US$50 or so into French bills; this will save you time at the airport.

American Express: 11, rue Scribe, 9*ème* (tel. 47 77 77 07). Mo. Opéra or Auber. Across from the back of the Opéra. No commission on AmEx traveler's checks, 5F20 commission on all other transactions. Mediocre exchange rates. Cardholders can cash a personal check from a US bank account; bring your passport. Mobbed during the summer, especially Mon. and Fri.-Sat. They will hold mail for you free if you have their card or traveler's checks; otherwise 5F per inquiry. Open Mon.-Sat. 9am-5pm.

Change Automatique, 66, av. des Champs-Elysées, 8*ème*. Mo. George V. An automatic machine that accepts 5, 10, or 20 dollar bills and 50 or 100 German mark, 50 or 100 Swiss franc, and 50,000 or 100,000 Italian lire notes. Rates and commission posted above "insert bill" slot. Not the best rates in town. Open 24 hrs.

At Train Stations: Remember these offices offer less than attractive rates intended for impatient travelers. **Gare d'Austerlitz,** 13*ème* (tel. 45 84 91 40). Open daily 7am-9pm. **Gare de Lyon,** 12*ème* (tel. 43 41 52 70). Open daily 7am-11pm. **Gare de l'Est,** 10*ème* (tel. 46 07 66 84). Open Mon.-Fri. 9am-6:30pm, Sat. 9:30am-5:30pm. **Gare du Nord,** 10*ème* (tel. 42 80 11 50). Open daily 6:15am-11:30pm. **Gare St-Lazare,** 8*ème* (tel. 43 87 72 51). Open daily 7am-9pm.

At Airports: Also not the best place to change your currency. Exchange just enough to get to Paris and change the rest within the city. **Orly-Sud:** open daily 6am-11:30pm. **Roissy-Charles de Gaulle:** open daily 6am-11:30pm.

Traveler's Checks

Carrying around large amounts of cash, even in a moneybelt, is risky. Traveler's checks are the safest and least troublesome means of carrying funds. Several agencies and many banks sell them, usually for face value plus a 1% commission. American Express and Visa are the most widely recognized, though other major checks are sold, exchanged, cashed, and refunded with almost equal ease. Each agency provides refunds if your checks are lost or stolen, and many provide additional services. (Note that you may need a police report verifying the loss or theft.) Inquire about toll-free refund hotlines, emergency message relay services, and stolen credit card assistance when you purchase your checks.

Expect a fair amount of red tape and delay in the event of theft or loss of traveler's checks. To expedite the refund process, keep your check receipts separate from your checks and store them in a safe place, or with a traveling companion. To help identify which checks are missing, record check numbers when you cash them and leave a list

Don't forget to write.

Now that you've said, "Let's go," it's time to say, "Let's get American Express® Travelers Cheques." Because when you want your travel money to go a long way, it's a good idea to protect it. So before you leave, be sure and write.

of check numbers with someone at home. When you buy your checks, ask for a list of refund centers. American Express and Bank of America have over 40,000 centers worldwide. Keep a separate supply of cash or traveler's checks for emergencies.

Finally, consider purchasing traveler's checks in francs. Most companies offer their checks in several currencies. While U.S. citizens can easily exchange dollars for francs in France, New Zealanders and Australians may have difficulty exchanging their currencies. Dealing with double exchange rates (such as Canadian to U.S. dollars and then U.S. dollars to francs) can be expensive. In smaller French cities and towns, as in stores and restaurants, it is often easier to exchange checks in francs. In addition, you avoid the hassle of worrying about exchange rates. Most banks will cash French franc traveler's checks commission free (be sure to ask, however, *before* you give them your money). Depending on fluctuations in the value of the French franc, you may either gain or lose money by buying them in francs in advance.

American Express (tel. in the U.S. and Canada (800) 221-7282, in the U.K. (088) 52 13 13, collect to the U.S. from anywhere else in the world (801) 964-6665; in France, call toll-free (19) 05 90 86 00). Available in 7 currencies, commission-free for members of AAA. 1% commission. **Check for Two,** a pricey new option, allows for double signing with a travel partner. American Express has 22 offices in France, each of which will cash their checks commission-free, as well as providing a mail-holding service (see Communications) and assistance with lost travel documents, temporary IDs, and airline, hotel, and car rental reservations. Call and ask for their cute booklet, *Traveler's Companion,* which gives full addresses for all their travel offices, as well as stolen check hotlines for each European country. AmEx maintains a Global Assist hotline for travel emergencies (tel. (800) 554-2639 or collect (202) 783-7474).

Lost American Express Traveler's Checks: tel. (19) 05 90 86 00.

Bank of America (tel. in the U.S. (800) 227-3460, collect from elsewhere (415) 624-5400). Checks in US$ only. 1% commission. Checkholders get access to a Travel Assistance hotline (tel. in the U.S. (800) 368-7878, collect from elsewhere (202) 347-7113). Hotline offers services including free legal and medical assistance, urgent message relay, lost document services, translator/interpreter referral, and up to US$1000 advance to a medical facility to ensure prompt treatment (tel. (01) 629 7466).

Visa (tel. in the U.S. and Canada (800) 227-6811, in the U.K. (0800) 89 50 78 toll-free; collect to the U.S. from anywhere else in the world (415) 574-7111). Checks available in 13 currencies. Commission depends on individual bank.

Barclays Bank (tel. in the U.S. and Canada (800) 221-2426; in the U.K. (202) 67 12 12; from elsewhere call collect (212) 858-8500). 1% commission. Checks in U.S. and Canadian dollars, British pounds, and German marks.

Citicorp (tel. in the U.S. and Canada (800) 645-6556, collect from elsewhere (813) 623-1709). Checks available in U.S. dollars, British pounds, German marks, and Japanese yen at banks throughout the U.S. 1-2.5% commission. Checkholders are automatically enrolled for 45 days in Travel Assist Hotline (tel. (800) 523-1199), a slightly abridged version of Europe Assistance Worldwide's Travel Assist program.

MasterCard International (tel. in the U.S. (800) 223-7373, collect from anywhere else in the world (212) 974-5696). Traveler's checks available in 11 currencies at many banks and from **Thomas Cook** (tel. same as Mastercard). 1% commission.

Credit Cards

Credit cards in Europe do everything they do in America—and more. For one, major credit cards—**American Express, Mastercard,** and **Visa** are the most welcomed—instantly extract cash advances from banks and teller machines throughout Western Europe, in local currency (albeit with hefty interest charges). Nearly 800 banks in France, indicated by the sticker *CB/VISA ou EC,* will allow you to withdraw money at a teller with a Visa or AmEx card. Additionally, Visa cash machines proliferate in France. American Express cards work in ATMs at **Credit Lyonnaise** banks, as well as at AmEx offices and major airports. All such machines require a **Personal Idenitification Number (PIN),** which credit cards in the United States do not carry; ask American Express, Mastercard, or Visa to assign you one before you leave home. Keep in mind that Mastercard and Visa have aliases here (Eurocard and Carte Bleue, respectively); some cashiers may not know this until they check their manual.

Credit cards are also invaluable in an emergency—an unexpected hospital bill or ticket home or the more prosaic loss of traveler's checks—which may leave you temporarily without other resources. Try to pay for large purchases abroad by credit card: the credit card company gets a better exchange rate than you would have. Furthermore, credit cards offer an array of other services, from insurance to emergency assistance— these depend completely, however, on the issuer. Some even cover car rental collision insurance. If a family member has a credit card, an additional card can be effortlessly issued in your name, with bills (and an increased annual fee) going to your loved ones.

In addition, **American Express** cardholders can cash up to US$1000 in personal checks (US$5000 for gold card holders) at any of the AmEx offices in France. With someone feeding money into your account back home, this can be one of the easiest and cheapest ways to send money overseas. Call **American Express Travel Service** (tel. (800) 221-7282) for more information, as well as their *Traveler's Companion* booklet which lists full-service offices worldwide.

Lost American Express Cards: tel. 47 77 72 00.

Lost Visa Cards: tel. 42 77 11 90.

Cash Cards

Cash cards—popularly called ATM cards—are widespread within Europe, and in the last year huge advances have been made in the extension of the **Cirrus** network to Europe. The PLUS network has unfortunately not yet followed suit. In Paris, **Crédit Mutuel's Minibanque/24** teller machines are on the CIRRUS network, and are located at the following addresses:

1er: 10, rue de la Vrillière (Mo. Bourse); **4ème:** 8, rue St-Antoine (Mo. Bastille); **8ème:** 24, bd. des Malesherbes (Mo. Madeleine); **9ème:** 35bis, rue de Provence (Mo. Chaussée d'Antin); **10ème:** 94-96, bd. de Magenta (Mo. Gare du Nord); **11ème:** 19, Cité Voltaire (Mo. Boulets Montreuil); **12ème,** 82, bd. Soult (Mo. Porte de Vincennes); **13ème:** 53, av. des Gobelins (Mo. Place d'Italie); **15ème:** 2, rue de l'Arrivée (Mo. Montparnasse); **16ème:** 28, rued'Auteuil (Mo. Michel-Ange Auteuil); **17ème:** 30, av. Niel (Mo. Péreire); **18ème:** 13, rue des Abbesses (Mo. Abbesses); **19ème:** 7, place des Fêtes (Mo. Place des Fêtes); **20ème:** 167-171, av. Gambetta (Mo. St-Fargeau or Porte des Lilas).

Sending Money Abroad

The easiest way to get money from home is to use the American Express personal check service described above. Otherwise, money can be wired abroad through international money transfer services operated by **Western Union** or **American Express.**

American Express offers a MoneyGram service by which US$100-10,000 may be sent abroad. MoneyGrams sent from the US to France arrive in 10 minutes at the designated AmEx office. It costs US$45 to send US$500 and US$70 to send US$1000. The money is disbursed in traveler's checks (in American funds). For more information, call the American Express MoneyGram Customer Service toll-free number: (800) 543-4080. This service operates only between American Express offices proper, not their representatives, and is available for non-card holders. Not every office in France can receive MoneyGrams; check carefully.

Western Union offers a convenient service for cabling money abroad to any of 15 cities in France. In the U.S., call Western Union any time at (800) 325-6000 to cable money with your **Visa** or **MasterCard.** No money orders are accepted. It costs US$65 to send US$500 and $75 for $1000. The cabled money is handled by Citibank in France and can be retrieved with proper identification. It should arrive, in francs, within 2-5 business days. A new direct money service is available to send money to any of three offices in Paris within 15 minutes (US$40 to send US$500, US$50 for US$1000).

If you're staying in France long enough to have a personal bank account, a cheaper alternative may be to **cable money** from bank to bank. Tell your home bank by mail or telegram the amount you need and the name and address of the receiving bank, together with the destination account number. Give the same information to a friend or family member who is sending you money from their own account. Transfer can take up to a few days; the fee is usually a flat US$20-30. Outside an American Express office, avoid trying to cash checks in foreign currencies; they usually take weeks and a US$30 fee to clear.

In emergencies, U.S. citizens can have money sent via the State Department's **Citizens Emergency Center,** Department of State, 2201 C St. NW, Washington, DC 20520 (tel. (202) 647-5225; at night and on Sun. and holidays (202) 647-4000). For a fee of about US$25, the State Department will forward money within hours to the nearest consular office, which will then disburse it according to instructions. The center serves only Americans in the direst of straits abroad and prefers not to send sums greater than US$500. The quickest way to have the money sent is to cable the State Department through Western Union or to leave cash, a certified check, a bank draft, or a money order at the department itself.

Opening a Bank Account

If you are planning a long-term stay in Paris and have fairly liquid assets, consider opening a bank account. Foreigners can open non-resident bank accounts, but banks expect that these will be long-term (several years) and usually require a hefty opening deposit (50,000F), and that a high minimum balance (30,000F) be maintained. In any case, go to the main bank offices near the Opéra to inquire about such accounts—small neighborhood branches without a foreign affairs department are not equipped to provide such services.

Value-Added Tax

Value-Added Tax (in France, abbreviated TVA) is a varying sales tax levied especially in the European Economic Community. The French rate is 18.6% on all goods except books, food, and medicine. There is a 33% luxury tax on such items as video cassettes, watches, jewelry, and cameras.

If you spend more than 2000F (4200F for EC members) in a particular store, you can participate in a complex over-the-counter export program for foreign shoppers that exempts you from paying TVA. Ask the store for an official *formulaire de détaxe pour l'exportation* (detax invoice) and a stamped envelope. At the border, show the invoices and your purchases to the French customs officials, who will stamp the invoices. (Make sure you leave all the articles you have purchased near the top of your suitcase.) If you're at an airport, look for the window labeled *douane de détaxe,* and be sure to budget at least an hour for the intricacies of the French bureacracy. On a train, find an official (they won't find you) or get off at a station close to the border. Then send a copy back to the vendor. With this official TVA-exempt proof, they will refund the agreed amount. The refunds are sent to your bank account and not to your address, a process which may take as much as six months.) Upon returning to your country, you may have to pay customs charges if your purchases amount to more than the allotted amount (US$400), but this often falls short of the VAT refund.

Language

> *Il n'y a bon bec qu'à Paris (There is no good speech except in Paris)*
>
> —*François Villon, 1461*

Aside from a few former French colonies, it is hard to think of any nation more obsessed with language than France. And, in a nation obsessed with language, Paris is the official high-priest—the Moscow of Russian, the American Midwest and BBC of English. The northern *langue d'oïl,* based in Ile de France, was imposed on all of the barbaric provinces, evolving into modern French. Like the city itself, the language of Paris was instrumental in forging the political unity of the nation and in creating its image of a monolithic national culture. Yet Paris is also a city for tourists, highly adapted to the needs of the multi-lingual crowds it receives each year. You will find a wide variety of English-language signs, tours, and brochures, and should have no trouble finding your way around and making yourself understood. Try using French; you will be received more kindly if you at least make the effort. Don't be discouraged, however, if the reply to your question is given in English. Parisians are experts at picking out and identifying foreigners at a distance, and a large percentage have a slight knowledge of English. Most major sites offer guided tours in English; or at least printed English translations. In general, be polite; a simple *"bonjour, monsieur/madame,"* (hello, Mr.,Mrs.), *"s'il vous plaît"* (please) and *"merçi"* (thank you) will get you far. As for food, just check our six-page menu reader in the appendix, and all your culinary worries will be solved.

Communications

Mail

Post offices are marked on most maps of Paris by their abstract flying-letter insignia; if you don't have a map, look for the yellow and blue PTT signs. Streets with post offices are usually marked by a cheerful sign at the corner. Attendants at hotels, restaurants, and *tabacs* can point you to the nearest one. In general, post offices in Paris are open weekdays until 7pm (they stop changing money at 6pm) and on Saturday mornings. Avoid long lines by purchasing stamps at local *tabacs* or from the yellow coin-operated vending machines outside major post offices. Better yet, bring all your mail to the post office in one fell swoop, go to the window marked *"lettres et paquets,"* and have them deal with stamping and sending it.

Air mail between Paris and North America takes five to 10 days and is fairly dependable. Send mail from the largest post office in the area. Surface *(par eau* or *par terre)* mail is considerably cheaper, but takes one to three months to arrive. It's adequate for getting rid of books or clothing you no longer need; a special book rate makes this option more economical. If you send a parcel air mail *(par avion* or *poste aérienne),* you must complete a green customs form for any package over 1kg (2kg for letter-post rate). Airmailing a 25g (about 1 oz.) letter from France to the U.S. or Canada costs about 4F. Postcards *(cartes postales)* are slightly less. Special delivery is called *avec recommandation,* and express mail *exprès postaux.*

If you're writing from home to France and expect a reply (i.e., when making hotel reservations), enclose an International Reply Coupon (available at post offices for US$1) for a response by surface mail; send two for airmail.

If you do not have a specific address is Paris, you can receive mail through the **Poste Restante** system, handled by the 24-hour post office at 52, rue du Louvre, 1er (tel. 40 28 20 00 for urgent telegrams and calls; 42 80 67 89 for postal information; Mo. Châtelet-les-Halles). To ensure the safe arrival of your letter, address it: LAST NAME (in capitals), first name; Poste Restante; R. P. *(Recette Principale);* 52, rue de Louvre, 75001 Paris, FRANCE. You will have to show your passport as identification and pay about 3F for every letter received.

American Express also receives and holds mail for up to 30 days, after which they return it to the sender. If you want to have it held longer, just write "Hold for x days" on the envelope. The envelope should be addressed with your name in capital letters, and "Client's Mail" should be written below your name. Most big-city American Express offices provide this service free of charge if you have their traveler's checks, but some require that you be an AmEx cardholder. The free booklet *Traveler's Companion* contains the addresses of American Express offices worldwide, and can be obtained from any American Express office or by calling customer service at (800) 221-7282 (allow 6-8 weeks for delivery).

Telephones

Almost all French pay phones accept only **télécartes;** in outlying districts and cafés and bars, some phones are still coin-operated. You may purchase the card in two denominations: 40F for 50 *unités,* and 96F for 120 *unités,* each worth anywhere from six to 18 minutes of conversation, depending on the rate schedule. Local calls cost 1 *unité* each. The *télécarte* is available at post offices and most metro stations and *tabacs.* The best places to call from are **phone booths** and **post offices**. If you phone from a café, hotel, or restaurant, you risk paying up to 30% more.

You can make **intercontinental calls** from any phone booth or post office. The postal clerk will assign you to a phone from which you can usually dial direct, and will collect your money when you complete your call. One of the cheapest options is to dial directly overseas from a **phone booth,** and ask to be called back (the number should be written on a sticker inside the booth, prefaced by *ici le).* Ask the person to dial the international access code (011 from the US), 33 (France's country code), 1 (Paris's city code), and the eight-digit local number. Calling overseas can cost as little as 5F, and it's much cheaper this way, even if your friends make you pay them back (the French tax calls by as much as 30%). This technique is also cheaper than calling collect or via credit card. International country codes are posted inside most telephone booths.

Another alternative for Americans is **AT&T USA Direct** service, which allows you to be connected instantly to an operator in the U.S. Simply dial 19, wait for the tone, then dial 0011. Rates run about US$1.75-2 for the first minute plus about US$1 per additional minute. Calls must be made either collect (US$5.75 surcharge) or billed to an AT&T calling card (US$2.50); the people you are calling need not subscribe to AT&T service. For more information call (800) 874-4000. For **MCI,** call 05 90 28 22. **Canada Direct, Australia Direct,** and **New Zealand Direct** are similar to USA Direct, though not as extensive. For information in Canada, call (800) 561-8868; in Australia, dial 0102; and in New Zealand, dial 018.

If your itinerary is unplanned and you don't want to be constrained by the expense of phone calls, you might also consider **Overseas Access,** a telephone checkpoint service offered by EurAide. In its Munich office, an American staff relays messages to and from family, business, or other travelers. As a member, you can call the Munich office for news from home (US$15 initial registration, US$15 per week or US$40 per month). If you buy a Eurailpass from them, the initial registration fee is waived. In the U.S., contact EurAide, Inc., P.O. Box 2375, Naperville, IL 60567 (tel. (708) 420-2343). In Germany, contact Bahnhofplatz 2, 8000 München 2 (tel. (089) 59 38 89).

Telephone rates are reduced Monday through Friday 9:30pm-8am, Saturday 2pm-8am, and Sunday all day for calls to the Common Market and Switzerland; Monday through Friday noon-2pm and 8pm-2am, and Sunday afternoon to the U.S. and Canada; Monday through Saturday 9:30pm-8am and Sunday all day to Israel.

A brief **glossary:** A call is *un coup de téléphone* or *un appel;* to dial is *composer;* a collect call is made *en PCV* (pay-say-vay); a person-to-person call is *avec préavis.* Emergency or collect calls do not require coins or a *télécarte.*

A brief **directory:**

Operator *(Téléphoniste):* tel. 10.

International Operator: tel. 19 33 11.

Directory information *(Renseignements téléphoniques):* tel. 12.

International information: 19 33 12 + country code (Australia 61; Ireland 353; New Zealand 64; U.K. 44; U.S. and Canada 1).

Direct long-distance calls within France: To call from the Paris region to elsewhere in France, dial 16 + the number, To call the Paris area from elsewhere in France, dial 1 + the number. Within the Paris area, just dial the number; do the same to make a call to a region outside of Paris from a region outside of Paris.

Direct international calls: tel. 19 + country code (listed above and in most phone booths) + area/city code + the number.

AT&T operator: tel. 19 00 11.

Fire: tel. 18.

SAMU (Ambulance): tel. 15.

Police Emergency: tel. 17.

Minitel

Minitel is a computer system which provides telephone numbers, addresses, and professions of French telephone subscribers, as well as newspapers on screen (including the *International Herald Tribune),* shopping, the weather, train schedules, and information of all shapes and sizes. There are several coin-operated Minitels (2F per min.) for public use at the Bibliothèque Publique Information at the Centre Pompidou. Directory information in English: 3614 ED. If you have a listed telephone number, you can lease your very own from the phone company. This is not advisable for anyone on a budget; at 2F a minute, Minitel could break your budget before you're even aware of it.

Safety

Paris has much less violent crime than its American big-city equivalents, but crime on the whole is disturbingly on the rise, especially in the outer regions and suburbs of the city. Remember, this is a BIG city; be careful. A few precautions will see you safely through your travels more effectively than constant paranoia. Take as few valuables as possible; flashy jewelry and big cameras will draw unwanted attention. Keep all valuables with you whenever you leave your room, even if it has a lock, as others may have a pass-key. At night, sleep with valuables on your person; laying your pack alongside the bed won't deter thieves. In general, keep your money, passport, and other important documents with you in a pouch or **moneybelt** at all times. **Neck pouches** worn under the shirt prove the most theft-resistant; fanny packs worn over clothing are invitations to thieves. Look for packs that have zippers designed to accept combination locks.

Like so much else, **Pickpocketing** has been brought to a fine art in Paris. Parisian pickpockets are fast, practiced, and professional. Pros can unzip a bag in just a few seconds, so wear yours with the opening against your body. Threading a safety pin or key-ring through both zippers on a pack makes it difficult to open quickly and prevents it from slipping open accidentally. Thieves often work in pairs, one providing a distraction and the other grabbing your wallet or purse. Some street children will do anything to distract you, even pretend that they are being molested. In busy areas, walk quickly and purposefully. Stories of wallets being stolen in Notre-Dame or in the Mona Lisa room of the Louvre (both always crowded with tourists) are common. Thieves in metro stations may try to grab your bag as you walk through the turnstile or as you board the subway, just before the doors close.

Photocopy all important documents such as your passport, identification, credit cards, and traveler's checks serial numbers. Keep one set of copies in a separate, secure place in your luggage, and leave another set at home. Although copies can seldom substitute for originals, at least you'll have the relevant information. If you are robbed, check your surroundings carefully. Thieves may throw away your wallet after taking the cash, and you might be able to retrieve non-cash items such as credit cards. Report the theft to the police station in the area where it occurred. Be insistent; a police report may be necessary to claim stolen traveler's checks. To replace a stolen passport, head for your nearest consulate (see Consulates). They are surprisingly helpful, and a friendly (non-French) face will make you feel a hundred times better. The consulate can also provide the European numbers for canceling your credit cards and, in moments of true desperation, will lend up to 100F per day.

Traveling Alone

Traveling with other people can be emotionally taxing; at one time or another you may want to strike out on your own. There are many possible rewards, including a sense of adventure, freedom to go where and when you want, and the chance to reflect on your experiences without the stress of another person. The following safety precautions apply to all travelers, but people traveling alone should be particularly attentive.

Be sure that someone knows your itinerary, and check in with that person reasonably often. Steer clear of empty train compartments, and avoid large metro stations after dark. When on foot, stick to busy, well-lit streets. Ask the managers of your hotel, hostel, or campground for advice on specific areas, and consider staying in places with a curfew or night attendant. Some cheap accommodations may entail more risks than savings. Forego dives and city outskirts; remember that centrally located accommodations are usually safest. Never say that you're traveling alone.

Women Travelers

Women exploring any area on their own inevitably face additional safety concerns. In all situations it is best to trust your instincts; if you'd feel better somewhere else, don't hesitate to move on. You may want to consider staying in *foyers* or religious organizations that offer rooms for women only. Stick to centrally located accommodations and avoid late-night treks or metro rides. Remember that hitching is *never* safe for lone women, or even for two women traveling together. Foreign women in Paris are frequently beset by unwanted and tenacious followers. Try to exercise reasonable caution without falling prey to the notion that all French men are best avoided. To escape unwanted attention, follow the example of local women; the less you look like a tourist, the better off you'll be. Look as if you know where you're going, and ask women or couples for directions if you're lost or if you feel uncomfortable. Your best answer to verbal harassment is no answer at all. In crowds, you may be pinched, squeezed, or otherwise molested. Wearing headphones or a conspicuous wedding band may help prevent such incidents. If you are propositioned directly, a loud *"Non!"* or *"Laissez-moi tranquille!"* (lehsay mwah trahn-KEEL; "leave me alone") is best, with no further explanation. Seek out a police officer or a female passerby before a crisis erupts, and don't hesitate to scream for help (*"Au secours"*: oh suh-KOOR). *Always* carry a *télécarte* and change for the phone and enough extra money for a bus or taxi. Carry a whistle on your keychain, and don't hesitate to use it in an emergency. For additional tips and suggestions, consult *The Handbook for Women Travellers* (£7) published by Piatkus Books, 5 Windmill St., London W1P 1HF, England (tel. (071) 631 0710). **SOS Viol,** the national **rape hotline,** answers calls (in French) from Monday through Friday, 10am to 6pm; in August, Wednesday through Monday, 10am to 6pm (tel. 05 05 95 95).

All this should not discourage women from travelling alone. Don't take unneccessary risks, but don't lose your spirit of adventure either. A series of recent travelogues by women outline their sojourns; check a good library or bookstore for these and other books: *Nothing to Declare: Memoirs of a Woman Traveling Alone* and *Wall to Wall: From Beijing to Berlin by Rail* by Mary Morris (Penguin); *One Dry Season* by Caroline Alexander (Knopf); *Tracks* by Robyn Davidson (Pantheon); and *The Road Through Miyama* by Leila Philips (Random House/Vintage).

Drugs

Possession of drugs in France can end your stay immediately. Never bring any illicit drugs across any border, since drug laws and the severity with which they are enforced vary considerably among different countries. In France, police may legally stop and search anyone on the street. It is not uncommon for a pusher to increase profits by first selling drugs to a tourist and then turning that person in to the authorities for a reward. If you are arrested, your home country's consulate can visit you, provide a list of attorneys, inform family and friends, and tell you bedtime stories, but they cannot get you out of jail. You're virtually on your own if you become involved, however innocently, in illegal drug trafficking. Write the Bureau of Consular Affairs, Public Affairs #5807, Department of State, Washington, DC 20520 (tel. (202) 647-1488) for more information and the pamphlet *Travel Warning on Drugs Abroad.*

Emergency, Health, and Help

Police Emergency: tel. 17.

Police: Each *arrondissement* of Paris has its own *gendarmerie* to which you should take all your non-emergency concerns. Call the operator (tel. 12) and ask where your local branch is.

Fire: tel. 18.

Emergency Medical Assistance: Ambulance (SAMU): tel. 15. For house calls, call 45 67 50 50 at any time.

Hospitals: Hospitals in Paris are numerous and efficient. They will generally treat you whether or not you can pay in advance. Settle with them afterward and don't let your financial concerns interfere with your health care. Unless your French is exceptionally good, you'll have best luck at one of the anglophone hospitals. **Hôpital Franco-Britannique de Paris:** 48, rue de Villiers,

Levallois-Perret (tel. 47 58 13 12). Mo. Anatole-France. Considered a French hospital and bills like one. Has some English-speakers and a good reputation. **Hôpital Américain de Paris:** 63, bd. Victor Hugo, Neuilly (tel. 46 41 25 25). Mo. Sablons or bus #82. In a suburb of Paris. Employs English-speaking personnel, but much more expensive than French hospitals. You can pay in U.S. dollars. If you have Blue Cross-Blue Shield, your hospitalization is covered as long as you fill out the appropriate forms first. They can also direct you to the nearest English-speaking doctor and provide dental services.

Poison Control: tel. 40 37 04 04.

All-Night Pharmacies: Les Champs Elysées, in the Galerie des Champs, 84, av. des Champs-Elysées, 8ème (tel. 45 62 02 41). Mo. George V. Open 24 hrs. **Drugstore St-Germain,** 149, bd. St-Germain, 6ème (tel. 42 22 80 00). Mo. St-Germain-des-Prés or Mabillon. Open daily 9am-2am. Also, every arrondissement should have a pharmacie de garde, which, if not open 24 hrs., will open in case of emergencies. The locations change, but your local pharmacy can provide the name of the nearest one.

Alcoholics Anonymous: 3, rue Frédéric Sauton, 5ème (tel. 46 34 59 65). Mo. Maubert-Mutualité. A recorded message in English will refer you to several numbers you can call for help. Daily meetings. Open 24 hrs.

Birth Control: Mouvement Français pour le Planning Familial, 10, rue Vivienne, 2ème (tel. 42 60 83 20). Mo. Bourse. Open Tues. and Thurs. noon-3pm.

Emotional Health: Services and aid for the needy in Paris are provided by a number of organizations. Try calling **SOS Crisis Help Line: Friendship** (tel. 47 23 80 80). English-speaking. Support and information for the depressed and lonely. Open daily 3-11pm. For more personalized counseling (for anything from pregnancy to homesickness), go to the services based at the **American Church,** 65, quai d'Orsay, 7ème (Mo. Invalides or Alma-Marceau): the **International Counseling Service (ICS)** and the **American Student and Family Service (ASFS).** These 2 groups share the same staff and provide access to psychologists, psychiatrists, social workers, and a clerical counselor. Payment is usually 250-300F per session, but if you are truly in need, the fee is negotiable. The ICS keeps hours in the morning (Mon.-Sat. 9am-1pm), the ASFS in the afternoon (Mon.-Fri. 2-7pm). The office is staffed irregularly July-Aug., but will respond if you leave a message on their answering machine. Call for an appointment (tel. 45 50 26 49 for both) at the American Church.

Rape Crisis: SOS Viol, tel. 05 05 95 95. Call from anywhere in France for counseling, medical and legal advice, and referrals. Open Mon.-Fri. 10am-6pm; Aug. Wed.-Mon. 10am-6pm.

STD Clinic: 43, rue de Valois, 1er (tel 42 61 30 04). Mo. Palais Royal. Testing and treatment for sexually transmitted diseases. Free consultations, blood tests, and injection treatments. Syphilis tests free. Plasma and chlamydia tests usually around 175F each. AIDS tests are generally 145F. Tests are not given anonymously, but the clinic does not require ID to establish that the name you give is genuine. If you need a doctor, it's best to call for an appointment (also free). English spoken. Open Mon.-Thurs. 9am-7pm, Fri. 9am-6pm.

HIV Testing: 218, rue de Belleville 20ème (tel. 47 97 40 49). Mo. Télégraphe. Free and anonymous. Open Mon.-Fri. 4-7:30pm, Sat. 9:30am-noon. Also at 3-5, rue de Ridder 14ème (tel 45 43 83 78). Mo. Plaisance. Open Mon.-Fri. noon-6pm; Sept.-July Mon.-Fri. noon-7:30pm, Sat. 9:30am-noon.

Drug Problems: Hôpital Marmottan, 17-19, rue d'Armaillé, 17ème (tel. 45 74 00 04). Mo. Argentine. You're not always guaranteed an English-speaker. For consultations or treatments, open Mon.-Sat. 9:30am-7pm; Aug. Mon.-Fri. only.

Other

Lost Property: Bureau des Objets Trouvés, 36, rue des Morillons, 15ème (tel. 45 31 14 80). Mo. Convention. You can visit or write to them describing the object and when and where it was lost. No information given by phone. Open Mon.-Fri. 8:30am-5pm; Sept.-June Mon., Wed., and Fri. 8:30am-5pm, Tues. and Thurs. 8:30am-8pm.

Public Libraries: Bibliothèque Publique Information, in the Centre Pompidou, 4ème (tel. 44 78 12 33). Mo. Rambuteau, Hôtel de Ville, or Châtelet-Les-Halles. Many books in English. Record and video listening room. Novels are arranged alphabetically by century on the 1st floor (entrance to the library on the second floor), so you'll have to hunt for those in translation. Guide books and books about France and Paris abound. Books cannot be checked out. Open Mon.-Fri. noon-10pm, Sat.-Sun. 10am-10pm. If you just need a quiet place to read or write, the historic **Bibliothèque Mazarine,** 23, quai de Conti, 6ème (tel. 43 54 89 48; Mo. Pont-Neuf), provides handsome old volumes and perfect silence. If you plan to visit frequently, apply for a *carte d'entrée* (bring ID and 2 photos). Open Mon.-Fri. 10am-5:45pm. Closed Aug. 1-15. Free to the public.

Catholic Information Center: 6, pl. du Parvis Notre-Dame, 4*ème* (tel. 46 33 01 01). Information about religious activities, prayer, and pilgrimages. Open Mon.-Fri. 9am-noon and 2-6pm.

American Church in Paris: 65, quai d'Orsay, 7*ème* (tel. 47 05 07 99). Mo. Invalides or Alma-Marceau. As much a community center as a church. Bulletin boards with notices about jobs, rides, apartments, personals, etc, both in the lobby and downstairs. *Free Voice*, a free English-language monthly specializing in cultural events and classifieds, is published here; submit your ad with 60F by the 20th of the month before. Interdenominational services Sun. at 11am, followed by a ½-hr. coffee break and, during the school year, by a filling, friendly luncheon at 12:30pm (45F, students 30F). International counseling service. Come here for advice (tel. 45 50 26 49). Church open Mon.-Sat. 9am-10:30pm, Sun. 9am-8pm. Free student concerts Oct.-May Sun. at 6pm. Hosts meetings for AA, AL-ANON, ACOA and FAACTS (workshops for people affected by AIDS, ARC, or HIV-positive status).

St. Michael's Church, 5, rue d'Aguesseau, 8*ème* (tel. 47 42 70 88). Mo. Concorde. Holds Anglican services in English Sun. at 10:30am and 6:30pm. From Oct.-May lunchtime services are also held Thurs. at 12:45pm. On the first floor, outside the offices, bulletin boards list jobs offered and wanted, accommodations available and sought, as well as information on activities of interest. Office open Mon. 9:30am-12:30pm and 2-5:30pm, Tues. and Thurs.-Fri. 9am-12:30pm and 2-5:30pm. Even if the office is closed, the boards and pamphlets should be accessible.

Synagogue: Union Libéral Israélite de France, 24, rue Copernic, 16*ème* (tel. 47 04 37 27). Mo. Victor-Hugo. The multilingual, ever-jovial M. Ogorek presides over a welcoming staff. Sixty-min. services Fri. at 6pm and 90-min. services Sat. at 10:30am, mostly in Hebrew with a little French. English-speaking rabbi stays after the service to chat. Call for info about the large High Holy Days celebrations and religious groups. Secretariat open Mon.-Fri. 9am-noon and 2-5pm.

Weather: Allo Météo, 5-day recorded forecasts. Preferable to call from touch-tone phones. **Paris,** tel. 36 65 02 75; **Ile de France,** tel. 36 65 00 00; **France,** tel. 36 65 01 01; **mountain regions** (choice of northern Alps, southern Alps, Pyrénées, and Massifs), tel. 36 65 04 04; **marine conditions,** tel. 36 65 08 08. All in French. You can also check out a map of the day's predicted weather at the corner of Rapp and Université in the 7*ème*, posted by **Météorologie nationale.**

Laundromats: Ask your hotel or hostel for the location of the closest one. The average price is 28F per wash, detergent included, and 2F per 6min. dry. Most laundromats are open 8am-10pm; last wash 9pm.

Public Baths: 8, rue des Deux Ponts, 4*ème* (tel. 43 54 47 40). Mo. Pont-Marie. Shower 4F80, with soap and towel roughly 10F80. For the same price you can also rub-a-dub-dub at 42, rue du Rocher, 8*ème* (tel. 45 22 15 19; Mo. St-Lazare), and at 40, rue Oberkampf, 11*ème* (tel. 47 00 57 35; Mo. Oberkampf). They are clean, respectable, and quite popular in summer. All open Thurs. noon-7pm, Fri. 8am-7pm, Sat. 7am-7pm, Sun. 8am-noon.

Publications About Paris

On those heartbreaking and rare occasions when *Let's Go* falls just short, consult the following guides. *Gault Millau* is a well-respected guide to Parisian eateries. Patricia Wells's *The Food Lover's Guide to Paris* (US$13, about 100F in France) lists most of the city's greatest and most famous restaurants, cafés, bakeries, cheese shops, *charcuteries*, wine shops, etc. Gourmets may not share all of Wells's opinions (and budget travelers may not be able to verify them), but the guide is generally reliable. Both of the above are available at **Gibert Jeune** and other Parisian bookstores.

Your most important printed resource will invariably be a map (see Maps). The Office du Tourisme publishes a monthly booklet entitled *Paris Sélection* that highlights exhibitions, concerts, suggested walking tours, and other useful information (free). Similarly, the **Mairie de Paris** publishes the monthly *Paris le Journal* (10F) with articles and listings about what's on, touristically and culturally, around the city (available at the Mairie's Salon d'Acceuil, 29, rue de Rivoli, 4*ème* (tel. 42 76 42 42; Mo. Hôtel de Ville) and at most *arrondissement mairies*). Some *arrondissements* (like the 16*ème*) publish their own magazines.

The weeklies (published every Wed.) *Pariscope* (3F), *Officiel des Spectacles* (2F), and *7 à Paris* (7F) list current movies, plays, exhibits, festivals, clubs, and bars. While *Pariscope* is the most comprehensive, the articles and reviews in *7 à Paris* reflect *branché* (literally, "plugged in") Parisian tastes. The Wednesday edition of *Le Figaro* includes *Figaroscope,* a supplement about what's on in Paris. *Free Voice,* a monthly newspaper published by the Cooperative for Better Living at the American Church, 65, quai d'Orsay, 7*ème* (Mo. Invalides), is available there for free and at many student centers. *France-USA Contacts* (FUSAC), printed twice monthly and available free from English-speaking establishments (bookstores, restaurants, travel agencies) throughout Paris lists job, housing, and service information for English speakers. See Travelers with Special Needs for information on gay and lesbian publications.

To look like a true Parisan on the metro, disappear behind a copy of *Le Monde* (7F), the city's most respected newspaper, decidely centrist in outlook, albeit with a few socialist leanings. *Le Figaro* (6F) tends to fall more toward the conservative end of the spectrum and offers more diverse coverage than *Le Monde*. *La Libération* (6F) writes from the left. Those homesick for the *Washington Post* and *The New York Times* can get the best of both in the *International Herald Tribune* (8F50). *France Soir's* (5F) sports coverage is good but the rest of its efforts tend toward the McPaper view of the world. *L'Equipe* (6F), the sports and automobile daily, offers coverage and stats on most sports you can think of and some that you cannot. True hippofanatics will gallop to get *Paris-Turf* (6F50), the horse racing daily.

Weights and Measures

1 millimeter (mm) = 0.04 inch	1 inch = 25mm
1 meter (m) = 1.09 yards	1 yard = 0.92m
1 kilometer (km) = 0.62 mile	1 mile = 1.61km
1 gram (g) = 0.04 ounce	1 ounce = 25g
1 liter = 1.06 quarts	1 quart = 0.94 liter

Accommodations

There are three basic types of Parisian accommodations suitable to the budget traveler: hostels, *foyers,* and hotels. According to the Office du Tourisme, high season in Paris falls around Easter, May-June, and September-October (when trade shows—*salons*—take over the city.) Indeed many hotels in the 11*ème* and 12*ème* consider July and August to be the off-season. But for hostels and other truly budget accommodations high season is invariably summer (June-August) and most beds are perpetually full. If you are planning to show up then, try to make a reservation. But if you do arrive in Paris without one, don't panic. Although hotels near the place de la Bastille and the place de la République sometimes have space in the summer, visiting random hotels is not a good idea. Instead, try one of the following two booking services.

> **La Centrale de Réservations (FUAJ-HI),**4, bd. Jules Ferry, 11*ème* (tel. 43 57 02 60; fax 40 21 79 92). Mo. République. The best way to get a bed in a hostel and one of the best to find any budget accommodation in Paris. Near the Jules Ferry hostel, the centrale can provide you with same-day reservation in one of the youth hostels or budget hotels with which they are affiliated—a total of 10,000 beds in and around the city. The earlier you show up, the better, but they can usually help anyone, anytime. They open supplementary hostels in the summer (usually one at the Cité Universitaire) and can sometimes get you hotel rooms for hostel rates. Making a reservation requires an on-the-spot deposit of 10F, which is deducted from your bill at the assigned hotel. Also books beds throughout France and Europe and arranges excursions. Open daily 8am-10pm.

> **Accueil des Jeunes en France (AJF)** 119, rue St-Martin, 4*ème* (tel. 42 77 87 80). Mo. Rambuteau; open Mon.-Sat. 9:30am-6pm). Other offices are at 139, bd. St-Michel, 5*ème* (tel. 43 54 95 86; Mo. Port-Royal; open Tues.-Sat. 10am-12:30pm and 1:30-6:15pm); and Gare du Nord, 10*ème* (tel. 42 85 86 19; Mo. Gare du Nord; open June 1-Sept. 4 daily 7:30am-10pm). Even in the busiest months, the AJF guarantees you "decent and low-cost lodging with immediate reservation" for the same day only. You must pay the full price of the *foyer* room when you make your reservation, even before seeing the room. AJF can also help you find a hotel room, although not always for the full duration of your stay; you may have to use AJF more than once. Individuals must pay a fee of 10F per reservations.

The **Office du Tourisme** on the Champs-Elysées or one of its other bureaus should be able to find you a room, although the lines may be long and the selections not necessarily among the cheapest in Paris. Unless otherwise noted, we list hostel prices per person, prices elsewhere per room.

Hostels and Foyers

Paris's big-city hostels don't bother with many of the restrictions—sleep sheets, curfews, and the like—that characterize most hostels in the world, but they do have maximum stays, though even these are flexible. Accommodations usually consist of bunk beds in single-sex dormitories. To stay in a **Hostelling International (HI)** hostel, you must be a member. Prospective hostelers should become members of the HI affiliate in their country before they leave. But if you show up at an HI hostel without membership, the hostel should issue you a blank membership card with space for six validation stamps. Each night you'll pay a nonmember supplement (19F) and earn one Guest Stamp; get six stamps and you're a member. Membership purchased this way costs 114F. Most student travel agencies sell HI cards on the spot. or you can contact one of the national hostel organizations listed below. The **HI card** costs US$25 (over 54 US$15, under 18 US$10, family US$35). Also ask about the *Hostelling International Handbook, Vol. 1: Europe and the Mediterranean,* which sells for about US$11 and lists up-to-date information on HI hostels. As of summer 1992, the **International Youth Hostel Federation (IYHF)** has officially changed its name to **Hostelling International (HI)**, with the result that all signs, membership cards, and other products relating to the association will henceforth bear the HI initials and logo, as well as the symbols of the relevant national hosteling association.

> **Hostelling International** headquarters, 9 Guessens Rd., Welwyn Garden City, Herts, AL8 6QW, England (tel. (707) 33 24 87), is mainly responsible for international policy matters. Direct general inquiries to one of the following national associations: In France, the **Fédération Unie des Auberges de Jeunesse (FUAJ),** 27, rue Pajol, 75018 Paris (tel. 46 07 00 01; Mo. La Chapelle);

in the U.S., contact **American Youth Hostels,** 733 15th St. NW, Suite 840, Washington DC 20005 (tel. (202) 783-6161); in Canada, **Hostelling International—Canada,** Suite 608, 1600 James Naismith Dr., 6th Floor, Gloucester, Ottawa, Ont. K1B 5N4 (tel. (613) 748-5638); in England and Wales, **Youth Hostels Association of England and Wales (YHA),** Trevalyn House, 8 St. Stephen's Hill, St. Alban's, Herts AL 1 2DY (tel. (727) 552 15); in Ireland, **An Óige,** 39, Mountjoy Sq., Dublin 1 (tel. (01) 363 111); in Scotland, the **Scottish Youth Hostel Association (SYHA),** 7 Glebe Crescent, Sterling FK8 2JA (tel. (0786) 511 81); in Northern Ireland, **Youth Hostel Association of Northern Ireland (YHANI),** 56 Bradbury Pl., Belfast BT7 1RU (tel. (0232) 324 733); in Australia, **Australian Youth Hostels Association (AYHA),** Level 3, 10 Mallett St., Camperdown NSW 2050 (tel. (02) 565 1699); and in New Zealand, **Youth Hostels Association of New Zealand (YHANZ),** P.O. Box 436, 173 Gloucester St., Christchurch, 1, New Zealand (tel. (643) 79 99 70).

There are only two hostels in Paris, marked with 'HI' in their listings, that require HI membership (see above). The rest of the dorm-like accommodations in Paris are either non-HI hostels or *foyers. Foyers,* many of which are full-time dorm residences during the academic year, have their own characters, rules, and prices. Some cater to rowdy students; others are more sedate.

Centre International de Paris (BVJ). A relatively luxurious chain of youth hostels. **Paris Louvre,** 20, rue Jean-Jacques Rousseau, 1*er* (tel. 42 36 88 18; fax 42 33 40 53). Mo. Louvre. 200 beds in spacious, dormitory-style rooms. Lunch or dinner for 50F. Groups that book into this one have to pay for one meal a day. **Paris Opéra,** 11, rue Therese, 1*er* (tel. 42 60 77 23, fax 42 33 40 53). Mo. Pyramides. 68 beds in bigger rooms with fewer beds, and a more subdued atmosphere than Louvre. **Paris Les Halles,** 5, rue du Pélican, 1*er* (tel. 40 26 92 45, fax 42 33 40 53). Mo. Palais Royal. 55 beds. Cramped rooms, less common space, and toilets and showers on alternate floors. **Paris Quartier Latin,** 44, rue des Bernardins, 5*ème* (tel. 43 29 34 80, fax 42 33 40 53). Mo. Maubert-Mutualité. 138 beds. Beautifully designed with a modern decor, with large, spotless, but more densely packed rooms. All these hostels are open 6am-2am. Families not allowed. Singles available in all except Paris Louvre. Rooms available at 2:30 pm. Doubles, triples, and quads 100F per person, including breakfast and showers. Singles in Paris Opéra and Quartier Latin, 110F. Individual reservations not accepted—call or show up the same day, about 8am.

Auberge de Jeunesse "Jules Ferry" (HI), 8, bd. Jules Ferry, 11*ème* (tel. 43 57 55 60). Mo. République. About 100 beds in this wonderfully located hostel. Clean, large rooms. Slightly crowded. Noisy party atmosphere, and jovial, multilingual management. Most spaces filled by 10am. If you come and they are full, they'll point down the block to the Centrale (see above). Adequate kitchen facilities. 4-day max. stay. Open 24 hours. Lockout for cleaning 10am-1:30pm but reception staff is always present to answer questions or accept membership cards for reservations. No curfew. Rooms with 2-6 beds 92F per person. Showers and breakfast (self-serve 7-9:30am) included. Sheets 14F or use your own sleeping bag. Lockers 5F. Bike storage in the basement. Laundry, including dryer and soap, 33F.

Auberge de Jeunesse "Le d'Artagnan" (HI), 80, rue Vitruve, 20*ème* (tel. 43 61 08 75; fax 43 61 75 40). Mo. Porte de Bagnolet or Porte de Montreuil. The epitome of a mega-hostel. 7-floor complex with 411 beds, a restaurant, a bar, and even a small movie theater. Plenty of vending machines and free microwaves downstairs. Most of the rooms are triples, some have 8 beds, and a few are doubles. Rooms are ingeniously designed for maximum space utilization without creating an atmosphere that is too cramped. Groups are limited to 150 beds. Friendly English-speaking staff. Wheelchair access. Flexible 3-day max. stay. Reception open 24 hrs. Lockout 10am-2pm. Triples and dorms 100F per person. Breakfast and sheets included. Doubles 115-125F per person. Lockers 15F. Laundry 15F per wash, 5F per dry; soap 3F. Individual reservations can be made through HI member hostels: by telefax (which is *not* the same thing as fax), by HI voucher (ignore the instructions and write one voucher for each day you plan to stay), by HI postcard, or by the HI's IBN computerized booking network.

Hôtel Ste-Marguerite, 10, rue Trousseau, 11*ème* (tel. 47 00 62 00). Mo. Ledru-Rollin. Affiliated with the Jules Ferry hostel. 240 beds. Small but airy rooms with real mattresses, an atmosphere of happy chaos, and youthful enthusiasm. Most rooms 2-6 beds; those on the courtyard especially pleasant. Small showers. Some bathrooms in hall, others in rooms. Safe for valuables. Room downstairs to eat or just hang out in. Vending machine sells beer for 5F. Need we say more? 90F per person. Same-day reservations available through Jules Ferry. Otherwise, show up at 8am to get a room.

Hôtel des Jeunes (MIJE): "Le Fauconnier," 11, rue du Fauconnier (tel. 42 74 23 45). Mo. St-Paul or Pont-Marie. "Le Fourcy," 6, rue de Fourcy (tel. 42 74 23 45). Mo. St-Paul or Pont-Marie. "Maubisson," 12, rue des Barres (tel. 42 72 72 09). Mo. Hôtel de Ville or Pont-Marie. All in the 4*ème.* These star *foyers* are all located in former aristocratic residences *(hôtels particuliers)* of the Marais district, close to the sights and to one another. Le Fauconnier *is* luxury in modern hostelry. Rooms with 2, 4, and 8 beds are fairly spacious. Le Fourcy surrounds a large courtyard, ideal for meeting travelers from around the world. Rooms are smaller, but the atmosphere is friendly. Lively Maubisson, the smallest of the three, has newer and even smaller rooms. All three give priority to groups of 10 or more (but no group discounts). Individuals cannot make reservations at all, whereas groups can reserve up to one year in advance. There are no age specifications or limits to time of stay for groups, but individuals must be between 18 and 30 and can stay no longer than 7 days. Lockout noon-4pm. Curfew 1-6am. 105F per person. Showers and breakfast included (showers are always in the room, toilets down the hall). Lockers 2F. Within walking distance of all three hostels is the Restaurant la Table d'Hôtes, 16, rue du Pt. St-Louis-Phillipe, where you can get 3 courses for 40F, provided you live at one of the hostels and show up at 12:30, 6:30, or 7:30pm.

Maisons des Jeunes Rufz de l'Avison, 18, rue J.-J. Rousseau, 1*er* (tel. 45 08 02 10). Mo. Louvre, Palais Royal. From the Louvre metro stop (not to be confused with "Musée du Louvre"), take rue du Louvre away from the river, turn left on rue St.-Honoré, and then turn right on rue J.-J. Rousseau. During the academic year, this is a private residence hall for male university students, but in summer it is filled with tourists of both sexes. (Some rooms may be open during the school year as well.) Rooms are doubles, triples and quads; in the quads, beds are quite close together, so it is better to come here in a group or to book long in advance. Reserve by mail with one night's payment, or arrive early. Three-day min. stay. Reception open 7am-7pm. No curfew. 95F. Shower and breakfast included. No credit cards accepted.

Young and Happy (Y&H) Hostel, 80, rue Mouffetard, 5*ème* (tel. 45 35 09 53; fax 47 07 22 24). Mo. Censier-Daubenton. An average but clean youth hostel ideally located in the heart of the raucous student quarter on the rue Mouffetard. Rooms with 2-4 beds. Lockout 11am-5pm. Curfew 1am. 85F. Showers and sheets included. Reservations accepted with one night's deposit.

UCJF (Union Chrétienne de Jeunes Filles) or **YWCA,** 22, rue Naples, 8*ème* (tel. 45 22 23 49). Mo. Europe or Villiers. Accepts women for a 3-day min. stay June-Sept. in light, airy rooms with old wood floors and low-set beds. From Sept.-May caters to longer stays of women 18-24, with obligatory half-pension of breakfast and dinner (1900-2260F per month). All guests must pay 30F membership fee and 100F processing fee. Reception open for arrivals Mon.-Fri. 9am-6:30pm, Sat.-Sun. 9:30am-2:30pm. Curfew 12:30am. Singles 105F. Doubles and triples 82F per person. Showers and breakfast included. Sheets 30F, or bring your own. Self-service meals in cafeteria roughly 40F. If you're staying for a week, *forfait semaine* is a good idea: 5 breakfasts, 5 dinners, and 7 nights for 620F (singles) or 540F (doubles or triples). Make at least a phone reservation. Other locations at 65, rue Orfila, 20*ème* (tel. 46 36 82 80; Mo. Gambetta) and 168, rue Blomet, 15*ème* (tel. 45 33 48 21; Mo. Convention).

Foyer International des Etudiantes, 93, bd. St-Michel, 6*ème* (tel. 43 54 49 63), across from the Jardin du Luxembourg. Mo. Luxembourg. With wood floors, large windows, beautiful desks, and excellent facilities, this is one of the best. Oct.-June only for women on long stays; July-Sept. accepts men as well. TV lounge, piano, kitchenettes on each floor (bring your own equipment), irons, and hair dryers. International students galore, and a friendly director. Open Sun.-Fri. 6am-1:30am, Sat. all night. Singles 140F. Doubles 98F per person. Showers and breakfast (July-Sept. only) included. Written reservations should be made 2 months in advance and followed by 100F if confirmed. Call ahead or arrive around 9:30am to check for no-shows.

Maison Internationale des Jeunes, 4, rue Titon, 11*ème* (tel. 43 71 99 21; fax 43 71 78 58). Mo. Faidherbe-Chaligny. Well-located, exceptionally clean and tranquil, with a garden in the back. Mostly bright rooms with 2-8 beds for ages 18-30 (exceptions made), with especially beautiful new duplexes. Single-sex by room, but exceptions made for traveling buddies, couples, and consenting groups. Coed bathrooms. Some family housing. 3-day max. stay. They'll find you another place if they're full. Reception open 8am-1am. Lockout 10am-5pm. Curfew 2am. Quiet hours 10pm-8am. 110F. Showers and breakfast (served 8-9am) included. Bring your own sheets or rent them for duration of your stay, 15F.

Résidence Bastille (AJF), 151, av. Ledru-Rollin, 11*ème* (tel. 43 79 53 86). Mo. Voltaire. Recently renovated, airy rooms with wood bunks. 167 beds; rooms for 2-4 people. Triples and quads have bathrooms in the room; doubles use older hall bathrooms. Hair dryers in hall. Less crowded and more subdued, but friendly multilingual staff. Limited to ages 18-35. Reception open 7am-12:30pm and 2pm-1am. Curfew 1am. 105F.Showers, breakfast, and sheets included. No reservations, so arrive early in the morning.

Aloha Hostel, 1, rue Borromée,15*ème* (tel. 42 73 03 03), on a tiny side street across from 243, rue de Vaugirard. Mo. Volontaires. The outgoing management welcomes the hordes of weary backpackers that swarm here with tons of cheer and a cheap Heineken or two. The paint is peeling, but the kitchen facilities let you save more francs for beverages. Sunny and pleasant 4-bed rooms, 75F per person. Closed from 11am-5pm. Reservations accepted with one night's deposit.

Three Ducks Hostel, 6, pl. Etienne Pernet, 15*ème* (tel.48 42 04 05). Mo. Commerce. Turn 180° when you come out of the metro, and take a right on the rue du Commerce. The hostel is to the right of the church about 50m down the street. The dismal plastic flooring, dark rooms (4-, 6-, and 8-person rooms) and portable toilets are offset by the pleasant leafy courtyard, where the young raucous guests eat their dinners and then drink and sing late into the night. One-week max. stay. Small kitchen. Lockout 11am-5pm. Curfew 1am. 85F. Reservations accepted with one night's deposit. Mountain bike tours of Paris begin here.

F.I.A.P. Jean-Monet, 30, rue Cabanis, 14*ème* (tel. 45 89 89 15). Mo. Glacière. From the metro, follow your nose down bd. St-Jacques, hang a left at the first street (rue Ferrus), and then a right onto rue Cabanis. An international student center with 507 beds, most of which are full during the summer with visiting American tour groups. Comfortable and well-furnished rooms are impeccably maintained and come equipped with toilet and shower. The center offers a disco and jazz concerts at night (free) and stacks of tourist information, as well as a game room, laundry room, and a cheap cafeteria (54F for a full meal). Doubles 150F per person. Quads 130F per person. Eight-bed rooms 110F per person. April-Sept. 3-day maximum stay. Reservations essential. Mastercard, Visa.

Centre International du Séjour de Paris: CISP "Ravel," 6, av. Maurice Ravel, 12*ème* (tel. 43 43 19 01; fax 43 44 45 30). Mo. Porte de Vincennes. On the edge of the city. Large and professional in services, with numerous facilities, this hostel caters primarily to groups. Very imposing and professional reception desk. Ravel has large rooms (most of which have 4 or fewer beds; 216 beds total), a bar, restaurant, and access to the municipal pool next door (50% reduction for guests, 15F). Flexible 3-day max. stay. Some rooms available for guests with disabilities. Reception open daily 6:30am-1:30am. Self-service restaurant open 7:30-9:30am; noon-1:30pm, and 7-8:30pm. Singles 136F, rooms with 2-5 beds 116F, with 8-12 beds 93F. Reduction for ISIC holders: 125F80, 107F80, 87F10 respectively. Breakfast included. Reservations accepted no more than 36 hrs. in advance.

Association des Foyers de Jeunes: Foyer des Jeunes Filles, 234, rue Tolbiac, 13*ème* (tel. 45 89 06 42). Mo. Glacière. From the metro, take a right on rue de la Glacière and then a left on rue Tolbiac. A large, modern foyer for young women (ages 18-25) with excellent facilities—including kitchens on all floors, cable TV, washers and dryers, piano, excercise room, library, cafeteria, and garden. Run by an exceptionally friendly and helpful staff. Singles with attractive brick walls equipped with a sink and closet space, and get lots of sunlight. Reception open 24 hrs., offering excellent security. Sept.-June 1-month min. stay 2810F, plus 30F registration fee; breakfast and dinner included. July-Aug. 83F per night. Showers and breakfast included. Dinner 42F. Mailed reservations accepted, but there are usually vacancies during the summer.

Maison des Clubs UNESCO, 43, rue de la Glacière, 13*ème* (tel. 43 36 00 63). Mo. Glacière. From the metro, take a left on rue de la Glacière. Enter through the garden on the right. Small simple rooms—some newly renovated—run by a friendly management. Wheelchair access. Flexible 3-day max. stay. Reception open 8am-1am. Singles 140F. Doubles 130F per person. Triples 105F per person. Showers and breakfast included. Individual reservations not accepted.

Residence Luxembourg, 270, rue St-Jacques, 5*ème* (tel. 43 25 06 20). Mo. Luxembourg. Reception open 24 hrs. No curfew. Singles 95F. Breakfast included. Open July-Sept. for people 18-25, though some exceptions are made.

Franco-Libannais Foyer, 11, rue d Ulm, 5*ème* (tel. 43 29 47 60). Mo. Cardinal Lemoine or Luxembourg. An industrial-type residence sponsored by the Lebanese government that looks as wartorn as its country. The dank rooms and hallways are decorated with peeling paint, falling plaster, and a truly impressive array of stains. In some rooms aging pull-out couches covered only by a thin layer of foam masquerade as double beds. Min. age 18. Singles 100F, with shower 110F. Doubles 170F, with shower 200F. 20F surcharge levied on non-students. No reservations accepted for short stays, though they are likely to have space.

Hotels

Of the three classes of Parisian budget accommodations, hotels may be the most practical for the majority of travelers. There are no curfews, no school groups, total privacy, and often concerned managers—features that hostels and *foyers* usually can't offer. Most importantly, hotels routinely accept reservations, which will save you hours of bed-searching. Budget hotels in Paris are not significantly more expensive than their hostel/*foyer* counterparts. Larger groups (of 3 and 4) may actually find it more economical to stay in a hotel.

The French government publishes a comprehensive guide that classifies hotels with a star system: 4L (luxury), 4, 3, 2, and 1, depending on the services offered, the percentage of rooms with bath, and other such indicators. Most hotels in *Let's Go* are one-star or unclassified establishments, though two-star establishments offering inexpensive rooms are sometimes included. Most rooms come with double beds. In our listings, double refers to rooms with a double bed; twin refers to the rare room with two separate single beds. Expect to pay at least 150F for singles. If your room has no shower, you'll usually have to pay extra (12-25F) to get the key to the hall shower. Showers in your room are included in the room charge.

Many North Americans are surprised to discover a strange toilet-like apparatus located in all wash-closets. This is called a *bidet*. A *bidet* is a somewhat archaic device intended for the cleansing of the more private body parts. No matter how desperate you are, do not use your *bidet* as a toilet. You will cause yourself much embarrassment and force your unfortunate proprietor to spend a few hours bleaching the bowl and cleaning out the pipes. Another distinctly French practice to keep in mind when looking at hotels is that the French call the ground floor the *rez-de-chaussée,* and start numbering with the first floor *above* the ground floor *(premier étage)*. Many hotels serve breakfast for 12-20F. Since local cafés often serve croissants and coffee for less, you may want to eat breakfast out.

Remember that these budget hotels are not miniature Waldorfs. Don't expect a brightly colored bus to pick you up at the airport or a uniformed cleaning staff to make your bed daily, change your towels and leave you souvenir bars of soap. Many hotels listed in this section have only a few rooms in any category (e.g., single with shower). Request what you like, but you may be disappointed when you arrive. Most hotels are happy to change your room on the second day if they could not accommodate your wishes on the first, especially if you plan to stay at least one week.

These hotels all have their own certain charm. Appreciate them as yet another aspect of your immersion in a foreign culture. Remember that there are usually rules against bringing food into your rooms. Parisian law forbids hanging laundry from windows or over balconies to dry. Respect other guests' need for quiet at night.

Reservations

Do not reserve for more nights than you might possibly need. If you decide to leave Paris before you intended, or if you simply want to switch hotels, don't expect to get back all your money. Every year, *Let's Go* receives many letters from readers complaining that hotel managers would not refund the nights that went unused. If in doubt, reserve for just one night; you can usually extend your stay once you get to the hotel.

Although most tourists visit Paris in the summer, this is not necessarily the heaviest-booked time, since business travelers take up many rooms in May, June, September, and October. Since the high and low seasons are both complicated and counterintuitive, reserve as soon as you know when you will be in Paris. Make reservations at least two weeks in advance; a number of hotels claim that they are fully booked two months in advance for the summer. To guarantee that you have a room waiting when you arrive, the following process is advised:

1.) Call or write to the hotel asking for a reservation for a specific date and kind of room (single, double, with bathroom, shower, etc.).

2.) If you write, enclose an International Reply Coupon (sold at post offices), so that the hotel need not bother with postage expenses. Remember that the postal code for an address in Paris is 750 plus the *arrondissement,* so a letter to a hotel in the fifth should be addressed to the hotel's name and street address, followed by "75005 Paris, FRANCE."

3.) When you receive positive confirmation, send *les arrhès* (a deposit) for one night. Most hotels will confirm reservations only upon receipt of a check for the first night's rent, although some will accept a credit card number instead. The easiest way to send this deposit is to mail a traveler's check in francs, double signed. This is the equivalent of sending a personal check, and you'll avoid the hefty US$25-30 charge for an international money order. Include an International Reply Coupon (two for air mail) for a prompt reply. Without a deposit, most hotels will not honor a reservation for more than an hour or so, the time it might take to arrive after calling from a payphone somewhere in Paris.

4.) Call one or two days in advance to confirm (or cancel) and inform the manager of your intended arrival time.

Try your best to honor your reservation. Small budget hotels are of a nearly extinct breed. Their services are a kind of luxury the budget traveler cannot afford to abuse. These small family-run hotels cannot afford to hold a room, turn away potential guests, and then swallow their losses if you decide you don't want it.

First Arrondissement

The first is a great place to stay, and usually you end up paying bountifully for your fashionable Right Bank location. A number of small family hotels, however, still offer clean rooms at reasonable prices. In general, this is one of the safest areas of Paris, but stay away from Mo. Châtelet or Les Halles at night. In the day, this mile-long underground station is home to a constant flux of perfectly respectable commuters and tourists; at night it becomes a haven for drug dealers. If your hotel is near Mo. Châtelet/Les Halles, try taking a different metro line or stopping at the next station down the road.

Hôtel de Lille, 8, rue du Pelican (tel. 42 33 33 42). Mo. Palais Royal. Walk down rue St. Honoré until you turn left onto rue Croix des Petits Champs. Take the first right and you are on rue du Pelican. Clean and pleasant. Very good location in a quiet street that's very close to the Louvre. In case you haven't had time to buy a *télécarte* (necessary for almost all public telephones in Paris), you can use the coin-operated phone on the first floor. No credit cards, no breakfast. Singles 160F. Doubles 190-240F. Showers 30F.

Hôtel Saint-Honoré, 85, rue St.-Honoré (tel. 42 36 20 38 or 42 21 46 96; fax 42 21 44 08). Mo. Louvre, Châtelet, Les Halles. From Mo. Louvre, take rue du Louvre (away form the river) and turn right on rue St-Honoré. Most of the rooms have been renovated recently. Pleasant atmosphere, friendly staff, young clientele. In summer, confirm your reservations by phone or fax the night before, or by telephone as soon as you arrive in Paris. Singles or doubles 150-180F, with shower and toilet 280F. Triples or quads with shower and toilet 330-400F. Showers 15F. Breakfast 19F.

Hôtel du Palais, 2, quai de la Mégisserie (tel. 42 36 98 25). Mo. Châtelet. The location by the Seine, at the corner of place du Châtelet and quai de la Mégisserie, gives all rooms in the hotel (except on the top floor) splendid views of the Châtelet square or the Ile de la Cité. Renovated in 1990, the hotel is very clean and comfortable. Telephone in every room. Breakfast, served in your room, 25F. Singles on the top floor 180F. Doubles on the top floor 230F. Singles with shower, 280F, with shower and toilet 320F, with bath and toilet 350F. Doubles with shower 320F, with shower and toilet 350F, with bath and toilet 380F. One quint 550F. Extra bed 70F. Breakfast, served in your room, 25F. Eurocard, Mastercard, and Visa accepted.

Hôtel Montpensier, 12, rue de Richelieu (tel. 42 96 28 50; fax 42 86 02 70). Mo. Palais-Royal. From the metro, walk around the Palais Royal/Comédie Française buildings until you find yourself on rue Montpensier. Clean and hospitable atmosphere. Elevator. Eat breakfast downstairs or ask for it to be brought to your room. Since the sounds of the street can be fairly loud, it's worth asking for a room that faces the courtyard. To cancel your reservation, call 48 hrs. in advance. Singles 220F. Doubles 230F. Singles or doubles with toilet 250F, with shower and toilet and TV 365F, with bath, toilet, and TV 420F. Triples with bath, toilet, and TV 490F. Extra bed 70F. Shower 25F. Eurocard, Mastercard, and Visa accepted.

Hôtel de Rouen, 42, rue Croix des Petits Champs (tel. or fax 42 61 38 21). Mo. Louvre, Palais Royal. From the Palais Royal metro, place yourself on rue St. Honoré with the Palais Royal on your left; walk straight ahead and turn left onto the rue Croix des Petits Champs. Renovated in 1991, this hotel has shiny modern bathroom fixtures, new carpeting and wallpaper. Run by an exceedingly pleasant couple who are flexible about details. A phone in every room, but overseas calls must be made from the lobby. Singles or doubles 180F, with shower 240F, with shower and toilet and TV 290F. Triples with shower and toilet 290F. Quads with shower and toilet 350F. Extra bed free. Breakfast downstairs or in your room 20F. Mastercard and Visa accepted.

Hôtel Lion d'Or, 5, rue de la Sourdière (tel. 42 60 79 04; fax 42 60 09 14). Mo. Tuileries or Pyramides. Slightly worn, but clean. Singles 180F, with shower 220F. Doubles 220F, with shower 280F, with bath and toilet 360F. Showers 20F. Extra bed 40%. Breakfast 25F. For stays of more than 4 days, 5% discount; larger discounts for longer stays.

Hôtel du Centre, 20, rue de Roule (tel. 42 33 05 18, fax 42 33 74 02). Mo. Pont Neuf, Louvre, Châtelet, Les Halles. From the Pont Neuf metro, take rue de la Monnaie towards les Halles; it will take you straight onto rue du Roule. Recent renovation has given shiny modern plumbing and a phone in every room. Relatively spacious rooms. Pleasant management. If you plan to arrive after 7pm on your first night, send a deposit of one night's rent. Singles or doubles with shower and toilet 310F. Breakfast 26F. Extra double bed, available only for a few rooms, is 30% extra. AmEx, Eurocard, Mastercard, and Visa accepted.

Second Arrondissement

Although it is not blessed with many major sights of its own, the second *arrondissement* is within easy walking distance of the Marais, the Centre Pompidou, the Louvre, the Palais Royal, Notre-Dame, and more. Many little restaurants and hotels, often quite cheap, are to be found in this mostly working-class area, making it an excellent choice as a place to stay. Though the rue St-Denis, at the eastern end, is a center of prostitution and pornography, it is more unpleasant than unsafe, and its seediness does not spill over very far into neighboring streets.

Hôtel Chénier, 1, rue Chénier (tel. 42 33 92 32; fax 45 08 57 73). Mo. Strasbourg-St-Denis. Clean, comfortable, and recently renovated. Phone in every room. Run by nice people who don't speak English. Every room has a toilet. No elevator. Singles with shower 220F, with bath 300F. Doubles with shower 250F, with bath 300F, with bath and TV 330F. Triples with shower or bath 450F. Quads with bath 500F, with bath and TV 530F. AmEx, Mastercard, Visa.

Hôtel Vivienne, 40, rue Vivienne (tel. 42 33 13 26; fax 40 41 98 19). Mo. Bourse, Richelieu-Drouot, or Montmartre. From the Bourse metro, walk down rue Vivienne toward bd. Montmartre. This place isn't just comfortable, clean, and well-lit...it's actually kind of *plush.* Friendly staff, firm beds, TV, and phone in every room. Elevator. Singles or doubles with shower 330F, with shower and toilet 390F, with bath and toilet 410-420F. Smaller singles with shower 330F, with shower and toilet 370F, with bath and toilet 410F. Breakfast 40F. Extra bed 30F (free for kids). Visa accepted.

Hôtel Sainte-Marie, 6, rue de la Ville Neuve (tel. 42 33 21 61; fax 46 06 33 30). Mo. Bonne Nouvelle. This little hotel is simple but clean; distinctly superior to many other hotels in the same price range. Phone in every room. No elevator. Singles 150F, with shower and toilet 205F. Doubles 160-180F, with shower and toilet 220-240F. Showers 15F. Breakfast 20F. No credit cards.

Hôtel Tiquetonne, 6, rue Tiquetonne (tel. 42 36 94 58). Mo. Etienne-Marcel. Near the intersection of rue St-Denis and rue de Turbigo. An open-arms hotel this is not, but rooms are clean, and the price is right. Singles 120F, with shower and toilet 190F. Doubles with shower and toilet 220F. Showers 22F. Breakfast 22F.

Hôtel Zora, 4, rue Léopold Bellan (tel. 45 08 18 75). Mo. Sentier. Not particularly well-lit and somewhat worn, but clean, adequate rooms still make this a decent option. Unless you speak Serbo-Croatian, you may have difficulty making yourself understood. Unlike most Paris hotels, they do not require a deposit for reservations. Singles 120F, with shower and toilet 220. Doubles 160F, with shower and toilet 220F. Showers 20F. No credit cards.

Hôtel La Marmotte, 6, rue Léopold Bellan (tel. 40 26 26 51). Mo. Sentier. Pristine rooms with amazingly firm beds managed by very friendly people. Singles 160F, with shower and toilet 240F. Doubles 180F, with shower and toilet 260F. Showers 15F. Breakfast 20F.

Hôtel Bonne Nouvelle, 17, rue Beauregard (tel. 40 08 42 42, for reservations 45 08 87 71; fax 40 26 05 81). Mo. Strasbourg-St-Denis or Bonne Nouvelle. Cozy, clean hotel with a TV and phone in every room. Singles and doubles with toilet and bath or shower 245-300F. Triples with toilet and bath 375F. One triple/quad with toilet and bath 475F. Breakfast 25F. They require a one-night deposit only if you're arriving after 3pm. Visa.

Third Arrondissement

Absolutely *the* place to live in the 17th century, the labyrinthine Marais has regained its chic thanks to extensive renovations in the past 30 years. The one-time palatial mansions have metamorphosed into exquisite museums, as interesting for their collections as for their aristocratic elegance, and the tiny twisting streets have adopted fashionable boutiques and galleries. Fascinating and lively quarters, the third and fourth *arrondissements* shelter some terrific accommodations at reasonable rates. Prices tend to drop as you head north through the fourth and into the third.

Grand Hôtel des Arts et Métiers, 4, rue Borda (tel. 48 87 77 00; fax 48 87 66 58). Mo. Arts et Métiers. From the metro, take rue de Turbigo a few meters toward the Place de la Republique, turn left onto rue Montgolfier, then take the first right, placing you on rue Borda. The paint and wallpaper are peeling in places, but the central location compensates. There is a kitchen for guests with babies, and a fridge downstairs for all guests. Reception open 24 hrs. Singles 130-160F, with toilet 220F. Singles or doubles with shower 250F, with toilet and shower 280F. Showers 20F. No credit cards, no elevator. If you have trouble climbing stairs, ask for a room on a lower floor.

Hôtel Bretagne, 87, rue des Archives (tel. 48 87 83 14). Mo. République, Temple, or Filles du Calvaire. From the République metro, walk down rue (not *boulevard* du Temple), then turn left onto rue de Bretagne, and turn right on rue des Archives. A clean and pleasant hotel with a fancy mirrored entrance staircase. Two small lounges available to guests. The wide spread in room prices reflects the wide range in room quality: the cheaper rooms are quite simple, while the more expensive ones have TVs and snazzy new bathroom fixtures. Reception open 24 hrs., but the receptionist before 7pm doesn't speak English. Singles 140F, with bath, toilet, and TV 290F. Doubles 180F, with bath, toilet, and TV 340F. Triples 400F, with 3 separate beds and bath, toilet, and TV 600F. Showers included. Breakfast 25F. No credit cards accepted.

Hôtel Picard, 26, rue de Picardie (tel. 48 87 53 82). Mo. République or Filles du Calvaire. From the République metro, walk onto rue Beranger and then turn right on rue de Franche-Comte; keep going and you'll be on the rue de Picardie. This 2-star hotel is affordable through the generosity of its ever-friendly, ever-jovial proprietor and his polyglot daughter. Anyone armed with *Let's Go* gets a 10% discount. The family that runs this place actually *likes* American students, who make up the vast majority of their clientele. Charming, clean little rooms. Singles 200F, with shower 250F, with bath and toilet 320F. Doubles 240-260F, with shower 320F, with bath and toilet 390F. Triples 360F. Showers 15F. Breakfast 25F. Extra bed 90F. Eurocard, Mastercard, and Visa.

Hôtel France-Europe, 112, bd. de Sébastopol (tel. 42 78 75 33). Mo. Strasbourg-St. Denis. From the metro, walk a short distance down bd. de Sébastopol; the hotel is on the left side of the street. The beds and toilets are clean, and the rooms are reasonably large, but the paint is peeling in places and some of the bathroom fixtures look quite old. The location near a metro stop in the 3rd *arrondissement* is great, but traffic noise filters up from the bd. de Sébastopol. Singles with shower 220-250F. Doubles with shower 290F. Triples with shower and 2 double beds 370F. 80F per extra person). Breakfast 25F. No credit cards.

Hôtel de Roubaix, 6, rue Greneta (tel. 42 72 89 91; fax 42 72 58 79). Mo. Réamur-Sébastopol or Arts et Métiers. From the Réamur-Sébastopol metro, walk down bd. de Sébastopol towards Les Halles (the street numbers should be decreasing); turn left and you're on rue Greneta. This hotel is sparkling clean and tastefully decorated. Modern plumbing and amenities, including an elevator. There are two lounges, one of which is equipped with a TV. All rooms have a shower and toilet. Singles 300-330F. Doubles 360-380F. Triples 460F. Extra bed 40F, available only with the 360F double. Eurocard, Mastercard, Visa.

Hôtel Paris France, 72, rue de Turbigo (tel. 42 78 00 04, for reservations 42 78 64 92; fax 42 71 99 43). Mo. République or Temple. From the République metro, walk down rue de Turbigo; the hotel is on the left side of the street. The hotel is clean and well-lit. There is an elevator, and every room has a phone. Some rooms are invaded by noise from the busy rue de Turbigo. If you are thinking of taking a room without a shower, be warned that there are no showers in the hall. Singles or doubles 210F, with shower 260F, with bath, toilet, and TV 330F. Extra bed 100F. AmEx, Mastercard, Visa.

Fourth Arrondissement

Henri IV, 25, place Dauphine (tel. 43 54 44 53) Mo. Cité. The last outpost of cheap accommodations on the Ile de la Cité offers somewhat dilapidated, but clean and average-sized rooms with squishy beds. Includes friendly management, as well as one of the best locations in Paris. The biggest disadvantage is that the toilets are located outside, accessible only by a little staircase that curls around the building. Singles 185F. Doubles 210F. Reserve way ahead.

Grand Hôtel du Loiret, 8, rue des Mauvais Garcons (tel. 48 87 77 00; fax 48 04 96 56). Mo. Hôtel de Ville. Modest, fairly clean rooms in a well-located hotel, just blocks from the Hôtel de Ville. The helpful management speaks some English. Singles and doubles 160F, with shower 210F. Showers 15F. Breakfast 15F.

Hôtel de la Herse d'Or, 20, rue St-Antoine (tel. 48 87 84 09). Mo. Bastille, St-Paul. This hotel is built around a courtyard. Not the typical Parisian hotel courtyard—small, seldom-cleaned, and exposed to the elements and the pigeons—but a freshly painted, clean courtyard protected by a glass roof. Too bad the rest of the hotel doesn't quite live up to this; the rooms are a little worn. The area is reasonably quiet, but if you're a light sleeper and you mention it, they'll give you one of the rooms in the back. Phone in every room. Singles 150F, with toilet and shower 200F. Doubles 200F, with toilet and shower 250F, with toilet and bath 270F. Triples with shower and toilet 375F. Extra bed (in doubles only) add 50%. Breakfast 25F.

Hôtel de la Place des Vosges, 12, rue Birague (tel. 42 72 60 46; fax 42 72 02 64). Mo. Bastille. Tastefully decorated in what appears to be a late medieval style, but with the best modern standards of cleanliness and comfort. Elevator on 1st floor; not accessible to wheelchairs. Usually there is someone who speaks English at the reception. Singles with toilet and shower 275F. Doubles with bath and shower 380F (for these rooms, extra bed available for under 16 102F, free for under 3). 4-bed rooms 400F for 1 or 2 people, 502F for 3 or 4 people. Breakfast 32F. AmEx, Mastercard, Visa.

Grand Hôtel Jeanne d'Arc, 3, rue de Jarente (tel. 48 87 62 11). Mo. St-Paul or Bastille. Comfortable, relatively spacious rooms are tastefully decorated. Good location on a quiet street. Elevator too narrow for wheelchair access, but 2 rooms on *rez-de-chausée* are accessible. TVand phone in almost all rooms. Singles or doubles with toilet and bath or shower 330-390F. Triples with toilet and bath or shower 450F. Quads with toilet and bath or shower 500F. Breakfast 30F. Mastercard, Visa.

Hôtel Practic, 9, rue d'Ormesson (tel. 48 87 80 47). Mo. St-Paul or Bastille. Smallish rooms, more-or-less clean. The bathrooms can be quite damp. Pleasant location next to a cobblestone square in the Marais. Singles 100-135F, with shower 180F, with shower and toilet 250F. Doubles 190-200F, with shower 220F, with shower and toilet 295F. Extra bed 80F. Showers 15F. Breakfast 20F. Prices fall outside of summer months, depending on demand.

Hôtel Moderne, 3, rue Caron (tel. 48 87 97 05). Mo. St-Paul. Off rue St-Antoine on a quiet, centrally located street. Small rooms that could use quite a lot of cleaning. Dampness in bathrooms creates bad smells. Singles 130-150F. Doubles 160-170F; with shower 190F, with shower and toilet 220F. Shower 15F. No extra beds.

Hôtel du 7ème Art, 20, rue St-Paul (tel. 42 77 04 03; fax 42 77 69 10). Mo. St-Paul. What the French mean by "The 7th Art" is movie-making, and sure enough, this hotel celebrates Hollywood with a profusion of posters and photographs from old movie classics. They even screen the occasional old movie downstairs. Sounds like it could be a tacky gimmick, but it's really quite tastefully done; the staff seems to have a genuine (and contagious) love for the hotel's theme. A garrulous receptionist with a more-American-than-Don-Johnson accent will tell you how he hand made his desk to improve the hotel's look. The rooms can be a bit small, but are all well-equipped: phone, safe deposit box, cable TV. Understandably, the place is booked one or two months in advance—but if you show up at the door you have a reasonably good chance of getting a room due to someone's cancellation. Singles 260F, with shower and toilet 380-430F. Doubles with toilet and shower or bath 380-430F. Extra bed 100F. Breakfast 35F. AmEx, Mastercard, Visa.

Le Palais de Fes, 41, rue du Roi de Sicile (tel. 42 72 03 68). Mo. Saint-Paul or Hôtel de Ville. Large, sparsely decorated rooms; reasonably clean. The reception is at the bar of the Moroccan restaurant downstairs. Singles 150F, with shower 180F. Doubles 200F, with shower 250F, with shower and toilet 260-300F. Extra bed 80F. Showers 20F. Breakfast 25F. AmEx, Mastercard, Visa.

Hôtel de Nice, 42bis, rue de Rivoli (tel. 42 78 55 29; fax 42 78 36 07). Mo. Hôtel de Ville. This recently redecorated hotel is a rare find in the world of budget accommodations. Courteous management presents elegant rooms, an elevator (not large enough for wheelchairs), and a delightful lounge that will make you forget that you're on a budget. On the 6th floor is a particularly nice room, that can be rented as a triple (400F) or a double (350F), complete with a beautiful view of the Seine (including Notre-Dame). Phone in every room. Singles and doubles 220F, with toilet and shower 320-350F. Triples 270F, with bath and toilet 400. Showers included. Breakfast 27F.

Hôtel Andréa, 3, rue St-Bon (tel. 42 78 43 93). Mo. Châtelet or Hôtel de Ville. Clean, comfortable rooms with plenty of light. Phone in all rooms, TV in rooms with shower. It's just as well they have an elevator (not wide enough for wheelchairs), since the common showers are only on the 1st floor. Singles 170F, with toilet and shower 275F. Doubles 180F, with toilet and shower 290-330F. Extra bed 60F. Showers 15F. Breakfast 25F.

Fifth Arrondissement

Dhely's Hotel, 22, rue de l Hirlondelle (tel. 43 26 58 25). Mo. St-Michel. A one-star hotel commendable for its central location on a quiet street only a 30-second walk from the Seine. Singles 170F. Doubles 250F, with shower 320F. Showers 25F. Breakfast 25F.

Hôtel d Esmeralda, 4, rue St-Julien Le Pauvre (tel. 43 54 19 20; fax 40 51 00 68). Mo. St-Michel. Right next door to Shakespeare and Co. A charmingly well-kept establishment tucked into a small street overlooking the Seine on one side and a flowery park on the other. The cozy wooden interior complements the homey atmosphere and friendly, multilingual staff. Reserve at least a month ahead during the summer. Singles 130F, with shower 290F. Doubles with shower 290F. Triples with shower and toilet 490F. Quads with shower and toilet 550F. Breakfast 40F.

Hôtel des Carmes, 5, rue des Carmes (tel. 43 29 78 40; fax 43 29 57 17), off the bd. St-Germain. Mo. Maubert-Mutualité. Located on a quiet street, this amicable hotel offers clean, well-furnished rooms with an orange decor. Singles with bath and toilet 256F. Doubles with bath 412F. Two-bed triples with bath 546F. Breakfast included. Reservations accepted with one night's deposit.

Hôtel St-Jacques, 35, rue des Ecoles (tel. 43 26 82 53; fax 43 25 65 50). Mo. Cardinal Lemoine or Maubert-Mutualité. Bilingual management maintains a clean, professional, and quiet hotel, with a bit of peeling paint on the ceilings. Singles with shower 150F. Doubles with shower 275F, with shower and toilet 360F. Triples with shower and toilet 430F. Breakfast 30F.

Grand Hôtel Oriental, 2, rue d Arras (tel. 43 54 38 12; fax 40 51 86 78), off rue Monge. Mo. Cardinal Lemoine. Run by an amazingly patient and friendly proprietress, this hotel offers spacious rooms with firm mattresses and large closets. Bonaparte-sized elevator holds *either* you or your luggage. Singles 220F, with shower and toilet 240F. Doubles with shower and toilet, 320F. About 50F more for doubles with two separate beds. Breakfast 28F. Mastercard, Visa.

Hôtel des Médicis, 214, rue St-Jacques (tel. 43 29 53 64) Mo. Luxembourg. Don t despair when you see the entrance; the hotel cuts corners to keep the prices down, but the rooms are in much better repair than the lobby. The hotel is frequented by young and energetic clientele. Singles 75F. Doubles 140-160F.

Hôtel des Grandes Ecoles, 75, rue Cardinal Lemoine (tel. 43 26 79 23). Mo. Cardinal Lemoine. If you re comtemplating going all-out on a hotel in Paris, this is the place to do it. Built around a verdant and flowery garden, where guests breakfast in warm weather, this charming ivy-covered establishment maintains impeccably clean and tastefully decorated rooms to the great pleasure of their faithful guests, many of whom return year after year. Doubles 280-330F, with shower and toilet 420-550F. Breakfast included. Reserve well in advance, deposit required. Mastercard, Visa.

Hôtel des Allies, 20, rue Berthollet (tel. 43 31 47 52; fax 45 35 13 92). Mo. Censier Daubenton. Off bd. Port Royal. Not quite as scenic or centrally located as other hotels in the 5th, but a fantastic bargain of clean and comfy rooms for next to nothing. Singles 120F. Doubles 160F, with shower and toilet 270F. Triples available for a 30% supplement on the double rate. Showers 15F. Breakfast 25F. Reservations accepted with one night's deposit.

Hôtel Gay Lussac, 29, rue Gay Lussac (tel. 43 54 23 96), at rue St-Jacques. Mo. Luxembourg. The affable owner loves *Let's Go* readers and provides carefully cleaned sunlit rooms with sculpted plaster ceilings in an old but well-preserved hotel on a noisy street. Tour groups may limit available space. Singles 200F. Doubles (with two beds) 280F. Triples 320F. Showers 15F. Breakfast included. Reservations accepted with one night's deposit.

Grand Hôtel du Progres, 50, rue Guy Lussac (tel. 43 54 53 18). Mo. Luxembourg. An English- and German-speaking receptionist welcomes guests with open arms. Breakfast room complete with piano and a miniature library. Clean, bright rooms with beautiful windows and simple decor. Top floors, with charming garrett-like rooms, look out over the Panthéon. Singles 136-200F, with shower and toilet 295F. Doubles 220-275F, with shower and toilet 310F. Triples with shower and toilet 310F. Showers 15F. Breakfast included. A very steep *non-refundable* deposit required for a reservation: 300F for 1 person, 400F for 2 people, 600F for 3 people.

Hôtel de Nevers, 3, rue de l Abée de l Epée (tel. 43 26 80 83), off rue Gay Lussac. Mo. Luxembourg. Run by a sprightly retired couple, this six-story hotel offers clean rooms, renovated bathrooms, a view of the Pantheon and lots of quiet. Some beds are rather saggy. Singles 140F. Doubles with one bed and shower 230F, with shower and toilet 260F. Doubles with two beds 230F, with shower and toilet 320F. Showers 15F. Breakfast 25F. Reservations accepted with one night's deposit.

Hôtel Marignan, 13, rue Sommerand (tel. 43 54 63 81). Mo. Maubert-Mutualité. Located on a quiet street between and parallel to bd. St-Germain and rue des Ecoles. Spacious rooms, though some could use more sunlight. In summer, 3-day min. stay. Singles 150F. Doubles 250-290F. Triples 340-360F. Quads 420F. Breakfast included. Reservations highly recommended far in advance, but the management tries to save a few rooms for unexpected arrivals.

Hôtel le Central, 6 rue Descartes (tel. 46 33 57 93). Mo. Maubert-Mutualité or Cardinal Lemoine. Small, quiet hotel on a café-rich *place* that becomes party-central at night. Dark rooms with low, squishy beds. Singles 130F, with shower 150F. Doubles with shower 190F. Triples with shower 220F.

Hôtel Gerson, 14, rue de la Sorbonne (tel. 43 54 28 49). Mo. Odéon. Not to be cited for its appearance, this small, simple hotel offers reasonable rates in an excellent location. Singles 150F, with bathroom and shower 275F. Doubles 180F, with bathroom and shower 290-325F. Breakfast 30F.

Sixth Arrondissement

One of the greatest people-watching arteries in the world, boulevard St-Germain enlivens St-Germain-des-Prés, a lively left Bank neighborhood that has turned the sidewalk café into an art form. Jean-Paul Sartre existed in Aux Deux Magots and Le Flore, but such cafés now belong mostly to the beautiful and the wealthy. Budget hotels are sparse in this chic neighborhood, stretching from the Seine to the bd. Montparnasse, but the following exceptions provide surprising bargains. Expect crowds of Parisian youth at night, wandering the streets, going to the movies, relaxing at cafés. This may not be the quietest placest to stay in Paris, but its definitely one of the most exciting.

Hôtel Nesle, 7, rue Nesle (tel. 43 54 47 02), off rue Dauphine. Mo. Odéon. The impeccably clean rooms with wooden rafters and funky Egyptianesque frescoes, the warm, outgoing management, the gaggle of geese in the rose garden, and the outrageously low price of 125F, including breakfast and shower, make this charming little hotel in the heart of the 6th *arrondissement* without doubt the best place to stay on the Left Bank. Singles 125F. Doubles 150F. Reserve 3-4 days in advance, or just show up early.

Hôtel St-Michel, 17, rue Git le Coeur (tel. 43 26 98 70), near pl. St-Michel, just steps away from the Seine. Mo. St-Michel. Large, comfortable rooms with bright floral prints. Friendly management. Curfew 1am. Singles 170F, with shower and toilet 300F. Doubles 170F, with shower 265F, with shower and toilet 300F. Showers 12F. Breakfast 25F.

Hôtel Stella, 41, rue Monsieur le Prince (tel 43 26 43 49). Mo. Odéon. While the office can be a steam bath during the summer, the wood-trimmed bedrooms are pleasant and breezy. Singles with shower and toilet 178F. Doubles with shower and toilet 238F. No reservations accepted; just come early.

Hôtel St-André des Arts, 66, rue St-André des Arts (tel. 43 26 96 16). Mo. Odéon. This centrally located one-star hotel offers clean whitewashed rooms complemented by wood beams, though it is somewhat more expensive than other hotels in its category. Singles with shower and bath 250F. Doubles with shower and bath 370F, with two beds 400F. Triples 450F. Reserve at least 2 or 3 weeks in advance. Visa.

Hôtel Petit Trianon, 2, rue de l'Ancienne Comédie (tel. 43 54 94 64), tucked away in the busy corner of rue Dauphine and rue St-André-des-Arts. Mo. St-Germain-des-Prés. Centrally located, but somewhat worn. Singles 160F. Doubles with shower 250F, with shower and toilet 350F. Showers 25F. Reserve at least 1 week ahead with 1st night's deposit.

Hôtel du Dragon, 36, rue Dragon (tel. 45 48 51 05). Mo. St-Germain-des-Prés. The justifiably proud owner of this comfy hotel in the swankier part of the 6th personally decorates the rooms with flowered Laura Ashley wallpaper and carefully chosen antique furniture. Singles with shower 250F. Doubles with shower 275F, with shower and toilet 390F. Breakfast 25F. Closed Aug. Mastercard, Visa.

Hôtel des Balcons, 3, rue Casimir Delavigne (tel. 46 34 78 50), right of the pl. Odéon. Mo. Odéon. Although located in a rather drably dark and institutional hotel, the rooms are basically clean and well cared for, even if decorated in garish shades of blue and red. Doubles with shower and toilet 310-395F. Triples 520F. Breakfast 40F.

Seventh Arrondissement

Numerous hotels cluster around the western edge of the seventh *arrondissement,* all proudly advertising that the Eiffel Tower is indeed visible from their rooms. Don't stay in the seventh for the view or for the party atmosphere—this is civil servant heaven, with an allure for traveling business types. Try the seventh for slightly pricier, although space-challenged rooms (unless we say otherwise, expect smallish rooms).

Hôtel de la Paix, 19, rue du Gros Caillou (tel. 45 51 86 17). Mo. Ecole Militaire, up av. Bosquet and left on rue de Grenelle. The only true budget accommodations in the 7th and it shows. Worn carpets, soft mattresses, and peeling paint but fairly clean and very lively. Self-styled "shareholder" Noël will greet you in French, English, or Japanese. Baggage storage. Reception open 9am-9pm. Key gets you in after doors lock at 10pm. Check-out at noon. Singles 125F, with shower 183F. Doubles with shower 235F, with shower and toilet 302F. Twins with shower and toilet 267F. Triples with shower and toilet 390F. Shower 15F. Breakfast 28F, served 7-10:30am in lobby. Reservations recommended, deposit required depending on time of arrival.

Hôtel du Palais Bourbon, 49, rue de Bourgogne (tel. 45 51 63 32 or 47 05 29 26; fax 45 55 20 21). Mo. Cambres des Députés, Varenne, or Invalides. Down the road from the Palais Bourbon. Mme. Claudon has been fostering the family atmosphere in this 33-room hotel for 23 years. On-going renovations are producing ultra-modern, ultra-slick bathrooms. Direct line telephones in each room and high ceilings in some. Have breakfast or work in the beautiful salon full of elegant tables. English spoken. Reception open 24 hrs. Singles 200-227F, with shower 239F, with shower and toilet 339F, with tub and toilet 403-430F. Twin with tub and toilet 430F, with additional bed 569F. Showers 12F. Breakfast included, served in the salon or rooms 7-9:30am. Reservations recommended—call and confirm by letter or fax with credit card number. Mastercard, Visa.

Grand Hôtel Lévêque, 29, rue Cler (tel. 47 05 49 15; fax 45 50 49 36). Mo. Ecole Militaire or Latour-Maubourg. Off av. de la Motte Picquet. Faux-sandstone entry with white and blue floor leads the way to small rooms with beautifully tiled bathrooms. Direct line telephone with automatic wake-up in each room. Reception open 7am-7pm; night porter otherwise. Singles and doubles 195F, with shower 275F, with shower and toilet 300-320F. Twin beds 210F, with shower and toilet 335F. Triples 280F, with shower and toilet 395F. Extra bed 80F. Showers included. Breakfast 25F, served in salon or rooms 7-11am. Call for reservations and confirm in writing. Mastercard, Visa.

Hôtel du Champs de Mars, 7, rue du Champ de Mars (tel. 45 51 52 30). Mo. Ecole Militaire. Off av. Bosquet. Rustic lamps, wooden bedsteads, and subdued wallpaper give these cosy rooms an old-fashioned feel. Bathrooms very clean; direct line phone in each room. Wheelchair accessible once you overcome the first step. Singles and doubles with shower and toilet 350F. Doubles with tub and toilet 380F. Twins with tub and toilet 380F. Triples with tub and toilet 450F. Breakfast 32F, served in rooms or salon 7-10am. Reservations recommended: call, then confirm in writing with one night's deposit. Closed for 15 days in Aug., roughly Aug. 10-25. Mastercard, Visa.

Hôtel Muguet, 11, rue Chevert (tel. 47 05 05 93). Mo. Ecole-Militaire (off av. de Tourville) or Latour-Maubourg (off av. de la Tour Maubourg). Space...the final frontier...room enough for you and your extended family in these 43 enormous rooms and in the high, firm, silky spread covered beds. Clean, with nice wood paneling. Check-out at noon. Singles 200F, with tub or shower 230F, with tub or shower and toilet 300F. Doubles 230F, with tub or shower 270F, with tub or shower and toilet (and small sitting room) 350F. Showers 15F. Breakfast 30F, served 7-9:30am. Call first for reservations and confirm in writing with one night's deposit. Closed in Aug. AmEx, Mastercard, Visa.

Hôtel Kensington, 79, av. de la Bourdonnais (tel. 47 05 74 00; fax 47 05 25 81). Mo. Ecole Militaire. Not a lot of excess space in these well-lit, brightly decorated rooms. Firm mattresses, classy bedspreads, with mirror tile above the head of the bed. Direct line phone and TV in each room. First-floor rooms wheelchair accessible. Singles with shower and toilet 220-260F. Doubles with shower and toilet 320F, with tub and toilet 370F. Twins with shower and toilet 340F, with tub and toilet 420F. Extra bed (only in 420F rooms) 80F. Breakfast 26F, served 7:30-11am in dining room or bedroom. Reservations recommended—call first and confirm in writing with one night's payment (check or credit card number). AmEx, Mastercard, Visa.

Royal Phare Hotel, 40, av. de la Motte-Picquet (tel. 47 05 57 30; fax 45 51 64 41). Mo. Ecole Militaire. The ever-friendly M. Le Rouzic and his dog have carefully chosen designer wallpaper, rainbow curtains, and water drop tile to make their small rooms and friendly hotel even more cheerful. TV and telephone in each room (and hair dryer in some) will brighten your days. Reception open 24 hrs. Singles with shower and toilet 280F-300F. Doubles with shower and toilet 300-320F. Doubles (big bed or twin) with tub and toilet 350F. Breakfast 28F, served 7-9:30am in room and lobby. Reservations recommended—call, confirm by letter or fax with credit card number. AmEx, Mastercard, Visa, or traveler's checks in francs.

Hôtel du Centre, 24bis, rue Cler (tel. 47 05 52 33). Mo. Ecole Militaire or Latour-Maubourg. Off av. de la Motte Picquet. The dining room full of shiny copper pots reminiscent of a farmhouse is the brightest in the place. Dark decor shrinks small rooms further. Clean, if not new. Check-out at noon. Singles and doubles with shower 260F, with shower and toilet 330F. Twins with tub and toilet 350F. Triples with tub and toilet 430F. 200F singles and 220F doubles are sometimes available—ask. Breakfast 30F. Reservation confirmed in writing with check in French francs or with credit card number. AmEx, Mastercard, Visa.

Eighth Arrondissement

High property values for the homeowner make for equally high property values for the hotel owner, and the real estate in the eighth *arrondissement* is prime. The budget traveler, however, has not been entirely forgotten.

Hotel d'Argenson, 15, rue d'Argenson (tel. 42 65 16 87). Mo. St-Augustin or Miromesnil. From St-Augustin metro stop, exit to the odd-numbered side of bd. Haussmann, cross bd. Malesherbes and turn left on rue d'Argenson. The gregarious Katya and the chic Martine will welcome you to this homey, friendly, well-located hotel. Lumpy mattresses should not deter you—each room has a direct-line phone and plenty of cupboard space. Small 6th-floor rooms without toilet are cheapest. Reception open 24 hrs. but make arrangements for late arrivals. Check-out at noon. Singles 195F, with shower and toilet 265F, 295F, or 315F (depending on size), with bath and toilet 355F. Doubles 220F, with shower and toilet 330F or 350F, with bath and toilet 390F. 2 beds for 2 people with shower and toilet 380F, with bath and toilet 420F. Triples with shower and toilet 445F, with bath and toilet 485F. Showers 20F. Breakfast included. Reservations important, especially June-August; send 2 nights' deposit in francs or leave credit card number as guarantee, along with arrival time and departure date.

Hôtel d'Artois, 94, rue La Boétie (tel. 43 59 84 12), a stone's throw from the Champs-Elysées. Mo. St. Philippe de Roule. The rugs may be a little worn, the mattresses less than new, but the bathrooms are impeccable, the plant-filled lobby an urban greenhouse, and the breakfast room a scented far-Eastern delight. English spoken. Someone always at the desk. Singles 235F, with shower 365F, with bath and toilet 410F. Doubles 260F, with bath and toilet 410F. Showers 20F. Breakfast included, served downstairs 6:30-9:30am. Reservations recommended, with deposit for late-night arrivals.

Hôtel Wilson, 10, rue de Stockholm (tel. 45 22 10 85). Mo. St. Lazare. Walk up rue de Rome and turn left on rue de Stockholm. A no-frills hotel of 40 rooms, around the corner from the Gare St-Lazare. Soft mattresses, thin aged carpet, incomplete soundproofing, cracks in the wallpaper—but at this price, what did you expect? Bathrooms within the rooms are newer and the occasional velvet chair offsets a drab color scheme. Singles 165F-170F, with shower and toilet 210F. Doubles 190F-205F, with shower and toilet 230F. Breakfast included, served 7-10:30am. Telephone reservations accepted but not necessary.

Ninth Arrondissement

The ninth bridges some of Paris's wealthiest and most heavily touristed quarters—the second and the eighth—as well as the less tantalizing and less affluent 10th and 18th. There are plenty of hotels here, but many in the northern half of the area are used by prostitutes and their customers. Avoid the Anvers, Pigalle, and Barbès-Rochechouart metro stops at night; use the Abbesses stop instead. The southern half of the quarter, though no glamorous hot spot, provides several worthwhile accommodations not too far away from the sights (and sins) of Paris. A few nicer, but not-so-cheap hotels are available near the more respectable and central bd. des Italiens and bd. Montmartre.

Hôtel des Trois Poussins, 15, rue Clauzel (tel. 48 74 38 20). Mo. St-Georges. Managed by the wonderful Desforges family, this hotel has a lovely courtyard, clean rooms, and editions of *Let's Go* dating from 1982. No children under 15. Singles 140-150F. Doubles with shower 220-230F. Showers 15F. Breakfast 20F.

Hôtel d'Espagne, 9-11, cité Bergère (tel. 42 46 73 30; fax 48 00 95 69). Mo. Montmartre. Not elegant, but it has high ceilings and is relatively clean, with decent beds and lighting. Helpful reception; some English spoken. Telephones in every room; TVs in some. Singles with toilet 150F. Doubles with shower and toilet 300F; with bath and toilet 320F. Triples with shower and toilet 420F. Quads 510F. One common shower, 10F. Breakfast 22F. Reservations recommended. Credit cards accepted.

Hôtel Central, 6, cité Bergère (tel. 47 70 52 98 or 48 24 71 24; fax 48 00 95 69.) Mo. Montmartre. Very clean and pleasant rooms with lots of light, big, firm beds, and phones and televisions in every room. Elevator. All rooms also come with either shower or bath and toilet. Singles 280F. Doubles 350-420F. Triples 495F. Extra bed 100F. Breakfast 28F. Reservations recommended. English spoken. Credit cards accepted.

Hôtel Beauharnais, 51, rue de la Victoire (tel. 48 74 71 13). Mo. le Peletier. Very pretty rooms with flowered wallpaper and wooden frame beds. Rooms are sunny and very clean and many have flowers in the windows. Telephones in every room. Singles with shower 280F, with shower and toilet 300F. Doubles with shower and toilet 320F. Triples with shower and toilet 420F. Breakfast 25F.

Hôtel Modial Européen, 21, rue Notre-Dame de Lorette (tel. 48 78 60 47; fax 42 81 95 50.) Mo. Notre-Dame de Lorette. Newly renovated rooms are all very modern, with pleasant, light-colored paint, nice bathrooms, and TVs in every room. Elevator. Doubles with shower and toilet 340F-360F. Triples 460-480F. Quads 480F. Breakfast 25F. Credit cards accepted, except for AmEx.

Hôtel des Arts, 7, cité Bergère (tel. 42 46 73 30; fax 48 00 94 42). Mo. Montmartre. Nice rooms, decorated with posters and prints. All rooms have showers, TV, and phone. And if you hear someone whistle at you, it's the parrot out front. Elevator. Singles with bath 300-325F. Doubles with bath 325-350F. Triples 480F. Breakfast 25F. Credit cards accepted.

Tenth Arrondissement

In response to the voluminous traffic that pours through the Gare de l'Est and the Gare du Nord, quite a few inexpensive hotels have set up shop in the tenth. In fact, the supply often exceeds demand, making this crowded corner of Paris a decent turn if you've struck out everywhere else. Bear in mind that the ever-swelling cost of living in Paris has driven many of the city's poor to the outer *arrondissements,* often resulting in large crowds and visibly depressed areas. In addition, these hotels are far from the primary sights and nightlife, so you'll be forced to use taxis once the metro stops running. Anyone traveling alone might want to look elsewhere; areas near the train stations are often far from safe. Exercise special caution in the area stretching west from pl. de la République along rue du Château d'Eau.

Cambrai Hôtel, 129bis, bd. de Magenta (tel. 48 78 32 13; fax 48 78 43 55). Mo. Gare du Nord. Clean and airy rooms with high ceilings. Beds are wide and firm. Large clean showers. Telephones in every room, and just a step away from the Gare du Nord. Singles 110F, with shower 188F. Doubles 160F, with shower 208F. Triples 315F, with shower 330F. Two-room suite for four 335F, with shower 352F. Showers 20F. Breakfast included. Some English spoken.

Palace Hôtel, 3, rue Bouchardon (tel. 42 06 59 32). Mo. Strasbourg/St-Denis. A family affair with an assembly of children and pets around the reception desk. Small, cheerful rooms, many facing an attractive, plant-filled courtyard. Quiet back-street location. Television and drink machines on ground floor. Singles 100F. Doubles 130F, with bath and toilet 250F. Triples 180F, with shower and toilet 280F. One two-room quad 230F. Breakfast 20F. Visa accepted. English spoken. No reservations.

Hôtel Métropole Lafayette, 204, rue Lafayette (tel. 46 07 72 69). Mo. Louis Blanc. Small, somewhat dark rooms, offset by nice, firm beds. Very clean, with friendly reception. Singles 110F, with shower 150F. Doubles 130F, with shower 180F, shower and toilet 200F. Triples with shower 230F, shower and toilet 250F. Showers 25F. Breakfast 15F. AmEx, Mastercard, and Visa accepted. English spoken.

Hôtel Pierre Dupont, 1, rue Pierre Dupont (tel. 46 07 93 66). Mo. Louis Blanc. Decent-sized rooms, relatively clean, comfortable beds. A little bit out of the way, but on a nice, quiet street. Singles 155-168F, with shower 215F, with shower and toilet 235F. Twins 190F-205F, with shower 245F, with shower and toilet 305F. Free showers. Elevator. Breakfast included. Most credit cards accepted. English spoken. Reservations recommended.

Hôtel du Centre, 4, rue Sibour (tel. 46 07 20 74; fax 46 07 37 17). Mo. Gare de l'Est. Conveniently close to the Gare du Nord and Gare de l'Est, with small, clean and well-lit rooms. Renovations are expected to be completed by 1993. Singles 170F, with toilet 180F, wtih shower 230F, with shower and toilet 240F. Triples 250F, with shower 300F, with shower and toilet 310F. Quads 320F. Showers 15F. Breakfast 20F. Elevator. Credit cards accepted; AmEx discouraged. Some English spoken.

Hôtel des Familles, 216, Faubourg St-Denis (tel. 46 07 76 56). Mo. Gare du Nord. A little dark, a little modest looking, but decent with big beds and decent showers. Singles 120-150F, with shower 200F. Doubles 180F, with shower 200F. Triples 234F, with shower 286F. Quad 286F, with shower and toilet 325F. Showers 17F. Breakfast 18F.

Hôtel du Jura, 6, rue Jarry (tel. 47 70 06 66). Mo. Chateau d'Eau. Small, decently clean rooms and clean showers. On a quiet street, but a little bit out of the way. Singles 140F, with shower 170F. Doubles 185F, with shower 210F. Triples 220F, with shower 250F. Showers 15F. Breakfast included. Traveler's checks accepted.

Eleventh Arrondissement

Reasonably cheap places to stay line the streets surrounding the place de la République and place de la Bastille. Others dot the more interior streets of the *arrondissement.* Many of these hotels consider July and August the off-season; they're very likely to have space should you you call once in Paris or even show up unannounced. Five metro lines converge on République, three cross over at Bastille. Both places are on the western side of the *arrondissement,* neighbors to the fourth: the location is excellent, the atmosphere charged with an intriguing mix of youthful vibrance and working-class joviality. If possible, avoid place de la République at night, when prostitutes and pickpockets are ever present.

Hôtel Rhetia, 3, rue du Général Blaise (tel. 47 00 47 18). Mo. Saint-Ambroise, St-Maur, or Voltaire. From St-Maur metro stop, walk left on rue St-Maur, turn right on Lacharrière. Well-lit, tastefully decorated rooms overlooking the happy park Square Maurice Gardette. A quiet neighborhood, not too far from the Bastille. Direct-line phone in each room and nifty tile in most. Reception open Mon.-Fri. 7:30am-10pm, Sat.-Sun. and holidays 8am-10pm. Singles 160F, with shower or tub and toilet 200-220F. Doubles 180F, with shower or tub and toilet 220F. Triples 220F, with shower or tub and toilet 260F. Showers 10F. Breakfast included, served Mon.-Fri. 7:30-9am, Sat.-Sun. and holidays 8-9:30am.

Plessis Hôtel, 25, rue du Grand Prieuré (tel. 47 00 13 38; fax 43 57 97 87), off av. de la République. Mo. Oberkampf or République. M. and Mme. Montrazat are authentic *hôteliers* who love their business, and it shows: they speak English, serve drinks, and have menus and cards from local inexpensive restaurants. Some call it the *hôtel au chien tournant* (hotel of the turning dog—

he will chase his tail in the lobby if excited); all enjoy the 49 small but beautiful rooms. Great tile, nice bedspreads, firm mattresses. You can even tickle the ivories on the piano in the non-smoking lounge. Singles 200F, with shower, toilet, and TV 295F, with tub, toilet, and TV 320F. Doubles 200F, with shower, toilet, and TV 295F-320F, with tub, toilet, and TV 320F. Extra bed 75F. Showers 10F. Big breakfast 32F, served 7-9:30am. Closed late July and Aug. AmEx, Mastercard, Visa.

Hôtel de Belfort, 37, rue Servan (tel. 47 00 67 33). Mo. Père Lachaise, St. Maur, or Voltaire. From Père Lachaise metro stop, take rue du Chemin Vert. Take the 4th left onto rue Servan. Not exactly chic, but the patterned blankets are homey and the bathrooms, although worn, are as modern as they come. Breakfast served in a cool *cave;* staff will greet you in multiple languages, including English, and the Lizard King's tomb is a stone's throw away. What makes this place so attractive is the price for young backpackers: an excellent 100F per person per night for a bed in a double, triple, or quad, with shower, toilet, phone, and TV—a very good deal. Otherwise: singles with shower, toilet, and TV 300F. Doubles 190-220F (shower on hall included), with shower, toilet, and TV 320F. Twins with shower, toilet, and TV 350F. Triples with shower, toilet, and TV 420F. Extra bed 100F. Breakfast 30F, served 7:30-9:30am. AmEx, Mastercard, Visa.

Hôtel Baudin, 113, av. Ledru-Rollin (tel. 47 00 18 91; fax 48 07 04 66). Mo. Ledru-Rollin. A real find: 20 big rooms with patterned bedspreads; very clean with tranquil decor. Only a few blocks from the Bastille and direct-line phone in every room. Check-out at noon. Singles 120F. Doubles 170-200F, with shower 230F, with tub and toilet 270F. Extra bed 100F. Showers 20F. Breakfast 25F, served 7-9:30am. Mastercard, Visa.

Hôtel Notre-Dame, 51, rue de Malte (tel. 47 00 78 76). Mo. République. From the metro, exit to rue de Faubourg du Temple and turn right onto rue de Malte. 51 bright rooms—not brand-new, but quite clean. English-speaking staff. TV in more expensive rooms; direct-line phone in all. Check-out at noon. Singles 180F, with shower 210F. Doubles 180F, with shower 260F, with shower or tub and toilet 340F. Quads 440F. Extra bed 70F. Showers 20F. Breakfast 30F, served 7-9:30am. Mastercard, Visa.

Hôtel de Nevers, 53, rue de Malte (tel. 47 00 56 18; fax 43 57 77 39). Mo. Oberkampf or République. From Oberkampf metro stop, exit to Crussol, cross bd. Voltaire onto rue de Malte. Friendly owners have lived in the U.S. and love Americans; you'll enjoy their cute, comfortable, newly renovated rooms. Firm mattresses, towels, and face cloths in the bathrooms, and an appealing breakfast plate to boot. Singles 162F, with shower 232F, with shower and toilet 257F. Doubles 204F, with shower 254F, with shower and toilet 279F. Triples 366F. Quads 466F. Extra bed 50F. Showers 20F. Breakfast included, served 7-10am.

Hôtel de Vienne, 43, rue de Malte (tel. 48 05 44 42). Mo. Oberkampf or République. From Oberkampf metro stop, exit at Crussol and take rue de Malte. Peaceful, floral papered rooms with firm mattresses and clean bathrooms. Direct-line phone and safe, family atmosphere—but no hall shower for those without one in their room. Singles 100F, bigger bed 125F. Doubles 150F, with shower 210F. Breakfast 30F, served 7-9am. Closed Aug.

Hôtel de France, 159, av. Ledru-Rollin (tel. 43 79 53 22). Mo. Ledru-Rollin. Low prices and facilities to match—worn rug on stairs, shower caulking and plaster in need of redoing, and carpet that doesn't quite fit the rooms. But good location—and a Boston Bruins sticker on the door. Singles with shower 150F. Doubles with shower 200F, with tub 220F. Triples (with extra bed) with shower or toilet 260F. Breakfast 25F, served 7-9am. Call and confirm reservations in writing. Mastercard, Visa. Restaurant downstairs (tel. 43 48 11 69) run by same management. 49F *menu; plats du jour* 38-66F. Special deals for hotel guests.

Cosmo's Hotel, 35, rue Jean-Pierre Timbaud (tel. 43 57 25 88). Mo. République. Exit to av. de la République and turn left on rue J.-P. Timbaud. A pleasant hotel, with clean, comfortable rooms, each with TV and direct-line phone. Singles 155F. Doubles 170F, with shower 200F, with shower and toilet 230-260F. Showers 25F. Breakfast 25F, served 7-10am. Call for reservations between 7am and 7:30pm and confirm in writing. Mastercard, Visa.

Hôtel Beaumarchais, 3, rue Oberkampf (tel. 43 38 16 16; fax 43 38 32 86). Mo. Oberkampf or Filles du Calvaire. From Oberkampf metro stop, exit to rue de Malte and turn right on rue Oberkampf. Green and brown decor radiates reassuring order and cleanliness. TV, telephone,and artificial yet tasteful flowers in each room. Fluent English and German at reception. Singles with shower and toilet 290F. Doubles with shower and toilet 340F. Triples with sower and toilet 450F. Breakfast 30F, served 7-10am. AmEx, Mastercard, Visa.

Pax Hotel, 12, rue de Charonne (tel. 47 00 40 98; fax 43 38 57 81). Mo. Bastille or Ledru-Rollin. From Bastille metro stop, take exit onto rue du Faubourg St-Antoine, turn left on rue de Charonne. Immaculate rooms off long hallways, with TV, phone, and hair dryer, might fool you into believing you're at a Best Western in Kansas. Singles with shower 260F, with shower and toilet 280F, Doubles with shower and toilet 310-340F. Quads 520F. Mastercard, Visa.

Hôtel de l'Europe, 74, rue Sedaine (tel. 47 00 54 38; fax 47 00 75 31). Mo. Voltaire. Walk past the Mairie up bd. Voltaire and turn left on rue Sedaine. Spacious comfortable rooms, firm mattresses, and 2 fairly friendly dogs at reception. Doubles 175F, with shower or tub 200F, with shower and toilet 220F, with tub and toilet 240F. Breakfast 18F, served 7-9am.

Mary's Hotel, 15, rue de Malte (tel. 47 00 81 70). Mo. Oberkampf or République. From Mo. Oberkampf, exit at Crussol and take rue de Malte. 38 small, non-descript rooms have seen better days—mattresses old, paint chipped, tile mildewed, but livable. Singles 130-150F, with toilet 150-180F. Doubles 170-200F, with toilet 180-240F. Triples with tub and toilet 360F. Showers 12F. Breakfast 20F, served 8-10am in a nice dining room. AmEx, Mastercard, Visa.

Hôtel de la Nouvelle France, 31, rue Keller (tel. 47 00 40 74). Mo. Ledru-Rollin. Walk up av. Ledru-Rollin and veer off to the left onto rue Keller. Nothing spectacular, but livable. Eager, English-speaking manager welcomes travelers and longer-term residents—but don't expect great luxury: toilets on hall are Turkish—plant 'em and squat. Singles 100-120F. Doubles 150-180F, with shower and TV 250F. Triples with shower and TV 300. Weekly and monthly rates available. Showers included. No reservations accepted, so likely to have space early in the morning.

Twelfth Arrondissement

Budget hotels cluster in the blocks near the Gare de Lyon, and to the southeast of the Bastille, as well as near pl. de la Nation. A generally safe *arrondissement* (though be careful around train stations); the streets nearer the Bois de Vincennes offer some of the city's cleanest and most pleasant places to stay, making up somewhat for their distance from the city center. Far or near the madding crowds of the Bastille, many of these hotels have space during the summer months. Hotel managers are less likely to speak English than their downtown competitors, but they get by.

Hôtel du Stade, 111, bd. Poniatowski (tel. 43 43 30 38). Mo. Porte Dorée. On the edge of the city and far from the happening center, but in a relatively safe tree-lined neighborhood next to the soothing Bois de Vincennes and worth the trip. After a tiring day in the city, you'll feel like you're coming home. 39 small comfortable rooms with high ceilings, TV, and plenty of afternoon light. Singles and doubles 170F, with shower 220F, with shower and toilet 250F. Extra bed 70F. Showers 20F. Breakfast 25F, served in rooms 6:45-9:30am. Best to reserve in advance by calling between 7am and 8pm, but rooms frequently available. Mastercard, Visa.

Hôtel de Reims, 26, rue Hector Malot (tel. 43 07 46 18). Mo. Gare de Lyon or Ledru-Rollin. From Gare de Lyon, take a right on bd. Diderot and take a left onto rue Hector Malot. Owner from the Savoie has been keeping clean rooms and bathrooms for 23 years by declaring war on dirt. Pink or orange color schemes a little bright but mattresses firm and breakfast served in a fabulous, familial, am-I-really-away-from-home? dining room. Singles 170F. Doubles 210F, with shower 255F, with shower and toilet 270F. Triples with shower 320-360F. Showers 25F. Breakfast 30F, served 7-9am. Call and confirm in writing (no deposit necessary) to reserve. Also a good bet if you arrive in the city without reservations, but look respectable when you show up. Closed Aug.

Grand Hôtel Chaligny, 5, rue Chaligny (tel. 43 43 87 04; fax 43 43 18 47). Mo. Reuilly-Diderot. Move south on bd. Diderot (numbers should decrease) and take a right on rue Chaligny. Classy purple and blue designer bedspreads cover new, firm mattresses in each of the 43 rooms. TV, phone, and plenty of light, artifical and natural, in every room. Management speaks English. Singles and doubles 200F, with shower and toilet 280F, with tub and toilet 290F. Twins with shower and toilet 300F, with tub and toilet 310F. Quads 360F. Extra bed 50F. Showers 25F. Breakfast 25F in salon, 30F in room, served 7-10am. Mastercard, Visa.

Mistral Hôtel, 3, rue Chaligny (tel. 46 28 10 20). Mo. Reuilly-Diderot. Move south on bd. Diderot (numbers should decrease), and take a right on rue Chaligny. Comfortable hotel—firm mattresses, TV in each of the 20 rooms, and impeccable bathrooms. Exudes cleanliness—even the ten-year-old gray carpet doesn't look remotely stained. Singles and doubles 190F, with shower 235F, with shower and toilet 240F. Triples 300F. Quads 320F. Showers included. Breakfast 30F, served in rooms 7-10am. Call between 7am and 11pm to make reservations and confirm in writing. Often has space in July and Aug.

Hôtel du Centre, 112, rue de Charenton (tel. 43 43 02 94 or 43 43 06 40; fax 43 44 98 91). Mo. Gare de Lyon. Move north (numbers should increase) on bd. Diderot, and take a left on rue Hector Malot, then right onto rue de Charenton. Don't let the marble wall decor fool you—this is not a mislabeled luxury hotel. But if the decor is nondescript and sometimes stained, the rooms are spacious, the mattresses OK, and the lump in the middle of the bed is...just an extra pillow. English spoken. Singles 145F (no possibility of shower). Doubles with shower 205F, with shower and toilet 225F, with tub and toilet 245F. Extra bed 80F. Breakfast 25F, served 7-10am. Reservations by phone suffice, but room often available. AmEx, Mastercard, Visa.

Hôtel de l'Aveyron, 5, rue d'Austerlitz (tel. 43 07 86 86). Mo. Gare de Lyon, Quai de la Rapée, or Bastille. From Gare de Nord, take a left on bd. Diderot, a right on rue Bercy, and another right on rue d'Austerlitz. Nothing fancy, but small rooms are clean and comfortable. Staff speaks English, German, and Danish (yes!) and provides a welcoming, lively atmostphere. Singles and doubles 160F, with shower and toilet 240F. Triples 180F, with shower and toilet 280F. Quads with shower and toilet 310F. Hall showers included, making this a very good deal. Breakfast 15F, served 6:30-9:30am. Reservations with deposit recommended. Mastercard, Visa.

Nièvre-Hôtel, 18, rue d'Austerlitz (tel. 43 43 81 51). Mo. Gare de Lyon or Quai de la Rapée. From Gare de Lyon, take a left on bd. Diderot, a right on rue Bercy, and another right on rue d'Austerlitz. Floral wallpaper, nice bathroom tile, and a resident pussy cat make this hotel and its 30 small bedrooms a cheery place to be. High ceilings in some rooms, but no big groups, please. Singles 140-160F. Doubles 180-220F, with shower 240-280F. Showers 20F. Breakfast 20F, served 6-9am. Call for reservations and confirm in writing, but freqently space in summer.

Modern's Hôtel, 11, rue d'Austerlitz (tel. 43 43 41 17 or 43 44 51 16). Mo. Gare de Lyon or Quai de la Rapée. From Gare de Lyon, take a left on bd. Diderot, a right on rue Bercy, and another right on rue d'Austerlitz. While the hotel is worn and not especially new, the mattresses are firm. Manager Joseph Kouby, to whom your deposit check should be made out, speaks English, Arabic, and Hebrew. Singles 130-140F, with shower 196F, with shower and toilet 210F. Doubles 164-174F, with shower 230F, with shower and toilet 244F. Extra bed 40F. Bath 20F. Showers 15F. Breakfast included, served 7:30-9:30am. Call 7am-1pm for reservations and confirm in writing at least one week in advance, with deposit and hour of arrival. Usually 10 rooms free daily if you want to show up.

Hôtel Printania, 91, av. du Dr. Netter (tel. 43 07 65 13). Mo. Porte de Vincennes. Go left onto av. du Dr. Netter off the even side of Cours de Vincennes. 25 tastefully decorated rooms with impeccable bathrooms off long brown hallways, but on the edge of the city. Just off the bustling Cours de Vincennes. Some English spoken. Doubles 150F, with shower and toilet 210F, with shower, toilet, and TV 250F. Showers 25F. Breakfast 25F, served 7-9am in rooms. Call for reservations.

Hôtel Jules-Cesar, 52, av. Ledru-Rollin (tel. 43 43 15 88; fax 43 43 53 60). Mo. Ledru-Rollin or Gare de Lyon. From the Ledru-Rollin metro stop, exit onto av. Ledru-Rollin. TV, direct-line phone, fancy bedspread and airy, light bathrooms with tile halfway up the wall—and you pay for it. Rooms not huge and some showers are just curtained-off pieces of bathroom floor—but bedding excellent. Singles with shower and toilet 310F. Doubles with shower and toilet 330F. Extra bed 80F. Breakfast 25F, served from 7-10:30am. Reservations taken 24 hrs., in English, among a panoply of other languages. Mastercard, Visa.

Fourteenth Arrondissement

Renowned for its nightlife, this commercial district just south of the Latin Quarter attracted artists and literati in the 20s. Picasso and his contemporaries abandoned their traditional haunt of Montmartre for this livelier, more central location. Today, areas closest to the fashionable bd. du Montparnasse maintain their glamour while adjoining neighborhoods have become residential and calm. Be prepared for an abundance of sex-shops and sleazy nightlife at the Northern end of av. du Maine (Mo. Gaîté).

Hôtel de Blois, 5, rue des Plantes (tel. 45 40 99 48). Mo. Mouton-Duvernet. From the metro, swing right onto rue Brezin, cross av. du Maine, continue on rue Sablière, and take your first right onto rue des Plantes. Unquestionably one of the best deals in Paris, considering that these rooms, decked-out with full bathrooms, televisions, telephones, and a Laura Ashley decor, would go for twice the price if there were an elevator in the hotel, but who cares when the stairs are so well maintained? The gracious proprietress, a real jewel compared to the majority in Paris, offers tourist advice and travel directions to her appreciative guests. Doubles 250-300F with bath. Triples 320F. Breakfast 25F.

Hôtel du Midi, 4, av. René-Coty (tel. 43 27 23 25). Mo. Denfert-Rochereau. A large, professionally run hotel, with rooms that recall a Holiday Inn. Antique-style headboards doubling as closets frame the queen-size beds. All rooms come with TV, telephone and a spotlessly clean bathroom. Doubles from 200-320F. Breakfast 26F.

Hôtel Plaisance, 53, rue Gergovie (tel. 45 42 11 39). Mo. Pernety. From the metro, take a right on rue Raymond Losserand, and then a left on rue de Gergovie. On a quiet street in a working-class neighborhood, this hotel, although institutional, is adequately clean and comfortable. Some rooms have frayed drapes and bedspreads (an impalatable shade of yellow), but are in general livable. Singles 100F, with shower and toilet 210F. Doubles 150F, with shower and toilet 240F. Showers 20F. Breakfast 20F.

Hôtel du Parc, 6, rue Jolivet (tel. 43 20 95 54). Mo. Montparnasse-Bienvenue. A large, modern hotel decked out with a marble interior and self-opening doors. Elements of the decor are not always coordinated, but rooms are very clean. You won't feel like a deprived budget traveler at all. Doubles 210F, with bath 320F, with bath and toilet 380F. Breakfast 20F.

Ouest Hôtel, 27, rue Gerbovie (tel. 45 42 64 99). Mo. Pernety or Plaisance. See the directions for Hôtel Plaisance above. The thin wood paneling, institutional gray carpeting, and generally dark decor does little for your spirit; and the stained and cracked tiling don't help. Singles 120F. Doubles 160F, with shower 220F. Showers 20F. Breakfast 20F.

Central Hôtel, 1bis, rue du Maine (tel. 43 20 69 15). Mo. Montparnasse-Bienvenue. A modern hotel with space-age lobby done in glass and mirrors. Rooms are impeccably clean and well-decorated; some look out on a quiet little park that seems to be quite a favorite with local bums. Doubles with bath 300F. Triples with bath 330F. Breakfast 30F.

Fifteenth Arrondissement

The expansive Parc des Expositions, just outside of the Porte de Versailles at the southern end of the 15th, attracts businessmen throughout the winter months to car shows and the area's hotels. When the hall closes in the summer, the hotels go scrambling for business, and tourists can even at times bargain on the price of breakfast when their fellows have swamped the more central *arrondissements.*

Hôtel l Ain, 60, rue Olivier de Serres (tel. 45 32 44 33). Mo. Convention. From the mtro take a left on rue de la Convention, and then a right onto rue Olivier de Serres. On a quiet residential street, this hotel has a pleasantly furnished breakfast room and modern lobby. Adequately clean rooms with whitewashed walls and plaid bedspreads lie up just one flight of stairs. Singles 140F. Doubles 200F, with shower 240F, with shower and toilet 320F. Triples 360F with shower and toilet. Reservations accepted with a deposit for the first night.

Practic Hôtel, 20, rue l Ingenieur Keller (tel. 45 77 70 58). Mo. Charles Michels. From the metro walk towards the river on av. Emile Zola, take a right on rue des Peignot, and a left on rue Ingenier Keller. A cozy family-run hotel with absolutely spotless rooms with sturdy wood furnishings and sparkling tiled bathrooms. About half the rooms have TVs. Doubles 240F with toilet but no shower, 300F with full bath and shower. Triples 400F with bath and shower. Breakfast 28F. Reservations accepted with one night deposit.

Hôtel Mont Blanc, 11, bd. Victor (tel. 48 28 16 79). Mo. Porte de Verailles. From the metro, walk right down Bd. Victor. This hotel sports clean hallways, flowered wallpaper rooms, and a familial management. During the winter it fills with visitors to the exposition hall across the street but is likely to have vacancies in the summer. Singles 150F. Doubles 240F with shower. Triples 300F with shower. Breakfast 25F. Reservations accepted with one night's deposit, but just call ahead during the summer.

Hôtel Printania, 142, bd. Grenelle (tel. 45 79 23 97), south of the Champ de Mars. Mo. La Motte Piquet-Grenelle. The blood-red decor, including red wallpaper, red rugs and red bedspreads can make guests feel they ve stepped into Jack Nicholson's favorite Red Room from *The Shining.* Peeling wallpaper. Singles 195F, 230 with bath. Doubles 240F, 260 with bath. Breakfast 30F. Reservations accepted with first night's deposit.

Sixteenth Arrondissement

The 16th arrondissement will never be the first choice of the budget traveler: sedate and posh, it is better suited to the needs of the multi-star-hotel-seeking voyager. Bargains do exist; check the *Hôtels 1993* guide from the Tourist Office as well as the following.

Hôtel Ribera, 66, rue La Fontaine (tel. 42 88 29 50; fax 42 24 91 33). Mo. Jasmin. Exit on to rue Ribera and turn left on rue La Fontain). Newly renovated, vibrantly colored rooms with impeccable bathrooms in a safe, quiet neighborhood. Reception open 7am-midnight but key or buzzer will get you in before or after. Friendly owner. Mattresses replaced every 3 years. Singles 170F, with shower 200F, with tub or shower and toilet 250F. Doubles 190F, with shower 240F, with tub or shower and toilet 290F. Twin 220F, with shower 260F, with tub or shower and toilet 320F. Triples 240F, with shower 290F. Breakfast 25F, served 7:30-9:30am (excellent bakery next door has baguettes for 3F60, eclairs for 10F; market nearby). Rooms with shower or bath have TV. Reservations recommended 15 days-3 weeks in advance. Call, then confirm in writing by mail or fax. Credit cards accepted.

Villa d'Auteuil, 28, rue Poussin (tel. 42 88 30 37; fax 45 20 74 70). Mo. Michel-Ange-Auteuil. Exit on to rue Donizetti, and turn left on Poussin. Or Mo. Porte d'Auteuil, exit on to bd. Exelmans/

de Montmorency and turn right on Poussin. Magnificent marble entryway leads into high-ceilinged, airy rooms with floral feel and beautiful bathrooms. While some mattresses are newer than others, all rooms boast telephones and ample closet space. Nature lovers will ask for rooms overlooking the *jardin* (read: trees) and feline fearers will stay away from the place: the owner's cat is in permanent residence. Reception 7am-12:30am, but your key will let you in after hours. Singles with either tub or shower and toilet 270F. Doubles with same 310F. Breakfast included. Reservations helpful; always confirm in writing.

Hôtel Mobligado, 7, rue d'Argentine (tel. 45 00 25 61 or 45 00 89 98), near the Arc de Triomphe. Mo. Argentine or Charles de Gaulle-Etoile. Cross to av. de la Grand Armée odd-numbered side and turn left on rue d'Argentine. Worn carpets, porcelain and sloppy caulking, chipped paint on windows and less than polished furniture in twelve rooms, offset by excellent location, firm mattresses, and the occasional splendiferous velvet bedstand. Rooms (single or double occupancy) with shower 260F, with tub and toilet 300F. Breakfast 30F, served in small garden or downstairs mealroom. Reservations in writing. No credit cards.

Hôtel Résidence Chalgrin, 10, rue Chalgrin (tel. 45 00 19 91; fax 45 00 95 41). Mo. Argentine or Mo. Charles de Gaulle-Etoile . Cross to av. de la Grande Armée odd numbered side, turn left on rue d'Argentine, and right on rue Chalgrin. Embroidery-covered walls, creative sculpture, and carriage cab (about as cramped as the cheapest room) lend a homey feel to the lobby of this hotel; the rooms are a bit dim. Family-style breakfast (25F). Guests can get in 24 hrs. a day. Rooms with toilet 150-230F, with tub or shower and toilet (and TV) 270-430F. Direct line telephones in all rooms. Reservations confirmed in writing recommended, especially for April and September. Credit cards accepted (dogs too).

Seventeenth Arrondissement

The 17th probably isn't where you want to stay; its hotels are either expensive stops for executives or cheap places catering as much to drug addicts and people who want a room by the hour as they do to tourists. Even so, we list below some hotels in this neighborhood, for decent exceptions do exist, and they can be a good bargain if you don t mind the clientele next door.

Hôtel Belidor, 5, rue Belidor (tel. 45 74 49 91). Mo. Porte Maillot. Head north on Bd. Gouvion and take your second right onto rue Belidor. A charmingly polite proprietress shows obvious pride in her well-tended establishment, which includes a flowery courtyard and spotless rooms. Singles 128F, with shower 187F, with shower and toilet 235F. Doubles 155F, with shower 214F, with shower and toilet 262F; 80F extra for doubles with two separate beds. Closed Aug.

Hôtel l Avenir, 23, rue Jonquière (tel. 46 27 83 41). Mo. Guy Moquet. A real find in this part of town, with cheery flowered wallpaper and clean bathrooms, and not a derelict in sight. Singles 95F, with shower 125F, with shower and toilet 145F. Doubles 150F, with shower 220F, with shower and toilet 220F. Breakfast 25F.

Hôtel des Deux Avenues, 38, rue Poncelet (tel. 42 27 44 35). Mo. Ternes. From the metro head down av. Ternes, and take your first right on rue Poncelet. A bargain for the location only ten minutes from the Champs-Elysée and Arc de Triomphe; the nondescript rooms are kept clean and tidy. Doubles 220F, with shower 280F, with shower and bath 370F. Showers 20F. Breakfast 25F.

Hôtel des Batignolles, 26, rue des Batignolles (tel. 43 87 70 40). Mo. Place Clichy. The rooms overcome their drab brownness with the amenities of a TV and telephone. Doubles 190F, with shower 310F. Breakfast 25F.

Hôtel des Deux Acacias, 28, rue l Arc de Triomphe (tel. 43 80 01 85; fax 40 53 94 62). Mo. Charles de Gaulle-Etoile. A professional management maintains this primely located hotel only seconds from the Arc de Triomphe, where you have the privilege of paying slightly more than usual for the spotless but nonetheless run-of-the-mill brown wallpaper, brown bedspread combination. Singles 200F. Doubles 260-325F with shower and toilet, depending on size of the room. Breakfast 25F.

Eighteenth Arrondissement

Once a gathering place for artists and intellectuals, the neighborhood between Pigalle and the top of Montmartre now crawls with tourists. Prices have risen accordingly, especially as you approach Sacré-Coeur and place du Tertre. In the other direction, towards the southern border of the 18th *arrondissement* (Mo. Anvers, Pigalle, or Barbès-Rochechouart), the hotels are often brothels—stay away. The following hotels, however, are neither too expensive nor patronized by prostitutes and their clients. Be sure to use the Abbesses metro stop, where the streets are allegedly safer.

Hôtel Tholozé, 24, rue Tholozé (tel., 46 06 74 83). Mo. Abbesses. This small, family-run hotel is on a nice quiet street, away from the noise and "action" of Pigalle. The rooms are of a reasonable size, unadorned, but clean and well-lit. Singles 150F, with shower 200F. Doubles 170F, with shower and toilet 240F. Triples with shower and toilet 300F. Showers 20F. Breakfast 20F.

Ideal Hotel, 3, rue des Trois Frères (tel. 46 06 63 63). Mo. Abbesses. Rooms here are small and bare, but in good repair and clean. On a pleasant street, lively and lined with shops and restaurants, and not at all seedy. Telephone in lobby. Singles 120-130F, wtih shower 200F. Doubles with shower 200F. Showers 20F.

Hôtel André Gill, 4, rue André Gill (tel. 42 62 48 48; fax 42 62 77 92). Mo. Pigalle or Abbesses. A freshly renovated hotel with funky pastel stucco walls and nice modern bathrooms. Rooms are clean, each with its own telephone. Elevator. English spoken. Singles 210F. Doubles 240F, with shower and toilet 300F, with bath and toilet 330F. Triples with bath and toilet 440F. Showers 15F. Breakfast 20F. Credit cards accepted.

Hôtel Beausejour, 1, rue Lepic (tel. 46 06 45 08). Mo. Blanche. On a noisy, busy street, relatively close to the "hotspots" of Montmartre; generally safe area, but very crowded at night. Rooms are somewhat small and dark, but definitely livable. Singles 130-150F. Doubles 190F, with shower 290F. Triples 310F, with shower 370F. Showers 20F. Breakfast 25F.

Nineteenth Arrondissement

The 19th is by no means central; apart from La Villette, you will have to commute into the city to do your sightseeing. And whereas the streets in central Paris are lined with little restaurants and stores, you can find yourself walking significant distances in order to get a bite to eat. Despite these deficiencies, the 19th can be a quite pleasant place to stay: the streets are mostly wide and clean, and are often lined with trees.

Rhin et Danube, 3, place Rhin et Danube (tel. 42 45 10 13). Mo. Danube. Metro leaves you practically at the doorstep. Facing what looks for all the world like a village square, surrounded by little villas, this hotel has the feel of a country inn. Not that it is without modern amenities: every room has a TV, phone, and kitchenette (complete with stove, refrigerator, plates, and silverware). Pleasant decoration, clean rooms. Singles or doubles with bath and toilet 300-330F (with option of taking up to 2 extra people, 50F each). Triples with bath and toilet 380F. Quads with bath and shower (2 people on a large futon) 430F. Eurocard, Mastercard, Visa.

Atlas Hôtel, 12, rue de l'Atlas (tel. 42 08 50 12). Mo. Belleville or Buttes-Chaumont. Renovated in 1992, this clean and friendly hotel boasts new fixtures in all the rooms. English spoken. Singles with sink 130F, with shower and toilet 200, with bath and toilet 220-240F. Doubles with sink 160-170F, with shower and toilet 200F, with bath and toilet 220-240F. Triples with sink 230F. No extra beds. Breakfast not normally provided, but guests have access to a kitchen downstairs.

La Perdrix Rouge, 5, rue Lassus (tel. 42 06 09 53). Mo. Jourdain. Quite plush, really. All rooms have a phone, TV, and toilet. Good location next to a pretty church and a metro stop. Sometimes reception is attended by a person who speaks no English. Singles with shower 260F. Doubles with shower 290F, with bath 310F. Triples with bath 340F. No extra beds. Breakfast 26F. Dog 20F. AmEx (discouraged), Mastercard, Visa.

Crimée Hôtel, 188, rue de Crimée (tel. 40 35 19 57 or 40 36 75 29; fax 40 36 75 29). Mo. Crimée. Rather upscale—modern rooms, all with soundproofing, hair dryer, TV, radio, telephone, and alarm clock. Narrow wheelchair models can fit in elevator. One receptionist has a very limited command of English. Singles with shower and toilet 280F, with bath and toilet 300-310F. Doubles with shower and toilet 310F, with bath and toilet 320-340F. Triples with shower and toilet 380F. Quads with shower and toilet 420F. Extra bed 50F. Breakfast 30F. AmEx, Mastercard, Visa.

Hôtel Polonia, 3, rue Chaumont (tel. 42 49 87 15). Mo. Jaurès or Bolivar. Polish immigrants runs this modest but clean hotel. The restaurant downstairs is a bit of a Polish hangout, even though the 19th *arrondissement* hardly has any Poles. Singles 105F, with shower 235F. Doubles 155-170F. Extra bed 70F. Showers 25F. Breakfast 27F.

Hôtel du Parc, 1, pl. Armand Carrel (tel. 42 08 08 37, 42 08 86 89, or 42 08 55 12; fax 42 45 66 91). Mo. Laumière. Nice location next to a metro stop and the Parc des Buttes Chaumont. Spacious, clean, well-lit rooms, most of which have a view of the park or of the large square in front of it. Since there's an elevator, you might as well ask for a room on the 5th floor, where the view is finest. All rooms have phone, most have TV. Singles or doubles with shower 235F, with shower and toilet 310F, with bath and toilet 390F. Extra bed 100F. Breakfast 30F, served to your room, never downstairs. From Nov.-Feb. prices fall roughly 10%. Mastercard, Visa.

Hôtel des Sciences, 219, rue de Crimée (tel. 40 38 91 00; fax 42 78 25 29). Mo. Crimée. The bathrooms and corridors are somewhat narrow, but the rooms themselves are comfortable. All rooms are clean and equipped with minibar, TV, and phone. Double-glazed windows protect against the noise of the street. Elevator. Unlike most hotels, they don't require a deposit for reservation—simply a letter or fax stating your intention to come. Singles with toilet and shower 300F, with toilet and bath 340F. Doubles with toilet and shower 340F, with toilet and bath 380F. Extra bed 130F. Breakfast 30F. Animal 25F. AmEx, Mastercard, Visa.

Paris Villette, 56, rue Curial (tel. 40 37 50 74; fax 40 37 02 25). Mo. Crimée. From the metro, walk down the rue de Crimée to rue Curial, and turn left, about a 5-min. walk. Clean, comfortable rooms with TV, phone, and hair dryer. Bathrooms smell a bit musty, and the hotel is decorated with paintings that look like they were bought from sidewalk vendors in Montmartre. Wheelchair access. July-Aug. and Dec.-Feb.: singles 250F; doubles 310F. March-June and Sept.-Nov.: singles with toilet and shower or bath 230F; doubles with toilet and shower or bath 250F. Breakfast included.

Twentieth Arrondissement

The hotels situated in this bland expanse of offices and apartment blocks get most of their work from businesspeople. In summer, the slowdown in commercial activity leaves the hotels half-empty, which makes them a very good bet if you're having trouble finding a place to stay.

Hôtel Eden, 7, rue Jean-Baptiste Dumay (tel. 46 36 64 22). Mo. Pyrénées or Jourdain. Good value for your money. Recently renovated, clean, and equipped with wonderfully firm beds. All rooms have TV, phone, shutters, and double glazing. Some double rooms are fairly small, however—it's worth paying the extra 20F to get a bigger one. Elevator, but not wheelchair accessible. Singles 180F. Doubles 220F, with shower and toilet 260-280F. Prices are 20F higher Sept.-July. Breakfast 25F. Dogs 30F.

Hôtel Printana, 355, rue de Pyrénées (tel. 46 36 76 62). Mo. Jourdain. Nice, clean little rooms at very reasonable prices. Run by a pleasant couple who speak no English. Elevator provides wheelchair access. Singles with toilet 120F. Doubles with toilet 180F, with toilet and shower 220F. Triples with toilet and shower 260F. Showers 10F. Breakfast 25F. Downstairs phone 1F per Paris call.

Hôtel Dauphine, 236, rue des Pyrénées (tel. 43 49 47 66; fax 43 36 05 79). Mo. Gambetta. Modern rooms with telephone and TV, and in some cases with a minibar. Elevator, but no wheelchair access. Singles with shower 260F. Doubles with shower 300-340F, with bath 340-400F. Extra bed 70F. Breakfast 25F.

Hôtel Palma, 77, av. Gambetta (tel. 46 36 13 65; fax 46 36 03 27). Mo. Gambetta. Fairly plush modern rooms with TV, phone, and hair dryer. Hallways are narrow and a bit dark, however. Elevator not wide enough for wheelchairs, but 2 rooms on ground floor have wheelchair access. Singles with shower and toilet 330F, with bath and toilet 350F. Doubles with shower and toilet 330-360F, with bath and toilet 350-380F. Triples with bath and shower 435-455F. Breakfast 30F.

Hôtel Pyrénées-Gambetta, 12, av. du Père-Lachaise (tel. 47 97 76 57). Mo. Gambetta. Modern, well-lit, and tastefully decorated. Elevator can accommodate narrow wheelchairs. Rooms with bath have big, airy bathrooms. Singles with toilet and shower 311F, with toilet, shower, TV, and fridge 324F, with toilet, bath, TV, and fridge 337-350F. Doubles with toilet and shower 337F, with toilet, shower, TV, and fridge 350-376F, with toilet, bath, TV, and fridge 376-402F. Breakfast 26F.

Alternative Accommodations

Student Accommodations

Short-term student housing is available in summer in the dormitories of most French universities. Contact the **Centre Régional des Oeuvres Universitaires (CROUS)** (address above).

Cité Universitaire, 15, bd. Jourdan, 14ème (tel. 45 89 35 79). Mo. Cité Universitaire. Forty-four different nations maintain dormitories at the Cité Universitaire, where they lodge their citizens who are are pursuing higher eduction in Paris. During the summer, the dorms lodge anyone on a first-come, first-serve basis, and must be reserved months in advance, at least by April for the months of June and July. If you'd like to stay in the American House write to Fondation Des Etas-Unis, 15, bd. Jourdan, 75690 Paris-Cedex 14 (tel. 45 89 35 79), which rents rooms for 2850F per month during the summer, mostly to students. For information about other dorms, write to M. le Délégué Général de Cité Universitaire de Paris, 19 Bd. Jourdan, 75690 Paris-Cedex 14. No kitchen facilities, but the restaurant in the Maison Internationale offers decent institutional fare at rock-bottom prices. Open Mon-Fri. 11:30am-2:30pm and 6-8:30pm. Meal tickets 11F50.

Bed and Breakfast

Though B&B is not so common a form in France as it is in, say, England, it is still possible to find rooms in homes. **Bed and Breakfast 1,** 73, rue Notre Dame des Champs, 6*ème* (tel. 43 25 43 97; fax 43 54 47 56) arranges stays in Paris and its suburbs. Prices per night (2-night min. stay) range from 210-350F for singles and from 260-450F for doubles, depending on location (the cheaper rooms are all in the farther suburbs) and fanciness of the decor. B&B1 also rents furnished apartments for 400-1000F per night (1-week min. stay). There is a charge of 50F per person per year for using the service, and discounts for stays over 1 month.

Long-Term Accommodations

If you plan to stay in Paris for a longer period of time, consider renting an apartment. Call, fax, write, or visit **Allô Logement Temporaraire,** 4, pl. de la Chapelle, 18*ème* (tel. 42 09 00 07; fax 46 07 14 41; Mo. Chapelle). This helpful, English-speaking association charges a 100F commission for each month of rental if the rental exceeds 5000F. For less expensive apartments, the maximum commission is 600F. In addition, there is an annual membership fee of 250F. When you call or write, be sure to leave a phone or fax number where you can be reached easily. Vacancies come and go very quickly. (Open Tues.-Sat. noon-8pm.) To bypass such commissions, try the bulletin boards in the **American Church** (see Practical Information). Or, look in any of the English-French newsletters like *Free Voice* or *France-USA Contacts,* also available at the American Church. Short-term rentals, usually more expensive per month than longer rentals, can be difficult to procure, especially in winter months. Make sure to sign a contract with your leaser detailing the finances of the transaction, such as the deposit, phone charges, utilities, etc.

Food

"Paris is just like any other city, only people eat better...." Thus the gravelly voice of Maurice Chevalier opens the film *Love in the Afternoon.* It's not an overstatement. Of course, even Parisians don't eat *tournedos Rossini* every day; the human body is simply incapable of processing that much saturated fat. And yes, it's true, the Parisians are ga-ga about McDonald's and Burger King, not all that surprising considering that red meat and french fries have been a staple here for decades, if not centuries. But despite the occasional lapse, Parisians on the whole have a truly phenomenal respect for good food. The soup and salad the Parisian makes at home for dinner may not be fancy, but they are made from fresh ingredients carefully selected from specialized food stores, and are prepared with love and creativity.

French Cuisine

> For a list of French food terms and descriptions of some classic dishes, please consult the Menu Reader at the back of the book.

The aristocratic tradition of extreme richness and elaborate presentation known as **haute cuisine** is actually not French at all; Cathérine des Médicis brought it from Italy along with her cooks, who taught the French to appreciate the finer aspects of sauces and seasonings. In their work and writings, great 19th-century chefs made fine food an essential art of civilized life. To learn about the skills involved—such as preparing base sauces which are in turn combined with other ingredients to make the classic sauces— leaf through the *Larousse Gastronomiqué,* a standard reference for chefs, first compiled in the 19th century. Today, Lyon stakes a strong claim for being the cutting edge of cookery. But as the center of France, Paris attracts master chefs from all over the country. Even though the capital city cannot lay claim to a particular regional cuisine, its restaurants offer specialties from all of France's delectable provinces.

The style made famous in the U.S. by Julia Child is **cuisine bourgeoise,** quality French home-cooking. A glance through her books, *Mastering the Art of French Cooking I & II,* should give you a long list of dishes to try while in France. Both *haute cuisine* and *cuisine bourgeoise* rely heavily on the *cuisine des provinces* (provincial cooking, also called *cuisine campagnarde,* or country cooking), which creates hearty peasant dishes using refined methods. The trendy *nouvelle cuisine,* consisting of tiny portions of delicately cooked, artfully arranged ingredients with light sauces, became popular in the 1970s; since then, its techniques have been integrated with heartier provincial fare. Simple French country meals such as *steak-frites* (steak and fries) or *poulet rôti* (roasted chicken) are staples and can be found for quite reasonable prices at just about every corner in Paris. Parisians eat such food all the time; eating these dishes will give you a more "authentic" taste of Paris than the rich sauces and fine seasonings of *haute cuisine.*

As Captain Hornblower discovered when he was taken prisoner, French **meat** is not all frogs and snails, though those tasty morsels both make great first courses (frog is reminiscent of both chicken and crab; snails taste like succulent shellfish). It is true that the French tend to eat a wider variety of creatures than do most Anglo-Saxons. *Tripes* (stomach lining of a cow) cooked in herbs is well-loved by many; the sausage version is called *andouille* or *andouillette.* Rabbit is fairly common; pigeon, a succulent bird, shows up in casseroles and pastry shells. Skate is an unusual fish that is sometimes bland and tough but can be delectable *au beurre noir.* On rare occasions you might be confronted with horse meat, but it has lost the popularity it once enjoyed. Mostly, though, fine French food consists of less exotic fare: saltwater fishes from the Atlantic or Mediterranean, freshwater fish from the Loire, and grilled or sautéed meats, topped with unforgettable sauces—*bordelais, béchamel,* and their kin—and accompanied by potatoes. Though not all steaks are *tartatre* (raw), most red meat is served quite rare unless you request otherwise.

Vegetables may be overcooked by some standards. The asparagus and the favorite *haricots verts* (green beans) come out limp and buttery. Restaurants often serve *pommes frites* (french fries) or potato *gratins,* potatoes sliced, doused with cream, butter and cheese, and baked in an oven (how French—when in doubt, slather whatever you re making with at least a pint of *crème fraîche* and bake it). Other starches, such as rice, are pretty good, but stay away from the noodles, which are more of a hellish *al Dante* than a nice and firm *al dente.*

Bread is served with every meal. It is perfectly polite to use a piece of bread to wipe your plate (in extraordinarily refined circles, French diners may push their bread around their plates with a fork). The *baguette* is the long, crisp, archetypal French loaf. The *bâtard* has a softer crust, the smaller *ficelle* a thicker, harder crust. *Pain de campagne* is heavier inside than the baguette, and made with whole wheat flour. The *pain complet* is a whole grain loaf, and the *pain à six céréales* is made with six grains. Finally, some argue that the best bread in Paris is the *pain Poilâne,* a sourdough blend baked in a wood-burning oven and available from only a few *boulangeries*—ask around. The cheap, government-subsidized bread you buy from a nameless bakery in Paris may well be the best you have ever eaten; don't hesitate to make it your staple.

The **cheeses** of France are as varied as the wines, yet they fall under three main groups (which is like saying all human beings are either short, tall, or lumpy). Cooked cheeses include beaufort and gruyère. Veined cheeses, such as bleu and roquefort, gain their sharp taste from the molds that are encouraged to grow on them. Soft cheeses, like brie (the king of cheeses) and Camembert round out a basic cheese tray. Tangy *fromages de chèvre* (goat cheeses) come in two forms: the soft, fresh *frais* (fresh) and crumbly, sharp *sec* (dry). Within these broad categories there is much variation.

Among **charcuterie** (cold meat products), the most renowned is *pâté,* a spread of finely minced liver and meat. Often a house specialty, it comes in hundreds of varieties, some highly seasoned with herbs. *Pâté de campagne* (from pork) is chunky, while *pâté de foie* (liver) is soft and silky. (Technically, a *pâté* is baked in a pastry crust, and the variety without a crust is a *terrine.* In practice, *pâtés* with crusts are rare, and the terms are used interchangeably.) *Rillettes,* rich minced pork, is similar to *pâté,* but more greasy. Both *pâté* and *rillettes* are eaten on or with bread, and often garnished with *cor-*

nichons (gherkins). Though the sausages of France are not as famous as the *Wursts* of Germany or the salamis of Italy, dozens of varieties are quite worth sampling, either as a cold appetizer, or hot, as a main course.

French **pastry,** a term including any dough enriched with oil or butter, is one of the major arguments in favor of civilization. Breakfast pastries include the *pain au chocolat* (chocolate croissant) and delectable *croissant aux amandes* (almonds). More elaborate choices are fruit tarts and *flans* (open tarts), including the *chausson aux pommes,* a light pastry with apple filling. Many *gâteaux* (cakes) were invented in the 19th century, such as the chocolate-and-espresso *opéra,* the cream-filled-many-layered *mille-feuilles,* and the *forêt-noire,* a rich slice of fudge with a cherry topping. These can be eaten in the afternoon with tea, after dinner as a dessert—heck, eat pastry whenever you want to. Also good with tea are crumbly cookies like macaroons and *madeleines.*

And of course, **wine.** In France, wine is not a luxury; it is a necessity. During World War I, French infantry pinned down by heavy shellfire had only iron rations brought to them: bread and wine. And when France sent its first citizen into orbit on a Soviet spacecraft, he took the fruit of the vine with him. Wines are distinguished first by color—white wines are produced by the fermentation of the juice of red grapes. Rosés allow some of the red color from the skin to seep in before the skins are removed, and reds come from the fermentation of the juice, skins, and sometimes stems of black grapes. In general, red wine is served with red meat and white wine with fish, but it is the color of the sauce, not the color of the meat, that really matters. Different regions, due to soil, climate, types of grapes, and aging processes, produce widely different wines. Bordeaux wines, contained in bottles with round shoulders, are smokier than Burgundies, whose bottles have sloping sides. When buying wine look for the words *Appellation Controlée* surrounding the name of a region. Don't get too self-conscious about not knowing anything about wine. No one knows everything, and learning about wine is a lifelong process. Waiters can give recommendations, and wine bars (see below) let you sample expensive wines by the glass. Or fall back on the *vin ordinaire* (house wine) of the restaurant—it's usually pretty good.

Other **alcohol** comes before or after dinner. Among the major *apéritifs* (before-dinner drinks) are *kir,* made from white wine and *cassis,* a black currant liqueur *(kir royale* substitutes champagne for the wine); *pastis,* a licorice liqueur diluted with water; *suze,* fermented *gentiane,* a sweet-smelling mountain flower that yields a wickedly bitter brew; and *picon-bière,* beer mixed with a sweet liqueur. It is fairly rare for Parisians to drink these in restaurants; they prefer them at home or, if they are going out, to stop in a bar or café for their drink (this is a good way to kill time before restaurants start serving around 7:30pm). Hard liquor, which dulls the palate, is always reserved until after the meal. Popular *digestifs* are cognac and various brandies, such as Norman *Calvados.*

While Paris is no San Francisco, its general cosmopolitan atmosphere and its history as the capital of a vast empire have provided it with restaurants serving **ethnic cuisine** from all over the globe. Particularly common are North African restaurants, specializing in *couscous,* rice-like particles of semolina flour topped with all sorts of goodies. *Indo-chinoise* restaurants serving Cambodian and Vietnamese specialties are a reminder of the Eastern empire that collapsed at Dien Bien Phu. Other former colonies in the Caribbean and West Africa do their share. Of course, not all diverse gastronomy is the product of exploitative imperialism in the service of finance capital. Paris has attracted cooks from India, China, Japan, Italy, and the United States. You can often eat their cuisines for much less than what you'd pay for a comparable French dinner, perhaps because ethnic restaurants are in general less accepted than French restaurants and have to make their food better and cheaper to attract customers.

Vegetarians may be dismayed by the dearth of strictly vegetarian restaurants in Paris. And, while you should have little trouble finding tastefully prepared vegetables in Paris, they are often cooked with salt, butter, sugar, or meat stock. Furthermore, vegetarians will have trouble eating cheaply in restaurants, since *menus à prix fixe* almost always feature meat or fish. Ordering a salad may prove cheaper (be careful, however, of green salads with eggs, ham, tuna, or chicken in them). A *salade verte* is a green salad with lettuce only; a *salade de tomates* is a delicious tomato topped with vinaigrette. Served with a healthy basket of French bread, both make an inexpensive and surprisingly satisfying meal at a café or *brasserie*. *Viande* refers only to red meat. If you don't eat pork, chicken, fish, eggs, or dairy products, you should clearly state this to the server. Ethnic cuisine, especially Vietnamese and North African, often provide excellent vegetarian options. American-style health food merchandising is entirely un-French, but is nevertheless starting to catch on in Paris. Look for health food stores (*diététiques* or *maisons de régime*). Health food products are sometimes referred to as *produits à santé* and are often availabe in supermarkets. *Biologique* refers to organically grown food. For information about traveling as a vegetarian, consult the **North American Vegetarian Society,** P.O. Box 72, Dolgeville, NY 13329 (tel. (518) 568-7970), or the **Vegetarian Society of the U.K.,** Parkdale, Dunham Rd., Altrincham, Cheshire WA14 4QG (tel. (061) 928 07 03).

Kosher travelers and anyone else looking for a good deli should stroll through the Jewish neighborhood around rue des Rosiers, in the fourth *arrondissement,* where you'll find an assortment of delicious bakeries, groceries, and kosher restaurants. You might also ask at the synagogue for tips (see Practical Information). Given the large North African community that has settled in Paris, **halal** food should also be readily available, particularly in the fifth, 19th, and 20th *arrondissements.*

Breakfast *(petit déjeuner)* is usually light, consisting of bread and sometimes *croissants* or *brioches* and *café crème* (espresso with hot milk) or hot chocolate. Many people still eat **lunch** *(déjeuner)*, the largest meal of the day, between noon and 2pm. Most shops, businesses, and government agencies close for two hours during this time; Paris has four rush hours—morning, evening, and two in the middle of the day as people hurry home and back. But this tradition is slowly giving way as more working Parisians choose to take their two-hour lunches in restaurants with friends and colleagues.

Dinner *(dîner)* begins quite late, and goes on for hours as revelers extend their meals into the early morning. Traditionally, the complete French dinner includes an *apéritif, entrée* (appetizer), *plat* (main course), salad, cheese, desserts, fruit, coffee, and a *digestif.* The French generally take wine with their meals, but mineral water is an almost acceptable substitute. Order sparkling *(eau pétillante* or *gazeuse)* or flat mineral water *(eau plate).* Ice cubes *(glaçons)* are rare. To order tap water, ask for *une carafe d'eau.* Finish the meal with espresso, which comes in lethal little cups. Of course, few Parisians indulge in the entire ritual frequently; most eat only an abbreviated version in a restaurant.

French etiquette dictates keeping the hands above the table, not in the lap. As many a high school French teacher will attest, if you put your hands out of view, your companions may ask what you're doing with them. Elbows shouldn't rest on the table, but they often do. If you want to try eating in true French manner, hold your fork in your left hand, your knife in the right, and scoop food onto your fork with the sharp edge of the knife (not with the dull edge—that's British). A last word: don't say *"Je suis plein, "* meaning "I'm full." This phrase is used for cows, and means they're pregnant. A more polite way of refusing food: *"Je n'ai plus faim."* (I'm not hungry anymore.)

How to afford the food in Paris

With a little praticality, and lots of *savoir-faire*, it's possible to eat like an emperor in Paris, on a peasant's budget. At breakfast-time, head to the nearest *boulangerie* for croissants of all varieties, often still warm from the oven. *Boulangeries* also sell delicious sandwiches (12-25F) throughout the day, an excellent option for a cheap lunch. For the classic sandwich, ask for *jambon et gruyère* (ham and cheese); if you're starved for vegetables, the *crudités* sandwich is a delectable lettuce, tomato, and hard-boiled egg concoction. Although these are traditionally made with a fresh-baked *demi-baguette,* a few sandwiches with *pain americain* are often available for the philistines who prefer WonderBread to French panache. If you can't speak French, just point.

And, of course, if you get hungry at any point during the day, the *boulangeries* and *patisseries* have *lots* of options for heavenly snacking (see Pastries, above). For a more nutritional snack, stop at a fruit stand or buy some bread and cheese. Plan on splurging once a day on a real sit-down meal. This is important, for your health, sanity, and karma. After all, you wouldn't want to spend a whole day in Paris without using our fine six page menu-reader! And indeed, you only live once. Many restaurants have cheaper *menus* at lunch; consider following the French and having a long mid-day meal, followed by a heavenly afternoon siesta.

Finally, anyone with a student ID can buy meal tickets at each restaurant from 11:30am to 1:30pm and from 6 to 8pm. (Tickets 18F40, *carnet* of 10 100F.) University restaurants are often crowded with students, thus providing a good opportunity to meet some local friends. For more information, including summer and weekend schedules, stop at **CROUS**, 30, av. Georges Bernanos, *5ème* (tel. 40 51 36 00; Mo. Port-Royal). The following University Restaurants are most convenient but the list is not nearly exhaustive. In addition, all the following, except Citeaux, Grand Palais, and C.H.U. Necker are also *brasseries,* open between lunch and dinner for sandwiches and drinks.

Bullier, 39, av. Georges Bernanos, *5ème.* Mo. Port-Royal. **Cuvier-Jussieu,** 8bis, rue Cuvier, *5ème.* Mo. Cuvier-Jussieu. **Censier,** 31, rue Geoffroy St-Hilaire, *5ème.* Mo. Censier Daubenton. Closed for dinner. **Châtelet,** 10, rue Jean Calvin, *5ème.* Mo. Censier Daubenton. **Mazet,** 5, rue Mazet, *6ème.* Mo. Odéon. **Assas,** 92, rue d'Assas, *6ème.* Mo. Port-Royal or Notre-Dame-des-Champs. Closed for dinner. **Mabillon,** 3, rue Mabillon, *6ème.* Mo. Mabillon. **Grand Palais,** cours de la Reine, *8ème.* Mo. Champs-Elysées Clemenceau. **Citeaux,** 45, bd. Diderot, *12ème.* Mo. Gare de Lyon. **C.H.U. Pitié-Salpe-Trière,** 105, bd. de l'Hôpital, *13ème.* Mo. St-Marcel. **Dareau,** 13-17, rue Dareau, *14ème.* Mo. St-Jacques. **C.H.U. Necker,** 156, rue de Vaugirard, *15ème.* Mo. Pasteur. **Dauphine,** av. de Pologne, *16ème.* Mo. Porte Dauphine.

Restaurants

The world's first restaurant was born in Paris over 200 years ago. Ironically, its purpose was not to indulge its clientele with delicious foods and wines, but rather to restore (from the French verb *restorer)* over-fed party-goers (most of Parisian high society throughout history) to a state of physical health. Restaurants were a social respite from the high-calorie world of soirées, balls, and private diner parties. Here, one could be in a social atmosphere and eat nothing. Instead, one was served a single glass of a ghastly brew made from concentrated meat and vegetable products.

Happily, the only similarity between Parisian restaurants today and their primordial ancestors is that they remain highly social milieus. The following restaurants, arranged by *arrondissement,* are a sure bet for an authentically prepared French meal (or ethnic equivalent). Prices are high, and a memorable meal will cost 100F or more, though you can eat satisfactorily for 50F. Technically, a **bistro** is different from a restaurant in that it should have a bar and be less formal, but that distinction has largely been lost, and you can pay as much in a bistro as in a restaurant for the same food. **Brasseries** typically offer a wide selection of beers and lean toward a more hearty Alsatian cuisine—lots of *choucroute,* a sauerkraut and sausage meal. Usually crowded and lively, *brasseries* are best for large groups and high spirits.

Most people in **restaurants** will order multiple courses, but you are under no obligation to do so. Don't order more than you want simply because you are afraid of doing the wrong thing. If you do want two or three courses, you will almost always save money by ordering the *menu à prix fixe* (fixed-price meal) that costs less than ordering *à la carte* and includes an appetizer such as *pâté, crudités,* or soup; a main course; and cheese and/or dessert. *Boissons compris* on a menu means that wine is included in the price; *boissons non compris* means the opposite. Service is included in the check *(l'addition)* which may be a long time in coming—spending two hours in a restaurant is not unusual. If you are particularly pleased with the service, feel free to leave a small cash tip as a sign of your gratitude (anywhere from a few francs to 5% of the check) but don't feel obligated.

Wander around looking for the authenticly French restaurant, avoiding the many that concentrate on volume rather than quality. It's admittedly hard to tell how seriously a place takes its food just from the menu, but avoid the telltale signs of an unsatisfying meal, such as an advertised "tourist special," a menu in any language but French, or any place that offers you raw vegetable *crudités*—often just a mound of carrot shreds—as an entrée on a *prix-fixe menu.*

Restaurant Chains

Just because a restaurant has more than one location doesn't mean it's a fast-food franchise. Look for these around the city.

La Criée, 15, rue Lagrange, 5ème (tel. 43 54 23 57). Mo. Maubert-Mutalité. 31, bd. Bonne Nouvelle, 2ème (tel. 42 33 32 99). Mo. Bonne Nouvelle. 84, bd. Montparnasse (tel. 42 22 01 81). Mo. Montparnasse-Bienvenue. Except for the sushi bars that abound in Paris, this is one of the few places that you'll be able to afford eating anything that came out of the sea. The service is pleasant, and the prices are good considering the quality of the food. Two fish next to an item on the menu indicate that it is recommended by the chef. 2-course *menu* (main course plus appetizer or dessert) 79F. Grilled sardines 60F, salmon scallops 70F.

Léon de Bruxelles, 8, pl. de la République, 11ème (tel. 43 38 28 69). Mo. République. Also on the Champs Elysées, 8ème (tel. 42 36 18 50) and in Les Halles, 1er (tel. 42 36 18 50). Léon started selling his mussels in Brussels in 1893; his Paris versions are popular with the local crowd. Heaps of mussels—fried, with snails, with *crème,* with all kinds of sauces (45-75F)—served up in classy creamy-decorated surroundings. Mussels and fries from 59F. The *complet*—appetizer, beer, mussels, and fries—will indeed finish you off (98F). Wonderfully located in the always eventful pl. de la République (but beware of pickpocketers at night). Business cards and menus in the shape of a shell. Open daily 11:45am-12:30am.

Bistro Romain has over 40 locations around Paris. Chain or no, the combination of plush benches, tapestry-covered walls, and reasonably priced food is tough to beat—reliable if not exceptional. At lunch, their 59F *Les Express menu* gives a choice of filling dishes; another *menu* at 75F90 is more appropriate for dinner. In the summer, the 89F *menu* full of fruit and fish lightens up the day. Dinner a la carte is around 130F. Desserts are the Bistro's specialty, however—they offer a choice of 35. Chocolate addicts will die for the *Colisée,* alternating layers of bitter chocolate mousse and white chocolate mousse with a fine layer of milk chocolate shavings (29F90). Credit cards accepted. Open daily 11:30-1am.

Hollywood Canteen, 4, rue Pierre Lescot, 1er (tel. 42 33 56 30). Mo. Châtelet-Les-Halles. 8, rue de Berri, 8ème (tel. 45 62 35 97). Mo. Georges V. 53, rue de la Harpe, 5ème (tel. 46 33 89 33). Mo. St-Michel. 18, bd Montmartre, 9ème (tel. 42 46 46 45). Mo. Rue Montmarte. 25, rue de la Roquette, 11ème (tel. 47 00 18 28). Mo. Bastille. They also have their own *boutique traiteur* (food shop) at 29, rue de Charenton, 12ème (tel. 40 02 09 42). Mo. Bastille. More American than America itself. Neon-illuminated 1950s-style diner grills decent burgers named after American movie stars (24-44F) and serves 'em up with a miniature stars and stripes stuck in the top. Not even French pastry can beat their sumptuously huge brownies drowned in ice cream and chocolate sauce (30F). Open Mon.-Sat. noon-10pm.

Ile St-Louis

The restaurants on Ile-St-Louis are everything you'd expect: expensive, romantic, and full of charming half-timbered rooms and quaint brass-pot-dangling walls. Come here for classic French cuisine and look for the bargain *menu* that just might make it affordable.

Auberge de la Reine Blanche, 30, rue St-Louis-en-l'Ile (tel. 46 33 07 87). Mo. Pont Marie. A small, charming restaurant, full of the delicious aromas of French cuisine. Covers all the bases of traditional French cooking, with lots of veal, lamb, and beef served with heavy sauces. The walls are a light peach, covered with hand-carved dollhouse furniture; the clientele is a pleasant mixture of families and middle-aged couples. Dinner a la carte can be quite expensive, but *menus* of 85F and 130F provide an option for the budget traveler. Open daily noon-11:30pm. Credit cards accepted. Reservations recommended for dinner.

Au Gourmet de l'Isle, 42, rue St-Louis-en-l'Ile (tel. 43 26 79 27). Mo. Pont Marie. A dark, cozy restaurant, with walls covered by wooden grills and wine bottles. Traditional French cuisine, with a specialty of *Pavé de Saumon à l'Estragon* (salmon steak with tarragon). The clientele is local, as is the *Maître.* Dinner a la carte is expensive, but a 125F *menu* is quite reasonable, given the food and the location. Open Wed.-Sun. noon-2pm and 1-10pm. Credit cards accepted. Reservations recommended for dinner.

Restaurant Monte Cristo, 21, rue St-Louis-en-l'Ile (tel. 46 33 35 46). Mo. Pont Marie. A truly delightful restaurant that is long, narrow, and stylishly decorated with plants and Art Nouveau lamps. The specialties are pasta, veal dishes, and sorbets. Dinner *menus* at 98F and 118F. This place fills up early, so it is best to reserve ahead. Open daily 1-11:30pm. Credit cards accepted.

First Arrondissement

The small streets around Palais-Royal teem with small, traditional restaurants, each one worth a special visit. Plus, you'll find some truly awe-inspiring buys. For faster meals and a younger crowd, head toward Les Halles, at the eastern edge of the *arrondissement*, where you'll find everything from fast food to 4-course Italian and American follies.

La Mangerie, 17, rue des Petits Champs, not to be confused with rue Croix des Petits Champs (tel. 42 97 51 01). Mo. Bourse. Casual, understated refinement in a little restaurant with a view of the Palais Royal and its gardens. *Plat du jour* for around 60F, *entrecôte* 65F. Wonderful but expensive pastries. The room in the back is the one with the view; the room in front is where you should sit if you're in a hurry. The place fills up, so it's worth making reservations. Open Mon.-Fri. noon-2pm.

Lescure, 7, rue de Mondovi (tel. 42 60 18 91). Mo. Concorde. Lively ambience has accompanied hearty French cuisine for over 70 years in this popular restaurant. 98F *menu* (includes three courses and wine) offers a wide selection and huge servings. Open Mon.-Fri. noon-2:15pm and 7-10pm. Sat. noon-2:15pm. Closed in Aug.

L'Incroyable, 26, rue de Richelieu or 23, rue de Montpensier, (tel. 42 96 24 64). Mo. Palais-Royal. Certainly incredible, this intimate restaurant serves up a three-course *menu* at an *incroyable* 58F (in the evening 68F). *Foie de veau* 55F, *confit de veau* 70F. Choose between the little terrace and quaintly decorated interior. Open Tues.-Fri. 11:45am-2:15pm and 6:30-9pm, Sat. and Mon. 11:45am-2:15pm. Closed in late Dec. and for the first three weeks of Jan.

La Moisanderie, 52, rue de Richelieu or 47, rue Montpensier (tel. 42 96 92 93 or 42 96 93 98). Mo. Palais Royal. A two-level restaurant serving a pleasant 3-course *menu* for 68F. The decor is charming: the rue de Richelieu level has wood paneling and copies of medieval tapestries, while the rue Montpensier level has stone walls like a castle. The service can be rather slow, however, so don't come here if you're in a hurry. Open Mon.-Sat. noon-3pm and 7-10pm. AmEx, Diner's Club, and Visa accepted.Flunch, 5-7, rue Pierre Lescot. Mo. Châtelet-Les Halles. If you're around Les Halles and you want to eat quickly, be warned that the lines at the "fast food" chains can be very long. You might instead want to try this cafeteria-style self-service restaurant, which gives you quick access to reasonably good food in a clean and pleasant environment. Open daily 11am-3pm, 5:30pm-10pm.

Le Carpaccio, 6, rue Pierre Lescot (tel. 45 08 44 80). Mo. Les Halles. Conveniently located for visits to Les Halles or the Centre Pompidou, this restaurant offers outstanding Italian food at affordable prices. They have a variety of two-course *menus,* ranging in price from 52 to 89F. Don't think it's a 4-course *menu* that you're getting—the menu is confusing on this point. Better yet, try the namesake *carpaccio:* wafer-thin slices of beef (57F), tuna, or salmon (89F), served with a house sauce and fresh bread. Trust the waiter on the choice of wine to accompany this. If you feel like celebrating, note that the pastries, as well as the aperitif called "Bellini" (peach liqueur and wine), are memorable. Open daily 11:30am -12:30am.

Le Grand Echiquier, 30, rue de la Grand Truanderie. Mo. Les Halles. Because of the popularity of dining on a terrace, many restaurants in Paris try to pack too many tables into small open-air enclosures. Not so at the *Grand Echiquier*, whose spacious terrace contributes to its generally relaxed and pleasant atmosphere. A la carte items are fairly expensive (72F for Basque chicken, 89F for duck in mushroom sauce), but the two-course *menu* for 68F is a good value. Among the appetizers, the *salade melée aux gésiers de canard* (mixed salad with duck giblets) is particulary worth trying. Open daily 12:15-3pm, 7:15-11:30pm.

Au Petit Ramoneur, 74, rue St-Denis. Mo. Les Halles. Exceptional value for your money. 61F *menu* includes appetizer, main course, salad, dessert, and half a liter of wine. The food is hearty, and the restaurant has a solid, working-class feel to it. The only real drawback is that seating can be quite cramped. The restaurant's location is convenient if you're visiting St-Eustache or Les Halles, or if you want to see a porn movie. Sit on the terrace and watch businessmen in suits darting into gaudily lit sex stores where they watch videos or buy unique toys. Open Mon.-Fri. 11:30am-2:30pm and 6:30pm-9:15pm.

L'Epi d'Or, 25, rue J.-J. Rousseau. Mo. Les Halles. Expensive, but a meal to remember. The dignified interior is adorned with linen tablecloths and polished wood. Service is polite, the clientele refined. *Onglet à l'échalotte* (flank steak) 80F, heavenly *entrecôte Bordelaise* 95F, steak *tartare* 90F. Open Mon.-Fri. noon-2:30pm, 7:30-11:30pm; Sat. 7:30-11:30pm.

L'Emile, 76, rue J.J.-Rousseau. Mo. Les Halles. This charming little restaurant has a sophisticated but unpretentious atmosphere. Tastefully decorated and run by friendly people who take obvious pride in their work, it serves very good food at reasonable prices. If only they could all be like this. Three-course lunchtime *menu* for 78 F. A la carte, veal with green lemon is 88F, beef with onion preserves 78F. As in many of the best restaurants, the menu changes with the seasons, so a la carte items may vary. Open Mon.-Fri. noon-2:30pm, 8pm-midnight; Sat. 8pm-midnight.

The Front Page, 56-58, rue St-Denis. Mo. Châtelet-Les Halles. The menu declares "I must be suffering from a mental disease" to choose American over French cuisine. Nonetheless such follies have arisen in the past and are likely to recur. The Front Page is an expensive but lively restaurant which offers warm memories of the New World. Elaborate burgers for 56F and up. Open daily 11:30am-5am.

Second Arrondissement

If you're down near the Louvre and can't find anything cheap, consider walking a few blocks north for better values. You'll find lots of small establishments, spreading an eclecticism that in itself is a statement of defiance to the Louvre's classical façade.

A la Perdrix, 6, rue Mandar (tel. 42 36 83 21). Mo. Sentier. Great food at reasonable prices. The 57F *menu* includes 3 courses and a drink. A la carte: *entrecôte* 55F, *cassoulet au confit de canard* 75F. Succulent homemade desserts. The decor is rustic—wood paneling and a boar's head—but the crowd is urban office workers. Big windows and high ceilings stave off claustrophobia. Open Mon.-Fri. 11:30am-3pm and 6:30-10pm, Sat. 6:30-10pm.

Babylone, 34, rue Tiquetonne (tel. 42 33 48 35). Mo. Etienne-Marcel. Revelers streaming out of discos after midnight pour into this Afro-Caribbean restaurant for ethnic dishes like *gombo* and *maffé*. Banana leaves, bamboo, and drums hang from the ceiling, and the walls are adorned with zebra-skin wallpaper and African carvings. Dance music, much of it from the Caribbean, blares over the speaker system. Prices are fairly high: main course between 70 and 100F. Aperitifs 35-65F, punch 40F, cocktails 50F. Open nightly 8pm-8am.

Crémerie Louvois, 5, rue Louvois (tel. 42 96 64 05). Mo. Quatre-Septembre. Quick service, good simple food, low prices. A 3-course *menu* for 48F (2 courses for 42F). A 10cl glass of red wine only 3F. Open Mon.-Sat. 11:30am-2:45pm. Closed in Aug.

Robata, 60, rue Montorgueil (tel. 42 33 49 61). Mo. Sentier or Etienne-Marcel. Except for its all-Western clientele and location on a Paris market street, this restaurant might as well be in Tokyo. If you sit at the bar, you see a cook with a Japanese sweatband slaving over a charcoal grill; what he produces is certainly worth the sweat. Several *menus* with soup, rice, and grilled meat or fish are available, the cheapest being 42F (lunch only). Dinner *menus* 41-150F. Open Mon.-Sat. noon-2:30pm and 7-10:45pm.

Ma Normandie, 11, rue Rameau (tel. 42 96 87 17). Mo. Pyramides. Down from the Bibliothèque Nationale on the pl. Louvois. A crowded restaurant with a jovial, laid-back atmosphere. A 51F *menu* promises *service rapide* to a largely business crowd. The regulars clamor for *couscous* on the days they have it. The 105F dinner offers a variety of meat selections. Open Mon.-Sat. 11:30am-3:30pm.

Le Drouot, 103, rue de Richelieu (tel. 42 96 68 23). Mo. Richelieu-Drouot or Bourse. Situated near the Bourse des Valeurs, this restaurant has the busy atmosphere of a stock-market trading pit. Despite the hubbub, it's a pleasant place to eat: good food, low prices, and classy interior decoration from 1938. They print a new menu everyday, but some dishes are available most days: grilled steak 45F, fried chicken 33F, grilled fish 43F. Note that you don't save money by ordering the set of items called the "suggestion du chef." Open daily 11:45am-3pm and 6:30-10pm.

Au Lyonnais, 32, rue St-Marc (tel. 42 96 65 04). Mo. Richelieu-Drouot or Bourse. Pleasant food in a classy but relaxed environment. *Caille rotie* (roast quail) or *lapin aux echalottes* (rabbit with shallots) 70F. Two-course *menu* 51F. If you take a *cassoulet lyonnais* (white bean and meat casserole), have it with wine—as tradition prescribes, the dish is greasy. Open Mon.-Fri. 11:30am-2:45pm or 6:30pm-midnight, Sat. 6:30pm-midnight.

Aux Caves de Bourgogne, 3, rue Palestro (tel. 42 36 38 55). Mo. Réaumur-Sébastopol. Hanging from the walls are a horse harness, a few agricultural implements, and some wood carvings of country scenes. On top of this, reasonably good food and friendly service complete the impression of a tavern in rural Burgundy. Beef *bourguignon* 49F, trout *bourguignon* 55F, steak *tartare* 59F. Three-course *menu* 75F. Open Mon.-Fri. 11:45am-2pm and 7:30-10pm, Sat. 7:30-10pm. Closed in Aug.

Au Clair de Lune, 27, rue Tiquetonne (tel. 42 33 59 10). Mo. Etienne-Marcel. Friendly service and very large helpings of good French or Algerian food at moderate prices. *Couscous* 44-58 F. *Entrecôte* 52F. Three-course *menu* 62F. Open daily noon-3pm and 7:30-11pm.

Yadgar, 9, rue Tiquetonne (tel. 40 26 46 98). Mo. Etienne-Marcel. Very good value for your money. Generous portions of good, spicy Pakistani food for 20-30F. Very authentic: they speak bad French and no English. A 3-course *menu* is 49F at lunch, 59F at dinner. Try getting a student discount: at lunch this should entitle you to a dish with rice and bread for 20F, at dinner to a dish with rice only for 35F. Open Mon.-Fri. 11am-2:30pm and 7:30-11:30pm, Sat.-Sun. 7:30-11:30pm.

Country Life, 6, rue Daunou (tel. 42 97 48 51). Mo. Opéra. Vegetarian *haute cuisine* in a charming, wooded health food store. 58F buffet includes soups and salads as well as hot and cold entrees. Open Mon.-Fri. 11:30am-2:30pm. Store open Mon.-Thurs. 10am-6:30pm, Fri. 10am-3pm.

Donys, 8, rue Etienne Marcel, on the corner of rue St-Denis. (tel. 42 36 28 30). Mo. Etienne-Marcel. Huge, greasy, great-tasting Greek sandwiches for 22F; one of the best deals around. Those who want to avoid the grease should go for the tuna sandwich (12F). If you're coming here for a late-night snack, avoid walking down the rue St-Denis, which can get a little intimidating after midnight. Open daily 10am-2pm and 4pm-7am.

Third Arrondissement

The Marais offers classic Parisian restaurants with traditional food, a local clientele, and a quiet conversation-fostering atmosphere. Sound good? Even better, they cost much less than the "traditional" restaurants in more touristed areas.

Le Hangar, impasse Berthaud. Mo. Rambuteau. Tucked away in a dead-end street off Rue Rambuteau, this is a quiet haven to eat in before or after a visit to the Centre Pompidou. Very good French food; popular with people from the neighborhood. *Steak Tartare* 54F, *Andouillette de Chablis* (approved by the demanding A.A.A.A.A.) 64F, *Coquilles St-Jacques* 98F. Open Mon. 7pm-midnight, Tues.-Sat. noon-midnight. Between 3:30 and 7pm, they serve tea and cakes but no meals.

Les Arcades, 4, rue Charlot, (tel. 48 87 57 85). Mo. Filles du Calvaire. A small restaurant frequented mainly by people from the neighborhood. 58F *menu* includes a wide choice of 3 courses plus ¼liter of wine. Prices a la carte are not much higher: chicken with olives costs 40F; steak is 50F. Pleasant service. Avoid the chocolate mousse, but the chocolate cake is very good. Open Mon.-Sat. 8am-2am.

La Taverne, 5, place de la Republique. Mo. Republique. If you are a beer fan in search of something exotic, this place is for you. The menu features mussels cooked in beer (54F, plus 20F if you take a side order of *pommes frites*) and beer fondue. This is not a frat-party joke—the tavern is deadly serious about providing Belgian cuisine, which happens to rely heavily on Belgium's distinctive beers, *gueuze* and *kriek.* The prices are fairly high (the set *menu* is 105F), but the portions are generous. Seating is available in the back and in the basement, in case you want to avoid the noise and pollution on the terrace. Open daily 9am-2am.

Le Bourgeois Gentilhomme, 75, rue des Archives (tel. 42 78 59 08). Mo. Arts et Métiers. Pleasant neighborhood restaurant, serving reasonable food at good prices. A 3-course *menu* costs 62F. A la carte: fowl with lemon (57F), beef *Bourgeois Gentilhomme* (68F), and duck in honey sauce (94F). Open Mon.-Fri. noon-2:30pm, 7:30-9:30pm.

Fourth Arrondissement

Running through the fourth is the **rue des Rosiers,** the focus of the city's Jewish community. Here you'll find superb kosher delicatessens and Middle-Eastern *patisseries,* though their offerings can be costly. The area remains lively on Sundays, when many other districts shut down.

Le Petit Bain, 9, rue St-Merri (tel. 40 27 86 80). Mo. Rambuteau. Fine dining at resonable prices, just a few steps away from the Pompidou Center. Its location next to a public swimming pool has bequeathed this elegant, informal place its name—which means the little swim—and suggested its decor, as artsy seaside photographs of swimmers plaster the walls. Two-course lunch *menu* 55F. Cocktails 45-65F. Apéritifs 22-55F. 2-course *menu* 85F, 3-course 115F. All a la carte dishes 85F. Open Mon.-Sat. noon-2:30pm and 7pm-midnight.

L'Arbre Aux Sabots, 3, rue Simon Leclerc (tel. 42 71 10 24). Mo. Rambuteau. The decoration (a lot of Klimt, some temporary art exhibits), and a good location near the Pompidou Center may explain why this restaurant attracts such an artsy crowd. It can't hurt that the *menu* is a bargain: 65F for 3 courses of reasonably good food plus ¼liter of wine. A la carte mixed fish with wine sauce is 70F, *emincé* of fowl with liqueur 65F. Open Mon.-Fri. noon-midnight.

Aquarius, 54, rue Ste-Croix-de-la-Bretonnerie (tel. 48 87 48 71). Mo. Hôtel de Ville. Give your body a rest from the all-too-frequent Parisian combination of animal fats and smoke-filled rooms. Aquarius serves fresh and wholesome vegetarian food, and asks its customers not to smoke. The seating is at long tables, rather like a college dining hall, but the service is polite and discreet. *Plat du jour* 41F (51F including dessert). Fresh juice (fruit or vegetable) 17-18F. Herbal teas 9-15F.

Open Mon.-Thurs. noon-10pm., Fri.-Sat. noon-10:30pm. The *plats du jour,* cereals, and hot vegetable dishes are served only noon-2pm and 7-10pm. Closed Aug.

La Dame Tartine, 2, rue Bisemiche (tel. 42 77 32 22). Mo. Rambuteau. From the ample terrace, you can watch the sculptures in the Stravinsky fountain bobbing about. The restaurant itself has an atmosphere almost as lively as the fountain. A mostly young crowd. Good value for your money—main courses 20-36F. Open daily noon-11:30pm.

Chez Jo Goldenberg, 7, rue des Rosiers. Mo. St-Paul. A popular kosher delicatessen since 1920. In the heart of Paris's historic Jewish quarter, Goldenberg attracts a crowd with large servings of superb old-fashioned Central European cookery. Target of a 1985 terrorist attack that claimed the life of the owner's son, the restaurant seems to have recovered. Jewish-interest Paris papers available. *Plat du jour* 70F. Take-out section where you can buy borscht, sauerkraut, pickles, pastries, and other traditional foods. Deli open daily 8:30am-11pm; dining room open daily noon-midnight.

Le Trumilou, 84, quai de l'Hôtel de Ville (tel. 42 77 63 98). Mo. Hôtel de Ville. Pleasant bistro atmsphere right opposite the Seine. Good meals in a simple but pleasant dining room or on sidewalk tables. *Menus* with moderate choice at 60F and 78F. The helpful staff shows no sign of the condescension that characterizes the waiters at many restaurants that cater (as this one does) to a number of tourists. Open Tues.-Sun. noon-3pm and 7-11pm.

Chez Marianne, 2, rue des Hospitaliers St-Gervais (tel. 42 72 18 86). Mo. St-Paul. Nearly every Israeli specialty and many Eastern European ones served here. Known for falafel (30F), blini, pirogi, and *gâteau de fromage,* a delicious treat rather different from what Americans call cheesecake. Popular and friendly. Sit in a cozy dining room and order 4, 5, or 6 specialties (50F, 60F, or 70F) from options such as chopped liver, tabouli, and hummus. Take-out available. Open Sat.-Thurs. 11am-midnight.

Au Paradis du Fruit, 1, rue des Tournelles (tel. 40 27 94 79). Mo. Bastille. Creative health food café with an inviting, colorful interior. Delicious fresh juices 18F. "Paradise salads" 55-69F. Mostly lighter fare, but in autumn and winter they have stews called *"marmites."* Open daily 11am-2am; last service at 1am.

Fifth Arrondissement

A bustling street in a student and tourist neighborhood where a rainbow of ethnic restaurants compete for business through rock-bottom pricing, the **rue Mouffetard** indisputably constitutes the culinary heart and center of the fifth *arrondissement.* Spreading from the "Mouf," traditional and ethnic restaurants spill down through the rue Descartes, all the way to join the bd. St-Germain, attracting not only locals, but large crowds of tourists in search of a cheap and filling meal. The specialty on the Mouf is enormous shwarma sandwiches, which come with a side of crispy fries for only 22F, and can be bought at any of the numerous sandwich stands lining the sidewalks.

L Estrapade, 15, rue de l Estrapade (tel. 43 25 72 58). Mo. Luxembourg or Place Monge. This tiny bistro, decorated in non-traditional tones of salmon and green, specializes in exquisitely prepared traditional French cuisine. Lunch *menu* quite affordable at 75F. Dinner a la carte runs 70-90F. Open Wed.-Mon. noon-2:30pm and 7-11pm.

Chez Lena et Mimille, 34, rue Tournefort (tel. 47 07 72 47). Mo. Censier Daubenton. One of the only places in the neighborhood that really *cares* about its food. Truly elegant traditional French cuisine served in this small restaurant tastefully decorated in soothing shades of pale pink. In warmer months, try the terrace overlooking an exquisite tree-lined *place.* Soak up French *joie de vivre* when the festive sing-along begins.

Le Grenier de Notre Dame, 18, rue de la Bucherie (tel. 43 29 98 29). Mo. St-Michel. Macrobiotics and soybean-freaks delight! A truly crunchy restaurant that ladles up hearty helpings of vegetarian *cassoulet,* a stew-like concoction of beans, tofu and soy sausages, along with an appetizer and dessert, all for 70F. And who could resist their tantalizing seaweed-flavor-fruit or tofu cream desserts? (yum, yum!) Carnivores may want to look elsewhere. Open daily noon-2:30 and 7:30-11pm.

Le Paradis, 11, rue de la Mont Ste-Genvève. Mo. Maubert-Mutualité. If you were an oil tanker, you'd come here to fill up. It's not gourmet, but it is copious and cheap. The 55F lunch *menu* includes an hors d'oeuvres buffet, a main dish such as lamb chops, salad or fries, dessert, and wine. The dinner *menu* is the same for 90F. Open Mon.-Sat. 11:45am-2:30pm and 6pm-midnight.

Restaurant Perraudin, 157, rue St-Jacques. Mo. Luxembourg or Maubert-Mutualité. At this family-style bistro, individual coffee filters perched atop the coffee cups invoke a bygone era when dining was good, simple, and affordable. Very small, with delicate decor. Order the chef's daily suggestions, or try old favorites like *sautée d'agneau aux flageolets* (sauteed lamb with white beans, 55F). Come early; this place gets crowded. Appetizers 25F. Main dishes 50-60F. Open Tues.-Fri. noon-2:15pm and 7:30-10:15pm, Mon. and Sat. 7:30-10:15pm.

L'Apostrophe, 34, rue de la Mont Ste-Geneviève. Mo. Maubert-Mutualité. Tiny, unpretentious French restaurant situated on a lovely street that winds its way down the hill from the Panthéon. Somewhat garishly decorated with huge candles made to seem even larger by the collection of wax drippings that adorn their sides, this restaurant offers an excellent bargain. Three *menus:* 49F served until 8pm, 59F until 9pm, and 75F all night. Open Tues.-Sat. noon-2pm and 7-10pm.

Le Clos Descartes, 10, rue Descartes. Mo. Maubert-Mutualité. A miniscule restaurant in the heart of the Latin Quarter melts the best *raclette* around, including potatoes, *charcuterie,* and as much melted, runny raclette-cheese as you can scoop on top.

Ferme Ste-Suzanne, 4, Fossés St-Jacques (tel. 43 54 90 02). Mo. Luxembourg. A welcome refresher, this pleasant little restaurant puts a new twist on traditional dishes. Salads are a specialty, and the *Salade Fraîche,* made with goat cheese in an orange dressing is a delicious lunch at 57F.

Café Le Volcan, 10, rue Thouin (tel. 46 33 38 33). Mo. Cardinal Lemoine. A boisterous restaurant with a young clientele at home in the plain brick-floored interior. The 55F menu includes appetizer, main dish, and dessert; at lunch they throw in a glass of wine as well. Open daily noon-2:30pm and 7-11:30pm.

Randy and Jay's, 4, rue Thouin (tel. 43 26 37 09). Mo. Cardinal Lemoine. The perfect answer to your barbecue cravings. Two good ol' American boys smoke up the best ribs this side of the Atlantic in their rough and raucous restaurant. The 95F *menu* is expensive, but when you gotta have it, you gotta have it; it includes your choice of pork ribs or chicken, plus macaroni and potato salads, coleslaw and beans. For a cheaper snack, try the pecan pie—it'll make you feel like you're home again. Open Tues.-Sun. noon-2:30pm and 7pm-midnight.

Le Jardin des Pâtes, 4, rue Lacépède (tel. 43 31 50 71). Mo. Jussieu. Gourmet pasta made from organically grown grains and served in a variety of recipes ranging from sesame butter to duck and *crème fraîche.* Eight tables unassumingly set with paper tablecloths. Main course 48-70F.

Sixth Arrondissement

Tiny restaurants with rock-bottom *prix-fixe menus* jostle each other for space and customers in this *arrondissement,* making it an excellent area to wander around looking for a filling meal, whether it be French, Japanese, Italian, or Hungarian. The streets around the rue de Buci, including rue Dauphine and rue du Seine, offer excellent bargain restaurants as well as expansive and rambling daily street markets, where you can pick up anything from a whole roasted chicken and fries to fresh yogurts and cheeses. The rue Gregoire de Tours wins the area contest for the highest density of cheap restaurants, and makes a great place to start if you feel like doing a little menu browsing. Farther west toward the St-Germain-des-Prés area and closer to the seventh *arrondissement,* cheap restaurants fade fast and are replaced by immaculately elegant and horrendously overpriced cafés and restaurants, where most people come to watch and be watched rather than to enjoy the food.

Orestias, 4, rue Gregoire de Tours, off bd. St-Germain (tel. 43 54 62 01). Mo. Odéon. Their *menu* is a truly inspired bargain with copious first and second courses as well as cheese or dessert for only 44F, for lunch *and* dinner. Both the food and dark wood-paneled ambience run toward middle-of-the-road French, with lots of grilled meats (the lamb skewers are the best of the offerings) accompanied by fries and green beans. You can't eat more for the price anywhere in the area.

Restaurant Des Beaux Arts, 11, rue Bonaparte (tel. 43 26 92 64), across from the Ecole Des Beaux Arts. Mo. St-Germain-des-Prés. Extremely popular with the locals, this place features friendly service, a simple decor and festive frescoed walls. The 67F *menu* (wine or beer included) includes some favorites like *lapin à la moutarde* (rabbit with mustard sauce) as well as more eccentric choices like *maquereau aux pommes à l huile* (mackerel with apples in oil) and a daily vegetarian dish. This is where renowned food writer A. J. Liebling learned to eat as a "student" in the 1920s. Open daily noon-2:30pm and 7-10:45pm.

Kiotori, 61, rue Monsieur le Prince. Mo. Odéon or Luxembourg. A young, energetic crowd packs into this typical Japanese restaurant, decked out with the usual black sushi bar and tables, to gorge on the succulent skewers of grilled beef, chicken, and shrimp, or relish the visually stunning plates of sushi and maki, all from the variety of amazingly cheap *menus,* ranging from 45-85F. All *menus* include a bowl of soup and *crudités* salad along with the main dish. Open Mon.-Sat. noon-2:30pm and 7-11pm.

Così, 54, rue du Seine (tel. 46 33 35 36), off rue de Buci. Mo. Odéon. Strains of *Così Fan Tutte* eminate from this totally hip little sandwich shop where you can have a sandwich made to order from the myriad tantalizing ingredients such as curried turkey, goat cheese, and tomato and basil salad, all stuffed between two slices of piping hot freshly baked *focaccia* bread (30-40F). It may sound expensive for just a sandwich, but this isn't just a sandwich. Respectable wines (12F per glass) complement the gargantuan creations, making a truly satisfying meal.

Le Petit Vatel, 5, rue Lobineau. Mo. St-Germain des Prés or Mabillon. This tiny restaurant offers little in ambience—plastic tables adorned with simple bouquets of daisies—but provides delicious, inexpensive meals the way the Parisians like 'em. Choose an appetizer, main course, and dessert from the 64F *menu* scribbled on the chalkboard, including rotating daily specialties like *lapin au vin blanc* and vegetarian stews. Take-out available. Open Mon.-Sat. noon-3pm and 7pm-midnight, Sun. 7pm-midnight. Closed 1 week in Aug.

Restaurant Maroussia, 9, rue Eperon (tel. 43 54 47 02). Mo.Odéon. This tiny restaurant specializes in classic Russian dishes and hearty peasant fare. Dried flowers, rustic wooden tables, and heavy red print drapes (used as much on the walls as on the windows) recreate the feeling of the countryside. Come at lunch for an affordable 75F *menu,* which includes 2 courses and wine. Dinner specialties like the filling *chicken kiev* beckon at prices ranging around 70F. Open Mon.-Sat. noon-2:30 and 7:30-11pm.

Au Petit Prince, 2, rue Monsieur le Prince (tel. 43 26 43 49), just off the pl. Odéon. Mo. Odéon. This clean, straightforward restaurant with a sophisticatedly subdued interior, offers a taste of delicate but rarely filling *nouvelle cuisine* with creations such as grilled sole in orange butter. The 125F *menu* includes 3 courses but no wine. Open Mon.-Sat. noon-2:30 and 7:30-11pm.

Slice, 62, rue Monsieur le Prince. Mo. Odéon or Luxembourg. Bakes huge New York style pizzas dripping with fresh mozzarella (14-20F per piece). Munch on chocolate chip cookies (5F) and brownies (9F) for dessert. Open daily 11am-11pm.

Pizza Pino, 57, bd. Montparnasse (tel. 45 49 19 08). Mo. Montparnasse. An Italian pizzeria that bakes its pies in genuine wood-burning ovens. An excellent choice for a magisterial Italian Thanksgiving dinner. The greatest thing about this restaurant, though, is that it stays open from 11am-5am, 7 days a week.

Au Paradis du Fruit, 27 and 29, quai des Grands Augustins (tel. 43 54 51 42). Mo. St-Michel. See fourth *arrondissement,* above.

Seventh Arrondissement

Contrary to what you might expect, the military and ministerial seventh actually offers affordable food. Don't expect great variety—*crêpes* and traditional meat dishes are the order of the day—but the standards are well executed. The seventh is a good place to indulge in that 100F+ menu meal that you promised to do at least once in Paris.

La Pie Gourmande, 30, rue de Bourgogne (tel. 45 51 32 48). Mo. Varenne or Chambre des Députés. Families, jeans-clad friends, and civil servants mix happily in this comfortable *crêperie.* Sit at the counter or one of the floral-clothed tables and unwind to the sound of sizzling *galettes* (crêpe cousins, 35-45F) and *crêpes* (for dessert, 18-35F). A salad for openers (20-40F) rounds out a filling meal. Open Mon.-Fri. 11:30am-3pm.

Au Babylone, 13, rue de Babylone (tel. 45 48 72 13). Mo. Sèvres-Babylone. Jovial atmosphere—a faithful clientele enjoys coming back to this restaurant again and again. Classy red tablecloths lie under classic French food. 80F *menu* includes appetizer, steak or *plat du jour,* and drink or dessert. A la carte appetizers 12-20F. Main dishes 45-60F (try the *gigot d'agneau* 45F). Desserts 15-18F. Open Mon.-Sat. 11:30am-2pm. Closed Aug.

CROQ 100WICH, 23, av. de la Motte Picquet. Mo. Ecole Militaire or Latour-Maubourg. A quick bite at the lunch counter or to go: filling sandwiches (15-22F) or warm quiche (16F). Salads look small but are excellent—*la salade paysanne* is chock full o' potatoes, chicken, bacon, olives, and other good stuff. Vegetarian options. Open Mon.-Fri. 9am-8pm, Sat. 9am-5pm.

La Croque au Sel, 131, rue St-Dominique (tel. 47 05 23 53). Mo. Ecole Militaire. Good country cuisine in a charming restaurant with brightly painted windows and nifty ceramic lamps. Eat excellent *pavé de boeuf émincé* (roast beef) smothered in *sauce croque au sel* as one-third of the 68F *menu.* Salads 30-40F. Main dishes 60-70F. Desserts 20-30F. The difference between the 68F and the 98F *menus* is, as the waiter explains, more choice and 30F. Open Mon.-Fri. noon-2pm and 7-10:30pm, Sat. 7-10:30pm.

Fontaine de Mars, 129, rue St-Dominique (tel. 47 05 46 44). Mo. Ecole Militaire. Traditional French fare served on checkered tablecloths, outside near the fountain or inside under the old musical instruments. Kick back and enjoy, because everyone else sure is. Lunch *menu* at 85F, *plat du jour* 60-75F. Be exotic—try *filet de loup au céléri* (celeried wolf fillet) for 75F. Open Mon.-Sat. noon-2:30pm and 7:30-11pm.

La Poule au Pot, 121, rue de l'Université (tel. 47 05 16 36), near the corner of rue Surcouf. Mo. Invalides or Pont de l'Alma. Join the suits on the small terrace under the faded striped awning or venture inside to the soothing green decor. Why order anything other than the signature dish—the *poule au pot farcie* (stuffed chicken stew, 85F)? Appetizers 25-56F. Main dishes 85-110F. Dessert 20-30F. 110F *menu* is worth it. Open daily 12:30-3pm and 7-11pm.

Le Club des Poètes, 30, rue de Bourgogne (tel. 47 05 06 03). Mo. Varenne. This unique club/restaurant offers a rare combination of good food and fine poetry. See Entertainment—Highbrow Diversions, for more information.

Eighth Arrondissement

You should know better than to expect inexpensive restaurants amid salons of *haute couture* and embassies. The eighth *arrondissement,* elegant abode of many of Paris's finest and most famous restaurants, is the Michelin diner's dream come true. Alas, *Let's Go* diners might want to drift back to the first or second *arrondissements* for a bargain meal after strolling through the eighth's famous *grands boulevards*. Of course, resourceful city that it is, Paris does in fact offer a few select affordables amidst this marathon of opulence. The *pot au feu* (read: stew) is king at **Le Roi de pot-au-feu,** 40, rue de Ponthieu (tel. 43 59 41 62; Mo. Franklin D. Roosevelt) and will warm your tummy for 85F. **La Maison du Valais,** 20, rue Royale (tel. 42 60 22 72: Mo. Madeleine or Concorde), serves up *raclette* (a cheesy fondue relative) in upscale surroundings with prices to match (from 90F).

L'Aubergade, 122, rue la Boétie (tel. 42 25 10 60). Mo. Franklin D. Roosevelt. Chaos may reign a few steps away on rue la Boétie, but you will find peace through the stained-glass doors. Lacy tablecloths, arched mirrors, and a luscious dessert table will entice you to linger, as will the 55F lunch *menu:* a filling salad and meat or fish dish. The old leather-bound menu (in both English and French) offers more elaborate *menus* at 75F and 120F and the house duck at 75F. Open Mon.-Fri. 10am-3pm and 6-11:30pm, Sat. 6-11:30pm.

Persepoliss, 66, av. des Champs-Elysées in the basement of Galerie Point Show no. 69 (tel. 42 89 57 89). Mo. Franklin D. Roosevelt. Decorated with a tacky bronze-esque wall hanging with the mandatory door beads and scarves that double as tablecloths, this restaurant serves generous portions of Persian specialties. At lunch or dinner, 37F will get you a meat dish accompanied by a heaping plate of rice. *Menus* at 42F, 59F, and 79F get progressively more elaborate; try the *gheymeh polo* (47F). Open Mon.-Sat. 11am-3pm and 7-11:30pm.

Natu Resto, 66, av. des Champs-Elysées, in the Galerie Point Show (tel. 42 56 49 01). Mo. Franklin D. Roosevelt. *"Mangez juste!"* is this vegetarian eatery's motto and you will eat well, either at the appropriately green counter, or at the restaurant downstairs. Vitamin and protein shakes and fruity cocktails will pump you up without deflating your pocket, as will the tasty and tasteful dishes (37-47F). Try the "Caroline"—lettuce, carrots, sprouts, apples, raisins, cheese, and sunflower seeds mixed into one happy and healthy meal. Counter open Mon.-Fri. 11am-7pm. Restaurant, where you pay slightly more, open Mon.-Fri. noon-3pm.

Dynastie Thai, 101, rue La Boétie. Mo. St-Philippe du Roule. An acknowledged top choice among Paris's Asian restaurants. Take advantage of the bargain weekday *menu* (90F) to sample exquisitely prepared Thai cuisine in an ambience *de luxe.* Open daily noon-2:30pm and 7-11:30pm.

Le Fouquet's, 99, av. des Champs-Elysées. Mo. George V. "Created" in 1899 and located in the shadow of the Arc de Triomphe, this is the premier gathering place for the Parisian *vedettes* (stars) of radio, television, and cinema. Tourists, oblivious to the celebrities drinking inside, bask on the *terrasse.* James Joyce dined here with relish. Bank-breaking coffee and a chance to be seen 34F. Entrees from 92F. Open daily 9am-2am; food served noon-3pm and 1pm-midnight.

Ninth Arrondissement

Except for a few gems, meals close to the heavily touristed Opéra area can be quite expensive; for truly cheap deals, head farther north. Displaced by the projectile force of the city's skyrocketing prices, much of ethnic Paris has found itself here, providing the outer regions of the ninth with wondrous delicacies from former French colonies. Beware, however, of the Pigalle area at night, when hookers and thieves abound.

Le Vieux Pressoir, 30-32, bd. Poissonière (tel. 47 70 25 55.) Mo. Bonne Nouvelle. *Brasserie*-type restaurant with wood paneling, peach tablecloths, and mirrors and plants decorating the interior. Tables outside also. The food here is traditionally French, with specialties such as sole, lamb, and steak. Dinner a la carte about 200F, but 89F and 139F *menus* are available. Open daily noon-2:30pm and 7-10:30pm; Sat. until midnight. Credit cards accepted.

Le Chartier, 7, rue du Faubourg-Montmartre (tel. 47 70 86 29). Mo. Bonne Nouvelle. On a little courtyard, this huge restaurant is really in the grand old French style, with chandeliers and wooden booths. The waiters here are older and very jovial; the clientele is mainly an older, local crowd. Specialties include beef in a house tomato sauce; *pot au feu* (stew) and roast veal; portions are huge. A full meal will cost about 90F. Open daily 11:45am-3pm and 6:30-10pm. Credit cards accepted.

Sannine, 32, rue du Faubourg-Montmartre (tel. 48 24 01 32.) Mo. Montmartre. This small Lebanese restaurant specializes in Middle Eastern basics: kebabs, marinated beef, falafel, and tabouli. The decor is simple but pleasant and the service is very friendly. Dinner a la carte for around 90F; *menu* for 49F (lunch) and 62F (dinner). Open daily noon-3pm and 6pm-midnight. Take-out available.

Casa Miguel, 48, rue St-Georges. Mo. St-Georges. This self-proclaimed bastion of communism holds strongly to its ideology of asking each to pay according to his means. Dinner or lunch is still 5F (unless you're an oppressive capitalist), for plentiful portions of simple (and not fantastic) fare of *couscous*, macaroni, or the like. Go for the lively, friendly atmosphere, and go early—it fills up with students. Open Mon.-Sat. noon-1pm and 7-8pm, Sun. noon-1pm.

Hayne's Bar, 3, rue Clauzel (tel. 48 78 40 63). Mo. St-Georges. This restaurant bar specializes in downhome New Orleans cooking. Come here for some good old fried chicken, New Orleans-style red beans, BBQ chicken and the like. Portions are very generous and dinner comes out to less than 100F. On Fri. nights, a pianist plays New Orleans jazz. Drinks 30F. Open Mon-Sat. 8pm-12:30am.

La Franche-Comté, 2, bd. de la Madeleine (tel. 47 42 86 52). Mo. Madeleine. Half-restaurant, half-tourist office about this eastern French province, this elegant place offers tantalizing regional specialties. Lots of wine, mushrooms, and fish. *Menus* at 82F, 110F, and 175F. Brochures free. Open Mon.-Sat. noon-10:30pm. Credit cards accepted.

Taverne Kronenbourg, 24, bd. des Italiens (tel. 47 70 16 64). Mo. Richelieu-Drouot. Cheery waiters serve up healthy portions of heavy Alsatian favorites, including plenty of *choucroute*, in a huge comfortable café atmosphere perfectly designed for optimal people-gazing. 79F and 170F *menus*. Open daily noon-1am.

Au Boeuf Bourguignon, 21, rue de Douai (tel. 42 82 08 79). Mo. Pigalle. The checkered tablecloths and movie posters contribute to the happy atmosphere. Cheerful French family presents 3-course 92F and 160F *menus*, drinks included. Clearly the *boeuf bourguignon* comes highly recommended. Open Mon.-Sat. noon-3pm and 6:30-10:30pm.

Hard Rock Café, 14, bd. Montmartre (tel. 42 46 10 00). Mo. Richelieu Druot. What can you say? Loud music, hamburgers, and guitars on the wall. Seen it all before? What more can you expect? Serves hamburgers, ribs, steaks, you know, American stuff. You can buy T-shirts next door. Please don't. Open daily noon-2am. Credit cards accepted.

Jeremy's Sandwich and Coffee Shop, 43, rue Fontaine. Mo. Blanche. Straight out of the 50s, this diner-style restaurant serves up milkshakes (25F), hamburgers (30F), salad, and all your American favorites. And it has a jukebox! Open daily 9am-10pm. Take-out available.

Tenth Arrondissement

This area may not be an eating mecca, but it does have some unexpected finds. The *brasseries* around the Gare du Nord tend to have inflated prices, due to their convenient location. Even among these, however, there is the occasional prize with better food and ambiance at lower prices. Don't be afraid to explore. Ethnic foods abound and, in general, the farther you get from the train station, the more likely you are to find a good *brasserie* that won't empty your pocket.

Paris-Dakar, 95, rue du Faubourg St-Martin (tel. 42 08 16 64). Mo. Gare de l'Est. Run by a Senegalese family, this place is extremely popular among Parisians who keep coming back to what is heralded as "the most African of all African restaurants." Brochettes and curries abound and *Tiep Bou Dieone*—the "national dish of Senegal"—is recommended. Loosen your belts and prepare to feast. Dinner a la carte will cost up to 150F while a 59F lunch *menu* provides a more economical option. Open daily noon-4pm and 7pm-midnight. Credit cards accepted, except AmEx.

La Maison Blanche, 21, rue Dunkerque (tel. 48 78 15 92). Mo. Gare du Nord. This may seem like just one of the many *brasseries* across from Gare du Nord, but the food is especially tasty and plentiful, the crowd diverse and interesting, the service exceptionally amiable. Standard *brasserie* fare: steak *au poivre*, salads, mussels *provençale*. Full meal a la carte about 120F, 68F *menu*. Open 24 hrs. Credit cards accepted.

Le Brouet, 14, rue Fidélité (tel. 45 23 26 26). Mo. Gare du Nord. The emphasis is on wine, rather than food. Entrees are simple, but good and very French (*paté*, medallions of veal and duck, etc.), but all this is secondary to the primary attraction: good wine at good prices. The specialties are wines from Franche Comté, Savoie, Jura, and Alsace. This place has great ambience. 29 cl. glass for 9F, 45 cl. glass for 18F. Dinner a la carte runs120F. Open Mon.-Fri. 12:30pm-3pm and daily 7:30pm-1:30am.

Brasserie Flo, 7, four des Petits-Ecuries (tel. 47 70 13 59). Mo. Chateau d'Eau. Beautiful dining room, with dark wood paneling and mirrors. The waiters seem to have been working there their entire lives and the diners are full of cheer. Specializes in seafood, with every imaginable type of oyster. A *brasserie* in the grand style. Dinner a la carte can be somewhat expensive at 200F, but a 94F *menu* is a great buy. Open 7pm-2am. Credit cards accepted. Reservations recommended.

Chez Vania, 12, rue du Faubourg Poissonnière (tel. 45 23 50 28). Mo. Bonne Nouvelle. Good, solid Russian food in a bright, musical ambiance. Specialties include *blini* and stroganoff made with vodka. The service is friendly and the clientele local and lively. Lunch *menu* 90F, dinner *menu* 120F. Open Mon-Sat. noon-4pm and 7pm-12:30am.

Le Palais de l'Est, 186, Faubourg St-Martin (tel. 46 08 16 64). Mo. Chateau Landon. This exotically decorated restaurant specializes in Chinese and Vietnamese cuisine. More expensive than many of its counterparts, it serves up big servings of light, tasty food, including a wide variety of *dim sum*. Dinner a la carte for around 170F; lunch *menu* 48F, dinner 68F and 78F. Open daily noon-2:30pm and 6pm-5am. Takeout available.

Eleventh Arrondissement

Father from the monuments, but convenient to many hostels and hotels, the eleventh is a great place to stretch your francs.

A la Banane Ivoirienne, 10, rue de la Forge-Royale (tel. 43 70 49 90). Mo. Daidherbe-Chaligny. Run by a gregarious Ivoirian emigré who wrote his doctoral thesis on his country's banana industry, this cheerful place serves delicious West African specialties, such as *attieke*, made from cassava, and *aloko*, from bananas. Entrees 49-80F. *Menu* 89F. Open Tues.-Sat. 7pm-midnight.

Au Petit Keller, 13, rue Keller (tel. 47 00 12 97). Mo. Ledru Rollin. Traditional, working-class bistro in the heart of the vibrant Bastille district. Filling, wholesome food, extremely popular with locals of all backgrounds—everyone looks like a regular. 60F *menu* includes beer or wine. *Gâteau de riz* (rice cake) is the house specialty and far more than the dry air-bubble the name conjures up. Open Mon.-Fri. noon-2:30pm and 7-9pm.

Le Val de Loire, 149, rue Amelot (tel. 47 00 34 11). Mo. Filles du Calvaire or Oberkampf. Locals share tables with tourists from nearby hotels. Nondescript decor and standard French fare: 60F *menu* includes a kir and a phenomenal buffet of appetizers. *Menu* at 105F adds an opening *terrine*. Open Mon.-Sat. noon-2:30pm and 6:45-10pm. Closed Aug.

Chez Justine, 96, rue Oberkampf (tel. 43 57 44 03). Mo. St-Maur. Tasty provincial food in a rustic dining room organized around a sizable chimney. Lunch (66F) and dinner (82F) *menus* include fabulous appetizer spreads on the *table d'hôte*. Otherwise appetizers 45-60F, *plats* 58-100F. Open Mon.-Sat. noon-2:30pm and 7-10:30pm. Closed mid-July to mid-Aug.

Au Trou Normand, 9, rue Jean-Pierre Timbaud (tel. 48 05 80 23). Mo. Oberkampf. More than the hole in wall that the name indicates. Indeed, a veritable neighborhood institution, with its orange tablecloths and unbelievably low-priced no-fuss French food. The lunch crowd has clearly been here before. Not huge portions. Appetizers 9-13F, *plats du jour* 29-39F, tasty desserts 9-13F. Open Mon.-Fri. noon-2:30pm and 7:30-11pm, Sat. 7:30-11pm. Closed Aug.

Occitanie, 96, rue Oberkampf (tel. 48 06 46 98). Mo. St-Maur. Rough weave material over wood tables provides the perfect setting to indulge in specialties from the south of France. *Formules express* 46-55F offer varying combinations of salads, wine, tabouli, and the *plat du jour*. Entrees 30-50F, *plats* 45-92F. Open Mon.-Fri. noon-2pm and 7-10:30pm, Sat. 7-10:30pm. Closed mid-July to mid-Aug.

Chez Paul, 13, rue de Charonne (tel. 47 00 34 57). Mo. Charonne, Ledru-Rollin, or Bastille. You'll have to see the late-night crowds to believe that people can have so much fun eating. A wonderfully friendly staff serves perfectly prepared heaps of traditional fare. Don't come for intimacy. This restaurant never stops serving up the fun to a deliriously (drunkenly?) happy Parisian crowd. Appetizers 30-50F. Entrees 60-75F. Open Mon.-Sat. noon-2:30pm and 7:30pm-2am. Closed Aug.

La Courtille, 16, rue Guillaume Bertrand (tel. 48 06 48 34). Mo. Saint-Maur. Chic young professional crowd feasts in soothing peach surroundings. Named for the hamlet of Courtille to which 18th-century Belleville residents fled to replenish themselves during Ash Wednesday celebrations. Lunch *menu* 61F; 115F at night. Appetizers 34-50F, *plats* 66-82F, dessert 32F. Open Mon.-Fri. noon-2pm and 7:45-10pm, Sat. 7:45-10pm.

Twelfth Arrondissement

Au Limonaire, 88, rue de Charenton (tel. 43 43 49 14). Mo. Ledru-Rollin or Gare de Lyon. The light bulbs strung outside match the festive feeling that prevails inside this bistro/folk music venue. This place was founded in 1890 as the auspicious Au Pissenlair, and has changed hands several times since. Well used chairs and nifty pictures add to the ambiance created by tasty regional cuisine and fine wines from the Rhône Valley (the owner is happy to advise the uninitiated). Appetizer and main dish *menu* 55F. Dessert 23-28F. More than the lights shine Wed.-Sat. from 10-11pm, when folk musicians from all over perform live. Drop by to pick up a monthly schedule. Open daily noon-3pm and 6pm-midnight; Aug. Tues.-Sat. noon-3pm and 6pm-midnight.

Le Parrot, 5, rue Parrot (tel. 43 43 05 64). Mo. Gare de Lyon. High-ceilinged, wood-paneled, mirrored dining room welcomes a local crowd for good French food at good French prices. 54F *menu* includes appetizer, *plat,* and dessert. Open Mon.-Sat. 11:30am-2:45pm and 7-10pm, Sun. 7-10pm.

Thirteenth Arrondissement

It's Chinatown, Jake.

Cap St-Jacques, 105, av. d Ivry (tel. 43 86 06 72). Mo. Tolbiac. This new establishment, tastefully decorated in tones of salmon and gray instead of the usual oppressive red glitz, serves up the best authentic Vietnamese food in Paris, including specialties like their beautifully prepared and presented rice noodles loaded down with beef and vegetables (32F). Probably the best restaurant in Chinatown. Open daily noon-11pm.

L'Oiseau de Paradi, 44-46, rue Javelot, in the cement pagoda structure set back from the street at 101, rue Tolbiac. Mo. Tolbiac. A gourmet Chinese restaurant where you can dine outside in warm weather on fantastic creations like stuffed crab claws (60F); it's more expensive than some of the other restaurants in the area, but the food is worth it. Open Mon.-Sat. noon-2:30pm and 6:30-11pm.

Lao Thai, 128, rue Tolbiac. Mo. Tolbiac. A small Thai restaurant that fills up quickly with hordes of faithful Thai and French customers. Their 45F *menu* (lunch only) includes appetizer, main dish, rice, and dessert. Open Thurs.-Tues. noon-2:30 and 7-11:30.

Château de Choisy, 44-46, av. de Choisy (tel. 45 82 40 60). Mo. Porte de Choisy. Not the utmost in gourmet Chinese food, this restaurant relies on its specialty, an all-you-can-eat buffet (55F lunch and 72F dinner), to attract the hordes of customers that pack in here. Their offerings include spring rolls, beef lo mein, beef or chicken stir-fry, and other standard Chinese dishes. Open daily noon-2:30pm and 6:30-11pm.

Fourteenth Arrondissement

The Breton invasion of the turn of the century has left the 14th rich in *crêpes* and *galettes,* the larger, buckwheat version of the *crêpe,* served with anything that isn't sweet.

Le Jerobam, 72, rue Didot (tel. 45 39 39 13). Mo. Plaisance. An authentic, comfortable French restaurant serving superb traditional fare at unbeatable prices. Lunch *menu* at 65F includes delectably prepared dishes such as *Tagine de Poisson aux olives et citron confit* (a fish stew with preserved lemons and olives). Dinner *menu* 85F. Open Tues.-Sat. noon-2pm and 7-10pm. Mon. noon-2pm.

La Route du Château, 123, rue du Château (tel. 43 20 09 59). Mo. Pernety. A true diamond in the rough in a relatively working-class neighborhood. Memorable repasts in a charmingly decorated dining room in the style of a traditional bistro. Specialties include rabbit sauteed with cider. *Menu* 80F, and definitely worth it. Open Tues.-Sat. noon-2pm and 7-10pm. Mon. 7-10pm.

Crêperie St-Malo, 53, rue de Montparnasse (tel. 43 20 87 19). Mo. Edgar Quinet. The plethora of *crêperies* on this street testifies to Montparnasse's large population of Bretons, who introduced their pancakes when they flooded the neighborhood in the 1920s. This restaurant offers the most promising menu including a meat crêpe, a dessert crêpe, hard cider and coffee for 49F. Open Mon.-Sat. noon-2:30pm and 6-10:30pm.

Crêperie Le Biniou, 3, av. General Leclerc (tel. 43 27 20 40). Mo. Denfert-Rochereau. In this cheerful green and white restaurant you ll find a tasty innovation on a traditional idea; a non-traditional *crêperie* that whips up unusual pancakes filled with such delectable stuffings as squid and mussels. Top off your dinner with a killer pear, chocolate, and chantilly crêpe. Both main course and dessert crêpes at 20-35F. Open Tues.-Sat. 11:45am-2:30pm and 6:45-10pm.

Aquarius Café, 40, rue Gergovie (tel. 45 42 10 29). Mo. Pernety. A beautifully serene vegetarian restaurant, where light wood tables and an exceptionally friendly staff enhance a politically correct meal. The famous "mixed grill" includes tofu sausages, cereal sausages, wheat pancakes, wheat germ, brown rice and vegetables in a mushroom sauce for 65F. Now doesn t that just make your mouth water? Positively yummy desserts, such as their decadent chocolate cake, 30-40F. Open July-Sept. Mon.- Sat. noon-2:30pm and 6:30-10pm.

Restaurant au Rendez-Vous des Comioneurs, 34, rue des Plantes (tel. 45 40 43 36). Mo. Alesia. A low-key establishment, which puts more emphasis on the food than on decor (plain chairs and checkered tablecloths with not a mirror in sight), but which offers honest traditional fare at unbeatable prices. The 60F *menu* includes such delights as stuffed grape leaves and *civet de lapin* (rabbit stew). Open Mon.-Fri. 12:45-2:45pm and 6-9:30pm.

N'Zadette-M'foua, 152, route du Château (tel. 43 22 00 16). Mo. Pernety. A well-received break from traditional French fare can be had at this lively restaurant specializing in Congolese cuisine. You ll be smiling after a "Sourire Congolais," a fish, tomato, pineapple, and cucumber concoction (42F). *Menu* at 85F. Open Mon.-Fri. noon-2pm and 7-10:30pm. Sat. 7-10:30pm.

Kai Etsu, 18ter, rue du Maine. Mo. Montparnasse. A tantalizing array of sushi and maki at unbeatably low prices in a simple wooden dining room *(menu* at 50F). Grilled skewers of beef, chicken and shrimp are also not to be missed *(menu* at 48F.) Open Mon.-Sat. 11:30am-2:30pm and 6:30-8:30pm.

Restaurant Le Berbère, 53, rue Gergovie (tel. 45 42 10 24). Mo. Pernety. A serious selection of Moroccan specialties, including a hearty couscous with chicken or beef for just 42F. Be sure to save enough room to attack the glorious dessert tray at the end, which supports an amazing array of fantastic sugar creations, such as the killer honey-laden baklava (20F). Open Mon.-Sat. noon-2pm and 7-10pm.

Fifteenth Arrondissement

Although the restaurants in the 15th do not escape the general Parisian plague of overpricing, the eateries in this *arrondissement* remain treasured local establishments, where owners personally welcome their regulars to their usual tables and then lovingly detail the specials of the day. Here you'll discover the true Parisian bistro, where you can easily spend three hours in a richly decorated glass and oak wood dining room, savoring the creations of a local culinary genius.

Sampieru Corsu, 12, rue de l Amiral Roussin. Mo. Cambronne. Run by a Marxist Corsican separatist as the articles and posters on the walls attest. Simple tables which you might share with other visitors. You are expected to pay according to your means, though the sugested price for the simple, but copious, three-course *menu* is 36F (beer or wine included). On some nights there is entertainment, and you should give a little extra for the artist. Open Mon.-Fri. 11:45am-1:45pm and 7-9:30pm.

Bistro Bourdelle, 12 rue Bourdelle (tel. 45 48 57 01). Mo. Montparnasse-Bienvenue. A traditional small, dark bistro where dignified old men come to pass their lunch hour quaffing the decent house wine while feasting on the impeccably prepared dishes of meat and fish. *Menu* for 88F includes such house specialties as *salade de choux et champignons* (a warm salad with cabbage and mushrooms) and *quenelles de brochet* (a type of crepe stuffed with fish). Open Mon.-Fri. noon-2:30pm, 7-10pm.

Le Petit Parnasse, 185, rue de Vaugirard (tel. 47 83 29 52). Mo. Pasteur. A bustling small bistro with the classic wood and mirror decor and traditional bistro food to match, which the joyous customers down as quickly as it appears from the kitchen. Lunch *menu* 60F, dinner 80F. Be sure not to miss the steak with morel mushroom sauce if you come in the early spring to late summer. Open Mon.-Sat. noon-2:30pm and 7-10:30pm.

Café du Commerce, 51, rue du Commerce (tel. 45 75 03 27). Mo. La Motte Piquet-Grenelle. A Parisian institution known for its decent food, unusually low prices, spacious and leafy interior, and exceptional hours. Entire families, poodle included, come to eat on weekend afternoons. Lunch *menu* 58F, dinner a la carte, 50-100F for a full meal. Open daily noon-midnight.

Restaurant Les Listines, 24 rue Falguière, (tel. 45 38 57 40). Mo. Falguière. A bar with a cheerful pink and green restaurant on the side. A superb place to come for lunch when you want to escape the tourist hordes. Specialties include duck confit with acacia honey. *Menu* 70F. Open Mon.-Sat. noon-2:30pm.

Phetburi, 31, bd. Grenelle (tel. 48 58 14 88). Mo. Motte Piquet-Grenelle. Definitely the place to go if you're suffering from severe Thai food withdrawal, though not the place to go if you're averse to lemon grass, as specialties include lemon grass fish soup, lemon grass squid salad, lemon grass beef...well, you get the idea. Lunch *menu* 68F, dinner 85F. Open Mon.-Fri. noon-2pm and 7-11pm, Sat. 7-11pm.

Café Aux Artistes, 63, rue Falguière, (tel. 43 22 05 39). Mo. Falguiere. A cheap restaurant with an extensive menu, where you can eat with your compatriots (whether they be Canadian, Australian, British, German, or American), while perusing posters of Ronald Reagan in his younger, better days as a model for Camel cigarettes. The low prices and late hours attract less discriminating palates; gourmets may want to keep looking. Lunch *menu* 54F, dinner 72F. Open Mon.-Fri. noon-2pm and 7pm-1am, Sat. noon-2pm.

Bistro d André, 272, rue St-Charles. Mo. Pl. Balard. The same folks who brought Restaurant Perraudin in the fifth. 55F lunch *menu.* Open Mon.-Fri. noon-2:30pm and 7:30-10pm. Sat. 7:30-10pm.

Sixteenth Arrondissement

The 16th *arrondissement* is not the place to go for a cheap meal. Heading back to the student quarter for a less expensive meal may well be worth the trip. Alternatively, prepare for brasserie fare—the standard *croque-monsieur* (toasted ham and cheese) is always affordable at 25-27F. The **Boulangerie de Ranelagh,** 8, Chaussée de la Muette (tel. 42 88 21 50), Mo. La Muette, offers good sandwichs roughly for 21F50 and a delectable *tarte citron* (lemon tart) for 10F, en route to the Musée Marmottan. (Open daily 6am-8pm. Sit on the terrace or take-out). *A emporter* (take-out) is always least expensive. For sit-down meals, try the following.

Les Chauffeurs, 8, chausée de la Muette (tel. 42 88 50 05). Mo. La Muette. The checkered tablecloths will make you feel at home no matter where you're from, but the scenes of Paris sketched on the wall will remind you of where you actually are. The local professional crowd packs in at lunch for the 59F *menu* and 16F bottles of wine. Open daily 5:30am-11pm.

Man Lung, 10, bd. Delessert (tel. 45 20 47 17). Mo. Passy . Quality Pekinese dishes served at long wood tables both inside and on the terrace. A favorite of Yves Montand and Peter Ustinov, it can be yours too, for the price is right: 69F *menu* includes a starter, a main meal, dessert, and drink. Anything with duck is especially worth trying. Open daily noon-2:30pm and 7-11pm.

Seventeenth Arrondissement

Sangria Restaurant, 13bis, rue Vernier (tel. 45 74 78 74). Mo. Porte de Champerret. A budget traveler's dream of a restaurant, with a self-serve hors d'oeuvres buffet, truly copious and mouth watering main dishes—including juicy steaks and char-grilled swordfish—as much wine as you want (lunch only), and desserts like chocolate mousse to top it off, all for only 75F at lunch, 85F at dinner. Open Mon.-Fri. noon-2:30pm and 7-10:30pm, Sat. and Sun. 7-10:30pm.

Restaurant Natacha, 35, rue Guersant (tel. 45 74 23 86). Mo. Ternes. Another restaurant offering an extraordinary lunch *menu* with an hors d'oeuvres buffet (mostly raw vegetables), a filling second course, as well as dessert for only 75F. Dinner 95F. Open Tues.-Sat. noon-2:30pm and 7-10:30pm, Mon. 7-10:30pm.

Specialités Turques, 76, av. Clichy. Mo. Place de Clichy. Actually, this isn't the name of the place, but this tiny Middle Eastern stand complete with a couple of tables in the back doesn't have a name, so you'll have to identify it by what's emblazoned on the awning. The owner/cook bakes fresh bread for his gargantuan *shwarma* submarine sandwiches, which come with a side of fries, hot sauce, tomatoes, and onions. Together with a drink, this will cost you only 27F (and you'll have enough left over for your next two meals). Open Mon.-Sat. 11am-10pm.

Joy in Food, 2, rue Truffaut (tel. 43 87 96 79). Mo. Place de Clichy. A vegetarian restaurant dedicated not only to taking care of your body—with tasty quiches and brown rice (30-50F)—but also your mind: their card reads *"Chaque incarnation humaine est la continuation de l historie inachevée de Dieu."* (Every human incarnation is the continuation of God's incomplete history.) All are welcome to join the weekly meditation session Wed. at 8pm. Open Mon.-Fri. noon-4pm; Tues. and Fri.-Sat. 7-10:30pm.

Le Relais de Venise, 271, bd. Pereire (tel. 45 74 27 97). Mo. Porte-Maillot. Come here for lunch to experience traditional bistro atmosphere where well-dressed locals come to dine exquisitely in a luxurious atmosphere of white linens and dark wood. The lunch *menu* is expensive at 92F, but worth it; forget the dinner *menu.*

L'Epicerie Verte, 5, rue Saussier Léroy (tel. 47 64 19 68). Mo. Ternes. Formerly a restaurant, this literally green grocery sells vegetarian food and runs an excellent lunch counter. Even unyielding carnivores may want to make the trek to try their salads (15F) and quiche (40F). Two warm dishes served daily. Order and go or grab one of the nine spots at the long table. Open Mon.-Sat. 9:45am-8pm; food served Mon.-Sat noon-7pm. Closed in Aug.

Eighteenth Arrondissement

Montmartre abounds in relatively cheap places to eat. The trick is to stay away from the place du Tertre and walk down the *butte* to more interesting, cheaper, and less touristy places. Go in groups, because this area at night (especially close to the places Pigalle, Anvers, and Blanche) can be, if not dangerous, at least unpleasant, especially for women.

De Graziano, 83, rue Lepic (tel. 46 06 84 77). Mo. Blanche. A lovely little Italian restaurant, tucked behind a huge iron gate in a pleasant garden, overshadowed by the Moulin de la Galette. The food is mainly northern Italian, with such specialties as veal, seafood, and pasta; this is some of the best Italian food in Paris. Lunch *menu* 60F; dinner *menu* 189F. A la carte about 310F (including wine, dessert, and coffee). Reservations recommended for dinner. Credit cards accepted. Open daily noon-3pm and 7:30pm-midnight.

La Villa des Poulbots, 10, rue Dancourt. Mo. Anvers. Wondrously elegant, this restaurant with plush velvet chairs and tapestried walls looks as though it might break your budget. Happy surprise. The 41F, 68F, 95F, and 120F *menu*s let you dine like royalty for a smidgeon of what you'd expect. Specialties: *magret* (breast) of duck, seafood lasagna, chicken in banana sauce. Outdoor seating as well. Open Tues.-Sun. noon-3pm and 6-9pm.

Au Grain de Folie, 24, rue la Vienville (tel. 42 58 15 57). Mo. Abbesses. This is a vegetarian restaurant for everyone, with a vast array of dishes from *couscous* to salads to every kind of cheese. The atmosphere is simple and just a little granola, to remind us that we are vegetarians after all. On a quiet street. Dinner a la carte about 100F, 65F and 100F *menus.* Credit cards accepted. Open Tues-Sun. noon-3pm and 7:30-11:30pm, Mon. 7:30-11:30pm.

Le Petit Chose, 41, rue des Trois Frères (tel. 42 64 49 15). Mo. Abbesses. This little restaurant, whose name means "whatchamacallit," is located in a former artist's studio. The atmosphere is warm and familiar, and the phonograph plays hits from the 1920s. The house specializes in southwestern French cuisine, especially fish (fish *pot-au-feu,* etc.). 95F and 120F *menus;* dinner a la carte will run about 200F. Some credit cards accepted. Reservations recommended for dinner. Open Mon.-Sat. noon-2pm and 7pm to 11:30pm.

Le Refuge des Fondues, 19, rue des Trois Frères (tel. 42 55 22 65). Mo. Abbesses. Not the widest selection of food; in fact there are only two main dishes: *fondue bourgignonne* (meat fondue) and *fondue savoyarde* (cheese fondue). But what else do you expect? Or want? A small place; fun and crowded at night. The 80F *menu* includes appetizer, fondue, dessert, and half *pichet* (jug) of wine. Open Tues.-Sun. noon-2:30pm and 7-9:30pm, Mon. 7-9:30pm.

Chez Francis, 122, rue Caulaincourt (tel. 42 64 60 62). Mo. Lamarck-Caulaincourt. Perched on the corner of a pleasant street, this restaurant commands a panoramic view of the city below and winding streets toward the Sacré-Coeur above. Indoor and outdoor seating. The house cuisine is from southwestern France, with such specialties as filet mignon, filet of sole, and lamb. 110F *menu.* Dinner a la carte about 200F. Reservations for dinner recommended. Credit cards accepted. Open Thurs.-Mon. noon-3pm and 7pm-midnight, Wed. 7pm-midnight.

Nineteenth Arrondissement

Tai-Yien, 5, rue de Belleville (tel. 42 41 44 16). Mo. Belleville. The large size and simple decoration of this Chinese restaurant give it the atmosphere of an eating factory, but the excellent food compensates. Located in Belleville, one of Paris's Chinatowns, it has a high proportion of Asian customers. Pork chop suey 40F. Sautéed crab claws 58F. Rice is an extra 7F. 3-course *menu* 60F. Take-out available. Open daily 10am-2am.

Ay, Caramba!, 59, rue de Mouzaia (tel. 42 41 23 80). Mo. Botzaris. Tex-Mex food has become quite fashionable among young Parisians, with the unfortunate consequence that it is almost always overpriced. Not so at this lively restaurant whose brightly colored walls (inside and outside) make it visible from a mile away. Good food, fiesta atmosphere. Chili con carne 55F, enchiladas 59F, fajitas 75F. Open Mon-Thurs. 7:30-11pm, Fri.-Sun. noon-2:30pm. and 7:30-11pm.

Aux Arts et Sciences Réunis, 161, av. Jean-Jaurès (tel. 42 40 53 18). Mo. Ourcq. A neigborhood clientele and a *patron* with a Clemenceau mustache who speaks absolutely no English provide a very French atmosphere. The food comes quickly and is outstandingly good, traditional fare from southwestern France. Avoid the ice cream at dessert. 3-course *menu* with wine only 55F. Open Mon.-Fri. 6am-9pm, Sat. 8am-2pm; Sept.-June Sat. until 9pm. Closed Aug.

Twentieth Arrondissement

A la Courtille, 1, rue des Envierges (tel. 46 36 51 59). Mo. Pyrénées. Traditional French cuisine, served on a charming terrace on a cobblestone square. From the edge of the square, look past the uninspiring modern architecture to the lovely slopes of the Parc de Belleville. A new menu every day; prices for a main course start around 70F. Open daily 11am-11pm, although lunch service doesn't begin until noon.

La Papaye, 71, rue des Rigoles (tel. 43 66 65 24). Mo. Jourdain. The Caribbean in Paris. Friendly management serves up exotic dishes like tripe with green bananas (60F). Open Mon-Tues. and Thurs.-Fri. noon-2pm and 7pm until last customer, Sat.-Sun. open at 7pm, but if you call ahead they'll make you lunch.

Au Sancerrois, 39, rue Pelleport (tel. 43 61 49 19). Mo. Porte de Bagnolet. Michel Zolli, the proprietor and cook, is the finest chef in the 20th *arrondissement*. That, at least, is the opinion of the Confrèrie Gastronomique de la Marmite d'Or, a society of food connoisseurs that has existed since the time of Richelieu. Savor Zolli's rich, traditional cuisine with a glass of wine and you will acknowledge that they probably know what they're talking about. Despite the recognition the chef has gained, the restaurant retains an unpretentious, familial air. 3-course *menu* 130F. A la carte: *manchons de canard* 50F, *rognons de veau* 120F. The *confit de canard* (85F) is great but a little heavy in hot weather. Open Mon. noon-3pm, Tues.-Fri. noon-3pm and 7:30-10:30pm, Sat. noon-3pm and 7:30-11pm. Closed for 3 weeks in Aug.

Cafés

> The hours I have spent in cafés are the only ones I
> call living, apart from writing.
>
> —Anaïs Nin

Cafés entered Parisian society in 1675 when **Le Procope** opened its doors to an eager coffee-drinking, cigarette-smoking crowd that included such luminaries as Montesquieu, Diderot, and Rousseau. Ever since Voltaire wrote some of his greatest works to the tune of 40 cups of coffee a day at Le Procope, the café has been an integral force in French political, social, cultural, academic, and literary life. Although they make their money selling drinks, their real function is to provide a dry, comfortable place to write, think, meet friends, or plot revolutions in a city that has traditionally housed much of its population in dark, cramped apartments. While the world-famous cafés listed here were hangouts for the fashionable and the literati, hundreds of cafés across the city have catered to a widely varied clientele. Workers, students, and artists have always valued their meeting places, and individual cafés may represent a particular slice of society. Learn to nurse a tiny espresso for hours, to stare at passers-by without lowering your eyes if they stare back, to flaunt the title of an intimidating tome while pretending to read, or to buy round after round of beer as a lively conversation spins off into the night. Cafés near monuments charge monumental prices for minimal atmosphere. The best seats in the theater of Parisian culture are the cafés on fashionable thoroughfares, such as the Champs-Elysées, bd. St-Germain, bd. Montparnasse, or rue de la Paix. To be sure, they charge exorbitant prices (coffee 14-25F), but an intriguing crowd passes the sidewalk tables, providing hours of entertainment for the price of one cup.

More casual crowds frequent the more dilapidated, hidden spots where coffee is only 8F and the use of *argot* (slang) makes eavesdropping an educational challenge. Make sure the prices posted outside correspond to your budget, and be picky before you relax. Prices in cafés are two-tiered, cheaper at the counter (*comptoir* or *zinc*) than in the seating area *(salle)*. Both these prices should be posted. Coffee, beer, and wine are the staple café drinks, but there are other refreshing options. Consider the cool *perrier menthe*, a bottle of Perrier mineral water with mint syrup. *Citron pressé* (lemonade—*limonade* is a soda) and *diabolo menthe* (peppermint soda) are other popular non-alcoholic choices. Cafés also offer Coke, but be prepared to pay twice what you would in the U.S. If you order *café*, you'll get espresso; for coffee with milk, ask for a *café crème*. (The term *café au lait* has been rendered derogatory.) If you order a *demi* or a *pression* of beer, you'll get a pale lager on tap. You can also order bottled imported beer: Heineken is popular in Paris. A glass of red is the cheapest wine in a café (4-6F), with white costing about twice as much. Tips are not expected in cafés—except for the really fancy ones.

Cafés are not suited to cheap meals, but snacks are usually quite economical. A *croque monsieur* (grilled ham-and-cheese sandwich), a *croque madame* (the same with a fried egg), and assorted omelettes cost about 15F. A more popular choice is a salad. Try the *salade niçoise*, the French version of a chef's salad, or a *chèvre chaud*, a salad with delicious, warm goat cheese. Cheaper varieties are the *salade verte* (read: lettuce) and *salade de tomates*. Check the posted menu before you sit down; some cafés (particularly the ones near the big monuments) will charge you 50F for a salad, something no budget traveler can afford.

Café Costes, 4-6, rue Berger, pl. des Innocents, 1er. Mo. Les Halles. Opened in 1905, Philippe Starck's strikingly modern café is a fashionable people-watching spot between Les Halles and Beaubourg. Coffee 16F, sandwiches 26-40F. Open daily 8am-2am.

Café de la Paix, 2ème (tel. 40 07 30 12), at the corner of av. de l'Opéra and, rue de la Paix. Mo. Opéra. This institution on the rue de la Paix (the most expensive piece of property on French Monopoly) has served a wealthy clientele ever since its founding in 1862. The elegant café occupies the terrace; inside, in the same building, are two restaurants owned by the same people. You probably don't have enough money to eat at the restaurants (the Brasserie du Cafe de la Paix and the Restaurant de l'Opéra), but you may decide that 26F isn't too bad for a Coke on the terrace. The waiters are really friendly—a sign of true class. Snobbery is only for jumped-up hoi-polloi, you see. Open daily 10am-1am.

Le Flore, 172, bd. St-Germain, 6ème, next door to Les Deux Magots. It was here, in his favorite hangout, that Jean-Paul Sartre composed *L'être et le néant (Being and Nothingness)*. Apollinaire, Picasso, and André Breton, and even James Thurber also sipped their brew in this light and happy atmosphere. Coffee 22F. Open daily 7:30am-1:30am.

Les Deux Magots, 6, pl. St-Germain-des-Prés, 6ème. Mo. St-Germain-des-Prés. Sartre's second choice and Simone de Beauvoir's first—the two first spotted each other here. Home to Parisian literati since its opening in 1875, this place is now a favorite of Parisian youth, who used to swoon over Sartre as he wrote. This café has nothing to do with fly larvae, but rather is named after two Chinese porcelain figures *(magots)*. Before you go, buy your Roland Barthes and Derrida at **La Lune,** the *hyper-chic* bookstore across the street, and brood over it as you drink your espresso. Coffee 22F. Open daily 8am-2am.

La Closerie des Lilas, 171, bd. de Montparnasse, 6ème. Mo. Vavin. This lovely flower-ridden café was the one-time favorite of Hemingway (a scene in *The Sun Also Rises* takes place here), and the Dadaïsts and Surrealists before him. Picasso came here weekly to hear Paul Fort recite poetry. Exquisite decor and a *terrasse* in summer. Coffee 24F. Open daily 10:30am-2am.

Le Procope, 13, rue de l Ancienne Comedie, 6ème (tel. 43 26 99 20). Mo. Odéon. This quiet café/restaurant was once frequented by the famous philosophers and writers whose figurines line its back wall. Founded in 1686 as the first café in the world, le Procope has been the stage for such weighty moments as Voltaire drinking 40 cups of coffee per day while drafting *Candide* and Marat expounding revolutionary strategy. But history has a price—a 299F *menu*. Frugal diners might choose to visit the café, where less expensive *menus*—98F and 69F (until 8pm)—are served. Open daily noon-3pm and 7pm-2am.La Coupole, 102, bd. du Montparnasse, 14ème. Mo. Vavin.

Le Coupole, 102, bd. du Montparnasse, 14ème. Mo. Vavin. **Le Séléct,** 99, bd. du Montparnasse, 6ème (tel. 45 48 38 24). Mo. Vavin. Two of the most famous cafés in Paris, these lively and ever-chic establishments have served political exiles (Lenin and Trotsky), musicians (Stravinsky and Satie), writers (Hemingway, Breton, Cocteau), and artists (Picasso and Eisenstein), although today they're mostly for tourists. The same is true of the nearby, once-illustrious **La Dôme** and **La Rôtunde.** Coffee 12F. Both open daily 8am-2am.

Salons de thé

Less crowded and less famous than cafés, *salons de thé* are just as much a ritual of the Parisian *savoir vivre*. Here, sample a fresher, more extensive offering of light meals and exquisite pastries, and of course, the friendly pot of tea. For the panic-stricken traveler, *salons de thé* provide a multitude of relaxing *infusions* (herbal teas); try *menthe* (mint) or *verveine* (vervain).

A Priori Thé, 35-37, Galerie Vivienne, 2ème (tel. 42 97 48 75). Mo. Bourse, Palais Royal. Classy place to have a meal or just sip tea. Shielded from the city noise because it's tucked away in a pleasant *galerie* (see Sights). You can get to the *galerie* from 6, rue Vivienne, 4, rue des Petits Champs, or 5, rue de la Banque. Single-course meals in the 75-85F range. Tea 22F. Open Mon.-Sat. noon-7pm, Sun. 1-6pm. Tea service starts at 3pm.

L'Arbre à Canelle, 57, Passage de Panoramas, 2ème (tel. 45 08 55 87). Mo. Rue Montmartre or Bourse. Cakes and tarts baked fresh every morning and served in a pleasant *galerie*—a little less elegant, but rather more animated than the Galerie Vivienne. Tarts 26-30F; salads 39-54F. Open Mon.-Sat. 10:30am-6:30pm.

Marais Plus, 20, rue des Francs Bourgeois, 4ème (tel. 48 87 01 40). Mo. St-Paul. This teahouse has a pleasant, cultured feel to it, perhaps because it is the annex of a bookstore, or perhaps because it is surrounded by fine old buildings in the Marais. Fresh pastry 33F, coffee 15F, tea 23F. Open daily 10am-7pm.

Salon de Thé de l'Hôtel Sully, 62, rue St-Antoine, 4ème. Mo. Bastille. Quality salads (22F-100F) and other light fare in a sumptuous environment: the courtyard of the 17th-century Hôtel Sully. Gets crowded in sunny weather, so it's a good idea to come here on a cloudy day, when the garden has a slightly melancholy charm. Quiche 30F, small pizza 28F. Open Tues.-Sun. 9am-8:30pm. Closed Aug. to mid-Sept.

Le Loir Dans la Théière, 3, rue des Rosiers, 4ème (tel. 42 72 90 61). Mo. St-Paul. The name means "the dormouse in the teapot," an allusion to the Mad Hatter's tea party in *Alice in Wonderland.* Furnished with 1930s armchairs and tables assembled haphazardly from garage sales, "Le Loir" has a unique, comfortable atmosphere somewhere between an upper-crust *salon* and bohemian student lodgings. Tea 20F. Coffee 10-12F. Homemade cakes 35-45F. Breakfast and brunch on Sun.: breakfast of fresh juice, tea, chocolate, or coffee, croissants and toast is 60F; brunch with all of breakfast plus a savory tart is 100F. Open Mon.-Sat. noon-11pm, Sun. 11am-11pm.

Christian Constant, 26, rue du Bac, 7ème (tel. 47 03 30 00). Mo. Rue du Bac. On one of the tastiest streets in Paris, this tearoom offers over 30 flavors of tea as well as 5 varieties of sugar. Modern chic rather than elegantly refined, but the desserts and chocolate transcend mere prose (Opéra 18F). Fresh jams and jellies line the windows. Open Mon.-Sat. 8am-8pm.

Dalloyau, 2, pl. Edmond Rostand, 6ème (tel. 43 29 31 10). Mo. Luxembourg. The most chic *salon de thé* in the neighborhood, this patisserie serves up light salads and lunches, but is really known for its tantalizing array of handcrafted dessert pastries, 18-20F each. Get them to go and nibble in the Jardin du Luxembourg. Open daily 8am-8pm.

La Chocolatière, 5, rue Stanislas, 6ème (tel. 45 39 13 06), near bd. Montparnasse. Mo. Notre-Dame des Champs. This painfully cute *salon de thé* cooks up tasty light lunch salads and quiches. *Menu* 59F. The dessert specialty is, unsurprisingly, a deathly rich chocolate cake, which resembles a heap of different kinds of chocolate piled on top of each other, with a dusting of chocolate shavings to top it off, 25F. Open Mon.-Sat. 9am-7pm.

Ladurée, 16, rue Royale, 8ème (tel. 42 60 21 79). Mo. Concorde. The perfect spot for a sandwich (11F50-13F80), an omelette (35-40F), or an éclair (12F), digested under the painted ceiling in a bustling tea room, full of young and old alike. Lunch served Mon.-Sat. 11:30am-3pm. Open Mon.-Sat. 8:30am-7pm. Closed Aug.

Pény, 2, p. de la Madeleine, 8ème. Mo. Madeleine. For afternoon tea, *chocolat,* or *café viennois* (28F), sit with the older couples and feel *très raffiné.* Stay on the covered *terrasse* to watch the waitresses surveying the comings and goings in the Place.

René Saint-Ouen's salon de thé, 111, bd. Haussmann, 8ème (tel. 42 65 06 25), corner of rue d'Argenson. Mo. Miromesnil. Specializes in bread sculptures—bikes, horses, dogs, ducks, etc. Grab an edible Eiffel Tower for 45F.

Thé-Troc, corner of rue de Nemours and rue de Jean-Pierre Timbaud, 11ème. Mo. Parmentier. Call it the alternative *salon de thé*—non-smoking, environmentally conscious, with windows chock full o' teas, spices, and Asian figurines, as well as records, comics, and T-shirts, all on sale inside. Natural and perfumed teas 13-18F. Open Mon.-Fri. 9am-noon and 2-8pm, Sat. 10am-1pm and 4-8pm.

La Tarte Tempion, 195, bd. Voltaire, 11*ème.* Mo. Rue des Boulets. Beautiful pastries, chocolates, and sandwiches—made with American-style sliced bread. Try *Le Voltaire,* a delight of layered chocolate and cake with candied fruit in the middle and divine powdered chocolate on top. Sit on the terrace that juts into the busy roads out front. Open Fri.-Wed. 8am-8pm.

Wine Bars

Although wine bistros have existed since the early 19th century, the modern wine bar emerged only a few years ago with the invention of a machine that pumps nitrogen into the open bottle, thus protecting the wine from oxidation. Rare, expensive wines, exorbitant by the bottle, have become somewhat affordable by the glass, but this is still not the place for pinching pennies. Expect to pay 20-80F for a glass of high-quality wine. Add to that the requisite *tartine* and several more glasses of wine, and you'll find yourself on the streets, drunk and penniless.

Try to go with a friend who knows wine, a helpful guide book, or an open mind and inquisitive tongue. The owners personally and carefully select the wines which constitute their *caves* (cellars) and are usually available to help out less knowledgeable patrons. Over 100-strong, the wine shops in the **Nicolas** chain are reputed for having the world's most inexpensive cellars, though Nicolas himself owns the fashionable and expensive wine bar **Jeroboam,** 8, rue Monsigny, 2*ème* (tel. 42 61 21 71; Mo. Opéra). Enjoy your bottle or glass with a full meal or a *tartine* (cheese and/or *charcuteries*—French equivalent of cold cuts—served on *pain Poilâne* or *pain de campagne).* And don't hesitate to ask the waiters for advice on which wine best complements your order.

Le Bar du Caveau, place Dauphine, 1*er.* Mo. Cité. Stylishly dressed Parisians make a point of meeting for a liquid lunch at this traditionally brass and wood saloon where they can sample glasses from the vast selection of heavenly wines (14-35F) over a plate of grilled goat cheese and Poilane bread (40F). It's not cheap, but it is worth every *sous.* (Open Mon.-Sat. 10am-8pm).

L'Ecluse, 120, rue Rambuteau, 1*er* (tel. 40 41 08 73). Mo. Les Halles. 13, rue de la Roquette, 11*ème.* Mo. Bastille. 15, quai des Grand-Augustins, 6*ème.* Mo. St-Michel. 15, pl. de la Madeleine, 8*ème.* Mo. Madeleine. 64, rue Francois 1*er, 8ème.* Mo. Georges V. Rue Mondetour, 1*er.* Mo. Les Halles or Etienne Marcel. Possibly the best and certainly the most famous of Parisian wine bar chains. The food is prepared not in a kitchen but in a "laboratory." Elegant and trendy, this small chain defies the assumption that what is mass-owned must be bad. Fresh pasta 60F, sautéed lamb 86F. L'Ecluse specializes in wines from Bordeaux, starting at a healthy 85F per bottle.

Au Sauvignon, 80, rue des Sts-Pères, 7*ème* (tel. 45 48 49 02). Mo. Sèvres-Babylone. This wine bar offers a sublime sampling of Beaujolais (especially in early Nov.) and Alsatian wines. Caricatures praising the owner and his wines coat the walls. Wine from 25F a glass. Open Sept.-July Mon.-Sat. 9am-11pm.

Jacques Mélac, 42, rue Léon Frot, 11*ème* (tel. 43 70 59 27). Mo. Charonne. *The* Parisian family-owned wine bar. Also an excellent bistro, frequented by a friendly crowd. Stop by in Sept. when owner Mélac harvests his own vines and convinces some women to crush them with their feet. Call for exact date. *Tartines* from 16F, wine from 15F per glass. Open Mon., Wed., and Fri. 9am-7pm, Tues. and Thurs. 9am-10pm. Closed July 15-Aug. 15.

Le Val d'Or, 28, av. Franklin D. Roosevelt, 8*ème* (tel. 43 59 95 81). Mo. St-Philippe-du Roule. Just steps away from the Champs-Elysées, the ambience in this friendly wine bar provides a welcome respite from the fast-paced neighborhood. Wonderful wines from all across France, including a magnificent selection of Beaujolais in November. Wine 25-80F (10-15F per glass at counter). Excellent homemade quiche and pastries 30-50F. Open Mon.-Fri. 8am-9pm, Sat. 8am-6pm.

Sweets

Indulge your fickle foreign sweet-teeth on some real ice cream with one of Paris's renowned *glaces,* which are lighter, wetter, and less creamy than their American counterparts, or work off all those cardio-funk exercise classes with a sinfully exquisite French pastry at any number of *patisseries.*

Berthillon, 31, rue St-Louis-en-l'Ile, 4*ème* (tel. 43 54 31 61), on the Ile-St-Louis. Mo. Cité or Pont Marie. Berthillon is simply the best ice cream and sorbet in Paris. The ice cream, which is lighter, wetter, and less creamy than the American version, comes in every imaginable flavor, from numerous varieties of chocolate to *cassis* (black currant) and wild strawberry. Coconut and wild cherry are especially not to be missed. Lines can be quite long in mid-summer, but the wait is definitely worth it. Or try one of the many cafés on Ile St-Louis which also sell Berthillon ice cream—the *glace* is the same, the lines are often shorter, and they're open in August, when the main Berthillon is closed. Unfortunately, Berthillon's ice cream is not only Paris's best, but also its most expensive. Open Sept.-July Tues.-Sun. 10am-8pm.

Mandarine, 6, pl du Marché Ste-Catherine, 4*ème* (tel. 42 74 01 14). Mo. St-Paul. In a cobblestone square at the heart of the Marais, this little café sells superb ice cream from the legendary Glaces Berthillon. On the terrace, two (large) scoops for 32F; pastries 32F. Take-out service: two (smaller) scoops 18F. Open Fri.-Wed. 11am-midnight; in bad weather 3pm-midnight.

Le Nôtre hawks wonderful pastries all around the city. Join the local children pointing out their chosen treat to *maman* at one of the counters. Place your order, pay your bill at the *caisse* and then return to the same counter to pick it up. Quiche 16-19F, buttery croissants 4F70. Open daily 9am-9pm.

Peltier, 66, rue de Sèvres, 7*ème* (tel. 47 83 66 12 or 47 34 06 62). Mo. Vaneau or Duroc. Also: 6, rue St-Dominique, 7*ème* (tel. 47 05 50 02). Mo. Solférino. Also: Japan. This delectable sweet-tooth haven shows that *pâtisseries* too can have slogans: *Les gâteaux Peltier, un défi vers un goût nouveau* (Peltier cakes, a challenge toward a new taste). Sample their specialty, *tarte au chocolat,* with a gold drop in the middle, not overly rich but oh-so-gooey (16F). Sit at the tastefully decorated chairs in the *salon de thé* area or order, pay at the *caisse,* and pick up your treat to go. Homesick travelers will appreciate the sight of Peltier's "normally shaped" bread (24-32F). Open Mon.-Sat. 9:30am-7:45pm, Sun. 8:30am-7pm.

Maison du Chocolat, 4, bd. de la Madeleine, 9*ème* (tel. 47 42 86 52). Mo. Madeleine. Every imaginable kind of chocolate: bonbons, blocks, milk chocolate, dark chocolate. Plus delicious ice cream and sorbets. A place *not* to be missed.

Le Chocolat Viennois, 118, rue des Dames, 17*ème* (tel. 42 93 34 40). Mo. Rome. A cozy *salon du thé* where locals pack in to quaff steaming mugs of the house specialty, *Chocolat Viennois avec Creme Battue* (hot chocolate with fresh whipped cream, 16F). Salads 35-45F. A delicious assortment of pastries 30-40F. Open Mon.-Fri. 10am-11pm, Sat. 10am-4pm.

The Baker's Dozen, 3, pl. de la Sorbonne, 5*ème* (tel. 44 07 08 09). Mo. Luxembourg. Real live fudge brownies (10F) and chocolate chip cookies (4F50) are the specialty of this micro-bakery. Open Mon.-Fri. 8am-6:30pm

Groceries

When cooking or assembling a picnic, buy supplies at the specialty shops found in most neighborhoods. *Crémeries* (selling dairy products), *fromageries* (selling cheese), *charcuteries* (meats, sausages, *pâtés,* and *plats cuisine*—prepared meals, bought by the kilogram), and *épiceries* (groceries) are open in the morning until noon and then again from 2 or 3 to 7 or 8pm. *Epiceries* also carry staples, wine, produce, and a bit of everything else. *Boulangeries* sell several varieties of bread; get there in the morning, when the goods are still hot. *Patisseries* sell pastries, and a *confiserie* stocks candy and ice cream (though the border between these two kinds of stores is often scrumptiously unclear). You can buy your fruits and vegetables at a *primeur. Bucheries* sell all kinds of meat and poultry, as well as roast chicken. Look for small neighborhood stores—the ones where bottles are covered in five-year-old layers of dust—to unearth some truly incredible deals. Your hotel manager or any local can point you to the neighborhood *fromagerie, charcuterie, boucherie,* and *boulangerie.* Most are very good; their owners are an endless source of information about their respective food specialties. **Supermarkets** *(supermarchés)* are found in every neighborhood and feed the masses all day at comparable prices. Be careful; French people use shopping carts the way they drive. Avoid the evening scramble, lest you be trampled by rabid housemakers trying to get the last loaf of bread. Look for the small foodstore chains such as **Casino** and **Félix Potin.** If you're in the mood for a five-and-dime complete with a supermarket, go to any of the **Monoprix, Prisunics,** or **Uniprix** that litter the city. Open-air markets, held at least once a week in most *arrondissements,* remain the best places to buy fresh fruit, vegetables, fish, and meat. Competition here is fierce, and prices low. The **Nicolas** chain sells wines at inexpensive prices, but doesn't always carry the widest selections. No luck finding that special ingredient? Try the following:

Fauchon, 26, pl. de la Madeleine, 8ème (tel. 47 42 60 11). Mo. Madeleine. The supermarket to end all supermarkets. You can savor the scent from the *patisserie* at least a block away. But do not dare to pick your expensive tea off the shelf yourself—turn to the brown-clad salespeople with the ornate F on their breast to do the dirty work for you. The cafeteria downstairs serves hot dishes for 30-50F and desserts for 17-30F (and beyond). Indulge. Open Mon.-Sat. 9:40am-7pm.

Hédiard, 21, pl. de la Madeleine, 8ème (tel. 42 66 44 36). Mo. Madeleine. A store of spices and exotic products, founded in 1854. Their neighboring *cave* offers a fine selection of wines. Open Mon.-Sat. 9:30am-9pm.

Au Bon Marché, 3, rue de Babylone, 7ème (tel. 45 49 21 22). Mo. Sèvres-Babylone. Here, at Bon Marché's ever-popular food annex, you'll find all the necessities for *haute cuisine,* as well as lots of "gourmet" American fare. You're about 10 million steps above Monoprix and Uniprix. Well-wrapped chocolates and *bonbons* make mouth-watering souvenirs. Open Mon.-Fri. 9:30am-6:30pm, Sat. 9:30am-7pm.

Poilane, 8, rue du Cherche Midi, 6ème (tel. 45 79 11 49), off bd. Raspail. Mo. Sèvres Babylone. A tiny, rather sparse shop services a huge bakery which makes the city's most famous bread: fragrant, crusty sourdough loaves baked throughout the day in wood-fired ovens. Menus in the city's finest restaurants proudly declare that they serve *only* Pain Poilane. Unlike the faithful baguette though, these circular loaves don't come cheap, and you can pay up to 40F for a whole loaf; if you want a taste, just ask for a *quart* (a quarter), for about 10F. It's probably enough; they're extraordinarily filling. Try them with cheese. Open Mon.-Sat. 7:15am-8:15pm.

Paul, 4, rue Poncelet, 17ème. Mo. Ternes. Parisians from all over the 17th float in through the door of this bakery, following the overpowering scent that wafts from its crusty loaves, baked throughout the day in their wood-fired ovens. If you're not in the area, this place merits a special pilgrimage. Open Mon. and Wed.-Sat. 6:30am-7:30pm, Sun. 6:30am-1pm.

Thanksgiving, 13, rue Beautreillis, 4ème (tel. 42 77 70 83). Mo. Sully-Morland or Bastille. Homemade American delights including cheesecake and pecan pie, plus plenty of groceries like nacho chips, brownie mix, peanut butter, and ketchup. Prices are pretty high. Brownies 10F, cookies 5F, bagel with cream cheese 18F. They also have take-out dishes: chili 100F per kg, barbecue ribs 40F for 5 pieces.

Peanut Shoppe, 37 rue Dauphine, 6ème. Mo. Odéon. A gorgeous little Indian spice shop stocked with all those ingredients you'd almost given up on finding: cumin, cardomom, coriander, and curry powders, all in a sparklingly clean gem of a shop. Spices sold loose by weight. Open Mon.-Sat. 10:30am-7:30pm.

Alleosse, 13, rue Poncelet, 17ème. Mo. Ternes. An immense and exquisite selection of cheeses.

Charcuterie Coesnon, 30, rue Dauphine, 6ème. Mo. Odéon. Traditional homemade sausage and prepared foods.

Markets and Noteworthy Streets

For a complete list of food and other markets, pick up *Les Marchés de Paris* at the tourist office or your local mairie.

Marché Montorgueil, 2ème. Mo. Etienne Marcel. An old-fashioned market that extends from rue Réaumur to rue Etienne Marcel, along rue des Petits Carreau and rue Montorgueil. Come here to buy bread, wine, cheese, *pâté,* or just about any other French specialty. Lots of meat, fish, and fruit, and a convenient pair of nearby supermarkets. Gets crowded after office hours on weekdays. Many shops and stalls open until the early evening and on weekends.

Marché St-Germain, 3ter, rue Mabillon, 6ème. Mo. Mabillon. A large, covered market selling all sorts of yummie foods. Open Mon.-Sat. 8am-1pm and 4-7:30pm, Sun. 8am-1pm.

Rue Cler between rue de Grenelle and av. de la Motte-Picquet, 7ème. Mo. Ecole Militaire. *Fromagers, boulangers,* and *bouchers* sell their tasty wares side-by-side; fruit and vegetable stands abound.

Marché Europe, 1, rue Corvetto, 8ème. Covered food-market. Open Mon.-Sat. 8am-1:30pm and 4-7pm, Sun. 8am-1pm.

Marché St-Quentin, 85, bd. de Magenta, 10ème. Mo. Gare de l'Est. This market is a massive, elegant construction of iron and glass, built in 1866 with a glass ceiling as glorious as that of Gare du Nord. Inside you'll find an enormous variety of goods, from flowers to fresh produce and skinned rabbits for your delectable *lapin à la moutarde d'Irène*. Open Tues.-Sat. 8am-1pm and 3:30pm-7:30pm, Sun. 8am-1pm.

Rue du Convention at the intersection of rue de Vaugirard, 15*ème*. Mo. Convention. A bewildering array of fruits, vegatables, meat, fish, cheese and pastries every Tuesday and Sunday between 7am and 1pm.

Rue Poncelet, near the Arc de Triomphe, 17*ème*. Mo. Ternes. A good bet, both for its daily morning market and for the dozens of *charcuteries, fromageries, bûcheries,* and *boulangeries* that line the sidewalks.

Sights

It almost was not. By August 23, 1944, in obedience to direct orders from Adolf Hitler, *Wehrmacht* engineers had placed mines at the base of every bridge in Paris. More explosives were crammed into the basements of the Palais Bourbon, the Invalides, and Notre-Dame. The Opéra and the Madeleine were on the list, and the Eiffel Tower was rigged so that it would topple and prevent the approaching Allies from crossing the Seine. A brief order from German commander Dietrich von Choltitz would reduce every major monument in Paris—eight centuries of history—to heaps of rubble and anguished iron.

Though a loyal German, the cultured general could not bring himself to destroy one of the most beautiful cities in the world. Pestered by Hitler's incessant question, "Is Paris burning?" von Choltitz stalled until the Allies had entered the city and relieved him of his burden. His courage preserved some of humanity's greatest architectural achievements. It also left you, the sightseer, with a lot of work to do.

Wander around the city. Don't just look at the buildings, look at the signs of daily life around you. Try walking, rather than taking the metro. Spend a day strolling from the Arc de Triomphe to the Bastille and from the Panthéon to the Assemblée Nationale. Don't be fooled by the apparent architectural homogeneity of central Paris. Replastering and added stories have blurred the visible difference between 17th- and 19th-century residential buildings, but a keen eye can still distinguish them; older buildings tend to be narrower, reflecting the high premium placed on street frontage when the street was the center of life.

Wait until dark, when the city lights up—from the austere place de la Concorde to the lace-like Tour Eiffel. If you can afford it, take a nighttime taxi ride around the city; it's worth the money. Finally, don't try to see too much. Stop for a picnic in one of Paris's beautiful parks; relax in a café and watch the procession of people marching by. "Parisians don't walk; they run, they dash ahead," wrote one 18th-century commentator. Don't be like the Parisians. Enjoy the parade of life Paris represents, without being trampled by it.

Seine Islands

Ile de la Cité

> Paris was born on this small isle of the Cité, which
> is shaped like a cradle. The shore of the island was
> its first rampart, the Seine its first moat.
> —*Victor Hugo*

Thus Hugo begins his famous description of 15th-century Paris, seen from the tower of Notre-Dame. If any one location could be called the sentimental and physical heart of Paris, the capital of the capital, it is this slip in the river. Possessing a long and varied history, the island was first inhabited by a primitive Gallic tribe of hunters, sailors and fisherfolk called the Parisii, who immigrated to the island in the 3rd century BC in search of an easily fortifiable outpost to defend themselves against the marauding Romans. The first certifiable record left by this tribe was, sadly, their defeat by Caesar's legions in the year 52 BC. The island became the center of the Lutèce colony, languishing for four long centuries under the crumbling Roman empire. In the early 6th century, Clovis crowned himself king of the Franks and adopted the embattled island as the center of his domain. No kingdom being complete without an adequately glorious church, work was begun on St-Etienne, the island's first Christian church. The basilica, built into the wall which still surrounded the island-fortress, was finished in the late 6th century under Clovis's son, Childebert I, but completely destroyed only two centuries later by Norman invaders. It was rebuilt, but razed again to make room for Notre-Dame.

During the Middle Ages, the island began to acquire the features for which it is best known and loved today. In the 12th century work commenced on Notre-Dame and Ste-Chapelle under the direction of Bishop Maurice Sully. As Hugo proudly (if somewhat inaccurately) proclaimed, "the first stones were set by Charlemagne...the last by Phillipe-Auguste." Actually, Sully's cathedral was not completed until the 14th century, when it became one of the most fascinating examples of medieval architecture, a mixture of different styles and periods molded into one building. The cathedral became the focal point of the island—and the city—surrounded first by a royal palace and then by the tribunals of the Palais de Justice. As the industrial revolution lured workers into Paris, the narrow streets surrounding these buildings came to house more and more of the city's poor, until its slums were destroyed by Haussmann as part of his great program to "rebuild" Paris. The Baron left the buildings of the Middle Ages intact, but so altered the area around them that they were demoted from functioning elements in the urban fabric to anachronistic relics. Now the island sinks under the weight of countless tour buses whose passengers spill into the souvenir shops to buy the only berets you're likely to see in Paris.

Notre-Dame

In 1163, Pope Alexander III laid the cornerstone for the **Cathédrale de Notre-Dame-de-Paris** (tel. 43 26 07 39; Mo. Cité) over the remains of a Roman temple to Jupiter. The most famous and most trafficked of the Cité's sights, this massive structure was not completed until 1361. The exterior was gaily painted, making the now-somber cathedral as showy as any Italian church. During the Revolution, it was renamed *Temple du Raison* and dedicated to the Cult of Reason. The Gothic arches were hidden behind plaster façades of virtuous, Neoclassical design, immortalized in David's *Sacre*, which hangs in the Louvre. Although reconsecrated after the Revolution, the building fell into disrepair and was even used to shelter livestock. But Victor Hugo's 1831 novel, *Notre-Dame-de-Paris (The Hunchback of Notre Dame),* inspired King Louis-Philippe and thousands of citizens to push for restoration. The modifications by Eugène Viollet-le-Duc (including the addition of the spire, the gargoyles and a statue of himself admiring his own work) remain highly controversial. Is Notre-Dame as we see it today a medieval building, or a product of the 19th century? After the restoration, the cathedral became a valued symbol of civic unity. In 1870 and 1940 thousands of Parisians attended masses to pray for deliverance from the invading Germans—both times without immediate success. But the faithful do not demand results; on August 26, 1944, Charles de Gaulle braved sniper fire to give thanks for his victory. All of this turmoil seems to have left the cathedral unmarked; as do the hordes of tourists who invade its sacred portals every day. In the words of e.e. cummings: "The Cathedral of Notre-Dame does not budge an inch for all the idiocies of this world." One hundred years earlier, Victor Hugo expressed the same sentiment: "Time is blind, humanity stupid."

Today, thousands of visitors float in sweeping torrents past the doors of the cathedral, with the devastating speed of a photo-op current that sucks tourists inside and spits them out again just as quickly, depriving them of one the most glorious aspects of the entire structure: the **façade.** "Few architectural pages," Hugo proclaimed, "are as beautiful as this façade...a vast symphony in stone...an extraordinary product of the forces of an entire epoch...a human creation, in one word, as powerful and fecund as divine creation, of which it seems to have stolen the twin character: variety and eternity." Break away from the line of marching souls to admire the delicate, intricate curves that adorn the three central wooden portals. Although it was begun in the 12th century, the façade was not completed even in the 17th, when artists were still adding Baroque statues of dubious artistic value. Highly symbolic, the carvings were designed to instill a fear of God and desire for righteousness in a population of which less than ten percent were literate. The central and especially picturesque **Porte du Jugement** expounds on the Damned and the Saved. On the right hand sinners, including cardinals, kings, and peasants chained together, are snatched by gleeful demons to a hell populated by tortured souls and grotesque devils. On the left, the happy, virtuous souls of the three estates await entry into heaven. The lower panels tell the viewer how to get into group B, with twelve carvings of good deeds over twelve carvings of sins, including such favorites as faithful wife vs. disobedient children, humility vs. pride, and prudence vs. folly. You make the call. On the **Porte de Sainte Anne,** to the right, don't miss the woman lying in a casket, over whom a dragon is being slayed. Contrary to popular myth, which said that the dragon was but a horrible post-mortem manifestation of a generally annoying woman, it represents the passing of the plague that ravaged the population during the 13th century. Revolutionaries, not exactly your regular churchgoers, wreaked havoc on the façade of the church during the ecstasies of the 1790s; not content to decapitate Louis XVI, they attacked the stone images of his ancestors above the doors. The heads were found in 1977, hiding away in the basement the Banque Française du Commerce, and were installed in the Musée de Cluny (see Museums). Chips of paint on the heads led to a surprising discovery: like all medieval cathedrals, Notre-Dame was once painted in bright and garish colors, making its theological message even more clear for the illiterate passer-by. Replicas of the heads (unpainted) now crown the royal bodies.

Once you pass inside, you'll be overawed by the soaring light and seeming weightlessness of the walls. The magical verticality is created by the spidery flying buttresses that support the vaults of the ceiling from outside, allowing the walls to be opened up to stained glass. The effect is increased by a series of subtle optical illusions, including the use of smaller pillars to surround the bigger ones, diminishing their apparent size. The most spectacular feature of the interior, and certainly the cathedral's biggest attraction, are the enormous stained-glass **rose windows** that dominate the north and south ends of the transept. Fascinated by the number eight, the designers dedicated the entire north window to the number; notice the circles of eight, sixteen, thirty-two and sixty-four panels that emanate from the Virgin and Son. Originally, similarly masterful artistry adorned the windows on the ground level. But "Sun King" Louis XIV, trying to live up to his nickname, ordered all the windows on the ground level to be smashed. Louis's clear windows have since been replaced by stained glass that goes a long way towards imitating pastel wallpaper. Behind the altar you ll find statues of the king and his father kneeling in pious self-righteousness before a miserably Baroque Pietà. Compare their theatricality with the simple, but breathtaking Madonna and Child statue in the transept, one of the foremost examples of the International Gothic style—a late medieval movement emphasizing graceful curves and weightless elegance. Don't overlook the carved wooden panels surrounding the choir, presenting an expressive depiction of the life of Christ. Free **guided tours** of the cathedral are an excellent way to acquire a deeper understanding of its history and architecture; inquire at the information booth to the right as you enter. A rousing tour in English is led by Irving Levine, "the only non-Roman Catholic to give tours at Notre-Dame." A sixty-year-old psychiatrist from New York, he has been living in Paris for the last 26 years. (Tours in English Wed. noon. Tours in French Mon.-Fri. noon, Sat.-Sun. 2pm. Free.) The cathedral's **treasury,** to the south of the choir, contains a rather humdrum assortment of robes and sacramental cutlery from the stately and artistic period of 1949. (Open Mon.-Sat. 10am-6pm, Sun. 2-6pm. Admission 15F, students 10F, under 17 5F.)

Outside again, don t miss the opportunity to visit the haunt of the cathedral's most famous fictional resident, the Hunchback of Notre-Dame, with a hair-raising climb into the two **towers,** especially recommended for jocks in Stairmaster withdrawal. The perilous and claustrophobic, steep and twisting staircase emerges onto a spectacular perch, where a bevy of gargoyles survey a stunning view of the heart of the city. In a supreme act of sacrilege, people have been known to commit suicide by jumping off the towers, now hemmed in by a barricade of steel netting. The climb generally deters the bus-load tourists, and you may even have the towers relatively to yourself if you come early.

Continue on (if you can face the stair again) to the south tower, where a dwarf-sized door gives access to the thirteen-ton bell, which even Quasimodo on a night of wild partying couldn t ring, since it requires the force of eight full-grown men to move. (Open Aug. daily 10am-6:30pm; April-July and Sept. 9:30-11:30am, 2-5:30pm; Oct.-March 10am-4:30pm. Admission 31F, seniors and students 17F, under 17 6F.)

For the best view of Notre-Dame's magnificent backside, cross Pont St-Louis (behind the cathedral) to Ile St-Louis and turn right on quai d'Orléans. At night, the buttresses are lit up, and the view from here is breathtaking. Follow the *quais* to Pont de Sully, at the far side of Ile St-Louis, for an equally striking view of the cathedral. Come here at sundown for the perfect Parisian experience—the Seine, sunset, and Notre-Dame. (See Ile St-Louis.)

Other Sights

The Mémorial de la Déportation, behind the cathedral, across from pl. Jean XXIII, and down a narrow flight of steps, is a haunting memorial erected for the French victims of Nazi concentration camps. 200,000 flickering lights represent the dead, and an eternal flame burns over the tomb of an unknown victim. The names of all the concentration camps glow in gold triangles which recall the design of the patch that French prisoners were forced to wear for identification purposes. A series of quotations is engraved into the stone walls—most striking of these is the motto *"Pardonne; N'Oublie Pas"* (Forgive; Do Not Forget) engraved over the exit. The old men who frequently visit the monument might act as voluntary guides to the monument. If so, they ll explain the symbols, recall their experiences in the camps, and caution that they will neither forgive nor forget.

Far below the cathedral towers, in a cool and dark excavation beneath the pavement of the *Parvis* (the square in front of the cathedral), the **Archeological Museum,**place du Parvis du Notre-Dame (tel. 43 29 83 51), houses a remarkably preserved archeological dig of the Roman village that once covered the island. The museum results from a 1965 underground car park, whose construction uncovered the remains of Roman foundations. The sacred causes of History and Parking split the difference, and now the ruins and the car park share the underground terrain, the entrance of the garage just meters from the museum. Infinitely more interesting than the garage, however, the museum provides a self-guided tour through the dig, wandering through the old *quais*, baths and houses, as well as an exhaustive display of the history of Ile de la Cité through dioramas and accompanying text in both English and French. (Open daily 10am-6pm. Admission 25F, seniors and students 14F, under 17 6F.)

If you re hungry when you emerge again into the sunlight, buy a sandwich and wander into the garden of the **Hôtel Dieu,** a hospital whose original mission was the aid of foundlings, located just along the north side of the Parvis. The soothing gurgling of the fountain and beautifully manicured shrubbery complement the vibrant flowers, making the courtyard a perfect location to repose before continuing on to attack a few more sights on the *Ile.* Climb the steps at the far side for a charming view of the Left Bank. The hospital dates back to the Middle Ages, though then it was more a place to confine the sick than to cure them; guards were posted at the doors to keep the patients from getting out and infecting the city. Pasteur did much of his pioneering research inside. In 1871, the hospital's proximity to Notre-Dame saved the cathedral; the defeated *Communards* were only dissuaded from burning the latter by the fear that the flames could engulf their hospitalized wounded. Across the street is the **Préfecture de Police,** where at 7am on August 19, 1944, members of the Paris police force began the insurrection against the Germans that lasted until the Allies liberated the city six days later.

The Palais de Justice, spanning the western side of the island, harbors the infamous **Conciergerie,** prison of the Revolution, the ethereal **Ste-Chapelle,** St-Louis' private chapel, and numerous tribunals where you can still see the law in action. Since 52 BC, various forms of the French judiciary have been housed in a building occupying this site. Since the 13th century, the structures here have contained the district courts for Paris. All trials are open to the general public, but don t expect a *France v. Dreyfus* every day. *Chambre 1* of the *Cour d Appel* (up *escalier* K) witnessed Pétain's convictions after WWII. Even if your French is not up to legal jargon, the cool sobriety of the interior, along with the lawyers archaic yet stylish black robes, makes a quick visit interesting and worthwhile, especially since it's free. (Trials Mon.-Fri. 1:30pm until the day's agenda is completed, around 5pm.) Criminal cases are the most interesting; ask for the location of the criminal courtrooms (open Mon.-Fri. 1:30-4pm).

At the heart of the Palais, **Ste-Chapelle** (tel. 43 54 30 09) remains one of the foremost examples of 13th-century French architecture, though its imprisonment in the middle of the 19th-century Palais de Justice obscures its medieval flavor. Crowded into an interior courtyard, the beautiful exterior is lost to view; the random passerby sees no more than the iron steeple, a 19th-century addition. The church was begun in 1241 to house the most precious of King Louis IX's possessions, the crown of thorns from Christ's Passion. Bought from Emperor Baudoin II of Constantinople in 1239 along with a section of the Cross for an ungodly sum of 135,000 livres, the crown required an equally princely chapel. Although the crown—minus a few thorns which St-Louis gave away as political favors—has been moved to Notre-Dame, Ste-Chapelle still remains a masterpiece—"the pearl among them all," as Marcel Proust called it. A blissfully dark and serene interior and domed roof mark a room of golds, reds and blues in the lower chapel. In the upstairs chapel, reserved for royalty and their court, an overwhelming array of stained glass windows provides a miracle of color and lace-like delicacy; its melding of blues and reds lights the church with a hue of fine wine, giving rise to the saying "wine the color of Sainte Chapelle's windows." The windows are the oldest stained glass in Paris, tastefully restored in 1845; the glass you see is for the most part the same under which St-Louis prayed to his holy relic. Check weekly publications for the occasional concerts here, or ask at the information booth at the gate; tickets run 75-155F. (Open daily 9:30am-6:30pm. Admission 25F, students and seniors 14F, under 17 6F. Combined ticket for the Chapelle and the Conciergerie 40F.)

The Conciergerie (tel. 43 54 30 06), around the corner of the Palais from the entrance to the Chapelle, lurks ominously, jealously brooding over the souls and memories of the prisoners who died here during the Revolution. The northern façade, visible in its entirety from the shores of the Right Bank, is that of a gloomy medieval fortress. At the farthest corner on the right, a stepped parapet marks the oldest tower, the Tour Bonbec (the tower of babble), which once housed the prison's extensive torture chambers. The modern entrance lies between the Tour d'Argent (Silver Tower), stronghold of the royal treasury, and the Tour de César, which housed the revolutionary tribunal. Before entering, notice the clock tower on the outside. The bright, 16th-century face of Paris's first public clock ticked down the lasts seconds of the prisoners' lives inside. Its inscription reads *Machine quae bis sex tam juste dividit horas, Justiciam servare monet legesque tueri* (This machine, which divides the hours very precisely into twice six, exhorts us to observe Justice and to execute the law.)

Don t pause too long at the heavy-handed guard room at the entrance, but instead flee along the *"Rue de Paris"*—the corridor leading from the entrance, so named for the prisoners' destination, *"M. Paris,"* the executioner. At the end is the Great Hall, an enormous Gothic hall where you ll find four fireplaces big enough to toast a queen-size bed. Past the Great Hall, stairs lead to facsimiles of prisoners cells, now inhabited by glum-looking mannequins, especially in the *pailleux* cell, where prisoners who weren t rich enough to bribe their jailers were forced to sleep on straw. Next door, the wealthier mannequins, the *pistoliers,* sleep two to a cell in relative comfort. Farther down the hall is a cell where Maximilien de Robespierre, the brutal merchant of death, awaited the sensation of a short, sharp shock. It has been converted into a display of his letters, as well as an actual guillotine from 1836 (used to execute the assassin Lacenaire). Engraved on the wall are Robespierre's famous last words, *Je vous laisse ma Mémoire. Elle vous sera chère, et vous la defendrez.* (I leave you my memory. It will be dear to you, and you will defend it.) Beyond Robespierre's cell lies a small room dedicated to the memory of those who died in the Revolution, containing walls covered with the thousands of names and occupations of the executed. A surprising number of bakers, servants, peasants and other commoners are represented, testifying to the frenzy of death into which the Revolution degenerated during its final chapter. Marie-Antoinette's cell has been converted to a chapel (located downstairs on your way into the courtyard), but a rather homey and unsatisfying replica can be found upstairs. The Conciergerie is still used as a temporary prison for those awaiting trial in the Palais de Justice. (Open daily 9:30am-6pm; Oct.-March 10am-5pm. Admission including guided tour in French 25F, seniors and students 14F, under 17 6F. A combined ticket to the Conciergerie and Ste-Chapelle 40F).

Place Dauphine, behind the Conciergerie, was a delightful oasis in 1607, when Henri IV ordered its construction. Originally it was lined with buildings bearing unified façades, much like the place des Vosges. Throughout the 18th century, art exhibitions were held here on Corpus Christi, allowing many of France's young artists to gain recognition for the first time. But renovations in 1874 largely destroyed the symmetry of the square, leaving the park as just a patch of dirt for happy poodles. Surrealist André Bréton called it "one of the most profoundly withdrawn places that I know, one of the worst wastelands that exists in Paris. Every time I am there, I feel myself abandon little by little the wish to go anywhere else." Even if you can't sympathize with Bréton's fondness for devastation, the square offers a uniquely peaceful respite from the chaos of the *Ile,* a magnificent view of the rear façade of the Palais de Justice, and a positive jewel of a wine bar (see Wine Bars). As you leave Ile de la Cité from here, you'll walk over the oldest bridge in Paris, ironically named **Pont Neuf,** or "New Bridge." Completed in 1607, the bridge's radical design lacked the usual domestic residences lining its sides. Before the construction of the Champs-Elysées, the bridge was the most popular thoroughfare, attracting peddlers, performers, thieves, and even street physicians. L. S. Mercier described this bridge in his 1789 *Tableau de la vie parisienne* (Tableau of Parisian Life): "Pont-Neuf is to the city what the heart is to the human body, the center of movement and of circulation. The flux and reflux of inhabitants and visitors strikes this passageway so strongly that, in order to find someone you're looking for, it is enough just to walk here one hour each day." Although not of particular architectural interest, the bridge does have individual gargoyle capitals on its supports, which can be viewed by hanging your head over the edge, or better yet, from below while taking a *bateau-mouche* trip down the river (see Entertainment).

Ile St-Louis

> *It was not without regret that I left the beautiful*
> *quartier of Ile Saint-Louis, with its agreable quays*
> *and the tranquil riverbank on which I took the air in*
> *the summer evenings....*
> —Manon Roland (1754-1793)

A short walk across the Pont St-Louis, away from the long line of tour buses behind Notre-Dame, will take you to **Ile St-Louis,** one of the city's most charming and elegant neighborhoods. Originally two small islands used as a cow pasture, this area received its name in 1267 when St-Louis was baptized here before leaving on his last crusade. In the 17th century, under Louis XIII and Louis XIV, the islands were connected and built up with a series of mansions to house the elite of Paris. The charming streets hide the houses in which such luminaries as Voltaire, Mme. de Châtelet, Daumier, Ingres, Baudelaire, and Cézanne resided. Some of the most privileged of Paris's exceedingly privileged elite, including the Rothschilds and Pompidou's widow, now call this scrap of land home. But seclusion has its downside; constantly ignored, the inhabitants grew tired of the lack of press and whimsically proclaimed the island an independent republic in the 1930s. Today, Ile St-Louis remains one of the city's most expensive residential areas. Home to some of the oldest *hôtels* (private residences) of Paris, it provides an enchanting retreat from the constant movement of the boulevards and the crowded tourist traps of Ile de la Cité. At night, Ile St-Louis comes alive with the charm of cast-iron lamps, outlined against the shadows of the Seine. Sweeping arcs of light from *bateaux-mouches* highlight, as in a moving picture show, the 17th-century *hôtels* on the *quais* and the 19th-century buildings on either side of the island.

Begin anywhere on this island and follow the *quais* around the perimeter for beautiful views on every side, including a postcard-perfect Notre-Dame (flying buttresses and all). As you walk around the island, notice the harmony and uniformity of the 17th-century architecture, and read the plaques that indicate here and there where a famous artist, writer, or historical figure lived. Try to get a peek at the beautiful interior court-yards filled with flowers, plants, and fountains. These are some of the most chic residences in Paris, although living in them means constant invasion by lights of the *bateaux-mouches* passing in the night. Follow steps down to the newly renovated lower *quais*, a traditional hideout for couples and daydreamers alike. As with any of the remote spots in Paris, women should not explore the lower *quais* alone at night.

The Quai d'Anjou, between Pont Marie and Pont de Sully, houses some of the island's most beautiful *hôtels*, with massive wooden doors and dramatic, watchful lion's heads above the windows. No. 9 marks the house where Honoré Daumier, realist painter and caricaturist, lived from 1846-1863. To see the interior of one of these mansions, try No. 17, the Hôtel Lauzon. Built in 1657 by Le Vau, the Hôtel Lauzon is a masterpiece of Baroque architecture, decorated with gilding, tapestries, and beautiful *trompe l'oeil* paintings. In the 19th and early 20th century, it was home to a steady stream of Bohemian celebrities, from Théophile Gautier and Charles Baudelaire to Richard Wagner and Rainer Maria Rilke. (Open to visitors from Easter to Nov. Sat. 10am-5:30pm.)

Beginning at either end of the island, walk down the central **Rue St-Louis-en-l'Ile.** This is the "main drag" of Ile St-Louis, filled with a pleasant array of gift shops, art galleries and traditional French restaurants, as well as the famous **Berthillon** *glacerie* (see Sweets, Restaurants, and Shopping sections). The **Hôtel Lambert,** at No. 2, designed by Le Vau and built in 1640 for Lambert le Riche, has housed such luminaries as Voltaire and Mme. de Châtelet. **Eglise St-Louis-en-l'Ile,** at the corner of rue St-Louis-en-l'Ile and rue Poulletier, presents a humble exterior to the passerby, yet was designed by Le Vau in the finest of aristocratic traditions. Built between 1664 and 1726, the church is covered with a thick coat of soot which makes it look more like a prison than a house of worship. The dark and brooding exterior, however, opens to the airiest of Rococo interiors, magnificently decorated with gold leaf, marble, and graceful statuettes. (Open to the public Mon.-Sat. 9am-noon and 3-7pm.) On either side of rue St-Louis-en-l'Ile, small quiet residential streets lead back to the *quais*. Follow rue Budé to 6, quai d'Orléans, for the **Musée Adam Mickiewicz,** full of memorabilia from this 19th-century poet and his compatriots (see Museums).

First Arrondissement

The first *arrondissement* has one of the highest concentrations of interesting sights per acre in the world. Hugging the side of the Seine, the Louvre—world-famous art museum and former residence of kings—occupies about a seventh of the *arrondissement* (for a full description of the museum and its treasures, see Museums). The Jardin des Tuileries, a large formal garden attached to the Louvre, contains the small Musée de l'Orangerie, home to an Impressionist collection that includes Monet's *Nymphéas* (Water Lilies). Next to the Louvre but on a smaller scale is the Palais Royal, a palace that Cardinal Richelieu built for himself in 1632. It is worth visiting for its old-fashioned formal garden and futuristic courtyard sculpture. Northeast is Les Halles, a marvelous area to stroll. The Forum des Halles is an underground shopping mall with a park above it; around the park are a Gothic/Renaissance church (St-Eustache) and plenty of sidestreets full of restaurants and a few bars. With the Centre Pompidou just around the block (see fourth *arrondissement)*, what more could you ask?

The Jardin des Tuileries, at the western foot of the Louvre, celebrates the victory of geometry over nature. The views from the elevated terrace by the river, and along the central path of the park, are spectacular. From the terrace you can see the Louvre, the gardens, the Eiffel Tower, and the Musée d'Orsay (right across the river). From the central path, gaze upon the obelisk of Luxor (in place de la Concorde), the Arc de Triomphe, and (on a clear day) the Arche de la Défense in the distance; turn around to see the Arc de Triomphe du Carrousel and the Cour Napoléon of the Louvre. Sculptures are sprinkled throughout the park, including 18 bronze nudes by Auguste Maillol. Cathérine des Médicis, missing the public promenades of her native Italy, had the gardens built in 1564; in 1649 André Le Notre (designer of the gardens at Versailles) imposed his preference for straight lines and sculptured trees upon the landscape of the Tuileries. Once he completed his work, the gardens were made public and have since become one of the most popular open spaces in Paris. Along with the gardens, Cathérine ordered the **Palais des Tuileries,** which stretched along the west end of the Jardin du Carrousel, forming the western wall of the Louvre. Long after most of the Louvre had been converted into an art museum, the Tuileries remained the royal residence. Louis XVI and Marie-Antoinette attempted to flee from here in 1791. Napoleon lived here prior to his exile; Louis XVIII was chased out of here upon Napoleon's return in 1814. Louis-Philippe fled in similar haste in 1848, and in 1870, the Empress Eugénie scrambled out as the mob crashed in the main entrance. Nine months later, as Republican forces streamed into the city to crush the Commune, a vengeful Communard official packed the palace with gunpowder, tar, and oil. His preparations were effective, and the building erupted into flames, which fortunately did not spread to the Louvre. The burnt-out ruins of the Tuileries survived until 1882, when the Republican Municipal Council, unwilling to restore a symbol of the monarchy, had them flattened. Today, only the Pavillion de Flore and the Pavillion de Marsan remain.

In recent years, the government has allowed an amusement park to spring up seasonally. If you're with kids or simply want to nourish your inner child, come for the rides between the first weekend of December and the first weekend of January, or between the last Sunday of June and the first Sunday after August 15. At night, the huge Ferris wheel offers a magnificent view of nocturnal Paris. There are also some more traditional amusements for tiny tots, which operate year round (except for a few weeks in winter). These include some *oh so cute* little ponies that little kids can ride for 20F, and some sailboats in the round fountain (near the Louvre courtyard) that you can rent and push around for 5F. If you just want to relax, there are a few cafés (closed in winter), but these tend to be expensive. The park opens at 7am on weekdays, and on weekends and holidays at 7:30am. From the last Sunday of March to the Saturday preceding the last Sunday of September, closing time is 10pm; for the rest of the year it is 8pm. Don't tempt fate by trying to remain in the Tuileries after the gates are locked. If you manage to survive the large hounds that patrol the grounds, you might enjoy less luck with the people who frequent the park after dark.

The place Vendôme, three blocks north along the rue de Castiglione from the Tuileries, was begun in 1687 according to plans by Jules Hardouin-Mansart, who convinced Louis XIV and a group of five financiers to invest in the ensemble of private mansions and public institutions. The project ran out of funds almost immediately, as Louis XIV placed the entire state treasury into his military campaigns; for several decades, before it was finished in 1720, the theatrical and ostentatious place Vendôme remained no more than a series of empty façades. Many of the buildings were gutted in the 1930s; again, their uniformly dignified façades were protected, and place Vendôme, as it exists today, is a series of 17th-century façades masking 20th-century offices. In 1972, a huge underground carpark was installed, another major change that did not vary the outside appearance of the square. Under renovation in 1992, the *place* should be more beautiful than ever by 1993.

The **column** in the center of the square has acted as a barometer reflecting fluctuations in regime. Originally, the square held a 7m statue of Louis XIV in Roman costume. The statue was destroyed on August 10, 1792, and the square was renamed place des Piques. *(Piques* were long spears—weapons of the common people—used in the Revolution to carry guillotined heads and Phrygian bonnets.) In 1805, the aristocratic place Vendôme was reborn when Napoleon erected a central column modeled after Trajan's column in Rome. Cast from 1,250 Austrian and Russian bronze cannon captured in battle, surrounding a core of stone, the column showed a series of soldiers and military heroes; the emperor at the top was represented in the Roman toga that once covered Louis XIV. Nine years later, with the entry of the Allied troops into Paris, the statue of Napoleon was deposed—not without difficulty. (In order to remove it, the Royalist government had to arrest the maker of the statue and force him, on penalty of execution, to figure out how to get rid of it.) All this was for naught; the return of Napoleon from Elba brought the original statue back to its proud stance. Over the next sixty years this would be replaced by the white flag of the ancient monarchy, by a re-

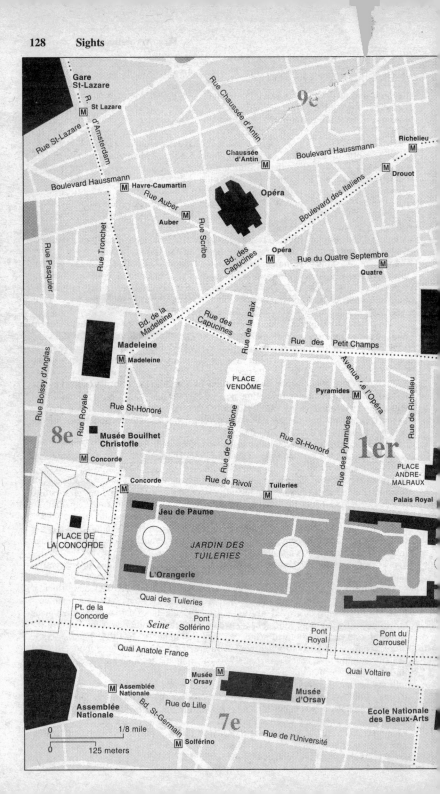

1er and 2e

N

Bonne
Nouvelle

Ⓜ Strasbourg
St-Denis

Boulevard Poissonniere

Ⓜ

Rue Monmartre

Rue Monmartre

Boulevard de Sébastopol

N
↑

3e

Rue Vivienne

Bourse
des Yaleurs

Rue de Cléry

Rue Réaumur

Réaumur-
Sébastopol

Ⓜ

Arts et Ⓜ
Métiers

Ⓜ

Bourse

Ⓜ Sentier

Rue d'Aboukir

Rue de Turbigo

Rue Beaubourg

2e

**Bibliothèque
Nationale**

Rue Montmartre

Rue Etienne Marcel

Etienne Marcel
Ⓜ

Rue St-Martin

ARDIN DU
PALAIS
ROYALE

Rue du Louvre

Rue Croix des Petits Champs

St-Eustache

Ⓜ Les Halles

Rue Rambuteau

Rue St-Denis

Rambuteau

Ⓜ

Forum

Ⓜ
Châtelet

**Centre
Pompidou**

Rue du Renard

**Palais
Royal**

Rue Berger

Rue St-Honoré

Sq. des
Innocents

4e

PLACE DU
PALAIS
ROYAL

Louvre

Ⓜ Louvre

Rue de Rivoli

Les
Halles
Ⓜ

Rue des Halles

Rue St-Denis

Bd. de Sébastopol

Rue de Rivoli

Hôtel
de Ville

Ⓜ

R. Amal.-de-Coligny

Pont Neuf

Rue du Pont Neuf

Châtelet

Châtelet
Ⓜ

Châtelet
Ⓜ

Ⓜ

PLACE DU
CHATELET

Quai de la Mégisserie

uai du Louvre

Pont
des Arts

Pont Neuf

Pont
au Change

Pont
Notre Dame

Pont
d'Arcole

Seine

Quai Malaquais

Quai de Conti

Quai des
Grands Augustins

Rue Dauphine

Conciergerie

**Palais
de Justice
Ste. Chapell**

Pl. Lépine

Ⓜ Cité

R. de
Lutèce

Ile de la Cité

Blvd. du Palais

**Notre
Dame**

PLACE
DU
PARVIS

**Institut
de France**

6e

**Hôtel
des
Monnaies**

PLACE
ST-MICHEL

Ⓜ St-Michel

Pont
St-Michel

Petit Pont

Pont au Double

newed Napoleon in military garb, by a classical Napoleon modeled after the original, and finally by the Red Flag of the Commune. Soon after, a committee headed by the artist Gustave Courbet toppled the entire war-like victory column, planning to replace it with a monument to the "Federation of Nations and the Universal Republic." Four years later, in Napoleon's final victory, the original column was recreated at Courbet's expense. New bronze reliefs were made from the original molds; the Emperor returned to the top where he still holds sway over the gracious square.

Today, the entire *place* shimmers with opulence; here are well-known bankers, perfumers, jewelers, and the Parisian branch of IBM. Savor the moments with a 50,000F watch from Cartier, or dress down with a pair of 100,000F earrings from Van Cleef & Arpels. Supposedly, Rothschild, instead of lending his friends money, would simply allow them to stroll with him around pl. Vendôme for a few minutes. The next morning the fortunate souls would be certain of credit at the most prestigious banks. Chopin died at no. 12; Hemingway drank at no. 15, the **Ritz Hotel.** (After riding into Paris with the U.S. Army, Hemingway gathered some Resistance troops and went off to liberate the Ritz. Greeted by his old chum, the assistant manager, Papa calmly ordered 73 dry martinis.) No. 11 and 13, identified by the proud flag, is the Ministry of Justice. At street level, to the left of the entrance, is The Meter, the mother of all rulers. Nowadays meters are defined using krypton 86 radiation, but this 1848 unit is a pretty reliable source. To the east, between the *place* and the Eglise St-Roch, no. 328, rue St-Honoré, is the former site of the **Jacobin convent,** which furnished a meeting-place for Robespierre, the brutal merchant of death, and his cronies and gave its name to the extreme republicanism of the Terror. Robespierre himself lodged at no. 398-400.

The Palais Royal lies across rue de Rivoli from the Louvre. Constructed in 1639 as Cardinal Richelieu's *Palais Cardinal*, it became a *Palais Royal* when Anne of Austria, regent for Louis XIV, set up house there. Louis-Philippe d'Orléans, the Duc de Chartres whose son became King Louis-Philippe, inherited the palace in 1780. Strapped for cash, in 1784 he built and rented out the elegant buildings that enclose the palace's formal garden, turning the complex into the 18th century's version of a shopping mall. It had boutiques, several restaurants, prostitutes, and—in lieu of a multi-screen cinema—theaters, wax museums, and puppet shows. On July 12, 1789, 26-year-old Camille Desmoulins leaped on a café table and, shouting "I would rather die than submit to servitude," urged his fellow citizens to arm themselves. The enthusiastic crowd filed out, and was soon skirmishing with cavalry in the Tuileries garden. The revolutions of 1830 and 1848 also began with angry crowds in these gardens. In the second half of the 19th century, the Palais recovered as a center of luxury commerce, preserving a serene aristocracy amid the "commercialism" of Haussmann's boulevards and the new, modern department stores.

Today, the galleries of the venerable buildings contain small shops and a few cafés, with a splendid view of the palace fountain and flower beds, both of which were re-landscaped in 1992. The levels above the cafés and shops, as well as the older parts of the palace, are occupied by government offices (including that of Jack Lang, France's dynamic Minister of Culture). A popular place to kiss, for couples with a large height disparity, are the *colonnes de Buren*—a set of striped pillars and stumps that completely fill the *cour d'honneur* (the main courtyard). Planted there in 1986, Daniel Buren's columns created a storm of controversy comparable to the one that greeted the Louvre pyramids. Separating this courtyard from the gardens are rather more staid columns, built in the early 19th century. (They served as the setting for the suspenseful climax of the Audrey Hepburn film, *Charade.*) On the southwestern corner of the Palais Royal, facing the Louvre, the **Comédie Française** is home to France's leading dramatic group. The theater was built in 1790 by architect Victor Louis, who created the other buildings, and was likewise sponsored by the Duc de Chartres. Molière, the company's founder, died here on stage; ironically, he was playing the role of the "Imaginary Invalid." A monument to the great playwright, "the Shakespeare of France," rises not far from here at the corner of rue Molière and rue Richelieu.

Stretching north from the Comédie into the second and ninth *arrondissements* is the glittering **Avenue de l'Opéra.** Haussmann leveled the butte de Moulins and many old homes to connect the old symbol of royalty, the Louvre, to the new symbol of imperial grandeur, the Opéra. The grand creation was intended to bear the mightiest name of all: avenue Napoléon, but the Franco-Prussian war interrupted this scheme, and when finally finished, the avenue was named for its terminus instead.

The Bourse du Commerce is the large round building between the rue du Louvre and the Forum des Halles. Not to be confused with the stock exchange (the "bourse des valeurs" or simply the "bourse"), the Bourse du Commerce is a commodities exchange where deals on agricultural produce are made. It's worth stepping inside (which you're allowed to do Mon.-Fri. 8:30am-7pm) to admire the iron-and-glass cupola and the paintings that surround it. In the Middle Ages, a convent of repented sinners occupied the site. Cathérine des Médicis threw out the penitent women in 1572, when a horoscope convinced her that she should abandon construction of the Tuileries and build her palace here instead. Cathérine's palace was demolished in 1748, leaving only the observation tower of her personal astrologer (a huge stone pillar that stands right next to the wall of the Bourse du Commerce) as a memorial to her superstition. Louis XV replaced the structure with a grain market on the site, which was transformed into a commodities market in 1889, when the current building was built.

St-Eustache (Mo. Les Halles, Châtelet les Halles), is the large Gothic/Renaissance church visible from all over Les Halles, right next to the Turbigo exit of the Les Halles metro. In front of the church is a large cobblestoned area with fountains and a distinctive sculpture of a huge human head and hand. Come to this area with a frisbee on a summer evening and you'll be sure to meet plenty of local youths and foreign backpackers who want to play. Eustatius was a Roman general who is said to have converted to Christianity upon seeing the sign of a cross between the antlers of a deer. As a punishment for his religious convictions, he and his family were locked into a brass bull which was then placed over a fire until it became white-hot. Construction of the church in his honor began in 1532, and dragged on for over a century. The church was finally consecrated in 1632, with its façade incomplete. In 1754, with the Neoclassical trend that swept the nation, the unfinished façade was knocked down and replaced with the Roman façade that it has today—terribly incongruous with the rest of the building, but entirely appropriate for the saint in question. You can get a nice view of the older parts of the church if you go down the stairs of the Porte St-Eustache (one of the entrances to the Forum des Halles). To visit the interior you can just look around, or take a guided tour (in French only). Perhaps the best way of taking in the architecture and the stained glass is to attend one of the organ concerts organized in June and July. The organ is one of the best in Paris; classical music lovers will not want to miss the experience of its thrilling baritone. For information on the organ festival, check *Pariscope*, call 45 22 28 74, or read the posters in front of the church. (Organ festival tickets 120F, students 80F. Church open Mon.-Sat. 8:30am-7pm, Sun. 8:15am-12:30pm and 3-7pm. Guided tours 3pm on Sun.; daily 2pm in June and July. Mass Mon.-Fri. 10am and 6pm, Sat. 6pm, Sun. 8:30am, 9:45am, 11am, and 6pm. On Sun., the 11am mass is with the choir and organ and the 6pm mass is with the organ.) The statue in front of the church was created in 1986 by sculptor Henri de Miller. Its apt title is *The Listener*.

Les Halles (Mo. Les Halles, Châtelet-Les Halles) was called *"le ventre de Paris"* (Paris's belly) by Emile Zola. Since 1135, when King Louis VI built two wooden buildings here to house a bazaar, Les Halles (pronounced "Lay Ahl") was the site of the largest food market in Paris. The Les Halles Zola described received a much-needed facelift in the 1850s and 60s, with the construction of large iron and glass pavilions that sheltered the vendors stalls. Designed by Baltard, the pavilions resembled the one that still stands over the small market at the Carreau du Temple in the third *arrondissement* (built in 1865). One hundred years later, the Les Halles market had again slipped into disrepair. This time, however, the authorities decided to solve the problem merely by sending the vendors off to a suburb near Orly.

After moving the old market in 1970, politicians and city planners debated how to fill *le trou des Halles* (the gap at Les Halles), 106 open acres which presented Paris with the largest urban redesign opportunity since Hausmannization. Most of the city adored the elegant pavilions and wanted to see them preserved. But planners insisted that only by destroying the pavilions could they create a needed transfer point between the metro and the new RER; demolition began in 1971. The city retained architects

Claude Vasconi and Georges Penreach to replace the pavilions with a subterranean shopping mall, the **Forum des Halles.** 200 boutiques (the most fashionable of which have floated to the uppermost levels) are crammed into the complex, along with a swimming pool (see Sports) and several museums: the Musée Grevin, the Musée d'Holographie, and the Martyrs of Paris/Rock 'n' Roll Hall of Fame complex (see Museums). There are movie theaters, as well as a small Videothèque de Paris which offers consultations on video and screenings of videos concerning Paris (tel. 40 26 34 30; open Tues.-Sun. 12:30-9pm; admission 20F). Watch your wallet inside Les Halles, and stay above ground at night. This is a good place to come for cheap clothes, but don't expect the high fashion world for which Paris is famous. Putting the mall underground had the advantage of allowing the vast Les Halles quadrangle to be landscaped with greenery, statues, and fountains.

Getting around the Forum can be quite confusing; computerized maps, scattered throughout the complex, tell you what's available and how to get there. The computers will even communicate with you in English—if you see a French screen, keep pressing the words *sommaire* or *fin* until you get to a display which features a button marked "change language." As with so much in life, a light touch yields better results than a hard shove. The Forum des Halles has wheelchair-access elevators.

South of the forum, along the rue St-Honoré, is the **Rue de la Ferronnerie.** In 1610, as he passed no. 11, Henri IV met his death at the hands of a man named Ravaillac, who lept into the king's carriage and stabbed him mortally. Ravaillac, who was upset that Henri was not persecuting the Protestants, was later seared with red-hot pincers and scalded with boiling lead in an effort to uncover his accomplices; finally, the tortuters concluded that Ravaillac acted alone. He was then torn to pieces and burned by an angry mob. Later, this street became the center of the metal trade in the city. Also nearby is the **Fontaine des Innocents,** built in 1548. It served both as an important water source and as a ceremonial marker along the royal route down the venerable rue St-Denis. Tucked behind the Louvre, near the Pont Neuf, is the Gothic church **St-Germain l'Auxerrois.** On August 24, 1572, the church's bell functioned as the signal for the St. Bartholomew's Day Massacre. Huguenots were rounded up by the troops of the Duc de Guise and slaughtered in the streets, while King Charles IX himself shot at the survivors out the palace window. **Pont Neuf** itself, the oldest and most famous of the Seine bridges, connects the first *arrondissement* to the Ile de la Cité (see Islands). At its left, **Samaritaine** is one of the oldest department stores in Paris. Founded in 1869, and named after the Samaritaine pump of Henri IV, it ushered in the modern age of consumption. The building you see today, with its tiled *Samaritaine* logo, began as a delicate iron and steel construction in 1906 and was revamped (some say massacred) in the Art Deco style of 1928.

Second Arrondissement

Galerie Colbert and **Galerie Vivienne,** near the Palais Royal, are the finest remaining examples of Parisian *galeries,* pedestrian streets inside city blocks, lined with cafés, restaurants, and quaint boutiques. Both arcades, recently restored, date from the early 19th-century, when developers searched for new opportunities in the already too-dense central district. Later, the indoor, glass-covered arcades provided a perfect showcase for the art of *flânerie*—strolling aimlessly amid the crowd—invented by Bohemians like Gérard de Nerval and Baudelaire. Their marbled colonnades, lined with elegant shops, brought the busy street indoors, becoming "a city, even a world, in miniature" (as described in an 1852 guide to the city). In more arcane terms, these two galleries, like the nearby Palais Royal (see first *arrondissement),* demonstrate the desperate folly of past ages as they groped through the darkness of ignorance before achieving the Nirvana of the shopping mall.

An entrance at 4, rue des Petits Champs reveals Galerie Colbert, an elegant passageway with a long row of marble columns. Actually, the columns are made of wood; place your ear against a column and listen for the hollow sound you produce by knocking the column with your knuckles. Yes, yet another example of mid 19th-century superficiality. At the end of this passage is a rotunda with a bronze statue from 1822. Turn right twice at the rotunda, thus making a U-turn into the Galerie Vivienne. Here again you'll find a pleasant Neoclassical decor and plenty of little boutiques; in addition, a number of large windows feature displays from the Bibliothèque Nationale, which uses this building as an annex.

The Bibliothèque Nationale, 58, rue de Richelieu (tel. 47 03 81 26) competes with the British Library for the title of largest library in Western Europe. Its collection of 12 million volumes includes two Gutenberg Bibles, countless first editions from the 15th century to the present, and unmatchable resources on Bohemian Paris and Rodolphe Bresdin. The private collections of the kings of France, collected long before the invention of movable type, provided the embryo, and the library has been growing ever since. Ever since 1642, the law has stipulated that every book published in France must be archived in the Bibliothèque Nationale; not surprisingly, the place is bursting at the seams. Annexes have been built nearby to house the ever-rising volume of books, notably the Annexe Vivienne (see above). In the late 1980s, however, the government decided that it could no longer expand the Bibliothèque Nationale and resolved to build a new library, the Bibliothèque de France (see 13th *arrondissement).* The collections of the Bibliothèque Nationale will be moved into their new home over several months, starting in late 1994; when this process is complete, the old Bibliothèque Nationale will become the Bibliothèque Nationale des Arts.

Foreigners are not allowed into the library's reading room, unless they can prove they're doing research that calls for publications unavailable elsewhere in Paris. Normally, they must be studying at a graduate level or higher to qualify. If you can get a letter from a university, publisher, or publication, call 47 03 81 02 for approval, or stop by at the library's main office. (Open Mon.-Sat. 9am-4pm.) Even for plebs who can't get into the stacks, the library is worth visiting. Temporary exhibitions highlight different portions of the library's priceless collection: if your French is up to it, call 47 03 81 10 to ask what's being shown. Also ask for the opening hours, since these vary depending on the exhibition. There is also a Musée des Médailles, displaying a wide mix of coins and medallions from various cultures and centuries, outshone by the Musée de la Monnaie in the sixth *arrondissement.* (Admission 20F, reduced 12F. Open Mon.-Sat. 1-5pm, Sun. noon-6pm.)

The Bourse des Valeurs (stock exchange), 4, place de la Bourse (tel. 42 33 99 83 or 40 41 10 00; Mo. Bourse), is housed in a sober building with an unmistakably financial air. Yet the generic Neoclassical building might as well be a church, a bank, or, as Hugo continued the list in *Notre-Dame de Paris,* "a royal palace, a house of commons, a town hall, a college, a riding school, an academy, a trade market, a tribunal, a museum, a barracks, a sepulchre, a temple, a theater." Massive Corinthian colonnades create a reassuring impression of stability, reinforced by four stone women in classical garb. To the right of the entrance is *Commerce* (sitting on a bale, with a money-chest at her feet). To the left of the entrance is *Justice,* supporting one arm on the Tables of the Law and holding a scale with her other hand. To the right of the back door is *Agriculture,* with a grapevine crown; she holds a wheat sheaf, and various agricultural tools provide support for her feet. And finally, to the left of the back door is *Industry:* sitting on an anvil, she rests her right hand on gear wheels and carries a hammer on her left shoulder.

The exchange was founded in 1724, long after those of Lyon, Toulouse, and Rouen. Through it flowed the ever more worthless bonds of the old regime, as the debts of the last, extravagant Bourbons multiplied to finance their debauchery and their wars. It was closed briefly during the Terror, due to Jacobin suspicion of profiteering traders, but it recovered under the regime of Napoleon, who first limited the number of seats. Construction of the present edifice began in 1808, according to plans laid by Alexandre Brogniart (who also designed Père Lachaise). Progress was slow and stopped entirely between 1814 and 1821 for lack of funds; only in 1826 were the stockbrokers able to move in from their temporary home on rue Feydeau (a workshop for opera props). Statues were ordered in 1825, but the contracts were abandoned during the Revolution of 1830. It was not until 1851 that the four allegories currently in place were installed. Almost immediately, with the growth of stock trading, Brogniart's palace became too small. As a stopgap measure, various parts of the market were moved elsewhere in Paris. Eventually, someone realized this could not go on forever; between 1902 and 1907, the wings to the left and right of the façade were added. The only way you can visit the interior is by taking one of the **guided tours** offered at least twice a day (be ready to show your passport as you enter). You get a little lecture about stock markets, complete with computerized audio-visuals, then a look at the trader's pit (which is pretty tame compared to London or New York). Unless markets fascinate you and your grasp of French financial vocabulary is fairly good, this probably isn't worth the 10F and the 45 minutes. (For daily times, call ahead or check the sign by the entrance.)

To the east of the Bourse, the **rue de Cléry** and the parallel **rue d'Aboukir** mark the line of the old rampart of Charles V. The buildings between the two streets were constructed after the destruction of the wall in the 17th century, and they illustrate the adaptation of the fanciest, Italianate forms to more inexpensive dwellings. Lintels and plaster were used instead of arches and stone, making handsome, serviceable abodes for hard-working professionals.

Far from this oasis of respectability, at the eastern edge of the *arrondissement,* the **Rue St-Denis** is home to a church, an elementary school, and lots of good restaurants. One of the oldest streets in Paris, it is home to the oldest profession. Prostitution is legal in France, and censorship of sexual material in store displays is very lax. At all hours of the day and night, high-heeled women stand around in doorways, watching the world go by and occasionally bargaining with fidgety men. Until quite late at night, dozens of little stores with lurid lights and explicit photographs advertise pornography, gadgets, and lingerie. A few have "hard couples" performing live on stage. What surprises many tourists is how openly all of this goes on, how easily average Parisians ignore this activity as they pass by on their humdrum errands. As someone said in Voltaire's *Candide, "L'homme s'habitue à tout. "* (One gets used to anything.) Actually, it might not be from *Candide.* Maybe it's from Camus's *The Stranger.* Either way, this street offers the ultimate in existential contrasts. The sidewalks are constantly patroled by plainclothes cops, so it's not particularly dangerous. It can, however, be intimidating, especially for a woman walking alone. During the daylight and early evening, this isn't much of a problem, because gawking tourists and blasé Parisians severely outnumber those interested in smut. After midnight, however, the sleaze factor is enough to make almost anyone uncomfortable.

Third Arrondissement: The Marais

The third *arrondissement,* together with the fourth, is called *le Marais* ("the swamp") because of its distinguishing quality of dampness before 13th-century monks drained it. With Henri IV's construction of the place des Vosges (see fourth *arrondissement)* at the beginning of the 17th century, the area became the center of fashionable living. Leading architects and sculptors were kept busy building the *hôtels particuliers* that still dot the Marais—discreetly elegant mansions nestled between large courtyards in front and gardens in the rear. Under Louis XV, the center of Paris life moved out of the Marais to the faubourgs St-Honoré and St-Germain, and construction of *hôtels* in the Marais slackened considerably.

The 19th and early 20th centuries were not kind to the old Marais. Many *hôtels* were destroyed or allowed to fall into disrepair. Narrow, medieval streets were widened at great architectural cost. Nineteenth-century planners who didn't want to widen a whole street at once tried to do it piecemeal; new laws specified that any new building had to be built some meters back from the curb. This has resulted in many streets having sawtoothed sides. (It turns out that given the longevity of some buildings, widening a street in this manner would take several hundred years. The idea was given up in 1974.) Recently the government has shown a greater interest in conservation: in 1964, part of the Marais was declared a historic neighborhood and protected from further destruction. In addition, museums such as the Musée de la Chasse, the Musée Picasso, and the Musée Cognacq-Jay have moved into and restored old *hôtels.* But there is much more to see than these handful of converted mansions; once you have seen a few *hôtels* you will find yourself noticing architectural traces of the old Marais on random walks through the neighborhood.

Les Archives Nationaux (National Archives) lie in the center of the architecturally rich southern part of the third. The archives are housed in the Hôtel Soubise, the Hôtel Rohan, and a few other old residences that all happen to be on the same city block. **The Hôtel Soubise** was built between 1705 and 1709 under the direction of Delamair, the same architect who designed the Hôtel Rohan (see below). The majestic courtyard provides a classic example of 18th-century aristocratic architecture. On two sides you are surrounded by Corinthian columns. The four statues standing between windows on the façade are copies; they represent the four seasons. The two women seated on top of the triangular portion of the façade represent Prudence and Fame; they were sculpted by Robert le Lorrain. If you choose to visit the Museum of French History (see Museums), you can see the very rich—some would say gaudy—interior decorations, executed between 1730 and 1745. The building's towered gate at 58, rue des Archives, is the only surviving portion of a mansion that was built in 1380. The unusual angle between the gate and the road was chosen to facilitate the entrance of litters and carriages. On the other side of the street from the entrance to the Hôtel de Soubise, notice the crack between nos. 57 and 59. The stone base of the red brick building in the background is a vestige of Philippe-Auguste's city wall, built 1180-1220. Using the ruins of such a wall as the foundation of a new building saved a great deal of work. On the side wall of no. 59 is a large piece of the 17th-century Hôtel de la Chataigneraye, which used to stand right next to here, at 52, rue des archives. This fragment was plastered onto the wall in 1885 to mitigate the architectural loss of demolishing the hôtel.

Hôtel de Rohan, one of the most famous *hôtels* in the Marais, reposes at no. 87, rue Vieille du Temple. It was built between 1705 and 1708 for Armand-Gaston de Rohan, Bishop of Strasbourg. During temporary exhibitions, you are allowed to visit the richly decorated interior of the palace (but only if you pay 10F or so for the temporary exhibit); otherwise, just tour the large, impressive courtyard. Whether or not you go inside the building, you should take a look at the small courtyard on the right. Above a gate you will see a vivid haut-relief sculpture by Robert Le Lorrain from 1738. The men are servants of Apollo, giving water to his fiery horses at the end of their daily gallop across the sky. Appropriately enough, this gate used to lead to the palace stable.

Across the rue des Quatre Fils from the archives is the the **hôtel Guénégaud,** built by Mansart in the 17th century and home of the **Musée de la Chasse** (See Museums). Nos. 16 and 18, rue des Quatre Fils, illustrate the city's piecemeal efforts to widen the streets in the Marais. The 17th-century gate of no. 16 used to stand forward of where it is now. The *hôtel* was destroyed, and the gate moved backward and stuck onto a newer building. At no. 18, a modern building with three arches occupies part of the courtyard of a 17th-century *hôtel*. Behind it, you can see the inner façade of the older building, which was spared by the street-widening policy.

The rue Vieille-du-Temple, which runs along the east side of the Hôtel Rohan, is lined with several stately residences. The little tower at the corner of the rue des Francs-Bourgeois belongs to the **Hôtel Hérouet,** built in 1528 for Louis XII's treasurer. Hérouet had to get special permission to add the bold angle turret to his house; normally such extravagances were reserved for the monarch. By the sixteenth century, such turrets were no longer needed for defense, and probably served as private studies. The building is in such good condition only because it has been restored quite heavily. Farther down at no. 75 is the 18th-century **Hôtel de la Tour du Pin.** No. 64 includes the remains of the façade of a 17th-century *hôtel*. Between rue des Coutures and rue de la Perle is the entrance to a park. A perfect place to have a picnic—you can buy a sandwich at a bakery on rue Vieille-du-Temple—the park adjoins the garden of the **Hôtel Sale,** home of the Picasso Museum (see Museums).

Rue de Sévigné (Mo. Chemin Vert) is a small street worth passing through on your way to the place des Vosges or the Eglise St-Paul-St-Louis. Near the top of the street, on the rue St-Gilles, is a pink *hôtel* from 1620; notice the more recent addition of the two upper stories. On the left side of rue de Sévigné at no. 52, an imposing gate is all that's left of the Hôtel de Flesselles, built in the 18th century and demolished in 1908. No. 48, the building with the French flag, houses an elementary school. The woman doing the breastfeeding is Charity, as sculpted by Fortin in 1806. On the right side of the street (no. 23), the **Hôtel Carnavalet** houses an enlightening museum of Parisian

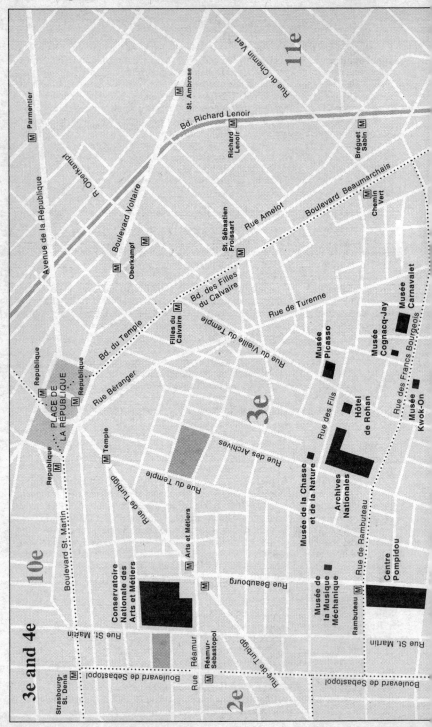

3e and 4e

10e

11e

2e

3e

Parmentier

St. Ambrose

Bd. Richard Lenoir

Richard Lenoir

Rue du Chemin Vert

R. Oberkampf

Avenue de la République

Boulevard Voltaire

Oberkampf

St. Sébastien Froissart

Rue Amelot

Boulevard Beaumarchais

Bréguet Sabin

Chemin Vert

Bd. des Filles du Calvaire

Rue de Turenne

Musée Cognacq-Jay

Musée Carnavalet

Filles du Calvaire

Bd. du Temple

Rue du Vieille du Temple

Musée Picasso

Rue des Francs Bourgeois

Musée Kwok-On

Republique

Rue Béranger

Rue des Fils

Hôtel de Rohan

Republique

PLACE DE LA RÉPUBLIQUE

Republique

3e

Republique

Temple

Rue des Archives

Musée de la Chasse et de la Nature

Archives Nationales

Republique

Rue du Temple

Rue de Turbigo

Arts et Métiers

Boulevard St. Martin

Rue St. Martin

Conservatoire Nationale des Arts et Métiers

Rue Beaubourg

Rue de Rambuteau

Centre Pompidou

Strasbourg-St. Denis

Réamur

Rue St. Martin

Musée de la Musique Méchanique

Rambuteau

Boulevard de Sébastopol

Réamur-Sébastopol

Rue de Turbigo

Boulevard de Sébastopol

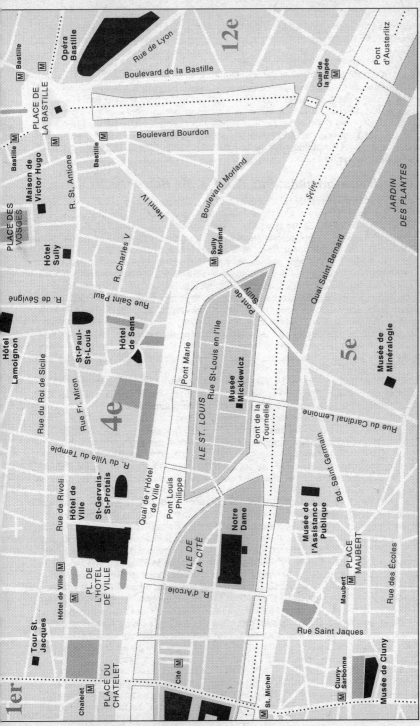

history in the *hôtel* that once housed the Marquise de Sévigné (see Museums). Even if you don't visit the museum, it's worth looking at the gate and courtyard of the building, built in the 1540s and 50s for Jacques des Ligneris, the ambitious president of the Parlement of Paris. The statue in the middle of the courtyard is Louis XIV; it used to be in front of the Hôtel de Ville. On the wall behind Louis, which dates from 1544, bas-reliefs represent the four seasons (the symbols above the people's heads are zodiacal signs). The walls to your right and left were added in 1655, as was the gate. To maintain architectural unity, these walls were given similar bas-reliefs: to the left are the four elements and to the right, the four winds. In the 1860s, architects tried to restore the building to its original appearance. Unfortunately, they mistook a 17th-century proposal to remodel the building for the original plans, and ended up carrying out the remodeling two centuries late.

Fourth Arrondissement: The Marais (lower half)

Paris's upper bourgeoisie rubs elbows with its traditional working class in this quiet *arrondissement,* where some of the oldest sites in Paris lie only a few blocks from the modern fantasy of the Centre Pompidou, where the ultra-conservative *garde républicaine* (together with a large percentage of Le Pen's support) exists side-by-side with an active gay and Jewish population. With the exception of the rue de Rivoli slicing through it, much of this area was left untouched by Haussmann's modernization; the fourth, with its mishmash of different social strata and political inclinations, will give you a sense of the old Paris, where aristocratic families lived next door to (or even downstairs from) the same workman who made their furniture and baked their bread. From place des Vosges on the north and Ile St-Louis on the south, to the Hôtel de Ville on the west and the boulevard Henri IV on the east, the fourth *arrondissement* offers an *épopée* (panoply) of elegant historic monuments, busy market streets, and sudden, fanciful extravagance, bisected by the busy rue de Rivoli and rue Saint-Antoine. The area around the Tour St-Jacques and the Hotel de Ville, in the southwest corner, was the setting for Hugo's *Les Misérables.*

The Hôtel de Lamoignon, 24, rue Pavée (Mo. St-Paul), directly south of the Hôtel Carnavalet (see third *arrondissement),* is one of the finest *hôtels particuliers* in the Marais. When it was built in 1584 for Diane de France, daughter of Henri II, the *hôtel* consisted only of the section immediately in front as you enter the courtyard. The noble façade, with its two-story Corinthian pilasters, is the first example in Paris of the "colossal" style of decoration. In the staid 16th century, these ground-to-roof pilasters were quite daring, but no one was going to tell that to the princess. The pediment overlooking the courtyard depicts huntresses amid the stags; Diane, named for the goddess of the hunt, possessed all the modesty typical of the French aristocracy. The wing at left, which blends rather clumsily into the original building, was added a generation later by Diane's heir Charles de Valois. The buildings of the small courtyard to the right date from 1968; added to make room for the library that moved here that year, they provide a surprisingly graceful counterpoint to Charles's wing. The unfortunate modern construction visible farther to the right, which detracts from the aesthetic balance that had been so thoughtfully created, dates from 1992. Through a door in the 1968 half-courtyard you can enter the **Bibliothèque Historique de la Ville de Paris** (tel. 42 74 44 44). This noncirculating library of Parisian history unbears its 500,000 volumes to anyone who can present a valid ID. This is not a tourist attraction; visit only if you want information. (Open Mon.-Sat. 9:30am-6pm.) To see the gardens of the *hôtel,* which are closed to the public, exit onto rue Pavée and turn right on rue des Francs Bourgeois.

Place des Vosges (Mo. Chemin Vert or St-Paul), Paris's oldest remaining public square and perhaps its most charming, provides one of the city's most refreshing strolls. The central square, now the site of a verdant, shadeful park, is surrounded by a series of 17th-century townhouses built in the height of French Renaissance style. Several kings lived in mansions occupying this lot, until the temperamental Cathérine des Médicis ordered the royal palace destroyed after the accidental death of her husband in a jousting tournament in 1559. In a drastic come-down from its formal royal glory, the newly vacant space became the site of a popular horse market. Yet the area was brought back to an even greater glory in 1605, when Henri IV expelled the horse market and decreed the construction of a new public square to be known as the *place royale*. Wishing to promenade himself in courtly opulence, he wanted a *place* both large enough and central enough to accommodate leisurely strolls. He also specified that all the buildings be constructed "according to the same symmetry," which explains the unusual unity of the square's architecture. All 36 buildings have arcades on the street level, surmounted by two stories decorated with pink brick, capped by a steep, slate-covered roof. (Actually, the decorative "brick" on most of the façades is just a layer of mortar painted to look like brick. This money-saving measure is most obvious on the south side of the square (nearest the Rue St-Antoine and the Seine), where the mortar has wrinkled and cracked.) The largest townhouse, forming the *place*'s main entrance on the south side, was the majestic King's pavilion; directly opposite, forming a smaller but equally gracious exit, is the pavilion of the Queen.

Unfortunately, Henri didn't live long enough to see his plans come to fruition; he was assassinated in 1610, two years before the *place royale* was completed. Its first great event, and official inauguration, was the marriage of the new king, Louis XIII, to Anne of Austria, an event said to have drawn 10,000 spectators and 150 buglers (many musicians still play in the arcades). Although Henri intended the *place* to house craftsmen and merchants (the ground-level arcades were ideal for shops), it was so expensive to build a house according to his regulations that only noblemen could afford to live there. Madame de Sevigné (born at no. 1bis), Cardinal Richelieu (no. 21), Molière, Racine, and Voltaire filled the grand parlors with their wit and philosophy. Mozart played a concert here at the age of seven. Even when the majority of the city's nobility moved across the river to the faubourg St-Germain, the *place royale* remained among the most elegant spots in Paris. Then, during the revolution, the 1639 Louis XIII statue in the center of the park was destroyed (the statue there now is a copy erected by the restored monarchy in 1818) and the park renamed place des Vosges, *not* after cows that did *not* graze there, but after the first department in France to pay its taxes (1800). Since then, successive liberal and right-wing regimes have changed the name back and forth from "Vosges" to "Royale" until 1870 and the Third Republic, when "Vosges" finally won out over its despotic competitor.

Follow the arcades around the edge of place des Vosges for an elegant promenade and some delightful window-shopping. Look for plaques that mark the habitations of famous residents. Théophile Gautier and Alphonse Daudet lived at no. 8; Romantics will not want to miss the former residence of Victor Hugo at no. 6, now an excellent museum with displays on his life, his work, and his contemporaries (see Museums). During summer weekends, these arcades fill with an array of talented musicians, playing and singing a variety of mostly classical music, from harp medleys to Mozart arias. For some first-class relaxation, stop at one of the many cafés for coffee and a delectable *tarte aux framboises* (raspberry tart) or head into the central park for a picnic lunch. You may even be able to avoid the park *gardiens* long enough to sit on the grass. Inside, under the shade of the tall trees and next to the peacefully whooshing fountains, visitors are entirely isolated from the traffic noises and fumes of central Paris. Come here at dusk for a romantic stroll, when the illuminated iron lamps and gracious silhouettes of the townhouses will put you in the middle of a 19th-century drama. The most scenic way of escaping the place des Vosges is through the little corner door at the right of the south face (near no. 5), which leads into the garden of the Hôtel Sully.

The Hôtel Sully, 62, rue St-Antoine (Mo. St-Paul), is the most congenial of all the Marais *hôtels* for a relaxing summer afternoon. Here, only a stone's throw from one of Paris's busiest streets, you'll find "a peace to end all earthly dignities." The small inner courtyard, with its elegant formal garden, offers all that a tired tourist could want: several stone benches (perfect for a mid-afternoon nap), a classy (if expensive) café, and even a few shade trees. What's more, if you're lucky, you'll come upon one of their frequent concerts—either the official, often free chamber music performances or the unofficial student musicians who croon away for extra money. Relax in the courtyard a moment, and look around you. The main building, adorned with allegorical statues of the four elements and the four seasons, was built in the 1620s and soon acquired by the duc de Sully, minister to Henri IV. At the opposite side of the garden, and now home to the cafe, is an extension known as the "Petit-Sully," added in the 1630s. The *hôtel* is occupied in part by the **Caisse Nationale des Monuments Historiques** (tel. 44 61 20 00), a government agency dedicated to preserving historic monuments. At the information office, you can pick up brochures about their excellent English-language guided tours of Paris monuments (32F, including the Hôtel de Sully). When you're tired of relaxation, culture, and people-watching (if ever), cross through the gardens to the **rue St-Antoine,** the major thoroughfare of the fourth *arrondissement,* on the other side. Walking along this boulevard, you'll find a variety of cafés, fruit and vegetable stands, *fromageries,* and boutiques, together with the more prosaic Monoprix supermarket. Buy food here for a picnic lunch in the Hôtel Sully.

The Eglise St-Paul-St-Louis, 99, rue St-Antoine (Mo. St-Paul), dates from 1627 and is one of the earliest examples of the Jesuit style in Paris. Its large dome—one of the trademarks of Jesuit architecture—is visible from afar, but hidden at close range by ornamentation on the façade. This architectural "mistake" was corrected in subsequent Jesuit constructions, such as the Sorbonne church (fifth *arrondissement).* Despite extensive pillaging during the Revolution, the church retains a rich Baroque interior, complete with three 17th-century paintings representing the life of Saint Louis. There used to be four, but one was lost and replaced by Eugène Delacroix's equally dramatic representation of *Christ in the Garden of Olives* (1826). (Open Mon.-Sat. 9:30am-7:30pm, Sun. 9:30am-12:30pm. Masses Sat. 6pm, Sun. 10am and 11:15am.)

The Hôtel de Sens, 1, rue du Figuier (Mo. Pont Marie), is one of the city's two surviving examples of medieval residential architecture. (The other is the Hôtel de Cluny in the Latin Quarter.) Built in 1474 for Tristan de Salazar, the archbishop of Sens (who, according to one text, had a "heart open to all evil and closed to all virtue"), its military features reflect both Salazar's life as a soldier and the violence of the day. The turrets on rue du Figuier and rue de l'Hôtel de Ville were designed to survey the streets outside, while the square tower at the far left corner of the courtyard served as a dungeon. An enormous Gothic arch for the entrance—complete with chutes for pouring boiling water on invaders and door-to-door salesmen—and steep chimneys and spires contribute to the mansion's intimidating air. Originally the exterior was festooned with the owner's noble escutcheon, but these were scraped off during the Revolution, together with the inscription that proclaimed de Salazar "a great man, whose memory will be celebrated everywhere by posterity."

The former residence of Queen Margot, divorced by Henri IV because of her illustrious sexual appetite, this magnificent edifice has witnessed some of Paris's most daring romantic escapades. One fine Sunday in 1606, the 55-year-old "Queen Venus" drove up to the door of her home, in front of which her two current lovers were arguing. One of them gallantly broke away to open the lady's carriage door, and the other pulled out a pistol and shot him dead. Unfazed, the queen demanded the execution of the other. She watched from a window as his head was hewn off with an axe in the courtyard the next day. Tours are conducted on the second Thursday of every month. Call 42 78 14 60 for tour information. The *hôtel* now houses the (peaceful) **Bibliothèque Forney** (tel. 42 78 14 60), a library that focuses on fine arts, decorative arts, graphic arts, and artisanry. The collection includes 200,000 books, 15,000 posters, and 1,000,000 postcards. Anyone with an ID can consult works in the library, but to check out books you must live in the Paris area. (Open Tues.-Fri. 1:30-8:30pm, Sat. 10am-8:30pm.)

Since the 13th century, when King Phillipe-Auguste so politely requested that the Jewish population living in front of Notre-Dame move to the Marais (then outside of city limits), this quarter has been the Jewish center of Paris. The area around rue des Rosiers and rue des Ecouffes still forms the spine of the Jewish community, with two synagogues (at 10, rue Pavée and 25, rue des Rosiers), one oratory (18, rue des Ecouffes), and dozens of kosher restaurants and delis. Down toward the river, at 17, rue Geoffroy de l'Asnier, the solemn 1956 **Mémorial du Martyr Juif Inconnu** (Memorial to the Unknown Jewish Martyr; Mo. St-Paul), commemorates the Parisian Jews who died at the hands of the Nazis and their French collaborators. In 1983, it was shot at by anti-Semitic gunmen. The threat of further violence explains why the curators now ask every visitor to step through a metal detector upon entering. The crypt downstairs has an eternal flame over human ashes brought back from concentration camps and the

Warsaw ghetto. (Open Sun.-Thurs. 10am-1pm and 2-6pm, Fri. 10am-1pm and 2-5pm. Free.) Upstairs, the **Centre de Documentation Juive Contemporaine** (Jewish Contemporary Documentation Center, tel. 42 72 44 72) has a small Holocaust museum (admission 12F), a library with more than 400,000 documents relating to the Nazi era, and frequent temporary exhibits. (Open Mon.-Thurs. 2-5:30pm.)

The Hôtel de Ville (Mo. Hôtel de Ville), Paris's grandiose city hall, dominates a large square with refreshing fountains and Victorian-style lampposts. The present edifice is little more than a century old, but Paris municipal government has been housed on this site ever since 1357, when it moved into what was called the "Maison au Piliers." In 1533, under King François I, the old Maison was destroyed and construction of a new, more spacious version was begun on the same spot. The newer building was designed by Boccadoro in a Renaissance style that recalled the châteaux of the Loire.

On May 24, 1871, despairing insurgents of the Paris Commune set Boccadoro's *hôtel de ville* on fire with the help of several barrels of petroleum. The fire lasted no less than eight days, at the end of which nothing remained but the frame. "It is a splendid, a magnificent ruin," wrote Edmond de Goncourt of the sight. "All pink and ash-green and the colour of white-hot steel...it looks like the ruin of an Italian palace, tinted by the sunshine of several centuries, or better still like the ruin of a magic palace, bathed in the theatrical glow of electric light...The irony of chance! In the utter ruin of the whole building there shines, on a marble plaque intact in its new gilt frame, the lying inscription: *Liberty, Equality, Fraternity.* " Goncourt thought the ruin should be preserved in all its "picturesque wonder;" the conservative regime of the Third Republic thought otherwise, and rebuilding of a virtually identical Hôtel de Ville began in 1872 on the same spot. Inaugurated in 1882, the new building is the one that stands today and governs the city of Paris from its jam-packed-with-ornament walls.

The only major change made to the exterior of the new *hôtel* was the addition of the bronze knights who strut on the roof of the building. The interior, however, is strongly marked with the ostentatious tastes of the 19th-century bourgeois officials who commissioned it. As with the Opéra Garnier and the Pont Alexandre III, the Third Republic used the decoration of the Hôtel de Ville to establish its own prestige. It spared not a *centime* for the finest of crystal chandeliers and gilded every possible interior surface, even creating a Hall of Mirrors in conscious emulation of the one at Versailles. In choosing painters, the officials in charge were suspicious of the new-fangled Impressionists: when Manet, Monet, Renoir, and Cezanne offered their services, they were all turned down. Instead, the Hôtel de Ville is decorated with heavy, didactic art that uses plenty of half-naked women to express lofty concepts. These paintings have names like *Philosophy* (in the Salon des Lettres), *The Triumph of Art* (in the Salon des Arts), and *Light Guiding the Sciences in the Heavens* (in the Salon des Sciences). To be fair, a few of the paintings are quite nice, and the opulent decoration can be quite impressive. Don't miss Rodin's unsmiling bronze bust of the Republic (in the Salon Laurens).

Foreign heads of state are welcomed with receptions at the Hôtel de Ville, but for most people the only way to visit the interior of the building is to take a guided tour. The tours are in French, and leave from the Information Office on 29, rue de Rivoli (tel. 42 76 40 40, open Mon.-Sat. 9am-6pm) every Monday (except for public holidays) at 10:30am. Thanks to an elevator, these visits are entirely accessible to people in wheelchairs. The Information Office also holds temporary exhibits in its lobby.

In front of the Hôtel de Ville, the **place Hôtel de Ville**, formerly the place de Grèves, has its own, uniquely Parisian history. During the Middle Ages, angry or unemployed workers gathered here, creating the expression *en grève* (on strike), now a staple of the French language (and the French way of life). The *place* also hosted many centuries worth of picturesque tortures and executions. Beheadings were a particularly popular diversion, and the executioner dressed in the most fashionable outfits. This was also the chosen spot for book-burnings. Voltaire, angered by the immolation of one of his tracts, wrote a pamphlet against the practice. The pamphlet, of course, was condemned and burnt. In 1789, the first Paris Commune was declared here, and later imitators declared the July Monarchy and the Second Republic on the same spot. The Third Republic, for a change, was proclaimed from a balcony of the Hôtel de Ville.

At night, the Hôtel de Ville is splendidly lit by rows of floodlights, and the *place* in front leaves behind its often-violent, always turbulent history. A line of illuminated fountains, attended by the stalwart iron lamps, provides an ethereal audience to the *hôtel's* magnificence. Yet the *hôtel* is at its most beautiful at sunset, when the sun's last rays cross the broad *place* virtually unobstructed, imparting beautiful pinks and oranges to the building's pale façade.

For a more intimate view of the Parisian sunset, walk to the Seine from the place de l'Hôtel de Ville, turn left and keep going until you come to a Batobus sign. Follow the ramp toward the river and turn right, where you'll find a small cluster of benches and trees. From this mini-park, you'll have a captivating perspective of the sun's rays making their way through the successive arches of the Seine bridges. Off in the distance, toward the sun, is the grandiose outline of the Louvre. Beside you, on the Ile de la Cité, you can distinguish the towers of Notre Dame. Bring a picnic supper or come earlier with a book for a relaxing afternoon on the edge of the Seine.

Cross quai de l'Hôtel de Ville to the backside of the city hall, where you will find the **Eglise St-Gervais-St-Protais,** one of the city's most beautiful examples of 16th- and 17th-century ecclesiastical architecture. The exterior is Neoclassical; the interior, with its intricate vaulting and stained glass, flamboyant Gothic. Look for the eminently Baroque wooden Christ by Préault, the less dramatic 16th-century Flemish Passion painted on wood, the beautiful 16th-century stained glass in the choir—which illustrates the life of Mary (including a troop of whimsical sheep)—and the strange Boschian misericords in the 16th-century choir stalls of the nave. François Couperin (1688-1733), together with eight other members of his family (spanning two hundred years of the church's history) was the main organist here; the organ on which they played is the same used in services today. St-Gervais-St-Protais is part of a working monastery, and if you come at the right time (check posted services) you will hear the nave filled with Gregorian chant and sung passages of the Bible.

Two blocks west of this area, the **Tour St-Jacques** (between 39 and 41, rue de Rivoli) stands strangely alone in the center of its own park. The flamboyant Gothic tower, whose silhouette seems to have lost all function or symbolic significance, is the only remnant of the 16th-century Eglise St-Jacques-la-Boucherie, which once stood here. (The rest of the church was destroyed in 1802.) Nor is it in truth without function: 52m high, the tower has a meterological station at its top, continuing a long, scientific tradition that began with Pascal's experiments on the weight of air performed here in 1648 (the statue of Pascal at the base of the tower commemorates this event). Until the second half of 1994, the bottom half of the Tour St-Jacques will be hidden by a construction site for the RER line D. If it weren't for that obstruction, you would see that the tower's elaborate decoration begins about a meter above ground. Baron Haussmann, in the role of the *artiste demolisseur* (artist-demolisher) that he envisioned for himself, insisted that his eastward extension of the rue de Rivoli be built on level ground. When the Baron leveled the modest hill that rolled through the quarter, he exposed part of the undecorated foundation. The tower marks the intersection of the rue de Rivoli and the boulevard Sébastopol, Haussmann's treasured *grande croisée* (great crossing). Here was the intersection of the builder's new east-west and north-south axes for the city, only meters away from where the Roman roads had crossed two thousand years earlier.

In the western section of the fourth, strollers stumble upon the startling **Centre Pompidou,** visible from afar (impossible to miss, in fact) with its famous inside-out architecture. Here it is: the most famous, roaringly idiosyncratic blemish in the uniformity of the city (even beating out the newer additions of the Louvre Pyramide and the Opéra Bastille). Haussmann, if he were still alive, would roll over in his grave. The center sits on the former site of a slum whose high rate of tuberculosis gained it the classification of an *îlot insalubre* (unhealthy block) and demolition in the 1930s. The lot remained vacant for many years, and two decades after the garish building's construction, some Parisians wish it still were. (For a fuller description of the center, see Museums).

In the afternoons and early evenings, the vast cobblestone *place* in front of the center is extraordinarily animated. Street performers, peddlers, and pickpockets try their hand at raking in the crowd's money. If you want an audience and a few francs in tips, you might try your hand here with whatever act you dream up—talent doesn't seem to be a prerequisite for drawing attention, and the police are quite tolerant just as long as you don't make too much noise. This is a classic performance area for Paris's street mimes, who show no reverance to personal dignity or natural shyness in choosing their victims among the crowd, a treat for everyone *except* the person thus chosen. For a safe view, watch the performances from the elevated area that's on your right as you face the building. (To find out how much time you have to use up all those checks marked 19__, consult the big numerical display, which is counting the seconds undtil the year 2000.) Late at night when the tourists have left, the square can get fairly dangerous, a function of the plethora of drunk men who hang around and occasionally pick fights.

On your right as you look at the Pompidou façade, an exuberant modern fountain, aptly named the **Fontaine Stravinski,** spurts and splashes amid an array of brightly colored shapes that will remind you alternatively of the stickers you used to collect, the Blue Meanies in *Yellow Submarine,* and your own peculiar surreal fantasy. Kinetic sculptures spouting water represent the atonal compositions of Russian composer Igor Stravinsky that offended the tender ears of the music world 80 years ago. The portions made of scrap metal—and it really is scrap, not new steel made to look like scrap—are the work of Jean Tinguely, whereas the brightly colored figures were created by Niki de Saint-Phalle. Next to the Stravinsky fountain, the **Eglise St-Merri** conceals some impressive Renaissance painted-glass windows behind its Gothic Flamboyant exterior. Ravaged during the Revolution, this church was known as the "Temple of Commerce" from 1796-1801, a sly reference to the flesh trade that has dominated this area since the 14th century. Free concerts are held here on Saturdays at 9pm and on Sundays at 4pm, except in August. After the concert on the first and third Sunday of each month, there is a guided tour of the church (in French).

Fifth Arrondissement: The Latin Quarter

Only one part of the Rive Gauche deserves a Bohemian reputation: the *quartier latin.* The Romans built some of the area's ancient streets, but the *latin* in the *quartier's* name refers to the language of scholarship and daily speech heard here until 1798. Home since the 13th century to the famed Sorbonne, the *quartier* symbolizes the romantic myth of the starving, shabby scholar, who shivers in winter and skips meals to save money to buy books. In fact, for most of the 19th century it was something of a slum, and any student who could spent as much time as possible on the Right Bank. The area has changed greatly in the last 20 years, imperiling its youthful and scholarly ambience. After the student uprisings of May 1968, the University of Paris was decentralized, and in one blow, the *quartier* lost many of its inhabitants. Then a tidal wave of tourist gold swept over the area and drowned many of its small booksellers and cafés. Much of the area now resembles any other Parisian commercial center, except for the tell-tale used book shops and repertory cinemas.

The Latin Quarter—bounded by the Seine to the north, the Jardin des Plantes to the east, bd. St-Michel to the west and the bd. de Port Royal and bd. St-Marcel to the south—still swarms with students of the University of Paris at the Sorbonne and the *grandes Ecoles,* prestigious exam-entry schools such as the Ecole Normale Supérieure and the Ecole Nationale des Sciences Politiques. And while the artists and hipper intellectuals are migrating to the Bastille, the Latin Quarter maintains an eternally youthful air. Untouched medieval streets remain tangled throughout the quarter, twisting their way through cafés, restaurants, and small neighborhood *patisseries* and *charcuteries.* The many dead-end streets ending in walls testify to Haussmann's demolition of the hills that used to roll through the neighborhood. The tiny rue Rollin (Mo. Monge), on a small hill untouched by Haussmann, drops down to rue Monge, a major thouroughfare.

The boulevard St-Michel, with its fashionable cafés, restaurants, bookstores and movie theaters, anchors the student life of the quarter. **Place St-Michel,** at the northern tip of this grand avenue, offers a microcosm of the entire quarter—the tourists, the students, and the street people (modern descendants of the Bohemians of yore). The majestically heroic fountain dates from 1860, yet includes a memorial to the liberation of France after World War II (the *place* was the scene of heavy student fighting against the Germans in August 1944). At the intersection of bd. St-Germain and bd. St-Michel at

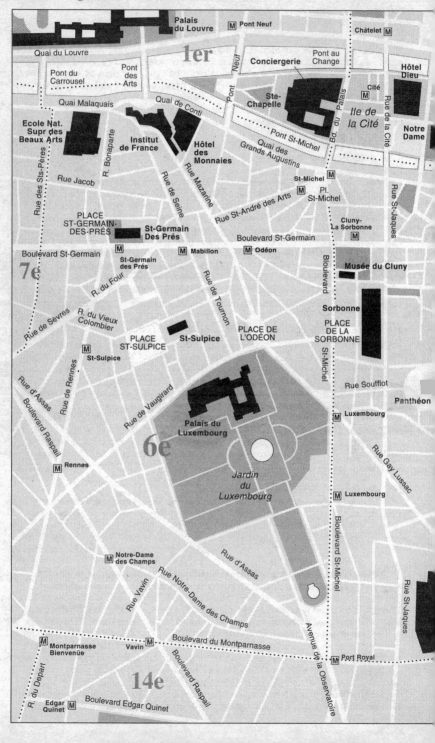

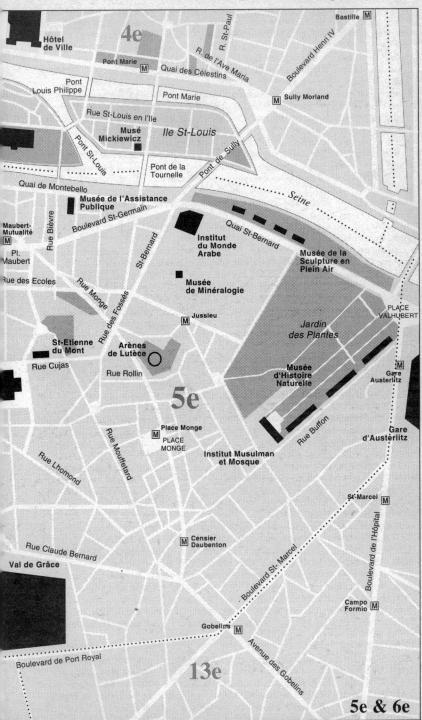

6, p. Paul Painlevé, the **Hôtel de Cluny** (Paris's second-oldest residential building still standing, built in 1330 and modified to its present flamboyant Gothic style in 1510), is now home to the **Musée de Cluny,** one of the world's finest collections of medieval art, jewelry, architecture, and tapestry (see Museums).

Farther south on bd. St-Michel, the **place de la Sorbonne,** (Mo. Cluny-La Sorbonne, RER Luxembourg), a square lined with cafés, lounging students, and bookstores, is the focus of student life in the Latin Quarter. **Librarie J. Vrin,** 6, pl. Sorbonne (tel. 43 54 03 47), is France's premier bookstore for philosophical dissertation. At the eastern end of the square stands the **Sorbonne,** 45-7, rue des Ecoles, Euope's oldest university. Founded in 1253 by Robert de Sorbon as a dormitory for 17 theology students (before which classes had been held in the open air), the Sorbonne soon became the administrative quarters for the University of Paris. Its scholars were treated as nobility; they could wear swords, waive taxes, and were not subject to arrest while on campus. Later, the University acquired papal sponsorship. Roger Bacon haltingly developed the scientific method, and Pierre Lombard assembled an early encyclopedia. It was here that the old curriculum of poetry and literature was rejected in favor of Aristotlean logic and science. As it grew in power and size, the Sorbonne often contradicted the authority of the French throne. During the Hundred Years War, it even had the gall to side with England over France.

All the original buildings have been destroyed and rebuilt, the last time in 1885, except for the **Ste-Ursule-de-la-Sorbonne** (the main building), commissioned in 1642 by Cardinal Richelieu. The Cardinal, himself a *sorbonnard,* lies buried inside, his hat suspended above him by a few threads hanging from the ceiling. Legend has it that when Richelieu is freed from Purgatory, the threads will snap and the hat will tumble down (don't hold your breath). Following the student riots of May 1968, the old University of Paris divided into 13 autonomous campuses scattered across Paris; the Sorbonne is No. IV. The public is allowed only in the chapel, which occasionally hosts art exhibits (open Mon.-Fri. 9am-5pm). Behind the Sorbonne is the considerably less exclusive **Collège de France,** an institution created by François I in 1530 to contest the university's supreme authority. Outstanding courses, given over the years by such luminaries as Henri Bergson, Paul Valéry, and Milan Kundera, are free and open to all. Check the schedules that appear by the door in September. (Courses run Sept.-May. For more information, call 43 29 12 11. If you re hooked on academic sightseeing, the **Ecole Normale Supérieur,** France's leading liberal arts college and home to notorious deconstructionist Jacques Derrida, is located southeast of the Sorbonne, on rue d Ulm. Don't try to analyze *Let's Go: Paris* as a Text; it has no structure, and its internal contradictions would take up ten years of your life.

The Panthéon, its proud dome visible from any point in the Latin Quarter, towers over the highest point of the Left Bank (tel. 43 54 34 52; Mo. Cardinal Lemoine, RER Luxembourg). The Panthéon is only the latest church to be built on this hill, the Montagne Ste-Geneviève. The Romans used it for a temple to Mercury, and Clovis built a shrine to the saints Peter and Paul, in celebration of his victory over Alaric at the Battle of Vouillé. The people of Paris, however, were much more faithful to their patron saint, Ste-Geneviève, whose prayers had deflected Atilla's hordes to Orléans, and soon renamed the church and surrounding hill in her honor. (Oddly enough, the Orléannais prefer Jeanne d'Arc, as saints go.) After being destroyed by Norman invasions in the late 9th century, the church was rebuilt and remained basically untouched until 1754, when it was requisitioned by Louis XV. As a sign of his gratitude to Ste-Geneviève for helping him recover from a grave illness in 1744, the king created this enormous, somber structure. Among the first in Paris to incorporate classical architecture, this church is largely responsible for the subsequent conversion of French art to classicism.

The Revolution converted the church into a mausoleum of heroes, designed to rival the royal crypt at St-Denis. On April 4, 1791, the great parliamentarian Mirabeau was interned, only to have his ashes expelled the next year when his correspondence with Louis XVI was revealed. Voltaire's body was moved here, amid a great ceremony, to the new Temple of Reason and Science. Over the next few centuries, the purpose of the Panthéon bounced between church and mausoleum, reflecting the history of France in its journey. In 1885, it became a national necropolis forever, or at least until France becomes a monarchy again. Visit the legendary writers, philosophers, and inventors buried in the **crypt** in the basement of the church. You ll find Voltaire, Rousseau, Hugo, Zola, Jean Jaurès, and Louis Braille decaying peacefully in their stone tombs, which can be viewed from behind locked iron gates at each of their niches. Léon Daudet, in his *Souvenirs littéraires,* recalled the pomp and circumstance of Hugo's interment here in 1885, when two million mourners, marching to the mournful tune of Chopin's *Marche funébre,* followed the coffin to its final resting place: "A cold crypt, where glory is represented by an echo which the *gardien* will make you admire. A room full of the leftovers of republican and revolutionary immortality. It's freezing in there, even in the summer, and the symbolic torch held up by a hand from Rousseau's tomb has the air of a cruel joke, as if the author of the *Confessions* could not even light a cigarette for the author of *Les Misérables.* "

From the crypt, a twisting staircase winds upward to the roof and dome, where you can get an upclose view of a horrifyingly garish set of Neoclassical frescoes proclaiming the glory and justice of France. While you can walk around the outside of the roof, the building is not quite high enough to afford anything but a view of the immediately surrounding rooftops. The dome's interior is an extreme example of Neoclassical architecture, replete with grand austere Corinthinian columns and expansive heights. As part of the transformation of the church to its new secular calling as mausoleum during the Revolution, the 42 tall windows of the exterior were walled over and all symbols of Christian worship were removed. During 1993 the interior of the church will undergo renovations, and most likely will be open only sporadically to visitors; call ahead. One ticket provides entry to both crypt and dome. (Open daily 10am-5:45pm. Admission 25F, students 14F, children 17F.)

While you're at the Panthéon, don't miss the unique, fanciful **Eglise St-Etienne du Mont** right next door. St-Etienne was built between 1492 and 1626—the resulting edifice is somewhere between a flamboyant Gothic cathedral and a gingerbread castle. The façade is a conglomerate of different aesthetic messages: delicate rose windows are outlined by broken Renaissance pediments, topped off by a clock tower that belongs more to a parish church in the Alps. Moving inside, feast your eyes on the huge 17th-century **rood screen;** this is the last place in Paris where you can still be preached at from on high (once a common custom). Delicate carving and double spiral staircases make the screen seemas if it might float up to the heavens (together with the sermon, priest, greenhouse gases, etc.). Walking down the right side of the nave, you will find epitaphs for Pascal and Racine, both of whom are buried farther down at the opening of the choir. Also on your right, don't miss the sanctuary of Ste-Geneviève, commemorating the patron saint of Paris with a chapel and reliquary of gilt copper that will remind you of a Van Eyck painting, even though they were only built in the 19th century. Ste-Geneviève's actual remains were burnt during the Revolution—the reliquary holds a piece of her original tombstone together with a few bones, fingers, and other scraps. A blank book placed in front allows you to render your homage to these fragments, as well as to ask for those few choice favors which such a well-known saint will be sure to grant. As you continue exploring the church, notice the lovely 16th- and 17th-century stained glass, in particular in the cloister (accessible through the back of the choir).

East of the Panthéon, at the intersection of rue de Navarre and rue des Arènes, rest the remains of the **Arènes de Lutèce,** a 100 by 130m oval Roman amphitheater, built to accommodate 15,000 spectators (far surpassing the needs of the still-tiny colony of Lutetia). The ruins were unearthed during the construction of rue Monge and were restored in the 1910s; all the seats are reconstructions. Benches on winding paths above the arena offer an oasis of calm. This is a great place for a picnic supper; try nearby rue Monge for a *fromagerie* where you can get bread and all the different types of cheese you've ever wanted.

People looking to kill a Sunday afternoon, but bored by the run of the mill walk in the park, will love the **Jardin des Plantes** (tel. 40 79 30 00; Mo. Jussieu). The main entrance is at 57, rue Cuvier. Leopards, bears, and 4m pythons stalk and slither, while 5cm-long diamonds, meter-high quartz formations, dinosaur skeletons, and rare tropical plants repose. The 45,000 square meter park, opened in 1640 by Guy de la Brosse, personal doctor to Louis XIII, was originally intended for the sole purpose of growing medicinal plants to promote his Majesty's health. Later it became a general garden for botanical research. Thomas Jefferson, an avid naturalist, loved this place, spending hours here hanging out, chewing the fat with its curators; he even donated the remains of several North American animals to its collection. The garden has since been converted into a conglomeration of museums, including a natural history museum, a mineral museum, an insect gallery, a hedge maze, an arboretum, a tropical-flower greenhouse, and a full-fledged zoo. While attractions such as the arboretum—a series of rare trees labeled with metal nameplates, scattered throughout the park—and the hedge maze, located at the northeastern end of the park, are free, all of the museums have separate tickets and hours (see Museums). Ask for a free park map, available at the two entrance gates. The Jardin des Plantes also has two exhibitions devoted entirely to botanical fascinations, including the **Jardin Alpin** and the **Serres,** both greenhouses full of rare flowers and plants, the first from the Alpine domain and the second from tropical and dessert regions. (Open Wed.-Mon. 1-5pm. Admission 12F, students 8F.)

The **Ménagerie,** also found in the Jardin des Plantes, surprises those who did not expect to find live jaguars roaming in downtown Paris. The cages are painfully small; the weather is cold and damp; the lions growl unhappily about their neighbors the leopards; and the general countenance of the animals is downtrodden and miserable. But there are a few pleasant exceptions. The reptile house, best of all, shelters 3m boa constrictors as well as an assortment of lethal pythons, cobras, and rattlesnakes, all of which spend their time sleeping peacefully in their tree displays—entirely oblivious to the crowds of admiring (and frightened) visitors. Next door, the insect house displays myriad unusual insects, much more appealing than their lifeless brethren in the *galerie d entomologie,* including camouflaged walking stick insects that are virtually indistinguishable from their twiggy environment, as well as a cage of two or three hundred copulating crickets...now that's the way to teach children about the birds and the bees! The Cutest Animals in the Zoo award most definitely goes to the bear cubs, on the left after the entrance, who stand on their hind paws and make puppy-dog eyes at anyone carrying food near their pit. During the siege of Paris in 1870, the zoo was raided for meat. Elephant became a great delicacy, but no one was brave enough to try slaughtering the lions. (Open Mon. and Wed.-Sat. 10am-5pm, Sat.-Sun. 11-6pm. Admission 25F, students and ages 6-16 13F.)

Walking west along the Seine back toward pl. St-Michel, stop to rest in the beautiful **Jardin des Sculptures en Plein Air,** quai St-Bernard, a lovely collection of modern sculpture on a long stretch of green along the Seine, with works by such artists as Zadkine, Brancusi, and Schéffer. Although this is a great place to catch some sun during the day, avoid this area at night; exhibitionists frequent this park to show tourists their own special parts of Paris. Across the street is the **Institut du Monde Arabe** (see Museums). Just next door to the institute, **La Tour d Argent,** 15, quai de la Tournell (Mo. Maubert), is Paris's most prestigious, most expensive restaurant.

Farther west along the Seine, square René Viviani (Mo. St-Michel), sequesters the oldest tree in Paris (a false acacia dating from 1693), one of the best views of Notre-Dame, and the **Eglise de St-Julien-le-Pauvre.** Though not the most beautiful in the city, this chuch, built in 1165, is the oldest in Paris. Okay, so Notre Dame was begun two years earlier, but St-Julien finished first. Oh yeah, some parts of St-Germain-des-Prés predate St-Julien-le-Pauvre, but that was back when St-Germain was a suburb of Paris. The obelisk? That's not a church, silly. This is *the oldest church in Paris.*

Sixth Arrondissement: St-Germain-des-Prés

Less frenzied and more sophisticated than its neighbors, the sixth *arrondissement* combines the vibrancy of the Latin Quarter to the east with the fashionable cafés, restaurants, and movie theaters of Montparnasse to the south. This area has long been the focus of literary Paris, and it remains less ravaged by tourists than other, more monumental quarters. Join the locals at one of the famous cafés on the bd. St-Germain, former haunts of the likes of Picasso, Sartre, Apollinaire, and Hemingway, and watch the hordes of well-dressed Parisians watch each other.

"There is nothing more charming, which invites one more enticingly to idleness, revery, and young love, than a soft spring morning or a beautiful summer dusk at the **Jardin du Luxembourg,** the respiratory center of the hard-working Latin Quarter," wrote Léon Daudet in 1928. (RER: Luxembourg.) Parisians don t take this park lightly—every chance they get, they are here, sunbathing, contemplating, writing, romancing, strolling, or just gazing at the delicious rose gardens and the still surface of the central basin. A mammoth task force of gardeners (1 per acre) keeps this most beloved of Parisian gardens looking like Paradise on earth; every year, they plant or transplant 350,000 flowers and move the 150 palm and orange trees back outside from winter storage. Thanks to the 12,000 Parisians who defended this park against Haussmann's wretched intentions to carve a street through it, you can now sail a toy boat on the pond, ride a pony, attend the *grand guignol* (puppet show—see Entertainment), shoot hoops, play *boules* or cards with the groups of old men, or simply soak up Paris.

The **Palais du Luxembourg,** within the park, was commissioned in 1615 by Marie des Médicis, who asked for an Italianate palace (and a garden, just a modest royal garden) to remind her of her native Tuscany. The palace was completed in a mere five years, gaining a symmetry and uniformity rare to the buildings of Paris. After housing various members of the royalty and high nobility, the Palais de Luxembourg served as a prison during The Terror, then as a prison for the proponents of The Terror. Jacobin artist Jacques-Louis David used his time confined here to paint the haunting, questioning self-portrait now displayed in the Louvre. Future Empress Joséphine was imprisoned in the palace together with her high-born republican husband, Beauharnais. Only half a decade later, Joséphine returned with her second husband, the new Consul Bonaparte, to the palace, now their official residence. Napoleon and Joséphine moved on to greater palaces, and to Waterloo. The Chamber of Peers met here under the Restoration and July Monarchy, when it judged many notorious trials of various traitors and assassins. The palace reached its current purpose, as the meeting place for the largely impotent French Senate, in 1852. The president of the Senate lives in **Petit Luxembourg,** a gift from Marie des Médicis to her nemesis, Cardinal Richelieu. The **Musée du Luxembourg** (tel. 42 34 20 00), next to the palace on rue de Vaugirard, displays temporary exhibitions, usually showcasing contemporary art and usually free.

Entering from bd. Saint-Michel and the Luxembourg RER station, you will be faced with the lovely gold-embossed wrought iron gates—closing off the busy city from Marie de Médicis's garden of Paradise. Go inside and wander. Sit at one of the folding chairs around the basin with a book or journal. Watch the parade of students and non-students walking by—a spectacular panorama of movement against the façade of the newly renovated Palais de Luxembourg. Follow the paths leading in each direction, moving past the statues of the queens to the garden's many secluded glens, each with monuments to different poets and heroes of French history.

The bust of Henry Murger, author of the 1851 bestselling *Scenes of Bohemian Life,* was set up in 1895, amidst a storm of controversy. An official banquet, to cost 6F and be presided over by the Minister of Education, was planned for the Café Voltaire, on the Right Bank. An alternative group—"True Bohemia"—accused the committee of possessing bourgeois values and arranged an alternate unveiling and a 2F banquet at the Café Procope (see below), to be held a day *earlier* than the official ceremony. Finally, a third group organized a third banquet to be held at the Cabaret de la Bohème, with a super-non-bourgeois 70 centimes meal made up of sausage, fried potatoes, and (for dessert) toothpicks. Meanwhile, a newspaper accused the mostly-Catholic Murger enthusiasts of anti-Semitism, and the unveiling of the bust of this quiet coffee-drinking melancholy turned into a violent riot that had little to do with Murger's literature and even less to do with the merry, starving artists and musicians he had described.

Don't miss the most beautiful spot in the garden, the **Fontaine Médici** in the northeast corner, at the end of a long alleyway and reflecting pool. Tall shade trees line the alley, giving the spot the verdancy and shade of an enchanted bower. A row of chairs along the reflecting pool provides a traditional spot for philosophical discussions and daydreaming. The fountain itself, with its heavy stone backdrop, complete with the Medici coat of arms (six balls), noble river gods pouring out their offerings on either side, and Pan and Diana surrounding a central niche below, was completed in 1624.

The three central figures—the bronze giant hovering on a rock over the marble lov-ers—were added when the fountain was moved here in 1863, yet blend elegantly into the Italian Baroque style of the site. The jealous cyclops, Polyphemus, sees his beloved nymph Galatea, "the exquisite, delicate, milk-white maid," in the arms of Acis and, be-ing a sensible, brawny cyclops, prepares to crush his rival with a rock. The contrast be-tween Polyphemus's coarseness and Galatea's beauty is emphasized by the different materials. On the backside of the fountain, a bas-relief illustrates the legend of Leda and the Swan. In such a bastion of heroic monumentality and forbidden love, you will think yourself in Italy, far from the heavily disciplined gardens and classically pure statues of the rest of the *jardin*. Here, above all, you will notice a phenomenon that one Parisian man of letters expressed eloquently in his 1852 description of the Luxembourg Gardens: "The soul still feels an involuntary impulse of sadness, a something melan-choly and subdued in the air you breathe there. One does not move, as in the Tuileries, with completely unfettered spirits; one feels oneself pursued by the ghosts of the past."

South of the Luxembourg stretch its elegant, linear annexes, the jardin R. Cavelier-de-la-Salle and the jardin Marco Polo, both forming the northern half of the **avenue de l'Observatoire.** The elaborate **fontaine de l'Observatoire** (1875) marks the halfway point between the observatory and the jardin du Luxembourg; its rearing horses, topped by an allegory of the "four parts of the world," provide a fittingly sumptuous perspective on the grand avenue that stretches at either side. Farther south, at the ex-treme southeastern corner of the sixth *arrondissement,* proudly stands Rude's statue of **Maréchal Ney,** *"le plus brave des braves"* and the greatest of Napoleon's marshals. Ney survived having five horses shot out from under him at Waterloo, only to be exe-cuted on this site by Louis XVIII's government for his support of Napoleon after his re-turn from Elba. After a lifetime as a soldier, the courageous marshal gave his last command to the firing squad lined up in front of him: *"Camarades, tirez sur moi et visez juste!"* (Comrades, fire on me, and aim well.) The present-day monument to Ney was erected in 1853, at the behest of another Napoleon. From the nearby **Closerie des Lilas** café, such notables as Baudelaire, Verlaine, Breton, Picasso, and Hemingway stared at the statue while listening to poetry and discussing their latest works (see Caf-és). Picasso, along with Matisse, found encouragement and financial support at 27, rue de Fleurus, west of the Luxembourg, where Gertrude Stein and her brother Leo lined the walls with paintings they had bought from some of the century's greatest artists.

Branching off from the avenue de l'Observatoire and moving back along the edge of the Luxembourg Gardens, the **boulevard Saint-Michel**—central axis of the Latin Quarter—marks the eastern boundary of the sixth *arrondissement.* Follow bd. St-Mich-el (or go back through the gardens) to the pl. Edmond Rostand, where a small fountain marks the end of the rue Soufflot. From this busy intersection, you'll have a majestic view (especially good at night) up the hill to the Panthéon—and the ever-popular Mc-Donald's, whose outside tables make it into an almost Parisian café. Almost.

Follow the arcades of the rue de Médicis around the edge of the Luxembourg Gar-dens to Paris's oldest and largest theater—the **Théâtre Odéon,** founded in 1770, hov-ering majestically over the place d Odéon, the nexus of six streets (Mo. Odéon). The Odéon company has competed with the rival Comédie-Française across the river (see first *arrondissement)* for centuries, sometimes in the political arena. Beaumarchais' *Marriage of Figaro,* after being nearly banned by the king, premiered here in 1784; aristocrats laughed wildly at the very jokes which ridiculed them; fist fights broke out on the street outside as poeple of all social classes struggled to get one of the last re-maining tickets. In 1789, the actor Talma staged a performance of Voltaire's *Brutus* in which he imitated the pose of the hero in David's painting (see Louvre). The rest of the-ater did not follow his leftist inclinations; the company was imprisoned for monarchist sympathies during the Revolution, and Talma fled across the river to the more liberal Comédie Française. The theater itself burned down twice in its early years; the present Greco-Roman incarnation dates from 1818 and was restored to its former glory under the advice of David. The Greek temple form is particularly compelling in the light of the recent discvovery that a Gallo-Roman temple stood less than 100m from here. Dur-ing the 19th century, the Odéon earned the title of *théâtre maudit* (cursed theater) after a chain of failures left it nearly bankrupt. All this changed in the 20th century, when the

1992 CATALOG

When it comes to
budget travel we know
every trick in the book
Discount Air Fares,
Eurailpasses, Travel
Gear, IDs, and more...

LET'S PACK IT UP

Let's Go Supreme

Innovative hideaway suspension with parallel stay internal frame turns backpack into carry-on suitcase. Includes lumbar support pad, torso and waist adjustment, leather trim, and detachable daypack. Waterproof Cordura nylon, lifetime guarantee, 4400 cu. in Navy, Green or Black.

A • • • • • • • • • • • • **$165**

Let's Go Backpack/Suitcase

Hideaway suspension with internal frame turns backpack into carry-on suitcase. Detachable daypack makes it 3 bags in 1. Waterproof Cordura nylon, lifetime guarantee, 3750 cu. in. Navy, Green or Black.

B • • • • • • • • • • • • • • **$119**

Undercover NeckPouch

Ripstop nylon with soft Cambrelle back. 3 pockets. 6 1/2 x 5". Lifetime guarantee. Black or Tan.

C • • • • • • • • • • • • • • **$9.95**

Undercover WaistPouch

Ripstop nylon with soft Cambrelle back. 2 pockets. 12 x 5" with 30 x 13cm waistband. Lifetime guarantee. Black or Tan.

D • • • • • • • • • • • • • • **$9.95**

Let's Go Backcountry

Full size, slim profile expedition pack designed for the serious trekker. Parallel stay suspension system, deluxe shoulder harness, Velcro height adjustment, side compression straps. Detachable hood converts into a fanny pack. Waterproof Cordura nylon, lifetime guarantee, main compartment and hood 6350 cu. in. extends to 7130 cu.

E • • • • • • • • • **$195**

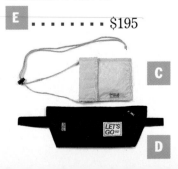

LET'S SEE SOME I.D.

1993 International ID Cards

Provides discounts on accomodations, cultural events, airfares and accident/medical insurance. Valid 9-1-92 to 12-31-93

F1	Teacher (ITIC)	$16.00
F2	Student (ISIC)	$15.00
F3	Youth (IYC)	$15.00

FREE "International Student Travel Guide."

LET'S GO HOSTELING

1993-94 Youth Hostel Card

Required by most international hostels. Must be a U.S. resident.

G1	Adult (ages 18-55)	$25
G2	Youth (under 18)	$10

Sleepsack

Required at all hostels. Washable durable poly/cotton. 18" pillow pocket. Folds into pouch size.

H	$13.95

1992-93 Youth Hostel Guide (IYHG)

Essential information about 3900 hostels in Europe and the Mediterranean.

I	$10.95

Let's Go Travel Guides

Europe; USA; Britain/Ireland; France; Italy; Israel/Egypt; Mexico; California/Hawaii; Spain/Portugal; Pacific Northwest/Alaska; Greece/Turkey; Germany/Austria/Swizerland; NYC; London; Washington D.C.; Rome; Paris.

J1	USA or Europe	$16.95
J2	Country Guide (specify)	$15.95
J3	City Guide (specify)	$10.95

LET'S GO BY TRAIN

Eurail Passes

Convenient way to travel Europe. Save up to 70% over cost of individual tickets. Call for national passes.

First Class

K1	15 days	$460
K2	21 days	$598
K3	1 month	$728
K4	2 months	$998
K5	3 months	$1260

First Class Flexipass

L1	5 days in 15	$298
L2	9 days in 21	$496
L3	14 days in 30	$676

Youth Pass (under 20)

M1	1 month	$508
M2	2 months	$698
M3	5 days in 2 months	$220
M4	10 days in 2 months	$348
M5	15 days in 2 months	$474

LET'S GET STARTED

Please print or type. Incomplete applications will be returned

International Student/Teacher Identity Card (ISIC/ITIC) (ages 12 & up) enclose:

1 Letter from registrar or administration, transcript, or
proof of tuition payment. FULL-TIME only.
2 One picture (1 1/2" x 2") signed on the reverse side.

International Youth Card (IYC) (ages 12-25) enclose:

1 Proof of birthdate (copy of passport or birth certificate).
2 One picture (1 1/2" x 2") signed on the reverse side.
3 Passport number   **4** Sex: M☐ F☐

Last Name	First Name	Date of Birth

Street	*We do not ship to P.O. Boxes. U.S. addresses only.*	

City	State	Zip Code

Phone	Citizenship

School/College	Date Trip Begins

Item Code	Description, Size & Color	Quantity	Unit Price	Total Price

Shipping & Handling		
	Total Merchandise Price	
If order totals: . . . . . . Add	Shipping & Handling (See box at left)	
Up to $30.00 . . . . $4.00	For Rush Handling Add $8 for continental U.S., $10 for AK & HI	
30.01-100.00 . . . . $6.00	MA Residents (Add 5% sales tax on gear & books)	
Over 100.00 . . . . $7.00	**Total**	

Enclose check or money order
payable to: Harvard Student
Agencies, Inc.

Allow 2-3 weeks for delivery. Rush
orders delivered within one week of
our receipt.

Harvard Student Agencies, Inc., Harvard University, Thayer B, Cambridge, MA 02138

(617) 495-9649   1-800-5LET'S GO (Credit Card Orders Only)

Prices subject to change

Odéon turned to contemporary playwrights and became *the* place to see modern drama. Leaders of the student revolt seized the building on May 17, 1968. It remained one of their strongpoints, until June 12, though at one point President de Gaulle seriously considered prying out the students with gunfire. Check posters and *Pariscope* for performance schedules (see Entertainment—Theater).

Nearby, the edifices at 49, rue Monsieur-le-Prince and 5, rue de Racine were home to Henry Wadsworth Longfellow in the 1820s before he returned to America to become a professor of German language, world-famous poet, and (together with his elder brother Stephen) progenitor of a long line of illustrious, myopic, and charmingly scatterbrained American scholars. Two blocks west of the theater, the awesome 17th-century **Eglise St-Sulpice** (Mo. St-Sulpice) contains Delacroix frescoes in the first chapel on the right, a stunning *Virgin and Child* by Jean-Baptiste Pigalle in one of the rear chapels, and an enormous Chalgrin organ, among the world's largest and most famous with 6588 pipes. All the great organists yearn for a chance to play at St-Sulpice. As with so many other Parisian churches (and football players), a fortress-like outer bulk conceals a serene, vaulted interior space. (Open daily 7:30am-7:30pm.) From St-Sulpice, move north to the **boulevard Saint-Germain,** the Left Bank's great transversal boulevard. This area, jam-packed with cafés, restaurants, cinemas, and expensive boutiques, is always crowded, noisy, and full of excitement. Follow the footsteps of Baudelaire, Apollinaire, Breton, Sartre, de Beauvoir, Picasso, and many, many others as you walk past such famous cafés as **Les Deux Magots** and **Le Flore** (see Food—Cafés).

The Eglise St-Germain-des-Prés (Mo. St-Germain-des-Près) watches benevolently over all this excitement. The first church on this site was founded in the fields outside Paris by King Childebert I in order to hold relics he had brought back from the Holy Land; it was finished in 558 and consecrated by Saint Germain, Bishop of Paris, on the very day of the king's death (conveniently, since he was to be buried inside the church's walls). Sacked by the Normans and rebuilt three times, St-Germain-des-Prés (St-Germain of the Fields) remained for a long time a heavily fortified abbey outside of Paris. Parts of the modern-day church date from 1163, making it officially the oldest standing church in what is now Paris, yet the building you see is a melange of eclectic architectural styles; each generation added to the church its own version of the "modern," and the result is a mixture of Romanesque, Gothic, and Baroque features. The last remains of the old abbey walls and gates were destroyed when Haussmann extended the rue de Rennes in front of the church and created the place St-Germain-des-Prés in front.

During the Revolution, the church was desanctified and even had a brief sojourn at the end of the 18th century as a saltpeter mill, which, of course, did wonders for the already badly deteriorating structure. In 1794, just after St-Germain-des-Prés was restored to its original function as a church, a major fire consumed its remaining (already severely depleted) collection of artwork and treasures. Yet the church as you see it today, a child of so many different eras and architectural philosophies, has an air of sanctity that bears its battle scars well. The painted interior—a memorial of sorts to the way all medieval churches once looked—was restored in the 19th century. Wander around, looking for the details: the Romanesque capitals on some of the pillars, the hidden stonework in the side chapels, the medieval shrines, the 17th-century vaulting—that attest to this building's near-millenium of history. In the second chapel on the right inside the church you ll find a stone marking the interred heart of Descartes and an altar dedicated to the victims of the September 1793 massacre, in which 186 Parisians were slaughtered by *sans-culottes* in the courtyard. Pick up one of their free maps of the church, with information in English on St-Germain's history and its artifacts. Come here for one of their frequent concerts, if you can afford it. As in most medieval churches, built to accommodate an age without microphones, the acoustics are wonderful, and the church at night has a somber air of mystery and devotion that will take you back several centuries. (Check posters and *Pariscope* for prices and schedule. Church open daily 9am-7:30pm.)

Moving north from Saint-Germain toward the Seine, you'll find some of the most tangled streets in central Paris. Haussmann retired before he could figure out a way to extend his rue de Rennes to the riverbank and across a bridge, to meet up with the Rue de Louvre. For years the impassable quarter presented a tempting morsel to urban designers wishing to improve circulation. But before they could decide on a plan, a new aesthetic of preservation kicked in; the neighborhood has been left as a largely unreconstructed maze. The streets near rue de Seine overflow with fashionable, expensive art galleries and boutiques. To see what local art students are up to, walk around the **Ecole des Beaux Arts,** 14, rue Bonaparte (tel. 42 60 34 57; Mo. St-Germain-des-Prés), at quai Malaquais. France's most acclaimed art school, the Ecole was founded officially by Napoleon in 1811 and soon became the bastion of French academic painting and sculpture. The current building for the Ecole des Beaux Arts was finished in 1838, in a gracious style much like that of the nearby Institut de France. Periodic exhibits showcase student work; check Parisian publications for up-to-the-minute information.

Just one block to the east on the *quais,* the **Palais de l Institut de France,** pl. de l Institut (Mo. Pont-Neuf), broods over the Seine beneath its famous *coupole,* the black-and gold-topped dome. This one-time school (1688-1793) and prison (1793-1805) was designed by Le Vau to house the college established in the will of Cardinal Mazarin. The glorious building has housed the Institut de France since 1806. Founded in 1795, in one of the last acts of a dying Convention before its replacement by the more conservative Directory, the Institute was intended to be a storehouse for the nation's knowledge and a meeting place for France's greatest scholars. During the Restoration, appointment to the Institute was more dependent on one's political position than one's erudition, but since 1830 things have been slightly more meritocratic.

One of the institute's branches is the prestigious **Academie Française,** which, since its founding by Richelieu in 1635, has assumed the task of compiling the official French dictionary and purging the sacred French language of dastardly foreign influence. (Dr. Johnson mocked the 40 members for taking 40 years to write their dictionary when he, working alone, was able to finish his in three. He concluded that a Frenchman was worth 3/1600s of an Englishman.) Already having registered its adamant disapproval of *le weekend, le parking,* and other "Franglais" nonsense, the Academy recently triumphed with the passing of a constitutional amendment that French is indeed the official language of France. Now the academy is gearing up for a battle with those government-sponsored infidels who want to eliminate the circumflex, that pointed hat of an accent capping words like *tête* and *crêpe.* But don't worry about speaking English near the Academy; bright yellow helmets make the Language Police detectable from quite a distance. So difficult is it to become elected to this arcane society, limited to 40 members, that Molière, Balzac, and Proust never made it, and only in 1981 was a woman, Marguerite Yourcenar, granted membership.

Next door, the **Hôtel des Monnaies,** once the mint for all French coins, still proudly displays its austere 17th-century façade to the heart of the Left Bank. Today, it mints only honorary medals. You can still tour its foundry and its significant coin collection by entering the **Musée de la Monnaie de Paris** (see Museums). The **Pont des Arts,** the footbridge across from the Institute, is celebrated by poets and artists for its delicate ironwork, its beautiful views of the Seine, and its spiritual locus in the heart of France's most presitigious Academy of Arts and Letters. Come here at dusk to watch the sun go down against the silhouette of Paris's most famous monuments.

Seventh Arrondissement: The Faubourg St-Germain

Architectural 18th-century Paris lives on in the seventh *arrondissement.* For several centuries, the faubourg St-Germain, roughly between the Invalides and rue des Saints-Pères around the bd. St-Germain, was the city's most fashionable place to live—the home of the elite and their families. Within its hallowed precincts, financiers and nobles built terribly grand *hôtels particuliers,* set back from the street behind high gates and elegant *cours d'honneur* (courts of honor). Many of these mansions are today ministeries and embassies, and if you hearken carefully when the wind dies down, you can just hear the sound of shuffling paper.

Some *hôtels* remain closed to the socially meek, for example, the **Hôtel Matignon.** This hogan, at 57, rue de Varenne, was owned by Talleyrand and Madame Adelaide, Louis-Philippe's sister. When it was built in 1721, the rue de Babylone was at the very edge of the city, and the mansion was built as a cross between an urban *hôtel* and a country *château*. Later it became the Austro-Hungarian embassy (not a great thing to be in late 19th-century Paris). That use collapsed with the empire. Today, complete with Fragonard murals, it is the official residence of the French Prime Minister. But unless M. Bérégovoy invites you in, it's off-limits. The neighboring **Hôtel Biron**, at number 77, was built by Gabriel in 1728. The state made it an artists' residence in 1904; sculptor Auguste Rodin rented a studio on its ground floor in 1908. When the Ministry of Education and Fine Arts evicted all tenants in 1910, Rodin offered to donate all of his works to make a museum—on the condition that he could spend his last years at Biron, where the museum was to be founded. Despite fierce debate, the state agreed to accept Rodin's gift, today called the **Musée Rodin** (see Museums). Up rue de Bourgogne and to the right, at no. 116, rue de Grenelle, the **Mairie du 7ème arrondissement** sits inside an *hôtel* built in 1709 for the Maréchal de Villars (Open Mon.-Fri. 9am-6pm). The imposing **Hôtel de Courteilles**, at no. 110, rue de Grenelle, houses the Ministry of National Education. Turning up rue de Bellechasse leads you toward the Seine and the elegant **Hôtel de Salm,** 2, rue de Bellechasse, built by Pierre Rousseau in 1786 for the German Prince of Salm Kyrbourg. The building remained untainted by his death by guillotine: in 1804, Napoleon chose the hôtel as the Palace of the Legion of Honor (the Palace of the Legion of Honor in San Francisco is an exact copy). As at the *Mairie,* average Joe Citizen can venture inside, in this case while visiting the **Musée de la Légion d'Honneur** (see Museums).

Across the street stands the now more famous rue de Bellechasse resident, the **Musée d'Orsay** (see Museums). The Gare d'Orsay, the train station housing the museuem, takes its name from the nearby *quai*. The façade borrows from the monumental grandeur of the Louvre, but the glass and metal roof heralded the arrival of the modern era when the building was completed in 1900.

Next door, the **Caisse des Dépôts et Consignations,** 3, quai Anatole France, operates on the site of the Count of Belle-Isle's 1730 mansion. Destroyed by Commune fires in 1871, the *hôtel* was rebuilt between 1872 and 1875, on the 18th-century foundations. The Caisse moved into the building in 1858 (it was created on April 18, 1816) and today continues to live up to its motto of "public trust" by letting people into its lovely courtyard and bustling lobby. The chunky sculpture *Réséda* by Jean Dubuffet (1901-1985) and the sharp primary-colored *Coups de Pinceau* by Roy Lichtenstein curve upward inside the courtyard and lobby respectively.

Exit at 56, rue de Lille, turn left and then right onto rue du Bac. In the 18th century, this (now food-rich) street marked the boundary between town and country. Quench tea thirst and satiate chocolate cravings at **Christian Constant,** 26, rue du Bac (see Salons de Thé) and the ever-present, ever-exquisite **Le Nôtre,** 44, rue du Bac (see Sweets). **Eglise St-Thomas-d'Aquin,** off rue du Bac on rue de Gribeauval, was originally dedicated to Saint Dominique when built in the 17th century. Its 1769 façade is based on Il Gesù in Rome. Ironically, in this *quartier* of military heroes and bellicose ministers, the Revolution made the church into a Temple of Peace. The irony continues today, for the church's closest neighbor is the Direction du Personnel Militaire de l'Armée de Terre (Administration of Military Personnel of the Land Army). Although under renovation, the 17th- and 18th-century paintings are still impressive and the central half dome is awesomely ornate. (Church open Mon.-Sat. 8am-noon and 4-7pm, Sun. variable.)

Just off to the left from rue du Bac, at 55-57 rue de Grenelle, the **Fontaine des Quatres Saisons** (the Fountain of Four Seasons) celebrates the city of Paris (the seated figure), who in turn controls the reclining Seine and Marne. Bouchardon sculpted the fountain between 1739 and 1745 not purely for aesthetic purposes: like most of Paris, the area was badly in need of water. At the eastern extremity of the seventh, university institutes begin peppering the streets, some accompanied by their specialist bookstores.

Square Boucicart, on the corner of bd. Raspail and rue de Babylone, has plenty of benches for adults and sand for kids, in addition to slides and something of a playhouse. Across from the back side of the Hôtel Matignon bizarre tiny trees sprout in the **Jardin de Babylone;** the green space is predictably calming. Past the **Caserne de la Garde Républicaine** (the yellow brick and funny hats give it away), stumble on the **Salle Chinoise** (corner of Babylone and rue Monsieur). Part movie theater but all Chinese palace, this building was once a welcoming chamber for the Chinese embassy. To-

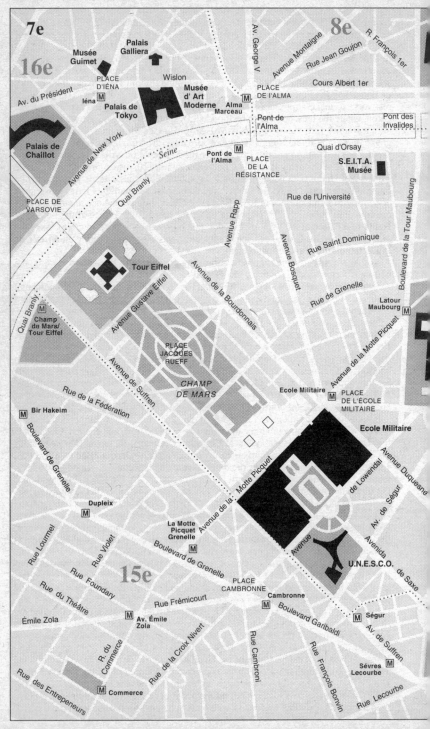

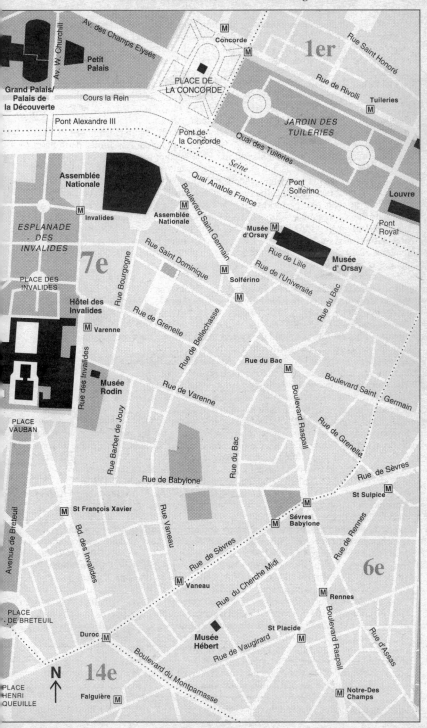

day, it livens up the architectural tedium of ministries and *conseils,* and offers a range of excellent movies, old and new (see Entertainment—Cinema). Walk down rue Monsieur, turn left on rue Oudinot, and take rue Rousselet down to **rue de Sèvres.** Restaurants line the streets of this busy road, itself full of *boucheries, marchés, pâtisseries,* and the like. Most food conceivable, cooked and otherwise, is available here.

The Palais Bourbon, 33, quai d'Orsay, challenges the Madeleine across the river for colonnaded supremacy of the place de la Concorde axis. Napoleon erected the present façade in 1807, but the *hôtel* itself was built in 1722 for the Duchess of Bourbon, daughter of Louis XIV and Mme. de Montespan. Allegorical sculpture festoons the palace, but the high iron gates and austere-looking machine-gun-laden police planted every few meters tend to be distracting. They're guarding the **Assemblée Nationale,** the French legislature, from a replay of the 1934 attempt by a mob to overthrow the government. French-speakers and govjocks may want to observe the assembly in session (if you are neither you won't understand and you won't care). A security check that lasts as least one hour must be run on all foreigners who want to enter the chamber—show up with your passport well in advance of the start of the day's sitting. Appropriate dress is required—shirt and tie and/or jacket for men. The guards admit that it's really only men's attire that matters but it can't hurt for women to wear dress pants or a skirt. (The Assembly sits Oct.-Dec. and April-June, although the session may last longer. Call 40 63 64 80 for the starting time of a particular day's meeting—the Assembly meets most weekdays in the afternoons of the above periods.)

Guided tours of the Palais Bourbon are offered in French—with a pamphlet in English—every Saturday at 10am, 2pm, and 3pm. Worth seeing is **Salon Delacroix** (Salon du Roi), decorated by Romantic painter Eugène Delacroix for Minister of the Interior Adolphe Thiers in 1834. Friezes depict Justice, Industry, Agriculture, and... Commerce? Labor? Science? No, the winner is *War.* The same team of Delacroix and architect Jules de Joly produced the spectacular **Library.** The ceiling paintings showcase moments and concepts from literary history, philosophy, and the like. (Socrates and his daemon appear in one spandrel.) Among the 700,000 books and documents are the transcripts of Jeanne d'Arc's trial, the basis for Carl Dreyer's 1928 film. The other standout on the tour is the **Salle de Séances** (the Assembly Chamber) itself. A red semi-circle with colonnaded gallery, the chamber is presided over by the *Président du conseil,* who sits in an ornate chair decorated by Lemot and Michallon. Behind him, a framed tapestry of Raphael's *School of Athens* presents an ideal of the republic of philosopher-kings (just so you know you're in France...). As the politicians pontificate, clerks scramble below to record the day's proceedings for publication in the *Journal Officiel.* Free tours are offered all year. Kiosque de l'Assemblée Nationale, 4, rue Aristide-Briand (tel. 40 63 61 21) has all kinds of information about the Assemblée Nationale, as well as the standard collection of souvenirs. (Open Mon.-Fri. 9:30-7pm, Sat. 9:30am-5pm.) Next door to the Palais Bourbon, the **Ministère des Affaires Etrangères** (Ministry of Foreign Affairs), usually metonymized as the Quai d'Orsay, contemplates global action.

The Esplanade des Invalides, a happy combination of benches, trees, and grass, stretches down to the river. This is no ordinary Parisian grass; people dare not only sit on it, but even engage in exuberant games of soccer on it. Of course, it's really just there to give you an unobstructed view of the fabulously huge **Hôtel des Invalides,** 2, av. de Tourville (Mo. Invalides, Latour-Maubourg, or St-François Xavier). In 1670, Louis XIV, wager of incessant war, decided to "construct a royal home, grand and spacious enough to receive all old or wounded officers and soldiers." The first stone was laid November 30, 1671; architect Libéral Burand's building accepted its first wounded in October of 1674, and veterans still live in the Invalides today. Jules Hardouin-Mansart finished the **Eglise St-Louis** and, in 1706, the imposing dome, which has been called superior to St. Paul's in London and St. Peter's in Rome. On July 14, 1789, a crowd raided the building for weapons; the mob then went to seek gunpowder, *and destiny,* at the Bastille. The Church of the Dome received Napoleon's body for funeral services in 1840, but the ostentatious tomb by Visconti was not ready for occupation until April 2, 1861. You can tour the Tomb, as well as the Musée de l'Armée, Musée d'Histoire Contemporaine, and Musée de l'Ordre de Libération, all housed within the complex (see Museums). Enter the complex either from place des Invalides to the north or place Vauban and avenue de Tourville to the south. Around the "back," to the left of the Tourville entrance, the **Jardin de l'Intendant** provides shade and benches in an ornamental setting, albeit next to a busy street. The big ditch, lined with foreign cannon captured in various wars, used to be a moat, and it still makes it impossible to leave by any but the official entrance.

A pleasant riverside walk awaits you to the east of the Invalides, on the quai d'Orsay. The **S.E.I.T.A.** (Société pour l'Exploitation Industrielle des Tabacs et Allumettes), on the corner of rue Surcouf and quai d'Orsay stands as a testament to the paradoxical approach of France to the government: tobacco and smoking are state-run, state-promoted activities that are sticking the state-run, state-promoted health system with increasingly large bills. Ah, socialism. Don't miss the nearby Musée-Galerie de la Seita (see Museums). The **American Church in Paris,** 65, quai d'Orsay (tel. 47 05 07 99), bustles with English speakers in search of accommodations and jobs (see Practical Information). The impossibly stern alien architectural nightmare at 59, quai d'Orsay is, not surprisingly, the South African Embassy; the popular republic's diplomatic importance is well-illustrated by its positioning next to the Qatar Embassy at no. 57. Appropriately named, the leafy av. Bosquet (Thicket Avenue) borders an area to the east rich in restaurants, hotels, and food stores. **Rue Cler** can satisfy any and all culinary needs. And you can join the sewer rats at the Musée des Egouts de Paris, entrance near pl. de la Résistance (see Museums).

And now, for the *pièce de résistance...*

At the opening of his impressive iron monument in 1889, Gustave Eiffel scrawled on the fan of an adoring spectator, "France is the only country in the world with a 300m flagpole." Still flying the tricolor, the skyline-piercing railroad bridge cut in half and put on its side that is the **Tour Eiffel (Eiffel Tower)** (tel. 45 50 34 56; Mo. Bir-Hakeim) is a globally admired symbol the City of Light. The Tour's design, actually concieved by engineers Emile Nouguier and Maurice Koechlin (who worked for Eiffel's bridge building company), was the winning entry in an 1885 contest. Judges chose the plans that bore Eiffel's name for the centerpiece of the 1889 World's Fair, held to celebrate the centennial of the French Revolution. Shockwaves of dismay reverberated around the city before the construction site at the end of the Champs-de-Mars even opened. Architects whined throughout 1886; one month into construction, in Feb. 1887, the artistic establishment published a scathing letter in *Le Temps*. Guy de Maupassant, Alexandre Dumas *fils,* Charles Garnier, and Sully Prudhomme joined countless other artists in condemning, in "the name of the belittled French taste," the erection "in the heart of our capital, of the useless and monstrous Eiffel Tower." Maupassant spoke of it elsewhere as a "giant and disgraceful skeleton;" after it was built he allegedly ate his lunch in the one-hectare expanse beneath it because it was the only place in Paris where he could avoid seeing the thing. It was even labeled with that most damning of epithets: "American." The condemnation was not altogether surprising. With its metal girders and boldly modern look, the tower was a triumph of engineering, seemingly cementing the split between science and art. Eiffel patiently responded to his critics by saying that his engineer's sense of beauty was delighted primarily by design that served a purpose, and that the grand curves of the tower would possess the beauty of wind resistance. The tallest structure in the world would be a monument to modern engineering and industry, comparable to the pyramids of Egypt.

Inaugurated March 31, 1889, the tower opened for visitors May 15, 1889 to great popular acclaim: nearly two million people went up in the tower during the fair. Numbers dwindled by comparison during the following decades and the entrepreneurial Eiffel began to confront the unpleasant prospect of tearing his masterpiece down: the lease on the property from the City of Paris expired on Dec. 31, 1909 and it was expected that the tower, like the other world fair buildings on the Champs de Mars, would be destroyed. But the so-called Tower of Babel survived because of its importance as a science and communications installation, which Eiffel had cultivated carefully in the 1890s. The radiotelegraphic center established on the top of the Tower worked full-time during World War I, intercepting enemy messages, among them the ones which resulted in the arrest and execution of Mata Hari. With another world exposition in

1937 and a new Trocadéro Palace built across the river in its honor, the Eiffel Tower again became a showpiece, firmly established as the ultimate symbol of Paris. Countless films have dwelled on its grace, including the hilarious *Lavender Hill Mob,* starring Alec Guinness. It has also been less skillfully depicted, notably on the cover of this book. Loving centennial renovations have made the tower look sparkling-new and Parisians and tourists alike have reclaimed the monument.

Seeing the Eiffel Tower, even for the umpteenth time, is inevitably breathtaking. The Tower is huge and, well, towers over its surroundings. It's also a soft brown, not the metallic steel gray that most visitors anticipate. And despite the 18,000 pieces of iron, 2,500,000 rivets, and 9,100,000 kilograms of sheer weight that compose the world's largest Gallic symbol, the Eiffel Tower appears surprisingly elegant, with many of the girders taking on a spidery, web-like elegance. This is especially true at night, when lines of light follow the delicate skeleton, turning it into a brilliant lace-like apparition—a modern counterpart to the heaven-reaching spires of Notre-Dame.

Judging by the range of services it offers, the Tour Eiffel might well be mistaken for an apartment building, with a mind-boggling number of visitors (the official visitor total had reached 142,914,619 on July 9, 1992, and they add to it every day). Buy exorbitantly priced souvenirs (including the unmissable green sponge Eiffel Tower) in the stores, eat good food at high cost in the restaurants, and even send mail with the only-available-here Eiffel Tower postmark. The *Cinemax,* a fun and relaxing stop midway through the climb on the first floor, shows hyperactive documentary movies about the tower. Informative posters about nifty and bizarre moments in the tower's history are literally everywhere—take the time to read them, both to learn and to rest your distended calves. The cheapest way to get up the tower is to walk up the first two floors (8F). This method also gives you an unbeatable, step-by-step tour of the Tower's complex structure. But you can't go to the Eiffel Tower and not go all the way. (Eiffel sure did. A true Frenchman, he designed a special room at the top of the tower where he could impress—and entertain—his lady friends.) The third floor/summit/tippy-top is accessible only by elevator. Tickets can be bought from the *caisse,* when open, or from the coin-operated dispenser in the east corner. (2nd-3rd floor elevator 17F, ages 4-11 7F, under 4 free. Ticket good for the day, when the third floor is open.) No matter what height you find yourself at, survey the city. Excellent aerial photographs point out significant landmarks and accompanying blurbs, in English, fill in the history. Whether you have trekked all over the city or are seeing it for the first time, a visit to the Eiffel Tower provides a lesson in Parisian sight-seeing. Try it at night—even the most blasé will be impressed by the beautiful, illuminated iron structure and the lights of Paris—its buildings, its traffic, its river—down below. For a splendid view of the tower, cross the river to the Palais Chaillot (see 16th *arrondissement).* (Tower open daily July 4-Sept. 9am-midnight; Sept. 7-Dec. and Jan.-March 20 9:30am-11pm; March 21-July 3 9am-11pm. Stairs open July 4-Sept. 6 and May 23-July 3 Fri.-Sat. and holidays until 11pm; Sept. 7-May 22 daily; May 23-July 3 Sun.-Thurs. until 6:30pm. Admissions to stairs and third floor elevator as above. Elevator to first floor 17F, ages 4-11 8F; to second floor 34F, ages 4-11 16F; to third floor 51F, ages 4-11 23F; under 4 free to all levels. Wheelchair accessible.)

For an area dedicated to the God of War, the **Champ de Mars** teems with a remarkable amount of peace and happiness. A green, flower-embroidered carpet stretching from the Ecole Militaire to the Eiffel Tower, the park is a veritable kid's heaven: jungle gyms, monkey bars, wood trains, and even abbreviated cement soccer fields line the southwest side. This does not stop anyone from picking up a game of *foot* (soccer) in front of obscure Egyptian statues. The park's name comes from its original function as a drill ground for the neighboring Ecole Militaire. During the Revolution and the First Empire, it hosted several ceremonies of great patriotic import. Particularly notable was Festival of Federation, held amid a drenching downpour on the first anniversary of the storming of the Bastille. To celebrate the nation's unity, 400,000 citizens approached a national altar to be blessed by the cynical bishop, Talleyrand, and the yet-untarnished Louis XVI. For the 1794 Festival of the Supreme Being, desgined to promote the new civic religion, Jacobin artist Jacques-Louis David built an artificial mountain out of plaster and cardboard. The field was used for various political demonstrations, the last being in 1851, when Louis Bonaparte distributed imperial eagles to the army, in an un-abashed imitation of his uncle. As Napoleon III, Bonaparte chose the field for the Great Exhibition of 1867, the crowning glory of his regime. An enormous glass pavilion sheltered the displays, which were visited by 15 million people from all over the world, including almost every crowned head of Europe. Other expositions followed in 1878, 1889 (for which the Eiffel Tower was built), 1900, and 1937, using the field as a com-bination fairground/construction site. After the 1900 Exhibition, the Municipal Council seriously considered parceling off the Champ de Mars for development, but was per-suaded that the dense city needed all the open space it had.

The Ecole Militaire was created by Louis XV at the urging of his mistress, Mme. de Pompadour, who wanted to transform "poor gentlemen" into educated officers. Jacques-Ange Gabriel's building accepted 500 students for three years of training only after funds raised from a tax on playing cards and a lottery allowed for its completion in 1773. In 1784, a 15-year-old Corsican named Napoléone Buonaparte arrived and within weeks presented the school's administrators with a comprehensive plan for its reorganization. The emperor later showed his fondness for his alma mater by founding a new academy at St-Cyr.

The Ecole's architectural and spiritual antithesis, **UNESCO (United Nations Edu-cational, Scientific, and Cultural Organization)** (tel. 45 68 17 13 or 45 68 17 18; Mo. Ségur) stands in the shape of a Y across the street at 7, pl. de Fontenoy. Estab-lished to foster science and culture throughout the world, the agency developed a repu-tation for waste, cronyism, and Marxist propaganda, which prompted the United States, the United Kingdom, and Singapore to withdraw in 1984, taking with them 30% of the agency's budget. The new head, Federico Mayor Zaragoza, is trying to persuade the U.S. to come back, especially now that the Soviet Union can't bankroll his organi-zation. But the White House is not enthusaistic about promising $50 million a year to a group of high-paid bureaucrats who spend 70% of their budget in Paris. Nine appropri-ately international pieces of art decorate the building and garden: ceramics by Miró and Artigas, a nameless painting by Picasso, a Japanese garden, and an angel from the façade of a Nagasaki church destroyed by the bomb among them. UNESCO frequently mounts temporary exhibitions of photography that make a visit more worthwhile. The library is open only to accredited researchers, but the bookstore is full of UNESCO publications. Bring your passport and call about conferences or lectures, when the place bustles with representatives from its 158 member countries. During especially important conferences when security needs are highest, you may have trouble getting in. (Open Mon.-Sat. 9am-6:30 pm. Bookstore open Mon.-Sat. 9:15 am-12:45pm and 2:15-5:45pm. Variable times for temporary exhibits. Free.)

Eighth Arrondissement: The Champs-Elysées

Almost as elegant as its neighbor to the southwest, the 16th, the eighth *arrondisse-ment* is home to Haussmann's *grands boulevards,* and the grandest street of all, the av-enue des Champs-Elysées. Salons and boutiques of *haute couture* pepper fashionable streets like rue de Faubourg St-Honoré with world-famous names. Embassies crowd around the Palais de l'Elysée, state residence of the French president. Already attrac-tive to the rising bourgeoisie of the early 19th century, the neighborhood took off with the construction of the swanky boulevards Haussmann and Malesherbes. The whole area bustles, and it should; within a very few blocks, the eighth provides you with all the resources necessary to dine exquisitely, dress impeccably, and accessorize magnif-icently. Moreover, you can indulge your esoteric music tastes, satisfy your *penchant* for sweets, and buy the ticket for your winter flight to Rio with the greatest amount of ease (and money). Most importantly, the eighth and its tree-lined streets provide you with the opportunity to show it—everything you are and everything you've purchased—off.

The Arc de Triomphe (tel. 43 80 31 31; Mo. Charles-de-Gaulle Etoile), looming gloriously above the Champs-Elysées in pl. Charles de Gaulle, commemorates France's victories, as well as its long obsession with military glory. The world's largest triumphal arch (49.546m high, 44.820m wide, and 22.210m thick) and an internation-ally recognized symbol of France, this behemoth was commissioned by Napoleon in

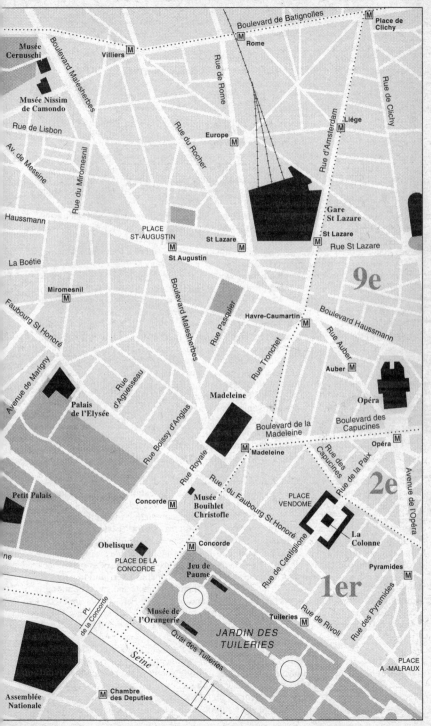

Boulevard de Batignolles

Place de Clichy

Musée Cernuschi

Rome

Boulevard Malesherbes

Villiers Ⓜ

Rue de Rome

Rue de Clichy

Musée Nissim de Camondo

Rue de Lisbon

Rue du Miromesnil

Rue du Rocher

Europe Ⓜ

Rue d'Amsterdam

Liége Ⓜ

Av. de Messine

Haussmann

Gare St Lazare

La Boétie

PLACE ST-AUGUSTIN

St Lazare Ⓜ

St Lazare Ⓜ

Rue St Lazare

St Augustin

9e

Miromesnil Ⓜ

Boulevard Malesherbes

Rue Pasquier

Faubourg St Honoré

Havre-Caumartin Ⓜ

Boulevard Haussmann

Rue Auber

Avenue de Marigny

Rue d'Aguesseau

Palais de l'Elysée

Rue Boissy d'Anglas

Rue Royale

Madeleine

Rue Tronchet

Auber Ⓜ

Opéra

Boulevard de la Madeleine

Boulevard des Capucines

Opéra Ⓜ

Madeleine Ⓜ

Rue des Capucines

Rue de la Paix

2e

Avenue de l'Opéra

Petit Palais

Concorde Ⓜ

Musée Bouihlet Christofle

Rue du Faubourg St Honoré

PLACE VENDOME

La Colonne

Obelisque

PLACE DE LA CONCORDE

Concorde Ⓜ

Jeu de Paume

Rue de Castiglione

Pyramides Ⓜ

1er

ne

Pt. de la Concorde

Musée de l'Orangerie

Tuileries Ⓜ

Rue de Rivoli

Rue des Pyramides

JARDIN DES TUILERIES

Quai des Tuileries

Seine

PLACE A.-MALRAUX

Assemblée Nationale

Ⓜ Chambre des Deputies

1806. When construction began, the Etoile (star) marked the western entrance to the city through the *fermiers généraux* wall; the surroundings were quite bucolic. Napoleon was exiled before the monument was completed, but Louis XVIII ordered resumption of work in 1823 and dedication of the arch to the war in Spain and to its commander, the Duc d'Angoulême. The Arc was finally consecrated in 1836, 21 years after the defeat of the great army of *"Le Petit Corporal."* There was no consensus on what symbolic figures could cap the monument, and it has retained its simple unfinished form. The names of Napoleon's generals and battles are engraved inside. The most famous of the Arc's allegorical sculpture groups depicting the military history of France is François Rude's *Departure of the Volunteers of 1792,* commonly known as *La Marseillaise,* to the right facing the arch from the Champs-Elysées.

Primarily, the Arc is a military symbol. As such, the horseshoe-shaped colossus has proved a magnet to various triumphal armies. The victorious Prussians marched through in 1871, inspiring the mortified Parisians to purify the ground with fire. On July 14, 1919, however, the Arc provided the backdrop for an Allied celebration parade headed by Maréchal Foch (hooray!). Then in 1940, the Nazis goose-stepped through (rats). But four years later, the Free French and Yanks came through the arch victorious (so there!). The Tomb of the Unknown Soldier has rested under the arch since November 11, 1920; the eternal flame is rekindled every evening at 6:30pm, when veterans and small children lay wreaths decorated with blue, white, and red. De Gaulle's famous cry for *Résistance* is inscribed on a brass plaque in the pavement under the Arc.

The Arc sits in the center of the **Etoile**, which in 1907 became the world's first traffic circle, where drivers were required to keep going right around the circle until they reached their chosen turn-off. Rather than risk an early death by crossing the traffic to reach the Arc, use the underpasses on the even-numbered sides of both the Champs-Elysées and av. de la Grande-Armée. Inside the arch, climb 205 steps up a winding staircase to the *entresol* and then dig deep for the 29 more that take you to the *musée.* (Or tackle the lines at the elevator for a muscle-pull-free ride.) The museum recounts the Arc's architectural and ceremonial history in French, complete with drawings and appropriately tacky souvenirs. The real spectacle lies just 46 steps higher—the *terrasse* at the top of the Arc provides a terrific view of the gorgeous avenue Foch (see 16th *arrondissement)* and the sprawling city. (Observation deck open daily 10am-5:30pm. Admission 31F, students 18-25 and seniors 17F, ages 7-17 6F, under 7 free. Lockers underneath the Arc for 5F a day. Phones too. Expect lines even on weekdays and buy your ticket before going up to the ground level.)

The avenue des Champs-Elysées is the most famous of the twelve symmetrical avenues radiating from the huge rotary of **place Charles de Gaulle;** it may even be the most famous avenue in the world. In a popular children's song, French youth are taught that you can do all you want on the Champs-Elysées. While this may not be entirely true, no one can deny that this ten-lane wonder, flanked by exquisite cafés and luxury shops and crowned by the world's most famous arch, deserves its reputation. Le Nôtre planted trees here in 1667 to extend the Tuileries vista, completing the work begun under Marie des Médicis in 1616. In 1709, the area was renamed the "Elysian Fields" because of the shade provided by the trees; it was also a reminder of the area's recent past and some of its present as field and swamp. In 1814, during the occupation of Paris, the Cossacks camped out underneath the trees of the Champs-Elysées. It was only under the Second Empire, after considerable repair, that this became an irrigation canal of luxury. First, mansions sprang up along its banks, then apartments and smart boutiques, making this strip of pavement the place to see and be seen in Paris. Balls, café-concerts, restaurants, and even circuses drew enormous crowds. In 1885, according to Edmond du Goncourt, the prostitutes of the city marked Victor Hugo's death by practicing "wholesale copulation...with all and sundry" on the avenue's lawns.

Today, you'll probably see more foreigners than Parisian aristocrats. Tourists and French film stars share the turf at **Fouquet's,** an outrageously expensive café/restaurant near the Arc de Triomphe. Paris's answer to Hollywood's Sunset Strip, this stretch of the Champs-Elysées bears golden plaques with names of favorite French entertainers. Street performers move in at night all along the Champs-Elysées, like the metal cloth-clad meccano men, moving in slow motion to an oppressive industrial beat. During the day, anyone can enjoy the potpourri of restaurants and overpriced stores, planted next to airlines and commercial offices. Six big avenues radiate from the Rond Point des Champs-Elysées. Av. Montaigne runs southwest from the point and shelters the houses of *haute couture* of **Christian Dior, Chanel** (no. 42), **Valentino** (no. 17 and 19). **St-Laurent, Nina Ricci,** and **Pierre Cardin** (pl. François 1*er)* hold sway nearby. Join the models who prance with their photographer, director, and reflector panel holder on the *trottoir* (sidewalk). Next to **Cartier's** (no. 51), at 49, Pierre Charron, stands **Pershing Hall,** a 113-year-old, five-story piece of America. Given to the U.S. federal government in memory of World War I General John J. Pershing and managed (or not) by the American Legion, the highly valuable building has allegedly been alternatively used as a brothel, a brawling bar, a gambling house, and a black-market money exchange. Refurbished and under the direction of the Deptartment of Veteran Affairs since 1990, the place now provides office space for respectable businesses like Council Travel and CIEE.

Like two big toes at the foot of the Champs-Elysées, the **Grand Palais** and the **Petit Palais** face one another on av. Winston Churchill. Built for the 1900 World's Fair, both *palais* are prime examples of art nouveau architecture; the glass over steel and stone composition of the Grand Palais makes its top look like a giant greenhouse (see Museums for exhibition information). Built at the same time as the palaces, the first stone of **Pont Alexandre III** was placed by the tsar's son, Nicholas II. It made quite a stir as the first bridge to cross the Seine in a single span. Today, as any *bateau-mouche* tour will tell you, this is considered the most beautiful bridge across the Seine, providing a noble axis with the Invalides (see seventh *arrondissement).* The statues on pilasters facing the Right Bank represent Medieval France and Modern France; facing the Left Bank, they show Renaissance France and France of the Belle Epoque.

North of the palaces, **Eglise St-Philippe-du-Roule,** 154, rue du Faubourg-St-Honoré (Mo. St-Philippe-du-Roule) was completed in 1779. Architect Jean-François Chalgrin mixed elements of a Greek temple and Roman basilica on a site where a church had stood as early as 1217. (Open Mon.-Fri. 8am-7pm, Sat.-Sun. 8am-12:30pm and 4pm-7pm. Free organ concert every Tues. at 1pm. Brief history and welcome posted in English.) The guards pacing around the house at the corner of avenue de Marigny and rue Faubourg St-Honoré are protecting the **Palais de l'Elysée.** The palace was built in 1718 but was embellished to its pleasant glory as the residence of the Marquis de Marigny, brother of Madame de Pompadour. During the Restoration, July Monarchy, and Second Empire, the Elysée was used to house royal guests. Since 1870, it has served as state residence of the French president. Although entrance requires a personal invitation, the persistent visitor can catch a quick glimpse of the luscious gardens. Socialist or not, President Mitterrand lives in style. Or ought to—in recent years Mitterrand has gained criticism from the French people by living in his own residence instead of the grandiose state palace (Mo. Champs-Elysées-Clemenceau). The Union Jack flying overhead at no. 35, rue du Faubourg-St-Honoré marks the British embassy. Closer to the Elysée Palace, predictably, is an equally large building flying the Stars and Stripes.

The place de la Concorde (Mo. Concorde), Paris's largest and most infamous public square, forms the eastern terminus of the Champs-Elysées. Like many sights in Paris, this immense *place* was built from pride—constructed between 1757 and 1777 to provide a home for a monument to Louis XV. Fittingly, as punishment for this royal hubris, the vast area soon became the place de la Revolution, the site of the guillotine which severed 1,343 necks. The celebrated heads of Louis XVI, Marie Antoinette, Charlotte Corday (Marat's assassin), Lavoisier, Robespierre (the brutal merchant of death), and others rolled into baskets here and were held up to the cheering crowds who packed the pavement. After the Reign of Terror, the square was optimistically renamed place de la Concorde. The gargantuan, rose-granite **Obélisque de Louqsor** was one of those monarch-pleasing gifts offered by Mehemet Ali, Viceroy of Egypt, to Charles X in 1829. Getting the obelisk from the Egyptian desert to the center of Paris was no simple task; a canal to the Nile had to be dug, the monolith had to be transported by sea, and a special boat built to transport it up the Seine. (A model of the flat-bed boat designed to transport it can be seen in the Musée de la Marine—see Museums.) Finally erected in 1836, Paris's oldest monument dates back to the 13th century BC and recalls the deeds of Ramses II. In 1944, the *place* was the site of a tank battle as the French 2nd Armored Division closed in on the German headquarters nearby. Although the area's architectural grandeur is somewhat obscured by a flood of traffic as deadly as any guillotine, a marvelous fireworks display recalls its history each July 14. (Be careful—during a fireworks display here in 1770, hundreds of people were trampled to death.) For a more peaceful display of light, walk (or better yet, drive) through here at night (it's worth the taxi fare): place de la Concorde, with the obelisk and fountains illuminated and the delicate turn-of-the-century cast-iron lamps glowing, is one of the most romantic spots in the unbeatable romance of nocturnal Paris. On each side, the viewer sees a frozen ballet of light, beginning with the obelisk at the cetner, moving out to the fountains, and then following the lines of the boulevards on each side: across the Seine to the Assemblée Nationale; down the Champs-Elysées to the Arc de Triomphe; up rue Royale to the Madeleine, and, finally, east to the Tuileries where, in the summer, the huge Ferris wheel presents its own ring of light. Don't be surprised if you see a commercial being shot on location here—and why not? What better way to create demand for your favorite product?

Directly north of the *place,* like two sentries guarding the gate to the Madeleine, stand the **Hôtel Crillon** (on your left) and the **Hôtel de la Marine** (on your right). Architect Jacques-Ange Gabriel built the impressive colonnaded façades between 1757 and 1770. Chateaubriand lived in the Hôtel Crillon between 1805 and 1807. On February 16, 1778, the Franco-American treaties were signed here, making France the first European nation to recognize the independence of the United States. The Americans came back in 1919, making the hotel the headquarters of their delegation to the Peace Conference. Today, topped with a line of flags from countries all over the world, it is one of the most expensive and elegant hotels in Paris. If you're dressed for the occasion (i.e., well) step inside and have an espresso in the plush salon, to the accompaniment of soft chamber music. The coffee will run you 30F, but it's worth it for a chance to experience Parisian life at its highest form. The businesses along rue Royale boast their own proud history. **Christofle** has been producing works in gold and crystal since 1830. (Call 49 33 43 00 to make an appointment to see their otherwise inaccessible museum. Or save yourself the hassle and just gawk at the store.) World-renowned **Maxim's** restaurant, 3, rue Royale, won't even allow you a peep in through the windows of what was once Richelieu's home.

The Madeleine, formally called Eglise Ste-Marie-Madeleine, is the commanding building ahead at the end of rue Royale. Screened for the present behind a construction barrier painted to resemble the façade, the church is nevertheless impressive. This architectural orphan was begun in 1764 at the command of Louis XV and modeled after a Greek temple. Construction was halted during the Revolution, when the Cult of Reason proposed making the generically monumental building into a bank, a theater, or a courthouse. In 1806, at the height of his power, Napoleon consecrated the partially completed building as a Temple of Glory, another monument dedicated to the achievements of his Grande Armée. Completed in 1842, the structure stands alone in the medley of Parisian churches, distinguished by its four ceiling domes, which light the interior in lieu of windows, 52 exterior Corinthian columns, and the lack of even one cross. (Open 8am-6:15pm. Occasional organ and chamber concerts; look for posters). Marcel Proust spent most of his childhood at 9, bd. Malesherbes, which runs northwest from the pl. de la Madeleine. Stretching out just below the Madeleine, roughly parallel to the Champs-Elysées, is the **rue de Faubourg St-Honoré.** Head west from rue Royale to rue Boissy d'Anglas where you can stare at the lavish, sparkly, refined, colorfully outrageous and oh-so-French decorated windows of **Hermès** (no. 24). **Pierre Balmain, Yves St-Laurent,** and **Karl Lagerfeld** boutiques all cluster nearby.

Square Louis XVI, on rue Pasquier, below bd. Haussmann, includes the improbably large **Chapelle Expiatoire.** The park's many benches make it a popular spot for lunch. Even more intriguing is the Chapelle, which holds monuments of Marie Antoinette and Louis XVI. A cemetery, affiliated with the Madeleine, was opened on the site in 1722; during the Revolution victims of the guillotine, Louis and Marie among them, were dumped here. Although Louis XVIII had his brother's and sister-in-law's remains removed to Saint-Denis in 1815, Charlotte Corday (Marat's assassin) and Philippe-Egalité (Louis XVI's cousin, who voted for the king's death, only to be beheaded himself) are buried on either side of the staircase. Statues of the expiatory ex-king and queen, displaced crowns at their feet, stand inside the Chapelle. Their last letters are engraved in French on the statue bases. (Open April-Sept. 10am-6pm; Nov.-Jan. 10am-4pm; Oct. and Feb.-March 10am-5pm.)

A few blocks north squats the **Gare St-Lazare,** whose platforms and iron-vaulted canopy are not to be missed by train riders and fans of Monet. To the north of the station is the place de Dublin, the setting for Caillebotte's famous painting, *A Rainy Day in Paris,* which hangs in the Art Institute of Chicago. To the west of the station, up bd. Malesherbes from the Madeleine, **Eglise St-Augustin** (Mo. St-Augustin) witnesses the meeting of science and religion. Designed by Baltard, who also created the pavilions at Les Halles (see first *arrondissement)* the 1868 church was the first large building in Paris to use cast iron. Stone is ornamental rather than integral. The cross on top of the cupola stands 84m above the ground. (Open Mon.-Fri. 9:45am-6:45pm, Sat. 9am-noon and 2:30-7:30pm, Sun. 9am-1:30pm and 6-7:30pm. Some history in English.)

The Parc Monceau, a bizarre preserve guarded by gold-tipped, wrought iron gates, borders on the elegant bd. de Courcelles. Whereas the Jardin du Luxembourg emphasizes show over relaxation, the Parc Monceau serves as a bucolic setting for children to play and parents to unwind in the shade—all in a series of false ruins and strange grottoes built in the best of the Romantic tradition. The painter Carmontelle designed the park for the Duc d'Orléans; it was brought to its present form in 1862 by Baron Haussmann. The Rotonde de Monceau, at the north end of the park, is a remnant of the Farmers-General wall of the 1780s. Designed to enforce customs duties rather than to keep out invaders, the wall and its fortifications reflected their creator's tastes in ornament more than the latest advances in military engineering. An array of architectural follies—a pyramid, a covered bridge, a pagoda, and picturesque Roman ruins—make this one of Paris's most pleasant spots for a *déjeuner sur* bench. Here, as elsewhere in Paris parks, frolicking on the grass is forbidden. Unlike most Parisian parks, however, this rule is not always strictly enforced. (Open 7am-10pm; Nov.-March 7am-8pm. Gates begin closing 15min. earlier.) For more release from Paris's architectural uniformity, skip down the rue Rembrandt to the **place du Pérou,** where a big red Chinese pagoda holds the Galerie C.T. Loo.

In the days of pre-revolutionary Russia, many Russian aristocrats owned vacation houses in France. Nice and Paris still retain a sizable Russian community. Though not as magnificent as the multicolored version in Nice, Paris's onion-domed **Eglise Russe,** 12, rue Daru (tel. 42 27 57 34; Mo. Termes), built in 1860, is an attractive church that continues to serve the quarter's Russian residents. (Open 10am-7pm.)

Ninth Arrondissement: Opéra

The ninth *arrondissement* goes by the name *"Opéra;"* the Opéra Garnier and the boulevards nearby form this area's central core. The Opéra lies on the southernmost border of the ninth, and this area is definitely the most prosperous and the most visited by tourists. Along the boulevards de Capucines, des Italiens, and Montmartre, many pleasant restaurants serve mouth-watering delicacies and cater to the post-theater and post-cinema crowd. This area also contains quite a few major movie houses showing big American and European box office hits. Near the Opéra, many large banks and chic boutiques greet their affluent clientele. Perhaps the busiest site of the ninth, however, is the American Express office at 9, rue du Scribe, where hordes of tourists come each day to change their traveler's checks commission-free.

Most tourists, willy-nilly, begin their tour with Opéra Garnier—on their way to the American Express office. Emerging from the huge underground den of the Opéra metro station, feast your eyes on Charles Garnier's grandiose **Opéra** (tel. 42 66 50 22), built under Napoleon III in the showy eclecticism of the Second Empire. This is Haussmann's most extravagant creation: an outpouring of opulence and meaningless allegory, not actually opened until 1875, five years after the Empire's collapse. Towering high above the *grands boulevards* of the southern 9th, the Opéra Garnier epitomizes both the Second Empire's obsession with canonized ostentation and its rootlessness; a

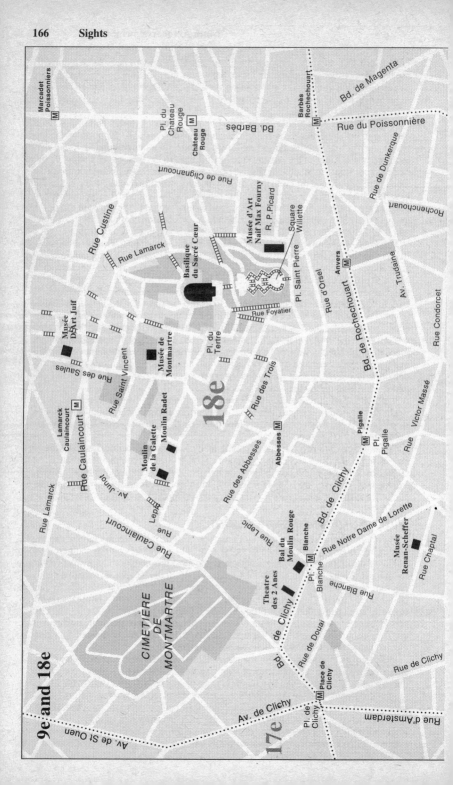

9e and 18e

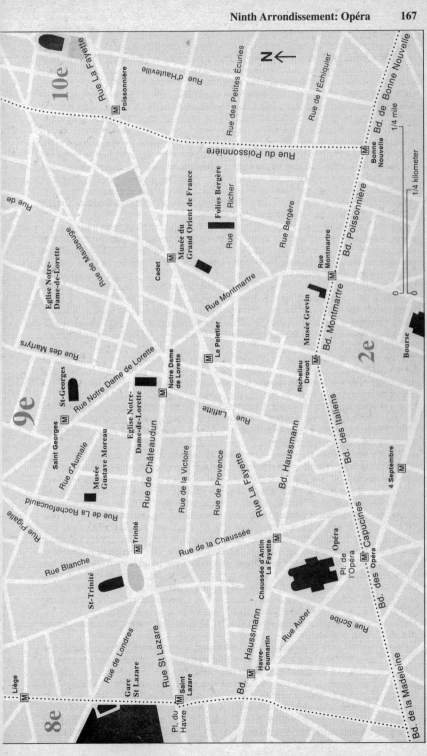

medley of styles and strange details tie it to no formal tradition or canon, other than the late 19th-century movement of modernism. Queried by the Empress Eugénie as to whether his building was in the style of Louis XIV, Louis XV, or Louis VXI, Garnier responded that his creation belonged to Napoleon III. The interior of the Opéra demonstrates the fabric of 19th-century bourgeois social life, with its grand staircase, enormous golden foyer, vestibule, and five-tiered auditorium—all designed so that the audience could watch each other as much as the action onstage. The entry hall, intentionally designed to be as huge as the stage, reverses roles to place the theater-goers on display as well. The grand staircase, which served as the model for the staircase at the Metropolitan Opera House in New York, provided the ideal vantage point to scope out the scene. As for the Phantom of the Opera, whom Gaston Leroux described so melodramatically in his 1910 thriller, decide for yourself. We suspect that the Phantom, frightened by the heightened cost of living in Paris, has emigrated; reliable sources report that he has been seen simultaneously in Boston, New York, and London, singing and dancing to the tunes of Andrew Lloyd Webber.

Garnier's elaborate design beat out hundreds of competing plans in an 1861 competition, outshining even the entry of the "Pope of Architects," Viollet-le-Duc. At that time, Garnier was a virtual unknown; the Opéra made him famous. The magnificent and eclectic interior is adorned by Gobelin tapestries, gilded mosaics, a 1964 Chagall ceiling (with a whimsical, Chagallian view of Paris and its major sights), and the sixton chandelier, which fell on the audience in 1896. Since 1989, when the new Opéra de la Bastille was inaugurated, most operas occur at the newer hall and Garnier's opera is used mainly for ballets, although a few operas and concerts still go up here. There is also a program of films on dance. Schedules for all performances and films are available in the entrance hall at the opera (for more information, please see Entertainment). Visits cost a hefty 28F, 15F for ages 10-16, and they include all public parts of the theater, except for the auditorium on performance days, and also the library and museum, which holds documents about costumes and objects tracing the history of opera and dance. Whether it's worth the money depends largely on your interest in theater or late 19th-century extravagance. To arrange for private tours, call 44 61 21 66 or 69. The Opéra is open for visits Mon.-Sat. 10am-4:30pm. Tickets for the ballet start at 30F; for the opera 50F; for the movies 60F. Rush tickets at reduced prices available at the box office 15 minutes before each performance. To reserve seats, call 7-14 days ahead at 47 42 53 71 between noon and 6pm.

Directly across from the Opéra is the **Café de la Paix,** a famous café from the 19th century, catering to the after-theater crowd and anyone else who doesn't mind paying 30F for an espresso (see Cafés). Behind the Opéra, at 9, rue du Scribe, hordes of tourists line up at the American Express office; it's probably not worth a special trip. All around this area, change bureaus advertise "No commission." Unless you're trying to change traveler's checks already in francs, they aren't lying, and the rates aren't bad. Of more historic interest, a bit farther down the bd. des Capucines, is the **Olympia** music hall, where Edith Piaf achieved her fame, along with Jacques Brel, Yves Montand, and many, many others. Popular artists still perform here; check posters for upcoming concerts. Following **bd. des Capucines,** you will arrive at **bd. des Italiens** and **bd. Montmartre.** Together, these three *grands boulevards* represent one of the busiest areas in the *quartier,* crowded with huge and popular restaurant/cafés (pricey but perfect for people watching), movie theaters and shops. Thomas Jefferson, in Paris in the 1780s as the American ambassador, lived near what is now the intersection of bd. Haussmann and rue du Helder. At no. 10, bd Montmartre, stands the carnivalesque **Musée Grevin** (see Museums).

West from this area along boulevard Haussmann, toward Mo. Chaussée d'Antin and Trinité, you'll find the largest clothes shopping area in Paris. Two of Paris's largest department stores, **Au Printemps** and **Galeries Lafayette,** are located on the bd. Haussmann, and the streets around here are littered with stores selling clothes and shoes (see Shopping). At the northern end of the rue de la Chaussée (Mo. Trinité), is the **Eglise de la Sainte-Trinité.** This church, built at the end of the 19th century in the style of the Italian Renaissance, has beautiful, painted vaults. It is surrounded by a very pleasant park with a fountain and tree-shaded benches. The quixotic **Musée Gustave Moreau** is also in this area, up the rue de La Rochefoucauld (see Museums). The museum is located in the painter's house and *atelier* (studio), on a quiet residential street.

A short walk west from here, on the place Kossuth, at Mo. Notre Dame de la Lorette, is the church **Notre-Dame-de-Lorette,** built in 1836 to "the glory of the Virgin Mary." This Neoclassical church is full of statues of the saints and frescoes of scenes from the life of Mary. Continuing up rue Notre-Dame-de-Lorette, one reaches the **place St-Georges,** one of the most pleasant parks in Paris, with benches, tall shade trees, and well-kept flower beds. This park attracts a vast number of mothers pushing babies in carriages, so if you're into the zero-to-three set, don't miss it.

North of the rue Châteaudun is a quiet, mostly residential area, with a large student population and many small, well-priced, ethnic restaurants. The streets are narrow and quiet, full of small shops, *tabacs,* little hotels and modest private residences. The **Musée Renan-Scheffer,** or Musée de la Vie Romantique, is up one of these charming narrow streets, the rue Chaptal, off the rue Fontaine (see Museums). The interior courtyard and garden of the house are representative of the layout of most of the residences on these streets. Farther north, at the border of the 18th *arrondissement* is the area called **Pigalle,** which Marcel Proust characterized as "almost another Paris in the heart of Paris itself." Pigalle is famous the world over, not only as home to the **Moulin Rouge** cabaret and many popular discotheques (see Entertainment), but also as the center of much of the city's prostitution. An array of "sex shops" advertises peep shows and the like to the manly. This area is quite fun, but tourists, especially women, should never walk around here alone at night and should be wary of pickpockets. Like humanity itself, which in the words of Dimitri Karamazov, spans from the insect to the divine, the ninth *arrondissement* spans from the most chic to the most sordid.

Tenth Arrondissement

"I live between two train stations, at the edge of a canal, in one of the *arrondissements* of Paris most rich in prisons, hideouts, pleasures, and hospitals. It is a rather vague *arrondissement*...much like one of those animal-molecules that can both expand and be cut in half. Half-worm, half-butterfly, one never knows which is the head and which the tail, and it is permanently caught at the mid-point of creation, straddling flight on the one side, abjectly crawling on the other." So wrote a resident of the tenth *arrondissement* in the 1920s, in terms still accurate today. Far from the normal tourist route, not the safest or most well-kept of areas, the tenth offers a few gems of its own to the adventurous soul. In the southern portion, along the Faubourg St-Denis, a curious and bustling market area offers an array of ethnic foods and spices. The rue de Paradis in the western section is home to some of the world's finest china and crystal. In the east, running north and south, the Canal St-Martin offers a pleasant place to walk and relax in the shade of trees, away from the noise and bustle of downtown Paris.

Outside of these interesting and pleasant walks, the tenth is a slightly rundown area which now houses a good portion of the city's minorities. There is some crime in areas around the place de la République; it is prudent not to walk the small sidestreets alone at night and single women should avoid this area entirely after dusk. In daylight, however, away from the bustling train stations, the tenth *arrondissement* is pleasantly free of loud, conspicuous tourists, and will give you a taste of another side of Parisian life.

The Gare du Nord (Mo. Gare du Nord) is generally encountered out of necessity rather than curiosity, but it is worth a look. Jacques-Ignace Hittorf created the enormous station in 1863, in the midst of the great re-building of Paris. The grandiose Neoclassical exterior is toppped by statues representing the great cities of France. Inside, the platforms are covered by a vast *parapluie* (umbrella), as Napoleon III called the glass and steel heaven which creates the giant vault of the train station. Across from the station a fringe of *brasseries* and cafés caters to the thousands of travelers who go through here very day.

Facing away from the Gare du Nord and walking one block down the rue de Compiègne takes you to the rue de Belzunce and the **Eglise St-Vincent de Paul,** a Neoclassical structure built in the first half of the 19th century by architects Hittorf and Jean-Baptiste Lepère. The entrance, in the shape of a temple with Ionic columns, is topped with a dramatic frieze sculpted by Leboeuf-Nanteuil. It stands on a flight of steps bordered by terraced gardens on both sides, offering a welcome rest and a pleasant view down the rue d'Hauteville. The church is open to the public Mon.-Sat. 7:30am-noon and 2-7pm; Sun. 7:30am-12:30pm and 3:30-7:30pm. There is a mass with Gregorian chant on Sundays at 9:30am.

Returning down rue Belzunce to the bd. de Magenta, you will arrive at the **Marché St-Quentin,** 85, bd. de Magenta. This market is a massive, elegant construction of iron and glass, built in 1866 with a glass ceiling as glorious, if smaller, as that of Gare du Nord. Inside you can find an enormous variety of goods, from flowers to fresh produce and skinned rabbits for your delectable *lapin à la moutarde d'Irène.* (Open Tues.-Sat. 8am-1pm and 3:30pm-7:30pm; Sun. 8am-1pm.) From the Marché St-Quentin cross bd. de Magenta and follow rue du 8 Mai 1945 until it arrives at the **Gare de l'Est.** More functional than beautiful, this train station is on a smaller scale than its neighbor *du Nord,* but conforms to the same Neoclassical style in which all six of Paris's train stations were originally built. Directly across from the train station, the place du 11 Nov. 1918 opens into the boulevard de Strasbourg, a hopping thoroughfare, as crowded with cafés, shops, fruit stands and people as St. Petersburg's Nevsky Prospect.

Close by, the small **rue de Paradis** offers a quaint and prosperous little area bordered by shops displaying fine china and crystal. The beautiful (and expensive) objects mark the road to the **Baccarat Co.** headquarters and the **Baccarat Museum,** housed in an 18th-century building at 30-32, rue Paradis (see Museums). Farther up the street, at 18, rue de Paradis, the art gallery **Le Monde de l'Art** displays a variety of exhibits, housed in what was once the headquarters of the Boulanger china company (see Museums).

Going south on the **rue du Faubourg St-Denis,** one walks through crowds of Parisians buying the components of their dinners in a very active market area. Individual stores, many owned by African, Arab, and Indian vendors, specialize in seafood, cheese, bread, or produce, rebuking supermarkets everywhere with the quality and selection they offer. At the end of the Faubourg St-Denis, the majestic **Porte Saint-Denis** (Mo. Strasbourg/St-Denis) welcomes the visitor into the inner city. Built in 1672 to celebrate the victories of Louis XIV in the Rhineland and Flanders, it is an imitation of the Arch of Titus in Rome. In the Middle Ages, this was the site of a gate in the city walls, but the present arch, characterized by André Bréton as *trés belle et trés inutile* (very beautiful and quite useless) served only as a ceremonial marker and a royal entrance on the old road to St-Denis. On July 28, 1830, it was the scene of intense fighting; revolutionaries scrambled to the top of the old Bourbon icon and rained cobblestones on the monarchist troops below. At its side, two blocks down the bd. St-Denis, the **Porte St-Martin** is a smaller copy, built in 1674 to celebrate yet another victory. On the façade, look for Louis XIV represented as Hercules (nude, except for the wig).

Going east from here along the bd. St-Martin, one arrives at the **place de la République** (Mo. République), at the meeting point of the tenth, the third and the eleventh *arrondissements.* This is a good place to avoid at night, when prostitutes and swindlers are ubiquitous. In the center a monument to the Republic of France celebrates the victories of the 23 years of intermittent republican rule between 1789 and the monument's erection in 1880. The statue of *La République* by Morice stands on a base by Dalou, with bronze reliefs representing various revolutions in French history.

A bit farther east lies the **Canal Saint-Martin,** 4.5km long and connecting the Canal de l'Ourcq to the Seine. The canal has several locks, which can be traveled by boat on one of the **canauxrama** trips (see Entertainment). You can also walk along the tree-lined banks, trying to avoid the many joggers. Again, it is probably a good idea to be careful in this area after dark. East of the canal, follow rue Bichat to the entrance of **hôpital Saint-Louis,** one of the oldest hospitals in Paris. Built by Henri IV as a sanctuary/prison for victims of the plague (the 17th century's version of a toxic waste dump), it was located across a marsh from the city, and downwind of both the smelly mess at Buttes-Chaumont (see 19th *arrondissement)* and a gallows (see below). Its distance from any source of fresh water confirms that it was intended more to protect the city from contamination than to help the unfortunates inside. The hospital is designed in two quadrilaterals: the inner one for victims, the outer one for functionaries, who communicated with the diseased through a tower in one of the pavilions. A cemetery inside

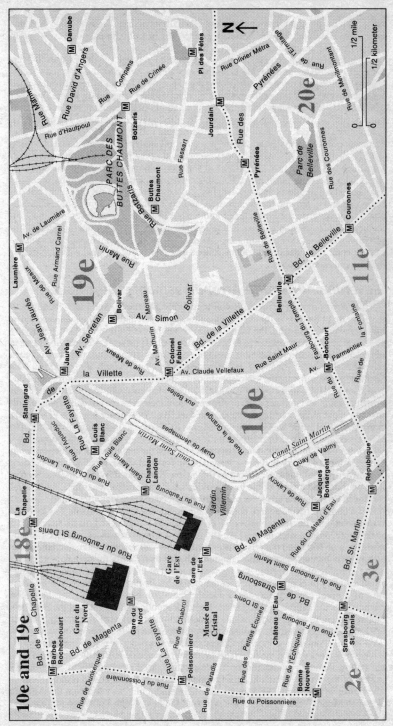

10e and 19e

the hospital walls made the complex entirely self-sufficient. Today, hôpital St-Louis specializes in dermatology, and offers a wonderfully peaceful Renaissance courtyard to those willing to brave any plague bacilli that might have survived the centuries.

Just north of hôpital St-Louis, in the area between the canal, rue des Ecluses St-Martin, rue Louis Blanc, and Rue de la Grange aux Belles, once stood the famous **Montfaucon Gallows**—famous for their hanging capacity of 60, an efficiency unrivalled until the invention of the guillotine several centuries later. The gallows were first constructed in the 13th century under the reign of Saint Louis; the first notable victim was a doctor of Phillip the Hardy, accused in 1276 of trying to poison the heir to the throne. In the early 14th century, the initial wooden structure was replaced by a two-story stone framework, designed by Pierre Rémy, treasurer to Charles IV. (Rémy had a chance to test his creation in 1328, when he was hanged with great pomp and circumstance.) A large ditch underneath provided a tomb of sorts for victims, together with the bodies of others who had been burnt alive, boiled, drawn and quartered, etc. Unless the space was needed for another hanging, dangling corpses were left to rot until they had decomposed and fallen into the ditch below—although sometimes, by way of "rehabilitation," they were *dependu* (unhung) and buried in nearby cemeteries. By the 17th century, the Montfaucon gallows had fallen into disuse, and today only memories linger. But in 1954, workers building the garage at 53, rue de la Grange aux Belles uncovered an eerie reminder of this area's former use: two of the original pillars, together with several human bones.

Eleventh and Twelfth Arrondissements: St-Antoine

As it courses eastward, rue de Rivoli transforms into rue St-Antoine, which runs to the **place de la Bastille** at the union of the third, eleventh, and twelfth *arrondissements*. Here squatted the Bastille, the famous fortress and prison built in the 14th century by Charles V at the eastern entrance to his new city walls. It served to defend this entrance and to imprison some of the most prestigious enemies of the state: religious heretics and political prisoners, many of them arrested on an arbitrary *lettre de cachet* and confined for years without trials. Notable inmates included Mirabeau, Votaire, and Fouquet, Louis XIV's unfortunate finance minister. Prisoners in the Bastille lived in perpetual damp and darkness, never allowed out of their cells for air, and supplied with only the most meager of food, water, and fuel. By 1789, under Louis XVI's gentle monarchy, the Bastille was largely unused, and its prisoners (including the imaginative Marquis de Sade) lived in relative comfort. But it remained a symbol of oppressive government and, more importantly, the warehouse of the largest stock of gunpowder in Paris. On July 14, angry Parisians cleaned out the arsenal of the Invalides and, needing gunpowder for the muskets, set out to the prison. Surrounded by a well-armed force, short on food, and unsure of the loyalty of his small garrison of Swiss merceneries and pensioned veterans, the governor of the prison agreed to surrender after a battle that left almost a hundred revolutionary corpses scattered outside the walls. As he was escorted to the Hôtel de Ville, the mob overpowered his captors and hacked off his head with a pocketknife, only to stick in on a pike and parade it around as a success symbol. Meanwhile the mob had freed the prisoners of the Bastille—all seven of them, including four forgers, two lunatics, and a noble committed by his own family for sexual depravity.

The storming of the Bastille was the first overt act of the French Revolution, and signified a victory of popular power over the monarchy. Its first anniversary was the occasion of a great celebration, and since the late 19th century, July 14th has been celebrated as the national holiday of the French Republic. Within a day of the Bastille's capture, ardent revolutionaries began the destruction of the hated edifice. By October 1792, they had completely demolished the prison. Some of its stones are now incorporated into the Pont de la Concorde. Others are stacked up in a memorial in the square H. Galli, a few blocks down the bd. Henri IV from the place de la Bastille. A certain Citizen Palloy, the main contractor for the destruction, used other stones to construct 83 models of the prison, which he sent to the provinces outside Paris to remind them of "the horror of despotism". For more Bastille memorabilia, travel across the Atlantic Ocean to Mount Vernon, where you will find the key, which Lafayette presented to

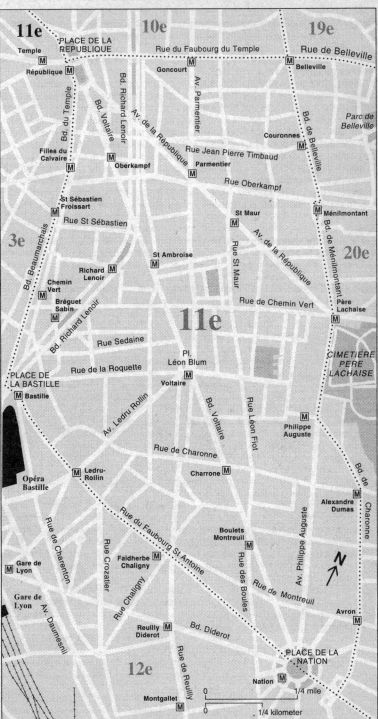

11e

10e

19e

Temple Ⓜ

PLACE DE LA RÉPUBLIQUE

Rue du Faubourg du Temple

Rue de Belleville

République Ⓜ

Goncourt Ⓜ

Belleville Ⓜ

Bd. du Temple

Bd. Richard Lenoir

Bd. Voltaire

Av. Parmentier

Av. de la République

Bd. de Belleville

Parc de Belleville

Filles du Calvaire Ⓜ

Oberkampf Ⓜ

Rue Jean Pierre Timbaud

Couronnes Ⓜ

Parmentier Ⓜ

Rue Oberkampf

St Sébastien Froissart Ⓜ

Rue St Sébastien

St Maur Ⓜ

Ménilmontant Ⓜ

Bd. Beaumarchais

3e

St Ambroise

Av. de la République

Bd. de Ménilmontant

20e

Richard Lenoir Ⓜ

Rue St Maur

Chemin Vert Ⓜ

Bréguet Sabin Ⓜ

Bd. Richard Lenoir

Rue de Chemin Vert

Père Lachaise Ⓜ

11e

Rue Sedaine

CIMETIÈRE PÈRE LACHAISE

Rue de la Roquette

Pl. Léon Blum

PLACE DE LA BASTILLE

Voltaire Ⓜ

Bastille Ⓜ

Av. Ledru Rollin

Bd. Voltaire

Rue Léon Flot

Philippe Auguste Ⓜ

Rue de Charonne

Opéra Bastille

Ledru-Rollin Ⓜ

Charrone Ⓜ

Alexandre Dumas Ⓜ

Bd. de Charonne

Rue du Faubourg St Antoine

Rue de Charenton

Boulets Montreuil Ⓜ

Av. Philippe Auguste

Gare de Lyon Ⓜ

Faidherbe Chaligny Ⓜ

Rue des Boules

Rue de Montreuil

Avron Ⓜ

Gare de Lyon

Rue Crozatier

Rue Chaligny

Av. Daumesnil

Reuilly Diderot Ⓜ

Bd. Diderot

PLACE DE LA NATION

12e

Rue de Reuilly

Nation Ⓜ

Montgallet Ⓜ

N

0   1/4 mile

0   1/4 kilometer

George Washington. Only the ground plan of the prison remains on its original site, marked by a line of stones. In 1831, King Louis-Phillipe laid the cornerstone for the **July column,** in the center of the *place,* as a memorial to the dead of the Revolution of 1789 and the Revolution of 1830, which had brought him to power. 504 martyrs of 1830 are buried in its vault.

President François Mitterrand, whose 1981 electoral victory was celebrated here with much ado, commissioned Canadian architect Carlos Ott to build a modern opera house on the *place.* Intended to be the largest in the world and to entertain over 960,000 spectators per year, this theater was conceived as a "People's Opera House." Inaugurated on July 14, 1989, and sitting in the square that symbolizes the spirit of republicanism, the **Opéra Bastille,** 120, rue de Lyon (Mo. Bastille) charges unusually low prices for performances of the highest caliber. Neighbors are outraged by this postmodernist's invasion of one of Paris's most hallowed square; others complain that the acoustics of the much-vaunted hall leave much to be desired. But the new is always greeted with suspicion. Tours (20F, students 10F), which take place every afternoon, are the only way to see the interior unless you attend a performance. (Tickets for tour sold 30min. in advance. Call 40 01 19 70 for information; stop in the box office for a free brochure describing the season's events. See Entertainment—Opera for more information.)

The flocks of students lounging on the steps in front of the oddly appealing metal and glass structure are tugging the youthful, artistic center of Paris away from the Latin Quarter and into this up-and-coming neighborhood; the Bastille has become, as had Montmartre, Montparnasse, and the Latin Quarter before it, the hip and happening quarter of Paris, the new bohemia, the new hang-out of the young, the eclectic, and the electric. Don't count on the *bcbg* glamor of the steadfast fifth or sixth; styles here change as quickly as new galleries open and close. Today's Beautiful People sport tattered miniskirts, bell-bottoms, platform shoes, and false eyelashes for both men and women. But tomorrow they might drape themselves in anything from monk's habits to Jean-Paul Gautier. The area has thankfully not entirely lost its former proletarian personality; some of Paris's more garrulous and crotchety old inhabitants create a strong and refreshing presence.

The area is east of the Bastille, on both sides of the *arrondissement* line, was, until its incorporation into Paris, the **faubourg St-Antoine.** Home of poor artisans in the 18th century, it was exempted by royal decree from certain duties and regulations. But the workers were not satisfied, and they became the *sans-culottes* (literally the "without-breeches"), the highly radical shock troops of the Revolution. Among these alleys, Madame Defarge of Dickens's *A Tale of Two Cities* quietly did her knitting. The faubourg rose up again in 1830 and 1848. More recently, on May 28, 1958, over 150,000 people marched to protest the expected takeover of the government by the armed forces. They followed what historian Jean Lacouture has called "the traditional left-wing route from the place de la Nation to the place de la République."

Beyond the pulsating activity of place de la Bastille and place de la République (see tenth *arrondissement),* the eleventh offers little in the way of sights. Drift back from the numerous *places* to smaller, less congested streets and remind yourself that real people, not rich, not chic, overworked like the rest of the world, do indeed live in Paris. There is a family presence in the eleventh that should be savored—kids romp all over neighborhood parks and parents shuffle to the local store to do their groceries.

To the southeast, the twelfth *arrondissement,* also made up mostly of businesses and quiet tree-lined boulevards, is pleasant but unexciting. The **Ministère des Finances** (Ministry of Finances) building on the quai de Bercy is the product of two of Mitterrand's *Grands Projets.* Having kicked his accountants out of what was perhaps the most prestigious office building in the world—the Louvre—he made it up to them by building this swanky new headquarters on the river. Topped with a big flat disk and stretching into the Seine itself, the ministry looks like a great place to dock the *Millenium Falcon.* Head east toward the Bois de Vincennes for an afternoon of zoo-going, greenery-watching, and trailblazing. On the way, **place de la Nation** (Mo. Nation), at the convergence of the nine streets and on the boundary between the eleventh and the twelfth, sports a classy statue of the *Triomphe de la République* (1899, by Dalou). This square was known formerly as place du Trône, in honor of the throne placed here in

1660 when Louis XIV returned to Paris with his new bride, Maria Teresa. During the Revolution, the throne was replaced by a guillotine that proudly chopped off over 1300 heads, and the square was renamed *"place du Trône-Renversé"* (Square of the Toppled Throne), a name which it held until July 14, 1880 when the place of the throne and the guillotine became the place of the nation. Just east of the *place,* twin tollhouses—part of Ledoux's 18th-century city walls—herald the Cours de Vincennes, the grand avenue toward the Château de Vincennes and the great park that surrounds it.

Thirteenth Arrondissement

A mostly residential *arrondissement,* the 13th maintains a small-town feel, despite its possession of many of Paris's taller apartment buildings and office towers (built before the imposition of the current height restrictions). Due to the presence of the Bièvre, an weak stream whose waters had been diverted into aqueducts and whose bed had been clogged with refuse and waste, this neighborhood was until the 1840s one of the worst-smelling areas in France. It can be neatly divided into three main neighborhoods, each with its own distinct group of residents and culture; the **Butte aux Cailles** district, in the heart of the 13th just south of the Corvisart metro stop, is the best preserved of the residential areas, and a stroll through this hilly neighborhood compares to a stroll through a small town in the provinces, with its deserted narrow streets and small cafés. **Chinatown,** located in the place d Italie area, running down avenue de Choisy and avenue d Ivry, is populated not only by thousands of Chinese, Vietnamese, and Cambodians, but hundreds of Asian restaurants and grocery stores. Like Chinatowns the world over, this one offers delicious Asian cuisines for about half the price of elsewhere in the city. Finally, the **Gobelins** tapestry factory, which transferred to the 13th *arrondissement* in the 17th century, brought with it hundreds of its artisan families and created an industrial district in the north of the *arrondissement,* centered around avenue Gobelins. All told, the 13th doesn t offer much for even the most dedicated tourist, except perhaps for a dinner-foray into Chinatown, or a fascinating tour of the still-functioning Gobelins factory (and, of course, the trains that depart non-stop from Gare d'Austerlitz to exotic destinations like Barcelona and Lisbon).

The Manufacture des Gobelins, 42, av. des Gobelins (tel. 43 37 12 60; Mo. Gobelins), is the workshop time forgot, where artisans, after being apprenticed by the factory for more than ten years, slave meticulously over complex tapestry weavings. Taken over by Louis XIV's finance minister, Colbert, in 1663, the Gobelins became a prison-like establishment, where whole families lived to produce tapestries the likes of which can now be found in the Cluny museum and in many of the châteaux near Paris. Still an adjunct of the state, the factory produces commission work for France's ministries and foreign embassies. Carefully chosen artists spend as much as one year weaving one square meter of colorful tapestry. Guided tours, the only way to get inside the factory, explain the intricate techniques that go into the weaving process. The two-hour tour is given in French only, but a free English-language handout translates the essential points of the tour and is in fact more complete than the tour itself in detailing the history of the Gobelins factory. (Wed.-Fri. 2pm. 25F.)

Farther south, the streets around the **place d'Italie** reveal the sad story of urban renewal. In the early 1960s, sociologist Henri Coing studied this area and found that despite the poor housing conditions, the residents of the neighborhood regarded this corner of Paris as their world, and could not conceive of living anywhere else. Decrepit apartments could be tolerated as long as the cafés were open; a journey across the city was like a trip abroad. But planners saw only slums without running water. The old buildings and their working-class tenants were swept away, replaced with sterile apartment buildings filled with the middle classes. It took immigrants from Asia and Africa to bring life back to the area.

Perhaps the largest attraction of the 13th *arrondissement* is yet to come—the huge **Bibliothèque de France,** which is currently in the planning stages. The project, designed to replace the Bibliothèque Nationale (see second *arrondissement)* and to create the largest library in Europe, is running into some very stiff opposition. The seven billion franc complex, located along the Seine facing the Ministry of Finances (see twelfth *arrondissement)* is supposed to consist of four L-shaped skyscrapers on the corners of a 7-hectare field. Critics claim this design will make the library very inefficient—imagine the difficulty facing a researcher who needs a book from the 15th story of tower A and another book from the 16th story of tower B, located all the way across a big field. Moreover, light streaming in through the large windows may damage precious books. Librarians' associations, as well as *ad hoc* committees of intellectuals (including such big names as Claude Lévi-Strauss) have written open letters to François Mitterrand to urge a radical redesign of the Bibliothèque de France. As of 1992, the government had only partly mollified its critics, by agreeing to build smaller skyscrapers and to put more books in the basement.

South of the library, at 12, rue Cantagrel, is Le Corbusier's **Cité de Refuge,** a Salvation Army shelter he designed in 1931. It is a fairly daring, Modernist structure—how did the staid Salvation Army choose so innovative and iconoclastic an architect? The fact that the chief donor of the project, the Princesse de Polignac, was a patron of the avant garde and a friend of Le Corbusier seems to have had something to do with it.

Fourteenth Arrondissement: Montparnasse

Like magnetic poles, most *arrondissements* attract only one type of person and utterly repel the rest; you d be hard pressed to find the *haute* bourgeoisie strolling the streets of Chinatown in the 13th, or recent African immigrants frequenting the cafés of the *bon chic, bon genre* 16th. Breaking this Parisian law of physics, the 14th draws immigrants from remote provinces in France, Europe, the United States, and even just the other side of the Seine. In the early 20th century, floods of Bretons, fleeing their failed crops, poured out of the Gare Montparnasse. They settled near the station that afforded them easy access back to their sunny shores on the Atlantic. Picasso, Gauguin, Whistler, and others set up *ateliers* here, and an equally august set of writers—such as Hemingway, Sartre, de Beauvoir—found themselves centered around the cafés of the bd. de Montparnasse, which later became the hotspot for literary pretenders and general hangers-on. Today, the 14th remains a conglomeration of different styles: business and tourism around Montparnasse, residential toward Mo. Denfert-Rochereau, and poor-student-dormitory in the Cité Universitaire.

Although the memory of Henry Miller picking fleas off himself and Mona in the Closerie des Lilas has receded along with Mitterrand's hairline, **boulevard Montparnasse** remains devoted to people-watching as well as to crêpes, the renowned Breton invention. Around this chic thouroughfare, the meeting place of the sixth, 14th, and 15th *arrondissements* has become one of the capital's most modern business centers, though dominated by the architecturally tragic **Tour Montparnasse** (see 15th *arrondissement).*

The Cimitière Montparnasse, 3, bd. Edgar Quinet (tel. 43 20 68 52; Mo. Edgar Quinet) is, let's say, less than romantic. Shrouded by the black pall of the Tour Montparnasse, crisscrossed by avenues, too crowded with tombs for grass, and occupied by chattering groundskeepers who appear to be doing their best not to disturb the final resting places of heaps of beer and mineral water bottles, Montparnasse cemetery is better left to the dead. Armed with a free *Index des Celebrités* (the detailed map available just left of the main entrance), determined sightseers thread their way through the unimportant to pay their respects to writers like Guy de Maupassant, Samuel Beckett, Julio Cortazar (whose slab sports a sculpted smiley face), Jean-Paul Sartre and Simone de Beauvoir (who share a grave), car manufacturer Andre Citroën, composer Camille Saint-Saens, editor Pierre Larousse (of dictionary fame), artist Man Ray, and loyal Frenchman Alfred Dreyfus.

Don't miss the tomb of Charles Baudelaire who, in his *Fleurs du Mal,* six years before he died, greeted Death willingly: "O Death, old captain, it is time! Lift the anchor! We wish, so much this fire consumes our brains, to plunge into the abyss, Heaven or Hell, what matters? To the very edge of knowledge in order to find something *new!"* Whether he found something new or not, it's anchors aweigh for him. Impressed by Baudelaire's eloquence? Plan for your own mortality at the tombstone shop across the street, or just pick up a marble remembrance for a friend. (Open Mon.-Fri. 7:30am-6pm, Sat. 8:30am-6pm, Sun. 9am-6pm; Nov. 6-March 15 closes ½-ho'r earlier. Free.)

Les Catacombs, 1, pl Denfert-Rochereau, (tel. 43 22 47 63; Mo. Denfert-Rochereau), crowds in five to six million lesser Parisians. These subterranean tunnels were originally excavated to provide stone for building the city. By the 1770s, much of the Left Bank was in danger of caving in, and digging stopped. The former quarry was then converted to a mass grave, to relieve the unbearable stench emanating from cemeteries around Paris. Near the entrance to the ossuary reads the ominous caution, Stop! Beyond Here Is the Empire of Death. Many have ignored the sign. In 1793, a poor Parisian got lost and was not found for nine years, at which point, he d become, so to speak, one with the pile of bones. In 1871, some of the last *communards* tried to hide in the passages, only to be hunted down and shot by torchlight. During World War II, this place was actually full of life—the resistance set up headquarters among these old and loyal Parisian bones. Bring a sweater, a flashlight, and a friend for support. (Open Tues.-Fri. 2-4pm, Sat.-Sun. 9-11am and 2-4pm. Admission 15F, students 10F.)

Parc Montsouris offers a sunny, sublime return to the land of the living. Begun in 1867 by the Baron Haussmann, this park remains one of his few pleasurable contributions to the populace of the city. Doubling as an arboretum, the park offers sanctuary to hundreds of rare and unusual trees, all well-labeled and cared for. An amazing variety of birds, ducks, and geese splash contentedly in the artificial lake at one end of the park. (The designer of this lake killed himself after the water mysteriously drained during the park's opening ceremony). Sunbathers, children, and bums are even allowed to stretch out on a 50m x 50m strip of grass along the street side of the lake; fantasize that you've escaped the city by closing your eyes and listening to the unbearable din of the assorted chirpings, quackings and honkings that rise from the lake. Don t experiment with petting the birds; first they hiss a warning, and then go right for the hiney. Across the boulevard Jourdan, hundreds of thousands of students rage the night away in the **Cité Universitaire,** a 40-hectare rompus park brimming with students from no less than 122 countries worldwide in no less than 44 different dormitories, two of them by Le Corbusier. The "vertical slab" called the **Pavilion Suisse** (1932) is adored by architects as a monument of his early career; its stark forms and blank surfaces anticipated his work at the United Nations headquarters in New York. With its *pilotis* (stilts) underneath and its garden on the roof, the building reflects the architect's dream of a vertical city, with life lived on several levels. During the German occupation, the roof garden housed a battery of anti-aircraft guns. Le Corbusier returned in 1959 with the **Maison du Brasil,** which reveals the influence of the time he spent in Rio di Janeiro. South and west of the dorms, the expansive greenery flaunts Parisian park customs, as hundreds of joggers, frisbee throwers, bikers, roller bladers and boom-box players run, sun, and fun themselves throughout the day, totally disregarding the signs to keep off the grass.

Hôpital St-Anne, 15, rue Cabanis, presents a more calming park experience. The psychiatric hospital first opened its doors to the nervous citizens of Paris in 1221, when this zone of Paris, now a bustling *quartier* renowned for nighttime male prostitution, was still a trip to the country. Lacking funds, the hospital languished, until the plagues of the 15th and 16th centuries, when people were just dying to get in. But it wasn t until Louis XIV took the throne that the hospital began to thrive with state funds, mostly earmarked for the imprisonment of "wanton girls and women." After a series of fires, the hospital went through several incarnations, including a dairy farm in the 18th century with a full complement of 140 cows, not to mention some 700 pigs, to be finally restored to its original life as a clinic by Napoleon III in 1863. Although access to most of the buildings is restricted to the medical staff and patients (neither of which you really want to visit), a tour of the grounds is a veritable medicine of its own. Secluded parks with weeping willows, statues, goldfish ponds and odiferous rose bushes will remind you of the Garden of Earthly Delights. (Open daily 7am-9pm.)

Fifteenth Arrondissement

Staid pensioners, yammering poodle clutched in one hand and the day's *baguette* in the other, pervade this southwestern arrondissement, more known for its population of

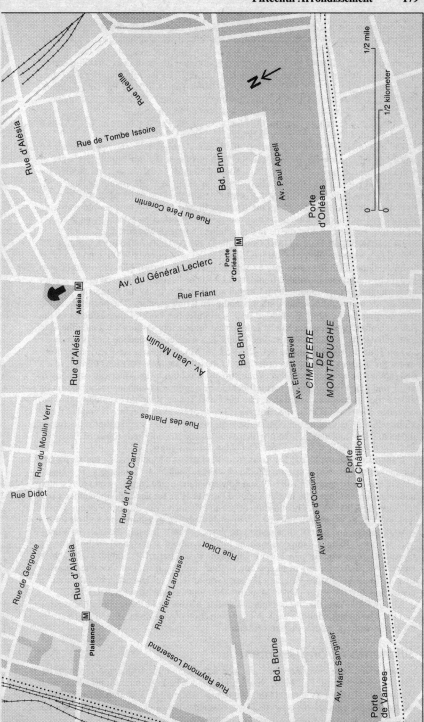

Rue Reille

Rue de Tombe Issoire

Rue d'Alésia

Rue du Père Corentin

Bd. Brune

Av. Paul Appell

Porte d'Orléans

1/2 mile

1/2 kilometer

Porte d'Orléans Ⓜ

Av. du Général Leclerc

Rue Friant

Ⓜ Alésia

Rue d'Alésia

Av. Jean Moulin

Bd. Brune

Av. Ernest Revel

CIMETIERE DE MONTROUGHE

Rue du Moulin Vert

Rue des Plantes

Rue de l'Abbé Carton

Rue Didot

Porte de Châtillon

Av. Maurice d'Ocagne

Rue de Gergovie

Rue d'Alésia

Rue Didot

Rue Pierre Larousse

Ⓜ Plaisance

Rue Raymond Losserand

Bd. Brune

Av. Marc Sangnier

Porte de Vanves

petit-bourgeois than for a hopping nightlife. Neither anachronistically antique nor oppressively modern, the architecture of the 15th mirrors its inhabitants; solid and staid, slightly uptight, and built about eighty years ago. Impressive sights are few, but the mostly residential district presents a view of quotidian life in the city; its little shops, restaurants and bars are frequented almost exclusively by the inhabitants, rather than by tourists disgorged by the busload near the Eiffel Tower. In 1973 Parisian planners, searching to renovate the 15th by transforming it into a new commercial and financial center, designed and built the much-disputed Tour de Montparnasse, a 210m monstrosity of steel and glass that disrupts the otherwise supine Parisian horizon, but acts as a center of little but the train station it houses.

The museums, the shopping districts, the famous concert halls and opera houses all belong to other *arrondissements,* but the 15th possesses the most important sight of them all, the true Paris, where people go about their daily lives, isolated from tourist invasions and busy traffic. Just breathing the air, drinking in a café among dedicated patrons, and watching children play in a nearby park is the kind of irreplaceable Parisian experience that you can't find on the Champs Elysées. For the best people-watching around, pop out of the Convention metro stop, where perfect cafés occupy each corner of the intersection between rue de la Convention and rue de Vaugirard.

La Ruche, 52, rue Dantzig (Mo. Convention), is a perfectly round brick building designed as a wine pavilion by Gustave Eiffel for the exposition of 1900, ten years after its more famous sibling came into existence. During the early 1900s the building was bought by the private charitable foundation La Ruche Seydoux, and used to house poor and struggling artists (among them Chagall and Soutine). Today the foundation still assists artists by providing grants, studios and even living quarters. The peaceful garden surrounding the building is studded with sculpture, the work of the residents of the house. Unfortunately, as La Ruche is a private foundation, visitors must call ahead to gain entry to the garden, though some people just wander in when the gate is open.

The Tour de Montparnasse (tel. 45 38 52 56; Mo. Montparnasse-Bienvenue) dominates the *quartier*'s northeast corner like a Godzilla that most Parisians think is just a bad movie, but won t end. The steel monstrosity was built by an American company in 1973, and indeed looks like it was left behind by a group of Manhattan skyscrapers on a field trip. Its builders hoped that, like the Eiffel Tower, it would eventually gain acceptance. That has yet to be the case; not all controversial architecture is good. An elevator whisks visitors to the observatory on the top floor (merely the 59th) for an indecent 34F, students 28F, from which you can see the only *real* tower of Paris, M. Eiffel's. (Open daily 9:30am-11pm, Oct.-March 10am-10pm.)

L'Institut Pasteur, 28 rue Dr. Roux (Mo. Pasteur), is a Montparnasse mecca for bovinophiles and infectious disease aficionados alike. Founded by Louis Pasteur, a champion of the germ theory, in 1887-89 and now an international conglomerate of research and treatment facilities, the Institute gained fame in 1983 for Dr. Luc Montagnier's isolation of the AIDS virus. The museum offers an exhaustive run-down of Pasteur's medical and artistic accomplishments, a tour of his laboratory equipment and preserved living quarters, and best of all, a visit to the crypt currently housing the scientist's maggotless corpse. Pasteur's son designed the highly symbolic fantasyland on the ceiling, a mosaic recalling Pasteur *père's* work with wine casks, butterflies, rabid dogs, rabbits, sheep, and of course, lots of happy cows. Tours in French with photocopied translations in English. (Should Pasteur's life spur you to some selfless act, a blood donation center is across the street.) Open Mon.-Fri. 2-5:30pm. Admission 12F, students 6F.

Also in the 15th is the surprisingly interesting **Musée de la Poste** (Postal Museum), and the **Musée Bourdelle,** a well-stocked collection of the works of the French sculptor Emile-Antoine Bourdelle (see Museums).

Sixteenth Arrondissement

Even if you have never been to Paris, you have been to the 16th *arrondissement* before. Londoners call it Pall Mall; New Yorkers call it Park Avenue; Montrealers call it Westmount. Every city has a 16th. The names, languages, and architectural styles change but the atmosphere generated by a concentration of old money is the same the world over. Magnificent buildings of the style found all over Paris stand majestically in the 16th: façades clean, balcony grilles intricate, and flower baskets bursting with color. An abundance of older ladies (for they are definitely ladies), wearing far too much or far too little make-up, pass serenely above the urban fray, devotedly exercising their compact dogs. To optimize your relations with the locals, try to resist the temptation to drop-kick the mutts.

The 16th *arrondissement* was created on January 1, 1860, when the three villages of Auteuil, Passy, and Chaillot banded together and joined Paris. History continues to loom large in this area, full of old aristocratic families who have held on to their heritage. Some of these families refuse to allow their children to sing *La Marseillaise* in the home because it was to this same tune that their ancestors were beheaded during the Revolution. Not surprisingly, this sumptuous neighborhood remains the nucleus of the city's conservative politics, fashion, and culture. Much social life here revolves around a uniquely French institution called a *rallye,* an exclusive group of children and young adults whose parents pay for the privilege of having their children *sortent* (go out) with other grand families of their class. Other less wealthy families crowd into small apartments to establish the residency that will allow them to send their children to the city's finest schools.

Lining the Right Bank from Avenue Grande-Armée in the north to Porte Saint-Cloud in the south, the opulent 16th spreads east from the immense Bois de Boulogne (annexed in 1929) to the nearly equally luxuriant eighth and the less plush 17th *arrondissements* north and east. Excellent museums abound and while it is money, even new, that talks in this *quartier* of grand avenues and huge mansions, it is always the culture of the BCBGs (*bon chic, bon genre*) that dominates.

Avenue Foch, one of Haussmann's finest creations, runs from the Arc de Triomphe (see eighth *arrondissement)* to the Bois de Boulogne. It was originally named for Napoleon III's consort, l'Impératrice, but was given the more neutral title, avenue du Bois de Boulogne, after her downfall. The current name, that of the universally admired victor of World War I, is hardly more controversial. Lined on either side by trees and parks, this is one of Paris's grandest boulevards, the 16th's widest, and reputedly the richest of them all. Not all mansions are created equal, however—those on the south side are even more prohibitively expensive because they receive better sun. To the north of Avenue Foch sits a quiet narrow-street residential area, where you can sit in the **Parc-Etoile Foch,** or easily happen upon one of the 64 embassies in the 16th.

Avenue Victor Hugo cuts southwest from the Arc and serves as one of the main places to shop, see and be seen in the 16th. You will know you've hit the (comparatively) rollicking **place Victor Hugo** when you see the line snaking out of the Haägen-Däzs store. Guarded by the dignified old **Eglise St-Honoré d'Eylau,** place Victor Hugo is the center from which most of this part of the *arrondissement's* roads radiate. At 24, rue Copernice, past the Lebanese Embassy, the **Union Libéral Israélite de France** synagogue remains a symbol of Jewish strength, in spite of the 1980 bombing that killed four people. **Rue Bugeaud,** leading out in the opposite direction from the *place,* runs through the impossibly beautiful **Pl. du Chancelier Adenauer.** South of Bugeaud, old and new meet comfortably as a perfect row of old classic Parisian buildings on one side of rue Spontini face their reflections in the glass FRADIM building across the street. Next to all—old and crumbling, old and classy, new and chic—squats the terribly posh Saint James Paris driving club.

Eglise St-Pierre de Chaillot, between av. Marceau and rue de Chaillot, while not intended for tourists, has a striking sculpture by Henri Bouchard over its front three arches and brilliantly lit stained glass. It is also a good place to find out about foreign language religious services around Paris. Just a few blocks from **place des Etats-Unis,** rue de Chaillot runs into **place Rochambeau**, another tiny monument seemingly designed to make Americans feel at home. Under a statue of Rochambeau, the general who commanded the French troops at Yorktown, and his permanent pigeon pals are engraved words of effusive praise from George Washington.

Across from the *place* stands the **Palais Galliera,** built for the Duchess of Galliera by Louis Ginain between 1878 and 1888, in Italian Renaissance style. Today it houses the **Musée de Mode et Costume** (see Museums). Wander around to the Palais's back garden off av. du Prés. Wilson and watch the kids happily frolicking under the gazes of *Painting, Architecture,* and *Sculpture*, allegorical figures framed by huge Romanesque arches. The **Palais de Tokyo,** home to the **Musée d'Art Moderne de la Ville de Paris** and numerous visual exhibitions (see Museums), was built for the International Exhibition in 1937 and was named after the quai de Tokyo that separated it from the Seine. The *quai's* politically incorrect name was a WWII casualty—it became the quai de New York—but the Palais has endured. George Washington reappears in the **place d'Iéna**, further along av. du Prés. Wilson, performing a difficult equestrian maneuver in front of the **Musée Guimet** (see Museums)

The **Palais de Chaillot** is the final product of a long string of attempts to build a palace on the heights of Chaillot. Cathérine des Médicis had a château here. Napoleon wanted to erect a residence for his son, but was interrupted by the bother called Waterloo. In the 1820s, the duc d'Angoulême built a fortress-like memorial to his victory at Trocadéro in Spain. In 1878, this was replaced by the Palais du Trocadéro, which in turn yielded to the present structure prior to the 1937 *exposition universelle* (world's fair). Architect Jacques Carlu's radical design features two curved wings with a gap where a central hall might be expected. Today the Palais houses the **Musées du Cinéma Henri-Langlois, de l'Homme, de Marine, et National des Monuments Français** (see Museums) as well as the **Théatre National de Chaillot** and the **Cinemathèque Française** (see Entertainment). The large terrace welcomes tourists, sun worshipers, souvenir vendors, and political demonstrators, and is watched over by the 1.5m-tall bronze Apollo by Henri Bouchard. It also provides the best view of the Eiffel Tower and the Champ de Mars, right across the Seine. Don't miss the inspiring inscriptions both on the buildings and the terrace.

The **Jardins du Trocadéro** bask beneath the palace, with cooling fountains (no bathing allowed) and much green grass. Toss a frisbee, flop on the grass, spin on the double carousel in the pl. de Varsovie (10F, kid or adult). Just don't get killed by the maniacal roller skaters who are jumping over barriers and slaloming on one foot around the fountains. Pre-teens and post-teens, they are good, albeit bandaged. Quench your thirst at the water fountain by the playground in the northeast section of the park.

One of the countless war monuments in Paris appears in the **place du Trocadéro** along one of the high walls of the **Cimetière de Passy.** Scheduled for erection in the 1930s, this tribute to the infantry was delayed by WWII and not built until 1954. The monument proudly proclaims "the glory of the French army," which by then had been a bit tarnished by Hitler's panzers. Buried in the Cimetière are Manet and Debussy, among others.

Passy (or **La Muette**), the region to the immediate south and southwest of the Trocadéro, has been known historically for its restorative waters, its châteaux, and its grand houses. The marks of its famous residents linger. You can visit the homes of a famed novelist and of a revered statesman by entering the **Maison de Balzac** and the **Musée Clemenceau** (see Museums). Jean-Jacques Rousseau lived on rue Raynouard and Benjamin Franklin, remembered today by street and statue, lived in this area for several years and built France's first lightning rod nearby.

Rue de Passy in modern-day Paris is another upscale shopping street—window-shop until it becomes Chausée de la Muette. Northwest of the La Muette Métro lies the former site of the Château de la Muette, where Louis XV went for his mistress-trysts. In 1783, Pilâtre de Rozier and the Marquis d'Arlandes became the first two humans to escape gravity as they lifted off from the château's lawn in a Montgolfier balloon, landing 20 minutes later in what is now the 13th *arrondissement*. (Though called a *montgolfier* in French after its inventors, the contraption got its English name from the nearby Bois de Boulogne.) Walk through the **Jardin de Ranelagh,** where kids (and the young at heart) will enjoy the old-style carousel. For 5F on a sunny afternoon, you can try to place the stick in the tantalizing brass ring. On the other side of the park, the **Musée Marmottan** offers an exquisite collection of impressionist paintings and medieval illuminations (see Museums).

The southernmost part of the 16th, **Auteuil** was once the meeting spot for poets and philosophers like Racine, Molière, and Boileau. Less oppressively ostentatious than its neighbors to the north, Auteuil has a charm linked in part to its *art nouveau* architecture. Who needs New York? A smaller replica of the **Statue of Liberty** can be found off Pont de Grenelle on Allée des Cygnes. Impossible to miss on av. du Prés. Kennedy is the circular **Maison de la Radio France,** the largest building in France and headquarters of the French national radio. Besides touring its Musée (see Museums), you can also attend one of Radio-France's concerts or appear in a studio audience, listening to a group of literati debate such classic French topics as *"Qu'est-ce que c'est qu'un intellectuel?"* ("What is an intellectual?") (Call 42 30 33 83 for details).

Rue La Fontaine is one of a number of streets to showcase the architectural *art nouveau* style of Hector Guimard. At 14, rue La Fontaine stands the famous **Castel Béranger** (1898) whose organically curving lines (called "noodle style" by one skeptical *hôtelier)* on balconies, staircases, and rooftops work to achieve the harmony of all of the building's elements. Guimard designed numerous buildings around Paris at the end of the 19th century and beginning of the 20th, as well as the green *Métropolitain* stations (Dauphine is a particularly good example of his work). Guimard lived for a while in the Castel Béranger, then moved to 122, av. Mozart, another of his creations. Several Le Corbusier structures lurk about in the architecturally rich 16th; the *mairie* may be able to provide a list.

L'Oeuvre des Orphelins Apprentis d'Auteuil (Society of Apprenticed Orphans), 40, rue La Fontaine, is a testament to the faith of two men. Abbé Roussel founded the institution on March 19, 1866, to provide a home and a future for local orphans. Despite financial obstacles, Roussel kept his organization going until his death in 1897. When the group seemed headed for disaster in 1923, Father Daniel Brottier (declared blessed by the Pope in 1984—the first step on the road to sainthood) became director and led the orphans into security. Today's orphans can perform apprenticeships in 30 occupations (the Auteuil "campus" does printing) and are an important part of the Auteuil community, as they are in communities all over France. Visit one of the churches or enjoy the gardens—carefully tended by the apprentice gardeners.

Seventeenth Arrondissement

The 17th suffers from the Dr. Jekyll and Mr. Hyde syndrome; its daytime personality near the Arc de Triomphe epitomizes bourgeois respectability, while its twisted nighttime personality, based around the place de Clichy, wades in a seemy underside of heroin, crime, and prostitution. Finding little but boredom on the one hand, or just a little too much adventure on the other, most visitors to Paris just avoid both sides of the 17th. The wealthier half of the *arrondissement,* extending west from the boulevard Malesherbes and south to the Arc de Triomphe, encompasses largely residential neighborhoods, as well as a number of overpriced hotels that cash in on their location near the place Charles de Gaulle. To the east, the place Clichy overflows with the *zonards:* junkies chased out of the place Pigalle by police intent on making the latter safe for busload tourists in for a little bare-breasted entertainment. While touring this *quartier* beware of the syringes that litter the doorsteps, and remember that dressing like a woman doesn t reveal anything about a person's actual gender.

Frankly, there isn t much to see in the 17th, apart from the unusual crowd of people that can be found around the place de Clichy towards the east end of the *arrondissement.* While barricades were erected, novels written, and mistresses wooed in the heart of the city, Les Batignolles was, until the mid-19th century, little more than farmers' fields. Though it has since been urbanized—many of the buildings were built using debris from Haussmann's demolitions in central Paris—it definitely does not merit a special excursion for the sole pupose of tourism. If you happen to be staying in a hotel in the area though, don t miss a visit to the **Musée Jean-Jacques Henner**, 43 av. de Villiers, a museum entirely dedicated to this late 19th-century painter (see Museums). Near the museum, at 1, place General Catroux, a building belonging to the **Banque de France** dominates a small garden with its huge mosaic brickwork; it's worth the detour. Built in 1884 as the residence of the bank's regent, the house features individualized gargoyle capitals leering out from the façade, divided neatly by serpentine iron drainpipes which slither down the sides of the building. The interior, open to the public but not for business transactions, contains a magnificent lobby with vaulted ceilings rising to impossible heights. Open Mon.-Fri. 8am-noon and 1:45-3:30pm.

Eighteenth Arrondissement: Montmartre

Soaring above Haussmann's flattened city, the heaven-kissing hill of Montmartre has a long and bloody history. A bishop named Dionysus, now known as St-Denis, came to this hill outside of Paris to introduce Christianity to the Gauls. The Romans, unappreciative of his efforts, swacked off his head in 272. Legend has it that he and two other martyred bishops picked up their noggins and carried them north to their final resting point, 7km away, where the Eglise St-Denis now stands. Thus the name *Montmartre* (Hill of the Martyrs), which this area has born ever since. In the 12th century, Louis VI brought a group of Benedictine nuns here to set up an Abbey—the origin of the area called "Abbesses" (around Mo. Abbesses). For the most part, Montmartre remained a farming area, covered with vineyards and wheat fields. The last of these vineyards, on the *butte* (knoll) behind the Musée du Vieux Montmartre (rue Cortot), is still operational. The wheat was processed in Montmartre's famous windmills, of which the Moulin de la Galette is one of the last remaining examples.

Montmartre gained particular attention during the siege of Paris of 1870 and the Commune of 1871. It was here, from the highest point in the city, that Minister of Interior Léon Gambetta ascended in a flimsy balloon, floating over the Prussian lines to the unoccupied provinces, where he mustered a new army in a desperate attempt to save Paris. After the capitulation of France, members of the National Guard dragged 170 cannon up the hill to keep them from the Prussians. The Republican government of Adolphe Thiers would not abide so strong a militia, and in the wee hours of March 18, 1871, Thiers's troops seized the guns. But they had forgotten to bring horses to pull the weapons down again. The radical Guards and citizens of Montmartre rallied, surrounded the troops, and killed the commanders, sparking a series of uprisings all over Paris. By the end of the day, the government had fled for Versailles, and ten days later the Paris Commune was proclaimed. On May 23, the Commune came to a bloody end; many captured *communards,* including women and children, were shot without trial by the victorious Republicans and buried in mass graves in the Montmartre Cemetery.

After the Commune, Montmartre recovered quickly. Untouched by Haussmann's demolitions, its narrow streets and sharp corners attracted such notable Bohemians as Gustave Charpentier, Toulouse-Lautrec, and Eric Satie, and performers like "La Goulue" and Aristide Bruant. Toulouse-Lautrec, in particular, immortalized Montmartre through his paintings of life in cabaret-concerts like the Moulin Rouge and the Lapin Agile. A generation later, in its last moment of glory before the devastation of World War I, Montmartre welcomed Picasso, Modigliani, Utrillo, and Apollinaire into its artistic circle.

Montmartre's heyday has since passed. Most of the places which were once so alive with art and conversation are merely shells for tourists to gape at and photograph. But there is still something magical about the *butte.* Perhaps it is the images from such classic films as *Le Balon Rouge* or *Les 400 Coups* of the stairways up its hillside and the benevolent façades of its half-crumbling houses. Maybe it is the dramatic views of the rooftops of Paris at one's feet. Perhaps it is the musicians and peddlers who gather in front of Sacré-Coeur at night, or the artists who sell their sketches of the *butte's* cobble-streets and narrow corners. Even with its hordes of tourists, this place can not fail to charm. Together with Montagne Ste-Geneviève (see fifth *arrondissement),* this is the only hill of Paris left intact by Haussmann's great uniforming plan. Come at dusk to watch the lights of Paris turn on below, and the famous gas lamps trace the line of the steps up the hillside.

One does not merely visit Montmartre; one ascends it. Enter this *quartier* at metro stops Barbes-Rochechouart, Anvers, Pigalle, Blanche, or Clichy, all along the southern boundary of the *arrondissement.* At nightime, it is best to use Mo. Abbesses instead; what's more, you'll enjoy the wildly colorful frescoes that decorate one of its staircases. You can take the direct route from Anvers up rue Steinkerque through sweaty, noisy crowds of tourists, and slimy "sex-shop" owners inviting one in for a voyeuristic orgy.

Or avoid these less desirable aspects of Montmartre altogether by taking less direct, more roundabout routes such as the rue Caulaincourt and the rue Lepic. Both are quiet, scenic streets, lined with trees, restaurants, bookstores, and antique stores, and both offer dramatic views of the city below and the Basilique du Sacré-Coeur above.

For the classic approach to Sacré-Coeur, climb up the switchbacked stairs leading up from the **Square Willette.** At night, crowds of students and tourists mingle in the square to play guitar music and sing and smoke and drink wine. The **Musée d'Art Naïf Max Fourny,** to the east of the square, is housed in a marketplace, an excellent example of late 19th-century iron and glass architecture (see Museums). A funicular offers a ride up for one metro ticket (5F50), but it may not be worth the wait or the price—the (free) climb up is not particularly taxing, and offers a splendid view of the receding metropolis below. The famous narrow cobblestone stairs of the rue Foyatier, just to the west (to your left as you look uphill), offer a more romantic climb, as well as an escape from the crowds and street peddlars on the white marble steps of the central park. To the east, a large park has winding paths that follow the slope of the hill, showcasing unexpected glimpses of strange grottoes and nesting couples, on your way up or down.

The Basilique du Sacré-Coeur (Basilica of the Sacred Heart), 35, rue du Cheval de la Barre (tel. 42 51 17 02; Mo. Anvers, Abbesses, or Château-Rouge), crowns the very top of the *butte* Montmartre like an enormous, puffy, white meringue. In 1873, the National Assembly selected the birthplace of the Commune to build Sacré-Coeur "in witness of repentence and as a symbol of hope." Politician Eugène Spuller called it "a monument to civil war." The basilica was not completed until 1914, after a massive fundraiser. It was consecrated in 1919, at the end of World War I. The style is pseudo Romanesque-Byzantine (mostly just strange), a hybrid of onion domes and arches. After taking in the majestic, white exterior, you may be disappointed by the gaudy mosaics and stained-glass windows inside. Much of the stained glass was blown out by bombers in World War II and replaced afterward. Climb the 112m bell tower for the highest point in Paris (yes, you *can* go higher than the Eiffel Tower) and a view that stretches as far as 50km on clear days. The crypt is open (for a price) and contains displays on the Basilica's history. (Basilica open daily 7am-11pm. Free. Dome and crypt open daily 9am-7pm; in winter 9am-6pm. Admission to dome 15F, 8F reduced; to crypt 10F, 6F reduced.)

The Eglise St-Pierre, one of the oldest churches in Paris, nuzzles up to this 20th-century monster. Built in 1134, St-Pierre is the last remaining mark of the old Abbey of Montmartre, which was demolished during the Revolution. Behind the church is the **place du Tertre,** the central square of the *butte.* Crowded with overpriced restaurants and souvenir shops, this area caters to the unwieldy masses of tourists that congregate here. A conglomeration of portrait and landscape painters offer so-so souvenir sunset Seine-scenes, often more of service to the artist's Pocket than to any higher Art. At 21, place du Tertre, the **tourist office** (tel. 42 62 21 21) gives free annotated maps and information about the area (Open daily 10am-10pm; Oct.-March daily 10am-7pm.) Nearby, the **Musée Montmartre, Musée du Vieux Montmartre,** and **Musée Salvador Dalí** highlight a variety of artistic and historical displays (see Museums).

Moving away form the crowded place du Tertre (which has its own noisy charm) you'll find narrow, winding streets, hidden walled gardens, sharp corners, and whimsical clues to the way life used to be when Montmartre was a center of Bohemian life and artistic extravagance. The area west of the *place,* including the rue des Abbesses, rue des Trois Frères, and rue Lepic, is littered with pleasant restaurants, antique stores, and *boulangeries.* Cobblestone roads twist around, moving down the hill; many of the 18th-century residences hide charming gardens behind their iron gates. Above the rue Lepic stands the **Moulin de la Galette,** one of the last remaining windmills from the days when Montmartre was covered with fields. Farther west, the **Cimitière Montmartre** makes for a nice stroll—don't miss the last resting place of such monumental figures as Emile Zola, Edgar Degas, Hector Berlioz, and Vaslav Nijinsky. In 1871, this cemetery was the site of huge mass graves from the Siege and Commune. Leaving this melancholy memory behind, follow the rue Caulaincourt, which circles around the base of Montmartre.

Along the boulevard de la Rochechouart, you'll find many of the cabarets and night-clubs that were the definitive hangouts of the Belle Epoque: the **Moulin Rouge,** for example, immortalized by the paintings of Toulouse-Lautrec and the music of Offenbach. (It wasn't all *can-cans;* one of the most popular entertainers of the turn-of-the-century Moulin Rouge made his living from controlled farting.) After World War I, the literati crowd mostly returned to the Left Bank, leaving behind what turned into a seedy red-light district centered around **place de Pigalle** (see ninth *arrondissement).* The Moulin Rouge, at place Blanche, still offers its risqué *revues,* but at a ridiculously high price. During the Belle Epoque, Paris's (otherwise respectable) upper bourgeoisie came here to play at being Bohemian; nowadays, the crowd is made up mostly of (otherwise respectable) tourists, out for a taste of Paris's flashiest experience (see Entertainment—Cabarets). Pigalle also has some discothèques, trendy nightspots for Parisian and foreign youth (see Entertainment—Discos). Other than that, it is the home of a large portion of Paris' seedy "sex-shop" industry, where one can see just about any sexual art either on screen or live. Women should never walk around this area alone at night. Farther down bd. de Clichy, at the edge of the 17th, the place de Clichy is filled with popular restaurants and cinemas, but also functions as a haven for drugs and crime.

Nineteenth Arrondissement

Apart from La Villette (see Museums), the 19th *arrondissement* has little to offer the ordinary pleasure-seeking tourist. Not part of Paris until the 19th century, it served as a home for the workers displaced by Haussmann's renovations of the city center. Instead of historical monuments, it flaunts a fair number of unaesthetic tower blocks. These HLMs *("habitations à loyer modéré,"* or "housing with moderate rent") provide subsidized, low-cost housing to a blue-collar crowd that includes many immigrants from France's former colonies.

The Parc des Buttes-Chaumont (Mo. Buttes-Chaumont) occupies the southern portion of the 19th. Now a fascinating melange of artificial scenery and transplanted vegetation, it once stank like an angered muishond. From the 13th century until the Revolution it was home to a gibbet, an iron cage in which the rotting, maggoty corpses of criminals were displayed on high in an effort to deter further crime. After the Revolution it was used as a garbage dump, then as a dumping-ground for dead horses. (In those days, the park was still outside of town, so the smells did not pose a problem except when the wind was in the wrong direction....) After a stint as a commercial breeding-ground for worms (sold to fishers as bait), it became a gypsum quarry, the source of "plaster of Paris." Then Napoleon III ascended to the throne. As a young man, he had been exiled in England, where he had been impressed by the grace of London's large public parks. As emperor, he decided to imitate them, creating four large public parks: the Bois de Boulogne, the Bois de Vincennes, the Parc Montsouris, and the Parc des Buttes-Chaumont.

Making a park out of this mess took four years and 1,000 workers. In order for trees to grow, all of the soil had to be replaced. Furthermore, designer Adolphe Alphand ordered the heavily quarried remains of a hill be built up with new rock to create fake cliffs surrounded by a lake. Workers made a fake waterfall, followed by a fake cave with fake stalactites. A pioneering suspension bridge leads to a fake Roman temple (a copy of a Sibyline temple in Tivoli) on top of the mountain. From this little temple, you have a view of the whole park and of the ugly skyscrapers that surround it. If all this sounds rather silly, remember that the urban proletariat in the 1860s had very little access to travel or greenery; the park provided the next best thing to seeing a real waterfall or Roman temple. And despite the kitsch, this low-tech Disneyworld makes for pleasant strolls and people-watching. The park is well-policed at night. (Open 7am-11pm; Oct.-April 7am-9pm.)

Twentieth Arrondissement: Belleville and Ménilmontant

As Haussmann's rebuilding expelled many of Paris's workers from the central city, thousands migrated east to Belleville (the northern part of the *arrondissement)* and Ménilmontant (the southern). By the late Second Empire, the 20th was known as a "Red" *arrondissement,* solidly proletarian and radical. In January 1871, just before the lifting of the siege, members of Belleville's National Guard stormed a prison to demand the release of some leftist political leaders—an omen of the civil war to come. Some of the heaviest fighting during the suppression of the Commune took place in these streets, as the *communards* made desperate last stands on their home turf. Caught between the *Versaillais* troops to the west and the Prussian lines outside the city walls, the Commune fortified the Parc des Buttes-Chaumont and Père-Lachaise cemetery, but soon ran out of ammunition. On May 28, 1871, the *communards* abandoned their last barricade on the rue Ramponeau and surrendered.

After the Commune, the 20th continued on as the fairly isolated home of those workers who survived the massacres. As historian Eugen Weber has written, "Many a workman's child grew to adolescence before World War I without getting out of Ménilmontant or Belleville." Today, locals freely admit that the only thing to see in the area is Père-Lachaise. The neighborhood is fairly safe, but avoid the area around the Belleville metro stop at night.

The Cimetière Père-Lachaise, bd. de Ménilmontant (tel. 43 70 70 33; Mo. Père-Lachaise), encloses the decaying remains of Balzac, Colette, Corot, Danton, David, Delacroix, la Fontaine, Haussmann, Molière, and Proust within its winding paths and elaborate sarcophagi. Nor is this, the most illustrious of Parisian cemeteries (named after Louis XIV's confessor), restricted to the French; foreigners inhumed here include Chopin, Jim Morrison, Gertrude Stein, and Oscar Wilde. Although so many famous people are buried in Père-Lachaise, it was never meant to be an all-star resting place like Westminster Abbey. Indeed, the land for Père Lachaise was bought in 1803 by Napoleon's government to create a "modern and hygienic necropolis" that would relieve the overcrowding of city cemeteries. This new concern with hygiene arose from the unpleasant experiences of the Revolution, when thousands of victims were stacked above ground in churchyards for lack of space—a public health hazard that created horrible smells and minor epidemics.

At first, Parisians were reluctant to bury their dead in a site which, at the time, was quite far from the city. To increase the cemetery's popularity, the ever-resourceful Napoleon ordered that the remains of a few famous figures be dug up and reburied in Père-Lachaise. Thus arrived the remains of Molière, Héloise and Abelard, La Fontaine, and several other pre-19th century figures. Since then, over one million people have been buried here. Yet there are only 100,000 tombs. The discrepancy is due to primarily because poor people used to be buried in unmarked mass graves and that old graves are usually dug up after a while to make room for new generations of the dead. This process of digging up graves, although it sounds grisly, is necessary in a densely populated city like Paris. The 44 hectares of Père Lachaise are filled to bursting point, so the government makes room by digging up any grave which has not been visited in a certain number of years. (In other words, if this likely event seems unattractive to the soon-to-be-dead, it's best to hire an official "mourner," much as wealthy patrons used to hire church choirs to sing their masses every year after their death.)

How did Jim Morrison and Oscar Wilde end up here? Simply by dying in Paris. Anybody who was born in Paris or who died in Paris has the right to burial in a Parisian cemetery. Because of overcrowding, however, city policy now requires a family to pay a hefty fee for a departed member to be inhumed in a popular cemetery like Père Lachaise. Cheaper, less desirable cemeteries are found farther away from the city center. Still, if you're looking for a unique gift for that special someone, a gravesite near a path is only 38,395F, one away from a path only 23,595F. If these prices are beyond your reach, but you still want your remains to be near those of Jim Morrison, your family can rent shelf space for your cremated ashes in the Columbarium: 50 years 9000F, 30 years 6000F, 10 years 2000F. What happens after your time runs out? Heck, by then you really won't care.

As thousands of tourists discover every year, Père Lachaise (with its huge variety of tombs, from the pompous and ornate to the charming and fanciful) makes for a pleasant, strangely surreal stroll. The cemetery is beautifully landscaped with winding paths and abundant trees. As for the graves, they are crowded with ornate funerary monu-

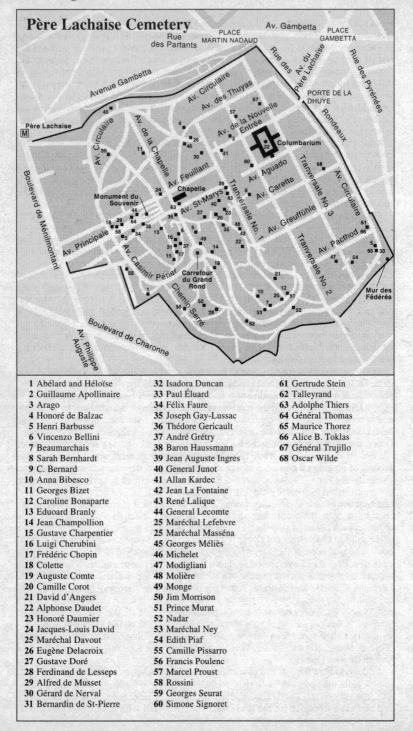

Père Lachaise Cemetery

1 Abélard and Héloïse
2 Guillaume Apollinaire
3 Arago
4 Honoré de Balzac
5 Henri Barbusse
6 Vincenzo Bellini
7 Beaumarchais
8 Sarah Bernhardt
9 C. Bernard
10 Anna Bibesco
11 Georges Bizet
12 Caroline Bonaparte
13 Eduoard Branly
14 Jean Champollion
15 Gustave Charpentier
16 Luigi Cherubini
17 Frédéric Chopin
18 Colette
19 Auguste Comte
20 Camille Corot
21 David d'Angers
22 Alphonse Daudet
23 Honoré Daumier
24 Jacques-Louis David
25 Maréchal Davout
26 Eugène Delacroix
27 Gustave Doré
28 Ferdinand de Lesseps
29 Alfred de Musset
30 Gérard de Nerval
31 Bernardin de St-Pierre

32 Isadora Duncan
33 Paul Éluard
34 Félix Faure
35 Joseph Gay-Lussac
36 Thédore Gericault
37 André Grétry
38 Baron Haussmann
39 Jean Auguste Ingres
40 General Junot
41 Allan Kardec
42 Jean La Fontaine
43 René Lalique
44 General Lecomte
25 Maréchal Lefebvre
25 Maréchal Masséna
45 Georges Méliès
46 Michelet
47 Modigliani
48 Molière
49 Monge
50 Jim Morrison
51 Prince Murat
52 Nadar
53 Maréchal Ney
54 Edith Piaf
55 Camille Pissarro
56 Francis Poulenc
57 Marcel Proust
58 Rossini
59 Georges Seurat
60 Simone Signoret

61 Gertrude Stein
62 Talleyrand
63 Adolphe Thiers
64 Général Thomas
65 Maurice Thorez
66 Alice B. Toklas
67 Général Trujillo
68 Oscar Wilde

ments vying with each other for attention. Among the most beautiful is that of Chopin, with a marble statue of a young girl, bedecked with fresh flowers; among the most interesting is that of Oscar Wilde, a whimsical gravity-defying bronze creation. Others seem abandoned and broken down, reminding you that the majority of the dead are soon forgotten. The most adored grave has to be that of **Jim Morrison** (lead singer of The Doors). Within a radius of at least 100m of the Lizard King, you might as well ignore your map: graffiti on all the tombs points in his direction. In summer, there are always dozens of young people hanging out at this cult tomb. Many of them bring offerings of flowers, joints, beer, poetry, or general Doors stuff to leave on Jim's grave. A few smoke joints quite openly. You're allowed to take photographs, but there's a rule against filming Morrison's grave.

Père-Lachaise's other big pilgrimage site is the **Mur des Fédérés (Wall of the Federals).** Nobody actually hangs out at this small wall (which you will find on the upper right hand corner of the map), but most French people have heard of it and will at least have a look. On May 24th, 1871, as the Republican forces were gaining back more and more of the city, a group of frustrated *communards* murdered the Archbishop of Paris, who had been taken hostage at the beginning of the Commune. They dragged his mutilated corpse to their stronghold of Père Lachaise, where they tossed it in a ditch. Four days later, on Whitsunday, the victorious *Versaillais* found the body. In retaliation, they lined up 147 *Fédéres* (an old term the *communards* had borrowed from 1789) against the eastern wall of the cemetery, shot them, and buried them on the spot. Ironically, Adolphe Thiers shares the same cemetery with them; he died of natural causes in 1877. Since 1871, the Mur des Fédérés has been a holy shrine and rallying point for the French Left, which recalls the anniversary of the massacre every Pentecost. Near the wall, a number of monuments containing human remains from concentration camps commemorate the victims of the Nazis. (Père Lachaise is open Mon.-Fri. 8am-6pm, Sat. 8:30am-6pm, Sun. 9am-6pm; Oct.-March Mon.-Fri. 8am-5:30pm, Sat. 8:30am-5:30pm, Sun. 9am-5:30pm.)

Bois de Boulogne

> *That sense of the complexity of the Bois de Boulogne which makes it an artificial place and, in the zoological or mythological sense of the word, a Garden...*
>
> —Marcel Proust

Spreading its leafy umbrella over 846 hectares at the western edge of Paris, the Bois de Boulogne (Mo. Porte Maillot, Sablons, Pont de Neuilly, Porte Dauphine, or Porte d'Auteuil) is a popular place for walks, jogs, and picnics. Formerly a royal hunting-ground, the Bois was given to the city of Paris by Napoleon III in 1852. The Emperor had become a dilettante landscape-architect during his exile in England and wanted Paris to have something comparable to Hyde Park. Baron Haussmann did a fair job of imitating the famous London park, filling in sand-pits and giving the Bois large artificial lakes and long, winding paths through thickly wooded areas. "He has often imitated nature very well," noted one contemporary. "It is almost a good likeness." This attempt to "copy nature" marked a radical break with the tradition of French formal gardens established by Le Nôtre (rectilinear paths framed by strictly disciplined lines of shrubs and flower-beds). The carefully landscaped "wilderness" is, of course, utterly artificial, yet it expressed a new urge to escape from Paris into a world of nature "outside the city"—the same urge captured by the Impressionists in their revolutionary school of *plein air* painting.

When Auteuil was annexed to the city in 1860, the park, though outside the city walls, became part of the 16th *arrondissement*. In 1871, it was the site of yet another massacre of *communards,* as General Gallifet performed a Mengele-like selection on the column of prisoners bound for Versailles. The hundreds he pointed out—men with gray hair, men with watches, men with "intelligent faces"—were shot that night. But bloodstains can be washed away, and during the Belle Epoque the park regained its status as a fashionable locale for carriage rides and horse-racing (and for the opening scene of Vincent Minelli's *Gigi*). The running of the Grand Prix at Longchamp in June was one of the premier events of the social calendar, comparable to the Ascot. The park became *the* place to see and be seen, and no family was fashionable unless they went to the Bois de Boulogne for their "Sunday afternoon in the country."

Although the park continues to fill its original purpose as a place for afternoon strolls, successive governments have added to its list of diversions. The Bois now has a number of stadiums, the most famous of which are Longchamp and Auteuil (horse-racing), Parc des Princes (mostly soccer), and the home of the French Open tennis tournament, Stade Roland Garros (see Sports). In addition, the Bois contains several separate parks, and boathouses that rent rowboats, allowing you to imitate your favorite Impressionist painting and go "punting" in the picturesque lakes. For a more exciting, albeit vicarious, ride, try renting the remote-control boats that zoom across the lakes in all varieties—from the classic tug boat to a fine replica of George Bush's cigarette boat.

There are some amusements, however, that the government has tried its best to discourage. Until a couple of years ago, the Bois de Boulogne by night was a bazaar for sex and drugs, where transvestite prostitutes would stand along the roads, and violent crime was quite common. Since 1991, however, the police have calmed things down considerably, closing the roads at night and stepping up motorcycle patrols. Nonetheless, it's a bad idea to come here for a romantic, moonlight stroll; it may not be as relaxing as you expect. In 1991, a flood of newly liberated Eastern Europeans visiting Paris camped out in the park, in an odd imitation of the Cossacks who bivouacked here after Waterloo. The Poles and Czechs have since been nudged out.

The Jardin d'Acclimatation, an amusement park at the northern end of the Bois (Mo. Sablons), lacks big, scary roller-coasters, but has plenty of neat stuff designed to appeal to little people. There's a small zoo, a mini-golf course, a carousel, and even a racetrack where kids can ride tiny motorcycles around in circles. And, for a little culture, try the **Musée en Herbe,** an art museum designed especially for children. The Jardin is lots of fun, really, with a certain old-fashioned charm. (Open daily 10am-6:30pm. Ticket office closes 45min. before park. Admission 9F, free for under 3 accompanied by their parents.) To get to the Jardin from the Porte Maillot metro, go to the big house marked l'Orée du Bois and follow the brown signs that point to the right of the building. Or you can go to the left of the building and take a cutesy little train. (Trains run Wed., Sat.-Sun., and public holidays, as well as daily during school vacations, every 10min. from 1:30-6pm. 8F, under 3 free.)

You can hear a pin drop at **Bowling de Paris** (tel. 40 67 94 00), near the rte. Mahatma Gandhi entrance of the Jardin d'Acclimatation. (Open daily 10am-2am. Games Mon.-Fri. 18F, after 8pm 22F, Sat.-Sun. 27F. Obligatory bowling shoe rental 9F.) After the park closes, you have to enter through the park's Mahatma Gandhi entrance, which remains open. Because the Bowling de Paris is inside the Jardin, you have to pay for admission to the Jardin even if you just want to go bowling. On the edge of the Jardin, the **Musée des Arts et Traditions** (tel. 44 17 60 00; Mo. Sablons) displays fascinating exhibits of tools and everyday artifacts illustrating French rural life before the Industrial Revolution. Enter from the Jardin or from rte. Mahatma Gandhi. (Museum open Wed.-Mon. 9:45am-5pm. Admission 18F, under 25 and over 60 9F, Sun. 9F.)

Pré Catelan is a manicured park whose paths wind through neatly clipped grass and lovely old trees. The enormous purple beech tree on the central lawn is almost 200 years old. You can sit on the grass, except where there are *pelouse interdite* signs. Inside the Pré Catelan, the **Jardin de Shakespeare** (created 1952-53) features all of the plants mentioned by the bard, grouped by play—thus there is a collection of Scottish highland vegetation in the *Macbeth* area, a Meditteranean section for *The Tempest,* etc. An unweeded garden that grows to seed, things rank and gross in nature possess it merely? Sadly, not. In the center, a lovely little open-air theater, the Théatre de Verdure du Jardin Shakespeare (tel. 42 76 47 72), gives popular performances of Shakespeare's plays (in French) during the summer (see Entertainment—Theater). Take the metro to Porte Maillot; then take bus #244 to Bagatelle-Pré-Catelan. (Pré Catelan open 7:30am-

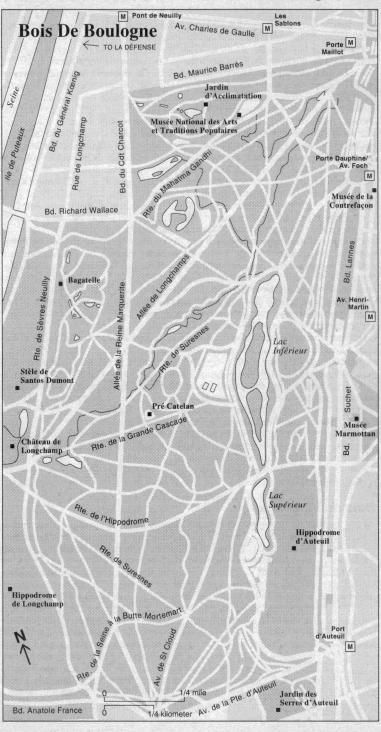

Bois De Boulogne

Pont de Neuilly Ⓜ

Av. Charles de Gaulle

Les Sablons Ⓜ

Porte Maillot Ⓜ

→ TO LA DÉFENSE

Bd. Maurice Barrès

Jardin d'Acclimatation

Musée National des Arts et Traditions Populaires

Bd. du Général Kœnig

Rue de Longchamp

Bd. du Cdt Charcot

Rte. du Mahatma Gandhi

Seine

Île de Puteaux

Porte Dauphine/ Av. Foch Ⓜ

Musée de la Contrefaçon

Bd. Richard Wallace

Rte. de Sèvres Neuilly

Bagatelle

Allée de la Reine Marguerite

Allée de Longchamps

Rte. de Suresnes

Bd. Lannes

Lac Inférieur

Av. Henri-Martin Ⓜ

Stèle de Santos Dumont

Pré Catelan

Rte. de la Grande Cascade

Château de Longchamp

Suchet

Musée Marmottan

Bd.

Lac Supérieur

Rte. de l'Hippodrome

Rte. de Suresnes

Hippodrome d'Auteuil

Hippodrome de Longchamp

Rte. de la Seine à la Butte Mortemart

Av. de St Cloud

N ↗

Port d'Auteuil Ⓜ

0   1/4 mile

Bd. Anatole France

0   1/4 kilometer

Av. de la Pte. d'Auteuil

Jardin des Serres d'Auteuil

8pm; shorter hours in winter. Shakespeare garden open daily 3-3:30pm and 4:30-5pm. Admission to Shakespeare garden 3F, under 10 1F50.)

The Parc de la Bagatelle (tel. 40 67 97 00; same bus stop as Pré Catelan) was once a private estate within the *Bois;* Bagatelle did not become a public park until 1905. The Count of Artois, the future Charles X, built the little Chateau de la Bagatelle in 64 days in 1777, because of a wager with Marie Antoinette, his sister-in-law. The garden is famous for its June rose exhibition and for its water lilies, which the gardener added in tribute to Monet. It frequently plays host to art exhibits—in 1992, for instance, the lawns were dotted with Henry Moore sculptures. Do *not* walk on the grass. They really care about this—enough to put up ridiculous signs in English shouting "GRASS PROHIBITED." Guided French tours of the castle at 3pm (25F) and of the castle and park at 4pm (35F) run from March 15 through October on weekends and public holidays. Meet at the castle. Call 40 71 75 23 to check these times. (Admission to park 6F, ages 6-10 3F. Open Jan. 16-31 9am-5:30pm; Feb. 1-15 9am-6pm; Feb. 16-28 9am-6:30pm; March 1-15 8:30am-7pm; March 16-April 30 8:30am-7:30pm; May 1-15 8:30am-8pm; May 16-July 31 8:30am-8:30pm; Aug. 8:30am-7:30pm; Sept. 8:30am-7pm; Oct. 1-15 9am-6:30pm; Oct. 16-Nov. 30 9am-6pm; Dec. 1-Jan. 15 9am-5pm. No, we don't know why they made it this complicated. Maybe it's because they're French.)

The two **artificial lakes** stretching down the eastern edge of the Bois de Boulogne make for a delightful promenade. Come on a weekday to avoid the crowds; come on a weekend to watch them. The manicured islands of the **Lac Inférieur** (Mo. Porte Dauphine) can be reached by rented rowboat only. Boats fit up to 5 people. (Boathouses open late Feb. to early Nov. Mon.-Fri. 9am-6pm, Sat.-Sun. 9am-7pm. Both daily and annual schedules depend on weather; in good weather they rent boats longer, in bad weather they shut down earlier. Boat rentals 41F per hr., 400F deposit; with insurance against damage to the boat 48F per hr., 200F deposit.)

Dedicated horticulturalists may want to stroll through the **Jardin des Serres d'Auteuil** (Greenhouse Garden), full of greenhouses, labeled trees, and semi-sickly flowers. (Open daily spring-summer 10am-6pm; autumn-winter 10am-5pm. Admission 3F.) Free, and prettier, although somewhat of a make-out spot (and what French garden is not?), is the neighboring (and quaint) **Jardin des Poètes.** Each cluster of flowers has an accompanying quote. Feeling saccharine? You can easily leave the poetry behind by attending a hard-fought and ardently cheered soccer or rugby match at the **Parc aux Princes,** one of several stadiums in the Porte d'Auteuil area.

Bicycles, a delightful way to get around the park, can be rented at two locations: across the street from the boathouse at the northern end of the Lac Inférieur and in front of the entrance to the Jardin d'Acclimatation. (Open Mon.-Fri. 1-6:30pm, Sat.-Sun. 9:30am-7pm; Sept.-June Wed. 1-6:30pm and Sat.-Sun. 9:30am-7pm. 27F per hr., passport or driver's license deposit.)

Bois de Vincennes

Like the Bois de Boulogne, the Bois de Vincennes (Mo. Château de Vincennes or Porte Dorée) was once a royal hunting forest, walled in to keep the exotic game from getting away. Outside the city limits, it was also a favorite ground for dueling. Alexandre Dumas, *père* was frustrated here in his duel with a collaborator who claimed to have written the *Tour de Nesle.* Dumas's pistol misfired, and the author had to content himself with using the experience as the basis for a scene in *The Corsican Brothers.* Along with its fellow *Bois,* the Vincennes forest was given to the city of Paris by Napoleon III to be transformed into an English-style garden. Not surprisingly, Haussmann oversaw the planning of lakes and pathways. Annexed to a much poorer section of Paris than the Bois de Boulogne, Vincennes was never quite as fashionable or as formal. As one *fin-de-siècle* observer wrote, "At Vincennes, excursionists do not stand on ceremony, and if the weather is sultry, men may be seen lounging in their shirt sleeves, and taking, in other respects, an ease which the inhabitants of the Boulevards, who resort to the Bois de Boulogne, would contemplate with horror." Today's *Bois*, officially part of the twelfth *arrondissement,* is less swanky and less well known than the Bois de Boulogne, making it arguably the far better and more peaceful park to visit.

Bois De Vincennes

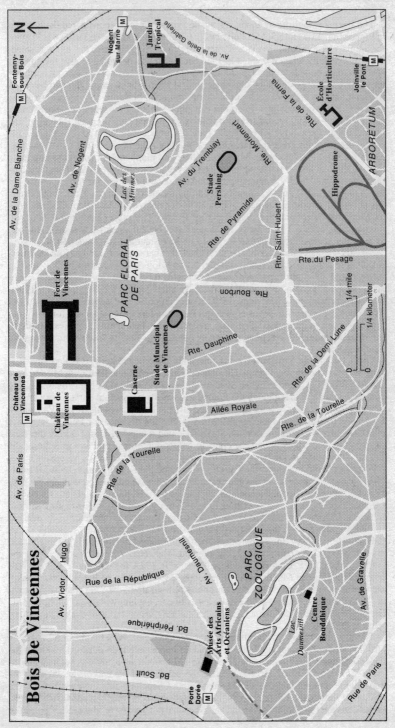

N

Fontenny-sous-Bois Ⓜ

Av. de la Dame Blanche

Nogent sur Marne Ⓜ

Jardin Tropical

Av. de la Belle Gabrielle

École d'Horticulture

Joinville le Pont Ⓜ

Av. de Nogent

Av. du Tremblay

Rte. de la Ferma

Stade Pershing

Rte. Morlemart

ARBORÉTUM

Hippodrome

Fort de Vincennes

Rte. de Pyramide

Rte. Saint-Hubert

PARC FLORAL DE PARIS

Rte. du Pesage

Château de Vincennes Ⓜ

Château de Vincennes

Caserne

Stade Municipal de Vincennes

Rte. Bourbon

1/4 mile

Av. de Paris

Rte. Dauphine

Rte. de la Demi Lune

1/4 kilometer

Allée Royale

Rte. de la Tourelle

0

0

Rte. de la Tourelle

Av. Victor Hugo

Rte. de la Tourelle

Rue de la République

Av. Daumesnil

PARC ZOOLOGIQUE

Av. de Gravelle

Bd. Périphérique

Lac Daumesnil

Centre Bouddhique

Bd. Soult

Musée des Arts Africains et Océaniens

Rue de Paris

Porte Dorée Ⓜ

The Parc Zoologique de Paris, 53, av. de Saint-Maurice, is considered the best zoo in France (tel. 43 43 84 95; Mo. Porte Dorée). Unlike their kin in the Jardin des Plantes, the animals strut around in relatively natural surroundings. Indeed, the zoo was something of a novelty when it opened in 1934 because it was designed to give the animals space to roam outside. While it's still disturbing to see waterbucks prance on hard, dry ground when the posted sign says their natural habitat is swampy, the zoo has been working hard to improve each animal's environment, building new indoor areas for greater comfort in the winter. Everyone can enjoy watching the western baboons interact, bonding over bug search and destroy missions in their hair, digging, frolicking, and squawking at one another. The *phoques* (yes, it's pronounced just like you think it is)—seals—are fed with great spectacle daily at 4:30pm. The otaries, their close relatives, eat at 4:35pm. Pandas, polar bears, ostriches, and elephants all roam around, none looking quite as sad or sounding quite as annoyed as the shrieking parrots in their barren cages. Don't feed the animals; the food stands and café are far too expensive for that. Don't miss the mountain goats assaulting the newly renovated 12m high Grand Rocher in the middle of the park. (Open Mon.-Sat. 9am-6pm, Sun. 9am-6:30pm; winter Mon.-Sat. 9am-5pm, Sun. 9am-5:30pm. Ticket office closes ½hr. before zoo. Admission 35F, ages 6-16, students 16-25, and over 60 20F, under 6 and disabled free. Wheelchair accessible. Train tour leaves from the restaurant: 10F, under 10 8F.)

Joggers, cyclists, and park bench sitters happily share the turf around **Lac Daumesnil.** People actually dare to sit on the grass and dogs chase thrown balls wherever they've gone. Unwind...and keep your eyes peeled for chimney swallows and Canadian geese, birds known to frequent the area. Navigate around the lake in a rented rowboat. (Boat rental daily May-Nov. 15 10:30am-5:30pm. 1 or 2 people 41F per hr., 3 or 4 people 47F per hr., 50F deposit, plus tip.) Penetrate farther into the park for good running and cycling paths and refreshing greenery. The **Vélodrome Jacques Anquetil,** the **Hippodrome de Vincennes,** and many other sports facilities lie within the sizable *Bois* (see Sports).

The Château de Vincennes, on the northern edge of the park, is called "the Versailles of the Middle Ages" (Mo. Château de Vincennes). French kings held court here as early as the 13th century, when St-Louis imitated the biblical Deborah by dispensing justice beneath a tree. Although the Louvre was royalty's principal home, every French monarch from Charles V to Henri IV whiled away at least part of his time at Vincennes. Charles V built up a true medieval fortress on the site his ancestor Philippe-Auguste chose for a royal hunting residence. Henri III found it a useful refuge during the Wars of Religion, and Mazarin and the court found its defenses useful in the wake of the Fronde. Château freaks will recognize the inimitable hand of Louis Le Vau in the buildings farthest from the entry; the Queen's palace and the King's palace, built for Louis XIV, face each other across the courtyard, bounded by an arch-filled wall. In the 18th century, Vincennes became a country-club prison for well-known enemies of the state. Mirabeau spent 3½ years here, killing time by writing lecherous letters to his (married) mistress. Diderot was imprisoned in the château; Rousseau, the lover of nature, enjoyed the walk through the forest necessary to visit his friend.

In the 19th century, the complex resumed its military functions, serving as fortress, arsenal, and artillery park. In 1917, the infamous Mata Hari, convicted of spying for the Germans, faced the firing squad within its walls. In 1940, the château served as headquarters for General Maurice Gamelin, Supreme Commander of French Land Forces. De Gaulle later criticized Gamelin for holing himself up in the *Thébaïde*—ivory tower—of Vincennes, without even a radio tower to connect him with the front. Today, the Services Historiques des Armées and other military historical institutes are headquartered at the château.

The **donjon** (keep) was built between 1360 and 1370. At a height of 52m, it is a striking piece of medieval architecture and an impressive hide-out for any king. The **Sainte-Chapelle** was founded as a church in 1379 but the building was not inaugurated until 1552. Dainty in its decor and especially beautiful at the end of the day with the sun shining through the rose window, the Sainte-Chapelle is looking even better these days after restoration of the exterior. (Open daily 9:30am-7pm; Oct.-April 10am-5pm. Guided visits of the Sainte-Chapelle and Keep daily at 10:15am, 11am, 12:30pm, 1:30,

2:45, 3, 3:45, 4:30, 5:15, and 6pm are the only way to get inside. In French, but guides have written English translations. Admission 25F, students under 26 and seniors 14F.) Have a look at the archeological digs in the main courtyard (purchase a guide to make the visit more meaningful). Wander around the ramparts, for a pleasant, if unexciting, view of the surrounding area. If you go on the appropriate day, drop by the **Musée des Chasseurs,** dedicated to the liberal, if non-PC, art of hunting. (Open Wed. 10am-5pm and Sat. 9am-3pm.)

One of the gems of the Bois de Vincennes is the **Parc Floral de Paris,** esplanade du Château (tel. 43 43 92 95; Mo. Château de Vincennes), reached by walking down rue de la Pyramide from the castle. Aside from magnificent horticultural displays, the park has miniature golf and all kinds of games (10 that cost, 60 that don't) for kids. Picnic areas, restaurants, and open-air concerts make it a center of summer entertainment. (Open daily 9:30am-8pm; hours shorten in winter. Admission 10F, children 5F.)

La Défense

Paris has laws governing the size and shape of buildings within the *boulevard périphérique;* these were instituted to prevent repeats of the architectural mistakes of the 1960s (ugly tower blocks which are not only an aesthetic disaster, but also contribute to traffic congestion). La Défense, just outside city limits, forms a sharp contrast to this regimentation. Clustered around the Grande Arche (a 35-story office block in the shape of a hollowed cube), elegant skyscrapers show off the latest in Gotham-city-like modern architecture. Not that this growth has been unregulated—since 1958, a government agency known as EPAD has directed the development of La Défense as a business district at the gates of Paris. Today, La Défense boasts of the headquarters of 14 of France's top 20 corporations, each trying to outdo the other with its sleek modern architecture. Thanks to EPAD, shops, galleries, trees, and a liberal sprinkling of sculptures make the large pedestrian esplanade a pleasant place for a stroll. The major roads go right underneath this esplanade, and you'll feel far freer from pollution and cars than you'll ever feel in central Paris. Pretend you're in a modern day Utopia, and hope it's not a Brave New World instead.

La Défense is the current endpoint of the famous *axe historique de Paris* (the historical axis of Paris), also known as the *voie triopmhiale* (the triumphal way). This magnificent corridor began in 1664 as an extension of the path through the Tuileries garden; designed by Le Nôtre and lined by a gracious row of elm trees. Its purpose was to make it easier for the court to get from the Louvre to the hunting-grounds of St-Germain-en-Laye. In 1772, the construction of the Pont de Neuilly extended the path across the Seine to a hill called the Montagne du Chante-Coq. Back in Paris, the route became more and more elaborate. In 1808, the Louvre end saw the completion of a little arch, the Arc de Triomphe du Carroussel, built to commemorate Napoleon's victories in 1805. Then in 1836, the larger Arc de Triomphe d'Etoile was completed, aligned perfectly with the Arc de Carroussel. 40 years later, planners selected Chante-Coq for a memorial to the defenders of Paris during the Siege of 1870. The resulting statue, called La Défense, gave the area its current name.

The proliferation of office towers in the area began in 1956, as part of a scheme to provide office space for Paris without drastically altering the city center. Originally the planners intended to limit buildings to certain heights and styles to create a unified complex. By the late 1960s and early 70s, companies were allowed to build distinctive *gratte-ciels* (skyscrapers), "Manhattan-style." But this haphazard building threatened the dignity and grandeur of the *axe historique.* La Défense needed something more than a random assortment of office towers if it were to maintain the traditional monumentality of the line stretching down the avenue Charles de Gaulle, the avenue de la Grand Armée, the avenue des Champs Elysées, and the place de la Concorde all the way to the Louvre itself. In 1969, Ioh Ming Pei suggested the first plan for a monument to anchor the end of the axis. French Presidents Pompidou, Giscard d'Estaing, and Mitterrand all sponsored international contests for such a monument, though only Mitterrand acted on the results. Of 424 projects submitted, four were presented anonymously to the president, who chose the plan of previously unkown Danish architect Otto von Spreckelsen for its "purity and strength."

The Grande Arche de la Défense, Spreckelsen's winning design, now towers over the metro/RER stop bearing its name. It was inaugurated on the French Republic's bicentennial—July 14, 1989. The roof of this unconventional office building covers 2.5 acres, and Notre-Dame cathedral could fit within its hollow core. The plan is remarkably ingenious, and the walls are covered with white marble that shines blindingly in the (rare) sunlight. Most of all, its undeniably modern design blends into the centuries-old architectural context of the *axe historique,* though unlike the smaller arches, this one is aligned 6° off the axis. The addition of this third arch, coherent within the older row of monuments, makes the assertion that La Défense is *part of* Paris, not just a new-fangled project on the horizon. Encouraged by this success, EPAD plans to extend the *axe historique* further by building up the area behind the Grande Arche; most of the work should be finished by 1995. As for I. M. Pei, who first proposed a monument at the western end of the *voie triomphiale,* he was instead commissioned to redesign the eastern terminus: the courtyard of the Louvre.

As you approach the Grand Arche and walk around its perimeter, it shifts from a 2-dimensional paper-cut-out arch to a starkly three-dimensional cube. An unparalleled view and an entirely modernist aesthetic experience await at the top. But first go to the **Info Défense booth** (tel. 47 74 84 24), located near the arch in front of the shell-shaped CNIT building. Ask for the brochure *Du haut de ce monument, vous contemplez vingt siècles d'histoire* (From the top of this monument, you contemplate 20 centuries of history). You may not care about the centuries, but the multilingual brochure entitles you to a 20% discount on the ticket to the arch. If you are interested in sculpture, ask for the handsome *Guide to Works of Art in the La Défense District,* available in English. Tickets for the roof of the arch are sold at a booth near the elevator shaft. (Open Sun.-Thurs. 9am-8pm, Fri.-Sat. 9am-9pm; roof closes 1hr. after ticket office. 40F, under 18 30F. Wheelchair accessible.)

Even if you don't want to go through the roof, it's still worth climbing up the steps of the big white cube and admiring the view of the Arc de Triomphe across the river. Notice, on your left, the odd shape of the **Bull Tower,** which looks as if it's had a piece cut out of it. As you walk down toward Paris, the **CNIT building,** the oldest building at La Défense, a hale old survivor from 1958, is on the left. On the right is the **Colline de l'Automobile,** an auto museum (scheduled to open in late 1992) that includes a dome-shaped cinema. Near here, plans are underway to construct the **Tour sans fin** (tower without end)—a 400m structure that will be the highest skyscraper in Europe. The brightly colored play-doh-like sculpture at pl. de La Défense is by **Joan Miró,** and looks remarkably like one of his anthropomorphic paintings come to life, as in a B-movie *(Attack of the Killer Mirós).* Across the *place,* **Alexander Calder's** linear, spidery red steel sculpture provides a fitting counterpart. Calder, by the way, seems to have thought Miró's work resembled a popsicle: when he first saw a model of it, he asked, "Is that good to lick?"

Just past the little lawn in front of you is a white tube called the **galerie art 4** (tel. 49 00 15 96; open Wed.-Mon. noon-7pm; call to find out about temporary exhibits and tours of La Défense, in French only, 20F). To the right, standing on a high pedestal, is the bronze statue after which La Défense was named (formerly the area was known as Courbevoie). Louis-Ernest Barrias's statue beat 100 other proposals, including one by Auguste Rodin. It was moved while the district was constructed, then returned to its original place in 1983. The name "La Défense," by the way, has engendered some serious confusions. An official whose title was "Managing Director of La Défense" was not allowed off a plane in Egypt, because that country did not welcome military personnel during wartime. On another occasion, a young foreigner presented himself at the office of the same official, asking to join the Foreign Legion. Finally, there is the story of the Soviet general who came to inspect the military installations here....

On weekdays, the brightly colored **fountain** behind the defensive statue runs from noon to 2pm and from 4:30pm to 6:30pm. At 3pm and 9pm on weekends and public holidays, a *"ballet d'eau"* is performed here, with the fountain's spurting "choreographed" to music played from nearby speakers. Don't stress if you miss this sight. For more of the "mute" spurting, come between 4pm and 9pm on weekends and public holidays. Times are subject to change; check at the info booth. To the left of the fountain, a major construction project is working to replace the 1964 Esso building with the Coeur-Défense complex, to be completed in 1995. Built in 1964, the Esso building came to be something of an embarrassment for the company, dwarfed as it was by the Fiat and Elf headquarters nearby. Esso executives, mortified that other businessmen had bigger towers, crawled off to Reuil in 1992. The planned Coeur-Défense will provide zillions of acres of office space and a modern art museum. A staircase in front of the construction site leads down to another art gallery, the **Galerie de l'esplanade.** (Open for temporary exhibits daily noon-7pm.) A tree-lined path takes you the rest of the way to the Esplanade de la Défense metro stop. The low buildings on either side are apartment blocks. About 20,000 people, most of them with a fairly low income, live in the business area of La Défense. At the end of the path, the stark steel lamps rising out of water are the work of the Greek artist Takis. The metro stop is on your left.

If you want to eat or shop in La Défense, the best place to go is the huge **4 Temps shopping center**—one of the largest shopping malls in Europe, with 200 stores, 3 levels, 20 restaurants, and 9 cinemas, home to 50,000 people a day. This is it...Nirvana! You can enter from the Grande Arche metro stop, from doors behind the Miró sculpture, or from next to the Colline de l'Automobile. There's a computerized map in English and French; press *sommaire géneral* and then "change language" and the machine will do so, politely! (Shops open Tues.-Sat. 10am-8pm, Mon. 11am-8pm. Supermarkets—*hypermarchés*—open Tues.-Sat. 9am-10pm, Mon. 10am-10pm.) A good bet among the restaurants in the mall is **Le Bistrot d'Edmond** (tel. 47 73 73 88). Located at pl. de la Patinoire, level 1, it's a large place with a vaguely rural feel. (Two-course *menu* 72F. A la carte carpaccio 60F, cold filet 69F. Open Mon.-Sat. 7:30am-10pm.)

To get to La Défense from Paris you can take the metro or RER. Older maps do not show the La Défense metro stop that opened only in 1992. The RER is faster, but the metro is cheaper—La Défense counts as zone 2 for the metro but as zone 3 for the RER. If you do take the RER, be sure to buy the more expensive ticket before going through the turnstile—a normal metro ticket may get you into the RER station in Paris, but it won't get you out at La Défense. Though the deserted La Défense is eerily impressive at night, you really need a car to appreciate it, and a taxi would be quite expensive.

The **La Défense park,** accessible one stop farther west on the RER (Nanterre-Préfecture), offers a pleasant area to picnic and rest up after your visit to the modernist metropolis. This is the largest park built in or near Paris in the 20th century, and includes botanical gardens, numerous basins, and sand boxes for the little kids. Other than rolling hills and a *gazon remarquable* (remarkable lawn), it is also home to the **Ecole de Danse de l'Opéra de Paris** (Opéra Ballet Dance School) and the experimental **Théâtre des Amandiers.**

Museums

Paris is not a museum, but you could certainly spend all your time going from one to the next. Every institution, artistic movement, ethnic group, and custom seems to have a museum devoted to its history, art, and memorabilia. For listings of the often excellent temporary exhibits, consult the bimonthly *Le Bulletin des Musées et Monuments Historiques,* available at the central tourist office (127, av. des Champs-Elysées). *Paris Museums and Monuments* provides not only phone numbers, addresses, and hours, but also describes the museums (including wheelchair access) and lists them by *arrondissement. Pariscope, 7 à Paris,* and *l'Officiel des Spectacles* also list museums with hours and temporary exhibits.

Most museums stop admitting people 30-45 minutes before their listed closing times. Discounts for students or young people are nearly omnipresent. Indeed, many museums (including the Louvre, Orsay, and Pompidou) are free for those under 18. In accordance with a policy set by the Ministry of Culture, the number of such museums should grow in the next few years. Larger museums often offer group tours in various languages. Prices are typically around 500F for a group of adults, 250F for students and seniors. Seniors means 60 and over unless otherwise stated.

Frequent museum-goers may want to invest in a **Carte Musées et Monuments.** This pass covers admission to any of 65 museums in the Paris area for free *without waiting in line*—an important consideration in the summer, when the lines to museums like the Louvre or the Orsay are often more than half an hour long. The card is available at all major museums and metro stations (1 day 60F, 3 consecutive days 120F, 5 consecutive days 170F). The card is only economical for die-hard museum goers who do not qualify for student or senior discounts.

Besides the major museums included on the *carte,* Paris has dozens of tiny eclectic collections. You may get the feeling that people have discovered some weird stuff in their house, shoved it in a room, called it a "museum," and now sit hoping someone will take it seriously. Some of these one-roomers work, some of them don't. Houses of the now-dead rich, famous, and talented often make for the most enjoyable museums, with a homey setting and friendly staff.

Galleries are very popular among Parisians. These far more intimate exhibits generally feature only one or two showrooms, so they can easily be enjoyed in a short period of time. Most of the city's 200 galleries specialize in one type of art, such as naive painting, modern sculpture, prints, or sketches of Parisian scenes. The highest concentration of galleries is in the Marais; in a casual stroll through the third and fourth *arrondissements*, you're sure to pass by several. The St-Germain-des-Prés area also contains an assembly of small, enticing galleries. Walk right in and don't feel intimidated; you're not necessarily expected to buy. For a complete list, pick up a free poster in any gallery.

Musée du Louvre

Aside from some canvases smeared with paint and some stones hacked into unnatural shapes, there isn't much to see in the Louvre. Then again, how could you miss it? . Ever since 1793, when it first opened its doors to the public, the Louvre (tel. 40 20 50 50; Mo. Palais-Royal/Musée du Louvre) has been the world's most famous museum, a giant warehouse of art whose collection includes such cultural icons as the *Mona Lisa,* the *Venus de Milo,* and Delacroix's *Liberty Leading the People.*

The Building

Construction of the Louvre began in 1200, and still isn't finished. Every ruler who has left a major mark on Paris—including Philippe-Auguste, Henri IV, Napoleon III, and François Mitterrand—has also reshaped the Louvre. Like the city itself, it is a living edifice that belongs to no single era or architectural style, but remains an oddysey of passion, butch in hues, somber in disquietude.

The Louvre's history, like that of the United States, has been one of slow but steady westward expansion. The original Louvre was a fortress built by King Philippe-Auguste just outside his new city walls, meant to protect Paris while the king was off on a Crusade. A century and a half later, Charles V extended the city walls to what is now the Jardin des Tuileries, and the fortress sat useless in the middle of the city. Not one to let a good castle go to waste, Charles converted the austere defensive structure into a residential château. Later monarchs destroyed his palace out of a wish for more modern and more grandiose structures, and all that remains of the old Louvre are its foundations. Unearthed in the early stages of Mitterrand's ongoing renovation, they can be seen in a fascinating underground exhibit called "le Louvre Médiéval" (admission included in the museum ticket).

Philippe-Auguste's fortress sat in the southwestern quarter of what is now the **Cour Carrée,** or Square Courtyard. The western wall of this court is part of the **Renaissance wing,** begun by François I in 1546. Early in his reign, François tried to avoid the Louvre, which was narrow, dank, somber, murky, tenebrous, gloomy, and rat-infested. For a long time, he lived in elegant countryside mansions, particularly Fontainebleau. In 1527, however, he returned to the Louvre in an attempt to flatter the Parisian bourgeoisie, whom he hoped to distract from their raised taxes. As soon as he could afford it, François set about rebuilding the medieval palace in the open style of the Renaissance.

Except for the west wall, finished by Louis XIII, the Cour Carrée owes its ponderous, symbolically charged classicism to Louis XIV, who reconstructed its interior façades, along with the majestic colonnade facing the rue de l'Amiral de Coligny, in the hopes of transforming the Louvre into the grandest palace in Europe. At first, he commissioned Bernini, the greatest of Baroque architects, to coordinate this mammoth job. Bernini's plan, however, began with destroying the existing palace, and Louis XIV turned instead to a domestic trio: Le Vau, Le Brun, and Claude Perrault. These architects did indeed destroy what was left of the medieval palace, yet left François's gracious addition untouched. Notice how the Sun King represented himself, on the pediment of the eastern wall, as a sun illuminating the Arts and Sciences. With typical subtlety, Louis XIV's addition changed the palace's main entrance to the eastern side, so that, like the great medieval cathedrals, it would face the rising sun. Tired of Paris, Louis eventually abandoned the Louvre in favor of Versailles, and the grandiose transformation did not get past the Cour Carrée.

Through the passage in the Renaissance wing is the much larger courtyard known as the **Cour Napoléon,** begun conceptually by Cathérine des Médicis and completed by Napoleon III over 200 years later. Two wings stretch into the distance in front of you, forming a dignified line all the way to the edge of the Tuileries garden. These two wings were once connected by the Tuileries palace, a royal residence that was begun in 1563 in order to make a separate château for Cathérine des Médicis. Henri IV completed the Tuileries and embarked on what he called the Grand Design—a project to link the Louvre and the Tuileries with two large wings like the ones you see today. He only managed to build a fraction of the project before he was snuffed out in 1610.

With the departure of the court to Versailles, the buildings around the Cour Carrée (the **Sully** wing) fell into disrepair. Indigent artists, prostitutes, and soldiers occupied much of the palace, but some chambers were maintained as a storage center for the royal art collections. In 1725, the Academy of Painting inaugurated annual *salons* in the halls to show the work of its members. For over a century, French painting would revolve around the salons. In 1793, the Revolution made the exhibit permanent, creating the first Louvre Museum. The galleries quickly filled with artists, copying the works of the masters, their air of reverence forming a strange counterpart to the squalor of beggars and prostitutes that had taken over the rest of the palace.

The museum's fortune took a turn for the better when Napoleon I evicted the squatters and filled the Louvre with plundered art from all over Continental Europe. With the defeat at Waterloo, however, most of this art had to be returned to the countries it was, um, borrowed from. More durably, Napoleon built the **Arc de Triomphe du Carroussel** (beyond the glass pyramid), a copy of the Arch of Septimus Severus in Rome, to commemorate the victories of 1805. It was originally surmounted by four world-famous bronze horses, which had been taken from St. Mark's in Venice; but these were duly returned in 1815 to their place of outlook over the Venetian bay.

In 1857, Napoleon III finally instituted Henri IV's Grand Design, extending the two wings of the Louvre to meet the Tuileries palace. In order to give architectural unity to the newly dubbed Cour Napoléon, "Crapulinski" (as Marx called him) ordered his architects to redo the façades of all the older buildings. The result is that the François I wing gained a new façade on its west side while retaining it original design on the Cour Carrée side. Only 14 years after the completion of the Grand Design, the Tuileries palace was burned to the ground by the Paris Commune. Ever since, the Louvre has had two large wings **(Denon and Richelieu)** that reach out to grasp only empty space.

As for the glass **pyramid** in the middle of the courtyard, it made its goose-dazzling appearance in 1989. The new entrance to the Musée du Louvre, the pyramid was the crucial step in Mitterrand's campaign to make the Louvre into a museum that welcomes visitors instead of sending them away cursing the French. How? By hiring an American. Previous entrances, each leading to separate areas of the museum, were hobbled by huge lines and utter disorganization. I. M. Pei, designer of the sleek East Wing of the National Gallery of Art in Washington, came up with a remarkable proposal: create one underground entrance at the center of the Cour Napoléon, "the Louvre's new center of gravity." At first, Pei's proposal met with intense disapproval, and many still lament its stark contrast with the courtyard's Baroque façades. Most, however, acknowledge Pei's pyramid as a stroke of genius. An enlarged reception area has solved the problem of an unstructured welcoming service, and escalators provide ready access to each of the palace's wings. Equipped with a bookstore, a cafeteria, and even an auditorium, this **Hall Napoléon** glows in the sunlight streaming through the glass pyramid overhead. With its cavernous openness and gleaming, unornamented expanses of marble and stainless steel, this is a somehow *American* space, reminiscent of the bustling efficiency of the New World's banks, fast-food restaurants, and airport terminals.

The second major step of Mitterrand's Grand Louvre project, scheduled to be completed in November 1993, will be the incorporation of the Richelieu (north) wing into the museum. The Ministry of Finance, which had "temporarily" occupied this space since 1871, has already moved to new offices in Bercy (see 12th *arrondissement*). Between Richelieu and the second floor of Sully (also being opened in 1993), the Louvre will double its display area. The curators plan to display only 20% more works (taken out of storage); the extra space will alleviate the legendary overcrowding of art on the Louvre's walls. It should also reduce the overcrowding of tourists on the Louvre's floors. Also in 1993, a new underground parking lot and *shopping mall* will open under the Arc de Triomphe du Carroussel, linked both to the Hall Napoléon and the metro.

The Museum

The last stage of the Grand Louvre project, currently underway, will be tough on tourists trying to find their way around. The curators plan to move 80% of the museum's art to new positions by the end of the project in 1997; at any given time over the next four years, a few rooms will be closed because of this work. More importantly, all of this juggling means that no guidebook can give you an adequate walking tour of the museum. For the current scheme, pick up a map (available in several languages) in the entrance hall. Even with a map it's easy to get lost. Enjoy the Dungeons & Dragons-style treasure-hunt-through-a-maze-like-castle for what it is, or take one of the guided tours of the museum (details below). Alternatively, make use of the racks of plastic-coated information sheets that stand in corners of many of the Louvre's chambers. These sheets, which most visitors seem not to notice, provide intelligent commentaries on the works nearby (usually available in English).

Though best known for its European paintings, the Louvre contains seven departments. **Oriental Antiquities** has nothing to do with East Asia, and everything to do with ancient Mesopotamia: Babylonians, Hittites, Assyrians, etc. (Paris hoards its East Asian treasures in the Musée Guimet.) Its collection includes the world's oldest legal document, a basalt slab from the 18th century BC on which is inscribed the code of King Hammurabi—the first written set of laws from one of the world's earliest civilizations. The **Egyptian Antiquities** section is stocked with statues of jeweled cats and interesting tools, and keeps several world-class mummies under wraps. Only a tiny fraction of the **Graphic Arts Collection** is displayed at one time. The 140,000 pieces are rotated through a series of exhibits in the Pavillon de Flore (for 1993's exhibits, see below). **"Objets d'Art"** refers to a grab-bag of furniture, jewelry, porcelain, and other tchachkes created to satisfy the derived demand of wealthy patrons.

The **Greco-Roman Antiquities** department includes two of the Museum's most famous pieces: the *Venus de Milo* and the *Winged Victory (Nike) of Samothrace.* The *Venus de Milo* was discovered in fragments by a Greek peasant on April 19, 1820, 500 steps from the theater of Mélos (Milo), and subsequently bought by the Comte de Marcellus and given to Louis XVIII for the Louvre. A 2nd century BC piece copied from a 4th century BC statue, Venus's harmonious proportions and sensuous curves quickly became world-famous as the ideal of classical female beauty. *Winged Victory,* standing aloft atop a flight of stairs, provides the museum's most stunning display. Sculpted around 190 BC to commemorate a naval victory, Nike—Greek goddess of victory—presides over the Louvre with the same majesty with which she once presided over the bow of a stone ship, set in a fountain. Her windblown draperies conform dramatically to her body, disguising the fact that she is made from a single block of marble. Her eloquent silhouette emphasizes the pride of her stance and the dramatic upswelling of the wind she confronts. This is the height of Hellenistic sculpture; spend a long time with it. The right wing and left torso were redone before the Nike was displayed in 1866; fragments of her right hand are visible on a display at the side.

The Sculpture department picks up where the Romans left off, and runs until the 19th century. The undisputed stars of the collection are two of **Michelangelo's** *Slaves,* originally planned for the tomb of Pope Julius II (the other four can be found in the Florence Accademia). Michelangelo—a workaholic notorious for sleeping in his boots— said that he attempted to free each of his sculptures from the marble block in which it was imprisoned; his tormented *Slaves* are the physical embodiment of this sentiment. In the context of the huge tomb, they were designed to represent "art enchained by the Death of their patron, Julius II." Given to Henri II in 1560, the *Slaves* were subsequently awarded to the valorous Constable de Montmorency, who moved them to his château at Ecouen. With Montmorency's death, the noble statues passed through Richelieu's soiled hands before ending up back in the Louvre.

Paintings

Having lost some of its former glory to the Musée d'Orsay and the Centre Pompidou, the Louvre's painting collection begins in the Middle Ages and stops in the early 19th century. But there's plenty within that interval, to say the least. **Hieronymous Bosch'**s small *Ship of Fools,* hidden away in the Flemish art galleries, provides a strangely surreal allegory of greed and folly. **Jan Van Eyck's** *Madonna and Chancellor Rolin* is one of the finest products of the late Gothic period, with its sharp contrast between the haughty face of the chancellor and the serene innocence of the Virgin and her rotund child—all three rendered with the same minute attention to naturalistic detail. Most captivating of all is the center of the painting, marked not by any of its principal characters, but by two mysterious figures in the background, looking over the castle walls into the distant landscape. Moving ahead several centuries, the soft light and human interaction of **Rembrandt's** *Supper at Emmaus* vie Nike in flawlessness. Meanwhile, the height of Baroque spectacle, **Peter Paul Rubens'** *Medici Cycle* (1621-5) unfolds in its very own room. Returning from exile imposed by her son, Louis XIII, Marie des Médici hired Rubens, the ultimate allegorical propagandist, to retell her personal history to the world (or at least to the treacherous French court). Swirling with vivid colors and high drama, the large canvases portray Marie as a student of the gods, a regent of great judgment, and a woman whose portrait alone could bring peace to war-torn Europe.

The Italian Renaissance collection is rivalled only by the Uffizi in Florence. **Mantegna's** *Calvary* presents a complex, choreographed ballet of glances and lines, focused on the crucified figure at its center. For the height of Renaissance potraiture, turn to **Raphael's** *Portrait of Balthazar Castiglione*—one of his closest friends—and **Titian's** strikingly textile *Man with a Glove,* held up as a model by the great portraitists of the Baroque era. Titian's *Fête Champêtre,* long attributed to his student Giorgione, presents a quietly atmospheric feast of the Gods, later reinterpreted scandalously by Manet's *Déjeuner sur l'Herbe* (see Musée d'Orsay). Compare this work to Mantegna's *Calvary* for the differences not only between early and high Renaissance, but also between the sharply intellectual Florentine school and the atmospheric Venetian school, famous for its colors and poetic quality.

And, of course, the most famous painting among the Italian Renaissance works is perhaps the most famous painting in the world. **Leonardo da Vinci's Mona Lisa** (a.k.a. La Giocanda, 1503), bought by François I in order to hang over his bathtub, smiles mysteriously at millions of guests each year. Are you sad because you're lonely, Mona Lisa, or is this the way you hide a broken heart? Actually, she's fortunate to be here at all. Louvre curators discovered her missing one August morning in 1911. Guillaume Apollinaire warned his friend Pablo Picasso, who owned two statues stolen from the Louvre, that a search for the *Mona Lisa* might uncover the contraband sculptures. The pair panicked, and at midnight struck out into the darkness with the statues packed into a suitcase, intending to dump them in the Seine. Near the *quais* they suspected they were being followed and decided instead to leave the statues anonymously with a local newspaper. But the police soon tracked down and jailed Apollinaire as a suspect in the *Mona Lisa* heist. After two days of intense questioning, Apollinaire's resolve broke—

the loyal friend accused Picasso of stealing the painting. In spite of this treachery, Picasso cleared his name with a convincing plea. Only through the efforts of local artists, who attested to the fine quality of Apollinaire's character, was the poet released. The *Mona Lisa* turned up two years later in the possesion of a former Louvre employee, who had snuck it out of the museum under his overcoat, leaving behind only the frame and a fine impression of his left thumb. Unfortunately, the museum recorded only its employees' right thumbprints. The joyful, albeit embarassed, museum directors returned the smiling lady to her proper place, where it now resides securely within a glass enclosure. Recent cleaning reveals the secret of her fame—what Walter Pater called "beauty wrought out from within upon the flesh." Look at the *Mona Lisa*, but don't forget to look at her remarkable neighbors as well. Leonardo's *Virgin of the Rocks* is unequestionably one of his most beautiful paintings, illustrating the rocky landscapes and *sfumato* (smoky) technique for which he is famous. And ponder da Vinci's quirky *St. John the Baptist,* which Kenneth Clark called "the most idiosyncratic of his paintings."

The French works are intimidating by their sheer numbers. Hundreds of still-lifes, portraits, genre paintings, and allegories are crammed together on the walls. Remember, they may be in the Louvre, but they aren't necessarily masterpieces. Don't linger on each one; just try to pick out a few that strike your fancy.

The reign of Louis XIV and the high Baroque are almost synonymous. **Nicolas Poussin** developed his highly structured "classical" theories of painting. His *Et in Arcadia Ego* (an allegory of Virgil's reminder that death stalks even the pastoral wonderland of Arcady) takes a traditionally grim theme and, ignoring the exigencies of Latin grammar, transforms it to an essay on the beauty of sorrow and a past when "I too was in Arcadia." Meanwhile, portraits of the Louis XIV and other notables show nothing but pure, undiluted, absolute power. The decadent court of Louis XV abandoned the Baroque in favor of the pastel colors and cloying cupids of the Rococo. **Antoine Watteau, Jean-Honoré Fragonard,** and **François Boucher** delighted the aristocracy with their tender, delicate visions of festivals, Venuses, and garden flirtations. The delicate colors, soft lines, and clear light of Boucher—first painter of the academy and a close friend of Louis's mistress, Mme. de Pompadour—appealed to courtiers. Paintings like Watteau's *Gilles,* a portrait of a harlequin clown, hint at a tragic emptiness behind the gay theatricality of his *Departure for the Isle of Cythera.* Even then, a powerful bourgeoisie found such pampered crapulence disgusting. Enlightenment leaders like Diderot gravitated to the more serious scenes of daily life by **Jean-Baptiste Greuze.** *The Village Bride* (1761) received lavish praise from both crowds and critics for its harmonious arrangement of twelve figures and sensitive handling of a tender moment: the signing of a marriage contract. But Greuze disgraced himself when he sought prestige by painting Romans. His *Septimus Severus* (1769), clumsily drawn and generally insipid, made him the laughingstock of the Academy.

Jacques-Louis David (1748-1825) was more successful. No matter how lost you get in the Louvre, you are unlikely to miss the movie-screen-sized canvases and quivering compositions of the greatest Neoclassical painter. David was more than an artist; he was an active participant in the politics of his day. As a young man, he rejected the Rococo puffiness of Boucher (his cousin and one-time instructor), seeking to illustrate moments of classical history in a fashion as austere and virtuous as the great Roman heroes themselves. He succeeded so well that Classical art could not progress beyond him; instead, it had to find a new direction—Romanticism. In 1785, the young artist electrified Paris with the *Oath of the Horatii,* which shows three Roman brothers swearing loyalty to their father, each other, and most of all, the *patrie.* Such paintings jibed perfectly with the republican ideals brewing on the eve of the Revolution. The follow-up, *Brutus* (1789), depicts an even greater sacrifice for country. Brutus, the founder of the Roman Republic, has ordered the execution of his sons, who attempted to restore the monarchy. As the bodies are brought in, Brutus glowers alone, while his daughters faint in their mother's arms. In both paintings, the cold, male world of politics is spatially separate from the emotional sphere of women.

When the Revolution did come, David was in the thick of it, as a prominent member of the Jacobin club. He served the regime with his art, arranging extravagant festivals (see Champ de Mars) and replacing the Romans of his earlier days with heroes of the

Revolution. He became administrator of the Louvre, living in the palace and controlling the museum's budget. Arrested in Thermidor, as part of the aftermath of the Terror, he vowed to give up politics. *The Intervention of the Sabine Women* (1799) was both a wish for peace (it shows women stopping a war before it starts) and a means by which David could replenish his fortune—he admitted thousands of people to see it at 1F80 a head. The chastened David mostly gave himself to painting portraits; look for several exquisite examples throughout the museum. But like so many others, David soon fell under the charismatic spell of General Bonaparte, a spell that would culminate in his collosal *Sacre* (Coronation). Each face in this room-sized scene is a specific person; David himself can be seen sketching in the gallery.

David's followers are also well represented. **Antoine-Jean Gros's** portraits of the emperor are even more adoring; look for Napoleon curing a plague victim with a touch of the imperial hand. **Jean-Auguste Ingres,** one of David's students, abandoned his mentor's devotion to classical physiques in favor of a more sensuous line. The proportions of his *Odalisque* (1814) are quite impossible, but they achieve the intended effect of sinuous luxury. **Théodore Gericault's** *Raft of the Medusa* (1819) uses David's classical physiques and formal composition, but the story it tells is one of disaster and brutality, not moral heroism. After a French frigate ran aground, 150 of its passengers lashed together a raft. Over the next 13 days, the castaways on the raft fought each other with sabers, stole provisions, and, by the third day, resorted to cannibalism. (They found that human flesh is more palatable when combined with a bit of fish and served with a hearty red wine.) To conserve food and water, the strong tossed the weak into the sea. Géricault spent eight months on the painting, keeping his head shaven so he wouldn't be tempted to leave the studio. **Eugène Delacroix,** one of the models for Géricault's work, was one of the last French painters to successfully carry off a big canvas showing a heroic action; his *Liberty Leading the People* is the 19th-century's most eloquent expression of the heroism of violent uprising. Louis-Philippe thought the painting so dangerous that he immediately bought it and kept it from view for the duration of his reign. Rather than imitating the severe colors and polished drafting skill of David, Delacroix founded the Romantic School, with an emphasis on dramatic movement, flashy colors and swirling lines. Later salon painters kept trying to go back to David's Classicism—a few of their miserable efforts hang in the Musée d'Orsay.

Practical Information

Many tourists show up at the Louvre on a fine summer afternoon and try to see all of it. They usually come away feeling frustrated and bored. The Louvre is simply too big for anyone's intellectual stamina, especially when (as on summer afternoons) it's crowded and hot. Try to take in a few galleries over the course of several days. The extra admission charges are a small price to pay for the satisfaction. To avoid heat and crowds, visit on Monday and Wednesday evenings, when the museum stays open until 10pm. If you can't afford to spend more than one day at the Louvre, at least give yourself a couple of breaks; your ticket is valid for the whole day, and entitles you to leave the museum and come back. Holders of a **Carte Musée** can skip the line by entering the Louvre from the Rivoli entrance, normally reserved for journalists, art students, and VIPs. (The Rivoli entrance is on the passage connecting the Cour Napoléon to the rue de Rivoli. For Carte Musée prices, see the introduction to Museums.)

Guided tours, in English, of the Louvre's permanent collections last 90 minutes, and start Monday and Wednesday-Saturday every half-hour from 10-11:30am and 2-3:30pm. Meet at the "Accueil Groupes" (enter between the bottoms of the Denon and Sully escalators). You should show up at least 30 minutes early and buy your ticket (30F) immediately to be assured of getting a place. Also available at the top of both Denon and Sully escalators are **cassette tours** of the museum, which focus on a short list of highlights. The tapes are more-or-less attuned to the changes in the location of works, since they are re-recorded every few months. The commentary lasts 50 minutes, but the tour takes about 2 hours when you include the time it takes to get from place to place (25F; 500F, driver's license, or passport deposit).

The Louvre is entirely wheelchair accessible; ask for free access guides in English at the Information desk under the pyramid. Speak to employees at the same desk if you want to borrow a wheelchair (free with passport or driver's license deposit).

(Open Mon. and Wed. 9am-10pm, Thurs.-Sun. 9am-6pm. Last entry 45min. before closing, but they start asking people to leave the museum 30min. before closing. Admission 31F, ages 18-25 and Sun. 16F, under 18 free.) If you are buying full-priced tickets, save time by using coins or a credit card in one of the automatic ticket machines; most tourists seem scared of them. The **Hall Napoléon,** the area under the pyramid, is open Wednesday-Monday 9am-10pm. The bookstore sells a wide range of postcards and posters of the museum's collection, as well as various guides that will deepen your understanding of the works on display. (Open 9:30am-10pm.)

Frequent temporary exhibits in the **Pavillon de Flore** and **Hall Napoléon** are free with admission ticket and often focus on drawings in the museum's collection. Temporary exhibits in the **Salle des Etats** (35F, ages 18-25 22F) will include: Oct. 2 1992-Jan. 25 1993: *Les Noces de Cana* (about Veronese's *Marriage of Cana* and its restoration, a process that included unintentionally dropping the thing and ripping a meter-long tear in the canvas). (Temporary exhibits open Wed.-Mon. 10am-10pm; as always ticket office closes before exhibition space.) The Hall Napoléon also has an **auditorium** that plays host to concerts, movies, and lectures and colloquia. For information on lectures and colloquia, call 40 20 51 12. For movies and concerts, see Entertainment.

The Musée d'Orsay

The Musée d'Orsay, 1, rue de Bellechasse, 7*ème* (tel. 40 49 48 14; RER Musée d'Orsay; Mo. Solférino) is often thought of as the Impressionist museum, but it is in fact devoted to French art in all forms from 1848-1914. Contrasting architecture, sculpture, painting, and furniture are all showcased beneath the breathtaking ceiling of a former train station, the **Gare d'Orsay.** Construction began in 1897 on the site of the former Palais d'Orsay, destroyed during the Commune in 1871. Victor Laloux, professor of architecture at the Ecole des Beaux-Arts, won the design competition and planned the building and its decoration down to the last detail. Although steel supports the structure, Laloux used stone, stucco, and liberal artistic touches to construct a station worthy of its refined setting in the seventh *arrondissement.* Because the station was designed for smokeless, electric engines, Laloux was able to lavish attention on an area that in traditional stations would be left to soot and noise. The Gare d'Orsay was inaugurated on July 14, 1900, in time for the Universal Exposition. For several decades, it was the main departure point for trains to the southwest, but newer trains were too long for its platforms, and it closed in 1939. Between April and August of 1945, the station and its attached hotel served as the most important French repatriation center, receiving and temporarily housing thousands of concentration and work camp survivors. Both the station and the hotel were scheduled for demolition in 1970, but amid the uproar following the destruction of Les Halles (see first *arrondissement),* they were instead declared protected landmarks. The movement to transform the *gare* into a museum begin in 1973. Unlike most of Paris's modern monuments, the Musée d'Orsay was a collaborative effort; after its inception under Pompidou, the Giscard d'Estaing presidency fostered the young project by setting up a public institution to run it. François Mitterrand saw the effort to its conclusion on December 1, 1986, when the museum opened.

Multilingual **Audioguides** provide analysis of 30 masterpieces throughout the museum. The tape lasts 50 minutes, but you need at least 90 minutes to do the path. (25F, driver's license or passport deposit. Tapes must be returned by 6pm.) Countless **guides** are on sale at various points in the museum, ranging in price from 50F-135F. The best guide, which merges excellent color plates with historical and artistic explanation is the *Guide to the Musée d'Orsay* by Caroline Mathieu, the museum's curator—more than worth the 100F price. For 15F, you can buy the interesting, if rushed, pamphlet, *Guide to the Visitor in a Hurry.* (See below for information on **guided tours.)**

The last preparatory step to take before plunging in to the sensory orgy is a quick stroll through **L'Ouverture sur l'Histoire,** underneath the main staircase. Its displays of newspapers, photos, and posters remind the visitor that the period from 1848 to 1914 was full of turmoil and upheaval, and that the 19th century was a time of intense indus-trialization. An adjoining room explains the history of the station and the museum.

The Musée d'Orsay puts on **temporary exhibits** every few months. Seven areas throughout the museum have been designated "dossier exhibits." Ever-changing, they tackle themes with a multi-disciplinary approach. Take the time to enjoy everything this museum has to offer. It is worth returning simply to appreciate as much as possible without frying your brain. Leave your camera at home and enjoy seeing masterpieces live. This may well be the most user-friendly large museum in the world.

Ground Floor: From Classicism to the proto-Impressionists

Academic and eclectic painting from the Second Empire adorn the rooms along the right-hand side of the ground floor. *Venus at Paphos* (1852-3) shows the soft, rounded curves, and crisp lines that defined **Ingres's** "Classical" style. Representing the oppo-site and highly controversial "Romantic" school, **Eugène Delacroix** focused on bril-liant colors, swift movement, and dramatic landscapes; in doing so he became the hero of a younger generation of artists, who decried Ingres's superficiality as "decorative art." Other, more convential artists achieved great success and the Salon's appropria-tion by following in Ingres's footsteps. The result—with ever greater heights of faint-ing women and "classical" sensuality—is best symbolized by **Alexandre Cabanel's** *Birth of Venus* (1863). The painting itself—so symbolic of the flawless technique, the balanced composition, the historical or mythological subject, that were needed to re-ceive a commision or show at the all-important salon—was bought by Napoleon III. The result, to modern eyes (and to the eyes of contemporaries like Manet and Courbet), was not only artificial and schematic, but utterly absurd.

The paintings by **Jean-François Millet, Jean-Baptiste-Camille Corot,** and **Théodore Rousseau** illustrate the spirit of the Barbizon school of painting, named for the village on the edge of the Fontainebleau forest to which they retreated in 1849 (see Daytrips—Fontainebleau). Fascinated by landscape and light, deeply influenced by the Dutch tradition, their intense study of peasant life and country simplicity is palpable in paintings like Millet's *The Gleaners* (1857) and Rousseau's *The Wagon* (1863).

Claiming to "translate the customs, the ideas, the appearance of my epoch, according to my own estimation...in short, to create a living art," **Gustave Courbet** began a school of Realist painting, rooted in the socialist-utopian ideas of philosophers like Charles Fourier. Courbet's monumental *Burial at Ornans,* displayed in the Salon of 1850-1851, caught flak for its unflattering depiction of 50 people from his native vil-lage attending an unnamed funeral. Critics were perplexed by the painting's traditional "grand history" format, tied to its mundane, nondescript subject. It seemed to be cari-cature and even (where the bulbous red noses of the curates were concerned) sacrilege. One critic whined: "M. Courbet is no longer just portraying truth, he is portraying *ug-liness.*" Courbet's equally grandiose *Allegory of an Artist's Studio* (1855) was refused by the Salon; Courbet defiantly set up a separate "Pavilion of Realism" outside the Sa-lon grounds. See if you can find your own meaning in the "allegory," which has kept art-historians busy for over a century. The face at the far right is, of course, Baudelaire.

For the most controversial of paintings—and the artist whom many consider to be the first modern painter—look to **Edouard Manet.** His *Olympia* (1863) caused an up-roarious scandal when exhibited at the 1865 salon. Manet had taken the format of Titian's *Venus of Urbino* (1538), *the* standard for female nudes in Western art, and transformed it to the contemporary age of Realism and objectivity. As his model, he used a high-salaried prostitute whose compact body, olive skin, and tied-back hair put her as far as possible from the classical standard of female beauty (soft curves, flowing tresses, perfectly sculpted features). Viewers objected to Olympia's fuzzy slippers and the ridiculously awake black cat (taking the place of the sleeping dog in Titian's paint-ing) stretching in the right foreground; Olympia's hands and feet were too big, she was too thin and too muscular, and her skin was the wrong color. Caricatures of the painting covered the pages of Paris's newspapers and art journals; Manet was met with catcalls and insults as he walked down the street. Why the uproar? Manet's painting destroyed the cultural icon that Titian had created. Whereas the *Venuses* of both Titian and Ca-banel seem entirely passive and vulnerable to the spectator's gaze, *Olympia* stares boldly back, comfortable with her nudity, rebuffing the bourgeois observer who might, after all, be her next client. This was pornography, cried the critics, not art. (Sound familiar?) Taken together with her entirely non-classical body, this stare invalidates the concept of art as Beauty, while opening the way to modern art, with its acknowledgment of "art for art's sake" and its awareness of the relationship between viewer and model. Manet himself was bewildered by the scandal; the ever-optimistic Baudelaire told him by way of support, "you are only the first in the decrepitude of your art."

Upper Level: Impressionism and Post-Impressionism

Upstairs, on the top floor, the Impressionist celebration begins in earnest. The location is ideal; soft light, filtered through the station's glass ceiling, illuminates the paintings to highlight the interplay of colors and the spontaneity of brushstrokes without producing a glare off the canvases.

Manet's *Déjeuner sur l'Herbe* (Luncheon on the Grass, 1863) caused yet another brouhaha. Once again (actually, two years before *Olympia),* Manet has taken an icon of Western art, Titian's *Fête Champêtre* (then attributed to Giorgione—see Louvre), and brought it scandalously into the everyday, contemporary world. *Why,* critics asked, were two perfectly respectable bourgeois gentlemen (the artist's brother and future brother-in-law) picnicking with a nude female? In a mythological context (so ably handled by Cabanel!), this situation was entirely acceptable and would have won Manet the highest of honors; in the context of modern-day Paris, and an afternoon picnic at the Bois de Boulogne...Never! Not surprisingly, *Le Déjeuner* was refused by the official Salon and subsequently shown in the famous *"Salon des Refusés"* (Salon of the Rejected), where Manet and contemporary "rejected" artists proudly showed their work, independent of the stifling strictures of the Academy.

Stand close to the Impressionist canvases to admire each seemingly haphazard brushstroke. But be sure also to stand back, squinting slightly—admire the genius that allows the mash of paint to become something coherent, not only portraying a scene, but creating wind, conveying emotion, and drawing the viewer into a moment of vibrant liveliness. Paintings like **Claude Monet's** *Gare St-Lazare* (1877) and **Renoir's** *Le bal du Moulin de la Galette* (1876) capture modern-day Paris—the iron train stations, the huge, crowded boulevards, and balls—while also rendering the graceful line of rising smoke at the train station and the excitement of swirling colors and light. Paintings by **Alfred Sisley, Camille Pissarro,** and **Berthe Morisot** provide a tranquil expression of daily life, especially in the countryside around Paris. Monet indulged in an almost scientific endeavor to capture the changing effects of light, as in his stunning series on the Rouen cathedral (1892-3), which demonstrates how intensities of light can overwhelm a classic structure, even altering its form.

Edgar Degas, who said that "No art is less spontaneous than mine," represents an alternative side of Impressionism, focusing on lines, patterns, and simple human expressions. His sculptures and paintings of ballet dancers are set not on stage, but in rehearsal or backstage. The *Petite danseuse de quatorze ans* (1881) adopts a tight fourth position, thrusts her nose in the air, and juts her groin forward. The dancers in *La classe de danse* (1874) scratch their backs, massage their tense necks, and cross their arms while vaguely listening to the ballet master. Deeply influenced by Japanese prints, Degas's figures are realistically ungraceful and off-balance; his tendency to cut off their straining limbs implies that the scene exists beyond the mere confines of the canvas. Paintings like *l'Absinthe* and *The Ironers* highlight the loneliness and isolation of life in the city, especially among the female working class.

Pushing on through history leads to the Post-Impressionists. Everyone inevitably crowds around **Vincent Van Gogh's** tormented *Portrait of the Artist* (1889). The bold colors and distorted perspective of *The Room of Van Gogh at Arles* (1889) were planned "to be suggestive of *repose* or of sleep in general...in this room with nothing but the closed shutters." The stunning *Doctor Paul Gachet* (Van Gogh's doctor) and *The Church at Auvers-sur-Oise* are two of the last works Van Gogh painted before he shot himself in the corn fields of Auvers-sur-Oise on July 29, 1890. Meanwhile, **Paul Cézanne,** preoccupied bythe relations of form, space, and color, painted his famous still-lifes, portraits, and landscapes, experimenting with soft colors and broken-down geometric planes that would open the door to cubism. Compare his *Woman and the Coffeepot* (1890-1895) to Van Gogh's *l'Italienne* (1887) for an understanding of the radically different approaches these two contemporaries fostered.

As you're leaving this area, just past the café, don't to miss the pastels displayed in a special, darkly lit room. Inside, the strange creations of **Odilon Redon,** yet another queer-potato student of Rodolphe Bresdin, represent a unique strain of mysticism among his more conventional contemporaries. His *Bouquet of Wildflowers* (1912) glows against the brown paper on which it is drawn, while his *Bouddha* (c. 1905) captures the spirit of Eastern art far more than any of the Orientalist works downstairs.

Moving into the north wing, you arrive at the chaos of the late 19th-century avant-garde. Pointillists like **Paul Signac** and **Georges Seurat** strayed from their Impressionist beginnings to a theory of painting based on tiny dots—a proto-version of the TV-screen. **Henri de Toulouse-Lautrec** left his aristocratic family background behind to paint the dancers and prostitutes who alone accepted his physical deformity. **Paul Gauguin's** *chef d'oeuvre, La belle Angèle* (The Beautiful Angel) (1889) pictures the title figure—a Breton peasant woman—in a circle reminiscent of Japanese art, amid the flattened objects and pure colors that have become his signature style.

On the way down the middle floor, swing through the **Passage of the Press,** showing the development of newspapers in the 19th century. **The Passage of Dates** highlights important events between 1848-1914, placing all of this art in its historical context.

Middle Level: Belle Epoque and Art Nouveau

After taking you through the ornate Neo-Rococo **Salle des Fêtes,** once the elegant ballroom of the Hôtel d'Orsay, the middle level displays late 19th-century sculpture, painting, and decorative arts. Wander through several decades of sculpture on the balcony. A display on **Salon painting** from 1880-1900 shows what was going on in the official world, while Impressionists were gaining their separate victories away from the Academy. (Most of the world's art museums display only the Impressionists and not their traditionalist rivals, depriving viewers of the chance to see why the Impressionists were so revolutionary.) Naturalism that carried an almost photographic realism, as in **Jules Bastien-Lapage's** *The Hay* (1877), was one of the most favored forms of art under the Third Republic. The regime gloried in the authentic depictions of peasant and country life; paintings like Léon Lhermitte's *Payment of the Harvesters* (1882) gave a dignity and nobility to the workers of rural France. Other artists tried to depict Biblical and historical scenes in the heroic tradition of David (see Louvre) but their attempts seem archaic in comparison with the bold techniques and attention to real life upstairs.

Even if you're utterly museum-exhausted at this point, don't miss a walk through the furniture, lamps, and general extravaganza of the whimsical *art nouveau* displays. Finally, walk forward into the 20th century, with brilliantly colored works by the Nabis artists, as well as the more familiar paintings by **Henri Matisse** (1861-1954) and **Gustav Klimt** (1862-1918). And, providing perhaps the clearest tie to our own age, end your tour with the fascinating "Birth of Cinema" display.

Practical Information

Feeling exhausted? Experiencing complete sensory overload? Try going to the museum early, leaving to explore the seventh *arrondissement,* and coming back later in the afternoon (keep your ticket stub and they'll let you right in). For a break while you're inside, unwind in the **Café des Hauteurs,** nestled artistically behind one of the train station's huge iron clocks. The adjoining balcony offers a beautiful view of the Seine and Right Bank across the huge stone figures that decorate the *gare's* façade. Climbing the stairs next to the café leads to the **Salle de consultation** (documentation room). Serene and usually uncrowded, the *salle* has books about many of the featured artists and the official guide book on hand for consultation. You can watch videos (of varying length) about different artists and their work. Remarkable computer terminals provide on-line access to information about any artist or painting, complete with video replica. Downstairs, browse in the **bookstore,** which offers excellent reproductions and postcards, as well as every 19th-century art book imaginable. (Open Tues.-Wed. and Fri.-Sun. 9:30am-6:30pm, Thurs. 9:30am-9:30pm.)

Contrary to what you might expect, the food at the **Restaurant du palais d'Orsay** (tel. 45 49 42 33), on the middle floor, is both good and affordable. Dining in the exquisite white and gold *salle à manger* underneath the ceiling decorated with the days and seasons by Gabriel Ferrier (1847-1914) isn't exactly a hardship either. *Formule rapide* at 69F provides all-you-can-eat access to the bottomless buffet table and a dessert (pay the extra money for the magnificent *profiterolles*). (Open Tues.-Sun. 11:30am-2:30pm, Thurs. 7-9:30; Open Tues.-Sun. as a *salon de thé* 4-5:30pm.)

Guided tours, which leave from the group reception desk, highlight the major artistic currents, and discuss certain paintings in more detail. (Tues.-Sat. 11:30am, Thurs. also at 7pm; in summer, additional tour at 2pm.) Inquire at the information desk for all details. (90 min., 30F.) Other tours are offered exclusively in French: a *visite stylistique* (Tues.-Fri. 12:15pm, 90min., 30F) showcases one stylistic feature of a school of art; a *visite monographique* (Tues.-Fri. 2pm, 90min., 30F) focuses on the life and work of one artist; *une oeuvre à voir* (Tues.-Fri. 12:30pm, 60min., 20F) provides an in-depth discussion of one work and its place within an artist's career. The booklet *Nouvelles du Musée d'Orsay,* available for free from the info desk, gives all the details about current tours, conferences, debates, concerts, and temporary exhibits. (Museum open June 20-Sept. 20 Tues.-Wed. and Fri.-Sun. 9am-6pm, Thurs. 9am-9:30pm; Sept 21-June19 Tues.-Wed. and Fri.-Sat. 10am-6pm, Thurs. 10am-9:45pm, Sun. 9am-6pm. Last tickets sold 5:15pm, Thurs. 9pm. Admission 31F, ages 18-25, over 60, and all on Sun. 16F, under 18 free. Wheelchair and stroller accessible. Nursery for kids ages 1-6 July 1-Aug. 30 Tues.-Sun. 10:30am-5pm; April 19-Dec. 27 Sun. 10:30am-5pm. Payment required.)

Centre Pompidou

Often referred to as the Palais Beaubourg, the Centre National d'Art et de Culture Georges-Pompidou, 4ème (tel. 42 77 12 33; 42 77 11 12 for recorded information in French on the week's events) has inspired architectural controversy ever since its inauguration in 1977. (Mo. Rambuteau, Hôtel de Ville, or Chatelet-Les Halles. Wheelchair accessible: enter through the back on rue Beaubourg.) Chosen from 681 competing designs, Richard Rogers and Renzo Piano's dazzlingly shameless building-turned-inside-out bares its circulatory system to all passers-by. Piping and ventilation ducts in various colors run up, down, and sideways along the outside (blue for air, green for water, yellow for electricity, red for heating). Framing the structure like a cage are the huge steel bars supporting all of the building's weight. Apart from its aesthetic shock value, this inside-out architecture has the advantage of creating enormous flexibility of interior design: each floor is a plateau of 7,500 square meters, unencumbered by any need for supporting walls or circulatory ducts. Rogers and Piano have achieved the ultimate goal of Gothic architects: function has become design.

The Pompidou Center attracts more visitors per year than any other museum or monument in France—more than Versailles, and more than the Louvre and the Eiffel Tower combined. The views from the escalator (bolted to the building's façade) and from the fifth-floor terrace are as dizzying as from the Arche de la Défense, but without the cost. An English-language tour of the building leaves every day at 4pm (50F, under 26 25F).

The Musée National d'Art Moderne, the center's main attraction, houses a rich selection of 20th-century art, from the Fauves and Cubists to Pop and conceptual art. The captioning leaves something to be desired, and not everything is translated into English. The entrance to the museum is on the fourth floor, which is particularly strong on modernism: Matisse, Derain, Picasso, Magritte, Braque, and Kandinsky. Three terraces display sculptures by Miró, Tinguely, Ernst, and Calder. Don't miss the penguin who looks as though he's preaching a sermon to his vastly diverse audience. The lower level of the museum (which can only be reached by a small escalator from the floor above) houses works from 1960 to the present. To reflect current developments in the art world, the museum frequently modifies this display. In addition to the permanent collections of the Musée National d'Art Moderne, the Pompidou Center has temporary display areas on the *rez-de-chaussee,* the mezzanine and the fifth floor. (Open Mon. and Wed.-Fri. noon-10pm, Sat.-Sun. 10am-10pm. Admission 28F, under 26 18F, under

18 free, Sun. 10am-2pm free. Prices for temporary exhibits varies with show. Buy your tickets downstairs; they are not available at the museum entrance.)

Most visitors are unaware that displaying art is only one of the four functions of the Centre Pompidou. The **Bibliothèque Publique d'Information** (tel. 42 77 12 33), a free, non-circulating library, is open to anyone who walks in (entrance on the second floor). The computerized card catalog and large holdings (including many English books) make this a place where you can do serious research. But that's not all: there are video and microfiche facilities, a computer room, a lounge with newspapers from around the world, a stereo center, and a language lab. Creative use is made of the little rooms scattered through the library: you may be able to catch a debate on women's issues, or see a video movie about Dire Straits or La Traviata. Twenty photocopiers are available, charging 50 centimes per copy. To avoid crowds, come before 2pm or after 7pm. (Open Mon. and Wed.-Fri. noon-10pm, Sat.-Sun. 10am-10pm.) The third permanent department of the center, the **Centre de Creation Industrielle (CCI),** studies the relationships between humanity, architecture, and technology. Although the resources of the center are closed to the public, its gallery is open to visitors for 16F. Finally, the **Institut de la Recherche et de la Coordination Accoustique/Musique (IRCAM)** is an institute of musical research housed (appropriately enough) next to the Stravinsky fountain. Except in summer, the institute organizes concerts: for inquiries, call 42 60 94 27. The director of the institute is composer/conductor Pierre Boulez.

While you're there, move up to the fifth floor for coffee or a meal. The Pompidou restaurant offers two courses plus a drink and a dazzling view for 95F and coffee for 9F. The cafeteria has lighter fare, including excellent tarts: for 54F you get a little pizza, a tart, and a drink (but not the view). (Restaurant and café open Mon., Wed.-Thurs., and Sun. noon-3pm, Fri.-Sat. noon-3pm and 7-11:30pm. Tea and ice cream service available in the restaurant Wed.-Mon. noon-6:30pm.) For those low on time and money, look for a self-service part of the restaurant, to the left of the cafeteria counter. (Open Mon.-Fri. 1:30-2:40pm and 6:20-9pm, Sat.-Sun. 1-3pm and 6:20-9pm.)

Musée Rodin

The Musée Rodin, 77, rue de Varenne, 7*ème* (tel. 47 05 01 34; Mo. Varenne), located both inside and outside the elegant 18th-century Hôtel Biron, highlights the work of France's greatest sculptor. During his lifetime, Auguste Rodin (1840-1917) was among the country's most controversial artists, classified by many as sculpture's Impressionist (Monet was a close friend and admirer); today, almost all acknowledge him as the father of modern sculpture. Born in a working-class district of Paris, Rodin began study at the Petite Ecole, a trade school, of sorts, for technical drawing. He tried three times to get into the famous Ecole de Beaux-Arts, and failed each time, on the basis of his far-from-academic sculptures. Frequenting the Louvre to study Classical sculpture, he later began work as an ornamental carver, eventually setting up a small studio of his own. His travels away from Paris allowed him to articulate a definitive, powerful style, completely unlike the flowery academic style then in vogue. One of his first major pieces, *The Age of Bronze* (1875), was so anatomically perfect that he was accused of molding it directly from the body. While working at the Sèvres Factory in decoration, he sculpted *St. John the Baptist Preaching* (1877), now in the lobby of the museum as you enter. The saint is in full stride, mouth open, body perfect, a purposeful air to his carefully sculpted hands. The plaster version was only given an honorable mention from a panel of judges at the Salon of 1880. But his work gained recognition.

As you wind through the *hôtel,* take advantage of the placement of the statues to study them from all sides. Rodin's training in drawing is evident everywhere: as he said, "my sculpture is but drawing in three dimensions." Fascinated by drama and movement, Rodin believed that "beauty in art is solely expressive truth," that honesty of representation and not necessarily ideal form should be the artist's goal. The first room casts some doubt on Rodin's reputation as a misogynist—the care put into the completely endearing expression of *Young Woman in a Flowered Hat* (1865-70) cannot be ignored. *The Hand of God* (902), holding an embracing couple, conveys a holy aura of creation. In *The Kiss* (1888-98), Rodin contrasts the smoothness of the figures with the roughness of the base and surrounding material to emphasize the emergence of form from marble—and to express the power and mystery of erotic love. In Rodin's later work, the contrast between smooth and rough becomes even more powerful: in *Mother and Dying Daughter* (1910), the rough texture of the hair and clothing dominates the figures to the point where smooth features, and thus life, barely remain.

In addition to temporary exhibits in the small building to the right upon entering, the museum has several expressive works by Camille Claudel, Rodin's muse, model, student, collaborator, and lover. Her *Chatterers,* in onyx and bronze, shows a scene in which even the benches on which the figures are seated lean in to hear the gossip.

The pleasant **garden,** sprinkled with sculptures and fountains, is a whole museum unto itself. If you're short on time or money (or just want to avoid the crowds of people inside), consider paying the smaller admission fee for the grounds only. You won't miss the stars of the collection: just inside the gates sits Rodin's most famous work, *The Thinker* (1880-1904). Some say this is Dante contemplating his *Inferno;* others insist it is any man pondering his existence. Either way, the tautness of the musculature, the intensity of the facial concentration, and the tension of coiled energy present a remarkable portrait of a man actively engaged in thinking. *Balzac* (1891-1897), behind *The Thinker* was commissioned in 1891 (41 years after the writer's death) by the Société des Gens de Lettres, but a battle royal over Rodin's design and his inability to meet their deadlines raged for years. (At one point the Société demanded, rather ridiculously, that Rodin deliver the statue within 24 hours.) Unlike the portrait the Société expected, the finished product shows a dramatic, haunted artist—a personification of genius, whose hollow eyes have a visionary quality. But the plasticity of the body and the distortion of the author's well-known face enraged countless artists and non-artists. Rodin cancelled the commission and kept the statue for himself, claiming proudly, "I have the formal wish to remain the sole owner of my work." Later in his life, he noted, "Nothing which I made satisfied me as much, because nothing had cost me as much; nothing else sums up so profoundly that which I believe to be the secret law of my art."

On the other side of the garden, the stunning *Burghers of Calais* (1884-1895) somberly recreates a near-tragic moment in the Hundred Years War, recorded in Froissart's *Chronicles.* In 1347, when Calais was starved into surrender after courageous resistance, England's King Edward III offered to spare the lives of the inhabitants if the keys to the city were brought to him by six burghers (prominent citizens), wearing the nooses which would hang them. The burghers agreed, and their heroism prompted the impassioned and successful intervention of Edward's pregnant queen, Philippine. The city of Calais had asked Rodin for a monument to Eustache de Saint-Pierre, the first burgher to volunteer his life. Rodin chose instead to depict all six, including Saint-Pierre, the bearded man in the center. The fascination of the work lies in the group's collective anguish and determination, despite the very different emotions recorded by each individual. They march inexorably onward on contorted feet, ropes around their necks, keys weighing heavily on their oversized hands (created by Claudel). Each face bears its own reaction to its destiny—from fear and desperation to stoic pride.

Beyond The Burghers of Calais stands Rodin's largest and most intricate sculpture, *The Gates of Hell* (1880-90). What you see is actually a prepatory model, planned as the portal to the then-soon-to-be-built Musée des Arts Decoratifs. The statue was never completed in its planned immensity; the planned site for the museum was used instead for the Gare d'Orsay—which, ironically, has become today the Musée d'Orsay. Among the 186 figures decorating the unopenable Gates of Hell are small versions of Rodin's most famous sculptures, many of them designed originally as studies for this portal. *The Thinker* contemplates the chaos from above while *Adam and Eve* flank the door. Lovers snatch *The Kiss* while *The Old Courtesan* sits looking impossibly wretched. Below, the man falling off the upper left ledge is the anguished figure of Ugolino, about to devour his own children. Inspired by Dante's Divine Comedy and conceived as a counterpart to Ghiberti's *Gates of Paradise* in Florence, Rodin's model shows the torment of the human condition in all of its chaos, meaninglessness, and sensuality. If you're hungry, grab a bite at the cafeteria (quiche 32F, buffet plate 30F). (Museum open Tues.-Sun. 10am-5:45pm; Oct.-March Tues.-Sun. 10am-5pm. Last admission ½hr. before closing. Admission to museum and park 21F, students, seniors, under 18, and Sun. 11F. Park open Tues.-Sun. 10am-7:45pm; April-June and Sept. 10am-5:30pm; Oct.-March 10am-4:45pm. Last admission ½hr. before closing. Admission to park alone 4F. Cafeteria closes 15min. before park.)

Hooked on Rodin's sculpture? Take the RER out to the smaller Musée Rodin, 19, av. Auguste Rodin (tel. 45 34 13 09) in **Meudon.** The "country" house where Rodin spent the final years of his life now contains most of his minor works and the plaster models for The Thinker, The Gates of Hell, The Burghers of Calais, and his other major bronze casts. In the garden, The Thinker sits contemplatively above the tombs of Rodin and his wife, Rose Beurat (the model for *Young Woman in a Flowered Hat,* whom he married the year of her death—after 53 years of cohabitation). (Open Sat.-Sun. 1:30-6:30pm. Admission 12F, students 10F.) (RER line C to Meudon-val-Fleury. Be sure to take a train that stops at all stations; some express trains zoom right by.)

The Invalides Museums

The Invalides complex guards a series of museums, revolving around French history and above all, France's martial glory. (Mo. Invalides, Latour-Maubourg, or Varennes. Also see Sights—Seventh Arrondissement.)

Pacifists beware! The **Musée de l'Armée** (tel. Mon.-Fri. 45 55 37 70; Sat.-Sun. and holidays 45 55 37 68) celebrates centuries of French military history. The main entry, on the east side (to the left as you enter) is located in the middle of the ground floor exhibit. Don't miss the line-up of bronze Napoleonic eagles, all looking very brave and Roman. One particularly stalwart eagle has a BIG HOLE in his breast and is proudly entitled, *"Aigle Blessée"* (Wounded Eagle). As you cross the gallery, and the line-up of eagle heros, ask for an English brochure at the coat room (all labels are in French). If you like, grab a free afternoon war documentary at the cinema (tel. 45 55 37 70). Otherwise head upstairs to rooms full of documents, weapons, and military leaders gazing down from the walls all-knowingly. The first room on the right contains one of the few condemnations of war in the entire Invalides complex—copies of Jacques Callot's (1592-1635) finely crafted engravings about the Thirty Years War, aptly named *Les Misères et les Malheurs de la Guerre* (The Miseries and Misfortunes of War).

The east side of the museum inevitably culminates in the First Empire exhibit on the second floor. See Napoleon's sword, his death mask, his charger Le Vizir (stuffed and branded with an N), a recreation of his death room, and the big files that he kept on enemy armies, whose accompanying tiny pieces eerily resemble those in the game Risk.

If Napoleon reigns over the East Wing, it is his successor (reincarnation?), Charles de Gaulle who looms large over the west side's 20th-century exhibits. Electronic maps trace troop movements during the First and Second World Wars. The General's *képi,* letters, and exhortations to his fellow citizens from London join an elaborate model of one of the D-Day beaches. The incongruity of peppy martial music floating over numerous swastikas—on flags, hats, and documents—and pictures of work camps can be nauseating. Escape by leaving, or go upstairs to the temporary location of the **Musée des Plans-Reliefs,** a collection of a hundred models of fortified cities, some of them enormous. As military historian Alistair Horne has pointed out, "from Vauban's day [as military engineer under Louis XIV] until the Maginot Line, the French have been unrivalled in the building of fortifications." Spanning the period from 1668 to 1870, the exhibit is a one-of-a-kind, of considerable architectural and urban-planning interest.

The same ticket admits you to **Napoleon's Tomb,** lovingly placed under Jules Hardouin-Mansart's royal dome. A painting of God giving St. Louis the sword to slay the infidels adorns the inside of the dome, below which are portraits of the four Evangelists, the twelve apostles, and twelve kings of France. Six chapels dedicated to different saints lie off the main room, sheltering the tombs of Famous French Marshals—Foch, Lyautey (extravagantly eulogized as "creator of Morocco"), and Turenne, famous imperial Bonaparte brothers—Joseph (king of Spain) and Jerome (king of Westphalia and once governor of the Invalides), and the hearts of Vauban and La Tour d'Auvergne.

Finished in 1861, Napoleon's tomb itself is actually six concentric coffins, made of materials ranging from mahogany to lead. If that weren't enough, the tomb is placed on the lower level and viewed first from a round balcony above, forcing everyone who visits to bow down to the emperor even in his death. This riot of bombast delighted Adolf Hitler on his visit to Paris in 1940. You can actually approach the sacred sarcophagus by descending the stairs beside the baldachino, an impressive rip-off of the Bernini masterpiece in the Vatican. Over the entryway, an inscription records the last line of Napoleon's will: "I wish that my ashes repose on the shores of the Seine, in the midst of the French people whom I have so loved." Twelve sculpted figures stand watch over the tomb, each representing one of Napoleon's campaigns. Names of significant battles are engraved in the marble surrounding the coffins—note Waterloo's absence. Ten bas-reliefs recall the institutional reforms of law, education, and the like under Napoleon, who is depicted wearing that most typical French attire: a toga and laurels. The Roi de Rome, Napoleon's son, is buried at his feet. Bring a 5F coin to the Tomb for a 5-minute recorded explanation in English.

On our way out, peer across the glass partition into the **Eglise St-Louis des Invalides,** also known as the Eglise des Soldats. Berlioz's Requiem was first played on this organ. Famous standards (battle flags) have always decorated the church, although the collection was depleted when the *hôtel's* governor burned 1400 of them upon learning of the enemy arrival in Paris on March 30, 1814.

To get the most out of any visit to the Invalides, invest in a 38F guide to the dome, tomb, and *hôtel* at the gift shop (to the left if you enter by av. de Tourville). (Musée de l'Armée open daily 10am-6pm; Oct.-March 10am-5pm. Napoleon's Tomb open daily 10am-7pm; Sept. and April-May 10am-6pm; Oct.-March 10am-5pm. Eglise des Soldats open daily, in theory, 10am-6pm; Oct.-March 10am-5pm.) Last admission ½hr. before closing. Admission 30F, reduced 20F. Ticket valid for 2 days, admitting you to the tomb, the church, the Musée de l'Armée, and the Musée des Plans Reliefs. Visit the Musée de l'Armée twice but the tomb, like heaven, is only entered once.)

The Hôtel des Invalides also houses the (completely unrelated) **Musée de l'Histoire Contemporaine** (tel. 45 55 38 39). M. et Mme. Henri Leblanc decided in 1914 to create a library and museum to hold documents about the history of the unfolding world war. Their humble efforts grew into the Bibliothèque de Documentation Internationale Contemporaine, located in Nanterre. The three-room museum mounts two temporary exhibits per year (March-June and Oct.-Dec.) using posters, magazines, pictures, and other documents from the library to probe recent history. Most of the posters and all of the labels are in French, but the visual nature of the exhibits helps transcend the language barrier, as does the general enthusiasm of the staff. Sharpen your political analysis and your French—the exhibits are meant to engage you and the staff is eager to hear your opinions, reactions, or questions. "La Course au Moderne" about the modernization of France and Germany in the interwar period opens in October of 1992; "Femmes photographes dans la guerre" (Female Photographers in Wartime) opens in March 1993. (Open, when exhibit is on, Tues.-Sat. 10am-1pm and 2-5:30pm, Sun. 2-5:30pm. Admission 20F, students and seniors 19F.)

One of the least celebrated, but most worthwhile parts of the Invalides is the **Musée de l'Ordre de la Libération,** 51bis, bd. de Latour-Maubourg (tel. 47 01 35 15). This museum conveys the pathos of World War II just as surely as the Musée de l'Armée fails to do so. Charles de Gaulle founded the order on November 16, 1940 to recognize civilian and military organizations and individuals, as well as cities that had distinguished themselves in the liberation of France and its Empire. Quiet and uncrowded, the museum tells the story of those who fought for the liberation of France, believing, like de Gaulle, Grandmaster of the Order, that although France had lost a battle, she had not lost the war. Linger over well-labeled cases of the General's letters and speeches, among them his response to an arrest notice from the French government: "I would be obliged if you would tell those who sent it that their communication presents, in my eyes, absolutely nothing of interest." Beyond the room dedicated to "the man of June 1940," full of his medals and possessions, lie tributes to the fighters of Free France. Their flightbooks and false passes present telling reminders of how they lived. The South Gallery salutes those who fought for liberation from within. Like de Gaulle's *Médaille de Résistance,* the display recognizes the "remarkable acts of faith and courage" in France and abroad that contributed to the French Resistance. Samples of machinery sabotaged by the Resistance stand chillingly close to Nazi diagrams depicting, so far as they knew, Resistance organization. Scrawlings believed to be Hitler's notes from a meeting with Chamberlain (Hitler was considering an alliance with the English for a while), next to the ever-popular swastika cookie-cutter, recall an all-too-real past. Many of the objects in the museum are accompanied by letters from the donors, creating a personal, as well as a national, context. The staircase and upstairs gallery, dealing with deportation, present by far the most devastating message. *"N'oubliez jamais!"* (Never Forget) cries the newspaper article next to the heartbreaking picture of a five-year-old girl, in concentration camp uniform, clinging to her teddy-bear. Guarded by two weeping angels, the exhibit juxtaposes forbidden journals and prisoner drawings with camp uniforms and instruments of torture, in an attempt to capture the mental and physical horror endured by so many. (Open Mon.-Sat. 2-5pm. Admission 10F.)

Musée de Cluny

The Hôtel de Cluny, 6, pl. Paul-Painlevé, 5ème (tel. 43 25 62 00; Mo. Cluny-La Sorbonne), not only houses one of the world's finest collections of medieval art, jewelry, and tapestries, but is itself a perfectly preserved medieval manor, built on top of restored Roman ruins. In the 3rd century, Romans built a complex configuration of *Thermae* (baths), a *frigidarium* (storage room), and houses on this site. After World War II, careful excavations directed by Paul-Marie Duval uncovered the ruins, which were then incorporated into the 15th-century mansion that had been built on the spot. The 1300-year gap between the architectural periods is particularly evident as you pass through the medieval courtyard and museum entry, replete with pointed arches and a cobblestone courtyard, into the Roman baths, Rooms IX and X, possessing grand spaces sparsely decorated with capitals and sarcophagi. Most of the building dates from the 1480s and 90s, when it was built for the Order of Cluny, a religious order then led by the powerful Amboise family, whose fondness for Italian forms is evident in their home. The house was converted to a museum in the 1850s, when restorers added some windows, marring the symmetry of the architecture.

Most visitors to the museum rush right upstairs to Room XIII on the second floor to gawk at the *Lady and Unicorn* cycle, consisting of six oversize tapestries dating from the end of the 15th century. Jean Le Viste, a merchant aiming at knighthood, commissioned the works. His upwardly mobile desires are revealed by the sprinkling of his would-be three-crescent coat of arms on all the tapestries. While the unicorn (resembling more a large white golden retriever than a horse) remains unexplained, art historians agree that five of the tapestries depict the senses. The sixth tapestry, *My Only Desire,* shows the Lady giving up her jewelry, or overcoming her worldly senses, for her lover. Le Viste hoped to show that he was a wise and self-controlled man, ready to sacrifice all for his king, and worthy of social promotion. But the real beauty of these tapestries comes from their rich portrayal of the Lady's garments, and the subdued color scheme that time has given them.

Upstairs you'll find an entire room (Room XVI) devoted to medieval royal jewelry and crowns. The gold rush continues down the corridor in Room XIX, with an enormously rare and valuable gold altarpiece, a finely worked ornament from Basel, Switzerland. Those longing to show the bygone years of knighthood and chivalry will love Room XXV, packed with sets of armor, shields, and swords; the rare display of iron chastity belts once proudly exhibited by the museum has, unfortunately, been removed. Downstairs, the *Galerie des Rois,* Room VII, proudly displays a set of 21 stone heads of Judean and Israelite kings, dating from 1210 to 1230. These heads (attached to statues) sat atop Notre-Dame's portals until the revolutionaries of 1793 separated them from their bodies, mistaking them for statues of the French kings. Found in 1978 in the bowels of the Banque Française du Commerce Exterieur, which was undergoing renovations at the time, the royal heads were moved to the Cluny while copies were made to once again complete the façade of Notre Dame. David's head still sports traces of red paint on his lips and cheeks—proof that at one time the cathedral's entire façade was brightly painted. Just down the hall, Room VI glows with colorful light from its eye-level display of medieval stained glass, including some of the original windows that adorned Ste-Chapelle. On Friday afternoons, the museum sponsors concerts of medieval chamber music performed on original instruments. (Fri. at 1pm—call ahead to confirm the time. Free with admission to the museum. Open Wed.-Mon. 9:30am-5:15pm. Admission 17F, students and Sun. 9F.)

La Villette

La Villette, 19ème (Mo. Porte de la Villette or Porte de Pantin), is a highly succesful urban renewal project in the northeastern corner of Paris. Its 55 hectares enclose a huge science museum, a landscaped park, and an Omnimax cinema. Previously the area had been home to a nationalized meat market-*cum*-slaughterhouse compound that provided most of Paris's beef. With the advent of refrigerated transport in 1969, it became more economical to kill cattle in the countryside and deliver the meat directly to butchers; the government closed down the La Villette slaughterhouse and market in 1974. In 1979, plans began for the new and modern La Villette that you can visit today.

The Cité des Sciences et de l'Industrie (tel. 40 05 80 00) perches on the northern end of La Villette, next to the Porte de la Villette metro stop. Inaugurated in 1985, this establishment is dedicated to making science more accessible to the lay person. It is housed in a vast building originally intended for use as an auction hall. The star attraction, located on the top two stories, is the **Explora** science museum, packed with a rich collection of interactive exhibits that can fill just about anyone with a sense of childlike wonder. Even when you know the scientific principles behind a particular display, you'll be surprised by the ingenious way it is presented. The inertial merry-go-round, on the first floor, spins you around on an axis. The voice on the public address system asks you to walk in a straight line, and you find yourself walking in an odd curved path. They ask you to throw a ball at a target, and the ball bends away from the direction you throw it in. Great fun, explained afterwards in terms of inertial frames of reference. (An English translation of what the p.a. voice is saying is pasted to the wall of the spinning chamber; there is in fact quite a lot of English throughout the museum.) Another highlight of the museum is its sophisticated optical illusions, in Sténopé (first floor) and Jeux de Lumière (second floor). The Cité-Pass ticket allows you to enter the museum's **planetarium** (second floor) as well as temporary exhibitions, the 3-D movies in the Cinéma Louis-Lumière (floor 0, tel. 40 35 79 40), and the rather modest aquarium (floor S2). (Museum open Tues.-Sun. 10am-6pm.) Floor S1 of the building houses the *médiathèque*—a multimedia, open-stack library with more than 300,000 scientific and technical works. (Open Tues.-Sun. noon-8pm. Free.)

The submarine *Argonaute,* now parked in front of the Cité, served for 25 years in the French navy until it was decommissioned in 1982. (Open Tues-Fri 10am-6pm, Sat.-Sun. 10am-7pm. Children under 3 not allowed inside.)

La Géode (tel. 40 05 80 00), the enormous mirrored sphere mounted on a water basin in front of the Cité des Sciences, will undoubtably remind you of an enormous extraterrestrial golf ball caught in a tiny water trap. The exterior is coated with 6433 polished stainless-steel triangles, which reflect every detail of the surroundings. Inside, Omnimax movies are shown on a 1000 square-meter hemispheric screen, "the largest in the world" (or so they say). Come here for tremendously exciting 3-D documentaries where you truly will feel like you're in the movies. (Showings Tues.-Sun. on the hour 10am to 9pm. There are also showings on Mondays during French school holidays; last showing at 7pm. Get your ticket early; they sell out.)

Tickets: A one-day "Cité-Pass" covers entrance to all exhibits of the museum, including the planetarium and the *Argonaute.* Passes cost 45F, under 25 35F, under 7 free. Buy tickets for Géode shows at the Géode entrance, at the level of the moat in front of the Cité. 50F, students and under 18 37F. (No reduced-price tickets between 1 and 7pm on weekends or holidays.) Combined tickets, good for admission to the museum, the submarine, and a movie at the Géode, are available only at the Géode ticket office: 85F full price, 72F reduced price. Admission to the *Argonaute* alone is 20F, ages 3-7 free.

If you're traveling with children, you may wish to leave them with other kids in the care of the Cité's innovative **children's programs.** The Inventorium (for kids 3-6) costs 15F for a 90-minute session (free for 1 or 2 accompanying adults per family). The Cité des enfants (for kids 5-12) costs 20F for a 90-minute session (no adults admitted).

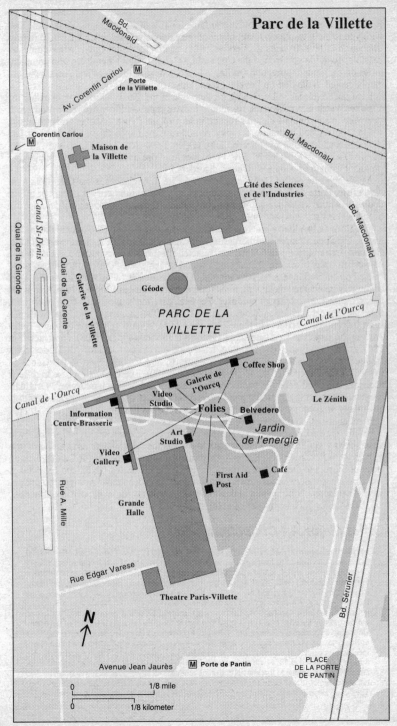

Parc de la Villette

Bd. Macdonald

Av. Corentin Cariou

M Porte de la Villette

M Corentin Cariou

Bd. Macdonald

Maison de la Villette

Cité des Sciences et de l'Industries

Bd. Macdonald

Quai de la Gironde

Canal St-Denis

Quai de la Carente

Galerie de la Villette

Géode

PARC DE LA VILLETTE

Canal de l'Ourcq

Canal de l'Ourcq

Coffee Shop

Galerie de l'Ourcq

Video Studio

Folies

Belvedere

Le Zénith

Information Centre-Brasserie

Art Studio

Jardin de l'energie

Video Gallery

First Aid Post

Café

Rue A. Mille

Grande Halle

Rue Edgar Varese

Theatre Paris-Villette

N

Avenue Jean Jaurès   M Porte de Pantin

PLACE DE LA PORTE DE PANTIN

Bd. Sérurier

0   1/8 mile
0   1/8 kilometer

Both programs are in French, but are suitable for kids of all languages. Or take the kids with you to the Explora museum; many of the exhibits will fascinate the whole family. The *vestiare* (level 0) rents strollers and wheelchairs; the entire Cité is **wheelchair**-accessible. To guide you around the Cité and La Géode (below), **headsets** with commentaries on each major attraction (in English; stand next to the sight and press a button) can be rented in the Cité on Level 0 (Tues.-Sun. 10am-5pm).

Between the Canal St-Denis and the west side of the Cité is a little marvel called the **Cinaxe.** Watch one of several 10-minute movies representing what you would see if you were in a Formula 1 car, in a rocket, in an airplane flying low over mountains, etc, while sophisticated hydraulic pumps jerk and spin the movie theater, so that you feel the curves and bumps as you see them. (Open Tues.-Sun. 11am-7pm; shows every 20min. Tickets 27F, under 18 24F. Forbidden to those under 6; not recommended to pregnant women or people with heart disorders.)

At the opposite end of La Villette from the Cité des Sciences is the **Cité de la Musique** (Mo. Porte de Pantin). At the moment only the conservatory is open, but by the end of 1994 the whole project will be completed—featuring a concert hall, a museum of musical instruments, and housing for music students.

The Parc de la Villette is a vast open area separating the two Cités, cut in the middle by the Canal de l'Ourcq and bordering the Canal St-Denis on its southwestern side. Bernard Tschumi, the park's designer, rejected the 19th-century notion of a park as a non-urban oasis of nature, attempting instead to achieve a 20th-century urban park, "based on cultural invention, education, and entertainment." Unifying this space, a set of roughly cubical red metal structures form a grid of squares 120m x 120m. Known as *folies,* they serve a variety of purposes. For example, one houses a fast-food restaurant, three are day-care centers, and one, right on Canal L'Ourcq, next to the Canal St-Denis, is an **information office.** Go there for a map of la Villette. (Open daily 10am-7pm.) Also in the park, the steel-and-glass **Grande Halle** (tel. 40 03 39 03), constructed in 1867 as the La Villette beef building, has become a cultural Jack-of-All-Trades, with frequent plays, concerts, temporary exhibitions, and movies. Next to the Canal de l'Ourcq is the **Zénith** (tel. 42 40 60 00 or 42 08 60 00), a concert hall whose high-tech acoustics and 6400-person capacity make it a favorite among rock musicians. Originally intended as a stopgap until a more permanent concert-space was built, the Zénith is essentially an enormous dome tent; the roof is made out of fabric and supported by peripheral columns, so that no internal supports block the view of the stage.

Finally, the park encompasses a number of thematic **gardens,** which you are likely to miss unless you follow the winding path known as the *"promenade cinématique"* (the map in the information office helps). Of particular interest, the Mirror Garden uses an array of mirrors to create optical illusions, while the Garden of Childhood Fears takes you through a little wooded grove resonant with spooky sounds. At night the *promenade cinématique* is lit up, and makes for quite an interesting walk. (Reasonably safe, too, because the park has plenty of security guards.)

Other Major Art Collections

Musée Marmottan, 2, rue Louis-Boilly, 16ème (tel., 42 24 07 02). Mo. La Muette. Collector Jules Marmottan purchased this hunting lodge in 1882; his son Paul, fascinated by the art and history of the Napoleonic period, turned it into a mansion and bequeathed both buildings and collections to the Académie des Beaux-Arts. Miniatures from around Europe, Empire furniture, and Italian Renaissance works are all tastefully arranged, but the Claude Monet sign outside the Musée is not there for nothing. The lower level of the museum displays roughly 100 Monet canvases, mostly donated by the artist's second son. The resulting display of blues and greens—waterlilies, reeds, willow trees by the edge of a river—make you feel as though you're at the bottom of the ocean. Unobtrusive yet effective lighting and well-placed couches enhance this effect, and you may have difficulty tearing yourself away. Of course, Mssrs. Renoir, Pissarro, and Gaugin also figure prominently. But do not miss the crown jewel of the Marmottan, *Impression: Soléil Levant* (Impression: Sunrise). Displayed in 1874 with eight other paintings, it led one critic to refer derisively to those *impressionistes,* a name Monet and his colleagues enthusiastically embraced. It was stolen in 1985 but was recently recovered in Corsica together with eight others stolen at the same time. Open Tues.-Sun. 10am-5:30pm. Admission 30F, students 15F, under 8 free.

Musée National des Arts Asiatiques (Musée Guimet), 6, pl. d'Iéna, 16ème (tel. 47 23 61 65). Mo. Iéna or Boissière. The largest collection of Asian art in the western world. Named for erudite industrialist Emile Guimet (1839-1918), traveler and collector of Japanese art, it is also one of the best organized and most peaceful of the 16th *arrondissement* museums: the benevolent smiles of Buddha, Jina, and Vishnu from around the continent welcome visitors. Admire the detail of the 19th-century model of a Burmese monastery, made out of teak wood, and the sheer breadth of Khmer art. *Midi l'Asie* (Asia Noon) is an informative conference in French focusing on some aspect of Asian culture, e.g. Sacred Mountains of India and China. Aug.-Sept. Mon. and Wed.-Thurs. 12:30-1:30pm; Oct.-July Mon. and Wed.-Fri. 12:30-1:30pm. Admission 20F. No reservation required. 90-minute conferences in French are devoted to summer-long themes July-Aug. Mon., Wed., and Thurs. 3:30-5pm. Admission 30F. Reservation required. Museum open Wed.-Mon. 9:45am-5:15pm. Admission 26F, students and seniors 14F. When temporary exposition is showing 32F, students and seniors 20F, grants admission to everything. Inquire about group visits, workshops, and concerts—activities, some free, abound. A few steps away, perched as calmly as the numerous Buddhas it houses, is the Musée Guimet's annex, the **Hôtel Heidelbach-Guimet,** 19, av. d'Iéna. Devoted to Buddhist pieces from China and Japan, some of them 14 centuries old, the Hôtel also offers a Japanese garden whose flowing water and bamboo shroud the visitor in tranquility. Open same hours as Musèe Guimet. Admission to one ensures entry to the other. Both museums are wheelchair accessible, but call ahead.

Musée d'Art Moderne de la Ville de Paris, 11. av. du Président Wilson, 16ème (tel. 47 23 61 27). Mo. Iéna. One of the world's foremost collections of 20th-century art. The permanent exhibit includes works by Matisse *(La Danse),* Picasso, Delaunay, and a piece by Thomas Schütte that looks like a few dozen black lemons on steroids and that is acually entitled *Citrons noirs.* Don't miss Niele Toroni's colored dots on the wall. Temporary exhibits display recent bizarreries of the avant-garde. Less complete and not as accessible to novices as its competitor at the Pompidou Center, this museum may not be the best place for an introduction to modern art. Open Tues. and Thurs.-Sun. 10am-5:30pm, Wed. 10am-8:30pm. Admission to permanent collection 15F, students and seniors 8F50. Admission to temporary exhibits varies, usually 20-35F, students and seniors 15-20F. Admission to all parts of the museum 40F, students and seniors 30F.

Musée de l'Orangerie, 1er (tel. 42 97 48 16). Mo. Concorde. Nestled in the southwest corner of the Tuileries, the Orangerie welcomes visitors to its small collection of Impressionist painting. Though less spectacular than the Orsay, this museum is also less crowded, so you can admire the Cezannes, Renoirs, Matisses, Picassos, and other greats in comfort. The crown jewel of the Orangerie's collection is Claude Monet's *Les Nymphéas* (The Water Lilies), occupying two rooms of the underground level. Each is paneled with four large curved murals that were created specifically for these chambers. It was on the day of the Armistice—Nov. 11, 1918—that Monet decided to give to France, like a bouquet of flowers, these paintings of the lilies in his garden at Giverny (see Near Paris). He spent the rest of his life working on them, finishing in the year of his death (1926). As a life-work, and a final summation of Impressionism, the result—a nearly abstract outburst of deep colors and swirling brushstrokes—is stunning. Open Wed.-Mon. 9:45am-5:15pm. Admission 26F, ages 18-25 and over 60 14F, Sun. 14F.

From Art Africaine to Zadkine

Musée des Arts Africains et Océaniens, 293, av. Daumesnil, 12ème (tel. 43 43 14 54), on the western edge of the Bois de Vincennes. Mo. Porte Dorée. One of Paris's best non-Western museums, housing several millennia of African and Pacific art. Particularly beautiful are the wedding dresses, jewelry, and decorated tile from the Maghrib—Morocco, Tunisia, and Algeria. Nifty displays that show that the Tunisians knew about platform soles long before Edie Sedgwick. All explanations are in French, but the historical interest transcends the language. The tropical fish aquarium downstairs is immensely popular with Parisian families and school children. The sawfish, determined to hack his way out of the tank, swims near adorable sea horses. The alligators repose lazily, oblivious to the centimes on their backs. Brightly colored fish abound, some small and swift, others fat and slow. Kids will be in heaven and big people just might enjoy watching the fishies too. Open Mon.-Fri. 10am-noon and 1:30-5:20pm, Sat.-Sun. 12:30-5:50pm. Last admission 30min. before closing. Aquarium and superb temporary exhibits open daily 10am-5:20pm. Admission to museum and aquarium 17F, students and seniors 9F, under 18 free. Combined admission with temporary exhibit 23F, students and seniors 15F, under 18 free.

Musée des Arts Décoratives, 107, rue de Rivoli, 1er (tel. 42 60 32 14). Mo. Palais Royal. Enter through a side door of the Louvre building. The definitive collection of interior decoration. Tapestries, china, paintings, and furniture from the late Middle Ages to the avant-garde fill five stories. Come here for the true meaning of "changing fashions." Admission 23F, under 25 14F, under 5 free. Open Tues.-Sat. 12:30-6pm, Sun. noon-6pm.

Musée d'Art Juif, 42, rue des Saules, 18ème (tel. 42 57 84 15). Mo. Lamarck Caumartin. On the northern face of the *butte* Montmartre, this museum is housed on the third floor of the Jewish Center. Founded after the war, the collection includes objects used during Jewish rituals, as well as an enormous model of Jerusalem. The library displays a variety of beautifully illustrated Jewish texts and a collection of works by popular artists from North Africa and Eastern Europe. Open Sun.-Thurs. 3-6pm. Closed on Jewish holidays. Admission 15F, students and children 10F.

Cristalleries Baccarat, 30-32, rue Paradis, 10ème (tel. 47 70 64 30). Mo. Gare de l'Est. The building at 30-32, rue Paradis houses both the Baccarat crystal company headquarters and the Baccarat museum (on the second floor). The building itself is impressive, built under the Directory between 1798 and 1799. Since its founding in 1764, Baccarat has become one of the most prestigious and expensive of crystal makers, patronized by kings, czars, and shahs. The museum houses an array of every imaginable crystal object, including a life-size chandelier-woman at the entrance. A tour makes a calm respite from the bustle of bd. de Strasbourg. Open Mon.-Fri. 9am-6pm and Sat. 10am-noon and 2pm-5pm. Free.

Maison de Balzac, 47, rue Raynouard, 16ème (tel. 42 24 56 38). Mo. Passy. Honoré de Balzac (1799-1850), one of France's greatest novelists, lived here from 1840-47, penning the last part of la Comédie Humaine. He was a quirky man, who denied himself the pleasure of orgasm during sex for fear that the loss of sperm would diminish his capacity to write. (After accidentally going too far one day, he exclaimed, "I lost a book this morning!") The house gives a feel for Balzac's entire life with portraits, samples of his work, and caricatures of him amid his fellow 19th-century literati. Starting in April 1993, a temporary exhibition will explore the theme of Balzac and Russia, including his Ukrainian wife. Open Tues.-Sun. 10am-5:40pm. Admission 12F, students and big families 6F50, seniors free. When temporary exhibition is showing 25F, reduced rate 18F.

Atelier-Musée Henri Bouchard, 25, rue de l'Yvette, 16ème (tel. 46 47 63 46). Mo. Jasmin. The cluttered workshop of Henri Bouchard (1875-1960), sculptor of the Palais de Chaillot's 7.5m bronze Apollo, illustrates not only his range of media (copper, plaster, clay, stone) and subjects (huge monuments, religious decoration, personal portraits), but also the complex technique involved in sculpture. Temporary 3-month exhibits in the front hallway bring out Bouchard's fascination for the ordinary, his attention to detail, and his skill at portraying human effort. The summer of 1993 will focus on women and children. Bouchard's son (who speaks English) and daughter-in-law act as exceptionally knowlegeable curators. On the first Sat. of each month at 3pm, Mme. Bouchard conducts a tour (free with admission). Open Jan. 1-March 14, April 1-June 14, July 1-Sept. 14, and Oct. 1-Dec. 14, Wed. and Sat. 2-7pm. Admission 25F, students and seniors 15F. Call about conferences on sculpting technique.

Musée Bourdelle, 16, rue Antoine Bourdelle, 15ème (tel. 45 48 67 27). Mo. Montparnasse Bienvenue. Even people who don't yet appreciate the raw aggressive style of Antoine Bourdelle (1861-1929) will become the most die-hard of fans after spending the afternoon wandering the rooms of Bourdelle's studios-turned-museum. Room after room packed with statues overwhelms the casual visitor with the sheer productivity and genius of the sculptor,a longtime friend and artistic contemporary of Rodin. The energetic and masculine Heracles the Archer, an arrow about to fly from his taut bow, conveys a power seldom witnessed in modern sculpture. Unfortunately, the lack of space, especially in the miniscule garden where the sculptures are literally piled on top of each other, makes the display crowded at best, and some of the works seem lost in the shuffle of hundreds of figures. Open Tues.-Sun. 10am-5:40pm. Admission 12F, students 6F50, Sun. free.

Musée Nissim de Camondo, 63, rue de Monceau, 8ème (tel. 45 63 26 32). Mo. Villiers or Monceau. This building tells the story not only of 18th-century decorative arts but of a family that met tragedy. Comte Moïse de Camondo built this hôtel particulier between 1911 and 1914, on the model of the Petit Trianon at Versailles, to house his exquisite collection of 18th-century furniture, paintings, tapestries, and porcelain. Camondo's will left the house to the Union des Arts Décoratifs, dedicated to the memory of his son, Nissim, who died in aerial combat in 1917. The rest of the family died at Auschwitz. On a visit in 1990, Barbara Bush—overcome by the combination of Savonnerie carpets, Sèvres porcelain, and a ravishing 1780 mahogany roll-top desk—in a rare burst of strong language exclaimed, "Isn't this the dárnedest place you ever saw?" Taking one of the 45-min. audio-guides (25F for 1, 35F for 2, available in English) or buying a 20F general explanation brochure (more detailed guide for 60F) will supplement the otherwise meager explanations. Open Wed.-Sun. 10am-noon and 2-5pm. Admission 18F, students under 25 and seniors 12F.

Musée Carnavalet, 23, rue de Sévigné, 3ème (tel. 42 72 21 13). Mo. Rivoli or Carnavalet. Housed in a 16th-century hôtel, the former residence of the Marquis de Sévigné, this is Paris's main display of its own history. Beginning with some bones and stones from prehistoric Paris, it continues with a series of paintings, engravings, and other memorabilia, arranged chronologically and telling the story of the "City o' Light" and how it came to be the world-famous capital it is today. Inside, the bloodthirsty will find plenty of gory details. The collection includes many portraits of Parisian notables whom you probably haven't heard of, but anyone familiar with Paris will enjoy the engravings and paintings of how the city used to look. Here you will find a step-by-step chronology of the French Revolution; don't miss the room that details the royal family's fate, complete with a rather graphic painting of the beheading of Marie-Antoinette. Enthusiasts of

French decorative art will appreciate the period rooms, with furniture from Louis XIV to Louis XVI styles. The museum is particularly popular with large groups of French schoolchildren and their teachers, who get in free. Current renovations will close small parts of the collection. See Sights--third *arrondissement* for comments on the museum's entrance courtyard. Open Tues.-Sun. 10am-5:40pm. Admission 16F, Sun. free. Temporary exhibits extra. Wheelchair access.

Musée Cernuschi, 7, av. Vélasquez, 8*ème*, just outside the gold-tipped gates of Parc Monceau (tel. 45 63 50 75). Mo. Villiers or Monceau. A magnificent and charmingly personable collection of Asian art is housed in a villa that belonged to Henri Cernuschi (1820-1896), a financier of Milanese descent who took off on a trans-world tour after being "affected" by the Commune. Second to the Guimet as an Asian art museum, the Cernuschi nevertheless contains some very impressive pieces. The 18th-century Japanese 3-ton, 3.5m-high bronze Buddha, seated on lotus petals, makes hand gestures symbolizing confidence and wisdom. Open Tues.-Sun. 10am-5:40pm. Admission to permanent collection 12F, reduced 6F50. When temporary exhibit on display, admission to both permanent and temporary exhibits 20F, reduced 15F.

Musée de la Chasse (Museum of Hunting), 60, rue des Archives, 3*ème*. Mo. Rambuteau. A delightful, bloodthirsty little museum about hunting, featuring exotic animal heads alongside hunting weapons from various ages and cultures. The first two floors are reasonably intriguing, with their narwhal tusks and oversize muskets. Things get really exciting on the third floor. On the right is the African room, featuring enormous stuffed animal heads, including rhinos, gorillas, and dozens of antelope, along with a number of African masks and weapons. Look out for the spear/blowpipe from the Malaysian rainforest, much more eco-friendly than any European firearm. Don't miss the beautiful antler chandelier hanging from the ceiling, or the Monet in the last room. *People who are squeamish, or who have a strong love of animals, may wish to avoid this museum. A few of the paintings of bleeding animals, and a dead cat hanging upside down on the third floor, can be a little upsetting.* Open Wed.-Mon. 10am-12:30pm and 1:30-5:30pm. Admission 25F, students 12F50, children 5F. You have to pay 10F in order to take photographs.

Musée du Cinéma Henri-Langlois, in the Palais de Chaillot, 16*ème* (tel. 45 53 74 39) Mo. Trocadéro. The history of sound and light in film starting with magic langerns and shadow theaters. Sets, costumes, scripts, and posters tell the tale of modern cinema. You can only see the Musée by 1hr. tour, however, and it is conducted in French. Open Wed.-Mon. for tours at 10am, 11am, 2pm, 3pm, and 4pm. Tours canceled if fewer than 8 people. Admission 22F, students and seniors 14F.

Musée Clemenceau, 8, rue B. Franklin, 16*ème* (tel. 45 20 53 41), through a small courtyard. Mo. Passy. The four rooms in which Georges Clemenceau (1841-1929), the mustachioed mayor of Montmartre, prime minister, *Président du Conseil,* Minister of War (1917-20), expert duellist (sword and pistol), accomplished journalist, and hero to the French people, lived for thirty-five years has not been changed since his death: the yellowed calendars are all hauntingly torn off at November 24, 1929. Explanation sheets in French or the bilingual guide point out details like the painting *Le Bloc,* done for Clemenceau by his friend Monet, or the withered bouquet of flowers given to him by a soldier at the front, the other half of which lies in his coffin, at his personal request. Other interesting details include sculptures by Rodin and Clemenceau's collection of Eastern and Greek art. The upstairs display of pictures and documents fills in *Le Tigre*'s early history. Open Tues., Thurs., Sat.-Sun., and holidays 2-5pm. Admission 20F, students and seniors 12F.

Musée des Collections Historiques de la Préfecture de la Police, 1bis, rue des Carmes, second floor, 5*ème* (tel. 43 29 21 57). Mo. Maubert-Mutualité. Founded in 1909, this one-room gallery is devoted to the preservation of police paraphernalia, both the curious and the mundane. Guarded by a group of hauntingly life-like wax *flics*, the cases protect an extraordinary number of wholly uninteresting writs and warrants, as well as a goodly number of police awards and metals. More interesting are the two cases of exotic weaponry, including a number of rather harmonica-like 6- and 8-barreled guns; what they lack in accuracy they make up in sheer number of simultaneous shots fired. Near the weapons the museum proudly displays a Revolutionary-era guillotine, along with a 15cm stuffed doll tied and prepared to undergo the guillotine treatment. You can also peruse bounteous cuffs, including a ghastly 2kg iron neck- and handcuff combination. While the museum is mostly a favorite with retired officers visiting Paris from the provinces, it can be an amusing diversion for anyone, especially since it's free. Open Mon.-Fri. 9:30am-4:30pm. Free.

Musée Cognacq-Jay, 8, rue Elzevir, 3*ème* (tel. 42 74 33 66). Mo. St-Paul, Chemin Vert or Rambuteau. The city of Paris acquired this collection of Enlightenment art, which belonged to Ernest Cognacq and his wife, Marie-Louise Jay, upon the death of M. Cognacq in 1929. Since 1990, the museum has been housed in the 16th-century Hôtel Denon. Highlights include works by Watteau, Tiepolo, and Canaletto. Works are grouped together in a natural and uncrowded manner, combining furniture and paintings to produce a "total" picture of a wealthy 18th-century household. People don't seem to have caught up with this museum's new location: you won't have to contend with the overcrowding of the Louvre. Open Tues.-Sun. 10am-5:40pm. Admission 12F.

Musée de Contrefaçon (the Counterfeit Museum), 8, rue de la Faisanderie, 16*ème* (tel. 45 01 51 11). Mo. Porte Dauphine. I can't see the difference. Can you see the difference? Is there a difference? You will ask these questions about the assembled bottles, logos, hand bags and their illegal counterfeits for about two minutes. Wow, you'll think. Obviously these people didn't get in to those college plagiarism lectures. Then you'll ask: Who cares? Absence of brochures and insufficient labeling turns what could have been a novel presentation into a trivial look-but-don't-buy garage sale. Open Mon. and Wed. 2-4:30, Fri. 9:30-noon. Free.

Musée Salvador Dalí (Espace Montmartre), 11, rue Poulbot, 18ème (42 64 40 10). Mo. Anvers, Blanche, or Pigalle. Right off pl. du Tertre, on the rue Poulbot, this space dedicated to the "Phantasmic world of Salvador Dalí" is chock full of drawings and sculptures by the Spanish surrealist. Don't miss the bronze sculptures of the famous droopy clocks, expressing the fluidity and irregularity of time. Other works include drawings of the costumes designed by Picasso for the Manuel de Falla ballet, *El Sombrero de Tres Picos* (The Three-pointed Hat) and several sculptural versions of the *Cabinet Anthropomosphique,* or the human body as a collection of empty half-open drawers. The museum is well laid out, with interesting lighting and slightly ridiculous "space-music" in the background. Good explanations of the often disconcerting works. Open daily April-Sept. 10am-10pm, Oct-March 10am-7pm. Admission 35F, students 25F.

Musée Delacroix, 6, rue Furstenberg, 6ème (tel. 43 54 04 87). Mo. St-Germain-des-Prés. This small museum, located in Eugène Delacroix's house and studio, contains works spanning the duration of the painter's highly productive career. Delacroix (1799-1863) was one of the leaders of French Romanticism—the fine arts counterpart of Victor Hugo. Some works by Delacroix's friend and contemporary Pierre Guerin are also displayed, though Guerin's heavy-handed Neoclassicism possibly detracts more than adds to this otherwise delightful museum. Open Wed.-Mon. 9:45am-5pm. Admission 12F, students 7F, under 18 free.

Musée des Egouts de Paris (Museum of the Sewers of Paris), actually inside the sewers, at the corner of the quai d'Orsay and pl. de la Résistance, 7ème (tel. 47 05 10 29). Mo. Pont de l'Alma. This unique (to say the least) museum details the history of the City of Light's fascinating subterranean avenues. In *Les Misérables,* Victor Hugo wrote, "Paris has beneath it another Paris, a Paris of sewers, which has its own streets, squares, lanes, arteries, and circulation." "It's a city beneath a city," screams the exhibit at the museum. Both are right. Each Parisian street over 20m wide has at least one sewer tunnel beneath it. More than 2000km of gravitational galleries, all visitable, wind beneath the city—if you stretched out the entire network, it would reach Istanbul. Aside from taking you over countless gallons of very smelly rushing water, a visit to the *égouts* exposes you to machinery used to "clean" the sewers—like the massive, Indiana-Jones-esque ball, slightly smaller than the pipes, used to roll the grit along. The actual museum exhibit filters through Parisian sewage from the days of Lutetia when the Roman Arcueil Aqueduct brought 1500 cubic meters of water to the town daily, up until 1989, when 800,000 cubic meters were pumped into Paris daily and 26,000 manholes dotted the city. In English, French, German, and Spanish, the display tells of the advances made after Napoleon asked a doctor what he could do for Paris and was told *"Donnez-lui de l'eau"* (Give her water). M. Bruneseau plotted the entire existing system of sewers and drains; an engineer, M. Duleau, developed the network of vaulted sewers. The cholera epidemic of 1832 reminded all that waste levels and water contamination were reaching intolerably high levels. By the mid-19th century, balls of methane 1m in diameter were bubbling out of the Seine, forcing the wealthy to move away from the river because of the awful smell. Napoleon III hired an engineer, M. Belgran, to take charge of water supply and treatment. His sewer cleaning techniques—boat and wagon valves, pump batteries, and gravity sewers—are still used today. The brochure and thorough historical panels explain the sewer sights well, but a guided tour with a real live *égoutier* (sewer worker) brings the place to life. These are organized informally throughout the year—if enough people are present, a tour is started. Although the tours are not as gross as one might imagine, the odor is quite powerful. During the summer, students make foreign-language tours available to visitors. Ask at the *caisse* about guided visits or call ahead. At the end of the visit, catch the narrated French slide show about sewer history and don't miss the display of decorated toilet seats. You can even use their toilet, where your waste will have a minimal distance to travel. Open Sat.-Wed. 11am-6pm; winter Sat.-Wed. 11am-5pm. Last ticket sold 1hr. before closing. Admission 22F, students and under 10 17F. Closed for 3 weeks in Jan. for maintenance.

Musée d'Ennery, 59, av. Foch, 16ème (tel. 45 53 57 96). Mo. Porte Dauphine. This collection of Chinese and Japanese decorative art, numbering close to 7000 pieces, was assembled under the Second Empire by author and librettist Adolphe d'Ennery (1811-1899). Open Thurs. and Sun. 2-5pm. Closed in August. Free. On the first floor of the same building, you'll find the interesting **Musée Arménien** (tel. 45 53 57 96), which displays jewelry, paintings, and religious decoration of the past and the present, from Armenia. Open Thurs. and Sun. 2-5pm. Closed in August. Free.

Galerie d'Entomologie (Insect Museum), in the Jardin des Plantes, 5ème. Mo. Censier Daubenton or Gare d'Austerlitz. Scrutinize the *Titanus Gigantus,* an 18cm-long brown and black beetle monster from South America, with the comforting knowledge that it's quite dead, secured to the display by a pin hammered through its back. Most of the one-room gallery is dedicated to various specimens, in different colors and sizes, of this one beetle, with a small concession to butterflies, displayed in two cases. Open Wed.-Mon. 1-4:45pm. Admission 12F, students 8F.

Musée du Grand Orient de France et de la Franc-Maçonnerie, 16, rue Cadet, 9ème (tel. 45 23 20 92). Mo. Cadet. A delightful museum designed just for you, provided you have a strong interest in French freemasonry. The dark hall holds medals, portraits, and busts of renowned freemasons, including Voltaire and Talleyrand. The museum is housed in the Hôtel Cadet, built in 1852 and designed as the headquarters for French freemasonry. During World War II, Vichy officials used it as a headquarter to identify and persecute masons. Open Mon.-Sat. 2-6pm. Free.

Grand Palais, av. Franklin D. Roosevelt, 8ème (tel. 42 89 54 10). Mo. Champs-Elysées-Clemenceau. Most of the building houses the Palais de la Découverte (see above), but the other 2 entrances lead the way to temporary exhibitions. Call to see what's on. Open, when an exhibit is there, Thurs.-Mon. 10am-8pm, Wed. 10am-10pm. Last entry 45min. before closing. Admission varies with the exhibit, but anticipate something like 40F, reduced and Mon. 26F, under 13 free.

Musée Grevin, 10, bd. Montmartre, 9ème (tel. 47 70 85 06). Mo. Montmartre. This wacky wax museum is rather light fun, but it's definitely worth a visit, if you don't mind the screaming and running of hundreds of over-enthusiastic French kids on field days or the disturbing stares of life-like figures from all sides. The super-ornate halls are filled with illustrious personages from the present and the past. Woody Allen hangs from the ceiling in his pressure suit from *Sleeper;* Marie-Antoinette awaits her execution in the Conciergerie; the cannibals from Géricault's painting *The Raft of the Medusa* reach out for the rescue ship on the horizon. And, of course, Michael Jackson poses in mid-moonwalk. Open daily 10am-7pm; Oct.-May 1-7pm. Admission 48F, ages 6-14 34F. The smaller subsidiary at level "-1" of **Forum des Halles,** near the Porte Berger, 1er (tel. 40 26 28 50; Mo. Châtelet-Les Halles) presents a fascinating spectacle of Paris in its "Belle Epoque" (1885-1900). A terrific sound and light show recreates the turn of the century through wax figures of Hugo, Verne, Renoir, Pasteur, Eiffel, and many others. If you don't speak French, however, you'll miss most of the action. Open Mon.-Sat. 10:30am-7:30pm, Sun. and holidays 1-8pm. Ticket office closes 45 min. before museum. Admission 38F, ages 6-14 28F, under 6 free.

Musée Jean-Jacques Henner, 43, ave. Villiers, 17ème (tel. 47 63 42 73). Mo. Villiers. This small musuem displays the paintings of Jean-Jacques Henner (1829-1903), who, in a tumultuous era for French painting, developed his own uniquely non-partisan style. Especially noteworthy are the haunting series of nymphs (on both the first and fourth floors), weeping or hunching pensively in the darkness by their stilled lakes and ponds. Henner's carefully studied portraits, on the ground floor, honestly portray their bourgeois subjects, while at the same time conveying the discomfort and anxiety of their class. Open Tues.-Sun. 10am-noon and 2-5pm. Admission 14F, students 9F.

Musée de l'Histoire de France, 60, rue des Francs-Bourgeois, 3ème. Mo. Hôtel de Ville or Rambuteau. Housed in the hôtel Soubise, this museum overflows with important French documents-- Napoleon's will, a letter by Jeanne d'Arc, and *the* Edict of Nantes. Labels are in French only and, unless you love (French) history and are able to read some French, you may not get much out of it. But if you've had a passionate urge to see a copy of Napoleon III's plebiscite ever since you finished Weber's *Economy and Society,* this is the place for you! Open Wed.-Mon. 1:45-5:45pm.

Musée d'Histoire Naturelle (Museum of Natural History), in the Jardin des Plantes, 5ème (tel. 40 69 30 00). Mo. Gare d'Austerlitz. Schoolchildren, teachers in tow, romp through the collection of dinosaurs, which includes the skeleton of a massive 7m iguanodon, as well as the more modern mastadon. Therest of the museum is devoted to more mundane though equally large skeletons, such as rhinoceroses, elephants, and whales, as well as the omnipresent necessary *homo sapiens.* Open Mon. and Wed.-Fri. 10am-5pm, Sat.-Sun. 11am-6pm. Admission 18F, students 12F.

Musée de l'Historial, 11, rue Poulbot, 18ème (tel. 46 06 78 92). Mo. Anvers, Blanche, or Pigalle. A little wax museum dedicated to scenes from Montmartre's past—from the decapitation of St-Denis to the defense of the Commune in 1871. The historical scenes are set up in caves with special lighting and sound effects. Open daily 10am-6:30pm. Admission 35F, students 25F.

Musée de l'Holographie, level "-1" of Forum des Halles, between porte Berger and porte Lescot, 1er (tel. 40 39 96 83). Mo. Châtelet-Les Halles. A small, moderately interesting set of holograms. Don't miss the one of a woman who blows a kiss at you and winks as you walk by. Open Tues.-Sat. 10:30am-7pm, Mon. and Sun. 1-7pm. Admission 30F, students 25F.

Musée de l'Homme (the Museum of Man), in the Palais de Chaillot, 16ème (tel. 45 53 70 60). Mo. Trocadéro. A painted cart from Sicily, a chock-full-o'-stuff Turkish store, a 2½m tall cylindrical drum from the New Hebrides, and the requisite polar bear leading into the Inuit display... The museum's multi-media presentation begins in pre-historic times and branches out into the different customs of the world. Current renovations will update the layout by 1995. Labels are in French only, but exhibits are often self-explanatory. Open Wed.-Mon. 9:45am-5:15pm. Admission 25F, reduced 15F, disabled and children under 6 free.

Maison de Victor Hugo, 6, pl. des Vosges, 4ème (tel. 42 72 16 65). Mo. Chemin Vert. A small museum, dedicated to the "father of the French Romantics,"and housed in place des Vosges, in the building where he lived from 1832 to 1848. The illustrious poet, novelist, and politician occupied the third floor only, but the museum in his honor takes up the entire house with an assortment of Hugo memorabilia, including his own highly expressive graphic art—many sketches, and a display of photographs he took while in exile at Guernsey. You'll also find works by Rodin, Delacroix, and Bonnat. Francophones can read his elegant love letters on the first floor. And *Les Miz* fans will recognize the drawing of Cosette that became the musical's logo, displayed in one of the blue rooms on the first floor. Open Wed.-Sun. 10am-5:40pm. Admission 12F, students 6F50.

Musée Jacquemart-André, 158, bd. Haussmann, 8*ème* (tel. 45 62 39 94). Mo. St- Philippe-du-Roule. Closed for renovation in 1992 but expected to reopen by 1993. Works from the Italian Renaissance (Donatello bronzes, Della Robbia's terra-cottas) and the French 18th century (Fragonard, Watteau) join pieces by Rembrandt and Rubens under Tiepolo's fresco. The collections belonged to the Jacquemart family, the *hôtel particulier* to Edouard André, a 19th-century collector; hence the name. Open Wed.-Sun. 1:30-5:30pm. Closed holidays and Aug. Admission 10F

Musée du Jeu de Paume, 1*er* (tel. 42 60 12 69). Mo. Concorde. The Jeu de Paume (tennis court), in the northeast corner of the Tuileries, was originally constructed under Napoleon III as a court on which to play *jeu de paume*, an ancestor of tennis. In 1909, it was converted into a display area, mostly for art exhibits. When the Nazis took over Paris, they used the Jeu de Paume for their own purposes: plundered art was sent here, where much of it was labelled "degenerate" and burned. Between 1947 and 1986, the building housed an Impressionist collection which has subsequently been transferred to the Musee d'Orsay. Since June 1991, the Jeu de Paume has been a showcase for contemporary art. To find out what's exhibited, call 42 60 69 69 (answering machine, in French), or just go there and take a look. Open, when exhibits are on, Tues. noon-9:30pm, Wed.-Fri. noon-7pm, Sat.-Sun. 10am-7pm. Admission 30F students, reduced 20F, under 13 free.

Kwok On Museum, 41, rue de Francs-Bourgeois, 4*ème* (tel. 42 72 99 42). Mo. St-Paul. M. Kwok On was a private collector of Chinese Opera costumes who left his collection to the city of Paris in 1971. Since then, the museum has acquired masks, marionettes, and garments from many other Asian countries. Displays are rotated every year. Ask about their extensive collection of documentation on Asian theatrical traditions. Open Mon.-Fri. 10am-5:30pm. Admission 10F, students 5F.

Musée National de la Légion d'Honneur et des Ordres de Chevalerie, 2, rue de Bellchasse, 7*ème* (tel. 45 55 95 16). Mo. Solférino. Inaugurated on March 25, 1925, this museum is housed in an 18th-century mansion built for the German Prince of Salm-Kyrbourg. Displays highlight innumerable medals, ribbons, and dress costumes associated with the French Legion of Honor, created by Napoleon in 1802 to reward civilian and military virtue. The cloak of the Order of the Holy Ghost, one of the most prestigious, makes an appearance, both live and in a painting. And of course, keep your eye out for the legendary *Chevalier de l'Ordre de la Tuile*. But unless Jerome Bonaparte's wedding reception glass or such foreign orders as the Laotian Order of a Million Elephants is guaranteed to thrill you, consider admiring the architectural view from across the street at the Musée d'Orsay. Open Tues.-Sun. 2-5pm. Admission 10F, students and seniors 5F.

Musée des Lunettes et Lorgnettes (Spectacles Museum), 2, av. Mozart, 16*ème* (tel. 45 27 21 05). Mo. La Muette. Fittingly, the display is squeezed into the office of *Pierre Marly, opticien*, because it was Marly himself, eyeglass designer to the King of Morocco and the Dalai Lama, whose private collection of historical eye pieces gave birth to the museum. Exhibits show the development of eye gear in all forms and from all cultures, from the 17th century to the present. Dog glasses, suspiciously resembling Snoopy's WWI flying ace helmet, and glasses of the rich and famous help to make this museum fun even if you—unlike the best of us—don't have four eyes with which to see it. Open Tues.-Sat. 9:30am-7pm. Free.

Musée de la Marine (Museum of the Navy), in the Palais de Chaillot, 16*ème* (tel. 45 53 31 70). Mo. Trocadéro. The collection of model ships has been growing since 1748, when Louis Henri Duhamel du Monceau, Inspector General of the Navy, placed his private holdings in the Louvre for study by students at the new school of naval architecture. Several revolutions later, the museum moved to the Palais in 1943. Today, naval nuts can pore over the detailed scale models of historical French ships. While torpedos, paintings, and the ornate *Canot de l'Empereur* in which Napoleon inspected Antwerp (built in a record 21 days), can be impressive, explanations are brief and chronology only loosely traced. A semi-informative brochure is available in English at the ticket counter. Open Wed.-Mon. 10am-6pm and on holidays. Tickets issued until 5:30pm. Admission 28F, seniors, ages 5-12, and big families 14F, under 5 free. No student discount. Mini-conference held every Mon. at 2:30pm to discuss in French some aspect of the museum.

The Museum of Marine Life, 195, rue St-Jacques, 5*ème*. (tel. 46 33 08 61). Mo. Luxembourg. Under renovation in 1992, this museum plans to exhibit tanks of tropical fish, along with films by Jacques Cousteau. Films shown Wed., Sat., and Sun. (in French, no subtitles), free with admission. Call for times. Open Tues.-Fri. 10am-12:30pm and 1:15-5:30pm, Sat.-Sun. 10am-5:30pm. Admission 20F, students 12F.

Les Martyrs de Paris, porte du Louvre of the Forum des Halles, 1*er*. Mo. Les Halles. A macabre museum of torture and cruelty, with a heavy emphasis on the medieval. Realistic waxwork representations of people being branded, burned, and abused in ways you would never have dreamed of, while signs in English and French explain the historical details. Heavy Metal fans will be delighted to see a model of the "Iron Maiden" torture machine from Nuremberg Castle. Every so often, a man dressed as an executioner comes after the tourists swinging an axe or thumping the ground, and screams are played on the stereo. All of it is most appropriate for the city that brought you the Bastille, the Guillotine, and the St. Bartholemew's Day Massacre. Admission 40F, students 29F. Martyrs of Paris and Rock 'n' Roll Hall of Fame, 66F, students 48F, groups of more than 10 adults 48F per person. Open daily 10:30am-6:30pm.

Musée Adam Mickiewicz, 6, quai d'Orléans, 4*ème* (tel. 43 54 35 61), on the Ile-St-Louis. Mo. Pont Marie. During the 19th century, this *hôtel* was a meeting place for Polish exiles and the residence of Adam Mickiewicz, one of Poland's greatest poets (1798-1835). Left as it was during the poet's lifetime, the museum is bursting with memorabilia about Mickiewicz and compatriots like Chopin. Displays highlight the poet's correspondence with other writers of the Romantic period. Paintings by Polish artists provide an interesting accompaniment. The building also houses a large Polish library. (Open Sat. 3-6pm. Free.)

Musée de Minéralogie (Museum of Mineralogy), Jardin des Plantes, 5*ème*. Mo. Gare d'Austerlitz. Precious minerals--diamonds, rubies, emeralds and sapphires--are eclipsed by the *objets d art* created with these minerals, including two Renaissance Florentine marble tables, inlaid with lapis lazuli, amethyst, and other semi-precious stones. What the minerals in the upstairs gallery lack in value per gram, they make up in sheer size. Meter-high rose quartz formations poke out of piles of crystal rubble, and amethyst geodes large enough to grow internal stalagmites dominate the exhibit. Open Mon. and Wed.-Fri. 10am-5pm, Sat.-Sun. 11am-6pm. Admission 25F, students 16F.

La Musée de la Monnaie de Paris, 11, quai de Conti, 6*ème* (tel. 40 46 55 33). Mo. Pont.-Neuf. Housed in the Hôtel des Monnaies, once the mint of all money in France, this museum displays an impressive array of French coins from the 9th century to the present. Today, the Monnaie manufactures medals of special honor, some of which are for sale on the ground floor. Tues. and Thurs. at 2 and 2:45pm, a guided tour of the workshops takes you past artisans at work. If you miss the tour, don't worry; the movie room on the first floor shows a dramatized film (in French only), where you can see a boy and girl lustily staring at each other across a display of coins. The bulk of the coins are exhibited on the 1st floor, all cleverly mounted in free-standing glass cases to permit a 360° view and all accompanied by small video or slide shows explaining their history (in French). Upstairs, a reproduction of an antique press, complete with wax dummies, illustrates how these coins and medals were made. Open Tues.-Sun. 1-6pm. Admission 15F, students 10F.

Musée de la Mode et du Costume (Museum of Fashion and Clothing), in the Palais Galliera, 10, av. Pierre 1er-de-Serbie, 16*ème* (tel. 47 20 85 23). Mo. Iéna. With over 12,000 ensembles in its possession, this museum mounts temporary exhibitions showcasing fashion throughout the past three centuries. Van Cleef, Arpels, and Givenchy have all been the foci of recent expositions. Revel in the splendor of yet another domain of Parisian pre-eminence. Open Tues.-Sun. 10am-5:40pm, when an exhibition is on. Admission 30F, students and seniors 20F.

Institut du Monde Arabe (Institute of the Arab World), 23, quai St-Bernard, 5*ème* (tel. 439 78 01 97). Mo. Jussieu. One of Paris's newest museums, a cooperative project between 27 Arab nations and the French government to promote education about Arab history, art, culture and language, the institute opened in 1987. The riverside façade is shaped like a boat, representing the migration of Arabs to France. On the courtyard side, the windows are blinded with automatic irises, mimicking the *Moucharieb Arab* blinds of the Arab world, which permit someone to look out between the cracks in the blind without permitting anyone else to see in. Notable for its displays of Arabic rugs and ceramics, the museum compares the art from the three Arab regions of Maghrib/Spain, the Near East, and the Middle East from the 3rd through the 18th centuries. Level 4 is devoted entirely to contemporary Arab artists, much of whose work comprises political statements about their desire for peace in the Middle East. The library contains over 45,000 volumes of Arabic literature in Arabic, French, and English, as well as over 900 periodicals, all of which are open to the public. At night, the auditorium provides a space for Arab movies (subtitled in English and French; 22F, students 18F) and theater (free). Call for a schedule of events. On Level 9, a delightful cafeteria cooks up 3-course lunches, including many Arab specialities, for only 60F. Take your tray to the rooftop terrace outside for a terrific view of the Seine. (Museum and Library open Tues.-Sun 1-6pm. Museum admission 40F, students 20F, under 18 free. A 90-min. guided tour of the museum is included with the full ticket price, Tues.-Fri. at 3pm, Sat.-Sun. at 2:30 and 6:30pm. Institute open Tues.-Sat. 8am-8pm. Cafeteria open Tues.-Sun. 11am-4pm.)

Galerie Le Monde de l'Art, 18, rue Paradis, 10*ème* (tel. 42 46 43 44). Mo. Gare de l'Est. The airy and light-filled interior of this gallery is decorated with beautiful tiles, holdovers from the days when the building was headquarters for the Boulanger China Company. The tiles are of every possible style and color, arranged in a variety of motifs, from African designs to Portuguese frescoes and art nouveau landscapes. The exhibits themselves rotate every few months and usually highlight modern dissident artists (ex-Soviets, Cubans, and others). Exhibits are set up to work perfectly with the architecture. Definitely a very cool place. And, unless you're planning to buy some artwork, it's free. Open Mon. 2-7pm, Tues.-Sat. 1-7pm.

Musée National des Monuments Français (National Museum of French Monuments), in the Palais de Chaillot, 16ème (tel. 47 27 35 74). Mo. Trocadéro. Just about everything in this warehouse-like structure is a copy of something else, lending the museum a fellowship with the Counterfeit Museum, also in the 16th. Cavernous ceilings stretch above moldings of monumental religious French sculpture (such as the north façade of Chartres Cathedral) and reproductions of famous French murals. The originals are probably more impressive and certainly better explained (there are few labels, no brochures, and the staff knows little). Open Wed.-Mon. 9:30am-5pm. Admisssion 17F, students 18-25, seniors, and on Sundays 9F. Conferences explaining parts of the museum free with admission Wed. at 1 and 3pm. Some parts of museum closed until March 1993.

Musée Gustave Moreau, 14, rue de La Rochefoucauld, 9ème (tel. 48 74 38 50). Mo. Trinité. This museum is a gem; located in the house of the 19th-century symbolist painter Gustave Moreau, it contains thousands of his drawings and more paintings than the walls can hold—all of which he willed to the creation of a museum in his former studio. The house itself is charming, and the rooms are lined with works in all stages of completion, from sketches and half-painted canvases—revealing the intricate base drawings that Moreau worked from—to fully complete works, including the celebrated painting of Salomé dancing before the severed head of John the Baptist. Open Wed-Mon. 10am-12:30pm and 2-5pm. Admission 17F, students and children 9F.

Musée Naïf Max Fourny (Halle St-Pierre), 2, rue Ronsard, 18ème (tel. 43 43 14 54). Mo. Anvers. Housed in a large turn-of-the-century iron structure that was once a marketplace, this museum displays "naive" paintings from the Caribbean, South America, and Europe, mostly imaginary and childlike visions of cities. The collection is interesting, but won't knock your socks off. More of a warehouse than an art gallery. Open Tues.-Sun. 10am-6pm. Admission 22F, students 16F.

Palais de la Découverte (Palace of Discovery), in the Grand Palais, entrance on av. Franklin D. Roosevelt, 8ème (tel. 43 59 18 21 answering machine). Mo. Champs-Elysées-Clemenceau. More central, less flashy than the Cité des Sciences. Within one enormous section of the art nouveau Palais, interactive exhibits run the gamut of scientific subjects and run it remarkably well. Kids will (and do) tear around at a manic pace to turn wheels that teach about complementary colors, press buttons that start comets on their celestial trajectories, spin on seats to investigate angular motion and glare at all kinds of cleverly camouflaged creepy-crawlies. Even big people with a more cerebral approach can have fun with fractals, nuclear physics, and anatomy. Open Tues.-Sat. 9:30am-6pm, Sun. 10am-7pm. Admission 20F, students, seniors and under 18 10F. Planetarium show 13F extra, students, seniors, and under 18 9F extra. Planetarium shows Tues.-Fri. 11am, 2pm, 3:15pm, 4:30pm, Sat.-Sun. and holidays 11:30am, 2pm, 3:15pm, 4:30pm and 5:45pm. Call 40 74 81 06 for information about free conferences in French dealing with scientific subjects.

Palais de Tokyo, 13, av. du Prés Wilson, 16ème (tel. 47 23 36 53). Mo. Iéna. Temporary exhibits of groups such as the Centre National de la Bande Dessinée (National Center of the Comic Book). Film, photography, and video reign in this palace with simultaneous displays as random as storyboards and the pictures of Annie Leibovitz. The *Cinemathèque Française* shows a wide range of films daily at 6:30 and 9pm. Get there while you can—the Palais closes in June 1993 for a year and a half of renovation that will transform it into the **Palais de l'Image,** an enormous film library. Open Wed.-Mon. 9:45am-5pm, cashier closes at 4:30. Admission to exhibitions varies, generally 25-30F, students 12-22F. Cinemathèque admission 22F.

Petit Palais, also called the Palais des Beaux-Arts de la Ville de Paris, av. Winston Churchill, 8ème (tel. 42 65 12 73). Mo. Champs-Elysées-Clemenceau. A display of sparking gems from ancient art through 19th- and 20th-century painting and sculpture. Each of the rooms of the permanent collection focuses on a theme: 17th-century Flemish and Dutch painting or canvases depicting the French Revolution. History buffs will enjoy the model sculptures and paintings drafted by artists in 1848 for a contest to pick the new symbolic embodiment of the Republic. This is a comfortable museum, so enjoy the devilish smile of Jean-Baptiste Carpeaux's *Young Fisher with the Shell;* gleefully stumble on Camille Claudel's bust of Rodin, Monet's *Sunset at Lavacourt* (spiritual counterpoint to *Impression: Sunrise),* as well as the occasional Rubens, Rembrandt, Cézanne, Pissarro, and Renoir. From Oct. 16 1992 to Feb. 14 1993, a temporary exhibit will highlight Fragonard and 18th-century French drawing ; "Splendors of Russia: 1,000 Years of Goldsmithery" (April 16-July 18 1993) will showcase 200 pieces from Moscow, never before seen in France. Open Tues.-Sun. 10am-5:40pm. Admission to permanent collection 15F, students 8F50, seniors free. Admission to temporary exhibits roughly 35F, reduced 20F. Conference visits (60-90min.), focusing on a special theme, held in French in the afternoon; admission 24F. Wheelchair accessible by the door at 1, av. Dutuit—call ahead.

Musée Picasso, 5, rue de Thorigny, 3ème (tel. 42 71 25 21). Mo. Chemin Vert. In France there is a hefty tax on inherited wealth. When the great cubist Pablo Picasso died in 1973, his heirs opted to pay this tax in artwork rather than money, which is why the French government owns the collection in this museum. (The 17th-century mansion that houses this collection did not, however, belong to Picasso. It happened to be a conveniently located building the French government chose to convert into a museum.) Many of the works are of minor significance, but the collection as a whole is fascinating, thanks largely to the tasteful and informative layout of the museum. It illustrates the artist's development through the several stages in his career, grouping works together by period. Alongside Picasso's paintings and sculptures are works by various artists who influenced him, including Braque, Cezanne, and (anonymous) African and Oceanian sculptors. Open Thurs.-Mon. 9:15am-5:15pm, Wed. 9:15am-10pm. Admission 21F. Wheelchair access.

Musée de La Poste, 34, bd. de Vaugirard, 15*ème* (tel. 42 79 24 24). Mo. Montparnasse. O.K., so a museum dedicated to the history of the French postal system since the year 1820 may not be the reason you came to Paris, but it does deliver a pleasant surprise. Most impressive are the several thousand stamps, every one produced by the post office since 1817, which adorn the walls of an entire floor. Also of note are the various mailbox designs on display, including a conceptionally original hollow cannonball, which was stuffed with letters and then floated downstream to Parisians during the Prussian siege of 1870 (most ended up deep in the mud of the Seine). Nascent bureaucrats thrill to a scale replica of a post office window; everyone else suffers mysterious waves of impatient anxiety. Open daily 10am-4pm. Admission 19F, students 9F.

Musée de la Maison de la Radio-France, 116, av. du Prés. Kennedy, 16*ème* (tel. 42 30 33 83). Mo. Passy, Mirabeau, RER (C) Av. du Pt. Kennedy/Maison de la Radio France. The museum can be visited only by guided tour in French, which hastily covers the history of the Maison, of radio, and of television, with the appropriate bias toward contribution of the French to all three. Childhood radio builders will enjoy the chance to look at classic specimens. Linger if you can but this is something of a whirlwind tour through communications history. Open Mon.-Sat. Tours at 10:30am, 11:30am, 2:30pm, 3:30pm, and 4:30pm. Admission 12F, students and seniors 6F.

Rock 'n' Roll Hall of Fame, porte du Louvre of the Forum des Halles, 1*er.* Mo. Les Halles. Right next to the Martyrs of Paris, and sharing the same ticket office, the Hall is considerably less interesting than its neighbor. Wax dummies of stars like Madonna, Prince, and the Beatles; video clips and piped-in music. If you think that can't be any more exciting than staying at home and watching MTV, well...you're right. Admission 40F, students 29F. Martyrs of Paris and Rock 'n' Roll Hall of Fame 66F, students 48F. Open daily 10:30am-6:30pm.

Musée Renan-Scheffer, also called the **Musée de la vie romantique,** 16, rue Chaptal, 9*ème* (tel. 48 74 95 38). Mo. Blanche or St-Georges. This small museum is housed in the former residence of 19th-century painter and *salonnier* Ary Scheffer, a close friend of George Sand. Busts, portraits, letters, and even personal belongings (rings, books, locks of hair) recall Scheffer, Sand, Ernest Renan, Franz Liszt, and many others who belonged to this salon. The house is lovely,--down a tree-lined lane and surrounded by a pretty garden--and never crowded. Open Tues.-Sun. 10am-5:40pm. Admission 12F, students 6F50.

Musée-Galerie de la Seita (Société d'exploitation industrielle des Tabacs et Alumettes), 12, rue Surcouf, 7*ème* (tel. 45 56 60 17). Mo. Invalides or Latour-Maubourg. Tobacco and cigarettes are state-managed commodities in France and the number one propaganda center sits here, right next to corporate headquarters. This very politically incorrect museum tells the story of tobacco from Jean Nicot's 1561 presentation of its medicinal qualities to the court, through Napoleon's 1810 imposition of a state monopoly, all the way up to the present day era of mass-marketed, filtered cigarettes. Meanwhile, 61,000 French citizens die annually from illnesses relate to smoking. Explanations in English and French dissect the anatomy of the cigar, trace the evolution of the pipe, and discuss the popularity of snuff, with ample historical samples. The bad effects of smoking? "Periods of tolerance and repression of varying degrees of vehemence have succeeded one another. In fact, smoking and anti-smoking go back equally far in time." Entertaining films of *gitanes* and *gauloises* TV commercials (in French) run continually in the small amphitheater. Temporary exhibits come and go, one devoted to tobacco, the other to something completely unrelated. Open Mon.-Sat. 11am-6pm. Free, usually: some exhibitions may require a small fee. Nice free bathrooms too.

Musée des Techniques, 292, rue St-Martin, 3*ème* (tel. 40 27 23 31). Mo. Réamur-Sébastopol or Arts et Métiers. In 1794, French revolutionaries decided to create a national collection of new technology to be housed in the 12th-century priory, Saint Martin-des-Champs. Umberto Eco called it "a conspiracy in which the sublime universe of heavenly ogives and the chthonian world of gas guzzlers are juxtaposed." With new exhibits being added to the collection over the years, the museum has become an often quaint record of progress over the past two centuries. Here you can find Volta's original battery, vintage cars and airplanes, wooden telescopes, and brass models of the solar system, as well as a roomful of 18th-century automata—activated on the first Wed. of each month at 2:30pm. Two billion francs are earmarked for renovating the museum in time for its 200th anniversary (Oct. 1994), but in its present condition it has a certain flea-market charm. Strewn around the priory nave is a dusty hodgepodge of treasures, including models of the Statue of Liberty, vintage cars and bicycles, and plenty of engines from various machines. Hanging from the ceiling are Blériot's 1907 airplane and Foucault's original pendulum. Created by the inventor of the gyroscope, it provided the first proof of the rotation of the earth on its axis. Another curiosity nearby is a white bust of Carnot, which, you will notice, has an opera mask on his face. Why? The museum curators wanted to commemorate this automobile pioneer, but couldn't find a portrait of him. So they did a portrait of a generic middle-aged guy in period costume, and slapped a mask on his face to keep from straying too far from veracity. Open Tues.-Sun. 10am-5:30pm; closed public holidays. Admission 20F, Sun. 10F.

Musée du Vieux Montmartre, 12, rue Cortot, 18*ème* (tel. 46 06 61 11). Mo. Camarck Caumartin. A museum dedicated to the political, artistic, cultural, and religious past of the *butte* Montmartre. The beautiful 17th-century house, overlooking a pleasant garden and Montmartre's only vineyard, once housed one of Molière's actors and, in more recent times, has been the residence of such artistic luminaries as Renoir and Utrillo. The museum's collection includes old maps, paintings, photographs, and a wooden moldel of the *quartier.* One room recreates the ambiance of a turn-of-the-century café owned by M. Buillot, with counter and tables set up under posters of artists and cabarets. Open Tues.-Sun. 11am-6pm.

Musée du Vin, rue des Eaux or 5-7 sq. Charles Dickens, 16*ème* (tel. 45 25 63 26). Mo. Passy. Nestled in the cool, damp vaulted cellars of the 14th-century Abbey of Passy, this museum tries to explain the process of wine production through wax dummies, old tools, and many barrels. Of interest, perhaps, only to the oenologists among you, it is at its most compelling when offering tasty tidbits of trivia—you should only fill a wine glass to its widest point so as to better release the vintage's bouquet. The mystery of champagne is unveiled and so is the wine classification system—it worked in 1855, so why not today? Don't miss your free tasting. Anyone allergic to dust might consider other options for a rainy afternoon. A short guide sheet to the exhibit is available in primitive English. Open daily noon-6pm. Admission 37F, seniors 25F, students 21F.

Musée Zadkine, 100bis, rue d Assas, 6*ème* (tel. 43 26 91 90), just across from the Jardin du Luxembourg. Mo. Notre Dame des Champs. After the more famous, overwhelmingly large museums, with exhibits packed in so tightly that masterpieces seem to be jumping off the walls, this human-sized museum is the perfect antidote to Parisian aesthetic overload. Complete with a charming sunny garden and tastefully maintained house, the museum highlights the work of master sculptor Ossip Zadkine (1890-1967). Zadkine's work spans the major developments in modern sculpture, moving from the extremes of Cubism to a renewed Classicism, and the exhibits display the fascinating development of his sculpting techniques. Especially striking are the *Woman with the Fan* (1923), a Cubist rendering of a woman's torso, and later, *The Birth of Forms* (1947), a study in shapes and spaces in which two vaguely human forms struggle to disentangle themselves. Even if you don t want to pay the admission to the museum, a visit to the garden is both free and worthwhile; a good selection of the artist's most important works, including his two-faced *Woman with the Bird,* reside in the verdant space and you can relax on the benches in peace while you contemplate Zadkine's work. Open Tues.-Sun. 10am-5:30pm. Admission 12F, students 6F50.

Entertainment

Paris after dark—you've heard a lot about it. The sun has set over the City of Lights and now you wait for things to happen. The city has much to offer, but don't expect the whole shebang of glamorous options to fall into your lap. The hottest spots in town change at the whim and fancy of elite Parisian party-goers. "In" spots are usually hard to find and frequented by a moderately exclusive crowd that will not go out of its way to accommodate newcomers. Meeting a local may be your only chance to enter a highly private culture that loves to disappear behind intolerably smoky air to stomp, shimmy, sing, or mellow out until dawn. Although nightclubs, jazz *caves,* theater, even opera don't have to cost an arm and a leg, they grow more expensive in geometric proportion to their exclusivity.

The first thing to do is buy an entertainment weekly, of which the best are the glossy magazine **Pariscope** (comes out on Wed., 3F) and the Entertainment section in the Thursday **Figaro** (Paris's major newspaper, 6F). These give listings of everything going on, from theater and films to concerts, discothèques, and late-night bistros. Look here for your Godard festival, your tango party, your free Mozart requiem. Even if you don't understand French, you should be able to decipher the listings of times and locations. These are the publications that hip Parisians use, so look through and get a feel for what's up. You can also contact **Info-Loisirs,** a multilingual recording that keeps tabs on what's up in Paris (in English tel. 47 20 88 98; in French tel. 47 20 94 94; in German tel. 47 20 57 58; in Japanese tel. 47 23 63 84).

Fortunately, the most traditional Parisian entertainment—*la flânerie,* strolling and observing other passers-by—is free. Hit the streets, walk around, and seek out your own adventures. Parade along the banks of the Seine or weave your way through the Latin Quarter—and join the many Parisians doing so already. The area around Beaubourg (the Pompidou Center) fills with fire-eaters, sword-swallowers, Chilean guitar bands, and other performers. Around pl. St-Germain, you'll find throngs of people parading by in the latest fashions and a few bars where unlimited jazz comes with the price of one drink. At Ile St-Louis you'll find more refined tourists strolling the banks of the Seine. To see a movie or linger in the more fashionable cafés, wander around Montparnasse, the touristy Champs-Elysées, and the streets radiating from bd. St-Michel, bd. St-Germain, and bd. Sébastopol.

Every evening from sunset until midnight (1am in the summer), Paris literalizes its reputation as the City of Light. Bright lights flood the Arc de Triomphe, Notre-Dame, the Tour Eiffel, place de la Concorde, the Hôtel de Ville, Madeleine, Sacré Coeur, the Bastille, and the Panthéon. Walk around to experience the unique magic this phenomenal electric display brings to the centuries-old monuments; better yet, splurge on a taxi tour of **Paris by Night** for some stunning perspectives on some of the most famous sites in the world. In summer, the historic buildings of the Marais and some of the buildings and gardens of Montmartre are also illuminated.

Keep in mind that several sections of Paris have developed entertainment businesses of a different sort. The areas around Pigalle, Gare St-Lazare, and Beaubourg fill nightly with prostitutes and drug dealers. Everyone, men and women alike, should avoid the Bois de Boulogne after dark.

Cinema

Paris is famous the world over for a movie scene that rivals—and some say, surpasses—that of New York. Movies, which the French call *cinéma,* are a national obsession, more of an activity than a passive form of entertainment. Sitting in the dark need not be a vacation from the Parisian experience. After all, cinema was invented here, by the Lumière brothers, Auguste and Louis. The first moving picture (featuring a train and workers returning home) flickered to life on December 28, 1895, in the basement of the Grand Café at 14, bd. des Capucines. Although proud of the short movie, Louis claimed that "the cinema is an invention without a future;" obviously, he was wrong.

Movie-going here, like everything from choosing cheese to wearing perfume, is distinctly French. Lines are often long, particularly for the eagerly anticipated flicks. Before the feature comes the *séance*—a collection of commercials and previews that roll for as much as a half hour. Don't be surprised if a sultry, skin-filled perfume-type commercial turns out to be an ad for the local coffee. After all, a recent study shows that coffee-drinking prolongs one's sexual drive. Also amusing are the cigarette ads, which by law aren't allowed to show anyone smoking. Hmm... During the *séance,* a vendor with a basket of chocolate, ice cream, and cookies will pass your way. These are expensive, but part of the experience. Make sure you tip the man or woman who points you to your seat (about 2F). An old law assuring service workers 12-15% inadvertently bypassed ushers and taxi drivers. Most foreigners are not aware that they are expected to tip ushers and often encounter hostility when they don't.

The entertainment weeklies list show times and theaters. Film festivals are listed separately. The notation "V.O." (for *version originale)* after a non-French movie listing means that the film is being shown in its original language with French subtitles; watching an English-language film with French subtitles is a great way to pick up new (and sometimes very interesting) vocabulary. "V.F." (for *version française)* means that it has been dubbed—an increasingly rare and entirely avoidable phenomenon. If you're in Paris during its annual (short) hot spell, make sure the movie theater advertises *"climatisé."* If not, you'll regret it: although air-conditioning is becoming more customary in France, many theaters preserve a traditional, overpowering (and energy-conserving) heat. Most cinemas grant students a 10F discount off the regular 35-50F admission on weekdays and sometimes before 5pm on weekends. Many theaters lower their prices by several francs on Mondays.

In addition to the latest European and North American big-budget features, Parisian cinemas screen classics from all countries, avant-garde and political films, documentaries, and little-known or forgotten works. In the 1940s, French critics discovered the wonderful crime films being made in Hollywood and elevated them to an art form with the fancy title, *film noir*. And ever since the New Wave crested in the early 1970s, French interest in American movies has been phenomenal; in fact, many American films play here that have not been shown in U.S. cinemas for years. On the Left Bank, in particular, you'll find more old Hollywood movies—from Alfred Hitchcock to Roman Polanski—than you ever knew existed. Many American movies that never make it to the big American theaters are shown here; don't be surprised to find a 1993 "blockbuster" hit that never played your home town. Often these are great movies that just didn't fit into some Hollywood executive's general plan.

You will find that French have an odd taste in Hollywood fare; Mickey Rourke is an icon here, as is Rosanna Arquette, and, of course, master *auteur* Jerry Lewis. French audiences show far more respect for film directors than their American counterparts. Feature films play in the grand theaters on the Champs-Elysées, bd. St-Germain, bd. Montparnasse, and bd. St-Michel. Artsier flicks roll in the little theaters on the sidestreets of the Left Bank. The options below are some of the most interesting, most unusual, and most popular theaters in Paris.

Cinémathèque Française, at the Musée du Cinéma in the Palais de Chaillot, on av. Albert de Mun at av. Président Wilson, 16ème (tel. 47 04 24 24). Mo. Trocadéro. Answering machine lists all shows. A must for serious film buffs. This government-supported theater shows 1-2 films per day, many of them classics, near-classics, or soon-to-be classics. Foreign films almost always shown with French subtitles. Expect long lines. Screenings also at the Palais de Tokyo just down the street. Open Tues.-Sun. Last show 9pm. Admission 22F.

Le Grand Rex, 1, bd. Poissonière, 2ème (tel. 42 36 83 93). Mo. Bonne-Nouvelle. This 2800-seat behemoth is the largest theater in Paris. Well worth a visit just to experience the phenomenon of "privatized" viewing amid thousands. Primarily first-runs, but the atmosphere is unique. Last show around 9:30pm. Admission 45F, students 31F.

La Géode, 26, av. Corentin-Coriou, 19ème (tel. 40 05 80 00). Mo. Corentin-Coriou, in La Villette. Mostly scientific documentaries on this huge hemispherical screen. A 3-D sound, light, and comfortable chair extravaganza. Shows daily on the hour 10am-9pm. Admission 45F, students 35F (Mon.-Fri. only).

La Pagode, 57bis, rue de Babylone, 7ème (tel. 47 05 12 15). Mo. St-François-Xavier. No tremendous screen, and not even Dolby sound, but the intimate *salle chinoise* and the oriental architecture make this Paris's most charming cinema. A *salon de thé* serves up delicious (if pricey) goodies for the pre-show wait. Current films, usually in the original language. Admission 45F, students 35F.

Le Cosmos, 76, rue de Rennes, 6ème (tel. 45 44 28 80). Mo. St-Sulpice. Once the actual property of the Soviet Union, with appropriately Soviet films—Russian, Armenian, Georgian, etc.—this theater has responded to the "end of the Cold War" by expanding to generally artsy, foreign film festivals. Admission 35F, students 25F.

L'Entrepôt, 7-9, rue Francis-de-Pressensé, 14ème (tel. 45 43 41 63). Mo. Pernety. Organizes a wide variety of week-long festivals, sometimes with director-debates. Two branches project high-quality independent, classic, and foreign films. **Les Trois Luxembourg,** 67, rue Monsieur-le-Prince, 6ème (tel. 46 33 97 77) Mo. Odéon. **Le St-Germain-des-Prés,** pl. St-Germain-des-Prés, 6ème (tel. 42 22 87 23). Mo. St-Germain-des-Prés. A big, beautiful theater. Open noon-midnight. Admission 35F, students 28F.

Action Ecoles, 23, rue des Ecoles, 5ème (tel. 43 25 72 07). Mo. Maubert. **Action Rive Gauche,** 5, rue des Ecoles, 5ème (tel. 43 29 44 40). Mo. Maubert. Both on a large street parallel to bd. St-Germai. **Action Christine,** 4, rue Christine, 6ème, off rue Dauphine (tel. 43 29 11 30). Mo. Odéon. Superb, innovative festivals, from Marilyn Monroe to the Marx Brothers. Admission 38F, students 28F.

Racine Odéon, 6, rue de l'Ecole de Médicine, 6ème (tel. 43 26 19 68). Mo. Odéon. Mostly film festivals of such greats as Godard and Truffaut. Very studenty crowd. Admission 38F, students 28F (Mon.-Thurs. only).

Musée du Louvre (tel. 40 20 52 99). Mo. Palais Royal/Musée du Louvre. Various series. Nov.-Dec. 1992: *Rétrospective Peter Greenway,* and *Music on Film: Honegger-Milhaud-Rossini.*

March 1993: *Le Siècle de Titien* (Titian's Century) and silent movies in concert. Movies 22F, except for the silent movies in concert, which are 100F, youth 80F. Call for schedule. For the silent movie concerts, reserve by calling 40 20 52 29.

Theater

Theater in Paris is not limited to Molière, Corneille, or Racine. The classics are there if you want them, but so are modern masterworks by Beckett and Genet, Broadway-type comedies and musicals, experimental plays, and political satires. Aside from the intimate *café-théâtres, cafés chansonniers,* and the Las Vegas-style *revues,* theater in Paris takes two main forms: the national theaters, such as the Comédie Française, and the private theaters, which concentrate on newer and more experimental works. Although intended for children, the famous *guignol* (traditional puppet show) may offer the most comprehensible text for Anglophones.

Theater tickets typically start at 130F, but there are usually a few tickets from 20 to 80F. Some theaters sell standby tickets a half-hour before the performance. Most theaters close at least for August. *Pariscope* prints complete listings of current shows.

Plays and concerts are often quite expensive, but discounts exist for most events. Far and away the best place to get reduced-rate theater tickets is at the **Kiosque-Théâtre,** 15, pl. de la Madeleine, 8ème (Mo. Madeleine). This splendid little kiosk sells tickets at half-price the day of the show. (Open Tues.-Sat. 12:30-8pm, Sun. 12:30-4pm.) For more advanced planning, the student organization **COPAR** (Service des Activités Culturelles), whose ticket agency is at 39, av. Georges Bernanos, 5ème (tel. 40 51 37 13; Mo. Port-Royal), sells discounted tickets and publishes a monthly list of plays for which these tickets are available. The agency also sells reduced-price concert tickets, even in summer. They accept any student ID. (Open Sept.-July Mon.-Fri. 9am-4:30pm.) Another useful service is **Alpha FNAC: Spectacles** at 136, rue de Rennes, 6ème (tel. 45 44 39 12; Mo. Montparnasse-Bienvenue); 26, av. de Wagram, 8ème (tel. 47 66 52 50; Mo. Charles de Gaulle-Etoile); and Forum des Halles, 1-7, rue Pierre Lescot, 1er (tel. 42 61 81 18; Mo. Châtelet-Les Halles). They sell tickets for theater and a variety of concerts and festivals. Their *Carte Alpha* (50F for 1 year) or Carte FNAC (100F for 3 years, students 50F) entitles you to discounts of up to 40% on classical music and theater tickets. (Open Tues.-Sat. 10am-7pm.) Another place to get tickets to concerts and shows is at the **Virgin Megastore,** 52, av. des Champs-Elysées, 8ème (tel. 40 74 06 48; Mo. George V). Look for the ticket office below the first floor. Finally, contact the theater itself—many offer last-minute rush tickets and can give you updates on availability.

National Theaters

Supported by the French government, the national theaters are the brightest stars of Parisian theater. With the advantages of giant auditoriums, superb acoustics, veteran actors, and, in some cases, several centuries of history, these companies stage superlative and extremely popular productions. Although modern pieces appear occasionally, expect Molière, Racine, Goethe, and Shakespeare (all in French). Unless you're trying to get last-minute rush tickets, make reservations 14 days in advance.

La Comédie Française, 2, rue de Richelieu, 1er (tel. 40 15 00 15). Mo. Palais Royal. Founded by Molière, this is the granddaddy of all French theaters. Guaranteed pomp and prestige, with red velvet and chandeliers. Expect over-acted slapstick farce in the typical and much parodied *"style Comédie Française."* You don't need to speak French to understand the jokes. 892 seats. Open Sept. 15-July. Box office open daily 11am-6pm. Admission 45-195F. 20F rush tickets available 1/2hr. before show; come 11/2hr. ahead to wait in line.

Théâtre National de Chaillot, in the Palais de Chaillot, pl. du Trocadéro, 16ème (tel. 47 27 81 15). Mo. Trocadéro. Mostly plays but occasional musicals as well. 1000 seats. Box office open Mon.-Sat. 11am-7pm, Sun. 11am-5pm. Admission 140F, under 25 and over 60 100F. Student standby tickets 70F.

Odéon Théâtre de l'Europe, 1, pl. Odéon, 6ème (tel. 43 25 70 32). Mo. Odéon. Eclectic programs running the gamut from classics to avant-garde. 1042 seats. Also **Petit Odéon,** 82 seats. Open Sept.-July. Box office open daily 11am-6:30pm. Admission 30-150F; Petit Odéon 48F.

Théâtre Nationale de la Colline, 15, rue Malte-Brun, 20ème (tel. 43 66 43 60). Mo. Gambetta. 760 seats. Also **Petit Théâtre,** 200 seats. Open Sept.-July. Box office open daily 11am-7pm. Admission 110-140F, under 25 and over 60 75F.

Private Theaters

Although private theaters don't carry the reputations or historical baggage of the national theaters, some stage outstanding productions. Poor showings are much more common than in the national theaters; check the reviews before investing in a seat.

Athénée-Louis Jouvet, 4, sq. de l'Opéra, 9ème (tel. 47 42 67 27). Mo. Opéra or Auber. 687 seats. Hard-to-find, with an unremarkable exterior, but a magnificent 18th-century interior and outstanding classical productions. Open Oct.-May. Box office open Mon.-Sat. 11:30am-6pm. Admission 80-110F.

Théâtre Mogador, 25, rue Mogador, 9ème. Mo. Trinité. For info, call 48 74 33 74; for reservatons call 48 78 75 15. With 1792 seats, one of the largest theaters in Paris. Grandiose comedies and musicals on a colossal stage. Open Oct.-May. Box office open daily 11am-7pm. Admission 80-240F.

Théâtre de la Ville, 2, pl. Châtelet, 1er (tel. 42 74 22 77). Mo. Châtelet. 1000 seats. Excellent productions of all sorts, with a heavy emphasis on the musical. Box office open Tues.-Sat. 11am-8pm, Sun.-Mon. 11am-6pm. Admission 70-120F, students 60-85F.

Théâtre Renaud-Barrault, 2bis, av. Franklin D. Roosevelt, 8ème (tel. 42 56 60 70). Mo. Franklin D. Roosevelt. 920 seats. Also **Petite Salle** (tel. 42 56 08 80). 150 seats. Large stage allows for some outlandish musicals and comedies. Open Sept.-July. Box office open Tues.-Sat. 11am-6pm, Sun. noon-5pm. Admission 120-200F, students and seniors 80F.

Théâtre de la Huchette, 23, rue de la Huchette, 5ème (tel. 43 26 38 99). Mo. St-Michel. 100 seats. Tiny theater whose productions of Ionesco's *La Cantatrice Chauve (The Bald Soprano)* and *La Leçon (The Lesson)* are still popular—after 33 years. Shows Mon.-Sat. Box office open Mon.-Sat. 5-9:30pm. Admission 100F, students 70F; for both shows 130F, students 90F. No discounts Sat.

Jardin Shakespeare du Pré Catelan, at the end of the Bois de Boulogne (tel. 42 71 44 06). Take bus #244 from Porte Maillot. Summertime Shakespeare in French. Tickets at the door or at FNAC. Shows Fri.-Sat. 7:30pm, Sun. 5pm. Buses won't be running after the show, and whatever you do, don't try walking. Take a taxi to Porte Maillot; some find rides among audience members. Admission 80-120F.

The Sweeney, 18, rue Laplace, 5ème (tel. 46 33 28 12). Mo. Maubert-Mutualité. This Irish pub hosts the Gare St-Lazare players, an English-speaking, Chicago-based theater company under the direction of Bob Mayer. One-hour productions Sun. and Mon. at 8pm. Admission 25F. Call for more information.

Experimental Theater Wing Studio, 14, rue Letelier, 15ème. Mo. Emile-Zola. Six-year-old extension of New York University's theater program. Interesting and unusual productions in English. Prices vary with performance.

Maison de la Poésie, 101, rue Rambuteau, 1er (tel. 42 36 27 53). Mo. Châtelet or Rambuteau. This small theater shows interesting plays by or about poets, done by domestic and foreign companies. After the show, use the Rambuteau metro stop. Shows Tues.-Sat. around 8pm. Admission 60-80F.

Lucernaire Centre National d'Art et d'Essai, 53, rue Notre-Dame-des-Champs, 6ème (tel. 45 44 57 34). Mo. Notre-Dame-des-Champs. 130 seats. Plays by classic authors like Chekhov, Tennessee Williams, St-Exupéry. Box office open 2-7pm or call for reservations 9am-5pm. Admission 140F, reduced price 71F.

Café-Théâtres

Continuing the European showtime tradition, *café-théâtres* deliver caustic, often political satire through skits and short plays. Puns and double-entendres galore: those who aren't up on French slang and politics may miss most of the fun. Despite the name, not all *café-théâtres* have tables with waiter service.

Au Bec Fin, 6, rue Thérèse, 1er (tel. 42 96 29 35). Mo. Palais Royal. Usually 2 different shows per night in this tiny place (60 seats). Dinner and 1 show from 220F. Dinner and 2 shows from 300F. Shows at 7, 8:30, and 11:30pm. Auditions sometimes open to the public (40F). Admission for show only 75F, students (Sun.-Fri.) 60F. Two shows 115F.

Le Point Virgule, 7 rue Sainte-Croix-de-la-Bretonnerie, 4*ème* (tel. 42 78 67 03). Mo. Hôtel-de-Ville. Often features works of special interest to gays and lesbians. Reservations suggested, available 24 hrs. Mon.-Fri. 2 shows, 130F; 3 shows 150F. Admission 75F, students 50F. Open 3pm-midnight.

Théâtre de l'Arlequin, 13, passage du Moulinet, 13*ème* (tel. 45 89 43 22). Mo. Tolbiac. Experimental and classic works—and plenty of uncanned laughter. Shows Tues.-Sat. at 8:30pm. Admission 45-75F.

Café de la Gare, 41, rue du Temple, 4*ème* (tel. 42 78 52 51). Mo. Hôtel-de-Ville. Comedy and satire about social and political issues. Shows start at 8 and10pm. Admission 50-100F.

Chansonniers

The *chansonnier* is the musical cousin of the *café-théâtre*. In the spirit of old Paris, the audience is invited to sing along to French folk songs. Again, the better your French, the better you'll follow the proceedings. Admission usually includes one drink (but only one).

Au Lapin Agile, 22, rue des Saules, 18*ème* (tel. 46 06 85 87). Mo. Lamarck-Coulaincourt. Picasso and his friends used to hang out here during the heyday of Montmartre. Get here before 7pm for a good seat. Usually crowded with tourists. Shows at 9pm. Admission and first drink 100F, students 75F. Subsequent drinks 32F. Open Tues.-Sun. until 2am.

Caveau de la République, 1, bd. St-Martin, 3*ème* (tel. 42 78 44 45). Mo. République. A more Parisian crowd fills the 100 seats. Tickets sold 6 days in advance from 11am. Shows Tues.-Sat. 9pm, Sun. 3:30pm. Admission 150F, students 80F.

Deux Anes, 100, bd. de Clichy, 18*ème* (tel. 46 06 10 26). Mo. Blanche. 300 seats. Shows Mon.-Sat. 9pm. Reservations by phone 11am-7pm, 2 weeks in advance. Admission 120F, students 95F. Closed July and Aug.

Caveau des Oubliettes, 11, rue Satin-Juline-le-Pauvre, 5*ème* (tel. 43 54 94 97). Mo. St-Michel. This club is located in what were once the bowels of the Petit-Châtelet Prison. The dark wood paneling and *"musée avec guillotine,"* together with the old French folk songs, give this place a medieval, self-flagellating feel. Drinks 130F. Open 9pm-2am.

Guignols

These renowned traditional puppet shows entertain adults as much as children. Go to them for your badly needed dose of slapstick humor—a veritable (and uniquely French) Oliver and Hardy in wood. The puppets speak French, but you'll have no problem understanding their outrageous antics. And even if you miss the joke, seeing rows of schoolchildren roar with laughter is as amusing as the show itself. Almost all parks have *guignols,* but check out these three in particular, and look in *Pariscope* for others that change their location weekly.

Guignol du Parc Choisy, 149, av. de Choisy, 13*ème* (tel. 43 66 72 39). Mo. Place d'Italie. *The* classic *guignol* with life-sized puppets from Lyon. Wed, Sat.-Sun., and holidays at 3:30pm. Admission 10F, groups 8F.

Marionettes du Luxembourg, Jardin du Luxembourg (tel. 43 26 46 47). Mo. Odéon. Roofed-in theater. Such wonderful stories as the *Adventures of Pinocchio* and the *Three Little Pigs.* Usually Wed. and Sat.-Sun. 3pm. Call ahead or look in *Pariscope* for program and time changes. Admission 20F, groups 16F.

Théâtre de la Petite Ourse, Jardin des Tuileries, 8*ème* (tel. 42 64 05 19). Mo. Tuileries or Concorde. A classic marionette show in walking distance from the Louvre, for the ultimate in aesthetic contrasts. Call for times and titles. Admission 8F.

Cabarets

Contrary to popular tourist belief, Parisian cabarets (officially called *revues*) are not exclusively for foreigners. The big names—the Moulin Rouge and the Folies Bergère—are frequented by as many cameras as people, but some of the less-publicized cabarets lure Parisians as well; stampedes of well-hoofed locals unwind at The Crazy Horse after work. Although the complete dinner package is forbiddingly expensive, you might be able to watch from the bar while hanging on to your cash.

Le Bal du Moulin Rouge, pl. Blanche, 9ème (tel. 46 06 00 19). Mo. Blanche. The most famous of them all, this *revue* celebrated its centennial in 1989. Unfortunately, tourists—of the money-burning-a-hole-in-their-pocket variety—have replaced Toulouse-Lautrec and his leering disciples, who carefully selected their models from the comely performers on stage. Still, an impressive show with 100 dancers, singers, and castanet players. Shows daily at 10pm and midnight. Reserve by phone 10am-7pm. Dinner and show from 640F. Show 445F.

Crazy Horse Saloon, 12, av. George V, 8ème (tel. 47 23 32 32). Mo. Alma-Marceau. More Parisians, fewer tourists; more flesh, less glamor. Shows Sun.-Thurs. at 9 and 11:35pm, Fri.-Sat. at 8pm, 10:30pm, and 12:50am. Reserve by phone 11am-6pm. Seats 195F-520F, seats and 2 drinks 390F-520F, seats and 1/2-bottle of champagne 450F-580F.

Les Folies-Bergère, 32, rue Richer, 9ème (tel. 42 46 77 11). Mo. Cadet or Rue Montmartre. Over 60 dancers and musicians in the music hall Manet immortalized with his strangely disturbing *Bar aux Folies-Bergère.* Don't expect to find the same crowd Manet painted, although the feeling of alienation may stay the same. 105 years running. Shows Tues.-Sun. at 9:30pm. Reservations at box office daily 11am-6pm or by phone 11am-6:30pm. Seats 98F-399F.

Music

Classical Music, Opera, and Dance

Classical music, opera, and dance are as alive in Paris as in Vienna, Berlin, or New York, but since the musicians aren't as well-known as in these cities, fewer visitors attend performances here. The spirit of French socialism has made these wonders available to even the most constricted budget traveler. Many churches sponsor free or nearly free organ and choral concerts, usually of superb caliber. Check at FNAC for hours and locations.

Orchestre de Paris, in the Salle Pleyel, 252, rue du faubourg St-Honoré, 8ème (tel. 45 43 96 96). Mo. Ternes. The internationally renowned orchestra delivers first-class performances under the baton of music director Semyon Bychkov. Their season runs Sept.-May; call or stop by for the concert calendar. Tickets 50-250F.

Opéra de la Bastille, pl. de la Bastille, 11ème (tel. 43 43 96 96). Mo. Bastille. The much-hallowed Opéra de la Bastille staged its first performance on July 14, 1989, the bicentennial of the French Revolution. Hailed by some as the hall to bring opera to the masses, decried by others as offensive to every aesthetic sensibility (including hearing), this huge postmodern theater features classic opera scores amid lavish costumes and sceneries. The 1992-93 season features such delights as Tchaikovsky's *Swan Lake* (yes, the ballet; we realize this makes no sense, but this is Paris), Mozart's *The Marriage of Figaro,* Arthur Honegger's *Jeanne d'Arc au Bûcher,* and Bizet's *Carmen.* Subtitles in English and French during impossible-to-understand lyrical performances. Tickets range from 50-560F. The Opéra de la Bastille also holds concerts by the **Orchestre Philarmonique de Radio-France,** directed by Marek Janowski, tickets for concerts 50-290F. Call, visit, or write to obtain a free brochure of the season's events. Tickets can be purchased by writing and enclosing a check (foreigners can pay on arrival in Paris by presenting their letter of confirmation), by calling 44 73 13 00 Mon.-Sat. betwen 11am and 5:45pm, through minitel 3615 code THEA then Opéra Bastille, and at the opera house itself Mon.-Sat. 11am-6:30pm. Tickets go on sale on site 14 days before show. Opera reserves right to limit the number of tickets you can purchase. Reduced rush tickets for under 25, students, and over 65, often available 15min. before show. The Opéra-Bastille is wheelchair accessible. Call 44 73 13 73 to make arrangements at least 15 days before the show. Visa accepted.

Opéra Garnier, pl. de l'Opéra, 9ème (tel. 40 17 35 35 for information; 47 42 53 71 for reservations). Mo. Opéra. The historic Opéra Garnier now hosts the Ballet de l'Opéra de Paris and visiting ballet troupes, as well as occasional operas and concerts by foreign companies and orchestras. Tickets available at the box office 2 weeks before each performance Mon.-Sat. 11am-6:30pm. Tickets 30-350F.

Opéra Comique, 5, rue Favart, 2ème (tel. 42 86 88 83). Mo. Richelieu-Druot. Operas on a lighter scale—from Rossini to Offenbach. Tickets can be purchased at the box office Mon.-Fri. 11am-6pm or can be reserved over the phone. Tickets 40-430F.

Théâtre Musical de Paris, pl. du Châtelet, 1er (tel. 42 33 00 00). Mo. Châtelet. A superb 2300-seat theater normally reserved for guest orchestras and ballet companies. Magnificent acoustics. Call for a schedule. Tickets run 70-300F.

Musée du Louvre, 1er (tel. 40 20 52 99 for information; 40 20 52 29 for reservations). Mo. Palais Royal/Musée du Louvre. Classical music in a classy auditorium. Sept. 1992-March 1993: *Musiques de Chambre* (7 chamber music concerts, series price 600F); Jan. 1993: *Mitsuko Shirai,*

Harmut Holl, and friends (5 concerts—420F); May-June 1993: *D'Après le Maîtres* (According to the Masters, 4 concerts—260F). Tickets for individual concerts 100-250F, youth 80-200F.

Free concerts are often held in churches and parks, especially when summer festivals scatter music throughout the city. These are extremely popular; get there early if you want to breathe. Check any of the entertainment weeklies and the Alpha FNAC offices (see Entertainment introduction) for concert notices. *Pariscope* has day-by-day concert listings in its "Musique" section. **AlloConcerts** maintains a 24-hour hotline that provides information in French on free open-air concerts in the parks (tel. 42 76 50 00). The **American Church in Paris,** 65, quai d'Orsay, 7ème (tel. 47 05 07 89; Mo. Invalides or Alma Marceau), sponsors free concerts (Oct.-June Sun. at 6pm). **Eglise St-Merri** is also known for its free concerts, which take place Saturdays at 9pm and Sundays at 4pm, except in August; contact Accueil Musical St-Merri, 76, rue de la Verrerie, 4ème (tel. 42 76 93 93; Mo. Châtelet or Hôtel de Ville).

Other churches, such as **Eglise St-Germain-des-Prés,** 3, pl. St-Germain-des-Prés, 6ème (Mo. St-Germain-des-Prés); **Eglise St-Eustache,** rue du Jour, 1er (Mo. Les Halles); and **Eglise St-Louis-en-l'Ile,** 19, rue St-Louis-en-l'Ile, 4ème (Mo. Pont Marie), stage frequent concerts that are somewhat expensive (70-100F for students), but feature fantastic acoustics and unbeatable atmosphere. For information about all church concerts, call 43 29 68 68. **Ste-Chapelle** hosts concerts a few times per week in summer (sometimes free on Sun.). Contact the box office at 4, bd. du Palais, 1er (tel. 46 61 55 41; Mo. Cité; open daily 1:30-5:30pm; admission 110F, students 65F). Weather permitting, Sunday concerts take place in the band shell of the **Jardin du Luxembourg** (tel. 42 37 20 00). Infrequent concerts in the Musée d'Orsay are free with a museum ticket.

Jazz

Some critics mourn that Paris is no longer the jazz center it once was. Although the big names find it more profitable to play the huge summer festivals in southern France and Switzerland, Paris still nourishes dozens of interesting clubs. Not only do many fine, lesser-known American musicians play here, but the variety of music—including African, Antillean, Brazilian—is astounding. For the most complete listings, pick up a copy of the monthly *Jazz Magazine* or check in one of the entertainment weeklies.

New Morning, 7-9, rue des Petites-Ecuries, 10ème (tel. 45 23 51 41). Mo. Château d'Eau. 500 seats in a former printing plant. Attracts big names like Wynton Marsalis and Bobby McFerrin. All the greats have played here—from Chet Baker and Archie Shepp to Miles Davis. Come here if you want a larger, less crowded and less smoky atmosphere (although you'll lose the intimacy and grittiness of a smoky *cave).* Open Sept.-July from 9:30pm; times vary—check *Pariscope.* Admission around 110F.

Le Petit Opportun, 15, rue des Lavandières-St-Opportune, 1er (tel. 42 36 01 36). Mo. Châtelet. A relaxed and unpolished pub, where you can hear some of the best modern jazz around, inluding a lot of American bands and soloists. 200 plaques in the entrance hall commemorate internationally renowned artists who have performed here. There's a catch: the club is tiny (60 seats), and so popular that it ought to seat 500. Come early. Open Sept.-July daily from 11pm; bar open until 3am. First drink 100F, 50F thereafter.

Au Duc des Lombards, 42, rue des Lombards, 1er (tel. 42 33 22 88). Mo. Châtelet. French jazz groups, with the occasional American singer or soloist. Great ambiance—dark and smoky—and a clientele that gets into what's going on on stage. Call for prices. First drink about 60F. Open daily from 10:30pm.

Le Petit Journal St-Michel, 71, bd. St-Michel, 5ème (tel. 43 26 28 59). Mo. Luxembourg. A crowded, intimate establishment. New Orleans bands and first-class performers play in this Parisian center of the "Old Style," classic big-band jazz. Music Sept.-July Mon.-Sat. 10pm-2:30am. Obligatory first drink 100F, 40F thereafter.

Slow Club, 130, rue de Rivoli, 1er (tel. 42 33 84 30). Mo. Châtelet. Miles Davis's favorite jazz club in Paris. Big bands, traditional jazz, and Dixieland in a wonderful old-time setting. Expect dancing and a crowd in the 30s. Weekday cover 65F. Weekend cover from 95F. Women and students 5F less during the week. Drinks from 18F. Open Tues.-Thurs. 9:30pm-2:30am, Fri. 9:30pm-3:30am, Sat. 9:30pm-4am.

Caveau de la Huchette, 5, rue de la Huchette, 5*ème* (tel. 43 26 65 05). Mo. St-Michel. The one-time tribunal, prison, and execution rooms here were used by Danton, Marat, St-Just, and Robespierre—the limited partnership of death—during the Revolution. Now just a traditional jazz hotspot. Maxim Saury often whistles dixie. Moving and breathing difficult on weekends. Min. age 18. Cover Sun.-Thurs. 55F, students 50F. Fri. and Sat. cover 60F. Drinks from 35F. Open Sun.-Thurs. 10pm-2:30am, Fri. 9:30pm-3am, Sat. 9:30pm-4am.

Théâtre Dunois, 28, rue Dunois, 13*ème* (tel. 45 84 72 00). Mo. Chevaleret. A newly renovated theater with 200 seats specializing in American avant-garde jazz. The bar serves drinks from 15-40F. Cover 80F. Open daily 10pm-2am.

Jazz O' Brazil, 38, rue Mouffetard, 5*ème* (tel. 45 87 36 09). Mo. Monge. Excellent samba guitarists and new groups. Try the house drink *caitirissa* (lime juice and vodka). No cover. Drinks 55F. Open daily 9:30pm-2am.

Chica, 71, rue St-Martin, 4*ème* (tel. 48 87 73 57). Mo. Châtelet. Primarily an excellent Brazilian restaurant (first courses 45F, main dishes 90F). Devoted clients reserve tables downstairs in the *cave* for late-night samba action. Live bands tune up at midnight. Fruit drinks 45F. Open Tues.-Thurs. and Sun. 8pm-2am, Fri.-Sat. 8pm-4:30am.

Discos and Rock Clubs

Paris is not Barcelona, Montréal, or Buenos Aires; you won't find entire streets filled with young people waiting and struggling to get into discos. Instead, the clubs are small, private, and nearly impossible to find out about, unless you're a native. The discos that are "in" (or even in business) change drastically from year to year; only a few have been popular since the 1960s. Many Parisian clubs are officially private, which means they have the right to pick and choose their clientele. The management can evaluate prospective customers through peepholes in the handle-less front doors. Parisians tend to dress up more than North Americans for a night on the town; haggard backpackers might be wise to try a bar instead.

In general, word of mouth is the best guide to the current scene. Some of the smaller places in the Latin Quarter admit almost anyone who is sufficiently decked out. To access one of the more exclusive places, you need to accompany a regular. Otherwise, plan to look good, very good, don't publicize your foreignness, and be prepared to shell out a good amount of money. Many clubs reserve the right to refuse entry to unaccompanied men. Women often get a discount or get in free, but don't go alone unless you're looking for lots of amorous attention.

The French dance any way they please and often alone. The music is often mediocre at best, with fast-paced disco and new wave pop. Weekdays are cheaper and less crowded so you'll have a better chance of moving, but most of the action (by force of inevitable body contact) happens on weekends. **Les Bains** (see below) is still the best, but also the most expensive and most exclusive. Other clubs have good and bad nights, but by going to them you might meet people who can suggest the current hot spot.

Les Bains, 7, rue de Bourg l'Abbée, 3*ème* (tel. 48 87 01 80). Mo. Réaumur-Sébastopol. Ultra-selective and ultra-expensive, but worth it—if you can get in past the fearless bouncers. Prince established the joint's reputation with a surprise free concert a few years ago. Not only that, but it used to be a public bath, that welcomed the likes of Marcel Proust into its midst. Lots of models and super-attractive people dressed to those proverbial nines. Cover and first drink 140F, second drink 100F. Can you stand a third? Open Tues.-Sun. midnight-6am.

La Locomotive, 90, bd. Clichy, 18*ème* (tel. 42 57 37 37). Mo. Blanche. Shaped like a huge choo-choo, this place has already had its heyday. You won't find Paris's most chic here; rather a younger, less hip bunch who couldn't or didn't try to get into Les Bains. A pick-up scene. Women—be prepared for annoying and persistent men trying to pick you up. Tues.-Thurs. and Sun. First drink 60F, Fri.-Sat. 100F. Second drink 50F. Open Tues.-Sun. 11pm-5am.

Le Palace, 8, rue du faubourg Montmartre, 9*ème* (tel. 42 46 10 87). Mo. Montmartre. A funky disco, although its days as the hottest club in Paris have gone by. If you hit a private party and still get in, the music and crowd can be very cool. Otherwise, the music is all too top-40 and the people a mix of happy high school students wanting to "get together" and some older people wanting to get in on the action. Still, the place is huge (up to 2000 people per night), with multi-level dance floors, each with separate bars and different music. American cocktails and occasional rock concerts. Cover and 1 drink Tues.-Thurs. 100F, Fri.-Sat. 130F, Sun. 130F for men, women free. Subsequent drinks 85F. Open Tues.-Thurs. and Sun. 11pm-6am., Fri.-Sat. 11pm-10am. The British owners also run **Le Central**, 102, av. des Champs-Elysées, 8*ème* (Mo. George V). Same prices, with older clientele and a higher percentage of foreigners.

Scala de Paris, 188bis, rue de Rivoli, 1*er* (tel. 42 60 45 64). Mo. Tuileries. Not as well-known or trendy as some of the other clubs, but becoming more and more popular as the others decline. Youngish (18-24) crowd dances to house and techno. Atmosphere changes a bit every night. Lots of foreigners. Cover Sun.-Thurs. 80F, women free, Fri. 80F, Sat. 90F. Open daily 10:30pm-dawn.

Le Tabou, 33, rue Dauphine, 6*ème* (tel. 43 25 66 33). Mo. Odéon. An older, very chic crowd of habitués make this club somewhat difficult to get into. Being in pairs, and very well dressed (not clubby, more elegant) will give you a fighting chance. Music ranges from reggae to rock to house, depending on the DJ. Cover and first drink Mon.-Thurs. 70F, Fri.-Sat. 80F. Drinks from 50F. Open daily from 11pm to dawn.

Le Balajo, 9, rue de Lappe, 11*ème* (tel. 47 00 07 87). Mo. Bastille. Formerly the favorite stage of Edith Piaf. Founded in 1936 by Jo France, hence the *Bal à Jo*. Jammed with a youthful crowd with a clear love of excitement. Cover and first drink 110F. Open Thurs.-Mon. 10pm-dawn.

Flash Back, 18, rue des Quatre Vents, 6*ème* (tel. 43 25 56 10). Mo. Odéon. Two levels of unusual secluded lounges and a small dance floor complete with mirrored walls and a shiny disco ball. Tuesday nights is retro—70s and early 80s tunes. Comfortable, easy atmosphere among Paris's beautiful youth. Cover 65F, Sun.-Thurs. women free. Drinks 65F. Open daily 11pm-6am.

For **folk music,** try the restaurant Au Limonaire (see Restaurants—Twelfth *arrondissement)*. Also popular in France are clubs specializing in **Brazilian samba** and **African music:**

Chez Félix, 23, rue Mouffetard, 5*ème* (tel. 47 07 68 78). Mo. Monge. Eat on the top level; sway to the excellent Brazilian beat in the *caves.* Music 11pm-dawn. Cover and first drink 100F, subsequent drinks 50F. Open Sept.-July Tues.-Sat. 8pm-5am.

La Plantation, 45, rue Montpensier, 1*er* (tel. 42 97 46 17). Mo. Palais-Royal. A friendly place playing mostly African, Antillean, and salsa music. M. Yaffa, the owner, is dedicated to improving race relations. Dress well. Doesn't pick up until 2am. Cover and first drink 90F, subsequent drinks 50F. Open Tues.-Sun. 11pm-dawn.

Le Tchatch au Tango, 13, rue au Maire, 3*ème*. (tel. 42 72 17 78). Mo. Arts et Métiers. Crowd dances to Antillean, African, Salsa, and Zouk music. Regulars all know each other. Wed. is salsa night; Fri., Sat., and the eves of holidays are mostly Zouk. Cover Wed. 50F, Fri. 40F, Sat. and eves of holidays 60F. Drinks 25-40F. Open Wed., Fri.-Sat., and eves of holidays 11pm-5am.

Bars

Almost as common as cafés, the bars are places for heavier drinking and heavier socializing. Expect to meet new people and engage in absurd conversation. Law dictates a price increase after 10pm, but no one really ventures out to drink before this wee hour.

Le Bar sans Nom, 49, rue de Lappe, 11*ème*. Mo. Bastille. There's nothing cooler than this bar—cavernous, deep crimson, and packed with the hippest of the hip. Now if it only had a name...Beer 20F. Cocktails 44F. Open daily 8pm-2am.

Finnegan's Wake, 9, rue Boulangers, 5*ème* (tel. 46 34 23 65). Mo. Jussieu. A boisterous Irish pub set in a renovated 14th-century wine cellar, that pours not only the best pints of Guinness in the city (15-30F), but also hosts a variety of Irish cultural events. Poetry readings Mon. 7:30-9pm; call for times for jig and Gaelic lessons. Open daily 8:30am-12:30am.

La Micro Brasserie, 106, rue de Richelieu, 2*ème* (tel. 42 96 55 31). Mo. Richelieu-Drouot. Possibly the best place for beer in Paris. You can choose from over 60 kinds, but the best deals are on the beers they brew themselves. The Morgane in particular should not be missed: slightly reddish, it is called in French a *bière rousse*. They also serve food; try mussels and fries with your drinks (40F). You can visit the brewery downstairs Tues. and Thurs. 10am-8pm without paying extra. Before 10pm you get 25cl of house beer for 11-12.50F at the bar or 13-14F at a table; after 10pm both beers go for 20F. Between 5 and 7:30pm, buy 1 beer and get 1 free. Open Sun.-Mon. 7am-2am, Fri.-Sat. 7am-9pm.

Le Violon Dingue, 46, rue de la Mont. Ste-Geneviève, 5*ème*. Mo. Maubert-Mutualité. Reminiscent of an American frat party with its American waiters, stuffed interior, and cheap, fast-flowing beer. Bottled beer starts at 25F, on tap 32F. Cocktails from 30F. Open daily 6pm-2am.

Polly Magoo, 13, rue St-Jacques, 5*ème* (tel. 46 33 33 64). Mo. St-Michel. When the Violon Dingue closes at 2am, Polly's gets going. Super-friendly, amazingly lively crowd often bubbles over into the street, providing nights of endless amusement and adventure. Beer 18-35F. Open noon-4am.

Café L'Entre Pots, 14, rue de Charonne, 11*ème*. Mo. Bastille. This authentic little bar pulsates with an electric Parisian crowd. A real pool table and loads of atmosphere—chic, yuppy. Drinks from 50F. Open Mon.-Sat. 5pm-3am.

Pub St-Germain-des-Prés, 17, rue de l'Ancienne Comédie, 6*ème*. Mo. Odéon. Perhaps the largest and least interesting pub in Europe, this 7-room mammoth bar is a long-time favorite for American students looking for a good time. Parisians go elsewhere. 100 types of whisky. 450 different types of bottled beer, with 24 on tap. The 3 underground rooms look like opium dens and are the most fun, especially when you can hear anything over the cheesy renditions of American pop music. Beers and cocktails start at an outrageous 75F per bottle. Open 24 hrs.

Au Diable des Lombards, 64, rue des Lombards, 1*er*. Mo. Châtelet. A fashionable and bustling restaurant by day and early evening, this joint metamorphoses into a raucous hangout by early morning. Exciting selection of delicious and unusual cocktails. Coke 19F. Michelob 28F. Vodka Sunrise 55F. Open 9am-1am.

Gay and Lesbian Entertainment

While not quite the gay Mecca that is London or Berlin, Paris has a lively and venerable gay and lesbian scene. There is a particular concentration of restaurants, cafés, and bars between the Rambuteau and Hôtel-de-Ville metro stops. The gay discos scattered throughout Paris change more rapidly than *hétéro* spots, so check *Gai Pied* (summer guide 50F from kiosks) for up-to-date information and an English introduction. *Lesbia's* ads are a good gauge of what's hot, or at least what's open (22F from kiosks).

Club 18, 18, rue du Beaujolais, 1*er* (tel. 42 97 52 13). Mo. Bourse. A happy, hopping place with a mirrored dance floor. Mostly men, but friendly to women as well. Cover 40-50F. Open daily 11pm-dawn.

La Champmeslé, 4, rue Chabanais, 2*ème* (tel. 42 96 85 20). Mo. Opéra. Intimate women's bar in a relaxed atmosphere. Comfortable couches, dim lighting, and an eclectic assortment of music for dancing or hanging out. Come Thurs. night for the wild cabaret show. Few men. No cover. Drinks from 25F. Open Oct.-Aug. Mon.-Sat. 6pm-2am.

Le Boy, 6, rue Caumartin, 9*ème* (tel. 47 42 68 05). Mo. Havre-Caumartin. Young crowd. 50F cover includes one drink. Open daily 11pm-dawn.

Le Bar Central, 33, rue Vieille du Temple, 4*ème* (tel. 42 72 16 94). Mo. Hotel de Ville. Small and crowded, this friendly bar is a favorite among locals and tourists alike. Mostly men. Drinks from 20F. Open daily 4pm-2am.

Le Swing, 42, rue Vieille du Temple, 4*ème* (tel. 42 72 16 94). Mo. Hôtel de Ville. Bar with 50s decor and happy hour 9-11pm. Cocktails from 50F. Open Mon.-Sat. noon-2am, Sun. 2pm-2am.

Le Piano Zinc, 49, rue des Blancs Manteaux, 4*ème* (tel. 42 74 32 42). Mo. Rambuteau. Campy downstairs piano bar with Liza-Minnelli-Judy-Garland-style decor is very crowded. Lots of physical contact. Mostly men. Drinks from 15F; after 10pm drinks 35-65F. Open daily 6pm-2am.

Le Petit Prince, 12, rue de Lanneau, 5*ème* (tel. 43 54 77 26). Mo. Maubert-Mutualité. Superb dining in this casual restaurant for lesbians and gay men. *Menus* 85 and 110F. Delicious white-chocolate mousse 18F. Make reservations. Open daily 7:30pm-12:30am.

Au Petit Cabanon, 7, rue Sainte-Apolline, 3*ème* (tel. 48 87 66 53). Mo. Strasbourg-St-Denis. Classic French cuisine for women. 120F *menu*. Open Sun.-Wed. noon-2pm; Thurs.-Sat. noon-2pm and 8pm-midnight.

Highbrow Diversions

If your French is good, Paris still offers the same range of intellectual pursuits that it did when Rousseau and Montesquieu jabbered about liberty and the state of nature. Many art museums sponsor conferences, lectures, and colloquia. See listings for individual museums. And for something truly unique...

Le Club des Poètes, 30, rue de Bourgogne, 7*ème* (tel. 47 05 06 03). Mo. Varenne. Dedicated to refreshing the stressed-out automata of Parisian society, former TV personality Jean-Pierre Rosnay hosts nightly *"spectacle de poésie."* Artists read from the poetry masters, French and foreign, known and obscure alike in a cozy, comfortable, country atmosphere. Dinner (appetizers 45F, *plats* 80F, desserts 35F) service begins at 8pm; the spectacle starts at 10:15pm. First drink 90F, students 60F, subsequent drinks 35F. 95F lunch *menu* served noon-2:30pm. Reservations not a bad idea. Open Mon.-Sat. Closed Aug. Call the *Etat d'Urgence* phone line for a different 5-min. message each day, complete with poem: 45 50 32 33.

Maison de Radio-France, 116, av. du Président Kennedy, 16*ème* (tel.42 30 33 83). Mo. Passy, Ranelagh, or Mirabeau; RER Line C Av. du Pt. Kennedy/Maison de la Radio France. Yes, you too can sit in the audience and listen while French intellectuals debate away on live, prime-time radio! Programming and schedule varies with season. Call above number for details.

Dumb Fun

The French have invented a new art form: take an impressive building, add a light show, superimpose a recorded message about the glorious history of the building, the region, or the country, *et voilà:* **son et lumière.** It's as tacky as it sounds, but that's half the fun. Check the three entertainment weeklies for listings.

A ride on the **bateaux-mouches** (tel. 42 25 96 10) river boats provides a classic, if highly goofy, tour of Seine-side Paris. Be prepared to laugh at the one-and-a-half hours of continuous sight-commentary in five languages and dozens of tourists straining their necks to peer over the next person. Why does the French version sound about twice as long? It's not your imagination—the translations are notoriously sparse. Once again, the ride is particularly worthwhile if taken at night. (Departures every 1/2hr. from 10am-11pm from the Right Bank pier near Pont d'Alma. 30F, under 14 15F.) Another option is **Vert Galant** boats. (Departures every 1/2hr. from 10am-noon and 1:30-6:30pm from the Pont Neuf landing. 35F, under 10 20F.) The **Canauxrama** (tel. 42 39 15 00) boat tours of Paris get excellent reviews. The shortest (3hr.) tour leaves at 9:15am from Bassin de la Villette, 9bis, quai de la Loire, 19*ème* (Mo. Jaurès) and at 2:30pm from Port de l'Arsenal facing 50, quai de la Bastille, 12*ème* (Mo. Bastille). (80F, students 65F, under 12 45F.) Day-long trips to the countryside leave the Bassin de la Villette at 8:30am Thursday through Tuesday (190F; reserve ahead). The **Batobus** (tel. 47 05 50 00) makes frequent stops along both sides of the river from April to September. A spin on this ridiculous form of transportation costs 10F. (Day pass 50F.) Buy tickets on board.

Festivals and Other Seasonal Events

The French love of celebration is most evident in Paris, where the slightest provocation brings masses of people into the streets to drink, dance, and generally lose themselves in the spirit of the *fête* (festival) or *foire* (fair). The gatherings in Washington on July 4, in Times Square on New Year's Eve, or in Auckland, ever, pale before the assemblages of humanity on hand for Bastille Day fireworks or the arrival of the New Year. The **tourist office,** 127, av. des Champs-Elysées, 8*ème* (tel. 47 23 61 72; Mo. Charles de Gaulle-Etoile), distibutes the multilingual *Saisons de Paris 1993,* a booklet listing all the celebrations. The English information number (tel. 47 20 88 98) reports a weekly summary on current festivals. *Pariscope* lists *fêtes populaires* for the coming week. You can also get a listing of festivals from the **French National Tourist Office** (see General Introduction).

March and April

Foire du Trône, Neuilly Lawn of the Bois de Vincennes. Mo. Porte Dorée. A gigantic amusement park with roller coasters, pony rides, fortune-tellers, funhouses, and enough caramel apples, *barbe à papa* (cotton candy), doughnuts, and waffles to keep the most gluttonous junk-food junkie smiling for days. Jammed on warm weekends. End of March-May. Open 2pm-midnight.

May

Festival de Versailles (tel. 30 21 20 20, *poste* 234). Ballet, operas, concerts, and theater. Prices vary radically from one event to another. Late May-late June.

Festival de Musique de St-Denis (tel. 42 43 72 72). Music in the Basilique. Late May-late June.

Festival de Paris, 38, rue des Blancs-Manteaux, 4*ème* (tel. 40 26 45 34). Mo. St-Paul. A harmonic convergence of some of the greatest orchestras and choruses. Mid-May to late June. Admission 50-500F.

Les Trois Heures de Paris (tel. 49 77 06 40). A day-long regatta on the Seine on a Saturday in May. Four classes of boats race between pont d'Austerlitz and l'Ile St-Louis, facing the quai St-Bernard.

Foire du Trône continues.

June

Fête de la Musique. On June 21, the city celebrates the first day of summer with major rock concerts and audacious partying in all the big *places.* Latin Quarter fills with anyone who can blow a horn, carry a tune, or watch others do so. Dancing all night. *Le Figaro* and *Pariscope* have listings of concert schedules—check out all nearby churches for organ fugues and general chamber music extravaganzas. Free and obvious to anyone who goes out.

Nuit de la St-Jean. For the Feast of St. John the Baptist, June 24, the city sponsors magnificent fireworks at 11pm in front of the marble dome of Sacré-Coeur, 18*ème.* Mo. Abbesses.

Fête du Cinéma, June 28. One movie ticket allows you to go from theater to theater until your head spins with movies.

Festival du Marais, 68, rue François Minon, 4*ème* (tel. 45 23 18 25). Mo. St-Paul. Classical and jazz music, theater, and exhibits. Many events are outside, in courtyards, or in renovated Renaissance buildings in the Marais. The classical concerts tend to be expensive, but other events are free. Early June-early July.

Festival Foire St-Germain (tel. 43 29 12 78). Antique fair in pl. St-Sulpice, concerts in the Mairie du 6*ème,* sports events in the Jardin du Luxembourg. All free. Mid-June to early July.

Festival d'Orgue à St-Eustache (tel. 45 22 28 74). Organ concerts in the beautiful St-Eustache church. Tickets 70-120F, on sale at ARGOS, 34, rue de Laborde, 8*ème* (Mo. St-Augustin). Mid-June to early July.

Musique en Sorbonne, at the Sorbonne Grand Amphithéâtre, 47, rue des Ecoles, 5*ème* (tel. 42 62 71 71). Mo. Maubert-Mutualité. Everything in classical music from chamber groups to grand opera. Late June-early July. Admission 60-140F.

Fêtes du Pont Neuf (tel. 42 77 92 26). Mo. Pont Neuf. The bridge is closed to traffic and opened for dancing, music, street artists, and minstrels. A weekend in late June.

Festival de la Butte Montmartre, 14bis, rue Ste-Isaure, 18*ème* (tel. 42 62 46 22). Mo. Jules Joffrin. Experimental drama, dance, and jazz performances. Master classes in jazz and acting. Mid-June to mid-July.

Foire du Trône, Festival de Musique de St-Denis, Festival de Paris, and **Festival de Versailles** continue.

July

Bastille Day, July 14. Big-time celebrations nationwide. *Vive la République,* and pass the champagne. The day starts with the army parading down the Champs-Elysées and ends with fireworks over the Arc de Triomphe, at Montmartre, the Parc Montsouris, and the Palais de Chaillot. Traditional street dances are held on the eve of Bastille Day at the tip of Ile St-Louis (the Communist Party always throws its gala there), the Hôtel de Ville, pl. de la Contrescarpe, and of course, pl. de la Bastille, where it all began. Dancing continues the next night. Unfortunately, the entire city also becomes a nightmarish combat zone of leering men cunningly tossing firecrackers (sometimes ignited inside bottles) under the feet of unsuspecting bystanders (and into the metro). Check the newspapers a few days before to see where the main *bals* will take place.

End of the Tour de France, Fourth Sun. in July. Thousands of spectators turn out along the Champs-Elysées to watch the finish of the month-long bicycle race, which attracts as much hype in France as the World Series does in the U.S. Get there early and expect a huge crowd.

Festival Estival, 20, rue Geoffroy-l'Asnier, 4*ème* (tel. 48 04 98 01). Mo. Pont Marie or St-Paul. Opera, chamber music, and recitals in churches, palaces, and concert halls throughout the city. Early July-mid-Sept. Admission 25-40F.

Festival de l'Orangerie de Sceaux. In the Orangerie of the Château de Sceaux (tel. 46 60 07 79). A mixture of chamber music, popular music, and piano recitals. Performances late July-early Oct. Sat.-Sun. at 5:30pm. Admission 60-110F.

Versailles Display (tel. 39 50 71 81) Spectacular fountain effects every Sun. 4-6pm. Early July-Aug.

Festival du Marais, Musique en Sorbonne, and **Festival de la Butte Montmartre** continue.

August

Festival Estival, Festival de Musique de Sceaux, and **Versailles Display** continue.

September

Festival d'Automne (tel. 42 96 12 27). In the Pompidou Center and other museums and churches. Drama, ballet, expositions, and chamber music concerts. Late Sept.-Dec.

Fête de l'Humanité, parc de la Courneuve. Take the metro to Porte de la Villette and then one of the special buses. The annual fair of the French Communist Party—like nothing you've ever seen. A million people converge to hear debates, ride roller-coasters, and collect Marxist-Leninist leaf-lets. *(Humanité* is the newspaper of the French CP.) Communist parties from all over the world distribute literature and sell their native food and drink. Entertainers in recent years have included Charles Mingus, Marcel Marceau, the Bolshoi Ballet, and radical theater troupes. A cross between the Illinois State Fair, the Republican Convention, and Woodstock; you don't have to be a Com-munist to enjoy it. Second or third week of Sept.

Festival de l'Ile-de-France (tel. 47 39 28 26). Gala celebratory concerts in the churches and mon-uments of the larger Paris area. Late Sept.-late Dec.

Festival Estival and **Festival de Sceaux** continue.

October

Rallye Paris-Deauville (tel. 46 24 37 38). More than 100 vintage cars assemble at the Trocadéro fountains across from the Eiffel Tower. 7am on a Fri. in early Oct. Race in Deauville on Sun.

Festival de Jazz de Paris, 5, rue Bellart, 15*ème* (tel. 47 83 33 58). Mo. Ségur. There's so much jazz in Paris that this is hardly necessary, but it makes things official. Everybody on the European circuit (Nice, Antibes, Montreux, etc.) should be here. At the Théâtre Musical de Paris and the Théâtre de la Ville. Late Oct.-early Nov.

Fête des Vendanges à Montmartre, rue Saules, 18*ème*. Mo. Lamarck-Caulaincourt. The cele-bration of the harvest of the vineyards on Montmartre. Though not France's best-known wine-pro-ducing region, Montmartre still bottles enough wine to merit a day to celebrate its accomplishments. First Sat. in Oct.

Festival d'Art Sacré, 4, rue Jules-Cousin, 4*ème* (tel. 42 77 92 26). Sacred music at churches around Paris (including Notre-Dame) by the Radio France Philharmonic Orchestra and the Choir of Cologne. Early Oct.-Dec.

Festival d'Automne, Festival de l'Ile de France, and **Festival de Sceaux** continue.

November

Armistice Day, Nov. 11. Military parade from the Arc de Triomphe to the Hôtel des Invalides.

Festival Internationale de la Guitarre (tel. 45 23 18 25). Concerts in many Parisian churches. Mid-Nov. to mid-Dec.

Concours International de Danse de Paris (tel. 45 22 28 74). Week-long dance competition in mid-Nov.

Festival d'Automne, Festival d'Art Sacré, Festival de Jazz de Paris, and **Festival de l'Ile-de-France** continue.

December

Christmas Eve. At midnight, with the celebration of the Christmas Eve Mass, Notre-Dame be-comes what it only claims to be the rest of the year: the cathedral of the city of Paris. Thousands of people fill the church. Many of the neighboring cafés stay open late for those who want to start celebrating Christmas early. Children's entertainment continues until the end of school vacation.

New Year's Eve. When the clock strikes midnight, the Latin Quarter explodes: strangers embrace, motorists find people dancing on their hoods, and for an hour bd. St-Michel transforms into a pedestrian mall, much to the dismay of the cops who still attempt to direct traffic. A similar scene occurs on the Champs-Elysées.

Festival d'Automne continues.

Participatory Sports

You may find it hard to believe as you trudge around inner-city pavement, but Paris and its surroundings teem with sporting opportunities. Your number one best resource for information is the Mairie de Paris's sports hotline **Allo-Sports** (tel. 42 76 54 54; open Mon.-Thurs. 10:30am-5:30pm, Fri. 10:30am-4:30pm). The helpful people at the other end can tell you anything you need to know about where, when, and how to practice a particular sport in Paris. Many of the nifty introductory courses (to sailing, rock climbing, rowing, *etc.*) offered by the city are for residents only, but if you're in town for an extended period, you may be able to talk your way into one (or more). Also for residents, the city coordinates summer introductory courses to a variety of sports for kids. All such courses are, of course, offered in French only. *Pariscope* (see Publications) has a 5-page *"Sports et Loisirs"* listing every week. If you want to take a day trek to a *"centre de loisir"* outside of Paris to revel in pools, mini-golf, tennis courts, horseback riding, and the like, Pariscope has some excellent suggestions.

The following are a grab-bag of activities and recommendations intended for the budget traveler. Sports facilities of all kinds form a ring around Paris, lining the inner and outer edges. While many house private clubs, specialized sports schools, or host pro events, some are open to the public. Call Allo-Sports for details, or wander into one intrepidly.

Jogging

Rather than trying to pick your way around congested city sidewalks, head to one of Paris' numerous parks. The **Champs de Mars,** 7*ème* (Mo. Bir Hakeim) is one of the most popular in-city jogging spots, with a 2.5km path around the outside. (You could pay 8F and run stairs up the first two floors of the Eiffel Tower to complete the workout.) The leafy **Luxembourg Gardens,** 6*ème* (RER: Luxembourg; Mo. Cluny-La Sorbonne) offers a 1.6km circuit inside the fence. **Parc Monceau,** 8*ème* (Mo. Monceau) crawls with kids but remains serenely green and has a pleasant 1km loop. The **Tuileries Gardens,** 1*er* (Mo. Concorde or Tuileries) provides a 1.6km route. The **Canal St-Martin** in the tenth is relatively safe and rather picturesque to trot around. Feel free, of course, to tackle the hard pavement around the Seine, whose harsh surface and sunlight is occasionally muted by trees and crushed gravel.

For more of the wilderness feel, seemingly fresher air, and longer paths, head to the outskirts of town. The **Bois de Boulogne,** 16*ème,* boasts 142,000 trees, 300,000 bushes, and 845 hectares of authentic park woods. According to official statistics, the Bois has 35km of walking and running trails, but any distance could be covered or concocted by the keen jogger. A nice 2.5km circuit takes you around Lac Inférieur and Lac Supérieur. Try to get a hold of a map before going in—the twisty routes can be endlessly confusing. Start the odyssey from any one of the last three stops on metro line #10 (terminus Boulogne—Pont de St-Cloud). Or venture to the heart of the Bois on bus #43 (terminus Neiully-Pl. de Bagatelle).

Less renowned and on the opposite side of the city is the **Bois de Vincennes,** 12*ème.* Even though they're sweating their glands out, the joggers who run faithfully around **Lac Daumesnil** (Mo. Porte Dorée) are visibly soothed by their distance from the city core. Less frequented trails await the runner who penetrates farther into the park. Or you can begin farther to the northeast at the medieval **Château de Vincennes** (Mo. Château de Vincennes) and work your way down.

For a 250F membership fee, you can join the **Association culturelle de sport de plein air (ACSP),** stade de la Muette, 60, bd. Lanneo, 16*ème* (tel. 45 25 74 87 or 43 79 23 72; Mo. Avenue Foch). Every Sat. and Sun. from 10am-noon, the ACSP organizes runs and other fitness activities in the Bois de Boulogne.

Swimming

The *Mairie de Paris* has created an incredible network of public-ac 'ess pools, most municipally owned, but some *municipale concédée* ("use granted to the municipality," an obscure bureaucratic side effect of a semi-socialist economy). Opening hours vary from pool to pool, but all are open during the summer Mon. 2-7pm, Tues.-Sat. 7am-7:30pm, and Sun. 8am-5pm. Call Allo-Sports to have a copy of *Les Piscines à Paris* sent to you, or pick one up at any one of the *mairies*. Aside from glossy pictures of each pool, it systematically lists hours throughout the year and services available at each of the pools.

Entry to any of the **municipal pools** costs 9F80; 4F90 for those under 17, over 64, or accompanying children without using the facility themselves. If you plan on using the pools for a long period, inquire about one-year passes and youth discounts. Children under age 8 must be accompanied by an adult. The last swimmers are admitted 30 minutes before closing; the pools are cleared 15 minutes before closing. Some pools have a *"nocturne,"* 1 or 2 nights a week, when they are open beyond 8pm. **Municipale concédée** pools grant public time to the municipality and are somewhat more expensive as a consequence. They include **Piscine des Halles,** 1*er* (tel. 42 36 98 44), a large, well-lit pool in the Les Halles complex. (Open Mon. 11:30am-8pm, Tues. 11:30am-10pm, Wed. 10am-7pm, Thurs.-Fri. 11:30am-10pm, Sat.-Sun. 9am-5pm. Last admission 45min. before closing; pool cleared 30min. before closing. Admission 21F, under 16 16F. Pass for 10 entries 190F, under 16 150F. Wheelchair accessible.) Another such pool is the **Piscine Pontoise-Quartier Latin,** 19, rue de Pontoise, 5*ème* (tel. 43 54 82 45; Mo. Maubert). This snazzy pool has a counter-current machine. (Admission 19F, children 15F.)

Neither municipally-owned nor *municipale concédée,* the **Piscine Deligny,** facing 25, quai Anatole France, 7*ème* (tel. 45 51 72 15; Mo. Chambre des Députés) is one of Paris's best-known and best-loved pools. Built near the turn of the century on the hulls of two ships floating on the Seine, this 50m pool becomes the centerpiece for the nightly fun and frolic at the rollicking Deligny club. (Open daily 9am-7:30pm. Admission 50F, students 40F, under 16 35F.)

A warning on swimming laps in France: lane lines are not marked. Be prepared for as much confusion as if you were driving around the Arc de Triomphe rotary at rush hour.

Tennis

While lugging tennis gear in a backpack is not particularly convenient, the abundance of municipal tennis courts in Paris may tempt you to haul the old racket along. Serious players should definitely bring their equipment; Paris boasts of 170 municipal tennis courts in 40 "tennis centers," each open to the individual player. Free introductory lessons offered to children. Call Allo-Sports for more information.

Consult the *"Sports et Loisirs"* section of **Pariscope** for other listings of tennis and squash clubs that can be joined for longer periods. Many such clubs exist around Paris, offering lessons to all skill levels and special introductory packages to kids. (Indoor courts 27F60 per 1/2hr., 55F20 per hr. Courts with lights 18F60 per 1/2hr., 37F20 per hr. Courts without lights 12F per 1/2hr., 24F per hr. Reserve at least 24 hrs. in advance.)

Gyms and Fitness

Looking for a good gym? Ask around. Allo-Sports (are you detecting a recurring theme?) will have suggestions. *Paris Pas Cher* (see Shopping) lists affordable clubs, geared more toward the long-term visitor. Hostels, hotels, and student services at the Université de Paris will have suggestions for students. *Pariscope* lists a number of health and beauty clubs. **Alesia Club,** 143, rue d'Alesia, 14*ème* (tel. 45 42 91 05; Mo. Alésia) has a gym, sauna, and other facilities and will sell you a membership for the day. Call for details. If you feel the need of a beach, or perhaps just a sauna, jacuzzi, wavepool, and waterslide, find them at **Acquaboulevard,** 4, rue Louis Armand, 15*ème* (tel. 40 60 10 00; Mo. Balard, Porte de Versailles). Come early in the morning to avoid the herds of people who crowd the place like sweaty camels watering at an oasis. (Open Sun.-Thurs. 9am-11pm, Fri.-Sat. 9am-midnight. Admission 68F for 4hr.; 75F on weekends. More facilities are available to club members: annual membership 1000F, classes supplement 100F per month.)

In the parks and gardens of the city, Sunday mornings (9:30am-noon) bring physical education monitors suggesting open-air exercises appropriate to your needs. Free! Call Allo-Sports at 42 76 54 54 to find out the designated meeting spot in the *arrondissement* nearest you.

Cycling

The city proper is not a good place for a leisurely afternoon pedal, but cyclists happily while away the hours in the **Bois de Vincennes,** 12*ème*, around Lac Daumesnil (Mo. Porte Dorée) or deeper into the woods. The **Bois de Boulogne,** 16*ème,* officially boasts of 8km of bike paths, but any cyclist can make up a wholly original route among the innumerable trees. The **canal de l'Ourcq** passes through the Parc de la Villette, 30, av. Corentin Cariou, 19*ème* (Mo. Porte de la Villette) and has a bicycle path alongside. For information on bike rental and cycling around the city, consult "Getting Around" in the Transportation section.

Long-distance cyclists who just missed an invitation to the Tour de France may want to attempt the 109km ride out to **Ferté Milon** in the province of Aisne. Just follow the canal as far as it goes. The real test, of course, is getting back. No matter how far you go, the canal is a lovely traveling companion. Also consider the **Forêt de Fontaineb-leau** (see Daytrips).

Roller Skating

Truly hip roller skaters perform slalom and other more death-defying feats in front of the Palais de Chaillot in the Jardins du Trocadéro. (Roller blades have yet to really hit Paris.) To rent your own pair and skate the night away, go to **La Main Jaune,** pl. de la Porte-de-Champerret, 17*ème* (tel. 47 63 26 47; Mo. Porte de Champerret). (Open Wed. and Sat.-Sun. 2:30-7pm, Fri.-Sat. 10pm-dawn. What a rockin' town! Admission Wed. and Sat.-Sun. 40F, skate rental 10F; admission Fri.-Sat. 70F, skate rental 15F.

Fishing, Golfing, and Bowling

The legendary, imperturbable Seine fishermen are gone, but sewer authorities hope to have the river fishable in a few years. For now, write to the **Annicale des Pêcheurs de Neuilly, Levallois, et environs,** Base Halientique de la Jatte, 19, bd. de Lavallois prolongé, 92000 Levallois-Perret or call them at 43 48 36 34. They'll fill you in on angling in the Bois de Boulogne.

Golfing opportunities abound in the countryside of Paris. Bowladromes are not uncommon within city limits. Talk to Allo-Sports for addresses and information. Then again, why the hell would you want to go fishing, golfing, or bowling while you're in the City of Light? Huh?

Spectator Sports

If you think that Parisians are obsessed with only the very highest of the high culture, think again. Parisians follow sports with fierce interest, reading between the lines of their own sports daily, *l'Equipe* (6F), as well as the sports section of other newspapers. Once again, Allo-Sports can tell you all you need to know. The **Palais Omnisports Paris Bercy,** 8, bd. de Bercy, 12*ème* (tel. 43 46 12 21 or 43 42 01 23) hosts everything from opera and beach volleyball to figure skating and horse jumping beneath its radical, sod-covered roof. Ticket prices vary wildly according to the event.

Soccer

Soccer (called *"football"* or simply *"le foot"),* France's hands-down national sport, consumes Paris, especially during the big championships like the World Cup (*Le Mondial).* The next one is in 1994, in the U.S. Michel Plantini, the former national-team hero, stepped down as coach after a disastrous French performance at the European Championship in June of 1992. Join the Parisian multitudes in waiting to see where *les bleus* will go from here.

The **Club de Football Paris St-Germain** (tel. 40 71 91 91) is Paris's own professional *foot* team, splitting its time between road games and matches at the enormous **Parc des Princes.** Located in the 16*ème* (Mo. Porte de Saint-Cloud), the Parc des Princes is the city's premier outdoor stadium venue. Call 42 88 02 76 for a recording of dates and times of upcoming events and to find out where tickets can be purchased. The finals of the Coupe de France take place in early May; the Tournoi de Paris is in late July. Tickets to all events can be purchased at the Parc des Princes box office and go on sale anywhere from two days to two weeks in advance. Games are held on weekends and some weekday evenings. Prices range from 50-170F depending on the seat and the event. With the more expensive tickets, you just might see the ball and avoid getting pummelled by some of the rowdier fans. (Box office open 9am-6pm when selling tickets for an event.) The Parc des Princes also hosts **rugby** matches, including the Tournoi des Cinq Nations (Feb.-March) and the final of the Championnat de France de Rugby in early June. Call the box office for details.

Cycling

Even non-fans have heard of a fairly impressive road race called the **Tour de France,** reaching the age of 80 in 1993. Held in July, *Le Tour* pits 200 of the world's best cyclists against the Alps, the elements, and each other for 21 gruelling stages. Call *l'Equipe* (tel. 40 93 21 92), one of the tour's sponsors, for information about the race's itinerary. Spectators turn out in droves along the way, making a day of heading out to an obscure bend in the highway to cheer their favorite cyclist to victory (or at least, survival). Parisians and tourists alike line the Champs-Elysées for the triumphal last stage, usually between noon and 6pm. Show up early, with food and a book, and be prepared for a mob scene; you may see more on your hotel's TV. The women's Tour de France leaves Paris in mid-August near the Eiffel Tower. Call 43 57 02 94 for information.

The **Grand Prix Cycliste de Paris** is an annual time trial competition held at the Vélodrome Jacques Anguetil, Bois de Vincennes, 12*ème* (tel. 43 68 01 27). Male and female cyclists of the highest caliber will race the clock on June 19, 1993. Tickets 50F, available on site. Other events here are free, but may be canceled by rain.

Tennis

The *terre battue* (red clay) of the **Stade Roland Garros,** 2, av. Gordon Bennett, 16*ème* (Mo. Porte d'Auteuil) has ended more than one champion's quest for a Grand Slam. Two weeks each year (May 24-June 6, 1993), **Les Internationaux de France de Tennis (The French Open)** welcomes the world's top players to Paris. Write to the Fédération Française de Tennis at the above address (tel. 47 43 48 00) in October, for information on tickets for the next spring's tournament. Also, ask your national tennis association; they sometimes have an extra supply of tickets. If in Paris and still out of luck, try your hotel, any ticket agencies, and the stadium itself. And pray, very hard.

Horse Racing

Elegant dress, sleek beasts, fine food, and a day of seeing and being seen...of course Parisians love the races. The numerous hippodromes in and around town host races of all kinds throughout the year. Far from seedy, an afternoon at the track is a family affair. The level of classiness climbs a notch or two for the season's championship races.

Hippodrome de Vincennes, 2, rte. de la Ferme, in the Bois de Vincennes, 12*ème* (tel. 49 77 17 17). Mo. Château de Vincennes. A hike through the woods from the metro stop takes you to the home of Parisian harness racing since 1906. Prix d'Amérique (late Jan.), Prix de France (early Feb.), and Prix du Président de la République (late June). Tickets 15-30F, even for the big races.

Hippodrome d'Auteuil, in the Bois de Boulogne, 16*ème* (tel. 45 27 12 24). Mo. Porte d'Auteuil. Steeplechases (obstacle courses) since 1873; the stands date from 1921. For the big races in June and July, shuttles run from the metro and RER stations. Tickets about 22F during the week, 37F on Sun.

Hippodrome de Longchamp, deeper in the Bois de Boulogne, 16*ème* (tel. 44 30 75 00). Mo. Porte d'Auteuil. On race days, shuttles run from nearby metro stops.

Hippodrome de Chantilly, Chantilly (tel. (16) 44 57 02 54). See Daytrips.

Shopping

In a city where everything is a "sight," where even walking becomes entertainment, where eating is a religion, one can only imagine what pleasures await the shopper—looking, walking, and eating all at the same time. That Parisians pride themselves on dressing well is obvious from a short stroll down any major boulevard. Truly Parisian items, however, embody the utmost simplicity. They are made to last, never to go out of fashion.

Until the mid-19th century, the bourgeoisie shopped at small, specialized boutiques. Because these stores abounded in every neighborhood, the Parisians never had to go far from home to supply their daily needs. Aristide Bouricaut opened **Le Bon Marché** in 1852, in a former lepers' hospital in the seventh *arrondissement*. Undeterred by the setting, shoppers flocked to the revolutionary store; its economies of scale resulted in prices far lower than those of the neighborhood boutiques. Most importantly, shoppers could browse through goods, and clothes were made *pret-à-porter* (ready to wear) instead of custom-ordered at the local tailor. Shopping became a social event, where middle-class women could converge for cordial chats while they browsed through a previously unknown wealth of merchandise. Today, French department stores are still going strong, though the shopping mall has already invaded Les Halles and La Défense (see Sights). As for the aristocrats, they turned their nose up at "ready-made" clothes, and continued to purchase exquisite, custom-made goods at ultra-expensive boutiques. These are the ancestors of the modern Hermès and Yves St-Laurent.

Although Paris is not a bargain hunter's paradise, even some of the most *haute* of the *haute couture* boutiques join in the twice yearly *soldes* (major sales) that sweep the city in January and late June-early July. Non-Europeans are eligible to receive a refund of the Value Added Tax (VAT) if you spend more than 2000F in one store (see Practical Information—Money for more information). Even if you don't spend 2000F, **souvenir**s are duty-free, and every Pierre, Jacques, and Etienne-Louis is selling them. Reasonable prices on T-shirts and the lovable mini-Eiffel Towers can be found on rue de Rivoli, near the Louvre, as well as on the Ile-de-la-Cité, near Notre-Dame. For quality perfume, watches, pens, clothing, and beauty products at a 30-40% discount, try **Honoré,** 316, rue St-Honoré, 1*er* (tel. 42 60 49 00; Mo. Tuileries; open Mon.-Sat. 9:45am-6:45pm). **Raoul et Curly,** 47, av. de l'Opéra, 2*ème* (tel. 47 42 50 10; Mo. Opéra), offers similar merchandise at similar prices, with an additional 20% discount for foreigners (open Mon.-Sat. 9:30am-6:30pm).

A word of warning: all stores close on Sundays in Paris. Some of the smaller ones will close over the lunch hour on weekdays. When you walk into a boutique or even a *papeterie,* many store owners will take that as a declaration of intention to buy. They will approach you immediately. If you want to browse, which they may not like, say, *"Merci. J'aimerais seulement regarder"* (Thank-you, I'd just like to look). Do not, of course, be coerced into buying something you don't want, but don't be surprised at reactions ranging from disdain to hostility should you leave without making a purchase.

Clothing

Paris gowns have been in demand across the world since the days of the Bourbon kings and wax fashion-model dolls. Today's swankiest shopping districts are scattered all around Paris. Probably the most famous of these areas surrounds the exquisite **rue du faubourg St-Honoré,** which runs northwest through the eighth *arrondissement*. This is the area of *haute couture* (custom-made, obscenely expensive clothing and accessories, as opposed to your normal, merely pricey, factory-made stuff). Gawk at the impeccably French scarves and bags at **Hermès** (no. 24), the outlandish solid knits at **Sonia Rykiel** (no. 70), the untouchables of all types at **Yves Saint Laurent** (no. 38), and the high fashion design of the Japanese **Ashida** (no. 34). **Karl Lagerfield, Pierre Balmain,** and **Versace** boutiques cluster nearby. Not far away, like webs ready to snag the oblivious passer-by, the streets projecting from the **place des Victoire** (1*er* and 2*ème*) harbor another galaxy of *haute couture* boutiques. Running southwest from the Rond Point des Champs-Elysées, **avenue de Montaigne** shelters the houses of **Chris-**

tian **Dior** (no. 32), **Chanel** (no. 42), **Valentino** (no. 17-19), and **Nina Ricci** (no. 39). The name **Pierre Cardin,** seemingly omnipresent in Paris, appears cn a regal house in place François 1*er.* The windows in **place Vendôme** and along **rue de la Paix** (north to the Opéra) glitter with the designs of **Cartier, Van Cleef & Arpels,** and other offerings from the jewelry overlords of Paris.

Across the river on the Left Bank, boutiques tend to be smaller and occasionally less expensive, though no less stunning. A slew of shops (including **Sonia Rykiel, Kenzo,** and **Claude Montana)** display their goods in large open windows surrounding the streets of rue Bonaparte, rue du Four, rue de Grenelle, rue de Rennes, and rue de Sèvres. Find what you like on bd. St-Germain, but hunt around for better bargains around rue de Seine and the top of bd. St-Michel. Once the preliminary sightseeing mission is accomplished and you're ready to buy, head away from the big names and look for the smaller boutiques that cater to one particular style. Boutiques in the Marais and the Bastille tend more toward the funky and the trendy.

A unique Parisian shopping phenomenon is the *magasin du troc,* a large store that resells clothes bought and returned at the more expensive stores. Don't expect dirt cheap prices, but given the retail prices of Chanel and Dior, bargains are astonishing nonetheless. Try **Troc Mod,** 230, av. du Maine, 14*ème* (tel. 45 40 45 93; Mo. Alesia; open Sept.-July Tues.-Sat. 10am-7:30pm; Aug. Tues.-Sat. 11am-7:30pm); **Troc'Eve,** 25, rue Violet, 15*ème* (tel. 45 79 38 36; Mo. Dupleix; open Tues.-Sat. 10am-7pm); and **Réciproque,** possibly the king of the genre with three outlets at 95, 101, and 123, rue de la Pompe, 16*ème* (tel. 47 04 30 28; Mo. Pompe; open Tues.-Sat. 10am-6:45pm). For the lowest prices on the newest shoe fashions, try the side streets surrounding pl. de la République and rue des Saints-Pères in the sixth *arrondissement.*

Department Stores

The department stores of Paris provide a more carefree, American-style of browsing than the smaller boutiques. You'll find many of the same fashions at equivalent prices, without the ever-present, often annoying sales people. Expect crowds, especially if you go in the midst of the intense winter and summer *soldes.* If you want a present, beautifully wrapped, *fast,* this is the way to go. But if you're looking for a cheap umbrella or alarm clock, turn around and go to Monoprix.

Galeries Lafayette, 40, bd. Haussmann, 9*ème,* (tel. 42 82 34 56). Mo. Chaussée d'Antin. Also at 22, rue du Départ, 14*ème* (tel. 45 38 52 87). Mo. Montparnasse. Prices are high, but not outrageous. Keep your eye out for posters in the metro, advertising sudden sale extravaganzas. Half of Paris, on seeing these posters, rushes to Galeries Lafayette. Clothes are organized by designer, so you can get a taste of the most recent styles. Unfortunately, you'll be sharing this experience with unbelievable masses of tourists. So many Americans come here that it was considered a highly unsafe place to go during the terrorist attacks of the mid-80s. Take the time to admire the ornate Belle Epoque dome in the main building on bd. Haussmannn. Main store open Mon.-Sat. 9:30am-6:30pm. Rue du Départ branch open Mon.-Sat. 9:45am-7:15pm. All major credit cards accepted.

Au Printemps, 64, bd. Haussmann (tel. 42 82 50 00). Mo. Chaussée d'Antin. Also at 30, av. Italie, 13*ème* (tel. 45 81 11 50). Mo Italie. 25, cours Vincennes, 20*ème* (tel. 43 71 12 41). Mo. Porte de Vincennes. 10, pl. de la République, 11*ème* (tel. 43 55 39 09). Mo. République. 30, av. des Ternes, 17*ème* (tel. 43 80 20 00). Mo. Ternes. Anything you could possibly want (but not necessarily need) at typical (high) department store prices. You will also find more people than you could possibly want to see in a lifetime. Haussmann store open Mon.-Sat. 9:30am-6:30pm. Check with branches for slightly different opening and closing times. All major credit cards accepted.

Au Bon Marché, 3, rue de Babylone, 7*ème* (tel. 45 49 21 22). Mo. Sèvres-Babylone. This is Paris's oldest department store, and perhaps its best. As chic as Galeries Lafayette, but on the Left Bank and minus the tourists. A great place to come for gifts, from fancy soaps to classy French notebooks and paper. (They'll wrap them up for you in brightly colored tissue paper as well.) You'll find all the big designers, from Laura Ashley to Cachet. Look for sales (advertised in metro stations)—they may be the only way you can afford these clothes. If you're hungry, go across the street to the food annex (see Groceries). Open Mon.-Fri. 9:30am-6:30pm, Sat. 9:30am-7pm.

Samaritaine (tel. 40 41 20 20). Mo. Pont-Neuf, Louvre, or Châtelet. Spread in four large buildings between rue de Rivoli and the Seine, interconnected by tunnels. Although not as chic as Galeries Lafayettes or Au Bon Marché, Samaritaine makes for great browsing, and you might just see more French people than Americans. For VAT refunds, inquire in the basement of building 2. Open Mon.-Wed. 9:30am-7pm, Thurs. 9:30am-10pm, Fri.-Sat. 9:30am-7pm.

BHV, 52, rue de Rivoli, 4ème (tel. 42 74 90 00). Mo. Hôtel de Ville . The initials stand for Bazar de l'Hôtel de Ville, logical enough for a department store across the street from the Hôtel de Ville. One notch less chic than Samaritaine. Open Thurs.-Tues. 9:30am-7pm, Wed. 9:30am-10pm.

Tati, 11, pl. de la République, 3ème (tel. 48 87 72 81). Mo. République. The original bargain basement store (bermudas 20-80F, dresses 80-150F, T-shirts 15-40F, nightgowns 40-60F). In the cheapest department store in Paris, you must meet mayhem with an attitude, prepared to push through cramped displays and dig to the bottom of the bin for the elusive something-or-other-you-might-want-to-buy. With consistently low prices, it's a good place for T-shirts and cheap clothes, but not a mecca for designer clothing. Get your sales slip made out before heading to the cashier. Open Mon. 10am-7pm, Tues.-Fri. 9:30am-7pm, Sun. 9:15am-7pm. Eurocard, Mastercard, Visa.

Books

Books in Paris, in either English or French, are much more expensive than in North American bookstores. English-language books sell for about US$20 a novel (paperback). Bibliophiles on low budgets should stay away, crossing the street to avoid the enticing window displays, beckoning you to monetary ruin.

Galignani, 224, rue de Rivoli, 1er (tel. 42 60 76 07). Mo. Tuileries. A marvelous, wood-paneled bookstore, in the best of upper crust literary traditions. "The First English Bookshop Established on the Continent," as the bookmarks—complete with a Redcoat admiring the window display—proudly declare. Coming here, as des Esseintes showed, is as good as going to London itself. An excellent collection of beautiful British books you definitely can't turn down. Don't miss the brilliant and exhaustive *Let's Go: France* at only 180F! The upstairs floor is devoted to children's literature. Open Mon.-Sat. 10am-7pm.

Shakespeare and Co., 37, rue de la Bucherie, 5ème, across the Seine from Notre-Dame. Mo. St-Michel. Run by George Whitman (alleged great-grandson of Walt), this cozy shop seeks to reproduce the atmosphere of Sylvia Beach's establishment at 8, rue Dupuytren and, later, at 12, rue de l'Odéon, an extraordinary gathering-place for expatriates in the 1920s. Beach published Joyce's *Ulysses* from these quarters in 1922; avant-garde composer George Antheil wrote music for pianos and airplane propellers in his room upstairs. Whitman's new and used selection is quirky, and battered paperbacks cost as much as 50F. Still, the profits support impoverished writers who live and work in this literary cooperative. The first *Let's Go* writer stayed at Shakespeare's; so did beatniks Allen Ginsberg and Lawrence Ferlinghetti. Open daily noon-midnight.

Brentano's, 37, av. de l'Opéra, 2ème (tel. 42 61 52 50). Mo. Opéra. An extensive selection, especially of American literature, and a wide display of guidebooks. Open Mon.-Fri. 10am-7pm, Sat. 10am-noon and 2-7pm.

The Village Voice, 6, rue Princesse, 6ème (tel. 46 33 36 47). Mo. Mabillon. An English bookstore with a terrific sci-fi section and a decent collection of feminist literature. Pick up *Let's Go:Europe* for 179F, the Good Book, or *Lets Go:France* for 169F. Open Mon. 2-8pm, Tues.-Sat. 11am-8pm.

W.H. Smith, 248, rue de Rivoli, 1er (tel. 42 60 37 97; fax 42 96 83 71). Mo. Concorde. Here you'll find the latest publications from Britain and America, including many scholarly works. And, of course, quality guides from the *Let's Go* series. Buy a magazine to read in the pleasant but pricey English tea room upstairs. They will order books for you, but the cost of mailing books from America can be apoplexy-inducing. Open Mon.-Sat. 9:30am-7pm.

Gibert Jeune, 5, pl. St-Michel, 5ème, near the Seine (tel. 43 25 70 07). Mo. St-Michel. *The* bookstore near bd. St-Michel, and also *the* place to go for French classics. Lots of reduced books for the short-on-cash. The same variety of books and stationery abounds at the branch at 15bis, bd. St-Denis, 2ème (tel. 43 26 82 84). Mo. Strasbourg-St-Denis. The store at 27, quai St-Michel (tel. 43 54 57 32; Mo. St-Michel), sells university texts.

Librairie Gallimard, 15, bd. Raspail, 7ème (tel. 45 48 24 84). Mo. Rue du Bac. The main outlet of this world-famous publisher of French classics, this *librairie* offers a huge selection of Gallimard books at reasonable, if significant, prices. Open Mon.-Sat. 10am-7pm.

Librairies Ulysse, 26, rue St-Louis-en-l'Ile, 4ème (tel. 43 25 17 35). Mo. Pont-Marie. Funky bookstore specializing in travel books. Used and out-of-print books. Open Tues.-Sat. 2-8pm.

Les Mots à la Bouche, 6, rue Ste-Croix-de-la-Bretonnerie, 4ème (tel. 42 78 88 30). Mo. Hôtel-de-Ville. A serene bookstore with French and English titles, magazines, postcards, and newsletters of interest to both gay men and lesbians. Open Mon.-Sat. 11am-11pm.

La Librairie des Femmes, 74, rue de Seine, 6ème (tel. 43 29 50 75). Mo. Odéon. The one-time home of feminist collective MLF; now a large, peaceful place to browse through the collection of women's literature. The *librairie,* together with the press it supports, has lost much of its former radical edge. Open daily 10am-7pm; late July-Aug. sometimes closed 12:45-2pm.

Chantelivre, 13, rue de Sèvres, 7*ème.* Mo. Sèvres-Babylone. This literary playland defines excellence in children's bookstores. Full of old favorites for the young (Puss-in-Boots*)* and not so young (Dumas, Jack London), this place even vaunts an alcove where kids can draw or read well-used books. Everyone browses happily, poring over books, and the odd knapsack or game. Join the fun—this is better than F.A.O. Schwartz. Open Mon. 1-6:50 pm, Tues.-Sat. 10am-6:50pm. Closed 1 week in Aug. and on other Mon. in summer.

Music

Cassettes and compact discs are highly taxed in France, and are therefore *really* expensive. Expect to pay at least 100F for a compact disc, perhaps much more. The good news is that you'll find a much better sampling of certain types of music (especially French and African) than in North America. Look for the rare but priceless recordings that never made it across the Atlantic. Each of the following megastores has helpful clerks, decent prices, and a huge selection.

Virgin Megastore, 52-60, av. des Champs-Elysées, 8*ème* (tel. 40 74 06 48). Mo. Franklin Roosevelt. This music mecca on the Champs-Elysées includes an affordable restaurant and countless headphones that let you listen to the latest and greatest hits. If it has been recorded, it's likely to be at Virgin. Beware of the free listening stations: since they invariably have recordings you've never heard of, but find you can't live without, they can be lethal for your pocketbook. Open Mon.-Thurs. 10am-midnight, Fri.-Sat. 10am-1am.

FNAC (Fédération Nationale des Achats de Cadres): Several branches. **Montparnasse,** 136, rue des Rennes 6*ème* (tel. 49 54 30 00). Mo. Rennes. **Etoile,** 26, av. de Wagram, 8*ème* (tel. 44 09 18 00). Mo. Charles de Gaulle-Etoile. **Forum des Halles,** 1, rue Pierre Lescot, 1*er* (tel. 40 41 40 00). Mo. Les Halles. Not only a huge selection of tapes, CDs, and stereo equipment, but also books and tickets for concerts and the like (see Entertainment). Montparnasse store open Mon. 1-7pm, Tues.-Sat. 10am-7pm. Etoile branch open Mon.-Sat. 10am-7:30pm. Les Halles branch open Mon. 1-7:30pm, Tues.-Sat. 10am-7:30pm.

Odds and Ends

Paris is crawling with specialized boutiques, selling imports from the world over and hand-crafted goods representing centuries of tradition. For a cluster of these, try Ile St-Louis and the rue du Pont Louis-Philippe, both in the fourth *arrondissement.*

Galerie Bamyan, 24, rue St-Louis-en-l'Ile, 4*ème* (tel. 46 33 69 66). Mo. Pont Marie. Specializes in exquisite objets d'art and carpets from central Asia. Open daily 11am-8pm.

Clair de Rêve, 25, rue St-Louis-en-l'Ile, 4*ème* (tel. 43 29 81 06). Mo. Pont Marie. A winsome boutique with hand-crafted jewelry and beautiful, curious marionettes. Open daily 2:30-5:30pm.

St-Louis Posters, 23, rue St-Louis-en-l'Ile, 4*ème* (tel. 40 46 91 65). Mo. Pont Marie. A classy shop with an array of *affiches,* old and new, postcards, prints, and cards. Open daily 11am-8pm.

Pylones, 57, rue St-Louis-en-l'Ile, 4*ème.* Mo. Pont Marie. Also at 7, rue Tardieu, 18*ème.* Mo. Anvers. Lots of colorful and funky gadgets: clocks, funny ties, weird pens, and pins. A unique place.

Markets

For a complete list of the locations and hours of Paris's 84 markets, ask for the brochure *Les Marchés de Paris* at the tourist office or your local mairie. For food markets, see Groceries in the Food section.

Carreau du Temple, on the angle of rue Dupetit Thouars and rue de Picardi, 3*ème.* Mo. Temple. This structure of blue steel and glass, built under Baron Haussmann, is a neighborhood sports center in the afternoon and a clothes market in the morning. The market is especially strong in leather—coats, bags, and shoes—but also sells fur and plenty of clothes that are less "animalistically exploitative." This is one of the last places in the capital where you can still bargain—usually you can get the price down by about 25%. Even if your French isn't up to bargaining, the starting prices are quite low. As in any public market, watch your wallets and pocketbooks. It gets crowded on weekends, so it's best to come during the week. Open Tues.-Sat. 9am-12:30pm, Sun. 9am-1pm.

Quai de Mégisserie, 1*er.* Mo. Pont-Neuf or Châtelet. The shops in this section of the waterfront sell all manner of strange pets. Plenty of birds, turtles, and little mammals, in cages that spill out from the storesonto the sidewalk.

Marché de Vanves, av. de la Porte-de-Vanves and av. Georges-Lafenestre, 14*ème*. Mo. Porte de Vanves. General flea market merchandise. Sat.-Sun. 7am-7:30pm.

Marché aux Timbres (Stamps), on the Champs-Elysées at av. de Marigny. Thurs. and Sat.-Sun., during daylight hours.

Puces de St-Ouen (St-Ouen Flea Market)

You may not find fleas at the **Puces St-Ouen** (St-Ouen Flea Market), but you *will* find everything else, from spangled 1920s dresses to 18th-century wooden armoires and even used kitchen sinks (really!), plus of course, plenty of pickpockets and con artists. The prices and quality of the merchandise vary as widely as the products, beginning at the dirt cheap, low-quality bargains found among the renegade stalls. At the other end of the spectrum, astronomically expensive, high-quality antique dealers use buzzers to ring in their preferred customers while keeping out the riff-raff. Antique itself, the market was formed during the Middle Ages, when merchants resold the cast-off clothing of aristocrats (crawling with the market's namesake insects) to peasant-folk on the edge of the city, and it has gradually developed into a highly structured regular market alongside a wild, anything-goes street bazaar.

If you take the metro, you'll encounter the street bazaar first. The 15-minute walk to the official market is jammed with tiny **unofficial stalls.** Most of these sell flimsy new clothes at exorbitant prices, but the leather jacket stalls have some good buys (suede jackets for as little as 275F). Don't be turned off by the raucous hurriedness of the stalls; once you pass through to the real market you'll be able to browse leisurely. Pickpockets especially love this crowded area, and Three Card Monte con artists positively proliferate (don't be pulled into the game by seeing someone win enormous sums of money—they're part of the con, there just to attract suckers to the crooked game).

The regular market comprises six markets, located on the rues des Rosiers and Jules Vallès. Rare finds linger at the Marché Malik (new and used clothing), Marché Vernaison (antique bric-a-brac), and Marché Paul Bert (antique bric-a-brac). The remaining three—Marché Biron (used valuable tableware: crystal glasses, etc., plus some gold and silver jewelry), Marché Dauphine (expensive antique furniture stores), and Marché Serpette (expensive antique furniture stores) may be good for dreaming about what you'll do with your money when you're rich and famous. Wherever you shop, be prepared to negotiate the price; the starting price isn't what sellers expect to get, and on rainy days when business is slack you can really get them to come down in price. The market is open three days a week—Saturday, Sunday, and Monday from 8am-sunset. To get there by metro, ride the Porte de Clignancourt line all the way to the end, take the bd. Ornano exit from the station, cross the street to the Burger King side, head right down the main street (passing the Credit Lyonnais bank on your left), go straight through the unofficial market stalls until you cross under the overpass, and you'll be in the official market area, around the rue des Rosiers.

If you want to stop for lunch while at the flea market (and you probably will, since browsing there is an all-day affair), try a steaming bowl of *Moules Marinière* with *frites,* the uncontested specialty of restaurants in the area. Two restaurants in particular stand out: **Chez Louisette,** 130, av. Michelet (tel. 40 12 10 14), inside the Marché Vernaison, all the way at the back, where cigarette-puffing singers further enliven the already boisterous atmosphere. It's an eclectically decorated restaurant (no more than six of the hundred or so chairs in this restaurant match each other) with classic French café *chansons.* Unfortunately, the secret is out, and you'll hear as much English and German as French. *(Moules* 58F. Open Sat.-Mon. 8am-8pm.) A younger, less-touristy clientele frequents **Au Baryton**, 50 av. Jules Vallès (tel. 40 12 02 74), outside the Marché Malik, where people slurp up the *Moules-Frites* combo for only 49F while taking in the free live jazz and rock concerts. (Open Sat.-Mon. 8am-10pm. The music starts at 4:30pm.)

Daytrips from Paris

Parisian, get up, get up, come out and picnic in the
country, and take a boat on the river, under the
trees, with a pretty girl; get up, get up!
                                        —Marcel Proust

Having taken all the time and expense to get to Paris, who would want to leave? Louis XIV, for one. Louis XVI, even more. Whether you are in Paris for a year or only a week, it's well worth your time to get out of the city for a few hours, a day, or a weekend. Fast trains can zip you past the urban sprawl to some of the greatest monuments in France and to villages that will give you a sample of the country beyond the metropolis—providing a much-needed perspective on an immense city that, for all its pretensions, does not contain all that is worth seeing or doing in France.

Châteaux

Venture forth to the many châteaux that surround Paris for a vision of the French aristocracy—and the French love of disciplined, ordered beauty—at its height. Although a château is literally a "castle," the magnificent structures that ring Paris are by no means the heavy defensive weapons that stud the hills of Wales and the Rhône Valley. Rather, they represent the greatest conspicuous consumption in European history, all paid for by onerous taxes inflicted on the long-suffering peasantry and townsfolk of France. Everything in these châteaux is intentional—from the carefully planned *parterres* and the "natural" English gardens, to the restrained symmetry and Neoclassicism of the architecture and the idyllic "rural" quality of Marie-Antoinette's famous hamlet. Each of these buildings is a political statement in itself, a statement of wealth and power. They reflect the age of divine-right kings and their aristocratic courts—more theatrical than the famous dramatists, from Racine to Molière, which they sponsored. At the same time, they embody all the grievances that the French people had against their monarchs—grievances that exploded in 1789, when châteaux like these became a favorite target for rioting peasants.

Some helpful hints on *châteauing:* in general, weekends are far busier than weekdays, although Tuesdays (when most museums in Paris are closed) can also get a bit hairy. On special occasions—such as the fountain displays at Versailles on Sundays, it may be worth braving the crowds. Beware of groups of schoolchildren on weekdays in June, although if you understand French, you might get the benefit of their guided tour by latching on. The morning is **always** a better time to arrive than the afternoon. Don't start a visit 45 minutes before the château closes for lunch—the guards will rush you by locking the door behind you each time you walk into a room. PLEASE leave your cameras alone while you're inside the building. Flash pictures are forbidden for a good reason; they slowly kill furniture, paintings, curtains, tapestries, etc. Besides, unless you're a professional with a tripod and James Stanfield's lighting equipment, your pictures won't look nearly as good as the postcards you can buy for less money than it would cost to develop your film. In addition, all people with video cameras should be shot. A huge number of tourists are so busy snapping pictures or taking "live footage" that they don't stop to see, ponder, or experience any of the wonder of these spectacular buildings.

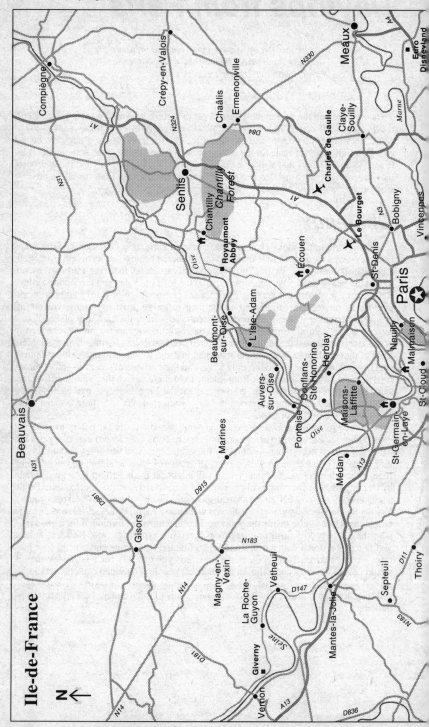

Ile-de-France

N←

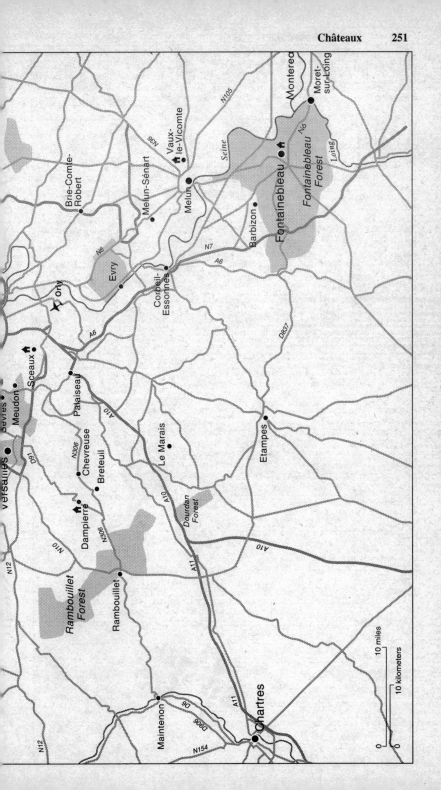

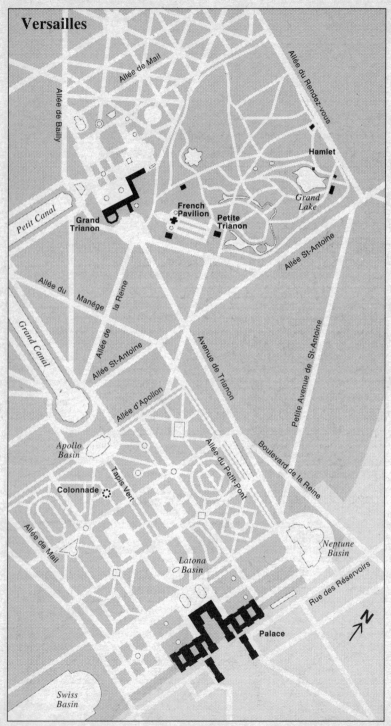

Versailles

Allée de Mail

Allée de Bailly

Allée du Rendez-vous

Hamlet

Grand Lake

French Pavilion

Petite Trianon

Petit Canal

Grand Trianon

Allée St-Antoine

Allée du Manége

Allée de la Reine

Grand Canal

Allée St-Antoine

Petite Avenue de St-Antoine

Avenue de Trianon

Allée d'Apollon

Apollo Basin

Colonnade

Tapis Vert

Allée du Petit-Pont

Boulevard de la Reine

Neptune Basin

Allée de Mail

Latona Basin

Rue des Réservoirs

Palace

N

Swiss Basin

Versailles

The magnificent palace of Louis XIV, Versailles perfectly embodies the Sun King's absolute power and his famous statement, *"L'Etat, c'est moi."* (I *am* the State.) Shunning Paris for its association with the power struggles of his youth, Louis XIV turned his father's hunting lodge (20km from Paris) into his royal residence, built and decorated mainly by Le Vau, Le Brun, and Le Nôtre, the team stolen from Vaux-le-Vicomte. The court became the center of noble life and more than a thousand of France's greatest aristocrats vied for the king's favor. In turn, Louis was able to keep the nobility away from Paris and their provincial power-bases and under his watchful eye in what Harold Nicolson called a "vast and glittering concentration camp." Busy vying for roles in the Sun King's wake-up *(levée)* and bed-going *(coucher)* rituals, including the inestimable privilege of passing the king his shirt, the French aristocracy had no time for subversion. Ever the clever politician, Louis also successfully destroyed their financial independence by forcing them to pay crippling taxes, which he used to support his own extravagant expenditures.

The ostentatious rooms and endless gardens at Versailles represent the pinnacle—and highest extravagance—of classical Baroque orchestration. No one knows just how much it cost to build Versailles; Louis XIV himself burned the accounts so no one would ever find out. At the same time, life there was considerably less luxurious than one might imagine—courtiers wearing rented swords urinated behind statues in the parlors, wine froze in the drafty dining rooms, and dressmakers invented the color "puce" (literally, "flea") to camouflage the insects crawling on the noblewomen of the palace. Although Louis XIV and his palace number among the few monarchical successes of 17th-century Europe, the kind of mass extortion that Versailles represents would spark the French Revolution a century later. On October 5, 1789, 15,000 fish-wives and National Guardsmen marched out to the palace and brought the royal family back with them. The intimidating grandeur of monarchy had failed at last. In 1871 the château regained its limelight as Wilhelm of Prussia became Kaiser Wilhelm I of Germany in the Hall of Mirrors, beneath the ceiling depicting Louis XIV, conqueror of the Rhine. That same year, as headquarters of the Thiers regime, Versailles sent an army against its old rival, Paris, then ruled by the Commune. And in 1919, a vengeful France forced Germany to sign the ruinous Treaty of Versailles in the very room of its birth.

Visiting Versailles is a mammoth undertaking; you may want to take two days to do it. **Arrive early in the morning** to avoid the worst of the crowds and the crowds of the worst—every country seems to hand-pick its most obnoxious tourists to send to Versailles. Pick up the orientation guide in English at one of the two tents on the way in. Then venture into the **courtyard.** The magnificent recessed façade, towering over the marble courtyard and the equestrian statue of Louis XIV, will draw you inward. Molière's *Tartuffe* debuted on this terrace. The clock on the pediment used to be set to the time of death of the previous king. Above what appears to be the main entrance is the balcony of the **King's bedroom,** at the center of the east-west axis along which the château and gardens are laid out. Although some might like to underplay the symbolism, the placement of the room was no mistake—the Sun King's place was at the center of the château system (thus Louis XIV adopted the once subversive ideas of Copernicus) and he rose each morning, to great ritual, in the east.

But where does the mere tourist begin the day? A frightening number of entrances, all lettered, assault the helpless visitor. **Entrance A,** on the right-hand side in the North Wing as you enter, is the main entry for individual visitors. Lines can be long, especially on summer afternoons. This door leads to the **State Apartments of the King** and **Queen** and the **Galerie des Glaces** (the famed Hall of Mirrors). Most of these rooms are now a self-guided museum of French history, full of portraits and engravings of the French aristocracy (see Main Tour, below, for more information). Invest in a guide of some kind—without explanation, the symbolic freight of the architecture and artwork will pass you by. Cassette guides last roughly one hour (25F, ID deposit; open 9am-5pm). Curator Danile Meyer's comments on the gardens and the Trianons constitue the best written guide to Versailles. At 50F, it's a worthwhile investment.

Guided Tours

A better place to start your visit is at Entrance D, where you can reserve a place on a guided tour, the only way of accessing many of the most interesting parts of the castle. Moreover, the admission ticket that you purchase at Entrance D allows you to bypass Door A and enter at the uncongested A2. (If the guards give you trouble, tell them the people at the D cash register told you to enter there. You should not have to wait in the A line if you already have a ticket.) Seven tours of different parts of the château are offered; only three are given in English and the English of the tour guides is of variable quality. The visit not to miss is that of the Opera and Chapel, offered a few times a day. The **Chapel** is visible from the general access area but you won't be able to appreciate the Rococo sculpture, the fresco of the Holy Ghost above the King's balcony, or the marble design on the floor unless you see it up close. Church services were held regularly in this chapel dedicated to Saint Louis; here Louis XV, far from a saint, yet not hypocritical enough to take communion while indulging with his mistresses, abstained from the rite for thirty years. In the chapel's last royal marriage, Marie-Antoinette and the sixteen-year-old Dauphin (future Louis XVI) were married here in 1770.

The architect Jacques-Ange Gabriel had been working on plans for the **Opera** for 20 years when Louis XV demanded it be finished in a mere 21 months, in time for the marriage of the Dauphin. With 20,000 people working, it was finished the day before and held its first performance on the royal wedding night. The pink and blue oval room is a marvelous fake; not marble or bronze as it appears to be, the restored Opera is actually made of wood. A series of mirrors around the galleries reflect the chandeliers, making the theater seem far larger than its actual size. Gabriel's 20 years of planning did not go to waste—many consider this one of the most beautiful theaters in the world.

Most of the other tours take you through a series of seemingly empty, if historically important, rooms. The tour of **Louis XV's Apartments** showcases a small collection of furnishings, instruments, and tapestries, while providing a history of Versailles under that monarch. You can see the room where Mozart played on his youthful visits (at ages 7 and 22) to Versailles and learn the origin of the name of the "voyeuses" chair. The visit to **Marie-Antoinette's Apartments** does not trail through as many lavishly decorated rooms as you would think and some of the smaller rooms are hard to appreciate in a large group. Much of the tour is spent in rooms filled with portraits, learning the who's whos for the Habsburgs, Bourbons, and their ministers. True French Revolution buffs will not want to miss the door and passageway through which the Queen fled to rejoin her king on October 6, 1789, when a crowd of bloodthirsty Parisians flooded into her bedroom, demanding the head of the "Austrian whore."

Other tours are fairly uninspiring. Unlike the Opera and Chapel tour, expect empty rooms with limited decoration—Versailles was completely sacked during the Revolution and only a tiny portion of its original glory has been restored. More portraits populate the visit to the **Apartments of Mesdames,** Louis XV's daughters, and in the other French-only tours, including tours of the **Apartments of Mme. de Pompadour, Mme. du Barry,** and the **Dauphin and Dauphine.** So you get to see the salon in which Mozart played for Mesdames. So what. Take these tours only if you are an addicted buff of the French aristocracy, or if you're looking for an oral history lesson, full of neat anecdotes, with some nifty backgound decoration. Tours last one hour and cost 20F each (under 18 15F). Brace yourself for some tortured English accents and very odd translations ("Welcome to Vairsiz"). Check in at Entrance D for specific times, mandatory reservations, and tickets. Tours leave from entrance F, across the courtyard. (Tours of the Apartments Tues.-Sun. 10:15-4:15pm; Opera and Chapel 10:45-4pm.)

Longer "field trip" tours go to the **Gardens and Groves** and to the **Petit Trianon and English-Garden.** The Gardens and Groves tour, with considerable walking, provides the history and explanation of Le Nôtre's gardens and the innumerable fountains that populate them. (June-Oct. Sat.-Sun. 11:30am. 2hr. Admission 40F, under 18 30F.) Guided visits to the **Petit Trianon and the Jardin Anglais** illuminate this favored hang-out of Marie-Antoinette. (July-Sept. 1-hour tour at 11am. Admission 20F, under 18 15F. Two-hour French-only tour 4pm. Admission 40F, under 18 30F. Both tours leave from the entrance to the Petit Trianon.)

The **King's Bedchamber** is the only other part of the château with a separate entrance. Don't feel compelled to make this cassette-guided visit (it's on the expensive side). However, it does yield a look at the Sun-King's gold bed and balustrade, and more than a passing glance at Nocret's beautiful family portrait, featuring Louis XIV as Apollo and his brother, Philippe d'Orléans, as holder of the morning star (Philippe was the first after the morning chaplain to see the Sun King—he was also kept in skirts until he was 18). (Tickets sold Tues.-Sun. 9am-5pm at Entrance C. Admission Tues.-Sat. 37F, ages 18-25 and over 60 29F, under 18 15F; Sun. 29F, under 18 15F.)

The Main Tour

The general admission ticket starts your visit in the **Musée de l'Histoire de France,** created in 1837 by Louis-Philippe to celebrate the glory of his country. Against the backdrop of richly textured walls are hung portraits of the men and women, aristocrats and artists, generals and ministers, who shaped the history of France. Expect to be spooked by the ever-present face of Louis XIV, and wonder if he spent his entire life sitting for portraits. Of particular interest are the perceptive portraits by Philippe de Champaigne, pre-eminent court artist under Louis XIII. These 21 rooms, arranged in chronological order, attempt to construct a historical context from which to understand the château. The North Wing ground floor, in Louis XIV's day, was a piece of road with open windows, a bustling open air market where men bought wigs and women ribbons. Thousands of people lived at Versailles, preoccupied by the court ritual rigorously set and re-set by the king. As you head into the (crowded) state apartments, try to imagine what living in this monolith as a not-so-elevated courtier would be like.

Each of the **Drawing Rooms** in the **State Apartments** is dedicated to a mythological god—Hercules, Mars, Mercury, and the ever-present Apollo, among others. Although less brilliant than you would expect, the gilt wood is still splendid, fresh from the 5-year, $70 million restoration that ended in 1989. Pay attention to the abundant detail, and especially to the integration of painting with bas-relief, sculpture, and furniture—as Le Brun's paintings meld with Le Vau's architecture. Be sure to shift your marble-mesmerized eyes toward the **Louis XIV statue** by Bernini in the **Diana Drawing Room.** A glimpse of his armor visible underneath the quintessentially Baroque frenzy of clothing, the luxuriously coiffed Louis looks into the sun unflinchingly, because he *is* the sun.

Framed by the **War and Peace Drawing Rooms** is the **Hall of Mirrors.** Originally, the hall was a dark, somewhat gloomy passageway, until Mansart (of roof fame) added the mirrors and doubled the light. Although many of the mirrors are old and cloudy, nothing quite compares to the visual impact of standing at one of the Hall and gazing down past the mirror-filled arches, gold figures, and countless chandeliers. Le Brun's ceiling paintings tell the history of Louis XIV's heroism, culminating in the central piece entitled *The King Governs Alone.* Don't expect a wall of seamless mirrors—the Hall of Mirrors is actually a series of mirrored panels joined together and set in wooden frames. Each of these panels was the largest mirror that 17th-century technology could produce; the ensemble represented an unbelievable, stunning extravagance. (One begins to understand why the Sun King burned his accounts....)

The **Queen's Bedchamber,** which saw the public births of 20 members of the royal family, sports its floral summer decor. A second version of David's huge painting depicting Napoleon's self-coronation dominates the **Salle du Sacré** (also known as the Coronation Room), in which the king used to wash the feet of 13 poor children on Holy Thursday. The **Hall of Battles,** 120m long, 13m wide, and 2 stories high, is a more modern tribute to France's military prowess.

(Château open Tues.-Sun. 9am-6:30pm; Oct.-April Tues.-Sun. 9am-5:30pm. Last admission 1hr. before closing. Admission to State Apartments and Hall of Mirrors 31F, ages 18-25, over 60, and Sun. 16F, under 18 free. For general information, call 30 84 76 76 or 30 84 74 00.)

The Gardens

The immense expanse of park behind the château is in the process of restoration, which will bring it back to its appearance in the days of Louis XIV. Even with work in progress, even mobbed with crowds of tourists, the gardens at Versailles are a breath-taking sight, providing the perfect complement to the Sun King's huge palace. Numerous artists—Le Brun, Mansart, Coysevox—executed pools, statues, and fountains here, but it is the hand of master gardener André Le Nôtre that you see all over the grounds. Louis XIV, an amateur enthusiast of landscaping, wrote the first and definitive guide book to the gardens entitled the "Manner of presenting the gardens at Versailles." Start, as he suggests, on the terrace, pausing to study the layout of the gardens—undoubtedly the jewel in the ostentatious crown that is Versailles. During the summer, the grounds at Versailles have an overwhelming impression of green rare to this area of France. Even more rare are the wide paths and tall trees—you can feel quite alone, even with lots of people around, and then you stumble upon a clearing with a fountain that seems a little piece of heaven. During the summer, the grounds are open until dusk (around 8:30pm). Come in the evening to see the immense château without people, like the empty stage of a grand opera. With only the occasional jogger to mar your view, you will see the entire panorama of Versailles as it was originally conceived—a single work of art, bringing together all artistic and natural media as a backdrop for the aristocrats who lived beneath its rigid, controlled beauty.

To the left of the terrace, the **South** and **Orangery Parterres** decorate the area in front of Mansart's **Orangery.** The temperature inside never drops below 6°C (42.8°F) and was once home to 2000 orange trees. In the center of the terrace, the **Water Parterre** boasts statues by the *ancien regime's* greatest sculptors; among the works are four figures representing France's main rivers.

Below, the **Latona Parterre** holds one of the most extraordinary fountains, alive with Baroque transformation, the **Fountain of Latona.** Latona, mother of Diana and Apollo, is seen shielding her children from the attack of peasants, whom Jupiter is turning into frogs. Part-human, part-frog figures belch water into the air when the fountains are turned on (see Special Events, below). The fountain can also be read as a thinly veiled political allegory—Latona represents Anne of Austria, fleeing Paris and the Fronde with her children, Louis XIV (Apollo) and Philippe d'Orléans (Diana). Louis XIV appears as both victim (Apollo) and savior (Jupiter).

Past the Latona Parterre and to the left is the **Rockwork Grove,** built between 1681 and 1683. Once known as the ballroom because courtiers danced on the long-gone marble floor, the Grove shows off odiferous water cascading over shell-encrusted steps. The south gate of the grove leads to the magnificent **Fountain of Autumn,** one of four seasonal fountains marking the intersection of pathways on either side of the main alley. The gilt lead of the benevolent Bacchus contrasts strikingly with the dark grapes spilling over the surrounding satyrs. The **Mirror Fountain,** unadorned, spurts near the peaceful **King's Garden** and the **Fountain of Winter,** an old man. Seemingly transported out of ancient Greece, the **Colonnade** is a 32-column peristyle, decorated by sculptures and 28 white marble basins, in the center of which the king used to take some light meals. The north gate to the Colonnade exits on to the **Tapis Vert (Green Carpet),** the central strip of grass linking the château to the much-photographed **Fountain of Apollo.** Pulled by the vigorous prancing of four horses, Apollo/Sun God/Louis XIV (as God of the Arts—the greatest of all patrons) rises out of dark water to enlighten the world. Don't forget to look back up at the château from the Apollo Fountain.

On the north side of the garden (to your left as you head back) is Marsy's incredible **Fountain of Enceladus.** One of the giants who attempted to unseat Jupiter from Mount Olympus, Enceladus cries out in agony under the weight of the rocks that Jupiter has thrown to bury him. When the fountains are turned on, Enceladus' cry is tangible in the form of an 25m jet that sprays from his mouth. Flora reclines more peacefully on a bed of flowers in the center of the **Fountain of Spring,** while Ceres luxuriates in sheaves of wheat in the **Fountain of Summer.** More endearing is the group of children frolicking on the **Children's Island.** The artificial grotto that houses the **Baths of Apollo** was, surprisingly, not built under Louis XIV, but in 1778 under Louis XVI and shows, not surprisingly, nymphs fluttering around Apollo.

The **North Parterre,** full of sculpted trees, flower beds, and triangular lawns, overlooks some of the most spectacular fountains in the garden. The **Water Avenue,** lined with a series of fountains held by child statues, allows for the best view of the **Bathing**

Nymphs Fountain. At the end of Water Avenue roars the **Dragon Fountain.** The drag-on is undergoing a transformation into a python, which Apollo slew with the force of his light at Delphi. A symbol of civil war, the dying beast vomits water 27m into the air, the highest of any jet in the gardens. The culmination of any visit to the gardens must be the **Fountain of Neptune,** the largest of all the fountains. Ninety-nine jets burst out from urns and seahorses surrounding the fierce figure of Neptune, trident thrust in front of him. (Gardens open sunrise-sundown. Free; May-Sept. Sun. 18F.)

Beyond the Petit Parc of Le Nôtre's classical gardens stretch wilder, more natural woods and farmlands. The **Grand Canal,** a large rectangular (and, like most of the park, entirely artificial) body of water, calm in the midst of wilderness, lies like a giant doormat beyond the Apollo Fountain. Rent a bike to the right (north) of the canal, just outside the garden gates to appreciate the vast grandeur of Louis XIV's concoction. (17F per ½hr., 28F per hr.). A *bateau-mouche,* smaller than those that skit along the Seine, tours the Canal (21F, under 16 16F).

The Trianons and Marie-Antoinette's Hameau

Also within the grounds of Versailles are the two Trianons—cozier palaces that at-tempted to give the royal family some privacy—and the Petit Hameau, an idyllic peas-ant village where Marie-Antoinette liked to milk the cows. Trianon was the name of the village the Sun King bought in 1668 in order to expand his estate. Built by Mansart, the single-story, marble-decorated **Grand Trianon** was intended as a meeker château in which, if need be, the king could reside alone with his family. Stripped of its furniture during the Revolution, the château was restored and inhabited by Napoleon and his second wife. Today past meets present as important state meetings, including the one that passed the constitutional amendment for Maastricht, are held at the Grand Trianon, and Versailles briefly becomes the capital of France once again. (Open Tues.-Sun. 11am-6:30pm; Oct.-April Tues.-Fri. 10am-12:30pm and 2-5:30pm, Sat.-Sun. 10am-5:30pm. Last admission ½hr. before closing. Admission 17F, ages 18-25, over 60, and Sun. 9F, under 18 free.)

The **Petit Trianon,** built for Louis XV and Mme. de Pompadour by Gabriel, was presented to Marie-Antoinette by Louis XVI. Restoration has closed off all but four rooms to the public—their cozy feel may not be worth the price of admission. (Open same hours as Grand Trianon. Admission 12F, ages 18-25, over 60, and Sun. 7F, under 18 free.) The English Garden, made for Marie-Antoinette, and the Grand Trianon gar-dens provide calm away from the madding crowds closer to the château. Quainter still and the opportune spot for a walk or rest is **Le Hameau** (the Queen's Hamlet), a collec-tion of Normandy cottages built for Marie-Antoinette. The young queen of "Let them eat cake" fame liked to play peasant here, to the great disgust of the people who actual-ly fit that description. None of the buildings are open to the public but they once con-tained drawing rooms of considerable, un-peasant-like elegance. Trains to the Trianons leave from behind the main château most of the day (26F round-trip, children 15F; last departure at 5:45pm in summer). The train does a 35-minute circuit that allows you to get off, tour the Trianons, and get back on another train. But the much-touted commen-tary on the gardens only repeats what is written on the pamphlet. If you are at all ambu-latory, save your pennies and walk (15-20min.).

Special Events and Practical Information

Brave the crowds on Sundays from May through September to see (and hear) the **Grandes Eaux Musicales,** the only time the fountains are in full operation. Seeing Versailles with the fountains on completes the sensual experience that the palace was designed to be; the entire park comes alive with spouting water. A *grande perspective* is offered between 11:15 and 11:35am; the best time to circulate and visit each fountain is between 3:30 and 5pm, when the fountains spout and appropriately inspirational mu-sic plays. A free pamphlet lays out a suggested walking path; a more expensive 20F guide in English will not give you much more info than that already found in the Meyer guide. (Admission to park during *Grandes Eaux* 18F.)

The **Grand Fête de Nuit,** a theatrical musical and firework extravaganza, imitates the huge *fêtes* of Louis XIV. The garden at Versailles had to be finished in 1664 in time for one such party, the Fête of the Enchanted Isle, for which Molière wrote an up-to-the-minute *masque*. (Fêtes held at the Neptune Fountain July and Sept. Sat. nights rain-or-shine. 80min. 50-170F, reduced rates for children.) Call the tourist office at 39 59 36 22 for exact dates and ticket info. Tickets go on sale at tourist office and certain agencies within Paris. Doors open 90 minutes before the show; enter at 2, bd. de la Reine.

The **Centre de Musique Baroque de Versailles** gives concerts at 5:30pm on Saturdays from May through early September (tickets 50-100F). Musical Thursday concerts by the Maîtrise Nationale of Versailles are held in the Royal Chapel at 5:30pm on Thursdays from November to June (tickets 20F). For more information on these events call 39 49 48 24; for reservations call Théatel at 42 72 77 72.

You will probably have little reason to venture into "greater Versailles;" the château even offers a cafeteria, open 9:30am-5pm. (Sandwiches 17F, *plat du jour* 38-45F.) But the **Office de Tourisme de Versailles,** Les Manèges, rue du Général de Gaulle, across the street from the train station (tel. 39 53 31 63), can offer basic information about all château events, other sights, restaurants, and accommodations. The caravan at 7, rue des Réservoirs (tel. 39 50 36 22), just outside the château gates, can do the same.

Reach Versailles by RER Line C5 to the Versailles Rive Gauche station from one of the downtown Paris stations (roughly every 20min., 35min., 8F there, 12F back). From the Invalides metro stop, take trains whose four-letter label begins with V. You may be allowed only to purchase a one-way ticket. Buy your RER ticket *before* going through the turnstile to the platform, despite the fact that your metro ticket will get you through. Your metro ticket won't get you through the turnstiles to exit at Versailles.

Vaux-le-Vicomte

Some might consider **Vaux-le-Vicomte** a mere hut compared to Versailles. Better to think of Le Vau, Le Brun, and Le Nôtre's first masterpiece as playing St. John the Baptist to Versailles's Christ. Nicolas Fouquet, Louis XIV's Minister of Finance, a man whose proud motto was *Quo non ascendet,* ("What heights will he not scale?") assembled Le Team of architect, artist, and landscaper to build Vaux for him between 1656 and 1661. In so doing, he financed the creation of a new standard of country château, in a uniquely French, Neoclassical Baroque style. To show off his new pad, Fouquet threw a *fête* to end them all on August 17, 1661. Louis XIV and Anne d'Autriche were but two of the witnesses to a sensual orgy that provided poetry by La Fontaine, a new ballet by Molière, and concluded in a fireworks extravaganza featuring the King and Queen's coat of arms and pyrotechnic squirrels (Fouquet's symbol). All conceivable elements—fire, music, air, light, water—had been harnessed to showcase Fouquet's—and humanity's—dominance over nature and subsequent molding of garden and stone into a disciplined aesthetic creation.

The celebration of Fouquet's impeccable grace, sophistication, and culture—he was surrounded by a circle of the finest artists and intellectuals—did not last long. Furious at being upstaged by his first minister, the young Louis ordered Fouquet arrested. Three weeks later, at Nantes, d'Artagnan, the captain of the Musketeers immortalized by Dumas, arrested the hapless man for speculation. Behind Fouquet's downfall were hidden causes. Colbert, another minister, had been turning the monarch against Fouquet for years; Fouquet's ill-advised expression of affection to Mme. de Lavallière, beloved of the king, didn't help matters either. And someone, even the man who had kept the French treasury solvent by raising funds against his own fortune, needed to be the fall guy for the state's abysmal financial condition. In a trial that lasted for three years, the judges in Fouquet's case voted narrowly for banishment over death; Louis XIV trumped them all, overturning the judgment in favor of life imprisonment. Pignerol, a dreary citadel, housed the fallen minister until his death in 1680, leading some to speculate that he was the famous man in the iron mask. But Louis did appreciate Fouquet's tastes: soon after the minister's arrest, the King confiscated many of Vaux's finest objects and hired the same trio—Le Vau, Le Brun, and Le Nôtre—who would take their crafts to (arguably) greater heights at Versailles.

Everything has been orchestrated to create an impressive whole. The designers integrated painting and sculpture, architecture and decor, building and garden to please the viewer with ideal forms and harmony. At a moment when the Spanish court had lost power, Charles I had been executed in England, and the Fronde had just threatened the monarchy in France, the focus of the Baroque movement had changed drastically. Instead of the dramatic, movemented forms of Italian Baroque and the Counterreformation, Vaux's Neoclassicism showed the stability and restraint of an aristocracy powerful enough to control nature itself.

The Château

The château itself (tel. 60 66 97 09) recalls both the grandeur of a Roman past, with its rusticated columns, and a French fort, complete with squat walls and moat. Walk over the moat, invisible from the road, and appreciate Le Vau's sense of symmetry and his use of water to set off the building. The recessed façade of the château intentionally pulls the visitor inward, beneath the pediment guarded by Apollo, god of arts, and Rhea, armed with a cornucopia of plenty. With the Spanish war ended, Fouquet's entrance sends the message that peace unites art and prosperity. Although the tour begins to your left, upon entering, peek up at the dome in the Oval Room ahead and then out to the gardens. Vaux was designed to draw people inside, contain them within the cupola, and expel them into the seemingly infinite space of the gardens.

A thorough pamphlet, available in English, guides the visit to the château. For more detail and a brilliantly colored souvenir, buy the glossy guide in the gift shop (40F). Notice the ornate scripted Fs all round the château, and keep an eye out for the ever-present squirrel, Fouquet's industrious symbol, and for the tower with three battlements, his second wife's crest. The **Minister's Bedchamber** may lead you to wonder who was the monarch in this kingdom. The opulent red and gold bed stands under an allegorical ceiling in which Apollo (read: Fouquet) bears the lights of the world. (One begins to understand why he was arrested....) **Mme. Fouquet's Closet** once had walls lined with small mirrors, the decorative forerunner of Versailles's Hall of Mirrors. Le Brun's portrait of Fouquet, whose penetrating look overrides his general appearance of humility, hangs over the fireplace. Tear your eyes away from the beautiful 1877 billiard table in the **Square Room** to admire the exquisite beams of the Louis XIII-style ceiling. The vivid colors and engaging expressions of the nine muses in the **Room of the Muses** make this one of Le Brun's finest decorative schemes. Le Brun planned to crown the Oval Room (or **Grand Salon**) with a fresco entitled *The Palace of the Sun*, but Fouquet's arrest halted all activity. The tapestries once bore Fouquet's squirrel, but Colbert seized them and replaced the rodents with his own adders. The ornate **King's Bedchamber** (the balustrade gives it away) boasts an orgy of stucco, angels, cherubs, and lions fluttering around the centerpiece of *Time Bearing Truth Heavenward*. But don't miss the squirrels perched in every second palm leaf of the cornice. (Talk about audacity!) Needless to say, King Louis didn't spend a single night in this bedroom. The bright and cozy **Dining Room** will make you hungry—scurry down to the **Basement** for a reminder of where all the toil of food preparation took place.

The Gardens

Vaux-Le-Vicomte presented André Le Nôtre with his first opportunity to create an entire formal garden. Three villages, a small château, and many trees were destroyed to open up space, though countless trees were later replanted to draw the all-important constrast between order and wilderness. Even a river was rerouted to provide the desired effect. With Vaux, Le Nôtre gave birth to a truly French style of garden—shrubs were trimmed, lawns shaved, bushes sculpted, and pools of water strategically placed to produce a kind of embroidered tapestry exuding classical harmony.

Start by considering the impressive panorama from the steps behind the château. The garden seems perfectly symmetrical and the grottoes appear to be directly behind the large pool of water, known as the water mirror. Closer inspection reveals otherwise. The right-hand *parterre* was a flowerbed in its original incarnation, but today is dominated by a statue of Diana. Its matching green area on the left side is actually wider and sunken. The **Pool of the Crown**, named for the gold crown at its center, is the most ornate of the garden pools. The **Round Pool** and its surrounding 17th-century statues marks an important intersection: to the left, down the east walkway, are the **Water**

Gates, likely backdrop for Molière's performance of *The Annoyances* before Louis XIV. **The Water Mirror,** farther down the central walkway, was designed to reflect the château perfectly, but you may have some trouble positioning yourself to enjoy the effect. The Mirror also hides the sunken canal, known as **La Poêle** (the Frying Pan), fed by the Anqueuil River. Stand across from the grottoes and appreciate Le Nôtre's genius: the statues on the other side seem so close, but unreachable. Well, not entirely: walk for about ten minutes around the left-hand side (east end) of the canal to see river gods Anqueuil and Tiber. Although somewhat smelly and scum-covered today, the canal was and is a not-so-subtle reminder that Fouquet made his fortune in shipping. Climb to the **Farnese Hercules** (the vanishing point when you look out from the castle), and survey the land and imposing château before you. Feel like the master of all you see and realize how well Le Vau and Le Nôtre accomplished their goal. The old stables today house a carriage museum, **Les Equipages.** Magnificent carriages of all kinds come complete with piped-in music, dressed-up party-goers, and liveried footmen. Picnicking in the gardens is prohibited, but **L'Ecureuil** (squirrel—ha!) on the castle grounds provides good salads (35-40F) and cooked meat and vegetables (54-58F).

Vaux is exquisite; getting there is exquisite torture, which may explain the absence of crowds. Your best and cheapest option, if traveling with other people, is to bite the bullet and rent a car (see Getting Around in the City). Take Autoroute A4 or A6 from Paris and exit at Val-Maubée or Melun, respectively. Head toward Meaux on N36 and follow the signs. The alternative is taking the train to Melun, a fairly large center on the SNCF *banlieue* line. (Every 15-30min. from Gare de Lyon, 45min., 62F round-trip.) Unfortunately, the station is a smug 6km from the château. You can take a bike on the train free of charge, but riding on the undivided highway without shoulder next to big trucks is not advisable. It might be worth it to splurge and take a taxi. The 6km ride will cost you at least 66F one way (pick one up at the train station; call 64 52 51 50 from Vaux). Many weary travelers have been known to ask other respectable tourists how they're getting back; they often get rides to the station or even to Paris; these travelers have the sense not to buy a round-trip ticket from Paris. Fit troopers might not mind the 70- to 90-minute hike for at least one part of the trip. Walk up rue Gallieni from the station and then walk straight on av. Thiers, which becomes rue St-Ambroise, rue Ste-Etienne, rue St-Aspais, av. Charles de Gaulle and av. de Meaux in turn. Then stay on Route N36 (direction: Meaux) until you see the turn off for Vaux, at which point you will have only 1.5km left. Whether you decide on physical or financial exertion, rest assured that Vaux is worth it. The effort may pay off most handsomely on Saturday evenings from May to October from 8:30-11pm when candle-lit visits make the château seem cozy and homey, if this is possible....The fountains in Le Nôtre's gardens are turned on from 3-6pm every second and last Saturday of the month from April to October. (Château open Mon.-Sat. 10am-12:30pm and 2-5:30pm, Sun. and holidays 10am-6pm; Feb.-March, Nov. and Dec. 19-Jan. 4 Mon.-Sat. 11am-12:30pm and 2-4:30pm, Sun. and holidays 11am-5pm. Equipages open same hrs., but remain open during lunch and for ½hr. after the château closes. Gardens open same hrs. as the équipages, except Sun., when they remain open an additional ½hr. Admission 42F, students with ID and under 16 34F, under 6 free. Entire estate open May-Oct. Sat. 8:30-11pm for candle-lit evenings. Admission 55F, students with ID and under 16 46F. Admission to gardens 20F.) The closest **tourist office,** 2, av. Gallieni, by the train station in Melun (tel. 64 37 11 31), can help you with accommodations, restaurants, other sightseeing opportunites in the area, and give you a free map—essential for those planning on walking. (Open Tues.-Sat. 10am-noon and 2-6pm.)

Fontainebleau

Like its name, believed to come from M. Bliaut who owned a local fountain, Fontainebleau is a composite of architectural and decorative styles. In close proximity to the famous forest of the same name, it has been a glorified hunting lodge for nearly 500 years, presenting a radically different architectural statement from the unity of Vaux-le-Vicomte and Versailles. Kings of France have lived on these grounds since the 12th century, when the exiled Thomas à Becket consecrated Louis VII's manor chapel. In

1528, François I tore down and rebuilt the castle, to bring him closer to the "red and black furred animals" he so loved to hunt (he actually said this). Italian artists designed and decorated the palace and their paintings, the *Mona Lisa* and the *Virgin in the Rocks* among them, filled his private collections. Under François, Fontainebleau peaked, as nobility from around France built their own palaces, no longer standing, near the king. Subsequent kings had varying degrees of affection for the château, depending generally on their love for dead and dying furry animals. Most used their favorite designers to add at least one magnificent room, while some attached whole new wings. The château remained a happening place throughout: Louis XIII was born here in 1601, Louis XV was married here in 1725, and Louis XIV revoked the Edict of Nantes here in 1685. The building remained intact during the Revolution, although the standard oversized garage sale of its furniture took place. The Emperor redeclared it a state residence, refurnishing many apartments to suit his own sumptuous Neoclassical style. Fontainebleau was also the perfect place to welcome the Pope, who had come to crown Napoleon in 1804, and to imprison His Holiness between 1812 and 1814. Napoleon popped in to Fontainebleau frequently and it is presented as one of his main residences; in reality he only spent 194 days in the building whose eclectic blend of architecture led him to dub it *"La Maison des Siècles"* (the House of Centuries). **Cour des Adieux** was so named after serving as the scene of his dramatic farewell in 1814. Also known as the **White Horse Court,** it is used as the main entry to the château.

The **Grands Appartements,** the standard visitors' circuit, provides a lesson in the history of French architecture and decoration. Guides available in English will make the whole visit more meaningful: 15F will get you a pamphlet about the château and some of the gardens or one describing the Grands Appartements alone; 25F buys the glossy booklet with more complete descriptions. All labels in the rooms are in French. Dubreuil's **Gallery of Plates** tells the history of Fontainebleau on a remarkable series of porcelain plates, fashioned in Sèvres between 1838 and 1844. In the **Gallery of François I,** arguably the most famous room at Fontainebleau, muscular figures by Mannerist artist Il Rosso (known in French as Maître Roux) tell mythological tales of heroism and bravado, brilliantly illuminated by light flooding in from courtside windows. The **Ball Room's** magnificent octagonal ceiling, with complementary floor, reminds the visitor that much of Fontainebleau should be observed with craned neck. The bacchanalian orgy of decorative frescoes, designed by Francesce Primaticcio, amaze with their intricacy. The ensemble of the decorative scheme in each room, successfully incorporating furniture and paintings from different eras and styles, overwhelms the visual faculties everywhere at Fontainebleau. Note the decorated beams on the Louis XIII ceiling in the **King's Guard Room.** The **King's Cabinet** (also known as the **Louis XIII Salon),** decorated under Henri IV, was the site of many an important meeting, as well as *le débotter,* the king's post-hunt boot removal. Gobelin tapestries and Savonnerie carpets line walls and floors throughout the palace—the four seasons, with floral hoops, are depicted on the wall of the **Empress's Antechamber.** Every Queen of France since the 17th century slept in the gold, green, and leafy **Queen's** (later **Empress's) Bed Chamber;** the gilded wood bed was built for Marie-Antoinette, who was headed off before she made it here. The *N* on the throne is another testament to Napoleon's enduring humility; the red and gold velvet meets in a crown above the throne and under the coat-of-arms-of-France-and-Navarre-ridden ceiling. **Napoleon's Bed Chamber** boasts predictably fancy decor, but the **Emperor's Small Bed Chamber,** complete with camp bed, seems more in a military man's style. In the **Emperor's Private Room,** known today as the **Abdication Chamber,** Napoleon signed his abdication in 1814, before stepping outside to say farewell to the Guard and sob into the tricolor. (Grands Appartements open Wed.-Mon. 9:30am-12:30pm and 2-5pm. Last entry 11:45am and 4:15pm. Admission 26F, students, seniors, and Sun. 14F, under 18, teachers with ID, unemployed, and art students with ID free. 90-minute guided tours available in French and possibly English Wed. and Sat.-Sun. 30F, students, seniors, and Sun. 20F. Call 64 22 27 40 for details. Château is wheelchair accessible.)

The same ticket admits you to the **Musée Napoléon,** a collection of paraphernalia including His tiny shoes, His tootbrush, His field tent (the most elaborate you've ever seen) and His son's (the Roi de Rome's) toys. A regular Napoleon love-in. Not to be missed are the not-so-great busts of Napoleon looking pseudo-Roman, as well as the gifts (don't you wish you had enemies like this?) from Carlos IV of Spain. (Same hrs. as Grands Appartements. Last entry noon and 4:30pm.)

The **Petits Appartements,** private rooms of Napoleon and the Empress Josephine, are accessible only by guided tours and only on certain days. If you are desperate to see these rooms, call ahead. (Admission 12F, under 26 and over 60 7F. Tours, on days they do take place, at 10am, 11am, 2pm, and 3pm. English-language tours may become available.) The **Musée Chinois de l'Impératrice Eugénie,** also in the château, offers a welcome respite from the sometimes crowded apartments upstairs. Reopened after restoration in 1991, these four rooms were remodeled in 1863 by the Empress to house the collection she herself called her *"Musée chinois"* (Chinese museum), a gathering of Far Eastern decorative art: porcelain, jade, and crystal. These pieces were brought to her after the 1860 Franco-English campaign in China and also by Siamaese ambassadors received by Napoleon III in 1861. The rooms are quietly decorated in green and maroon and are among the few in the château that seem to have anything to do with real people living comfortably. (Open same hrs. as château. Last entry 12:15 and 4:45pm. Admission 12F, students, seniors, and Sun. 7F.) The **Appartements des Reines Mères ou du Pape** (the Apartments of the Queen Mothers or the Pope), where the Pope was imprisoned, are currently under renovation.

Underkept and fairly unimpressive, the gardens at Fontainebleau still make for a pleasant stroll. If you throw some bread into the **Etang des Carpes,** the hundreds of carp that live in this pond, once they wake up, will battle to the death for the last soggy crumb. Big carp, little carp; some respond to thrown breads, some don't. You can cruise around the pond in a rented boat. (4-person max. per boat. Boat rental May 23-Aug. 31 daily 10am-12:30pm and 2-6pm; Sept. Sat.-Sun. 2-6pm. 35F per ½hr., 55F per hr; 50F deposit). Quieter and more refined are the **Jardin Anglais,** complete with rustic grotto and the famous Fontaine-belle-eau, and the **Jardin de Diane,** guarded by a statue of the huntress. In both gardens, Royal peacocks flaunt their feathers, desperately trying to impress uninterested peahens. The grass grows longer down by the canal, and provides a perfect picnic place. (Gardens open daily sunrise-sunset. Jardin Anglais and de Diane open variably.)

The **Forêt de Fontainebleau** is a thickly wooded 20,000-hectare preserve with hiking trails and the famous sandstone rocks used for training alpine climbers. If you're going to be around for a while and are up for it, you too can learn how to climb. Ask at the tourist office. Tamer tourists will prefer to rent a bike at **A la Petite Reine,** 14, rue de la Paroisse (tel. 64 22 72 41; fax 60 72 11 75). (Open Tues.-Sat. 9am-12:30pm and 2-7pm, Sun. 9am-6pm. Weekday rental 50F per ½-day, 80F per day. Weekend and holiday rental 80F per ½-day, 100F per day. 2000F deposit. Credit cards accepted; locks and pumps available.) Maps of hiking and bike trails are available at the tourist office. Fans of 19th-century art will recognize the thick hardwoods and sandstones made famous by Rousseau and Millet, painters of the Barbizon school (see below).

The **Musée Napoléonien d'Art et d'Histoire Militaire,** 88, rue St-Honoré, grew out of Louis Prost's (creator and conservator of the museum) childhood fascination with Napoleon and things military. This is the place to go if you've seen Fontainebleau but, like France, didn't get enough of Napoleon the first time. The exhibits could be entitled "Variations on a uniform," "Variations on a weapon," and "Napoleonic trivia." Military historians will enjoy strutting around to piped-in music. (Open Tues.-Sat. 2-5pm. Last admission 4:30pm. Admission 10F, under 2 free.)

Fontainebleau's **tourist office,** 31, pl. Napoléon (tel. 64 22 25 68), across from the **post office** and near the château, organizes tours of the village surrounding the château and can help you with accommodations. (Open Mon.-Sat. 9am-12:30pm and 1:45pm-7pm; Oct.-May slightly shorter opening times.) A caravan outpost of the tourist office sits in front of the château. A *petit train* (tel. 42 62 24 00 or 64 22 25 68) run by the tourist office, tours the city and the park, with multilingual commentary (Wed.-Mon. 10am-12:30pm and 2-6pm; 25F, children 15F). Hourly **trains** run to the town from the Gare de Lyon, *banlieue* level (45 min., 66F round-trip). The château is a pleasant 2km walk or bus ride. Take Car Vert A from the station (7F50).

Near Fontainebleau: Barbizon

On the edge of the Fontainebleau forest blossoms the rustic village of **Barbizon,** a favorite of 19th-century French landscape painters. Théodore Rousseau, Jean-François Millet, and Jean-Baptiste Camille Corot were the key figures in the Barbizon School, living and working in this artistic haven in the mid-1800s. They called themselves naturalists, interested in the land as it actually appeared, yet their work has deeply Romantic overtones. Influenced at once by the writings of Jean-Jacques Rousseau and the 17th-century Dutch landscapists, they were the spiritual and artistic predecessors of the Impressionists. They borrowed their somber palate from artists like Ruisdael and from the forest of Fontainbleau itself, with its deeply shaded glens and giant oak trees. Their work deeply influenced that of Van Gogh, although their dark shadows and earthy tones could not be farther from the vibrant explosion of color in his later paintings.

The **Musée Municipal de l'Atelier de Théodore Rousseau,** 55, rue Grande (tel. 60 66 22 38), showcases the work of the man who founded the Barbizon School and whose wooded scenes captured the dark beauty of the forest. (Open Wed.-Mon. 10am-12:30pm and 2-6pm; Oct.-March Wed.-Mon. 10am-12:30pm and 2-5pm. Admission 15F.) The town's other museum, the **Maison et Atelier de Jean-François Millet,** 27, rue Grande (tel. 60 66 21 55), shifts focus to Millet, the best-known of the Barbizon masters, famous for his portrayal of the French peasantry as the great, the proud, the victimized, the simple and the uncorrupted. (Open Wed.-Mon. 9:30am-12:30pm and 2-5:30pm. Free.) Galeries dedicated to the Barbizon School, as well as contemporary art, literally line the streets. The **Office du Tourisme,** 41, rue Grande (tel. 60 66 41 87), has all kinds of documentation on Barbizon and the surrounding area. (Open Wed. and Sat.-Mon. 10:30am-noon and 2-4pm, Fri. 2-4pm.) The tourist office at Fontainebleau (see above) sells a 5F map of Barbizon and can provide a schedule for the *autocars verts* that erratically connect the two towns. Biking to Barbizon is probably the cheapest option for those without a car; otherwise, a taxi from the Melun or Fontainebleau train station is the most practical (if highly extravagant) option.

Chantilly

Chantilly says a lot about unreality. The faux-Renaissance castle, built in the late 19th century, looms above a carefully-tended "natural" landscape, while a play village recalls the idealized view of peasant-life depicted by a medieval artist. An earlier age's attempt at Euro Disney, it testifies to an aristocracy a bit removed from the real world. Fittingly, during World War I, French commander-in-chief Général Joffre established his headquarters here, whence he plotted grand strategy in blithe and happy ignorance of the magnitude of the slaughter taking place on the front.

Set in the magnificent gardens Le Nôtre sculpted from the surrounding forest, the **château de Chantilly** drapes elegantly over its serene gardens, lakes, and canals. As one approaches from the huge stables and the town, the château rises like a fairy-tale castle. A Roman citizen named Cantilius built his villa here, leaving his name and a tradition of high property values. A succession of medieval lords constructed elaborate fortifications, but the palace of Chantilly did not come into its own until the Grand Condé, celebrated victor of Rocroi and cousin of Louis XIV, brought Le Nôtre to create the gardens and, eventually, commissioned the Grand Château. His château was razed during the Revolution; the building you see before you is a reproduction built in the 1870s by its then owner, the Duc d'Aumale, fifth son of Louis-Phillippe. As you approach, the dramatic Renaissance façade, the lush greenery, and the extravagant entrance hall whet your appetite for something truly remarkable.

Inside, the château houses the **Musée Condé** (tel. 44 57 08 00), crowded with the duke's private collection of elegant furniture and dusty paintings. For the castle's most sumptuous experience, head first to the beautiful wood-paneled library, with displays of medieval miniatures, a Gutenberg Bible, and a facsimile of the museum's most famous possession: the **Très Riches Heures du Duc de Berry,** a 15th-century manuscript showing the French peasantry and their noble counterparts, engaged in the labors of the different months. The **Salle de Gardes** displays two van Dyck paintings, along with a Roman mosaic of *The Rape of Europa* taken from a house in Herculaneum that was just the thing to hang over the duc d'Aumale's mantel. The crowded galleries contain paintings by Raphael, Titian, Poussin, Gros, Corot, Delacroix, Ingres, and Veronese...an impressive collection, unfortunately so crowded in the long halls that it's hard to appreciate the individual works. Think well before you pay the hefty 32F admission fee. For the dedicated royalist, it may be worth it, just to see the museum's collection of chairs taken from Marie-Antoinette's dressing room in Versailles.

Even if you skip the museum, consider taking a 15F-wander through the gardens, which are, in themselves, the château's main attraction. For another 6F, you can buy a map of the gardens with a suggested walking tour; free wandering, however, will lead you on a delightfully aimless tour of discovery. The central expanse, directly in front of the château, is in a typical French formal style, with neat rows of carefully pruned trees and calm statues overlooking geometrically shaped pools. To the right, hidden within a forest, the lovely "English" garden attempts to recreate the natural forms of nature, rendered more picturesque by the human element. Here, paths meander, seemingly without a set direction, through woods and round pools where lone swans float along. Windows carved out in the foliage allow you to see fountains in the formal garden. You'll also find a play village, the inspiration for Marie-Antoinette's infamous hamlet at Versailles. Elsewhere, a statue of Cupid encased in a lovely gazebo reigns over the "Island of Love" with Dionysian ardor. (Château open Wed.-Mon. 10am-6pm; Nov.-March Mon.-Fri. 1-5pm and Sat.-Sun. 10:30am-5:30pm. Admission 35F, reduced 25F. Admission to grounds 15F.)

The approach to the castle passes the **Grandes Ecuries,** enormous stables that housed 240 horses and hundreds of hunting dogs from 1719 until the Revolution. The stables were originally ordained by Louis-Henri Bourbon, who hoped to live in them when reincarnated as a horse. These immense stables now house the **Musée Vivant du Cheval** (tel. 44 57 13 13), a huge museum dealing with all things equine: on display are dozens of saddles, horseshoes, merry-go-rounds, horse postcards, and horse sculptures. Sad to say, the horses themselves are only here for your viewing pleasure—no touching, no riding. The museum also puts on magnificent horse-training demonstrations (in French) which are a must see for all horse lovers. (April-Oct. daily at 11:30am, 3:30pm, and 5:15pm. Museum open Mon. and Wed.-Fri. 10:30am-6:30pm, Sat.-Sun. 10:30am-7pm; May-June also Tues. 10:30am-5:30pm; July-Aug. also Tues. 2-5:30pm. Admission to museum and show 45F, students and seniors 35F. Special show Sun. 4pm. Admission 1-4:30pm 50F.) Two of France's premier horse races are held here in June—the **Prix de Diane** and the **Prix du Jockey Club.**

The **tourist office** is stabled at 23, av. du Maréchal Joffre (tel. 44 57 08 58). (Open Wed.-Mon. 10am-12:30pm and 2-5:30pm., Sun. 9am-2pm.) Hourly **trains** run to Chantilly from Paris's Gare du Nord (every hr., 35min., 70F round-trip). To reach the château from the station, take the shuttle bus (6F, ask at the station for times), or walk down rue des Otages and turn left in front of the tourist office (2km). Rent **bikes** at Chantilly VTT (tel. 44 57 57 25), straight ahead and to the left of the station (35-47F per day; open Sat. 1-8pm, Sun. 11am-8pm).

Near Chantilly: Senlis

Tiny **Senlis,** a 10-minute bus ride from Chantilly, basks in the ineffable glory of being the quaintest and best-preserved village in the Ile-de-France. Its cobblestone streets, friendly residents, and intimate atmosphere are the closest you'll get to the France of storybooks. The **Cathédrale de Notre-Dame,** begun in 1191, is a prime example of early Gothic architecture. Its Grand Portal influenced the designs of Chartres and Notre-Dame in Paris. Across the *place* from Notre-Dame, the **Eglise St-Frambourg,** founded around 900 by the merciful Queen Adélaïde, also deserves a quick look. Reconstructed in 1177 by Louis VII and ransacked during the Revolution, this beauty found its most recent savior in the great pianist Girogy Cziffra, who restored the church as an international music center, now called, appropriately, the Fondation Cziffra. Enter the park next to the tourist office to reach the **Château Royal,** a hunting lodge for monarchs from Charlemagne to Henri IV, now converted to a hunting museum. The remains of Gallo-Roman fortifications, with 31 towers, surround the town. (Open April-Sept. Thurs.-Mon. 10am-noon and 2-6pm, Wed. 2-6pm. Admission 15F, reduced 10F.) The old town is a network of medieval alleyways winding up and down cobblestoned hills between several of the original gates. Senlis's **tourist office,** pl. du Parvis Notre-Dame (tel. (16) 44 53 06 40), has information on concerts, exhibitions, and the rest of the local brouhaha. (Open March-Nov. Mon. and Wed.-Fri. 2-6pm, Sat.-Sun. 10am-noon and 2-6pm.) SNCF buses meet most trains to Chantilly for the 10-minute ride to Senlis (14F one-way; railpasses valid).

Malmaison

The **Château de Malmaison,** 1, av. du Château (tel. 47 49 20 07), represents the sentimental and familiar side of Napoleon's personal life, short and sporadic as that side was. After the heroic pretentions and dimensions of his residences at Fontainbeleau and the Tuileries, there is something more approachable about this château, bought in 1799 by Empress-to-be Josephine as a quiet hideaway for the newlyweds. Malmaison was always more hers than his; it was she who lived here to her death in 1814, after Napoleon had divorced her in 1809 because she had not produced an heir. The château was one of the several old Napoleonic sites restored by Napoleon III; as a boy, he had roamed the garden of his grandmother (Josephine), giving orders to the patient sentries.

The house was built in 1622 on the site of a former leper colony (thus its name *"Mal-Maison"* (house of sickness). Josephine furnished it in the height of the Empire style: chairs with Egyptian motifs, square tables, short, tentlike beds. Especially interesting is Napoleon's study, decorated to look like a tent, reminiscent of council-rooms on a Napoleonic campaign. One of the bedrooms has a dome above the bed, decorated with a beautiful *trompe-l'oeil* of sky with clouds and angels receding into the distance. The walls are covered with portraits by Neoclassical painters of the period: Gros, David, Gérard, and Prud'hon. The house itself overflows with Josephine memorabilia: her jewels, her shoes, her colossal dress bills, her harp, her perfumes (together, of course, with souvenirs of *"le petit corporal,"* including his death mask and the bed on which he died). This is the place to come for a modern-day enactment of *Napoleon and Josephine*—the miniseries in living color.

The most enchanting part of a visit to Malmaison is a walk through the carefully **landscaped gardens.** YES, you CAN sit on the grass! Bring a picnic lunch for a delightful afternoon outing. The gardens are neither as formal nor as geometric as the classic Baroque creations of Vaux-le-Vicomte and Versailles. Instead, they are livable, with a harmony and sense of freedom rare to the French countryside. Josephine took a personal interest in the grounds, and it shows. In the summer, her personal rose garden becomes a veritable bower of blooming color and wondrous perfume. On the grounds is a memorial to Eugène-Louis-Jean-Joseph Bonaparte, the Prince Imperial, son of Napoleon III. But for his death in the Zulu War of 1879, France might well have endured a Third Empire and a Napoleon IV.

To get to the château, take the RER or metro to La Défense. From there take bus #158A to "Château" or "Malmaison;" buses leave every 30 minutes. The château can only be visited with a guided tour, given in English, French, German, and Italian—they leave as soon as a group has formed. (Open Wed.-Mon. 10am-noon and 1:30pm-5pm. Last entry 11:30am and 5pm. Admission 26F, students and Sun. 14F.)

St-Germain-en-Laye

A swift RER ride from Paris, St-Germain-en-Laye is less remarkable for what it is now, than for who once was born, lived, and died within its boundaries. Louis VI le Gros built the first castle here in the 12th century, near the site where his ancestor Robert the Pious had constructed a monastery dedicated to St-Germain. Rebuilt by Charles V after destruction during that nasty Hundred Years War, the castle was transformed to its present appearance in 1548 by François I. Lover of all things Italian, François I ordered his architects Chabiges and Delorme to construct a luxurious Renaissance palace—the current *château-vieux*—on the foundations of the old church and castle. Henri IV added the *château neuf,* Louis XIII made it his home, and in 1638, his son, the future Louis XIV was born there. The Sun King retreated to St-Germain when the sky got cloudy, hiding out there during the Fronde and while waiting for Versailles to be finished. Even after the court moved to Versailles, St-Germain was used for important ceremonial occasions. An impressive list of famous names graced these two châteaux— among them Colbert, Mme. de Maintenon, St-Vincent de Paul, Mme. de Sévigné, Rousseau, Moliére, and Lully (the last two wrote many plays and poems performed at the châteaux). James II of England died here in exile in 1701. The 18th century was not kind to the estate. The *château neuf* was torn down; Revolution, Empire, and the July Monarchy used St-Germain alternately as a prison, a cavalry school, and a military prison. The Austro-Hungarian Empire was formally dismantled here in 1919. In 1955, the *château* saw the independence of Morocco agreed up within its hallowed halls.

Napoleon III, in the midst of sprucing the place up for Queen Victoria's visit to her dethroned predecessor's tomb, decided to make the castle into a museum of antiquity. Today, the **Musée des antiquités nationals** (tel. 34 51 53 65) claims to have the richest collection of its kind in the world. But Roman urns and early tools with little explanation, combined with an uncanny resemblance to museums like it in other major cities, make it memorable only for its inability to engage the semi-informed, mildly curious viewer. (Museum open Wed.-Mon. 9am-5:15pm. Admission 17F, sudents, seniors, and Sun. 9F. Wheelchair accessible.) A better bet is to wander along the **garden terrace** (open daily 8am-10pm), designed by the omnipresent Le Nôtre. His gardens were destroyed along with the *châteaux-neuf* at the end of the 18th century; the terrace (30m wide and 2400m long) survived. While lacking the extraordinary orchestration of Versailles, these gardens and the nearby forest make for a pleasant stroll and view of western Paris. A map of trails through the forest is available from the tourist office.

Across from the château stands the Roman-temple-resembling **Eglise St-Germain** consecrated in 1827 on the site of the 11th-century priory that gave St-Germain its name. The modern white pillars have a neo-American colonial feel and piped-in religious music inside gives the church a Southern evangelical atmosphere, but the 14th-century stone statue of Notre-Dame-de-Bon-Retour (Our Lady of the Safe Return) is not to be missed. (Church open daily 8:30am-noon and 2-7pm.) Anglophiles will appreciate a shrine to the memory of James II, erected by Queen Victoria.

Spend a fawning afternoon at the two-room museum of the **Maison Claude Debussy**, 38, rue Au Pain (tel. 34 51 05 12), the Impressionist composer's birthplace. An autographed copy of *Prélude à l'après-midi d'un faune* and a revealing survey he completed for a young girl—he wrote Hamlet down as his hero in fiction—are among the eclectic assemblage of documents and pictures about the man who said, "I want to dare to be myself and to suffer for my truth." (Open Tues.-Sat. 2-6pm. Free.)

The fascinating **Musée Départemental du Prieuré**, 2bis, rue Maurcie-Denis (tel. 39 73 77 87), is dedicated to the works of painter Maurice Denis (1870-1943), the Symbolists, and the Nabis. Built in 1678 for the Marquise de Montespand and used as a hospital, *Le Prieuré* (The Priory) was purchased by Denis in 1914. He decorated the chapel with his interpretation of the Beatitudes; today, you can visit his house and workshop and see the work of artists who, like Denis, received Gauguin's challenge to "risk everything." (Open Wed.-Fri. 10am-5:30pm, Sat.-Sun. and holidays 10am-6:30pm. Admission 25F, students 15F, children under 12 free.) Linger in the peaceful garden or over coffee in the tented *Salon de thé*.

You can grab a bite to eat at any one of a number of places. **Le Collignon**, 7, rue Collignon (tel. 34 51 48 56), serves tasty traditional French fare in a 65F *menu*. (Open Tues.-Sat. noon-3pm and 7-11pm, Sun. noon-3pm.) The **Office Municipal de Tourisme**, Maison Claude Debussy, 38, rue Au Pain (tel. 34 51 05 12) can provide you with lists of restaurants, hotels, and an English-language map. (Open Mon.-Sat. 9am-12:30pm and 2-6:30pm; June-Sept. also open Sun. 10am-1pm.) St-Germain is 45 minutes from downtown Paris by RER Line A1 (11F there, 14F50 back.)

St-Cloud

The **Château de St-Cloud**, 3km southwest of Paris, was the scene of the assassination of Henri III in 1589 and Napoleon's coup d'état in 1799, when troops loyal to the rising general invaded the chambers of the legislature in session there, leaving only a rump body willing to put Napoleon in place as consul. In 1870 marauding Prussians burned the château; nothing remains but Le Nôtre's magnificent park, which includes fountains, statues, arbors, and an English garden—well worth a visit on a sunny afternoon. The **Grande Cascade,** Hardouin-Mansart's fanciful 17th-century creation, was made to look like an enormous, tiered waterfall, with statues of the Seine and the Marne emerging from the water. Nestled by the park gates, the **Musée Historique** offers drawings, paintings, and a short film tracing the history of the château. (Grounds open daily 7am-9pm. Museum open Wed. and Sat.-Sun. 2-5:30pm. Free.) Stroll around the town of St-Cloud, built on a steep hill across the Seine from Paris. The quiet streets are lined with small shops and pretty houses, interspersed with the occasional modern apartment building. Nearing the top, the streets are so steep that some of them become stairways, leading to the *centre-ville,* a classic French town square with the Hôtel de Ville and the modest but charming Romanesque **Eglise St-Cloud.** To get to St-Cloud, take the metro, RER Line B, bus #72 from the Hôtel de Ville or bus #52 from Madeleine to "Boulogne-Pt. de St-Cloud." There you can take a local bus across the Pont de St-Cloud or walk (15min.) across. After you cross the river, the park is to your left, the town is straight ahead and up; look for the spire of Eglise St-Cloud.

Sceaux

The peaceful, upscale suburb of **Sceaux** (RER: Sceaux), 10km south of Paris, is one of the most fashionable places to live outside of Paris itself. Three hundred years ago, Sceaux was home to Colbert, Louis XIV's finance minister. His resplendent mansion, built by Claude Perrault, was destroyed during the Revolution: Perrault's Sceaux château was a no-go. Le Nôtre's gracious gardens remain. In the 19th century, the Duc de Trévise inherited this property and built the charming (if more humble) **Château de Sceaux** (RER: Bourg-la-Reine), which now houses the **Musée de l'Ile de France** (tel. 46 61 06 71), dedicated to the *haute culture* and *traditions folkloriques* of the region surrounding Paris. As you approach the château, notice the **Grande Cascade,** with 20th-century additions by Rodin. At its base, Le Nôtre's elegant **Octagon** pool leads into the requisite **Grand Canal.** A pleasant park surrounds these ornamental gardens. You'll know you're not in Paris anymore when you lie on the grass without a green-clad *gardien* whistling at you and yelling *"pelouse interdite."* (Museum open Mon. and Fri. 2-6pm, Wed.-Thurs. 10am-noon and 2-7pm; off-season until 5pm. Admission 10F, students and seniors 5F. Park open daily 6:45am-9:30pm. Free.)

Cathedrals

For some of the most inspiring aesthetic creations ever created by the human psyche, explore the magnificent cathedrals in the area around Paris. Although the band of great medieval cathedrals stretches from York to Florence, the Ile-de-France is the heartland of the Gothic. Gothic architecture was invented in the early 12th century at St-Denis, and the influence of the Gothic remained stronger in the Paris region than perhaps anywhere else. Cathedrals like Chartres and Notre-Dame defined the style; pilgrims to these religious centers, overwhelmed by what they had seen, returned to their homes throughout Europe to demand cathedrals equal in grandeur. And today, in spite of the tourists and electric lights, you can still experience that same feeling of amazement. Some of these cathedrals took centuries to build; each is lavished with detailed ornament. The entire building, from the flying buttresses to the smallest sculpted angel, expresses a complex theological function that tour guides and guidebooks will help you to uncover. If possible, bring binoculars or opera glasses. But most of all, give yourself enough time to examine not only the great space and immense towers, but also the all-important details—the highly expressive stone carving, the rose windows composed of thousands of pieces of hand-blown glass, the web-like lines of the vaulted nave.

Saint-Denis

In a small, blue-collar town 10km north of Paris lies one of France's most important historical monuments, the **Basilique St-Denis** (Mo. St-Denis-Basilique). Ever since 768, this beautiful church has been home to the remains of almost all of the kings and queens of France, whose funerary monuments form a progression from medieval simplicity to 19th-century extravagance. Even more importantly, its delicate 12th-century ambulatory (the cloistered passageway encircling the choir at the east end of the church) is *the* first example of Gothic architecture and the ethereal, vertical aesthetic that soon ruled all of Europe.

According to medieval legend, St-Denis gets its name from the 3rd-century missionary who converted Paris to Christianity. Decapitated by the Romans on Montmartre, Dionysus (later Frenchified to Denis) supposedly picked up his fallen head and, carrying it in his arms, walked to the area now called St-Denis. Before expiring definitively, he made known his wish to be buried there. Toward the year 475, a little church was built to honor the saint's grave. About two centuries later, that church was destroyed by King Pepin to make way for a larger version—perhaps because Pepin himself wanted to be buried there (which he was, in 768). Vestiges of both of these early churches can be seen in today's crypt. Other early Frankish kings followed Pepin's lead, and at the end of the 10th century the church became the official necropolis of French royalty.

In 1136 Abbot Suger began the rebuilding of the basilica in a new and revolutionary style that would open the hallowed area of the basilica to the "light of the divine." Suger was deeply influenced by his library's copy of the writings of Dionysus-the-pseudo-Aeropagite (a 6th-century theologian whom, with typical medieval confusion, Suger believed to be their very own St-Denis). Dionysus (the pseudo-Aeropagite) equated God, the "Superessential Beauty," with the "cause of the harmony and splendor in all things, flashing forth upon them, like light." Understandably, given this theory, Suger was dissatisfied with the dark, heavy appearance of Romanesque interiors, with their small windows and forests of thick columns. Instead, he brought together a host of already-known architectural elements to create an unprecedented openness in the suddenly spacious nave. In the final Gothic creation, function melded perfectly with aesthetic form—the vaulted arches of the nave, so essential to the cathedral's effect of verticality and weightlessness, funneled the weight of the roof into a few precise points, supported with long, narrow columns and flying buttresses outside. Freed from the burden of supporting the roof, the walls could be pierced with the huge stained-glass windows that became the style's trademark.

These developments had a complex theological counterpart: the play of light from the stained-glass windows in the vast, airy interior of the church became the symbolic presence of God, as expressed in the book of John: "In the beginning was the Word and the Word was the Light of the world." Suger's basilica church became the equivalent of the Solomon's Temple, bathed in a jewel-like splendor of colored glass; in a mutation as dramatic as the transubstantiation of the holy bread, the space of the cathedral became the mystical arena of the Heavenly and Pure. Thus, wrote Abbot Suger, "Thou uniformly conjoins the material with the immaterial, the corporeal with the spiritual, the human with the Divine." Mortal eyes, captivated by the brilliant colors of a stained-glass window, by light streaming into darkness, became the recipient of the divine Word—as Light. Appreciation of earthly beauty allowed the soul to elevate itself and commune with the Absolute. "Thus," declared Abbot Sugar, "when—out of my delight in the beauty of the house of God—the loveliness of the many-coloured gems has called me away from external cares...then it seems to me that I see myself dwelling, as it were, in some strange region of the universe which neither exists entirely in the slime of the earth nor entirely in the purity of Heaven; and that, by the grace of God, I can be transported from this inferior to that higher world in an anagogical manner."

Whatever opinion one may hold on Suger's metaphysics, there is indeed something uplifting and awe-inspiring in the church he created. In an age before skyscrapers and neon lights, the stained glass and human-dwarfing nave must have seemed like a miracle. Suger's contemporaries were flabbergasted and quickly worked to outdo him with their own new cathedrals, building ever more intricate interiors, larger stained-glass windows, loftier vaults, and higher towers—the age of the Cathedral had been born.

Suger himself died in 1151, well before most of his basilica had been rebuilt. His successors altered his plans, but did not stray from the Gothic pattern he had set. In particular, they created an unusually wide transept, complete with magnificent rose windows. The extra space was needed to accommodate the large and ever-growing number of dead monarchs. In 1593, underneath the newly spacious nave, Henri IV converted to Catholicism with his famous statement: *"Paris vaut bien une messe"* (Paris is well worth a mass). St-Denis's royal connection brought upon it the wrath of the Revolution. Most of the tombs were desecrated or destroyed, and the remains of the Bourbon family were thrown into a ditch. With the restoration of the monarchy in 1815, Louis XVIII ordered that the necropolis be re-established. The bodies of Louis XVI and Marie Antoinette were buried here with great pomp. The remains of the other Bourbons were dug out of their anonymous ditch and placed in an ossuary inside the crypt. The tombs that had survived the Revolution (none of them belonging to the Bourbons), were returned from the National Museum of Monuments (see Ecole des Beaux-Arts, sixth *arrondissement)*, where they had been displayed. Louis also added to the St-Denis collection a number of funerary monuments from other churches that had been completely destroyed during the Revolution.

Admission to the necropolis includes a pair of headphones with a recorded tour (in English, if you want). The headphones don't come with a tape recorder, but pick up infra-red signals from a number of "islands." If you stand next to island 3, for example, and press the green button, you hear intelligent commentary on the sights around island 3. Lights come on automatically to illuminate particular details as the commentator discusses them. This whiz-bang technology makes for a remarkably enjoyable visit. A couple of tips on how to use it best: 1) If you are unable to hear the commentary, try repositioning yourself relative to the transmitter island. 2) If you decide that you don't want to listen to the full 1 hour and 15 minutes of commentary, then skip the least exciting islands (7, 8, 9, and 17). Be sure not to miss the little room on the left side of the church (outside of the necropolis area). It contains the splendid funerary garments (literally, "regalia") of the royal family. **(Guided tours** in French daily 3pm; July-Aug. Sun. 12:15, 3, 3:30, and 4:30pm. Crypt open Mon.-Sat. 10am-7pm, Sun. noon-7pm; Oct.-March Mon.-Sat. 10am-5pm, Sun. noon-5pm. Ticket office closes 30min. earlier. Admission to crypt—including guided or recorded tour—25F, ages 18-24 14F, ages 7-17 6F, under 7 free.) There are free **organ concerts** on Sundays from 11:15-noon.

Near St-Denis: Ecouen

The only reason to go to Ecouen is for the **Musée National de la Renaissance** (tel. 39 90 04 04), housed in its demure 17th-century château built for the Constable de Montmorency, a significant patron of the arts and one of the 16th-century's most dashing (and wealthiest) knights. Niches in the outside façade, along the southern portico, were designed to hold Michelangelo's *Slaves* (a gift from Henri II to his most valuable knight, now in the Louvre). The museum holds an extensive collection of 16th- and 17th-century art from France and Italy, moved here in 1976 from the Musée de Cluny in Paris. Each of the rooms displays an array of decorative arts from different periods and crafts, creating an atmophere heavy with the daily accoutrements of the French aristocracy. The museum is especially noteworthy for its painted fireplaces of the fabulously famous Fontainebleau school and the huge Flemish tapestry of *The Love of King David and Bathsheba.* (Open Wed.-Mon. 9:45am-12:30pm and 2-5:15pm. Admission 15F, students 8F.) Take the metro to St-Denis—Porte-de-Paris and from there, bus #268C to the *mairie* of Ecouen. The château is 5 minutes from the *mairie.* Be careful at the St-Denis stop: this is a dangerous area with plenty of pickpockets.

Chartres

The Cathedral

Stunning **Cathédrale de Chartres,** spared by bureacratic inefficiency after being condemned during the Revolution, survives today as one of the most sublime creations of the Middle Ages. The existing structure is the fifth to occupy this site—three different churches stood here before the year 1000. In 876, Charlemagne's grandson, Charles the Bald, made a gift to Chartres of the *Sancta Camisia,* the cloth believed to have been worn by Mary when she gave birth to Christ. Pilgrims have been flocking to the cathedral ever since to see the sacred relic and perhaps benefit from its supernatural powers. In 911 its magic was confirmed when the citizens of Chartres, under attack from Vikings, placed the relic on view at the top of the city wall. The infidels ran away; their leader Rollin converted to Christianity and became the first duke of Normandy.

The cathedral became a foremost center of learning and scholasticism, led by the brilliant Fulbert who arrived in 990 and supervised the bulding of the fourth church, a magnificent Romanesque cathedral. Disaster struck in 1194 when the third fire in 200 years burned all but the enormous crypts, the new west tower, and the Royal Portal. When they discovered that Mary's relic (hidden in the crypt by three loyal priests who stayed with it, sweating out the fire) had emerged like the phoenix unsinged by the flames, the villagers took it as a sign of not only Mary's love but her desire for a more worthy cathedral. Clerics took advantage of the miracle to solicit funds on a grand scale and building proceeded at a furious pace: the majority of the cathedral was completed by 1223 and consecrated in 1260. Arguably the finest in the world, the stained-glass windows soon gained fame for their clarity and beauty, as did the magnificent sculptures adorning each of the main portals. Since then, in a series of miracles as great as the survival of the *Sancta Camisia* in 1194, Chartres Cathedral has emerged intact from Protestant iconoclasm, the clergy's decision to "modernize" in the 18th century, the Revolution's attempt to turn it into a Temple of Reason, and two world wars.

Few cathedrals rival Chartres in size and majesty and fewer reward time spent as generously. A masterpiece of finely crafted detail—architecture, sculpture, and glass—the cathedral is an extraordinary fusion of Romanesque and Gothic architectural elements. Built in a record-breaking 29 years (compared to 163 years for Notre Dame de Paris) the cathedral stands as one of the most unified and harmonious of medieval buildings. The famous twin-steepled silhouette is visible miles around the town, rising up above the flat wheat fields that surround Chartres. The flying buttresses, connected to the vaulting inside, fulfill both a functional and aesthetic role: they take the weight of the roof away from the walls (allowing the wall to open to the magnificent stained glass) and provide an elegant outside expression of the cathedral's interior structure. Towering over the surrounding town, Chartres Cathedral is a powerful embodiment of a time when the Church controlled every aspect of the daily routine and the tallest buildings in existence were its cathedrals. Today, the modern-day pilgrim, like the medieval counterpart, can see medieval theology "come alive" in glass and stone. The famous 12th-century statues of the Royal Portal present an assembly of Old Testament figures at the height of late Romanesque sculpture. The ones in the central bay, attributed to the "Master of Chartres," are especially beautiful: their elongated figures have a stillness and elegance that invites the visitor to leave the material world behind as they enter the divine space of the cathedral.

The 13th-century North and South Porch, representing the life of Mary and Christ triumphant, are highly expressive examples of Gothic sculpture. Notice, for example, the face of John the Baptist on the central bay of the North Porch: an expression of ineluctable sorrow is traced through the downcast eyes, the narrow cheekbones into the long curve of his beard, and finally the disc he holds with the lamb and cross, symbols of Christ's coming. In the left bay, the figures of Mary and Elizabeth turn to greet each other, silently telling the story of the Visitation and showing the extent to which their sculptors have broken free from the rigid style of the Romanesque Royal Portal. Inside, the process is continued in the beautiful Renaissance choir screen begun by Jehan de Beauce in 1514 and finished in the 18th century, telling Mary's story from her birth, through the life of Christ, to her death and ascension.

Most of the glass dates from the 13th century and was preserved through both world wars by town authorities, who dismantled over 3000 square meters and stored it piece by piece until the end of hostilities. The merchant sponsors of each window are shown in the lower panels, providing a valuable record of daily life during the 13th century. The famous "Blue Virgin" window, an object of pilgrimage and one of the few pieces of 12th-century glass to survive the fire, is visible at the first window of the choir, on the right. Note the contrast between the jewel-like brilliance of the windows that have been cleaned and the murkiness of the ones that have not. Bring binoculars if you can; many of the stories told by the stained glass are barely visible with the naked eye.

World-renowned tour guide Malcolm Miller, an authority on Gothic architecture, has brought the cathedral to life for English-speaking visitors for the past 35 years. Miller composes each tour individually to explain the cathedral's colorful history, as well as the fascinating symbolism in different segments of its windows and sculpture. As he rightly observes, the cathedral is a medieval text waiting to be read. Miller knows everything about the extraordinary religion and daily routine that the windows depict and his presentation is intelligent, witty, erudite, and enjoyable for all ages. He will tell you about the labyrinth on the floor, which provided a path for the penitent pilgrim to follow on hands and knees, as well as the sloping floor which permitted the cathedral to be washed after becoming a hostel for pilgrims every night. If you can, take both of his tours the day you are there. They are worth it, and Miller is careful to discuss different aspects of the cathedral on each one. You may want to invest in a 29-35F guide (pretty pictures included) as well. (11/4hr. tours run April-Jan. Mon.-Sat. at noon and 2:45 pm. Admission 30F, students 20F. Try to avoid Sat. and Tues.—busy days in the high season. Private tours available on request: tel. 37 28 15 58; fax 37 28 33 03.)

The sacred relic is now on display in the cathedral's **treasury,** at the east end, along with other significant garments and objects from the building's history. For all of you skeptics: a team of experts recently dated the cloth at about 2000 years old and named its place of origin as the Middle East.... (Open Mon.-Sat. 10am-noon and 2-6pm, Sun. and holidays 2-6pm; Oct. 16-March 15 Mon.-Sat. 10am-noon and 2:30-4:30, Sun. and holidays 2-5pm. Free.) Climb the north tower, **Tour Jehan-de-Beauce,** named after its architect and completed in 1513, for a magnificent view of the cathedral roof, the flying buttresses, and the city below. The tower itself is a wonderful example of flamboyant Gothic, a late medieval style named after the flame-like nature of its decoration. Built to replace a wooden steeple which continuously burned down, it provides a fascinating counterpart to its more sedate neighbor (and predecessor by three centuries), the octagonal steeple built just before the 1194 fire. (Open April-Sept. Mon.-Fri. 9:30-11:30am and 2-5:30pm, Sat. 9:30-11:30am and 2-4:30pm, Sun. 2-4:30pm; Nov.-Feb. Mon.-Sat. 10-11:30am and 2-4pm, Sun. 2-4pm. Admission 20F, students, big families, and seniors 13F, under 6 free.)

Parts of Chartres' **crypt,** one of the largest in Western Christendom, date back to the 9th century. You can only enter the subterranean crypt as part of a tour that leaves from *La Crypte,* the store opposite the south entrance of the cathedral. The tour (tel. 37 21 56 33 for info) is in French but information sheets are available in English. Even if you can't follow the narration you'll see the numerous old chapels, the staircase that allowed the relic to be saved from fire, a 4th-century wall, and the well down which a band of roaming Vikings tossed the bodies of their victims after an 858 raid. *Dommage.* Look for the slender, ethereal forms of statues from the Royal Portal, copied and transferred to the crypt after severe weathering had almost erased their features. (Tours last 30 min. and leave Thurs.-Tues. at 11am and daily at 2:15pm, 3:30pm, 4:30pm, and in summer 5:15pm. Admission 10F.)

The cathedral is open daily in summer from 7:30am-7:30pm and in winter from 7:30am-7pm. No casual visits are allowed on Sat. 5:45-7pm or Sun. 9-10:15am and 10:45am-noon because of religious services. If you want the true Chartres experience, however, try attending one of these services. Call the tourist office (see below) for information on concerts in the cathedral, as well as the annual student pilgrimage in late May and other festivals throughout the year.

The Town

The town of Chartres provides a refreshing change from the grand boulevards and cosmopolitan atmosphere of Paris. The charming *vieille ville* (old town) has the cobblestone staircases, gabled roofs, timbered houses, and iron lamps of a traditional French village. Old streets, named for the trades once practiced there—rue de la Poissonerie being home to the fishmongers—run into one another. Charming stone bridges cross the Eure River, providing an ideal spot for photographs. Although the town is surrounded by flat wheatfields, Chartres is built on a hill, and some of the best views of the cathedral are found by walking down along the well-marked tourist circuit. Maps are available from the tourist office (see below).

Le Musée des Beaux Arts (Museum of Fine Arts), 29, cloître Notre Dame (tel. 37 36 41 39), next door to the cathedral, resides in the former Episcopal Palace. Built mainly in the 17th and 18th centuries on the site occupied by bishops since the 11th century, the palace houses a rich collection of painting, sculpture, and furniture. Zurbaran, Holbein, and Vlaminck all figure prominently, as do local scenes and medieval wood polychrome statues from the 13th century on. (Open Wed.-Mon. 10am-6pm; Nov.-March 10am-noon and 2-6pm. Admission 10F, students and seniors 5F. For temporary exhibits 20F, students and seniors 10F.)

La Galerie du Vitrail (Gallery of Stained Glass), 17, rue du Cloître Notre-Dame (tel. 37 36 10 03), provides information on the cathedral's stained glass and showcases contemporary pieces. Films (8-25 min.) on the history and production of stained glass and Chartres in the Middle Ages are shown free upon request in English, French, or German. (Open Tues.-Sun. 9:45am-7pm; Nov.-March Tues.-Sat. 9:45am-1pm and 2-6:30pm. Free.) The **Centre Internationale du Vitrail**, 5, rue du Cardinal Pie (tel. 37 21 65 72) hosts temporary exhibitions on stained glass, both historical and contemporary. The 12th-century barn in which it is housed was once used to store wine and grains received by the clergy from surrounding farmers. Note the 14th-century wood rafters and the 12th-century vaulting downstairs. (Open 9:30am-7pm; Oct.-March 10am-12:30pm and 1:30-6pm.)

Eglise St-Aignan, on rue des Greniers, was rebuilt in the 16th century, but boasts feudal origins. The Romanesque **Eglise St-André** sits on a street by the same name overlooking the banks of the Eure River. Fires have ravaged it, but the church has been a part of Chartres since the 12th century. During the 16th and 17th centuries, its gallery was extended to cross the river; one of the arches on which it was supported is still visible. **Eglise St-Pierre** in the place St-Pierre is a delicate Gothic (13th-century) masterpiece. Once the church of the Benedictine monastery of Saint-Père-en-Vallée, St-Pierre was renamed during the French Revolution when the monastery was disestablished. (All churches open daily in season 9am-7pm; Oct.-June 10am-5pm.)

Worth the walk across the river (which offers the best view of the cathedral), up rue St-Barthelémy and down rue du Repos past the cemetery is the **Maison Picassiette**, 22, rue du Repos (tel. 37 34 10 78). Until you see it, you will not believe it; from 1938 to 1964, Raymond Isidore decorated his house and garden with mosaics made from broken china and colored glass. 25,000 hours of work yielded a wall of Chartres sites, another wall dedicated to Jerusalem, floral ceiling designs and a hauntingly holy chapel. (Open April-Oct. Wed.-Mon. 10am-noon and 2-6pm. Admission 10F, students 5F.)

Practical Information

Chartres is accessible by frequent **trains** from Gare Montparnasse (1hr., round-trip 122F. In Paris call 45 82 50 50 for info; in Chartres call 37 28 50 50. Many trains run only on certain days or occasions—make sure you don't get caught waiting for one that isn't coming.) The **tourist office** (tel. 37 21 50 00), opposite the cathedral's main entrance, helps find accommodations in Chartres or in the surrounding area (20F fee). They also have a list of restaurants, oodles of delectable brochures and an excellent map with a walking tour marked. For 35F, one or two people can use a headphone guide (in English, French, or German) to see the old city. (Tour lasts 90min.-2hr. and is worth it. Available while the office is open.) The tourist office staff speaks excellent English, as well as other languages. (Open Mon.-Fri. 9:30am-6:45pm, Sat. 9:30am-6pm, Sun. 10:30am-noon and 2-6pm; March-May and Oct. Mon-Sat. 9:30am-6pm, Sun. 10:30am-noon and 2-6pm; Nov.-Feb. Mon-Fri. 9:30am-6pm, Sat. 9:30am-5pm.)

The pleasant **auberge de jeunesse (HI)**, 23, av. Neigre (tel. 37 34 27 64), is 2km north of the train station. Follow the signs past the cathedral and over the river by Eglise St-André. Comfortable four- to eight-bed rooms run 59F per night for HI members; others pay an additional 19F for a guest stamp. Five minutes from all conveniences, with a spectacular view of the cathedral. Beware of the seatless toilets, but rejoice in the nice, new mattresses. Sleeping bags allowed. (Reception open 8-10am and 6-11pm; Sept. 30-Mon. before Christmas and Feb.-March 6-10pm. No lockers Once you leave between 10am-6pm, you're gone for the day. Curfew 11:30pm in summer, 10:30pm in winter. Breakfast included. Sheets 16F for stay. Wheelchair accessible and equipped. Reservations not a bad idea, but show up in early evening to make good on them.)

For **food**, try sandwich or *brasserie* fare in rue de Cygne or place Marceau, open air pedestrian areas with musicians and great atmosphere. **La Passacaille**, 30-32, rue Sainte-Même (tel. 37 21 52 10) offers filling pizza (28-53F) in a tasteful green, peach, and mural surrounding. (Open June-Aug. daily 11:30am-10:30pm; around mealtimes rest of the year.) **Le Pélage,** place Châtelet (tel. 37 36 07 49) serves ample portions of standard meat and potatoes fare (49-60F; menus at 68F50 and 79F50; open daily Mon.-Sat. noon-2pm and 7-11:30pm.)

Illiers-Combray

Proust fans should bite the cookie and take the half-hour train ride from Chartres to **Illiers-Combray,** the author's childhood vacation home and the setting for much of *A la recherche du temps perdu (Remembrance of Things Past).* This idyll remains much as Proust described it with his famous attention to detail (to say the least). Mementos of his life are displayed in the former home of his favorite aunt, the **Maison de Tante Léonie**, 4, rue Docteur Léonie. (Tel. 37 24 30 97. By tour only, Wed.-Mon. at 2, 3, 4, and 5pm—times subject to change. Call ahead to verify and to ferret out foreign language tours on weekday mornings. Admission 25F.)

Beauvais

Largely destroyed in the shelling of World War I, the town of Beauvais has not fully recovered. Originally known as Caesaromagus—Ceasar's market—the town was an important Gallo-Roman settlement until Germanic invasions destroyed it in the 3rd century AD. Things calmed down after the last Norman raids of the 9th century, and Beauvais grew wealthy enough to build its first cathedral. Along with the rest of the Ile-de-France, the city thrived in the fat 12th century, and decided to rebuild its cathedral in the trendy Gothic style. Survivor of world war destruction, the mammoth **Cathédrale Saint-Pierre** stands proud on rue Saint-Pierre. Its Gothic chancel, tallest in the world, is the product of architectural ambition pushed beyond reason and engineering principle. In the late Gothic race to build a tower (and a town's prestige) ever closer to heaven, this was the ultimate contender—and the most dramatic failure.

First begun in 1225, the chancel was finished in 1272 and collapsed dramatically in 1284. Rebuilding began immediately, but the repair was not finished until the end of the 14th century. Then, the misery of epidemics, the Hundred Years War, and civil discord brought work to a halt until the beginning of the 16th century. Before the transept was completed, the overly eager powers-that-be decided to build a 150m central spire. Transept and spire stood tall by 1569, but the tower of stone and wood began to sway almost immediately. Experts suggested that the nave be built to support the weight; the church had finally decided to do so when the spire collapsed on April 30, 1573. So much time and money was then spent on rebuilding and strengthening the chancel again (see the complex of flying buttresses around it) that construction of the nave never began; the slate-covered wooden panel that blocked off the opening from the transept has been "temporarily" in place for the past 400 years. A 35F guide, available in English, helps to illuminate the finer details of the church. The dainty sculpture of the exterior and the delicate network of buttresses amaze with their intricacy. But most awe-inspiring of all: stand back from the cathedral and try to imagine its even more immense proportions—the largest of any Gothic cathedral in the world—had gravity, technology, and funding ever allowed the nave to be built.

For a moment of peace, venture out the back door to the green, seemingly ancient cloister. The buildings that border the courtyard are known as the **Basse-Oeuvre** and are the only remains of the 10th-century Carolingian church that once stood on the site. Only the three western bays remain, made of *pastoureaux* (small cubic stones taken from Gallo-Roman structures). The rest of the church went through the classic medieval cathedral death—trial by fire. The cathedral also flaunts an impossibly complex **Astronomical Clock.** Crafted between 1865 and 1868 by local clockmaker Louis-Auguste Vérité, the clock is 12m high, 5.12m wide, and 2.82m thick. Ninety thousand pieces work synchronously to power one of the world's most complete and most beautiful astronomical timepieces. A 25-minute *son et lumière* highlights the different symbolic facets of the impressive decorative scheme. (Explanations of the clock daily at 10:40am except Sun. in summer, 2:40pm, 3:40pm, and 4:40pm. Admission 20F, children 5F. Call Association *"ESPACES"* at 44 48 11 60 for any further info. Cathedral open daily 9am-12:15pm and 2-6:15pm; winter 9am-12:15pm and 2-5:15pm.)

Next door, in the former Bishop's Palace, the **Musée Departemental de l'Oise,** 1, rue du Musée (tel. 44 84 37 37), displays an eclectic ensemble of painting, sculpture, furniture, and ceramics dating from the 16th century onward, plus a few fossils. The focus is on regional artists or on the depiction of the area. While the collections are not exceptional, occasional gems do surface: the seven canvases in Nabi painter Maurice Denis' *l'Age d'Or* series (1912) capture serenity itself in their soothing soft pinks and greens, winding up a spiral staircase. Any ceramic plate or statue constitutes a Beauvais specialty and deserves admiration, as does the 16th-century wood rafter sequence on the third floor. Take the time to admire the rest of the building: the two towers guarding the entry date from the 14th century, while the 12th-century main building was rebuilt in the 16th and restored in the 18th century. (Open Wed.-Mon. 10am-noon and 2-6pm. Admission 16F, ages 18-25 and over 65 8F, under 18 and Wed. free.)

On the other side of the cathedral, across from the ruins, the modern **Galerie Nationale de la Tapisserie,** rue St-Pierre, pays homage to the Gobelins factory built here in 1664 under the watchful eye of Colbert. Because it is a gallery and not a museum, the display is continually changing, but always constitutes an interesting collection of tapestries dating from the ancient and historical to the contemporary and abstract. *The King Visiting the Gobelins Factory,* woven between 1673 and 1680, features the Sun King, Colbert, Charles Le Brun—both the designer of the work and the first director of the factory—and countless workers scrambling to look occupied. Furniture sets and wall tapestries preserve this delicate art: look for the MNB (Manufacture Nationale Beauvais) monogram in the lower right-hand corner of the tapestries. Gallo-Roman ramparts and a tower dating from the late 3rd and early 4th centuries jut into the basement as an added historical touch. (Open Tues.-Sun. 9:30-noon and 2-6:30pm; Oct.-March Tues.-Sun. 10am-noon and 2:30-5pm. Last entry ½hr. before closing. Admission 18F, students and seniors 12F, ages 7-18 6F, under 7 free.)

The **Manufacture Nationale de la Tapisserie,** 24, rue Henri Brispot (tel. 44 05 14 28) spent 49 years in safe exile during and following World War II. Happily installed again in Beauvais, this time in a former slaughterhouse, modern artists and weavers continue the centuries-old tradition of producing stunning tapestries. You can see them at work and are even encouraged to question them about their craft. (Open Tues.-Thurs. 2-4pm. Admission same as to the Galerie.) The **Eglise Saint-Etienne,** on rue Engrand-Leprince, shows architectural elements from the 12th through the 16th cenuries and boasts the beautiful 16th-century stained-glass windows of d'Engrand Le Prince.

The **Office de Tourisme,** 1, rue Beauregard near the cathedral (tel. 44 45 08 18 or 44 45 25 26) offers countless brochures on the surrounding area, a list of hotels and restaurants and an invaluable map of the town. (Open Tues.-Sat. 9:30am-7pm, Sun.-Mon. and holidays 10am-1pm and 2-6pm; in winter closed Sun.) Places to eat and shop line the nearby **espace piéton** (pedestrian area). Try large but pleasant self-serve cafeteria **Inter Resto,** 5, bd. Saint-Jean (tel. 44 45 76 40 or 44 82 24 25). Traditional French cuisine—appetizer, *plat,* dessert, and cheese for 35F. Drink 4F, coffee 3F—buy your ticket at the cash register as you go in. (Open Mon.-Fri. 11:30am-2pm.)

On the last weekend in June (June 26-27 in 1993), the **Fête de Jeanne Hachette** celebrates the bravery of Jeanne Hachette (roughly Jean the Axe), the town's patron who led the resistance against the onslaught of Charles the Bold's Burgundian army in 1672. Townspeople trundle through the streets dressed in medieval garb and the central place Jeanne Hachette, in front of the 18th-century *hôtel de ville,* is transformed into a medieval market. Fireworks and the mandatory parade round off the occasion.

Roughly 15 **trains** daily head to Beauvais from Paris's Gare du Nord, *grandes lignes* platform (75min., 104F round-trip). For more information, call the Beauvais train station (tel. 44 21 50 50). To reach the cathedral from the train station, follow bd. du Général de Gaulle past the garden and turn left on rue des Jacobins. Walk through the pedestrian area and if you can't see it by now...

Other Daytrips

Euro Disneyland

It's a small world after all; it's a small, small world. Opening the pastel pink gates to tens of thousands of visitors on April 12, 1992, the fanfare of publicists touted Euro-Disney as a vast entertainment and resort center, the largest on the continent, covering an area one-fifth the size of Paris. But though Disney may eventually develop its 600 hectares, the current theme park doesn't even rank the size of an *arrondissement*. From the gate it takes only ten minutes to walk to the farthest point inside the park, nothing like the vasty reaches of Florida's Disneyworld. On the other hand, this Disney park is the most technologically advanced yet, and the special effects on some rides are enough to knock your Reeboks off.

Despite the whines of French intellectuals about a "cultural Chernobyl," the park has been a hit, and Disney has had to close the ticket windows repeatedly for hours at a time to keep lines down. Try to get there on a weekday--official statistics show Tuesday or Thursday to be the least crowded. Otherwise, expect to spend most of your time fighting to keep your place in line, rather than having fun. Masses of people practice the French national custom of line-cutting, as whole families duck under barriers and worm their way up front. (The small children are sent in first to make a small breach, then the parents rush in to exploit the gap—a clever adaptation of classic armored-assault tactics.) The management's apparent tolerance of the practice is perhaps the park's sole concession to European culture. To make things worse, devious architecture hides the true length of the lines. A line just emerging from a building may be just the tail end of a 90-minute wait inside. The crowds thin out toward 5pm, when the kiddies, all tuckered-out from a day of excitement, start crying to go home, reducing the wait in line to as little as 15 minutes. Saving the bigger rides for the evening is probably the best way to go, and considering that the park closes at midnight during the summer, you'll still have plenty of time to do all your favorite rides several times over.

There are a total of 14 rides—nine of them relatively sedate and suitable for small children—and 20 other attractions, such as dance shows and car displays. 58 stores, boutiques, and restaurants, and a plethora of food stands round out the park. You can buy a 52F cheeseburger, as well as Mickey Mouse pens and Minnie Mouse underwear, but it's practically impossible to meet the costumed characters; their only contact with the crowd comes when they float by during the two daily parades. WHERE'S MICKEY? Like everything in the park, Mickey doesn t come cheap.

Getting There

The easiest way to get to EuroDisney is by taking the **RER** A4 from Paris. Get on at either Mo. Gare de Lyon or Châtelet-Les Halles and take the train (direction: "Marne-La-Vallée") to the last stop, "Marne-La-Vallée/Chessy." Before boarding the train, check the illuminated electric boards hanging above the platform to make sure there's a light next to the Marne-La-Vallée stop; otherwise the train won't end up there. (Every 30min., 50min., 58F50 roundtrip.) The last train to Paris leaves Disney at 12:20am, but you may have trouble getting the metro at the other end. By **car,** take the A4 highway from Paris and getting off at exit 14, marked "Parc Euro Disneyland," about a 30-minute drive from the city. You can park for free in any one of the 1200 spaces in the parking lot, located next to the RER station. Finally, **Disney Buses** make the rounds between the terminals of both Orly and Roissy/Charles de Gaulle airports and the bus station near the Marne-La-Vallée RER (Every 45-60min., 40min., 65F). Buses run from Disney from 6:45am to about 10pm.

Orientation and Practical Information

Tickets: Instead of selling tickets, Disney issues *passeports,* available at the 50 windows located to the left after passing through the pink hotel that surrounds the front of the park. From the RER station, walk toward the right, and you'll see it. You can also buy passports at the Paris tourist office on the Champs-Elysées (see Paris Practical Information). Pursue this option if you plan on coming out on a weekend day, so you won t risk wasting a couple of hours while the windows remain closed due to the crowds. Admission 225F, under 12 150F. Open daily 9am-midnight, 8am-midnight for those staying in the on-site hotels. Hours subject to change during the winter.

Information and Lost & Found: City Hall, on the left side of Main Steet (tel. 64 74 28 82), just after you enter the park. Pick up free maps and entertainment schedules. The 4-hr. foot tours are probably not worth the 45F, because you still have to wait in line for the rides, just like everyone else (check with City Hall to see when it leaves). You can write messages in a book that can be read by anyone; convenient if you want to leave a message for a friend. Open daily 8am-midnight.

French Tourist Office: Maison du Tourisme, Festival Disney (tel. 60 43 33 33). Provides a 15-minute headphone-guided tour in French and English of the history of France, as represented by model châteaux and monuments scattered throughout the office. Rail and transport information, as well as museum schedules and lists of special events and holidays. Open daily 10am-midnight.

American Express: Hotel Disney Land, boîte postale 111, Marne La Vallée 77777, Cedex 4 (tel. 60 45 65 20). Outside the park gates to the right; follow the signs for *Relations Visiteurs* (Guest Relations), and you ll see it on your right before you get there. A full-service American Express office, including currency exchange and travel services. Open daily 9am-9pm.

Post Office: At Festival Disney. Take a left (away from the Park) at the RER station. A full-service post office. Open daily 10am-11pm. You can post mail at City Hall, but they don t sell stamps.

Lockers and Storage: both located on the right side of Main St., just after you enter the park. Check your bags or use a coin-operated locker, both 10F. Open 8am-midnight.

First Aid, Lost Children and Baby-Care: At the top of Main Street before the rotary, off to the right. Contact City Hall or come in person.They hand out bandages and aspirin; major problems are dealt with at an area hospital. If you ve lost a child, chances are you ll find the tot at the Lost Child Center, happily coloring away on a Disney drawing book while watching classic cartoons, all under the careful eyes of two staff nannies. The Baby Care center provides parents a room to nurse and change their infants, and sells baby food, diapers, and bottles. All open 8am-midnight.

Strollers and Wheelchairs: tel. 64 74 21 32. On f Main St., just after the lockers. Strollers and wheelchairs 30F per day. 20F deposit. Neither can leave the park. Open 8am-midnight.

Sights and Activities

The park can roughly be divided into five areas. **Main Street,** the first area you ll pass through after the gate, is home to City Hall and the highest concentration of stores. Take a quick peek into the **Main Street Vehicles** car store on the right side of the street, where classic horseless carriages from the 1890s are up for sale for only US$100,000 each. Also on Main Street you can hop on to a reproduction of these cars for a ride up to the **Château de la Belle au Bois Dormant (Sleeping Beauty's Castle).** If the line is long don't bother; it's only a two-minute walk. The château itself contains one stupendous high-tech smoke-breathing *dragon* in the dungeon, and a shop where you can buy the crown jewels (a gold-plated crown with colored stones) for a paltry 3200F. It makes one heck of a landmark, as well as a good meeting place for separated friends. Exiting out the back of the château, you fall into **Fantasyland,** a small world designed for small people. Although the rides are tame, **Peter Pan, Snow White and the Seven Dwarves,** and **It's a Small World** all merit a spin; Peter Pan swings you over a starry nighttime view of London before gliding into Never-Never Land. Bide your time while avoiding the lines at the rides at **Alice's Labyrinth,** a not too challenging, but peculiar hedge maze, replete with squirting fountains and a bong-smoking caterpillar.

Off to the left, **Adventureland** awaits both the intrepid explorer and the weary parent with a mix of themes from "adventurous" countries: Egypt, West Africa, and the Caribbean. **Pirates** presents 15 minutes of frighteningly lifelike corsairs and a fantastic water-dungeon set, where you occasionally get sprayed with the bilge water as your lifeboat rushes through. Unfortunately, the pirates prate in French, but even if you don't understand there is plenty to watch. Be warned: the line outside is only a fraction of the total wait. Mosey on down to the rough and ready zone of **Frontierland,** a honkey-tonk cowboy town. **Thunder Mesa,** a towering sunset colored reproduction of a New Mexican desert mesa, hosts the park's most breathtaking ride (and its only roller coaster), **Big Thunder Mountain.** At high noon, the line is almost as deadly as the ride, but the marvelous robot llamas and donkeys that border the track, and the bumpy trip itself, are superb. Set apart on a scraggly hill, the creaky **Phantom Manor** is the park's classic haunted house. Excellent special effects are enhanced by the enthusiastic staff, who delight in scaring their visitors. Walk back toward the château, and boldly go to **Discoveryland,** which beams you into the future. Fasten your seatbelt on **Star Tours,** a Star Wars-esque flight simulator that dizzies passengers with a combination of a high-tech video display and fast dips and turns. For a pop disco-rock dance show, with lots of dry ice and lip-synching, head to the **Videopolis,** a large theater-*cum*-snack bar (check the entertainment schedule at City Hall for times). **Visionarium,** another passive viewer attraction, pieces together footage from nine different cameras to create a 360° film about the human craving for flight.

In addition to the rides, Disney also puts on three daily special events: a **Disney character parade** with myriad elaborate floats including Snow White's castle, a fire-breathing dragon (as opposed to the smoke-breathing dragon in the château), and live doves; a nighttime **Electrical parade** (for the best view of the parades stand to the left at the top of Main Street near the pseudo-rotary—that's where the special effects on the floats are timed to go off); and a fantastic **fireworks** show, set against the background of the château. Check the daily entertainment schedule available at City Hall.

Beyond the park is **Festival Disney,** located to the left as you exit from the RER. Watch football and baseball games at the **Sports Bar,** or feel like a piece of meat up for auction at **Billy Bob's Saloon**—a country music pick-up joint. Both places offer beers starting at 25F a bottle; the Sports Bar sells Sam Adams for 30F. (Open daily 11am-2am.) Dancing starts after 10pm at **Hurricanes,** a Florida-theme disco, which is quite a rage not only with visitors, but with the resort staff and locals who come to Disney just to boogie here. (Open nightly 9pm-2am. Cover 100F, free for those staying at the on-site hotels.) Also at Festival Disney is **Buffalo Bill's Wild West dinner show,** a riding and shooting extravaganza where actors zealously play out such politically incorrect themes as good ole cowboys perforating the savage Native Americans, all to the delight of the thousand or so non-Americans in the audience. The two nightly shows are not worth the 300F ticket price. Prices in general are astronomical at Festival Disney, where just about the cheapest meal you can buy is a 59F burger and fries at **Annette's Diner,** a 1950s reproduction where all the waitresses wear roller skates.

Disney's resort hotels are cheapest for groups; all the four-person rooms are rented for a flat price, regardless of how many people stay there. Pitching a tent at the wooded **Camp Davy Crockett** (tel. 60 45 69 00) is the cheapest option. Take bus #3 from the RER station. (Campsites 270F, including electricity, showers, a barbecue pit, and access to a pool. Tennis courts are an additional 10F per hr.). Trailer cabins (750F per night) come equipped with a small stove in addition to the features mentioned above. The only other "budget" accommodations available at the resort is **Hotel Santa Fe** (tel. 60 45 60 80). Take Disney bus #2 from the RER station. The spotless rooms cost 550F per night, and are set up with two double beds, with little room for anything else.

Giverny

Halfway between Rouen and Paris, the small village of **Giverny** would have fallen off the map by now had Claude Monet not decided to purchase a small garden here. Sixty-seven years after his death, the then-impoverished painter surely would not recognize today his quaint pink and green house and his small, tangled garden. The Japanese-style bridge and water lilies are indeed quite beautiful, but the site has been methodically converted into a tourist trap of the first degreee, called the **Musée Claude Monet** (tel. 32 51 28 21). The steep admission fees now finance six months of continuous blooms, something Claude, who spent as much time writing rent-forgiveness letters to his landlord as he did painting, might well find incredible. The most famous paintings have been scattered around the world's museums, but with a little imagination, it's possible to disregard the freshets of tourists and appreciate the inspiration of

Monet's water lilies, which the master not only painted, but even addressed by name. Don't be surprised, however, if this seems more like a "Givernyland" than a real place.

Undoubtedly, the **gardens** are the main attraction—especially the lily ponds. Unfortunately, labels are scarce and maps nonexistent; unless you're a botany expert, you'll have no idea what's what. Among the flowers you might recognize: poppies and lilies of every variety, and lots of roses in the paths and alleyways in front of the house. A bit farther, the **water garden** is the definitive five-star attraction of Giverny, made famous by Monet's paintings of *Les Nymphéas,* now hanging in the Musée de l'Orangerie (see Museums). These are several connecting pools, fed by a tributary of the Epte River, full of water lilies of several varieties, and shaded by enormous weeping willows. A winding path around the pools, traversed at several points by the famous Japanese bridges over the water, reminds you of Monet's later paintings, as well as of the Japanese prints that inspired him both in his gardening and in his painting. You'll feel as if the Nymphéas room at the Orangerie or the lower level of the Musée Marmottan have come to life (thus proving Oscar Wilde's assertion that art fashions life). The house itself is lovely, with a façade of pink crushed brick. Inside, in the **Musée Claude Monet,** the walls of the small rooms are painted in cheerful pastels and lined with Monet's collection of 18th- and 19th-century Japanese woodblock prints. It is easy to see the profound influence that *ukiyoe* prints, imported en masse after the opening of Japan in 1853, had on Monet and his contemporaries. Adjacent pictures of Monet with his family and friends are unmarked and mostly indecipherable. (House and gardens open daily April-Oct. 10am-6pm. Admission 30F, students 20F. Admission to gardens 20F.)

Trains from Paris run to Vernon several times a day (45min. from Gare St-Lazare, 55F each way). From Vernon to Giverny is a 6km trek. Rental bikes are available at the station (44F per ½-day, 55F per day, 1000F deposit payable with Visa), or take a bus from the front of the station (3 per day each way, 10min., 10F, round-trip 16F). Unfortunately, the bus schedules are not as regular as they seem and not at all coordinated with the trains, leaving the traveler with long waits at either—or both—ends.

If you're not burdened by a frenzied itinerary, climb up the valley into the **Forêt de Vernon,** alongside Giverny, to see some Norman cows and beautiful poppy-covered countryside. The Vernon **tourist office,** 36, rue Carnot (tel. 32 51 39 60), distributes maps of hiking trails in the area. (Open Tues.-Sat. 9:30-12:15pm and 2:30-6:30pm, Mon. 2:30-6:30pm.) The tourist office also has information about the nearby **Château de Bizy** (tel. 32 51 00 82), where Gobelin tapestries drape the walls of a still-lived-in palace. Off the D181 (direction: Pacy-Evreux), Bizy is a 35-minute walk from the train station. (Open April-Nov. daily 10am-noon and 2-6pm. Admission 26F.) It may not be worth the price or the walk. The **Musée de Vernon,** 12, rue du Pont (tel. 32 21 28 09), exhibits an eclectic range of art objects, from the predictable series on Giverny (only one is a Monet), to a display of archeological relics found near Vernon and a room devoted to animal art. (Open Tues.-Sun. 2-6pm. Admission 25F, students free.)

Hotel beds in Vernon do not come cheap, but the excellent **Auberge de Jeunesse (HI),** 28, av. Ile de France (tel. 32 51 66 48), one block from the Seine, has immaculate four-person rooms. The walk along the green banks of the river takes 20 minutes. (Reception open daily 7-10am and 6:30-10:30pm. No lockout. Members only. 40F. Breakfast 15F. Open April-Sept. Reservations recommended at least a few days in advance.) You can also **camp** in back of the hostel on the wide lawn (22F per person).

Château-Thierry

On the train line from Paris to Strasbourg, Château-Thierry offers both a relaxing getaway from urban madness and a lesson in French (mainly military) history. The town on the Marne takes its name from the castle whose ruins stand atop the hill. Charles Martel built the first fortress here in 721. Martel, the powerful *maire du Palais,* ostensibly constructed the castle for seven-year-old King Thierry IV, son of Dagobert III, in whose name Martel in fact ruled. The fort became known as "Thierry's Castle"—hence Château-Thierry. Nowadays, locals call it **le Vieux Château,** and climb the hillside to walk their dogs and occasionally admire the view.

The ruins visible today, thanks to an ongoing archeological dig, date from the 11th-century military construction campaign of Hugues Thierry. The project was completed in 1140 by Thibaud le Grand, Count of Champagne and of Brie (and caterer to the world). The **ramparts** date from the 13th century, as does the **Porte Sainte Pierre,** one of the doors to the town. Built 50 years later, the **Porte Saint Jean** served as the main entrance to the castle. Walk through the first arch off rue de la Barre and imagine yourself trapped between two portcullises, at the mercy of a hostile castle garrison peering down from above while cranking their crossbows to finish you off. The **chemin de Roude** provides shaded silence under gnarled and knotty trees, but the best view of the surrounding area is found on top of the hill. Revel in the panoramic view and the abundant ruins. Henri II, Cathérine des Médicis, and Richelieu were among those who stayed at the castle; there was still a building standing in 1813 for Napoleon to present to the town. The archeological sites are labeled in French, but **guided tours** (sometimes available in English) are offered June 15-September 30, Monday-Saturday by the Unité Archaeologique, Hôtel Dieu, av. J. Latour (call 23 83 03 46 or the tourist office for information). The archeological laboratory at the Hôtel-Dieu also has an exhibit on the dig, its methods, and its finds to date.

Jean de La Fontaine, fabulous fabulist and Château-Thierry's favorite son, was born on July 8, 1621 at 12, rue Jean de La Fontaine (what a coincidence!). Built in 1559, the house serves as the **Musée La Fontaine** (tel. 23 69 05 60). Three rooms evoke the life and works of the man who composed poetry for Fouquet (see Vaux-le-Vicomte) and Louis XIV, as well as countless moral fables that have been passed down through the generations. Personal relics, including La Fontaine's signed letters to his uncle and his baptismal act (both hidden under brown cloth to protect them from the light), are supplemented with pictures of the author and editions of his works. Each room covers a different century, all the way up to some of Chagall's illustrations of the fables. (Open Wed.-Mon. 10am-noon and 2:30-6:30pm; April-June Wed.-Mon. 10am-noon and 2-6pm; Oct.-March Mon. and Wed.-Sat. 2-5pm, Sun. 10am-noon and 2-5pm. Admission 11F50, ages 4-18 6F50, under 4 free.) Unfortunately, the tower where La Fontaine did much of his work was destroyed in 1820. A **statue** of the man, myth and legend suffered its own war injury when battles wracked Château-Thierry: a bomb took a chunk out of one calf. Fontaine was baptized nearby in the **Eglise Saint-Crépin,** 1, rue la Madeleine, whose tower, rebuilt after destruction in 1421 under English-Burgundian rule, is the tallest in town. In need of repair, the church has surprisingly low ceilings but admirable vaulting.

Château-Thierry won its place in the historical atlas during the ordeal of World War I. In September 1914, as the Germans pressed forward, most residents fled. Only 180 of them stayed behind. On September 3, the Germans pillaged the city, but were forced to retreat after being repulsed on the Marne. (In the jingoistic words of the 1919 Michelin battlefield guide, a copy of which resides at the town library, "the Germans, as is their habit, destroyed for the pleasure of destroying.") The real hell arrived in 1918. German commander Erich Ludendorff had made one of the greatest gambles in history. He would take advantage of the Bolshevik Revolution to transfer troops from the Russian to the Western Front, to defeat France in one last offensive before the American troops could arrive. After attacking the British on the Somme in March, Lundendorff looked south toward Paris. On May 27, he launched a surprise assault and within days had crossed the Aisne at Soissons and was within 65km of Paris. The Allies decided that, as in 1914, they would stop the Germans on the Marne. To do so they would use the only troops at their disposal, the untested American Expeditionary Force.

On May 31, the first Americans arrived in Château-Thierry, whose two bridges made it an obvious target for the advancing Germans. Yank machine-gunners kept the Germans at bay while the French demolished the bridges. The next day, the Germans managed to capture the city after heavy street fighting, but the battle wasn't over. Doughboys barely off their transport trucks joined the battle that raged throughout June and into early July. The Allied counteroffensive of July 18 relieved Château-Thierry and the Germans left July 21. By then, the town was largely rubble. The bilingual **Monument** to the "Heroic Deeds of the Third Infantry Division, United States Army," along av. Jules Lefevre overlooking the Marne, is one reminder of the gratitude that the residents of Château-Thierry feel toward those who helped free them. The **Cimetière Militaire Franco-Britannique,** rue Léon Lhermitte, with its rows of simple, no longer whitewashed crosses provides a sober reminder of French losses during World War I.

Trains leave from Paris's Gare de l'Est for Château-Thierry (16 per day, 55 min., 133F round-trip). From the train station, walk up av. Wilson, turn left onto av. République and then right onto rue Carnot. Follow it over two bridges, up rue du Général de Gaulle to the **Office de Tourisme—Syndicat d'Initiative,** pl. de l'Hôtel de Ville (tel. 23 83 10 14 or 23 83 51 14), where you can get maps and pamphlets briefly explaining most of the sights, as well as lists of hotels and restaurants in the area and brochures about what to see in the region. (Open Mon.-Sat. 9am-12:30pm and 1:30-6:30pm, Sun. 9:30am-12:30pm; Oct.-May Mon.-Sat. 9am-12:30pm and 1:30-6:30pm.)

You can rent a bike at **Cycles Van Nimmen,** 4bis, av. de Château-Thierry (tel. 23 83 21 16), in Brasles, a 5- to 10-minute walk along the Marne east of the center of town. (Standard bikes 20F per ½day, 40F per day. Mountain bikes 40F per ½day, 80F per day. Scooters 125F. 1000F or ID deposit. Locks and helmets available. Open Mon. 2-7pm, Tues.-Sat. 8:30am-12:30pm and 2-7:30pm.) The **Au Tout Va Bien** brasserie, 13, rue du Général de Gaulle (23 83 02 13) serves a tart *citron pressé* (lemonade, 15F) and a filling cold meat plate (25F). (Open Thurs.-Tues. 8:30am-8pm.)

On the weekend in June closest to the 24th (St-Jean-Baptiste Day), Château-Thierry erupts into celebration of the Fêtes Jean de la Fontaine. The weekend features dances and bonfires, serenades and balls, a parade of flowered floats, and of course, fireworks. (Call the tourist office for more info. Sun. admission 20F, under 12 free.)

Near Château-Thierry

Three km west of Château-Thierry on the main Paris road (and worth the trek), the **Monument Américain de la Côte 204** honors the memory of the American troops who fought in the First World War. Perched on a hill 204m high, the monument was inaugurated in 1937 by General Pershing. Two statues, each a towering 7.6m high, represent America offering a helping hand to France. The colonnade is visible from quite a distance and, conversely, provides a spectacular view of the valley.

Belleau Wood (Bois de Belleau), 10km northwest from Château-Thierry, occupies an equally hallowed place in American military tradition, and with Château-Thierry, established the United States's prestige as a military power. There, the Second Division, composed of troops from both the Army and the Marine Corps, dislodged the Germans from an extremely strong position dug into the dense, tangled forest. On the first day of the assault, June 6, 1918, the Marine Corps suffered 1087 casualties, more than in all its previous campaigns combined. Many of the dead rest in the sprawling **American Cemetery** at the town of Belleau. With 2289 soldiers buried there, 250 of them unknown, the cemetery acts today as a memorial to those Americans who died during the First World War. (Open daily 8am-6pm; winter daily 8am-5pm.) There is no public transportation—hike, rent a bike (see above), or drive.

More cheerful and awe-inspiring in a completely different way are the medieval *caves* at **Champagne Pannier,** 23, rue Roger Câtillon (tel. 23 69 13 10). Carved out of rock as far as 30m under the ground during the 13th century, the *caves* stun with their grandeur. An excellent hour long guided tour is offered in three languages, complete with audiovisual presentation, tasting, and champagne flute as a souvenir. The *cave* is 1.5km out of town; buses sometimes pass by. (Tours March-Dec. every Sun. at 3, 4, and 5pm. Tours available any other time by appointment at least 2 or 3 days in advance. Admission 15F.)

Compiègne

Tranquil Compiègne (pop. 45,000) seems to have a knack for ending wars. The English captured Jeanne d'Arc here in 1430, and the armistice ending World War I was signed on November 11, 1918 in a forest clearing about 6km away. The town's luck, however, did not hold out against Adolf Hitler, who forced the French to surrender at the same spot in 1940. Under the German occupation, this little town was the site of one of France's largest detention centers for French Jews, sent here to wait in fear on their way to concentration camps farther east. In fact, it was from the train station in Compiègne that the "death train" to the concentration camps left—a train ride that resulted in the death of over half of its passengers. This dark period in the town's history is carefully neglected by most tour guides, and daytrippers from Paris can enjoy Compiègne's 17th-century château, three unusual museums, and a web of hiking trails in peaceful ignorance. The center is sufficiently compact that wandering mapless among its winding, cobblestone streets may well be the best way to explore this historic town.

Built for Louis XV as a summer "country cottage" and later serving as a second home for Napoleon, the **Palais National** contains 18th-century furniture and decorations and is surrounded by beautiful gardens. After declaring himself emperor in 1851, Napoleon III made it one of his residences, and stayed there—with up to a hundred of his closest friends, plus a mistress or two—for five or six weeks every autumn. Anyone who was anyone was there; each stayed in a particular room for a particular amount of time depending on social status. The atmosphere was tense, as the elite of Paris spent their days hunting in 16th-century costume and living in terror of making a *faux-pas*. As Théophile Gautier told the Goncourts, "everybody behaves very awkwardly: the whole atmosphere is one of embarrassment. They aren't used to it....The only people who are completely at their ease are the old servants, the remnants of dynastic varletry, handed down from Charles X and Louis-Philippe. They are the only people who look as if they knew what a court was like." But Compiègne was never as mentally distant from Paris as Versailles; ministers could make the trip from Paris in two hours.

This era is recalled by the **Musée du Second Empire** (tel. 44 40 02 02). Also within the palace is the **Musée de la Voiture** (Carriage Museum, tel. 44 40 04 37), crammed with antique bicycles, tricycles for two, and carriages, including the ostentatiously painted vehicles Napoleon and Marie-Antoinette used for joyrides. (Obligatory guided tours every 15min. Wed.-Mon. 9:30am-5pm. Last admission ½hr. before closing. Admission to palace and museums 26F, students, seniors, and Sun. and holidays 13F.) The château's manicured park is an excellent spot for picnics and trysts. Wander through the gilded gate to the edge of the gardens and the untamed **Forêt de Compiègne.**

Six km into the forest is the **Clairière de l'Armistice** (Armistice Clearing). The Ludendorff Offensive of 1918 put Compiègne on the frontline between the French and German forces, so it was here that the Supreme Commander of the Allies, Maréchal Foch, brought his railway carriage for the signing of the Armistice that November. On June 20, 1940, a gleeful Hitler ordered that Général Huntziger, the leader of France's delegation of surrender, be driven all the way from Tours so he could be presented with the German terms for peace in the very same railway carriage, in the very same clearing. Hitler himself arrived and sneered at the monument to French victory, showing, in the words of eyewitness William Shirer, his "burning contempt for this place now and all that it has stood for in the twenty-two years since it witnessed the humbling of the German Empire." After the capitulation was signed two days later, Hitler destroyed the monument and brought the railway carriage back to Berlin as a trophy. It was destroyed there by Allied bombing; a sturdy replica is now berthed here in a small museum with a simple monument. (Open daily 8am-noon and 1:30-6:30pm; Nov.-March Wed.-Mon. 9am-noon and 2-5:30pm. Admission 3F.)

The **Musée de la Figurine Historique,** in the annex of the Hôtel de Ville (tel. 44 40 72 55), contains a charming collection of toy kings, soldiers, and commoners reenacting highlights of French history. Its highlight is a fully staged battle of Waterloo. (Open Tues.-Sun. 9am-noon and 2-6pm; Nov.-Feb. 9am-noon and 2-5pm. Admission 10F50, students 5F, students on Wed. free.)

The **Auberge de Jeunesse (HI),** 6, rue Pasteur (tel. 44 40 72 64), is past the town hall at the end of rue des Cordeliers. (Reception open 7-10am and 5-10pm. Curfew 10pm. Members only. Bunk beds 33F. Showers included. Sheets 11F. Kitchen facilities.) Compiègne's friendly and helpful **tourist office** (tel. 44 40 01 00) is located in the Hôtel de Ville. (Open Easter-Oct. Mon.-Tues. and Thurs. 9am-noon and 1:45-6pm, Wed. and Sat. 9am-noon and 1:30-6pm, Sun. 9:30am-12:30pm and 2:30-5:30pm.) The town is easily accessible by **trains** from Paris's Gare du Nord (1hr., 55F). The train station is across the river from the center of town. To reach the center of town, cross pl. de la Gare in front of the station, turn right, and then turn left onto the bridge.

APPENDICES

Glossary

Here you will find a compilation of some of the French terms *Let's Go* has used, along with their pronounciations. The gender of the noun is either indicated in parentheses or by the article (feminine, *la;* masculine, *le)*. The glossary is followed by some phrases you might find helpful. The listed words or phrases which use the article "le" ("luh"), "la" ("lah"), "les" ("lay") indicate the pronounciation of the noun only. Eu and eue (pronounced the same) have a pronounciation in between the English "ew" and "uh." In this guide we have used "uh" to indicate this sound.

l'abbaye (f.)	abbey	lah-BAY
l'abri (m.)	shelter	lah-BREE
l'aile (f.)	wing	LEHL
l'allée (f.)	lane, avenue	lah-LAY
l'aller et retour	round-trip	lahLAY ay ruh-TOOR
aller simplel	one-way	ahLAY SEHM-pleh
les arènes (f.)	arena	ah-REHN
l'auberge (f.)	inn, tavern	loh-BEHRZH
la banlieue	suburbs	bahn-LEEH
le bateau	boat	bah-TOH
la bibliothèque	library	bihb-lee-oh-TECK
le billet	ticket	bee -YAY
le bois	forest	BWAH
la bourse	stock exchange	BOORS
la butte	hillock	BOOT
la cathédrale	cathedral	kah-tay-DRAHL
la cave	cellar	KAHV
le centre ville	center	SAHN-truh VEEL
la chambre	room	SHAHM-bruh
le champ	field	SHAM
la chapelle	chapel	shah-PEHL
le château	castle	shah-TOH
le cimetière	cemetery	see-meh-TYAYR
la cité	walled city	see-TAYh
le cours	tree-lined walk	KOOR
le couvent	convent	koo-VON
la croisière	cruise	kwahz-YAYR
la croix	cross	KWAH
la dégustation	tasting	day-GOOS-tah-SY SYOHN
le donjon	dungeon	dohn-ZHON
la douane	customs	DWAHN
l'école (f.)	school	lay-KOHL
l'église (f.)	church	lay-GLEEZ
l'escalier (m.)	stairway	lehs-kahl-YAY
l'evêché (m.)	bishop's palace; bishopric	lay-veh-SHAY
le faubourg	quarter	foh-BOOR
la fête	celebration	FEHT
les feux d'artifices	fireworks	FUH dahr-tee-FEES
la foire	fair	FWAHR
la fontaine	fountain	fohn-TEHN

282

la forêt	forest	foh-RAY
la gare	station	GAHR
la gare routière	bus station	GAHR root-YAYR
la halle	market hall, covered market	AHL
la haute ville	upper town	OHT VEEL
l'horloge (f.)	clock	lohr-LOHZH
l'hôtel (particulier) (m.)	mansion (town house)	loh-TEHL (pahr-tee-cool-YAY)
l'île (f.)	island	LEEL
le logis	lodging, dwelling	loh-ZHEE
la mairie	seat	meh-REE
le marché	market	mahr-SHAY
la montagne	mountain	mohn-TAHN
la mosquée	mosque	mohs-KAY
le mur	wall	MYUR
le palais	palace	pah-LAY
le parc	park	PAHR
la place	square	PLAHS
la plage	beach	PLAHZH
la pointe	headland, promontory	PWANT
le pont	bridge	POHN
la porte	gate; entry to the city	POHRT
le quartier	section (of town)	kahr-TYAY
la rue	street	RU
le salon	drawing or living room	sah-LOHN
la tapisserie	tapestry	tah-pees-REE
la tour	tower	TOOR
la trésorerie	treasury	tray-SOHR-uhree
la vieille ville	old town	VYAY VEEL

Helpful Phrases

please	*s'il vous plaît*	see voo PLAY
thank you	*merci*	mehr-SEE
hello	*bonjour*	bohn-ZHOOR
good evening	*bonsoir*	bohn-SWAHR
How are you?	*Comment allez-vous?*	KOH-mehn TAH-lay VOO
I am well.	*Je vais bien.*	ZHUH VAY BYEHN
goodbye	*au revoir*	OH ruh-VWAHR
Excuse me.	*Pardon.*	pahr-DON
(to get s.o.'s attention)	*Excusez-moi.*	ehks-KOO-ZAY MWAH
Do you speak English?	*Parlez-vous anglais?*	PAHR-lay VOO zahn-GLAY
I don't understand.	*Je ne comprends pas.*	ZHUH NUH kohm-PRAHN pah
I'm sorry.	*Je suis désolé.*	ZHUH SWEE day-soh-LAY
how much?	*combien?*	kohm-BYEHN
what?	*comment?*	koh-MOH
who	*qui*	KEE
how	*comment*	koh-MOH
why	*pourquoi*	poor-KWAH
when	*quand*	KAHN
What is it?	*Qu'est-ce que c'est?*	KEHS-kuh SAY
I would like	*Je voudrais*	ZHUH voo-DRAY
I need	*J'ai besoin de*	ZHAY buhz-WAN DUH

I want	*Je veux*	ZHUH VUH
I don't want	*Je ne veux pas*	ZHUH NUH VUH PAH
to rent	*louer*	loo-AY
The bill, please.	*L'addition, s'il vous plaît.*	lah-dees-YOHN, SEE VOO PLAY
Where is/are	*Où est/sont?*	OO AY/SOHN
the bathroom?	*les toilettes*	twa-LET
the police	*la police*	po-LEES
to the right	*à droite*	ah DWAHT
to the left	*à gauche*	ah GOHSH
up	*en haut*	ahn OH
down	*en bas*	ahn BAH
straight ahead	*tout droit*	TOO DWAH
a room	*une chambre*	oon SHAHM-bruh
double room	*une chambrepour deux*	oon SHAHM-bruh POOR DEUH
single room	*une chambre simple*	oon SHAHM-bruh SAYM-pluh
with	*avec*	ah-VECK
without	*sans*	SAHN
a shower	*une douche*	oon DOOSH
breakfast	*le petit déjeuner*	puh-TEE day-jhuh-NAY
lunch	*le déjeuner*	day-jhuh-NAY
dinner	*le dîner*	dee-NAY
shower included	*douche comprise*	DOOSH kohm-PREE
included	*compris*	kohm-PREE

Numbers

one	*un*	UHN
two	*deux*	DEUH
three	*trois*	TWAH
four	*quatre*	KA-truh
five	*cinq*	SANK
six	*six*	SEES
seven	*sept*	SEHT
eight	*huit*	WEET
nine	*neuf*	NUHF
ten	*dix*	DEES
twenty	*vingt*	VAN
thirty	*trente*	TRAHNT
forty	*quarante*	kah-RAHNT
fifty	*cinquante*	san-KAHNT
sixty	*soixante*	swah-SAHNT
seventy	*soixante-dix*	SWAH-sahnt DEES
eighty	*quatre-vingt*	KA-truh VAN
ninety	*quatre-vingt-dix*	KA-truh VAN DEES
one hundred	*cent*	SAHN

Menu Reader

à la	in the style of	*beurre blanc*	butter sauce with white wine, vinegar, and shallots
abatis	giblets	*beurre à la maître d'hôtel*	butter seasoned with parsley, lemon juice, salt, and pepper
abricot	apricot		
agneau	lamb		
aiguillettes	long, thin slices, usually of duck breast	*beurre noir*	butter with parsley and capers
		bigarade	bitter sauce made with orange peel
ail	garlic		
aile	wing	*bien cuit*	well done
aïoli	garlic mayonnaise	*bière*	beer
allemande	a white sauce with eggs	*bifteck*	steak
allummettes	matchstick potatoes	*bisque*	shellfish puree soup
alsacien	with sauerkraut	*blanc*	white
amandes	almonds	*blanc de volaille*	breast of chicken
ananas	pineapple		
anchois	anchovies	*blanquette*	stew in a white sauce with onions, mushrooms, eggs, and cream
andouillette	tripe sausage		
aneth	dill	*blette*	chard (white beet)
anguille	eel	*bleu*	very rare, blood red
à point	medium rare	*boeuf*	beef
artichaut	artichoke	*boeuf à la mode*	beef marinated and braised in red wine and served with vegetables
asperge	asparagus		
assiette de	plate of		
au	in the style of	*bouef bourgignon*	beef stewed in red Burgundy wine, onions, and garlic
aubergine	eggplant		
avec	with	*boissons*	drinks
avocat	avocado	*bombe glacée*	mixture of ice creams and flavored ices
baba au rhum	rich rum cake with currants		
baguette	long, crisp loaf of bread	*bordelais*	brown sauce with red wine, shallots, tarragon, and bone marrow
ballotine	a roll of boned and stuffed poultry, meat, or fish		
		bouchée	filled pastry shell
banane	banana	*boudin*	sausage
bar	sea bass	*boudin noir*	blood sausage
bardé	wrapped in fat and roasted	*bouillabaisse*	Marseillaise soup with chunks of saltwater fish and sometimes shellfish, with tomatoes, garlic, saffron, herbs, and olive oil
basilic	basil		
basquais	with ham, tomatoes, and red pepper		
bavarois	Bavarian cream: custard whipped with cream and gelatine		
		bouilli	boiled
		bourride	Provençal fish soup, with mayonnaise and bread
béarnaise	sauce made with egg yolks, shallots, white wine, vinegar, and tarragon		
		braisé	braised
		brioche	buttery bread, almost like pastry
béchamel	white sauce with butter, flour, milk, onions, and herbs		
		brochette	kebab (skewer)
		Bretonne, à la	with white beans
beignet	fritter: deep-fried dough or fruit	*brûle*	caramelized
		brunoise	shredded vegetables or a mixture of vegetables
bercy	with herbs and butter		
betterave	beet	*cacahouète*	peanut
beurre	butter	*caille*	quail

café	coffee	*clafoutis*	fruit pastry or crêpe
calamar	squid	*cochon*	pig
Calvados	apple brandy	*cochon de lait*	suckling pig
canard	duck	*cochonnailles*	platter of sausages and pâtés
carneton	duckling	*coeur*	heart
cannell	cinnamon	*compote*	whole fruit cooked in syrup and seasonings
câpre	caper		
carbonnade	beef stew with beer and onions	*concombre*	cucumber
		confit	duck or goose cooked and preserved in its own fat
carotte	carrot		
carpe	carp	*confiture*	jam
carré d'agneau	rack of lamb	*consommé*	clear meat or poultry broth
cassis	black currants	*contre-filet*	sirloin steak
cassoulet	casserole of white	*coq au vin*	chicken stewed in red Burgundy wine with mushrooms
céleri	celery		
cèpe	wild boletus mushroom		
cerf	venison	*coquillages*	shellfish
cerise	cherry	*coquilles St-Jacques*	sea scallops in a white sauce
cervelas	pork sausage with garlic		
cervelles	brains	*cornichon*	small pickle, served with pâtés
chair humaine	human flesh		
champignon	mushroom	*côte*	rib or chop
chanterelles	yellow mushrooms	*cotelette*	cutlet
Chantilly	whipped cream sweetened with sugar	*coulis*	meat juices, also a thick soup
		coupe glacée	ice cream sundae
charcuterie	prepared meats	*courge*	squash
charlotte	molded dessert, filled with cream or fruit	*courgette*	zucchini
		court-bouillon	a flavored broth in which poultry, fish, or meat is cooked
chasseur	sauce with wine, mushrooms, tomatoes, and shallots		
		crème caramel	caramel custard
chaud	hot	*crème fraîche*	fresh heavy cream
chèvre	goat cheese	*crêpe*	thin pancakes, but pancakes to die for. Served with jam, sugar, or other fillings
chevreuil	venison		
chiffonnafe	thin strips of lettuce or other vegetables		
		crêpe suzette	crêpes with fresh-squeezed orange juice and Grand-Marnier
chocolat chaud	hot chocolate		
choix	choice	*crépinette*	small, flat sausage
chou	cabbage	*cresson*	watercress
chou frisée	kale	*crevette grise*	shrimp
choucroute	sauerkraut with sausage and potatoes	*crevette rose*	prawn
		croque-ma-dame	toasted, open-faced ham and cheese sandwich, with an egg on top
chou-fleur	cauliflower		
choux	pastry; cream puff		
choux de Bruxelles	Brussels sprouts	*croque-mon-sieur*	toasted, open-faced ham and cheese sandwich
ciboulette	chive	*crôte*	crust
cidre	cider	*cru*	raw
citron	lemon	*crudités*	raw vegetables, usually with a dressing
citron vert	lime		
civet	stew made with red wine and blood	*crustacés*	crustaceans
		cuisset	haunch

cuit	cooked
darne	a thick slice of fish
datte	date
daube	red-wine stew
déjeuner	lunch
dinde	turkey
dîner	dinner
duxelles	chopped mushrooms and shallots sautéed and mixed with cream
eau	water
échalote	shallot
écrevisse	crayfish
émincé	thinly sliced meat
entrecôte	rib steak
entrée	first course (appetizer)
épaule	shoulder
épices	spices
épinard	spinach
escabéche	small fish fried in olive oil, boiled and then marinated in court-bouillon, and served cold
escalope	thinly sliced meat, cutlet
escargot	snail
estouffade	beef
estragon	tarragon
étouffe	stewed
faisan	pheasant
farci	stuffed
faux-filet	tenderloin steak
fenouil	fennel
feuilleté, en	puff pastry, in
fèves	broad beans
figue	fig
fines herbes	mixture of parsley and other herbs, such as chervil, chives, and tarragon
flageolet	small kidney bean
flambé	flamed
flan	open, round tart, usually filled with custard
flétan	halibut
fleur	flower
florentine	with spinach
foie	liver
foie gras	liver of a fattened goose
forestière	with mushrooms
four, au	baked
frais	fresh

fraise	strawberry
fraise des bois	wild strawberry
framboise	raspberry
fricassée	braised or stewed in white wine
frit	fried
frites	french fries
froid	cold
fromage	cheese
fromage blanc	sweet white cheese, served with jam
fruits de mer	seafood
fumé	smoked
galantine	cold meat, glazed in aspic
galette	thick crêpe made with buckwheat and topped with cream or eggs, nothing sweet
garni	garnished
gâteau	cake
gelée	aspic
génoise	sponge cake
gésier	gizzard
gibelotte	rabbit casserole
gigot	leg (of lamb or mutton)
girofle	clove
girolles	wild mushrooms
glace	ice cream
glacé	glazed
gratin	crust, made of bread and cheese
gratin dauphinois	potatoes boiled in milk and topped with a crust of cheese
grecque, à la	cooked in olive oil
grenouille	frog (legs)
grillé	grilled
groseille	red currant
hachis	hash
hareng	herring
haricot de mouton	mutton stew with turnips and potatoes
haricot rouge	kidney bean
haricot vert	green bean
herbes de Provence	parsley, sage, rosemary, and thyme
hollandaise	yellow sauce made of egg yolk, butter, and lemon juice or vinegar
homard	lobster
homard à l'Américaine	lobster with tomatoes, olive oil, shallots, and wine

homard Thermidor	lobster with butter, cream, brandy, and Madeira	*médallion*	round or oval piece, usually of meat
hors d'oeuvre	appetizer	*mélange*	mixture
huile	oil	*menthe*	mint
huître	oyster	*meunière*	dipped in flour and cooked in butter
île flottante	layered dessert of sponge cake, jam, custard, and cream	*meurette*	red wine sauce made with mushrooms, onions, bacon, and carrots, often served with fish
infusion	herbal tea		
jambon	ham	*miel*	honey
jambon cru	raw ham, salt-cured or smoked	*mignonette*	small cubes, usually of beef; also coarsely ground peppercorns
jambonneau	pig's knuckle		
jardinière	garnish of vegetables	*mille feuille*	"thousand-layered" pastry with cream; a Napoleon
jeune	young		
julienne	cut into strips	*mimosa*	with chopped hard-boiled egg
jus	juice	*mirabelle*	sweet yellow plum
knepfen	Alsatian dumplings	*mirepoix*	minced onions, celery, carrots, and sometimes ham simmered in butter and herbs
lait	milk		
laitue	lettuce		
langouste	spiny lobster (rock lobster)	*mixte*	mixed
langoustine	prawn	*monégasque*	with crushed walnuts, anchovies, garlic, and mustard in olive oil
langue	tongue		
lapereau	young rabbit	*mornay*	béchamel sauce with cheese
lapin	rabbit	*moule*	mussel
lardon	cubed bacon	*moule à la marinière*	mussels steamed in white wine and served in broth
léger	light		
légume	vegetable	*moule-frites*	steamed mussels, served with french fries
lièvre	wild hare		
limande	sole	*mousse*	literally "foam:" a whipped mixture containing eggs and cream
limousine, à la	with red cabbage		
lotte	monkfish, angler	*mousseline*	whipped whipped cream
loup de mer	Mediterranean sea bass, similar to striped bass	*moutarde*	mustard
		mouton	mutton
lyonnaise	with onions	*mûres*	blackberries
macédoine	mixture of raw or cooked diced fruit or vegetables	*nantua*	béchamel sauce with crayfish or shrimp
mâche	lamb's lettuce	*nature*	plain
madeleine	lemon-flavored tea cake	*navarin*	lamb or mutton stew with potatoes and turnips
magret de canard	breast of fattened duck		
		navet	turnip
maigre	lean	*niçoise, à la*	with tomatoes, onions, anchovies, and olives
mandarine	tangerine		
mange-tout	snow pea	*noisette*	hazelnut; slice of tender meat or potato
maquereau	mackerel		
marchand de vin	sauce with red wine, shallots, and meat juices	*noix*	nut
		noix de coco	coconut
marinée	marinated	*normande*	with cream, eggs, and mushrooms or cooked in cider or Calvados
marmite	a pot; also a thick soup made in a pot		
		nouilles	noodles
marron	chestnut	*omelet*	omelette

ouef	egg	*pied*	foot
oeuf à la coque	soft-boiled egg	*pintade*	guinea fowl
oeuf à brouillé	scrambled egg	*pipérade*	Basque dish of scambled eggs, pepper, tomatoes, and onions and ham, grilled meat, or grilled fish
oeuf dur	hard-boiled egg		
ouef à la neige	beaten egg whites poached in milk, served in a custard sauce		
		pistache	pistachio
oie	goose	*pistou*	sauce of basil, garlic, and olive oil
oignon	onion		
os	bone	*plat du jour*	daily special
oseille	sorrel	*plateau*	platter
oursin	urchin	*poché*	poached
pain	bread	*poêlé*	pan-fried
palourdes	clams	*poire*	pear
pamplemousse	grapefruit	*poireau*	leek
panaché	mixed	*poire belle Hélène*	half-pears with vanilla ice cream and chocolate sauce
pané	breaded		
papillote, en	cooked in parchment paper	*poisson*	fish
parfait	flavored-ice dessert	*poitrine*	breast
parisienne, à la	with scoops of potatoes, fried and doused in gravy	*poivrade*	peppercorn sauce with wine and vinegar
parmentier	with potatoes	*poivre*	pepper
pastèque	watermelon	*poivron*	bell pepper
pastis	anise (licorice-flavor) liqueur	*pomme*	apple
pâté	minced and seasoned liver or meat, baked in a crust and served hot or cold. This spread without the crust is technically a terrine, but is often called a pâté.	*pomme de terre*	potato
		pommes frites	french fries
		poppiettes de veau	stewed veal rolls stuffed with a mixture of ground veal and pork, herbs and sometimes prunes
pâté à choux	cream puff	*porc*	pork
pâté feuilletée	layered pastry	*porc salé*	salt pork
pâte	pasta	*potage*	soup
pâtisserie	pastry	*potage purée condé*	red-bean soup with bacon and wine
pavé	thick steak (literally cobblestone), usually very rare inside		
		pot-au-feu	beef boiled with vegetables in a ceramic pot
paysan, à la	with braised potatoes, vegetables and bacon	*potée*	rich soup with cabbage, pork, and potatoes
pêche	peach	*pouding*	pudding
pêche Melba	peach with vanilla ice cream and raspberries	*poularde*	fattened pullet (chicken)
		poulet	chicken
perche	perch	*poulet marengo*	chicken with tomatoes, mushrooms, wine, and crayfish
perdreau	partridge		
périgourdine, à la	with foie gras and truffles	*poulpe*	octopus
		poutine	french fries topped with gravy and cheese curds
persil	parsley		
petit déjeuner	breakfast	*pressé*	pressed
petit-fours	tiny, bite-sized cakes	*profiteroles*	small pastries filled with custard, cream, or ice cream and covered in chocolate sauce
petit pain	roll		
petit pain au chocolat	chocolate croissant		
		provençal	with garlic, olive oil, onions, tomatoes, parsley, and white wine
petit-pois	peas		

pruneau	prune
quenelle	dumpling, usually with fish, sometimes with poultry or meat
raclette	melted cheese served over boiled potatoes
ragoût	stew
raie	ray (skate)
raisin	grape
râpé	grated
ratatouille	sliced eggplant, zucchini, tomatoes, peppers, and garlic fried in olive oil
ravigote	white sauce made with oil, vinegar, and several herbs
redis	radish
rémoulade	mayonnaise with mustard and herbs
rhum	rum
rillette	coarsely minced pork
ris	sweetbreads
riz	rice
rognon	kidney
Romanoff	(fruit) with cream and liqueur
romarin	rosemary
rosé	pink, as in meat
rôti	roast
rouget	red mullet
sabayon	custard, flavored liquor or wine
safran	saffron
saignant	rare (bleeding)
saison	season
salade niçoise	lettuce, tomatoes, green beans, tuna, black olives, potatoes, spanish onions, and anchovies
salade verte	green salad
salé	salted
sanglier	wild boar
sauce vert	mayonnaise with pickles and capers
saucisse	fresh pork sausage
saucisson	large dried sausage
sauge	sage
saumon	salmon
savoyarde	with Gruyère cheese
sel	salt
soissonaise	white-bean soup
sorbet	sherbet
soubise	white onion sauce
soupe de poisson croisiçause	fish chowder with potatoes
sucre	sugar
suprême	white, creamy sauce
suprême de volaille	chicken breast
tartare	chopped raw meat topped with a raw egg
tartare (sauce)	mayonnaise with mustard and cayenne pepper
tarte tatin	caramelized upside-down apple pie
tartine	open-faced sandwich or buttered bread
terrine	baked minced liver or meat, served cold; see pâté
thé	tea
thon	tuna
tiède	warm
timbale	anything cooked in a metal casserole
tournedos Rossini	filet mignon with foie gras, truffles, and Madeira
tortue	turtle
truite	trout
vacherin	baked meringue with ice cream
vapeur	steamed
veau	veal
velouté	"velvety" cream sauce
véronique, à la	with white grapes
viande	meat
vichyssoise	cold cream soup with leeks and potatoes
vin	wine
vinaigre	vinegar
volaille	poultry
vol au vent	pastry shell
xérès	sherry
yaourt	yogurt

INDEX

292   Index